# The Cost of Conquest:
# Indian Decline in Honduras
# Under Spanish Rule

# Dellplain Latin American Studies

## The Cost of Conquest:
## *Indian Decline in Honduras Under Spanish Rule*
### Linda Newson

At the time of the Spanish conquest, Honduras was inhabited by two distinct social systems, which defined the boundary between the cultures of Mesoamerica and South America. Each system was administered in a different way, and subsequently the survival of each civilization varied markedly. This study examines the nature of each culture at the time of Spanish conquest, the size of the populations, and the method of colonization applied to each. Particular attention is focused on Spanish economic activities and the institutions that directly affected the Indian way of life. Dr. Newson bases her findings on extensive archival research conducted in Spain, Guatemala, and Honduras and on archaeological, ethnographic, and linguistic evidence found in secondary sources.

Linda Newson is lecturer in geography at King's College in London.

# DELLPLAIN LATIN AMERICAN STUDIES

PUBLISHED IN COOPERATION
WITH THE DEPARTMENT OF GEOGRAPHY
SYRACUSE UNIVERSITY

## EDITOR

David J. Robinson
Syracuse University

## EDITORIAL ADVISORY COMMITTEE

William M. Denevan
University of Wisconsin

John H. Galloway
University of Toronto

John Lynch
University of London

Robert McCaa
University of Minnesota

Linda Newson
University of London

## EDITORIAL ASSISTANT

Kay Steinmetz

# The Cost of Conquest:
# Indian Decline in Honduras
# Under Spanish Rule

## Linda Newson

Dellplain Latin American Studies, No. 20

Westview Press / Boulder and London

*Dellplain Latin American Studies*

Published in 1986 in the United States of America by Westview Press, Inc.; Frederick A. Praeger, Publisher; 5500 Central Avenue, Boulder, Colorado 80301

Library of Congress Catalog Card Number: 86-51457
ISBN: 0-8133-7273-9

Composition for this book was provided by the author.
This book was produced without formal editing by the publisher.

Printed and bound in the United States of America

∞ The paper used in this publication meets the requirements of the American National Standard for Permanence of Paper for Printed Library Materials Z39.48-1984.

6   5   4   3   2   1

# Contents

# Tables

# Figures

# Abbreviations

Unpublished Sources

AGCA    Archivo General de Centro América, Guatemala City

AGI    Archivo General de Indias

       AG    Audiencia de Guatemala
       CO    Contaduría
       EG    Escribanía de Camara
       IG     Indiferente General
       JU     Justicia
       MP    Mapas y Planos
       PAT   Patronato

AHNM    Archivo Histórico Nacional, Madrid

ANCR    Archivo Nacional, Costa Rica

       CC     Complementario Colonial

ANH    Archivo Nacional de Historia, Honduras

BM    British Museum, London

       Add.    Additional Manuscripts

BNM    Biblioteca Nacional, Madrid

BPR    Biblioteca del Palacio Real, Madrid

       MA    Miscelánea de Ayala

MNM    Museo Naval, Madrid

PRO    Public Record Office, London

       CO    Colonial Office

RAHM    Real Academia de la Historia, Madrid

        CM    Colección Muñoz

SHM    Servicio Histórico Militar

Published Sources

AEA    Anuario de Estudios Americanos

ASGH    Anales de la Sociedad de Geografía e Historia, (Guatemala)

BAGG    Boletin del Archivo General de Gobierno, Guatemala City

CDHCN    Colección de Documentos Referentes a la Historia Colonial de Nicaragua

CDHCR    Colección de Documentos para la Historia de Costa Rica

CDI    Colección de Documentos Inéditos Relativos al Descubrimiento, Conquista y Organización de las Posesiones Españolas en América y Oceanía

CDIU    Colección de Documentos Inéditos Relativos al Descubrimiento, Conquista y Organización de las Antiguas Posesiones Españolas de Ultramar

CS    Colección Somoza

HAHR    Hispanic American Historical Review

HMAI    Handbook of Middle American Indians

HSAI    Handbook of South American Indians

JLAS    Journal of Latin American Studies

LARR    Latin American Research Review

RABNH    Revista del Archivo y Biblioteca Nacionales (Honduras)

# Part I

Introduction

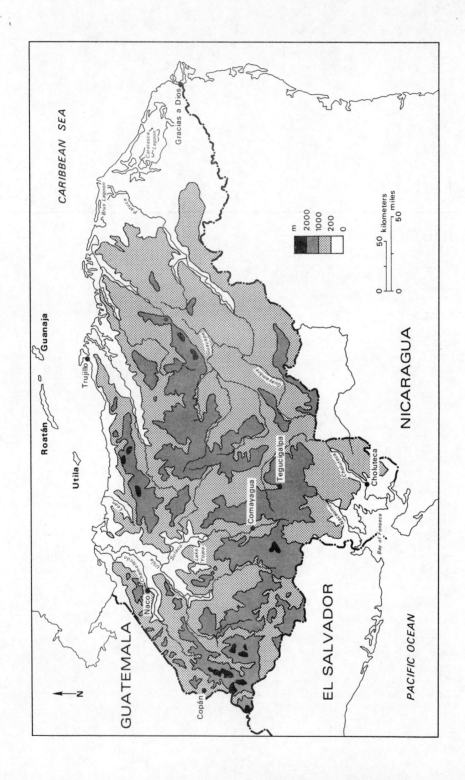

# 1
# Patterns of Conquest and Indian Populations

The conquest and colonization of Honduras was disastrous for its Indian population. In common with Indians in other parts of the New World, those of Honduras suffered a dramatic decline from which they have never fully recovered. Although Dobyns has suggested that the Indian population of the subcontinent declined by about 95 percent between the time of Spanish conquest and its population nadir,[1] it is clear that there were considerable regional variations in the decline and recovery of different Indian groups. Some groups became extinct at an early date, whilst many suffered a sharp decline followed by a slow recovery, and others continued to decline into the nineteenth century.

## DEMOGRAPHIC PATTERNS IN CENTRAL AMERICA

Demographically Central America is a microcosm of colonial Spanish America. There are areas where the Indian population declined dramatically at an early date, with any remaining Indians being gradually absorbed into an expanding *ladino* population. In geographical terms these areas comprised the Pacific coast south from Soconusco to Nicoya, as well as the lowlands of the Gulf of Honduras. In Soconusco and Zapotitlán the Indian population was reduced to about one-twentieth of its preconquest size by the 1570s, when its continued decline was checked by immigration from the highlands.[2]

---

[1]H.F. Dobyns, "Estimating Aboriginal American Population: An Appraisal of Techniques with a New Hemispheric Estimate," *Current Anthropology* 7 (1966):415.

[2]M.J. MacLeod, *Spanish Central America: A Socioeconomic History, 1520-1720* (Berkeley and Los Angeles: University of California, 1973), pp. 71, 77-78; idem, "An Outline of Central American Colonial Demographics: Sources, Yields and Possibilities," in *The Historical Demography of Highland Guatemala*, eds. R.M. Carmack, J. Early, and C. Lutz (Albany: SUNY, 1982), p. 7; P. Gerhard, *The Southeast Frontier* (Princeton: Princeton University Press, 1979), pp. 169-70, suggests an aboriginal population of 80,000 for Soconusco, which fell to 1,800 tributaries in 1569 and 800 in 1684.

Here intense economic activity, associated with cacao production, contributed to the rapid decline in the Indian population, whereas further south in El Salvador, Choluteca and Pacific Nicaragua similar activity focused on the cultivation of indigo, which largely supplanted that of cacao. The other major factor that contributed to the decline in the lowlands, particularly in the Caribbean lowlands of Honduras, the Bay of Fonseca, Pacific Nicaragua and Nicoya, was the Indian slave trade, which resulted in the latter two regions alone losing up to one-half million Indians.[3] By the end of the sixteenth century, Indian populations in Pacific Nicaragua and Nicoya had been reduced by over 97 percent, a depopulation ratio of nearly 40:1. Subsequent increases in the Indian population in the lowlands were retarded by miscegenation and later, particularly on the Caribbean coast, by tropical diseases, but some increases were registered in Soconusco and Pacific Nicaragua in the eighteenth century.[4]

In general the scale of depopulation in the highlands was lower than in the neighboring lowlands. In the highlands of Guatemala depopulation ratios calculated from population estimates for Totonicapán by Veblen and for the Cuchumatán highlands by Lovell for 1520 to 1570-80 are 8.1:1 and 5.5:1 respectively,[5] but if they are calculated to their respective nadirs in the late seventeenth century, the corresponding figures are 13.5:1 and 16.1:1. These figures are fairly comparable with those estimated for the central Mexican highlands. Cook and Borah have estimated that between 1532 and 1608 the depopulation ratio for the plateau of central Mexico was 13.2:1 and for the coast, 26:1.[6] Furthermore, in common with the central Mexico plateau and in contrast to the lowlands, Indian populations in the highlands of Central America generally experienced a sustained recovery. However, in most areas this increase did not begin until at least the middle of the seventeenth century and even then it was punctuated by epidemics.

A number of authors have drawn attention to the significant difference between the levels of decline in the highlands and lowlands, often attributing it to differences in the impact of disease, and in particular to the added impact of tropical fevers in the lowlands. Although the validity of this assertion can be questioned, other factors such as the Indian slave trade and the greater intensity of economic activity clearly contributed to the higher level of decline in the lowlands. In fact the simple division between highlands and lowlands masks regional variations with these broad areas. Clearly Indian populations in areas that attracted few outsiders, such as Totonicapán, the Chuchumatán highlands and Verapaz, declined at a slower rate and became less ladino in character than

---

[3]L.A. Newson, "Demographic Catastrophe in Sixteenth-Century Honduras," in *Studies in Spanish American Population History*, ed. D.J. Robinson (Boulder, CO: Westview, 1981), pp. 227-28; and idem, "The Depopulation of Nicaragua in the Sixteenth Century," *JLAS* 14 (1982):270-75.

[4]J. Gasco, "Demographic Trends in the Soconusco, 1520-1970" (Paper presented at the 44th International Congress of Americanists, Manchester, 1982); L.A. Newson, *Indian Survival in Colonial Nicaragua* (Norman: University of Oklahoma Press) (in press).

[5]T.T. Veblen, "Native Population Decline in Totonicapán, Guatemala," *Annals of the Association of American Geographers* 67 (1977):484-99; W.G. Lovell, "The Historical Demography of the Cuchumatán Highlands, Guatemala, 1500-1821," in *Spanish American Population*, ed. Robinson, pp. 195-216.

[6]S.F. Cook and W. Borah, *The Indian Population of Central Mexico, 1531-1610*, Ibero-Americana 44 (Berkeley and Los Angeles: University of California, 1960), p. 48.

other areas where commercial agricultural and mining enterprises were established.[7] This generalization does not hold true for areas of sparse Indian population, such as Costa Rica and the eastern Caribbean lowlands, where colonization, often initiated by missionaries, was delayed and the Indian population declined slowly through the colonial period. Meanwhile, at the subregional scale Indians located near major towns and ports also experienced a more rapid decline, which, although sometimes mitigated by Indian immigration from more remote areas, continued as the Indians were gradually absorbed into the growing population of mixed races.

## FACTORS INFLUENCING DEMOGRAPHIC CHANGE

From the time of Spanish conquest to the present day, the changing size of Indian populations during the colonial period has been attributed to a variety of factors, the relative importance of which has varied over time with the availability of evidence and interpretation of observers and researchers. Early commentators stressed the ill treatment and overwork of the Indians in explaining the rapid decline of the Indian population, but more recently researchers have emphasized the importance of disease.

Sixteenth-century observers blamed the rapid decline of the Indian population on the overwork and ill treatment of the Indians by conquistadors and colonists. There is no doubt that the Black Legend was a reality in the Caribbean, where the Indians became virtually extinct within a generation. Particularly important in Central America was the Indian slave trade, which resulted in the coastal regions of Pacific Nicaragua and to a lesser extent Honduras, being rapidly depopulated. The rapid decline of the Indian population and the concerned representations to the Crown, particularly by the Dominicans, resulted in the New Laws being introduced in 1542. Although the New Laws were often infringed, by banning Indian slavery, moderating personal service and calling for the regulation of tribute payments, they did lead to a general improvement in the treatment of the Indians. Since Central America was effectively colonized before the introduction of the New Laws, its Indian population received little legal protection from exploitation, such that overwork and ill treatment probably contributed more significantly to the decline in the Indian population there than it did on the South American mainland where colonization largely followed their introduction. But, as has already been demonstrated, different regions within Central America experienced different levels of decline and these cannot be satisfactorily explained by differences in Crown policy or in the activities of its officials. It was the Crown's intention that laws and institutions formulated in Spain should apply uniformly to all parts of the empire. Whilst laws might be interpreted differently by different administrators, officials were constantly changing and it is doubtful if personnel in any one area interpreted the laws consistently in a manner that might account for a smaller or larger decline in the Indian population in some areas than in others. Any spatial variations in Spanish-Indian relations that emerge are

---

[7]For similar ideas see M.J. MacLeod, "Ethnic Relations and Indian Society in the Province of Guatemala, ca.1620-ca.1800," in *Spaniards and Indians in Southeastern Mesoamerica: Essays on the History of Ethnic Relations*, ed. M.J. MacLeod and R. Wasserstrom (Lincoln and London: University of Nebraska, 1983), pp. 203-205; and L. A. Newson, "Indian Population Patterns in Colonial Spanish America," *LARR* 20 (1985):62-65.

6

better interpreted as reactions to local conditions than as expressions of differences in government policy or its interpretation by its officers.

Most recent writers on the historical demography of Latin America agree that disease was a major factor in the decline of the Indian population.[8] The most notable killers were smallpox, measles, typhus, plague, yellow fever, and malaria. In the documentary record there are numerous accounts of the populations of villages and whole areas being reduced by one-third or one-half as a result of epidemics, particularly of smallpox and measles. The devastating impact of these diseases on previously noninfected populations has been corroborated by historically more recent epidemics.[9] It is often assumed that the greater decline in the Indian population of the tropical lowlands was due to the greater impact of disease, mainly yellow fever and malaria, which only occur in climates where the mean temperature is over 20°C, and possibly due to the greater virulence of diseases in warmer climates. There are a number of difficulties with these proposals. First, it seems likely that malaria and yellow fever were relatively late introductions to the New World. It is generally held that malaria was introduced into the New World about the middle of the seventeenth century and the first agreed upon epidemic of yellow fever occurred in Yucatán in 1648, although a few would argue for its

[8]S.F. Cook, "The Demographic Consequences of European Contact with Primitive Peoples," *Annals of the American Academy of Political and Social Science* 237 (1945):108-109; J. Vellard, "Causas biológicas de la disaparición de los Indios Americanos," *Boletín del Instituto Riva-Aguero* 2 (1956):77-93; Cook and Borah, *Indian Population of Central Mexico*; H.F. Dobyns, "An Outline of Andean Epidemic History to 1720," *Bulletin of the History of Medicine* 37 (1963):493-515; W. Borah, "America as Model: The Demographic Impact of European Expansion upon the Non-European World," *35th International Congress of Americanists*, Mexico, Vol. 3 (1964), pp. 379-87; Dobyns, "Estimating Aboriginal American Population," pp. 410-11; A.W. Crosby, "Conquistador y Pestilencia: The First New World Pandemic and the Fall of the Great Indian Empires," *HAHR* 47 (1967):321-37; W.R. Jacobs, "The Tip of the Iceberg: Pre-Columbian Indian Demography and Some Implications for Revisionism," *William & Mary Quarterly* 31 (1975); A.W. Crosby, "Virgin Soil Epidemics as a Factor in the Depopulation of America," *William & Mary Quarterly* 33 (1976):289-99; W.M. Denevan, ed., *The Native Population of the Americas in 1492* (Madison: University of Wisconsin, 1976), pp. 4-6; H.F. Dobyns, *Native American Historical Demography: A Critical Bibliography* (Bloomington: Indiana University, 1976), pp. 22-57.

[9]Dobyns, "Estimating Aboriginal American Population," pp. 410-11; Jacobs, "Tip of the Iceberg," pp. 130-32; Dobyns, *Native American Historical Demography*, pp. 25-34; W.H. McNeill, *Plagues and Peoples* (Oxford: Blackwell, 1976), pp. 204-205.

presence at an earlier date.[10]  Hence, the early decline in the Indian population cannot be attributed to these diseases.  Second, although it is true that intestinal infections are more prevalent in the tropics and, although not contributing directly to the mortality rate, would have increased the susceptibility of Indians living there to more deadly diseases,[11] a number of other diseases introduced from the Old World were equally if not more virulent in the highlands.  Smallpox and pneumonic plague thrive in cool, dry climates, where unhygienic conditions are created that also favor the spread of typhus.[12]  Furthermore, the concentration of population in large nucleated settlements in the highlands would have enabled and facilitated the spread of disease, whereas in the tropical lowlands its spread was generally hindered by the dispersed character of the population and settlements.[13]  Despite these comments, it is important to recognize that many tropical coasts earned early reputations for being unhealthy, and it may be that there were other tropical diseases, as yet unidentified, which may have contributed to the higher mortality rate there.  At present, however, there is insufficient evidence to conclude that the lower level of Indian survival in the tropical lowlands can be accounted for wholly in terms of the greater impact of disease.  Whilst disease was clearly a major factor in the decline of Indian populations, the pattern of its impact is likely to have been much more complex than sometimes suggested, with the spread of diseases dependent not only on altitude and climate, but on a whole variety of other factors, including the presence of

---

[10]P.M. Ashburn, *The Ranks of Death:  A Medical History of the Conquest of America* (New York:  Coward-McCann, 1947), pp. 130-34; J.A. Vivó Escoto, "Weather and Climate of Mexico and Central America," in *HMAI*, ed. R.C. West, Vol. 1 (Austin: University of Texas, 1964), pp. 213-14; F. L. Dunn, "On the Antiquity of Malaria in the New World," *Human Biology* 37 (1965):385-93; C.O. Sauer, *Early Spanish Main* (Berkeley and Los Angeles:  University of California, 1966), p. 279; J.E.S. Thompson, *Maya History and Religion* (Norman:  University of Oklahoma, 1970), pp. 54-55; J. Duffy, *Epidemics in Colonial America* (Port Washington and London:  Kennikat Press, 1972), p. 140; C.S. Wood, "New Evidence for a Late Introduction of Malaria into the New World," *Current Anthropology* 16 (1975):93-104; McNeill, *Plagues and Peoples*, p. 213; Denevan, ed., *Native Population of the Americas*, p. 5; A.W.A. Brown, "Yellow Fever, Dengue and Dengue Haemorrhagic Fever," in *A World Geography of Human Diseases*, ed. G.M. Howe (London:  Academic Press, 1977), p. 390.

[11]These may have included typhoid, paratyphoid, bacilliary and amoebic dysentery, hookworm, and other helminthic infections most of which were water-borne and more prevalent in the humid tropics (G. Sangster, "Diarrhoeal Diseases," in *Geography of Human Diseases*, ed. Howe, pp. 145-74).

[12]Smallpox:  C.W. Dixon, *Smallpox* (London:  Churchill, 1962), p. 313; Z. Deutschmann, "The Ecology of Smallpox," in *Studies in Disease Ecology*, ed. J. May (New York:  Hafner, 1961), pp. 7-8; Crosby, "Conquistador y Pestilencia," p. 333. Plague:  P.H. Manson-Bahr, *Manson's Tropical Diseases* (London:  Cassell, 1948), p. 261; R. Pollitzer, *Plague*, WHO Monograph Series no. 22 (Geneva:  World Health Organization, 1954), pp. 256-57, 418, 451; J.F. Shrewsbury, *A History of Bubonic Plague in the British Isles* (Cambridge:  Cambridge University Press, 1970), pp. 1-6; MacLeod, *Spanish Central America*, pp. 8-9. Typhus:  Ashburn, *Ranks of Death*, pp. 81, 95-96.

[13]F.L. Black, "Infectious Diseases in Primitive Societies," *Science* 187 (1975):515-18; D.E. Shea, "A Defense of Small Population Estimates for the Central Andes," in *Native Population*, Denevan, ed., pp. 159-61.

vectors for transmitting the disease, population density, the degree of interpersonal contact, subsistence patterns, sanitation, and immunity.[14]

## INDIAN SOCIETIES AND RESOURCES

Although disease and the ill treatment and overwork of the Indians both contributed significantly to the decline in the Indian population, alone they cannot adequately explain its differential decline. The level of decline (and subsequent recovery) of Indian populations in different regions appears to have been influenced by two factors. First, it was influenced by the nature of Indian societies at the time of Spanish conquest and, related to this, the size of the aboriginal population. This factor influenced the type of institutions and mechanisms used to control and exploit the Indians. The second factor was the existence and desirability of resources to be found in the area.

### Indian Societies and Spanish Policies

The background of those who came from Spain to conquer and colonize America was essentially feudal, but one in which the Crown, supported by the Church, played a dominant role. The Spanish had two main aims with respect to the Indians of the New World: to effect their civilization and christianization and to exploit them as sources of profit and labor. From the beginning policies adopted towards the Indians attempted to reconcile these conflicting aims, which were perhaps most apparent in the *encomienda*. The encomienda was a grant of Indians to an individual who, in return for providing the Indians with protection and instruction in the Catholic faith, could levy tribute from them in the form of goods or money, and until 1549 could also demand labor services. However, the early years of conquest witnessed the dramatic decline of the Indian population in the Caribbean and demonstrated that not all Spaniards could be entrusted with the important tasks of civilizing and christianizing the Indians. Hence, from the mid-sixteenth century the custodial duties of *encomenderos* were gradually taken over by Crown administrators (*corregidores de indios*) and the secular clergy. Meanwhile, tribute revenue increasingly entered the royal coffers rather than the hands of encomenderos, and labor was organized under the *repartimiento*. The latter required each Indian village to make available a quota of its tributary population for approved work for specified periods and fixed wages. The encomienda and repartimiento were later superseded in many areas by free labor. Despite their shortcomings, the encomienda and repartimiento were initially considered appropriate for controlling and exploiting Indians in the highland states and chiefdoms of Middle America and the Andes for several reasons.[15] First, these Indians had paid tribute and had been subject to labor drafts in the pre-Columbian period,

---

[14]Shea, "Defense of Small Population Estimates," pp. 160-61.

[15]S. Zavala, *New Viewpoints on the Spanish Colonization of America* (Philadelphia: University of Pennsylvania, 1943), p. 68; E.R. Service, "Indian-European Relations in Colonial Latin America," *American Anthropologist* 57 (1955):413-14; M. Harris, *Patterns of Race in the Americas* (New York: Walker, 1964), pp. 3-13; J.A. Villamarin and J.E. Villamarin, *Indian Labor in Mainland Colonial Spanish America* (Newark: University of Delaware, 1975), pp. 24-30.

so that although the Spanish modified the systems by which they were exacted, such demands were not considered extraordinary. Second, the hierarchical structure of these societies permitted the Spanish to control and exploit large Indian populations through a relatively small number of native leaders; a closer means of control such as slavery was therefore unnecessary.[16]

The control and exploitation of essentially egalitarian tribes, who subsisted on the products of shifting cultivation supplemented by hunting, fishing, and gathering, could not be effected so easily by means of the same institutions. These Indians had not paid tribute or provided labor for extracommunal purposes in pre-Columbian times, so that no organizational structure existed for their exaction and the task was made even more difficult by the lack of effective native leadership.[17] Thus to impose the encomienda and repartimiento would have required considerable managerial input. Since these Indians produced only small surpluses, if any, and constituted only small sources of labor, the task was not generally considered to be worthwhile. Instead the initial conversion and civilization of tribal Indians were left to the missionary orders, who could supply the closer form of supervision required. Theoretically after ten years mission settlements were to be handed over to the secular authorities and the Indians were to pay tribute and provide labor in the same way as those Indians who had been granted in encomiendas. In practice, however, they persisted much longer.

The nomadic hunters, fishers, and gatherers provided even less in terms of surpluses and sources of labor, and they were more difficult to control than tribes, so that little effort was made to bring them under Spanish control. Where the Spanish exploited minerals and lands within the territories of these groups, they generally employed imported labor, and only when the Indians harassed their settlements did the Spanish attempt to control them by enslavement or extermination. In fact Indian slavery was forbidden in 1542, but it continued in remote parts of the empire, notably northern Mexico, southern Chile and Argentina, where the Indians proved exceptionally difficult to control.[18]

---

[16]For example, C. Gibson, *The Aztecs under Spanish Rule* (Stanford: Stanford University Press, 1964), pp. 220-21; C. Furtado, *Economic Development of Latin America: A Survey from Colonial Times to the Cuban Revolution* (Cambridge: Cambridge University Press, 1970), p. 10; M. Lucena Salmoral, "El Indofeudalismo Chibcha como explicación de la fácil conquista Quesadista," in *Estudios sobre política indigenista Española en América*, Vol. 1 (Valladolid: Universidad de Valladolid, 1975), pp. 111-60; Villamarin and Villamarin, *Indian Labor*, p. 29; M. Godelier, "The Concept of 'Social and Economic Formation': the Inca Example," in *Perspectives in Marxist Anthropology*, ed. M. Godelier (Cambridge: Cambridge University Press, 1977), pp. 68-69; I. Wallerstein, *Mercantilism and the Consolidation of the European World-Economy, 1600-1750* (New York and London: Academic Press, 1980), p. 174; S.J. Stern, *Peru's Indian Peoples and the Challenge of Spanish Conquest: Huamanga to 1640* (Madison: University of Wisconsin, 1982), pp. 27-50.

[17]H.E. Bolton, "The Mission as a Frontier Institution," *American Historical Review* 23 (1917):45; R. Benedict, "Two Patterns of Indian Acculturation," *American Anthropologist* 45 (1943):207-12.

[18]Service, "Indian-European Relations," p. 418; Harris, *Patterns of Race*, pp. 10-11. Slavery here means the right to dispose of an individual as a piece of property, not a condition of ill treatment or limited freedom of action.

Thus, although there were some exceptions, there was a fairly high degree of correlation between the nature of Indian societies and the institutions and mechanisms used to control and exploit them. These institutions disrupted the Indian way of life to varying degrees and thus had different demographic consequences. In general slavery was the most disruptive, followed by missionization and the encomienda-repartimiento.

Resources

The nature and degree of cultural and demographic change during the colonial period were also related to the intensity of contact between Indians and other races. This in turn was largely determined by the desirability of resources to be found in the area. Colonists settled in areas where there were mineral deposits, and where there were large sedentary Indian populations that could be employed in the development of commercial agriculture, and in particular in the raising of tropical crops. Indians employed in these activities were often overworked and ill-treated, whilst the demands the colonists made on Indian labor and lands undermined Indian communities, encouraged free labor, and fostered miscegenation. In the towns, mines and haciendas, miscegenation was rife, and the surrounding Indian communities experienced greater cultural and demographic changes.[19] Conversely, the lack of resources and the remoteness of Indian communities from centers of intense economic activity aided their survival.

THE STUDY AREA

Within the context outlined, the aim of this book is to study the demographic and cultural changes experienced by Indians in Honduras during the colonial period. The demographic history of Honduras is probably the least well known of all the Central American countries, and this study aims to identify trends in the Indian population, comparing them with those noted for other provinces of Central America, and focusing attention on regional variations within Honduras itself.

At the time of Spanish conquest Honduras was inhabited by Indian groups representative of two cultural types: chiefdoms and tribes (Figures 1 and 2). The nature of these societies at the time of Spanish conquest and the resources of the province directly influenced the pattern of conquest and colonization and thus the demographic and cultural changes experienced by the Indians.

The book is divided into three main sections by dates that are significant in terms of the process of demographic and cultural change: conquest and 1550. Reasons for choosing conquest are obvious and 1550 is considered appropriate since it marked the effective introduction of the New Laws, including the end of the Indian slave trade, and the loss of the seat of the *Audiencia*. A further division could have been made at 1720, which marked the beginning of the Bourbon administrative reforms, including the abolition of the encomienda, and the first signs of demographic recovery. However, since

[19]For example, Gibson, *Aztecs*, p. 144; F. Cámara Barbachano, "El mestizaje en Mexico," *Revista de Indias* 24 (1964):34; W. Jiménez Moreno, "El mestizaje y la transculturación en Mexiamérica," in *El mestizaje en la historia de Ibero-América* (Mexico: Instituto Panamericano de Geografía e Historia, 1961), p. 81; MacLeod, "Ethnic Relations," pp. 196-205.

these events did not significantly alter economic and social trends, a break at 1720 would not have illuminated the process of change, but rather would have broken its continuity. As such, although the book was originally divided into four major parts, it was later collapsed into three.

Within the two major sections of the book, the nature of Spanish conquest and colonization is outlined before the cultural and demographic changes consequent upon it are discussed. For the period up to 1550, the inadequacy of the evidence makes a precise comparison between the experiences of chiefdoms and tribes difficult, so that the nature of Spanish conquest and colonization and its impact on the Indian population is discussed for the country as a whole. Subsequently, Spanish activities within the regions occupied by chiefdom and tribal groups remained broadly distinct. In western and central Honduras the establishment of haciendas, towns and mines and associated activities directly affected Indian communities, as did the encomienda, repartimiento, and other exactions that made demands on Indian production and labor. In eastern Honduras, with the exception of the Olancho valley and Trujillo and its immediate hinterland, where Spanish activities were broadly similar though less intense than those in the central and western areas, the most important influences on Indian life were the missionaries and later the Zambos-Mosquitos who emerged on the Mosquito Shore. Following the discussion of the nature and distribution of outside influences, the cultural changes experienced by Indians in the distinct areas will be analyzed and finally the demographic trends in both regions described and compared. The fact that the activities of Spaniards and other non-Indian groups are described before the changes experienced by the Indians are considered, is not meant to suggest that the culture-contact process was unidirectional. Clearly the process was an interactive one in which innovative responses to the new economic, social, and political order accompanied Spanish demands for change. Nevertheless, many of the changes were precipitated by the arrival of the Spanish and it seems logical to describe the context within which the changes were occurring, before discussing the changes themselves.

The discussion of cultural changes experienced by the Indians in Honduras is uneven, reflecting the availability of documentary evidence, which in turn is related to the importance the Spanish attached to different regions. The larger Indian populations to be found in the chiefdom area attracted conquistadors and colonists from an early date and it was here that Spanish centers of administration and economic activity were located. Thus from the time of conquest there are accounts of these cultures by conquistadors, chroniclers, missionaries, and royal officials amongst others. For most of the tribal area, however, there is little evidence available until the end of the sixteenth century and even from that time onwards it is fragmentary, although it does improve during the colonial period as the area came into the sphere of European influence. As such, any reconstruction of Indian cultures in these areas at the time of conquest has to rely mainly on documentary evidence from the seventeenth and eighteenth centuries, prior to which they had undoubtedly experienced some degree of change as the result of intermittent and indirect contact with other races and cultures. Until more archaeological investigations have been conducted in this area, there is no alternative but to rely on the documentary evidence available. The analysis of the cultural changes experienced by Indians in eastern Honduras is made even more difficult by the variety of cultural influences to which they were exposed (Figure 1). Although the civilization and christianization of Indians in the tribal area were largely left to the missionary orders, on the western fringes of the area Indian communities were brought under Spanish administration and allocated in encomiendas. The picture is complicated even further by the settlement of the English on the Mosquito Shore and by the emergence of the Zambos-Mosquitos, who gradually extended their influence over the tribal groups from the east. Because of the variety of cultural influences to which Indians in the tribal area were exposed, the discussion of cultural changes experienced by them after 1550 will be divided into four sections: tributary Indian villages; the missions; Indians outside Spanish control; and residents on the Mosquito Shore. The last category poses a problem in terms of examining trends in the Indian population, because there were changes in the racial character of the population that involved the Indians in contributing to the emergence of a mixed race known as the Zambos-Mosquitos. As a mixed racial group the Zambos-Mosquitos as a whole cannot be classified as Indians any more than mestizos, and this is particularly true for the Honduran sector of the Shore, where the negro influence was strongest. As such, the Zambos-Mosquitos are not regarded as Indians at the end of the colonial period.

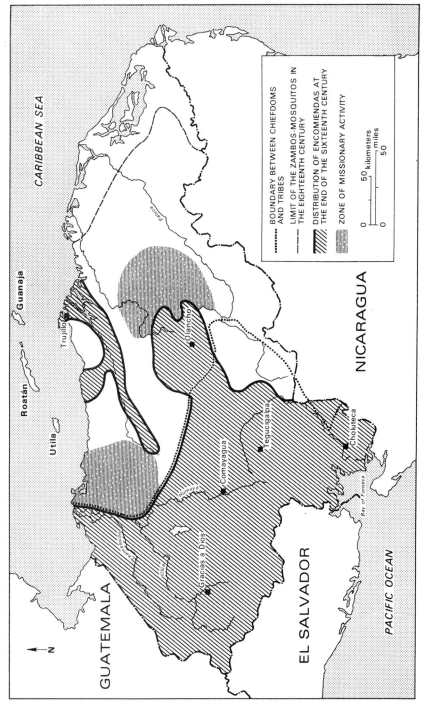

Figure 1. Zones of Cultural Influence During the Colonial Period

# Part II

Honduras on the Eve of
Spanish Conquest

# 2
# Indian Cultures and Environments

Recent attempts to classify the Indians of Spanish America have not always recognized the variety of cultural-linguistic groups that inhabited Honduras. Steward, in his original typology of South American cultures, identified a fourfold developmental sequence of Marginal, Tropical Forest, Circum-Caribbean and Sub-Andean, and Andean cultures. In this typology the whole of Central America, including Honduras, was classified as Circum-Caribbean.[1] Steward considered that the Circum-Caribbean culture was the foundation on which the Andean civilizations had been built. It was characterized by the presence of large sedentary farming communities, which were socially stratified and possessed some form of political organization, and had a priest-temple-idol complex.[2] According to Steward the origin of this cultural type was in the Andean area, from whence it spread to Central America, Colombia, Venezuela, and the Antilles. As it spread into the tropical forested lowlands it introduced new technologies, but it lost many of its sociopolitical, religious, and material elaborations. Hence the Tropical Forest type was seen as derivative from the Circum-Caribbean type, and was characterized by smaller villages formed by unstratified groups, who subsisted more on wild food resources, and whose religion was based on shamanistic practices.[3] A more recent analysis of cultural traits by Chapman using historical evidence has suggested that the tribes of eastern Honduras and Nicaragua should be classified as Tropical Forest cultures, since much of the cultural elaboration to be found there is the result of

---

[1]J.H. Steward, ed., *Handbook of South American Indians: The Marginal Tribes*, vol. 1, Bureau of American Ethnology Bulletin 143 (Washington, DC: Smithsonian Institution, 1946) pp. 4, 12.

[2]Ibid., pp. 6-9.

[3]J.H. Steward, ed., *Handbook of South American Indians: The Circum-Caribbean Tribes*, vol. 4, Bureau of American Ethnology Bulletin 143 (Washington, DC: Smithsonian Institution, 1948), pp. 11-15; idem, *Handbook of South American Indians: The Comparative Ethnology of South American Indians*, vol. 5, Bureau of American Ethnology Bulletin 143 (Washington, DC: Smithsonian Institution, 1949), pp. 769-71; J.H. Steward and L.C. Faron, *Native Peoples of South America* (New York: McGraw Hill, 1959), pp. 284, 453.

postconquest acculturation. She also rejects the proposed origin of the Tropical Forest culture as derivative from Circum-Caribbean culture and suggests that the Tropical Forest culture in Central America originated from a 'sweet manioc culture' that developed in northwest South America prior to and independent of any Circum-Caribbean culture. She suggests that the former was introduced to the area by Chibchan peoples a few thousand years before the Christian era.[4] In 1959 Steward modified his typology of South American cultures and changed the names of the types to give an indication of their characteristics; thus the Tropical Forest type was renamed Tropical Forest Farmers and the Circum-Caribbean type was called Theocratic and Militaristic Chiefdoms. He also recognized the presence of Tropical Forest peoples in Central America by indicating that northern and eastern Honduras was inhabited by Tropical Forest Farmers.[5]

The distinction between Indian groups inhabiting western and eastern Honduras was also effectively drawn by Kirchhoff, who in defining Mesoamerica on a cultural-linguistic basis, included within it western Honduras.[6] Kirchhoff's eastern boundary of Mesoamerica was later defined more precisely by Stone using archaeological, historical, and ethnological evidence. However, she admitted that the boundary was difficult to establish because of the natural blending of cultures at the margins of culture areas and the presence of cultural inliers and outliers within the major culture areas.[7] Similarly, Baudez maintains that there was no sharp break between Mesoamerican and other Central American cultures and that, although the cultures of the Pacific area possessed many traits characteristic of Mesoamerica, they were essentially marginal to the Mesoamerican civilization. As such, he prefers to talk of a zone of Mesoamerican tradition and a zone of South American tradition.[8] More recent writers, notably Sharer, Fox, and Henderson, have also suggested that the frontier of Mesoamerica should not be conceived as a sharp boundary, but as a broad zone of interaction between Mesoamerican and non-Mesoamerican peoples.[9] Since much of Honduras fell within this broad zone of interaction, the boundaries of cultural groups at the time of Spanish conquest are not easy to define. The following account is based primarily on historical sources, together with published archaeological and linguistic evidence. Although an attempt will be made to draw a line between the Maya on the one hand and the Lenca and Jicaque on the other, for reasons given above, this line should not be regarded as a sharp boundary defining Mesoamerica. Indeed the major distinction of interest for this study is between chiefdom

---

[4]A. Chapman, "An Historical Analysis of the Tropical Forest Tribes on the Southern Border of Mesoamerica" (Ph.D. diss., Department of Anthropology, Columbia University, 1958), pp. 158-67.

[5]Steward and Faron, *Native Peoples*, p. 13.

[6]P. Kirchhoff, "Mesoamérica," *Acta Americana* 1 (1943):92-107.

[7]D.Z. Stone, "The Eastern Frontier of Mesoamerica," *Mitteilungen aus dem Museum für Volkerkunde im Hamburg* 25 (1959):118-21.

[8]C.F. Baudez, *Central America* (London: Barrie & Jenkins, 1970), p. 227 n.2.

[9]R.J. Sharer, "The Prehistory of the Southeastern Maya Periphery," *Current Anthropology* 15 (1974):174; J.S. Henderson et al., "Archaeological Investigations in the Valle de Naco, Northwestern Honduras," *Journal of Field Archaeology* 6 (1979):191; J.W. Fox, "The Late Postclassic Eastern Frontier of Mesoamerica: Cultural Innovations Along the Periphery," *Current Anthropology* 22 (1981):322.

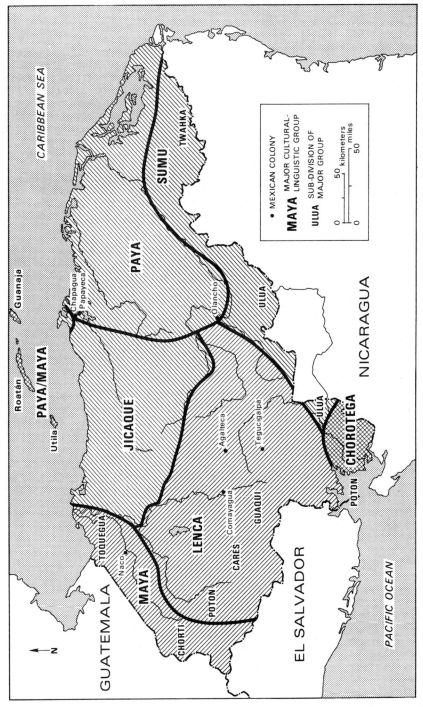

Figure 2. Distribution of Indian Cultures on the Eve of Spanish Conquest

and tribal groups, rather than between Mesoamerican and non-Mesoamerican peoples. Although there is a broad correspondence between the two classifications, they are not identical. Although the chiefdoms comprised a number of Mesoamerican groups--the Maya, Chorotega, Pipil, and Nahuatl--they also comprised the Lenca. Linguistically the Lenca are unaffiliated, although they show the least divergence from the Xinca in Guatemala and El Salvador;[10] culturally they appear to have been organizationally more complex than their neighbors to the east, and as such they are included amongst the chiefdom groups. The tribal groups comprised the Paya and Sumu (and later Mosquito), who belonged to the Macro-Chibchan linguistic stock, and the Jicaque. The latter are generally considered to belong to the Hokan stock found predominantly in North America, although the evidence for their affiliation is far from reliable.[11] The Jicaque are thought to have migrated to Central America at an early date--probably about 5,000 years ago--from whence they became acculturated to Chibchan culture.[12] Culturally they are most akin to the Paya and Sumu, and they are therefore regarded as a tribal group.

THE CHIEFDOMS

The Lenca

Although the Lenca inhabited the greater part of central Honduras at the time of Spanish conquest, there are few historical references to these Indians or their language. The earliest reference to the Lenca is contained in an account of an encomienda of the villages of Yngrigula, Renytala, and Alupare in 1543, which indicates that the latter two villages were Lenca.[13] Unfortunately the location of these villages is unknown. Stone suggests that the Lenca included a number of Indian groups known as the "Potón, Guaquí,

---

[10]J.A. Mason,. "The Native Languages of Middle America," in *The Maya and Their Neighbors*, ed. C.L. Hay et al. (New York: Appleton Century, 1940), pp. 74-75; D.Z. Stone, *The Archaeology of Central and Southern Honduras*, Papers of the Peabody Museum 49, no. 5 (Cambridge, MA: Harvard University Press, 1957)p. 4 n.8; idem, "Synthesis of Lower Central American Ethnohistory," in *Handbook of Middle American Indians*, vol. 4, ed. R. Wauchope (Austin: University of Texas Press, 1966), p. 210; T. Kaufman, "Mesoamerican Indian Languages," *Encyclopedia Britannica*, 15th ed., vol. 11 (of 24) (Chicago: Benton, 1974) p. 960; L.R. Campbell, "Distant Genetic Relationship and Diffusion: A Mesoamerican Perspective," *42nd International Congress of Americanists* (Paris) (1978) 4:595-605.

[11]Kaufman, "Mesoamerican Indian Languages," p. 960; L.R. Campbell, "The Linguistic Prehistory of the Southern Mesoamerican Periphery," in *Las fronteras de Mesoamerica*, XIV Mesa Redonda de la Sociedad Mexicana de Antropología, vol. 2 (Mexico, 1976), pp. 157-64.

[12]Chapman, "Tropical Forest Tribes," p. 48.

[13]AGI AG 52 Montejo 24.9.1543.

Cares, Chatos, Dules, Paracas, Yaras, possibly the Colo, and naturally the Guajiquiro if they are not already included under the term Guaquí."[14]

In 1576 Lic. Palacios recorded that Potón was spoken by Indians in San Miguel (Chiquimula) and Nicaragua, but he did not include it amongst the languages spoken in Honduras, which were "la ulba, chontal y pipil."[15] However, Herrera, following a letter written by Jerónimo de San Martín in 1537, recorded that "Potones" lived near Cerquín in the vicinity of Gracias a Dios, and in 1586 Fr. Alonso Ponce observed that "Potones" lived on the islands of Teca and Meangola in the Bay of Fonseca, as well as on the mainland in El Salvador.[16] In arguing that Potón was a Lenca language,[17] Stone indicates that Fr. Alonso Ponce clearly distinguished Potón from four known Maya dialects.[18] Fr. Alonso Ponce observed that "Potones" inhabited some islands in the Bay of Fonseca, which in the late seventeenth century fell under the jurisdiction of the convent of Amapala, where it was said that the Indians spoke "the Mexican language in general, and Lenca in some."[19] Other authors believe Potón was a Maya dialect; Sapper, for example, suggests that the Chol Maya called their language "Putum."[20] In a testimony presented by the Mercedarians in 1688 in support of their claim that they instructed the Indians in their native languages, witnesses testified that the language spoken in the partido of Aguanqueterique was Lenca and that this was distinct from the language

[14]Stone, *Central and Southern Honduras*, p. 4.

[15]CDI 6:5-40 ref. to p. 7 Palacios 8.3.1576.

[16]A. de Herrera y Tordesillas, *Historia general de los hechos de los castellanos en las islas i tierra firme del Mar Océano*, 17 vols. (Madrid: Real Academia de la Historia, 1934-57) 12 dec. 6 lib.3 cap.19:279; Fr. A. Ponce, *Relación breve y verdadera de algunas cosas que sucedieron al Padre Fray Alonso Ponce en las provincias de Nueva España* (Madrid: Viuda de Calero, 1873), pp. 381-82, 385-93.

[17]Stone, *Central and Southern Honduras*, pp. 84-85; idem, "Central American Ethnohistory," p. 213 n.21. Her conclusion is backed by Thompson (*Maya History and Religion*, p. 96).

[18]Ponce, *Relación breve*, pp. 383-84.

[19]Ibid., pp. 381-82; F. Vázquez, *Crónica de la provincia del Santísimo Nombre de Jesús de Guatemala*, vol. 4 (Guatemala: Sociedad de Geografía e Historia, 1937-44), pp. 62-63.

[20]W.E. Gates, "The Distribution of the Several Branches of the Mayance Stock," *Carnegie Institution of Washington Yearbook*, Publication no. 219 (Washington, DC, 1920), Appendix 12, p. 610; W. Lehmann, *Zentral-Amerika*, 2 vols. (Berlin: Dietrich Reimer, 1920), pp. 625-26, 643, 645-47, 823; Stone, *Central and Southern Honduras*, p. 84. Mason is more cautious; he refers to the Potón as "unclassified, probably Mayan" (Mason, "Native Languages of Middle America," p. 84).

spoken in Gracias a Dios and Tencoa, which most witnesses said was "Puttum."[21] It seems likely that the term "Puttum" referred to the Putun (Chontal Maya), who are thought to have inhabited the area around the Chamelecón valley.[22] However, the Potones found in southern Honduras were probably Lenca rather than Maya. This is supported by the fact that Lic. Palacios recorded that "Potón" was spoken in Nicaragua, which was certainly not inhabited by Mayan groups.

There is probably less controversy over the identification of the Cares, Guaquí, and Colo as Lenca groups, although it is largely based on historical evidence for their presence in areas which are thought to have been inhabited by the Lenca. In 1539 Bishop Pedraza noted that "the provinces of the cares and guaquí" were located in the jurisdiction of Gracias a Dios,[23] and Herrera recorded that they were to be found in the vicinity of Cerquín, near Gracias a Dios.[24] Since the Lenca leader Lempira combined with the Cares to oppose the Spanish and, since according to Herrera (following López de Velasco) Indians in this area "who were never at peace were those of a different tongue," Stone argues that the Cares must have been a Lenca group.[25] However, the same source makes it equally clear that the cooperation was only achieved by Lempira through the use of force; in fact his forces had to conquer "the Cares their enemies."[26] If Herrera's statement that those who were never at peace were those who spoke different languages is correct, then it is clear that the Cares and Potones cannot both be considered as Lenca groups, since just before the Spanish conquest these two groups had fought a bitter war. The evidence of a Lenca affiliation is slightly stronger for the Cares. Nevertheless, the Cares were clearly distinguished from the Lenca throughout the colonial period; in 1591 the Mercedarians had charge of four Indian parishes: Tencoa, de los Cares, Cururu, and de los Lencas.[27] Seventeenth century sources indicate that the centers of the partidos of the Cares and Lencas were Intibucá and Aguanqueterique respectively, with Lenca also spoken in the villages of Locterique, Curarén, Alubarén, and Reitoca.[28] Although the languages of the Cares and Lencas could be distinguished, the culture and distribution of the Cares suggest that they were probably a Lenca group.

---

[21]AGI AG 183 12.7.1683, AG 184 1688. The villages where it was spoken were: Telica, Yamala, Ylamatepeque, Teconalistagua, and Yguala. One witness suggested that the language spoken was "naguatle," which was used as a lingua franca throughout the area. Another said that in some villages in Tencoa "jucap" was spoken, the affiliation of which is unknown.

[22]Thompson, *Maya History and Religion*, pp. 6, 91.

[23]AGI AG 9 Pedraza 18.5.1539. Elsewhere he distinguishes the "Cares" from those of "Çarquín" (CDIU 11:400 Pedraza 1544).

[24]Herrera, *Historia General* 12 dec.6 lib.3 cap.19:279.

[25]Stone, *Central and Southern Honduras*, p. 5; Herrera, *Historia General* 9 dec.5 lib.8 cap.3:108--"los que no tenían paz eran los diferentes en la lengua."

[26]Herrera, *Historia General* 12 dec.6 lib.3 cap.19:279.

[27]AGI AG 164 Fr. Andrada, Bishop of Honduras 20.4.1591.

[28]AGI AG 184 Testimonio 1688; BNM 2675 f.453 Misiones de Mercedarias 1696; ANH P5 L68 Alcalde Mayor of Tegucigalpa and Choluteca 3.5.1698.

The province of "Guaquí" was also located in the vicinity of Gracias a Dios,[29] and it seems likely that it included the villages of Guajiquiro, Marcala, Chinacla, Yarula, Cacaoterique, and Opatoro, where the Indians today speak a language classified as Lenca.[30] Fr. Alonso Ponce observed that in Comayagua and Agalteca Colo was spoken,[31] which was probably a Lenca language. In 1553 the Mercedarians were given charge of the "*partido* de los Rencas (sic)," which included the villages of "Xeto, Comayagua, Lajamaní, Tencoxquín, Curucu and Orica."[32]

Evidence for the inclusion of the Chatos, Dules (Sules), Yaras, and Paracas as Lenca groups is even more problematic. In the eighteenth century the Chatos, Dules, and Yaras were living in the vicinity of Olancho El Viejo and in the headwaters of the Río Tinto.[33] It would appear that the Chatos and Dules were probably Lenca or perhaps Matagalpa, but the Yaras were almost certainly a Jicaque group.[34] The historical evidence that Stone presents for including the Paracas as a Lenca group is that Frs. Espino and Ovalle on a missionary expedition to the Olancho valley met "a family of Paraca Indians of the Lenca nation."[35] It is clear that the Paracas were less extensive in Honduras than in north-central Nicaragua, where Franciscan missionaries were active in converting them in the late seventeenth century. Lehmann believes that they were Matagalpan, a proposition that is generally supported by historical evidence of their location in the seventeenth century.[36]

---

[29]AGI AG 9 Pedraza 18.5.1539.

[30]F. Johnson, "Central American Cultures," in *Handbook of South American Indians*, vol. 4, Bureau of American Ethnology Bulletin 143 (Washington, DC: Smithsonian Institution, 1948), pp. 61-62; Stone, *Central and Southern Honduras*, p. 111. Squier identified the following villages as Lenca-speaking: Guajiquiro, Opatoro, Intibucá, and Similatón (E.G. Squier, "The Xicaque Indians of Honduras," *The Athenaeum*, no. 1624 (1858):760). D.G. Brinton (*The American Race* (New York: N.D.C. Hodges, 1891), p. 160), and Lehmann (*Zentral-Amerika* 2:668-70), accept this identification, the latter adding Chilanga to the Lenca dialects. However, Swadesh has recently suggested that Chilanga is a distinct language (M. Swadesh, "Lexicostatistic Classification," in *Handbook of Middle American Indians*, vol. 5, ed. N.A. McQuown (Austin: Texas University Press, 1967), p. 98.

[31]Ponce, *Relación breve*, p. 347.

[32]P. Nolasco Pérez, *Historia de las mercedarias en América* (Madrid: Revista 'Estudios,' 1966), p. 99.

[33]AGI AG 297 Fr. Betancurt 9.8.1698; AGCA A1.3 219 2466 Indians of Olancho El Viejo 6.6.1724; AGI AG 343 Rivera 5.4.1737; BAGG 1:29-39 ref. p. 32 Letona 20.7.1743; AGI AG 449 Navarro 30.11.1758 (Report 1744).

[34]Lehmann, *Zentral-Amerika* 2:631, 635. See the discussion of the Jicaque.

[35]Vázquez, *Crónica* 4:189; Stone, *Central and Southern Honduras*, p. 4.

[36]Lehmann, *Zentral-Amerika* 1:481-82, 2:631; Newson, *Indian Survival*.

Stone does not include the Popoluca as a Lenca group, although Brinton has suggested that they should be considered as such.[37] Popoluca is the Nahuatl word for a foreigner or one who speaks a different language, a term that could have been used by Mexicans to distinguish a distinct cultural-linguistic group.[38] In 1683 "Pupuluca" was spoken in the following villages: Tambla, Cururu, Opatoro, Cacaoterique, Guajiquiro, Similatón, Tatumbla, Jurla, Quelala, Reitoca, Chinacla, and Marcala--many of which have already been identified as Lenca villages.[39]

The distribution of the Lenca can be judged by place-name evidence. Lehmann has associated the Lenca with the following place-name endings: -tique, -quín, -aiquín, -guala, and -guara,[40] but clearly their distribution indicates their maximum extension rather than their location at the time of Spanish conquest. Archaeological evidence is also inconclusive. Stone has identified a variety of archaeological remains that provide evidence for a simpler indigenous culture than that associated with the Ulúa-Yojoa polychrome complex found further north in the Ulúa valley. These remains have been termed 'the Central American complex' and they are to be found throughout "the interior highlands, the area bordering the Comayagua Depression, the region of Tegucigalpa, the higher portions of the Choluteca Valley, and the Sierra and southwestern mountain area."[41] In addition Strong, Kidder, and Paul have attributed the Bold Animistic element of the Yojoa-Polychrome, found to the north of this area, to the Lenca.[42]

Due to the fragmentary and unreliable nature of the evidence of the distribution of the Lenca, many of the boundaries shown on the map are defined by the boundaries of other cultural-linguistic groups. To the west the Lenca bordered on the Maya and to the north they met the Jicaque. To the east, in the valley of Olancho they met the Paya,[43] whilst to the south and east they had the Sumu and Matagalpa as neighbors. The precise boundaries with these latter groups are difficult to define. The Lenca are known to have lived in the Olancho valley, along with the Taguacas,[44] who were a branch of the Sumu, the most extensive cultural-linguistic group in Nicaragua. On the basis of place-name evidence and the assumption that the Paracas can be identified as Lenca, Stone extends

---

[37]Brinton, *American Race*, p. 152.

[38]Ibid; F.V. Scholes and R.L. Roys, *The Maya Chontal Indians of Acalan-Tixchel: A Contribution to the History and Ethnography of the Yucatán Peninsula*, Carnegie Institution Washington, Publication no. 560 (Washington, DC, 1948), p. 92.

[39]AGI AG 184 Testimonio 1688 (Visita 1683).

[40]Lehmann, *Zentral-Amerika* 2:625, 636.

[41]Stone, *Central and Southern Honduras*, pp. 120-21.

[42]W.D. Strong, A.J. Kidder, and J.D. Paul, *Preliminary Report on the Smithsonian Institution-Harvard University Archaeology Expedition to North-Western Honduras 1936*, Smithsonian Institution Washington, Miscellaneous Collections 97, no. 1 (Washington DC, 1938), p. 123.

[43]Stone, *Central and Southern Honduras*, pp. 76-77, 80; and idem, "Central American Ethnohistory," p. 214.

[44]AGI AG 183 Frs. Ovalle and Guevara 4.3.1681, 22.3.1681; Vázquez, *Crónica* 4:123-24.

the area inhabited by the Lenca into northern Nicaragua.[45] There is some evidence to support this view in an account by Fr. Pedro de la Concepción in 1699, which records that in the area between the Olancho valley and the Río Segovia three languages were spoken: "Lenca, this is known by a few in the rivers of the Guaiape and is common in the river Segovia and that of the Tuma, the second is of Parrastas which is called Sampiz, the third of the Guaianes is called Guaiatuni."[46] Nevertheless, there are more frequent references to the Taguacas inhabiting this area.[47] It seems likely that in fact a number of Indian groups inhabited this eastern and southeastern region.

Similarly, in the south of the country a variety of languages were spoken. It will be demonstrated that the Chorotega were present in Choluteca, and that the Lenca were also to be found there in the seventeenth century at least. In 1689 Indians in Nacaome were regarded as Lencas and those of Guascorán and nearby villages of "Pororos, Amamoros, Zapigre, Aramesina, Langue, and Pipiri" were described as "Lencas and Mexicans who speak castellano," whilst a year later the convents of Nacaome and Tegucigalpa both contained friars who could speak "mexicana and lenca."[48]

## The Maya

From about AD 300 Maya cultural influences extended into western Honduras, probably reaching their maximum extension about AD 900. The origin of the Maya as manifested at Copán is difficult to determine, but, although some traits indicate close connections with the highlands, the general flavor of the whole stela complex found there is lowland Maya, and it seems likely that it originated in the Petén-Belize region passing through the upper Motagua and Copán valleys.[49] On the basis of archaeological evidence, Lothrop had placed the maximum extension of the Maya along a line following the Ulúa River and passing south to Lake Yojoa before swinging southwest to Gracias a Dios and the River Lempa.[50] Longyear places the eastern boundary of the Maya on the northern coast of Honduras at Santo Tomás de Castilla and argues that the boundary should not be placed further east than Los Higos on the Chamelecón, since this represents the furthest extension of the stela cult downvalley. Further south he places the boundary

---

[45]Stone, "Central American Ethnohistory," p. 213.

[46]AGI AG 223 and 297 Fr. Pedro de la Concepción 13.1.1699. The Tuma is a tributary of the Río Grande in Nicaragua.

[47]See the discussion of the Sumu.

[48]Vázquez, *Crónica* 4:31-32, 63-64.

[49]J.M. Longyear, *Copan Ceramics: A Study of Southeastern Maya Pottery*, Carnegie Institution Washington, Publication no. 597 (Washington, DC, 1952), p. 83; Thompson, *Maya History and Religion*, pp. 99-102.

[50]S.K. Lothrop, "The Southeastern Frontier of the Maya," *American Anthropologist* 41 (1939):49-53.

at the Jicatuyo River and the present-day boundary of the department of Copán.[51]  He maintains that although much of the Ulúa-Yojoa area came under Maya influence, the polychrome pottery to be found there comprises a distinct complex and that other features of the Maya "hierarchic" or ceremonial cult are absent in the region.

During the decline of the Maya civilization from AD 900 some of the ceremonial centers the Maya had possessed in Guatemala and western Honduras were abandoned and the boundary of the Maya area shifted westwards.  In the south the Maya probably only occupied the departments of Copán and Ocotepeque at the time of conquest,[52] although the boundary would have to be modified if the Potón were classified as Maya.  To the north the Maya probably did not extend further east than the Ulúa valley.  Archaeological evidence indicates that whilst Maya influence was strong in the area during the Late Classic period (AD 600 to AD 900), during the Postclassic period (AD 900 to AD 1500) it was replaced by southern influences with Chibchan or at least Central American affiliations.  Nevertheless, there is archaeological evidence for trading links between Utila Island and Maya sites in Belize in the form of Plumbate pottery and Red Ware.[53]  Using historical evidence, Thompson places the linguistic boundary of the Maya at the mouth of the Chamelecón.[54]  This is supported by an account in 1533, cited in Scholes and Roys, which recorded that "from Ulúa to the river of Copilco-zacualco [in western Tabasco] is all one language, and they all trade with one another and consider themselves to be the same...beyond the Ulúa river is yet another language."[55]  Although these sources clearly draw the boundary between the Maya and other languages at the Ulúa or nearby Chamelecón River, it has been suggested that at the time of conquest the Maya still extended as far as Trujillo.  Peter Martyr's account following Hernando Colón's description of Columbus's fourth voyage recorded that the north coast of Honduras was divided between the "Maia" and "Taia," and other documentary evidence suggests that

---

[51]J.M. Longyear, *Cultures and Peoples of the Southeastern Maya Frontier*, Carnegie Institution Washington, Division of Historical Research, Theoretical Approaches to Problems, no. 3 (Washington, DC, 1947), p. 9.

[52]Ibid., p. 9; Johnson, "Central American Cultures," p. 62.

[53]J.F. Epstein, "Late Ceramic Horizons in Northeastern Honduras," (Ph.D. diss., Department of Anthropology, University of Pennsylvania, 1957), p. 227, quoted in Chapman, "Tropical Forest Tribes," pp. 65-66; J.F. Epstein, "Dating the Ulua Polychrome Complex," *American Antiquity* 25 (1959):126, 128; P.F. Healy, "Los Chorotega y Nicarao: evidencia arqueológica de Rivas, Nicaragua," in *Las fronteras de Mesoamérica*, XIV Mesa Redonda de la Sociedad Mexicana de Antropologia, vol. 2 (Mexico, 1976), pp. 237-38, 240.

[54]Thompson, *Maya History and Religion*, pp. 89-102.  For other attempts at defining the linguistic boundary of the Maya, see C. Thomas and J.R. Swanton, *Indian Languages of Mexico and Central America and Their Geographical Distribution*, Bulletin of the Bureau of American Ethnology 44 (Washington, DC: Smithsonian Institution, 1911); Lehmann, *Zentral-Amerika*; and F. Johnson, "The Linguistic Map of Mexico and Central America," in *The Maya and Their Neighbors*, ed. C.L. Hay et al. (New York: Appleton Century, 1940), pp. 88-114.

[55]Scholes and Roys, *Maya Chontal*, p. 18.  The document cited is from AGI JU 1005-3-1, Petition on behalf of Montejo, 1533.

two distinct cultures were separated at Point Caxinas.[56] Whilst the Maya lived in the vicinity of Point Caxinas, further documentary evidence suggests that they formed trading colonies there, probably based on the production of cacao in the Aguan valley, and that they did not inhabit all of the north coast to the west. Lothrop cites Hernando Colón's account in support of his view that Maya traders were present on Guanaja and on the adjacent mainland.[57] Hernando Colón described how his brother, Bartolomé, met some traders on Guanaja, who said they were bound for New Spain, which Bartolomé later specified as "Maiam," which was probably Yucatán.[58] The traders could not have been Payas, since an Indian chief who subsequently went with them as their guide to the mainland to the west of Cabo de Gracias a Dios could not converse with Paya Indians there.[59] They are also unlikely to have been Jicaques, since there is no indication that this group was involved in seagoing trade at that time.[60] Hence, it seems likely that Maya traders were present on the Bay Islands and on the adjacent mainland near Point Caxinas. However, in the Bay Islands they were accompanied by the Paya and on the north coast from Point Caxinas to the Ulúa River the Jicaque were the dominant group.

It is unclear which Maya dialects were spoken in western Honduras. In 1535 Indians living in the hills around Naco were called Chontales, and in 1576 Lic. Palacios identified "Chontal" as one of the three languages spoken in Honduras, and more specifically from Chiquimula to Gracias a Dios.[61] Brinton and Thompson suggest that these Indians were Chortí Maya, and linguistic analyses indicate that Chortí was spoken around Copán, and that it was a branch of Chol.[62] Thompson, following the contemporary observation of Ximénez, also identifies the Toquegua as Chol Maya,

---

[56]J. Pinkerton, *A Modern Atlas* (Philadelphia: T. Dobson, 1812), pp. 126-27; P.H. Martyr D'Anghera, *De Orbe Novo*, ed. F. MacNutt, 2 vols. (London and New York: Knickerbocker Press, 1912): 1 dec.3 lib.4: 318; S.K. Lothrop, "The Word 'Maya' and the Fourth Voyage of Columbus," *Indian Notes*, Museum of the American Indian, Heye Foundation, 4 no. 4(1927):350.

[57]Lothrop, "The World 'Maya'," pp. 354-55.

[58]H. Colón, *Vida del Almirante Don Cristóbal Colón* (Mexico: Fondo de Cultura Económica, 1947), p. 274; Lothrop, "The World 'Maya'," p. 354.

[59]Pinkerton, *Modern Atlas*, p. 126; Colón, *Vida del Almirante*, p. 275; Chapman, "Tropical Forest Tribes," p. 51.

[60]Chapman, "Tropical Forest Tribes," p. 51.

[61]AGI AG 49 Celis 10.5.1535; CDI 6:5-40 ref. to pp. 7 and 35 Palacios 8.3.1576.

[62]E.G. Squier, *Notes on Central America* (New York: Harper & Bros., 1855), p. 385; Brinton, *American Race*, p. 149; Gates, "Mayance Stock," pp. 605-606, 610; A. Membreño, *Hondureñismos: vocabulario de los provincialismos de Honduras* (Tegucigalpa: Tip. Nacional, 1897), p. 193; J.E.S.Thompson, "The Maya Central Area at the Time of Spanish Conquest and Later: A Problem in Demography," *Proceedings of the Royal Anthropological Institute of Great Britain and Northern Ireland for 1966* (1967), p. 27; idem, *Maya History and Religion*, pp. 99-100; Campbell, "Linguistic Periphery," p. 176.

28

although Ximénez himself did not distinguish between Chol and Chortí.[63] Roys suggests that their name may have been derived from the Nahuatl word "toquaeuayo" meaning scalp, since many Mayan peoples shaved their heads.[64] In the seventeenth and eighteenth centuries these Indians lived along the coast of Honduras, particularly between Puerto Caballos and Santo Tomás de Castilla.[65] It would appear that Chol, Chontal, and Chortí are closely related variants of the same language, which at present is impossible to distinguish in the documentary record, although it is clear that they were all lowland Maya.[66]

## The Chorotega

The Chorotega probably represent the first definitely identifiable migration from the north into Central America.[67] On the basis of information collected from old Indian informants Torquemada relates that the Chorotega migrated south from Soconusco (Chiapas) as a result of oppression by the Olmecs.[68] When these groups arrived in Choluteca, an old man prophesied that the Chorotega would settle on the Pacific coast and would establish a good port near the island of Chira in the Gulf of Nicoya. Following the prophecy the Chorotega continued south and established themselves in western

[63]Fr. F. Ximénez, *Historia de la provincia de San Vicente de Chiapa y Guatemala*, 6 vols. (Guatemala: Sociedad de Geografía e Historia, 1929-71) 2 bk.4 ch.5:20; J.E.S. Thompson, "Sixteenth and Seventeenth Century Reports on the Chol Mayas," *American Anthropologist* 40 (1938):585; Scholes and Roys, *Maya Chontal*, p. 18.

[64]R.L. Roys, *The Indian Background of Colonial Yucatán*, Carnegie Institution of Washington, Publication no. 548 (Washington, DC: Carnegie Institution, 1943), p. 114.

[65]Ximénez, *Historia de la provincia* 2 bk.4 ch.5:20; Fr. A. de Remesal, *Historia general de las Indias occidentales y particular de la gobernación de Chiapa y Guatemala*, 2 vols. (Guatemala: Sociedad de Geografía e Historia, 1932-33) 2 bk.11 ch.20:582; F.A. Fuentes y Guzmán, *Historia de Guatemala: Recordación Florida*, vol. 2 (of 3) (Guatemala: Sociedad de Geografía e Historia, 1932-33), p. 302.

[66]Thompson, "Chol Mayas," pp. 584-90; Roys, *Indian Background*, pp. 113-14; Kaufman, "Mesoamerican Indian Languages," p. 959.

[67]Mason, "Native Languages," pp. 58-59; Johnson, "Central American Cultures," p. 63.

[68]Fr. J. de Torquemada, *Monarquía Indiana*, 3 vols. (Madrid: Nicholas Rodríguez, 1723) 1 lib.3 cap.40:332-33.

Nicaragua and Nicoya.[69] Torquemada states that the Nicarao left Soconusco at the same time, although later he refers to the Chorotega as those "who went first" (que iban en la delantera). The later arrival of the Nicarao in Central America is attested by historical and archaeological evidence, although it is not known by what time period. It has been calculated that the Nicarao arrived in Central America about AD 1200 and the Chorotega probably arrived in the ninth and tenth centuries AD.[70] It is possible, however, that, as Lothrop believes, they arrived much earlier. He suggests that the Chorotega were living in Honduras prior to Maya whose arrival caused their migration south.[71]

---

[69]The fact that the Nicarao had to fight the Chorotega to gain possession of lands they wished to inhabit on the isthmus of Rivas suggests that the Chorotega were already living there when the Nicarao arrived. Archaeological evidence supports the arrival of the Chorotega in Nicaragua and Nicoya about AD 800. The Chorotega have been associated with Nicoya polychrome wares, which exhibit influences from Mesoamerican cultures, including the Maya with whom they came into contact during their migration south. These pottery types have been dated between AD 800 and AD 1200 (S.K. Lothrop, *Pottery of Costa Rica and Nicaragua*, 2 vols., Contributions from the Museum of the American Indian, Heye Foundation 8 (1926), p. 390; W.D. Strong, "The Archaeology of Costa Rica and Nicaragua," in *Handbook of South American Indians*, vol. 4, Bureau of American Ethnology Bulletin 143 (Washington, DC: Smithsonian Institution, 1948), p. 141; Healy, "Chorotega y Nicarao," pp. 258-60; idem, *Archaeology of the Rivas Region, Nicaragua* (Waterloo, Ontario: Wilfrid Laurier U.P., 1980), pp. 336, 345). The Nicarao appear to have adopted Nicoya polychrome pottery, adding to it northern motifs often representing Mexican gods. Thus archaeological evidence gives backing to the proposition derived from historical accounts that the Chorotega arrived in Central America prior to the Nicarao. Although the evidence is inconclusive, it would appear that the Nicarao were arriving in Nicaragua about AD 1200 (Lothrop, *Pottery of Costa Rica*, p. 398; W.D. Strong, "The Archaeology of Costa Rica and Nicaragua," p. 141; Chapman, "Tropical Forest Tribes," p. 13; M.D. Coe, "Costa Rican Archaeology and Mesoamerica," *Southwestern Journal of Anthropology* 18 (1962):180; M. León-Portilla, *Religión de los Nicarao* (Mexico: Universidad Nacional Autónoma de Mexico, 1972), pp. 30-32; D.Z. Stone, *Pre-Columbian Man Finds Central America* (Cambridge, MA: Peabody Museum, 1972), pp. 171-72; Healy, "Chorotega y Nicarao," pp. 260-61; and idem, *Archaeology of the Rivas Region*, p. 339).

[70]For attempts to calculate the date of the migration based on historical accounts, see: Lothrop, *Pottery of Costa Rica*, p. 8; J.E.S. Thompson, *An Archaeological Reconnaissance in the Cotzumalhua Region, Escuintla, Guatemala*, Carnegie Institution Washington, Publication no. 574 (Washington, DC, 1948), p. 11; W. Jiménez Moreno, *Síntesis de la historia pre-Tolteca de Mesoamérica esplendor del México antiguo*, 2 vols. (Mexico: Centro de Investigaciones Antropológicas, 1959), p. 1077; A. Chapman, *Los Nicarao y los Chorotega según las fuentes históricas*, Serie Historia y Geografía 4 (San José: Universidad de Costa Rica, 1960), pp. 74-75; León-Portilla, *Religión de los Nicarao*, pp. 32-33.

[71]Lothrop, *Pottery of Costa Rica*, pp. 93-94, 394, 416. He suggests that some Chorotega moved north to Chiapas as a result of this displacement.

The Chorotega belong to the Oto-Manguean linguistic stock and the language they spoke in Honduras was referred to as Choluteca or Mangue.[72] In the sixteenth century the Chorotega were living around the Bay of Fonseca, where they bordered on the Ulúa and Lenca. The area was often referred to as Chorotega Malalaca or Chorotega Malaca.[73] In 1586 Fr. Alonso Ponce recorded that Mangue was spoken in Nicomongoya and Nacarahego in Choluteca, and it is possible that it may have been spoken further west in El Salvador.[74] It is not clear whether the Chorotega who were living there at the time of conquest were representatives of the original migration of the Chorotega south to Nicaragua or whether they had arrived there recently as a result of their displacement north from the Pacific coastal plain of Nicaragua by the Nicarao.

### The Pipil and Nahuatl

Central America was at various times influenced by the migration of Nahua-speaking peoples into the area. There appear to have been two migrations that affected Honduras: one of Nahuat-speaking peoples, known as Pipil, and a later one of Aztec traders who spoke a more recent dialect known as Nahuatl. The Pipil probably arrived during the ninth and tenth centuries AD, about the same time as the Chorotega, whilst Aztec traders began to establish colonies in the area between the fourteenth and sixteenth centuries.[75] Stone believes that there was an earlier migration of Nahuat-speaking peoples into Honduras between AD 300 and AD 600. Some scholars maintain that this migration did not extend to Honduras, but Stone argues that the presence of artifacts at Travesía and Playa de los Muertos in the Sula plain indicates more than just a mere

---

[72]Johnson, "Central American Cultures," pp. 63-64; Chapman, *Los Nicarao*, p. 79; Kaufman, "Mesoamerican Indian Languages," p. 959.

[73]AGI PAT 26-5 and CS 1:457-70 Cerezeda 20.1.1529, JU 1030-2 and CS 2:95-100 Diligencias . . . sobre poblar Chorotega Malaca 2.9.1529, PAT 26-5 and CS 2:283-7 Pedrarias 25.11.1529; G. Fernández de Oviedo y Valdés, *Historia general y natural de las Indias, islas y tierra firme del Mar Océano*, 5 vols. (Madrid: Ediciones Atlas, 1959) 4 lib.39 cap.3:347.

[74]Ponce, *Relación breve*, pp. 337-38; Lehmann, *Zentral-Amerika* 2:647; D.Z. Stone, "Los grupos Mexicanos en la América Central y su importancia," *Antropología e historia de Guatemala* 1 (1949):44.

[75]Lehmann, *Zentral-Amerika* 2:978-80; P. Rivet, P. Stresser-Péan, and C. Loukotka, "Langues du Méxique et de l'Amérique," in *Langues du Monde*, eds. A. Meillet and M. Cohen (Paris: Centre National de la Recherche Scientifique, 1952), pp. 1057-60; E. Wolf, *Sons of the Shaking Earth* (Chicago and London: University of Chicago Press, 1959), pp. 36-42; Chapman, "Tropical Forest Tribes," p. 13.

influence from central Mexico and may be due to the presence of Nahuat-Pipil in the area, or else to diffusion from Copán, which shows evidence of Nahuat culture at this time.[76] Although these migrations were distinct, the documentary record is sometimes confusing with respect to the languages that were spoken by these groups. Many documents just describe the language spoken as 'mexicana' or 'pipil,' which could refer to either of these two groups. Sometimes, however, the terms 'mexicana corrupta' or 'pipil corrupta' were used. These terms clearly referred to Nahuat dialects that were held in contempt by later Nahuatl speakers. Vázquez, for example, referred to "mexicana corrupta or pipil (as we would say the language of children or that spoken by those of little intelligence)."[77] Another problem in relating languages to specific Indian groups is that even where documents do refer to Indians speaking Nahuatl it does not necessarily mean that it was their native language. Nahuatl was used as a lingua franca in the early colonial period and in many cases was introduced by the Spanish.[78] Place-name evidence is also unreliable for the same reason. Whilst some villages with Mexican names may indeed have been inhabited by Mexicans in the pre-Columbian period, others were given those names during the early colonial period. Unfortunately there is little archaeological evidence for the presence of Mexican cultures in Central America that would help to clarify the picture painted in the documentary record; Lothrop suggests that Mexicans tended to adopt the culture of the Indian groups they met in the course of their migrations, and their intermarriage with them might explain the relative lack of material evidence of Mexican culture.[79]

## The Pipil

At the time of conquest Pipil were probably living in an area to the south and east of the Bay of Fonseca. In 1586 Fr. Alonso Ponce recorded that "indios navales" formerly lived at Ciuatepetl, but had recently moved to El Viejo; and that they spoke "mexicana corrupta and they call it naual, and those who speak it nahuatlatos."[80] Although the name of the language suggests that these people were descendants of early Pipil migrants,

[76]D.Z. Stone, "Nahuat Traits on the Sula Plain, Northwestern Honduras," *38th International Congress of Americanists* (Stuttgart-München) (1968) 1:532-33; idem, *Pre-Columbian Man*, pp. 112-15, 136, 142-51. She suggests that the second migration occurred between AD 700 and AD 900 and entered Honduras via a northern route through Tabasco, the Petén, and Golfo Dulce. Finally a third migration took place about AD 100 following the same route. Scharer, "Southeastern Maya Periphery," pp. 172-76, notes Pipil influences in El Salvador in the Classic (AD 600) and early Postclassic (AD 1100) but it is not clear that they were all the result of migrations; they may have been due to trade or diffusion.

[77]Vázquez, *Crónica* 4:81.

[78]Roys, *Indian Background*, p. 114; Wolf, *Shaking Earth*, p. 41; Kaufman, "Mesoamerican Indian Languages," p. 962.

[79]S.K. Lothrop, "South America as Seen from Middle America," in *The Maya and Their Neighbors*, ed. C.L. Hay, et al. (New York: Appleton Century, 1940), p. 427; Stone, *Central and Southern Honduras*, p. 127.

[80]Ponce, *Relación breve*, pp. 352, 379.

Oviedo's description of the town of El Viejo and the culture of the Indians living there suggests that they probably constituted an outlier of the Nicarao who migrated to the area at a later date and who did not establish permanent settlements in Honduras.[81]  In the seventeenth century Indians living in the vicinity of Guascorán were described as "indios lencas y mexicanos," whilst those who fell under the jurisdiction of the convent at Amapala in the Bay of Fonseca were noted as speaking "the mexican language in general and lenca in some."[82]  It is possible that these Indians were descendants of early Pipil migrants, however, the Mexican language could have been introduced during the colonial period.  Johnson has suggested that possible descendants of early Pipil migrants are to be found around Ocotepeque.[83]

Other descendants of early Pipil migrants were probably living near Trujillo at Papayeca and Chapagua.  These towns had eighteen and ten villages respectively under their jurisdictions and their inhabitants spoke to Cortés and his representatives in Culua, which was described as almost the same as Mexican, but with a slightly different pronunciation and vocabulary.[84]  In addition, later in the sixteenth century the Bishop of Honduras sent some "indios naguatatos" with some other caciques from around Trujillo to the surrounding hills in order to persuade Indians who had taken refuge there to return to their villages.[85]  These accounts suggest that the dialect spoken by some Indians in the vicinity of Trujillo was Nahuat.

At the time of conquest there was a Mexican colony at Naco, but it is unclear whether its inhabitants were Pipil or Aztec traders.  At the time of conquest it was reported that Naco had been settled by people who "came from the Southern Sea," which suggests that they were Pipil who had come from El Salvador or Soconusco.[86]  In 1535 Indians living in the valley of Naco were described as "cholutecas," who were said to have subjugated the Chontales who were living in the hills.[87]  Although it seems unlikely that the "cholutecas" were an outlier of the Chorotega, the evidence suggests that the area was inhabited by early Mexican migrants.  The presence of an elite group at Naco has been testified by archaeological evidence, and Henderson suggests that elements of Cortés Polychrome to be found in the Late Postclassic period may indicate the presence of a Pipil group, though he suggests that the town was basically Maya.  However, Strong

---

[81]Oviedo, *Historia general* 4 lib.42 cap.11:413-14.

[82]Vázquez, *Crónica* 4:32-33, 62-64.

[83]Johnson, "Central American Cultures," p. 62.

[84]D.E. de Vedia, "Cartas de relación de Fernando Cortés," in *Historiadores primitivos de Indias*, vol. 1 (Madrid:  Los Sucesores de Hernando, 1918), pp. 142-43 Cortés 3.9.1526 "y los torné a hablar con la lengua que conmigo llevé, por que la de Culua y esta es casi una, excepto que difieren en alguna pronunciación y en algunas vocablos."

[85]AGI AG 968B Bishop of Honduras, no date.

[86]CDI 14:244 Moreno 1525; Stone, *Pre-Columbian Man*, p. 190.

[87]AGI AG 49 Celis 10.3.1535.

considered the Mexican influence to be late and attributed it to the Nahuatl,[88] and Chapman has suggested that Naco was one of the 'ports of trade' that the Aztecs established in Central America.[89] Certainly the town was located in an important commercial area, for in 1535 the valley of Naco was described as "highly populated and of much trade on account of the cacao which is grown there."[90] It appears that Naco was located on a major trade route from Tabasco to Nicaragua, the Nito to Naco stretch of which was described by Díaz del Castillo.[91]

The Nahuatl

Apart from Naco, there is some evidence to suggest that Aztec traders may have established colonies in Honduras at Comayagua, Agalteca, Olancho, and Tegucigalpa, but it is inconclusive. Fr. Alonso Ponce recorded that Indians in villages around Comayagua spoke "colo and others mexicana or pipil," whilst at a later date Vázquez noted that five villages under the care of the convent of San Antonio in Comayagua were being administered in "naguatle."[92] The name of the town is thought to have been derived from the Aztec Comalhuacán or 'place of the comales,' *comales* being used in making *tortillas*.[93] In all these cases, however, the Mexican influence could have been introduced during the colonial period, and unfortunately there is no archaeological evidence to clarify the picture. Pottery similar to that found at Naco, which Strong has associated with the Aztecs, has been found at Agalteca about 30 miles east of Comayagua.[94] Stone sees further support for an Aztec colony at Agalteca in that it was one of the most important Indian villages in northern Honduras during the early colonial period and that it was located between Naco and the valley of Olancho, where it is suggested there may have been other Mexican colonies. In 1586, however, Fr. Alonso Ponce observed that the Indians living in Agalteca spoke colo, which was probably a

---

[88]J.S. Henderson, "The Valley de Naco: Ethnohistory and Archaeology in Northwestern Honduras," *Ethnohistory* 24 (1977):372-73; Henderson et al., "Archaeological Investigations," p. 190.

[89]Strong, Kidder, and Paul, *Preliminary Report*, pp. 9-10, 118, 123; W.D. Strong, "Anthropological Problems in Central America," in *The Maya and Their Neighbors*, ed. C.L. Hay et al. (New York: Appleton Century, 1940), p. 380; A. Chapman, "Port of Trade Enclaves in Aztec and Maya Civilizations," in *Trade and Market in Early Empires*, eds. K. Polanyi, C.M. Arensberg, and H.W. Pearson (New York: Free Press, 1957), pp. 114-53; Thompson, *Maya History and Religion*, pp. 74, 78-79. Roys, *Indian Background*, p. 118, suggests that the Mexicans may have been Olmecs.

[90]AGI AG 49 Celis 10.3.1535.

[91]Roys, *Indian Background*, p. 117; B. Díaz del Castillo, *Historia verdadera de la conquista de la Nueva España*, vol. 2 (Mexico: Editorial Porrua, 1960), p. 210.

[92]Ponce, *Relación breve*, p. 347; Vázquez, *Crónica* 4:355.

[93]J. Ypsilantys de Moldavia, *Monografía de Comayagua, 1537-1937* (Tegucigalpa: Tip. Nacional, 1937), p. 46.

[94]Stone, *Central and Southern Honduras*, p. 73.

Lenca language.[95]  Historical evidence from the seventeenth century suggests that Mexicans were living in the Olancho valley. Vázquez relates that Fr. Verdelete and Fr. Monteagudo on a missionary expedition to the Olancho valley met Lencas and Mexicans living together, and that the Mexicans conducted wars with the Taguacas.[96]  Finally another Aztec colony may have been located at Tegucigalpa.  Vázquez de Espinosa relates how Montezuma used to send down a delegation to the "province of Tegusgalpa" to collect tribute in gold and other valuables.[97]  Whilst the province of Taguzgalpa was a vast area comprising much of eastern Honduras and Nicaragua, Aztec objects have been found in the city of Tegucigalpa.[98]

## THE TRIBAL GROUPS

The areas of eastern Honduras and Nicaragua where unconverted Indians remained outside Spanish control were known as Taguzgalpa and Tologalpa.  The boundary between the two areas was generally taken to be the Río Tinto or Río Segovia, but occasionally the whole area as far south as the San Juan River was called Taguzgalpa.[99]  There appear to have been six major Indian groups inhabiting these areas, four of which were to be found in Honduras--the Jicaque, Paya, Lenca, and Sumu. Nevertheless in the documentary record there are a multitude of names for Indians living in this area not all of which can be assigned with any degree of certainty to any one of these major groups.  For example, in 1681 Frs. Ovalle and Guevara reported that the nations living in Taguzgalpa were "Xicaques, Paias, Taos, Aras, Guaulas, Taupanes, Lencas and Tagucas."[100]  The picture is further confused by the fact that a large number of these and other groups were often referred to by generic names such as 'Xicaque' or 'Caribe,' so that it is not always clear precisely which Indian group is being discussed. The situation is most confused for the area from the Olancho valley south to the headwaters of the Río Segovia, which was inhabited by a diversity of Indian groups whose location did not remain constant over time.  With these difficulties in mind an attempt will be made to identify the areas inhabited by the major Indian groups at the time

---

[95]Ponce, *Relación breve*, p. 347.

[96]Vázquez, *Crónica* 4:107; D. Juarros, *A Statistical and Commercial History of the Kingdom of Guatemala* (London, 1823), p. 350.

[97]A. Vázquez de Espinosa, *Compendium and Description of the West Indies*, Smithsonian Institution of Washington, Miscellaneous Collections No. 102 (Washington, DC, 1942), p. 247.

[98]J. Ypsilantys de Moldavia, *Monografía de la Parroquia del Señor San Miguel de Heredia de Tegucigalpa* (Tegucigalpa: Tip. Nacional, 1944), p. 12.

[99]AGI AG 371 Fr. Ximénez 9.9.1748; A.R. Vallejo, *Historia documentada de los límites entre la República de Honduras y las de Nicaragua, El Salvador y Guatemala* (New York, 1938), pp. 30-31; Vázquez, *Crónica* 4:78-79.

[100]AGI AG 183 Frs. Ovalle and Guevara 4.3.1681.

of Spanish conquest, although much of the evidence will necessarily be drawn from the documentary record of the seventeenth and eighteenth centuries.

## The Jicaque

During the sixteenth century the term Jicaque (sometimes spelt Xicaque or Hicaque) appears to have been used by Mexicans to describe the original non-Mexican inhabitants of Honduras,[101] but later it was applied more widely to any heathen or hostile Indian group as far south as Nicaragua and Costa Rica.[102] Thus in 1681 Franciscans were active in converting "indios infieles jicaques de las naciones payas, yaras y letas," in northern Honduras, whilst Vázquez relates how the "lencas and taguacas (who are all xicaques)" killed two missionaries in the valley of Olancho at the beginning of the seventeenth century.[103] Despite the confusion in the use of the terms Jicaque and Xicaque, Greenberg and Swadesh have identified Jicaque as a distinct language, which they maintain belongs to the Hokan-Sioux linguistic stock.[104] Most authors now use the term Jicaque to refer to the cultural-linguistic group, and the term Xicaque when they are using it generically.[105]

Archaeologically the Jicaque, together with the Paya, have been associated with the ceramic style known as North Coast Appliqué, which has been found with some variations from the Yoro mountains to the Patuca River.[106] This style has a definite 'South American' flavor of Chibchan character. Similar ceramics have been found by Stone at the historic Paya site of San Esteban de Tonjagua and at the historic Jicaque sites of Cangelica and Subirana, although there the ceramics appear to have degenerated from

---

[101]D.Z. Stone, "The Ulua Valley and Lake Yojoa," in *The Maya and Their Neighbors*, ed. C.L. Hay et al, p. 389; idem, "A Delimitation of the Area and Some of the Archaeology of the Sula-Jicaque Indians of Honduras," *American Antiquity* 7 (1942):376; Roys, *Indian Background* p. 118.

[102]For example, AGI AG 181 Bishop of Nicaragua 15.7.1683, AG 223 Testimonio . . . sobre reducir los indios jicaques 1712 (16.1.1699); MNM Bª-XII Cª-C n°2 late eighteenth century; Juarros, *Statistical and Commercial History*, p. 62.

[103]AGCA A1.12 161 1687 1.8.1681; Vázquez, *Crónica* 4:123.

[104]J.H. Greenberg and M. Swadesh, "Jicaque as a Hokan Language," *International Journal of American Linguistics* 19 (1953):216.

[105]Lehmann, *Zentral-Amerika* 2:631; Stone, "Sula-Jicaque Indians"; Chapman, "Tropical Forest Tribes," p. 40.

[106]W.D. Strong, *Archaeological Investigations in the Bay Islands, Spanish Honduras*, Smithsonian Institution, Miscellaneous Collections vol. 92, no. 14 (Washington, DC, 1935), pp. 169-70; D.Z. Stone, *Archaeology of the North Coast of Honduras*, Memoirs of the Peabody Museum, Harvard University vol. 9, no. 1 (Cambridge, MA: Harvard University Press, 1941), p. 42; W.D. Strong, "The Archaeology of Honduras," in *Handbook of South American Indians*, vol. 4, Bureau of American Ethnology Bulletin 143 (Washington, DC: Smithsonian Institution, 1948), pp. 114-15; Chapman, "Tropical Forest Tribes," p. 65; Epstein, "Dating the Ulua Polychrome," pp. 126, 128.

an earlier prehistoric form found in the Bay Islands and throughout the Paya country.[107] As yet there is no archaeological material that can definitely be identified with the Jicaque in preconquest times.[108]

The earliest historical reference to the Jicaque comes from a letter from a *vecino* of Trujillo in 1579, which described their attacks on both Indians and Spaniards along the coast saying that they had depopulated many Indian villages including those of Montexucar, Guacura, and Moaca.[109] Throughout the colonial period the terms Jicaque and Xicaque were applied to groups that have since been identified as Paya, Lenca, Sumu, and Matagalpa. In the eighteenth century it was most consistently applied to Indian groups inhabiting the area between the Ulúa River and Trujillo, and inland as far south as the Sulaco River.[110] In 1798 Governor Anguiano recorded that they lived in an area that measured 32 leagues north-south from the north coast, and 20 leagues east-west between the Ulúa and Cuero rivers.[111]

The western boundary of the Jicaque at the time of conquest was probably the Ulúa valley, although Chapman maintains that during the eighteenth century they extended further west.[112] She maintains that Fr. Fernández founded the Jicaque villages of San Josef de Guaima and Nuestra Señora de la Candelaria in the Ulúa valley. The document to which she refers makes no precise reference to the Ulúa valley and it seems more likely that the former settlement was established in the Guaimas valley, possibly at the present-day site of San José, where Jicaque Indians were living at the end of the eighteenth century.[113] The information relating to the settlement of Nuestra Señora de la Candelaria is more obscure. There are several villages with the name Candelaria either side of the Ulúa valley and it is not certain that the settlement founded by Fr. Fernández was in fact the same Candelaria to which she refers.[114] An account by the engineer Navarro in 1744 may help to clarify the picture. He reported that

---

[107]Stone, *North Coast of Honduras*, p. 20; idem, "Sula-Jicaque Indians," pp. 379-81.

[108]Longyear, *Southeastern Maya Frontier*, p. 10.

[109]AGI AG 55 López 1579.

[110]BAGG 5:59-75 Testimonio . . . misión de los indios jicaques 1752, BAGG 1:213-256 ref. to p. 219 Consulta de Fr. Ortiz 1768; AGI AG 449 Navarro 30.11.1758 (Report 1744), IG 1525 and AG 457 Anguiano 1.7.1798, AG 501 Anguiano 10.5.1804.

[111]AGI AG 457 Anguiano 1.7.1798.

[112]Lehmann, *Zentral-Amerika* 2:631; Roys, *Indian Background*, p. 119; Chapman, "Tropical Forest Tribes," p. 43.

[113]BAGG 7:74-79 Dictamen del Diputado 1813; AGI AG 457 Anguiano 1.7.1798 and accompanying map MP 272B 1798.

[114]AGI AG 546 Notes on a journey . . . by the President 1.11.1768; AGCA A1.73 390 3662 1771; Chapman, "Tropical Forest Tribes," p. 43.

the villages nearest to the coast are: in the *partido* of San Pedro Sula, Candelaria Viejo, which is a small Indian village distant from Omoa and Puerto Caballos by 12 leagues of reasonable road, these Indians are defenceless; in the *partido* of Lloro [Yoro] is the village of Candelaria Nueva next to the Lean river, which is very small and of Jicaque Indians converted a few years ago.[115]

The village located west of the River Ulúa was probably Nuestra Señora de la Candelaria Masca, which was in existence in the sixteenth century, if not before, and which was described by Cockburn in 1735.[116] There is no archaeological evidence for the Jicaque west of the Ulúa valley.[117]

Although it seems unlikely that the Jicaques were living to the west of the Ulúa River before the end of the eighteenth century, by the nineteenth century they had established themselves there. In 1813 the Guardian of the Recollects in Guatemala reported that the Jicaque inhabited the mountains inland from the north coast between Omoa and Trujillo, and that although they appeared as "one nation," their dialects were different.[118] In the middle of the nineteenth century about 1,000 Jicaques were living in the department of Santa Barbara, of which 400 were to be found on the Choloma River, and later in the century Membreño recorded a Jicaque vocabulary from the village of El Palmar, near San Pedro.[119] Linguistic studies have indicated that the Jicaque dialects spoken to the west and east of the Ulúa valley are distinct.[120]

There is some doubt as to whether the Jicaque extended to the north coast at the time of conquest. It has been shown that the Maya inhabited parts of the north coast as far as Point Caxinas and Stone suggests that in fact they may have pushed the Jicaque back from the coast or else inhabited the area with them.[121] In 1744 engineer Navarro reported that the Jicaque traded with the English along the coast at the ports of Puerto Caballos, Sal, River Lean, and Trujillo, and in 1798 it was stated that the Jicaque had formerly lived on the coast but that they had retired inland due to hostile raids by the Zambos-Mosquitos and English.[122] It seems most likely that Maya and Pipil or Nahuatl

---

[115]AGI AG 449 Navarro 30.11.1758 (Report 1744).

[116]For example, BAGG 10:5-19 ref. to p. 16. Relación de todos los pueblos 1582; J. Cockburn, *A Journey Overland, from the Gulf of Honduras to the Great South Sea* (London: C. Rivington, 1735), pp. 23-25.

[117]Stone, "Sula-Jicaque Indians," p. 386.

[118]AGI AG 963 Guardian of Recollects 10.1.1813 "en partes son diferentes sus dialectos e ingenio."

[119]E.G. Squier, "Xicaque Indians," p. 760; Membreño, *Hondureñismos*, p. 195.

[120]Membreño, *Hondureñismos*, p. 195; Lehmann, *Zentral-Amerika* 2:634; E. Conzemius, "The Jicaques of Honduras," *International Journal of American Linguistics* 2 (1921-23):163; Campbell, "Linguistic Periphery," pp. 157-58.

[121]Stone, *North Coast of Honduras*, pp. 15, 93.

[122]AGI AG 449 Navarro 30.11.1758 (Report 1744); AGCA A1.12 118 2487 Anguiano 13.4.1798.

traders were localized around Trujillo and on the Bay Islands, whilst the Jicaque were to be found along the coast to the west, and the Paya from there to the east.[123]

The southeastern boundary of the Jicaque is difficult to define. It may be placed too far south on the accompanying map, but there are a number of references suggesting that Jicaques were present in the Olancho valley. For example, in 1600 the President of the Audiencia of Guatemala, Alonso Criado de Castilla, reported that 500 "xicoaques indios de guerra" had been settled next to the village of Olancho, which was located at a site later identified as "the place which they call the river of the stones [rio de las piedras] in the Olancho valley."[124] However, it is possible that the President was using the term "xicoaques" generically. Throughout the seventeenth century Jicaques were active in attacking settlements in the valley of Olancho,[125] but it is unclear whether they lived there. The Olancho valley was clearly inhabited by a large number of tribes, for in 1674 a mission settlement was established in the Olancho valley of 200 Indians "of different nations and languages."[126] In 1698 there appear to have been three major Indian groups living in the Guayape and Guayambre valleys: "Lencas, Parrastas y Yaras."[127] The Parrastas were probably Sumu, and since it was noted that the Payas and Yaras were distinct, the Yaras could not have been Payas; they were probably Jicaques.[128] The mixed character of the Indian inhabitants of this region was also recorded by engineer Navarro, who noted that "the said river [Tinto] comes down from the mountains where the Chatos, Payas and Jicaques live which are in the area which borders on the jurisdictions of Tegucigalpa and Comayagua."[129]

The eastern boundary of the Jicaque will be defined by the Paya to be discussed next; the southern boundary was probably on the Sulaco River, where Stone has identified a Jicaque site, but with Mexican influence.[130] In the nineteenth century Brinton observed that the Jicaque had "their seats on the waters of the Río Sulaque and Río Choloma."[131]

---

[123]Chapman, "Tropical Forest Tribes," p. 52.

[124]AGI AG 11 Criado de Castilla 15.5.1600, AG 12 Criado de Castilla 30.1.1608.

[125]For example, CDHCN 170-5 Bishop of Guatemala 15.11.1677; AGI AG 39 Godoy y Ponce de León 15.3.1676; Vázquez, *Crónica* 4:123; Juarros, *Statistical and Commercial History*, p. 369.

[126]M. Serrano y Sanz, *Relaciones históricas y geográficas de América Central* (Madrid: Librería de V. Suarez, 1908), p. 373 Fr. Espino 17.9.1674.

[127]AGI AG 297 Fr. Betancurt 8.9.1698.

[128]BAGG 5:283-308 Fr. Ovalle 11.9.1675; AGI AG 183 Frs. Ovalle and Guevara 4.3.1681, AG 343 Teniente of Olancho 5.4.1737; Brinton, *American Race*, 163; Lehmann (*Zentral-Amerika* 2:629, 631, 635) considers the Yaras to be Jicaques.

[129]AGI AG 449 Navarro 30.11.1758 (Report 1744).

[130]Stone, "Sula-Jicaque Indians," p. 386.

[131]Brinton, *American Race*, p. 161.

## The Paya

*[the Payas] were never / that far east* (handwritten)
*Toponyms* (handwritten)
*Petroglyphs* (handwritten)

The Paya language is considered by ⟨...⟩ chan,[132] although some linguists believe it to be an ⟨...⟩ ibited the area immediately to the east and south of th⟨...⟩ rea to the east of Point Caxinas was inhabited by ⟨...⟩ been a corruption of Paia or Paya.[134]  According ⟨...⟩ ibited the area to the east of the Aguan River as far ⟨...⟩ ast as far south as Cabo de Gracias a Dios, but during the eighteenth century they were ousted from the coast around the Caratasca Lagoon by the Zambos-Mosquitos, to whom they became tributary.[135]  Many toponyms in the area now occupied by the Zambos-Mosquitos are Paya, and Girard suggests that there was a religious center on the Plátano River, where Paya petroglyphs have been found.[136]

In the documentary record the Paya are often confused with other Indian groups and often referred to as Xicaques.  At the end of the seventeenth century there were a number of missionary expeditions amongst Payas inhabiting the valleys of Agalta, Tinto, and Wampu (Guampu).[137]  Later Butucos Indians, who were also Payas, were settled at

---

[132]Lehmann, *Zentral-Amerika* 2:641; Chapman, "Tropical Forest Tribes," p. 53, personal communication with Greenberg; D. Holt and W. Bright, "La lengua Paya y las fronteras lingüísticas de Mesoamérica," XIV Mesa Redonda de la Sociedad Mexicana de Antropología (Mexico, 1976) 2:149-56.

[133]Brinton, *American Race*, p. 163; E. Conzemius, "Notes on the Miskito and Sumu Languages of Eastern Nicaragua and Honduras," *International Journal of American Linguistics* 5 (1929):57; F. Johnson, "Linguistic Map," p. 88; idem, "Central American Cultures," pp. 66-67; Rivet, Stresser-Péan, and Loukotka, "Langues du Méxique," pp. 1093-97.  Others are undecided: Mason, "Native Languages," pp. 175-77; Kaufman, "Mesoamerican Indian Languages," p. 61.

[134]Martyr, *Orbe Novo* 1 dec.3 lib.4: 318; Stone, *North Coast of Honduras*, p. 9.

[135]AGCA A1.12 134 1504 13.12.1722; AGI AG 501 Anguiano 10.5.1804; E. Long, *A History of Jamaica...An Account of the Mosquito Shore*, vol. 1 (of 3) (London: T. Lowndes, 1774), pp. 323, 326-27; Capt. G. Henderson, *An Account of the British Settlement of Honduras* (London: C.R. Baldwin, 1809), p. 190.

[136]R. Girard, *Los Chortís ante el problema Maya*, vol. 4 (of 5) (Mexico: Instituto Indigenista Interamericano, 1949), p. 1807.

[137]CDHCN 170-5 ref. to p. 171 Bishop of Guatemala 15.11.1677; AGI AG 27 3.3.1681, AG 223 President of Audiencia 20.8.1712, AG 223 Testimonio . . . indios de la nación Paya 1711; AGCA A1.12 50 511 1781; Fr. Goicoechea, "Relación sobre los indios gentiles . . . ", *ASGH* 13 (1937):301-15; Serrano y Sanz, *Relaciones Históricas*, pp. 380-85 Fr. Ovalle 11.9.1675; Vázquez, *Crónica* 4:89-201; E. Conzemius, "Los Indios Payas de Honduras: estudio geográfico, etnográfico y lingüístico," *Journal de la Société des Américanistes* 19 (1927):269-81; F. Lunardi, *Los Payas, documentos curiosos y viajes* (Tegucigalpa: Tip. Nacional, 1943); K. Helbig, *Antiguales (Altertümer) der Paya-Region und die Paya-Indianer vom Nordest-Honduras* (Hamburg: Hamburgische Museums für Volkerkunde und Vorgeschichte, 1956), pp. 34-35.

Telica in the Guayape valley, and later moved to Maniani near Comayagua.[138] The Paya were to be found in these eastern areas with other Indian groups, notably the Taguacas, Chatos, Sules, Yaras, and Cumajas (Cumages).[139] The Taguacas were Sumu, and the Chatos and Sules may have been also, although as already indicated Lehmann considered that they may have been Lencas or Matagalpas. Conzemius suggests that the Cumajas or Cumages were an independent group.[140]

Stone has identified archaeological rema_____l, Negro (Tinto), and Aguan as Paya,[141] but the_____n documentary evidence of their presence in these ar_____it is highly probable that the Paya did manufacture_____é style found at these sites, it cannot be indisputably_____t materials.[142]

Lehmann and others believe that the Bay_____ Paya.[143] The basis of this proposition is that in 16_____ employed as interpreters on a missionary expedit_____. Also, Stone and Epstein suggest that the artifacts f_____) those found in Paya territory on the mainland.[144] On the other hand, Conzemius identifies the inhabitants of the Bay Islands as Jicaques, but on no stronger evidence than their propinquity to the Jicaque on the mainland.[145] It seems likely that the islands were inhabited by the Paya, and by Maya traders whose presence there has already been noted.

To the west of the Paya were the Jicaque and to the southwest were the Lenca.[146] Conzemius maintains that Payas only inhabited the northeast of the department of Olancho, whilst the Sumu occupied the Olancho valley, but the documentary evidence already used in support of the presence of the Jicaque in the latter region also records the

---

[138]AGI AG 456 Governor of Honduras 30.8.1767; AGCA A1.12 50 511 12.3.1781; Conzemius, "Los Indios Payas," p. 277.

[139]AGCA A1.3 219 2466 Indians of Olancho El Viejo 6.6.1724; AGI AG 343 Teniente of Olancho 5.4.1737; BAGG 1:29-39 ref. to p. 32 Letona 20.7.1743; AGI AG 449 Navarro 30.11.1758 (Report 1744); AGCA A3.2 1075 19750 1761.

[140]Conzemius, "Los Indios Payas," p. 277.

[141]Stone, *North Coast of Honduras*, pp. 19-41.

[142]Strong, "Archaeology of Honduras," p. 115.

[143]Lehmann, *Zentral-Amerika* 2:629, 631 and map; Stone, *North Coast of Honduras*, pp. 9-10, 96; Strong, *Bay Islands*, p. 18; Roys, *Indian Background*, p. 119.

[144]Stone, *North Coast of Honduras*, p. 42; Epstein, "Late Ceramic Horizons," referred to in Chapman, "Tropical Forest Tribes," p. 65.

[145]E. Conzemius, "On the Aborigines of the Bay Islands," *22nd International Congress of Americanists* (Rome) (1928) 2:68.

[146]See the discussion of the Lenca and Jicaque; Stone, "Central American Ethnohistory," p. 214.

presence of Payas;[147] indeed there is evidence that they were living as far south as the area between Catacam⸏                    ⸏ by the fact that the dialect used in Catacamas an⸏                    ⸏ya vocabulary published by Membreño in 1897.[149]                    ⸏ce Nombre de Culmí and El Carbón.[150]

Finally, Stone r⸏                    ⸏g the northern coast and up the Sula valley. This                    ⸏e and the fact that around Choloma near Chamele⸏                    ⸏ftain.[151] She suggests that a colony of Paya settler⸏                    ⸏he area.

*[handwritten annotations: "I haven't seen the Mosquitos do this." "mosquito emergence was much sooner?"]*

<u>The Sumu</u>

The Sumu formed one of the most extensive Indian groups in Central America during the colonial period, extending south from the Río Patuca in Honduras through the central highlands of Nicaragua to the Río Rama. To the west they extended into southern Honduras and in Nicaragua they bordered on the Matagalpa and Lake Nicaragua.[152]

Lehmann considered that Atlantic Nicaragua was inhabited by four linguistic groups: Miskito, Ulua, Sumo-Tauaxha, and Matagalpa.[153] The Ulua and Sumo-Tauaxha have been considered by many to be subdivisions of a single group such that the languages spoken in eastern Nicaragua are often referred to as Misumalpan--<u>Miskito</u>-Sumu-Matagalpa--and are considered to be related to Chibchan, although the relationship is not so clear in the case of the Mosquito and Matagalpa.[154] The Mosquito and some branches of the Sumu, notably the Twahka (Taguaca) and Ulua, extended into Honduras.

The term Sumu was used by the Mosquito to describe Indian groups in the interior mountains areas. Since it will be demonstrated that the Mosquito did not emerge as a distinct cultural-linguistic group until the middle of the seventeenth century, there are no early documentary references to the Sumu.[155] There are, however, a number of references to Sumu subgroups, including the Twahka and Ulua some of whom lived in Honduras. At the beginning of the seventeenth century Frs. Verdelete and Monteagudo

---

[147]See nn. 128 and 129.

[148]AGCA A1.24 1556 10210 f.154 30.5.1681, A1.12 117 2473 Autos relativos . . . indio carive 1768, A1.12 50 511 1781, A1.12 51 517 4.4.1791.

[149]Membreño, *Hondureñismos*, pp. 229-32; Stone, *North Coast of Honduras*, p. 10.

[150]Conzemius, "Los Indios Payas," p. 254; Lunardi, *Los Payas*, pp. 18-42.

[151]Stone, "The Ulua Valley," pp. 389-90; and idem, *North Coast of Honduras*, pp. 9, 96.

[152]Chapman, "Tropical Forest Tribes," pp. 58-59; Stone, "Central American Ethnohistory," map opposite p. 216.

[153]Lehmann, *Zentral-Amerika* 1:461-62.

[154]Mason, "Native Languages," pp. 75-76; Johnson, "Linguistic Map," pp. 10-13; Stone, "Central American Ethnohistory," p. 210.

[155]Lehmann, *Zentral-Amerika* 1:471; Stone, "Central American Ethnohistory," p. 213.

encountered "Lencas and Taguacas" in the Olancho valley.[156] Their location in Honduras persisted into the eighteenth century, for in 1761 missionaries were active in converting "payas, sules, taguacas, and cumajas" in the valley of Agalta,[157] but by then they had been displaced from the coast by the Mosquito.[158] The Ulua were probably the most extensive of the Sumu subgroups, extending west into Honduras and El Salvador. At the time of Spanish conquest only remnants remained in the latter areas, the rest having been displaced by later migrations.[159] In the late sixteenth century Fr. Alonso Ponce observed that Uluas were living in the villages of Ola, Colama, Santiago Lamaciuy, and Zazacalí in the jurisdiction of Choluteca.[160] Chapman suggests that the widespread occurrence of the term Ulua in the northern Chibcha area suggests that it had a generic meaning in Chibchan, in which case it cannot be used as definite evidence for the presence of Ulua Indians.[161]

The Sumu were often referred to as 'Caribes.' For example, in 1674 Fr. Espino whilst converting Indians in the Olancho valley noted that in the "tierra adentro" were "some caribes called Taguacas."[162] However, it is clear that the term 'Caribe' was not restricted to the Sumu, but was applied to any Indian group within southeast Honduras and eastern Nicaragua.

### The Mosquito

There are no documentary references to the Mosquito in the early colonial period and it would appear that they emerged during the seventeenth century. The earliest reference to the Mosquito comes from the buccaneer Exquemelin who in 1672 observed that they formed a small nation of 1,600 to 1,700.[163] In 1681 Dampier, making a more conservative estimate of their numbers, observed that "They are but a small Nation or Family, and not 100 Men of them in Number, inhabiting on the Main on the North-side, near Cape Gratia Dios; between Cape Honduras and Nicaragua."[164] In 1684 Raveneau de Lussan identified two Mosquito groups: one at Cabo de Gracias a Dios and the other

---

[156]Vázquez, *Crónica* 4:123-24; AGI AG 183 Frs. Ovalle and Guevara 4.3.1681.

[157]AGCA A3.2 1075 19570 1761.

[158]Henderson, *British Settlement of Honduras*, p. 190; O.W. Roberts, *Narrative of Voyages and Excursions on the East Coast and in the Interior of Central America* (Edinburgh: Constable, 1827), pp. 116-18.

[159]Ponce, *Relación breve*, p. 393; Lehmann, *Zentral-Amerika* 1:471; D.Z. Stone, *Estampas de Honduras* (Mexico City: Impresora Galve S.A., 1954), p. 65.

[160]Ponce, *Relación breve*, pp. 339-40.

[161]Rivet, Stresser-Péan, and Loukotka, "Langues du Méxique," p. 1077; Chapman, "Tropical Forest Tribes," pp. 59-60.

[162]BAGG 5:283-308 Fr. Espino 16.9.1674.

[163]J. Esquemeling, *Buccaneers of America* (London: Routledge, 1924), p. 234.

[164]W. Dampier, *A New Voyage Round the World* (London; A & C Black, 1937), p. 15.

at Sandy Bay.[165] It has been suggested, and it seems probable, that the Mosquito are a purely historic group, whose origin lies in the miscegenation of Sumu Indians with negroes who were shipwrecked on the Mosquito Cays in 1641.[166] In 1711 the Bishop of Nicaragua described the origin of the "Zambos-Mosquitos" as follows:

> In 1641 a ship laden with negroes was shipwrecked on the Atlantic coast and in the part between the San Juan river, in the province of Nicaragua, and the city of Trujillo, in the province of Honduras . . . one third of the negroes were gathered together and the rest took refuge and settled in the foothills of those mountains occupied by carib Indians [indios caribes] . who suspicious and fearful of those new arrivals made war on them and for a few years it was very bitter and in time the negroes defeated the caribs and these retired into the mountains towards the lands of Segovia and Chontales. . . . With women of the conquered, the conquerors multiplied and because these first strangers are already dead, they call their descendants zambos because they are the sons of negroes and Indian women.[167]

There is some biological evidence to support the proposed mixed racial origin of the Mosquito. In an examination of the blood groups of Mosquito and Sumu Indians from the Río Segovia area, Matson and Swanson found that whilst the Sumu all belonged to blood group O, the distribution of blood groups amongst the Mosquito were 90 percent O, 8 percent A, 0.67 percent $A_2$, and 1.33 percent B.[168] The close association of the Sumu and Mosquito can be seen in their legends and language. For example, a Sumu legend relates how the tribal ancestors Mai-sahana and Yapti-Misri were born from a great rock near the River Patuca and they gave birth to the Mosquito, Twahka, and Ohlwa.[169] Similarly, the Mosquito language is most like the Bawihka dialect of Sumu, but its more recent origin is suggested by its insignificant dialectical variations compared to Sumu, whose dialects are so different that subgroups have some difficulty in

---

[165]S. Raveneau de Lussan, *Journal of a Voyage into the South Seas in 1684 and the Following Years with the Filibusters* (Cleveland: A.H. Clark, 1930), p. 15.

[166]E. Conzemius, *Ethnographical Survey of the Miskito and Sumu Indians of Honduras and Nicaragua*, Smithsonian Institution, Bureau of American Ethnology, Bulletin 106 (Washington, DC, 1932), p. 17; Chapman, "Tropical Forest Tribes," pp. 55-57; M.W. Helms, *Asang: Adaptations to Culture Contact in a Miskito Community* (Gainesville: University of Florida, 1971), pp. 16-19. One document gives the date of the shipwreck as 1652 (AGI AG 302 Malgarejo 3.4.1715).

[167]AGI AG 299 Bishop of Nicaragua 30.11.1711.

[168]G.A. Matson and J. Swanson, "Distribution of Hereditary Blood Antigens Among Indians in Middle America: Part V in Nicaragua," *American Journal of Physical Anthropology* 21 (1963):545-57.

[169]G.R. Heath, "Notes on Miskuto Grammar and on other Indian Languages of Eastern Nicaragua," *American Anthropologist* 15 (1913):48; Conzemius, *Ethnographical Survey*, pp. 16-17.

communicating.[170] In addition it possesses more foreign words, especially Spanish and English, and there is some evidence of African influence, although it is slight.

From a localized origin near Cabo de Gracias a Dios the Zambos-Mosquitos spread along the coast displacing and dominating Indian groups, particularly the Paya and Sumu. As early as 1699 M.W. observed that from Cabo de Camaron to Cabo de Gracias a Dios "the Mosqueto-men inhabit the sea-shore, pretty close to the sea-side, or on the sides of some lakes and lagunes hardby."[171] In 1711 the Bishop of Nicaragua confirmed their northern position by indicating that they were to be found "en las lagunas llamadas de mosquitos en frente casi de Trujillo."[172] Later documents and maps confirm that the Zambos-Mosquitos were living between the Río Tinto in Honduras and Punta Gorda in southern Nicaragua.[173] One account records that the Zambos-Mosquitos possessed 27 rancherías along the coast between the River Lean in Honduras and the River Matina in Costa Rica.[174] Although the Zambos-Mosquitos did carry out raids and contraband trading along the north coast of Honduras it is unlikely that they settled west of Trujillo; all other documentary and cartographic evidence is to the contrary.

Within the area delimited by the Río Tinto and Punta Gorda it is clear that the area they occupied inland from the coast varied in extension, as did their density and racial characteristics. In 1757 Hodgson suggested that on average the Mosquito extended 100 miles inland, but that they were established 200 miles up the Río Segovia.[175] In 1774 Long reported that the Mosquito were "most numerous near Cape Gracia a Dios, especially up the Wanks river, and about Sandy bay, where their king resides."[176] Similarly, there were spatial differences in the racial composition of the Zambos--Mosquitos with the negro influence being stronger to the north of Cabo de Gracias a Dios and Sandy Bay, and the Indian influence more dominant to the south.[177] This probably reflects the location of the shipwreck and the fact that the area to the north received a more continuous stream of negro slaves imported to work on English plantations. Thus, in 1773 a concentration of "Samboes" was noted between the Black River (Río Tinto) and

---

[170]Conzemius, "Miskito and Sumu Languages," pp. 59, 64, 67; Chapman, "Tropical Forest Tribes," p. 56; Helms, *Asang*, p. 19. For a recent analysis of African influences on the Mosquito language, see J. Holm, "The Creole English of Nicaragua's Miskito Coast: Its Sociolinguistic History and a Comparative Study of its Lexicon and Syntax" (Ph.D. diss., Department of Linguistics, University College London, 1978), pp. 314-23.

[171]M.W., "The Mosqueto Indian and his Golden River," in *A Collection of Voyages and Travels*, ed. A. Churchill, vol. 6 (London: T. Osborne, 1752), p. 300.

[172]AGI AG 299 Bishop of Nicaragua 30.11.1711; CDHCN 12-63 5.6.1713.

[173]AGI AG 449 Navarro 30.11.1758 (Report 1744) and accompanying map MP 49 1758; PRO CO 123/1 ff.55-79 Hodgson 1757; MNM Bª-XI Cª-B n°1 1782; BAGG 7:157-75 5.3.1800.

[174]AGCA A1.17 335 7088 Rivera 23.11.1742.

[175]PRO CO 123/1 ff.55-79 Hodgson 1757.

[176]Long, *History of Jamaica* 1:323.

[177]T.S. Floyd, *The Anglo-Spanish Struggle for Mosquitia* (Albuquerque: University of New Mexico, 1967), pp. 63-64.

Cape Gracias a Dios.[178] Despite these spatial variations in the racial character of the population inhabiting the Mosquito Shore, most documents refer to the mixed Indian and negro groups collectively as Zambos-Mosquitos. The latter term will be used here in preference to the term Miskito currently used by social scientists, primarily because it is more commonly found in the documentary record.

[178]B. Edwards, "Some Account of British Settlements on the Mosquito Shore," in *The History, Civil and Commercial of the British West Indies*, 5th ed., vol. 5 (London: 1819), p. 320.

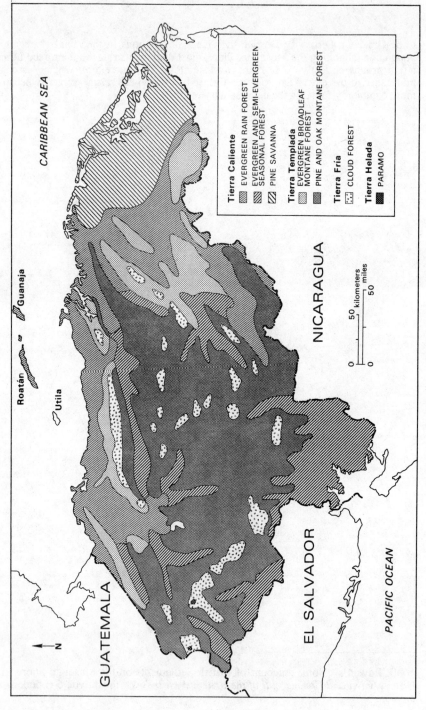

Figure 3. Ecological Regions of Honduras

ENVIRONMENTS

In describing Honduras Herrera wrote "the plains of this land are few, the highlands and mountain ranges very extensive."[179] Honduras is essentially a land of mountains fringed by narrow coastal plains to the north and south, and by a wider alluvial plain comprising the Mosquitia to the east. The country can thus be divided into three broad regions--the Caribbean lowlands, the Pacific lowlands and the Interior mountains or *serranías*.

The coasts of north and east Honduras may be divided into two at Cabo de Camarón. To the west of this point the coastal plain is narrow and backed by high mountains that rise as high as 2,451m in the case of Pico Bonito south of La Ceiba. The plain consists of alluvial deltas and plains, but it is broken by headlands where the

---

[179]Herrera, *Historia general* 9 dec.4 lib. 8 cap.3:104. The physical geography of Honduras has not been comprehensively studied. A few monographs exist dealing with distinct aspects of the environment and with different areas but these in no way add up to a complete picture. Amongst the most useful accounts that refer to Honduras are the chapters by Stevens, Vivó Escoto, Wagner and West (2) in the *HMAI*, vol. 1. Others include:

GENERAL: E.G. Squier, *Honduras; Descriptive, Historical & Statistical* (London: Trübner, 1870), pp. 16-44; K. Sapper, "Beiträge zur Physichen Geographie von Honduras," *Zeitschrift der Gesellschaft für Erdkunde zu Berlin* (1902):33-56, 143-64, 231-41; K.P. Schmidt, "Honduras," in *Naturalist's Guide to the Americas*, ed. V.E. Shelford (Baltimore: Ecological Society of America, 1926), pp. 601-602; V.W. Von Hagen, "The Mosquito Coast of Honduras and its Inhabitants," *Geographical Review* 30 (1940):238-59; A.F. Carr, "Outline for a Classification of Animal Habitats in Honduras," *Bulletin of the American Museum of Natural History* 94 (1950):563-94; K.M. Helbig. "Die Landschaft von Nordost-Honduras," *Petermanns Mitteilungen Ergänzungshaft* 286 (Gotha, 1959); C.F. Bennet, "A Review of Ecological Research in Middle America," *Latin American Research Review* 2 (1967):3-27.

GEOLOGY: C. Schuchert, *Historical Geology of the Antillean-Caribbean Region* (London: Wiley, 1935); R. J. Roberts and E.M. Irving, *Mineral Deposits of Central America*, US Geological Survey, Bulletin 1034 (Washington, DC, 1957.

CLIMATE: W.H. Portig, "Central American Rainfall," *Geographical Review* 55 (1965):68-90.

SOILS: R.L. Pendleton, "General Soil Conditions in Central America," *Proceedings of the Soil Science Society of America* 8 (1943):403-407.

VEGETATION: O.F. Cook, *Vegetation Affected by Agriculture in Central America*, US Department of Agriculture Bureau of Plant Industry Bulletin, 145 (Washington, DC, 1909); W. Popenoe, "Plant Resources of Honduras," in *Plants and Plant Science in Latin America*, ed. F. Verdoorn (Waltham, MA: Chronica Botanica, 1945), pp. 273-75; J.J. Parsons, "The Miskito Pine Savannas of Nicaragua and Honduras," *Annals of the Association of American Geographers* 45 (1955):36-63; W. Lauer, "Klimatische und Planzengeographie Grundzüge Zentralamerikas," *Erdkunde* 12 (1959):344-54; C.L. Johannessen, *Savannas of Interior Honduras*, Ibero-Americana 46 (Berkeley and Los Angeles: University of California, 1963); B.W. Taylor, "An Outline of the Vegetation of Nicaragua," *Journal of Ecology* 51 (1963):27-54.

ANIMAL LIFE: G.G. Goodwin, "Mammals of Honduras," *Bulletin of the American Museum of Natural History* 79 (1942):107-95.

mountains reach the sea. The alluvial deposits have been brought down from the interior highlands by rivers, such as the Chamelecón, Ulúa, Lean, and Aguan, which flow northwards in structural depressions to the Caribbean coast. The valleys and mouths of these rivers are covered with recent fertile alluvium, which also contains gold deposits brought down from gold-bearing strata in the highlands. These lands were intensely cultivated in pre-Columbian times. To the east of Cabo de Camarón the plain is much wider and the deposits that comprise it are much older. Here Pliocene gravels and sandy clays have been heavily leached, yielding very acidic soils that are considered unsuitable for the cultivation of maize.[180] The presence of lagoons and submerged forests[181] indicates that the coast is sinking fairly rapidly, but the two major rivers, the Patuca and the Segovia, have brought down deposits from the highlands building up alluvial levées and deltas. These areas of new alluvium constitute the best areas for cultivation in the region. In contrast to the north, the coastal plain of the Mosquito Shore rises gently from the coast and although the mountain slopes belong topographically to the interior mountain region, ecologically they have more in common with the Caribbean lowlands.

All of these areas have a mean annual temperature of over 25°C and they receive over 2,000mm of rain a year. There is a short dry season from February to May, and another from August to September, but the seasons are not marked, unlike in the rest of the country. The climate is clearly capable of supporting tropical rain forest, but the extent of the forest cover has been reduced largely by human activity. The coastal plains to the west of Cabo de Camarón were probably once covered with tropical rain forest, but they were used for cacao cultivation in pre-Columbian times and have since been almost entirely cleared for the establishment of banana plantations. To the east of Cabo de Camarón, and indeed as far south as Bluefields in Nicaragua, the coastal plain is largely covered with coarse grass savanna with clumps of Caribbean pine (*Pinus caribaea* Mor), chaparro (*Curatella americana* L.), and nance (*Byrsonima crassifolia* L.) DC. Although these pine savannas are closely associated with the Pliocene deposits, they are generally considered to be a fire disclimax possibly hundreds of years old.[182] The climax vegetation in these areas is thought to be tropical rain forest, with swamp forest on the coast, but now the former survives only on inland mountain slopes. The tropical rain forest extends up to about 600m and consists of three or four stories rising to 30m or 40m. The forest contains a great variety of species, among which the most notable are mahogany (*Swietenia macrophylla* King), ceiba (*Ceiba pentandra* [L.] Gaertn.), santa maría (*Calophyllum brasilense* Camb.), and cedar (*Cedrela* sp.). In addition strangler figs (*Ficus* sp.) and palms (*Palmae*) are common, whilst other lianes and epiphytes are abundant. The variety of plant species is paralleled by the diversity of animal life, which includes white-faced and howler monkeys, deer, white-lipped and collared peccaries, tapirs, anteaters, armadillos, agoutis, pacas, ocelots, jaguars, and a great variety of wild birds, including curassow. Many of these animals have been hunted since pre-Columbian times. In contrast to the forest, the savanna areas have a poor fauna, although the lagoons and larger rivers provide alternative sources of food in the form of fish and manatee, and at certain times of the year turtles are abundant offshore. In the sixteenth century the waters off Trujillo were said to abound in fish, which included "many groupers, small

---

[180]Pendleton, "Soil Conditions," p. 404.

[181]Von Hagen, "Mosquito Coast of Honduras," p. 238.

[182]Parsons, "Pine Savannas," pp. 45-47; Taylor, "Vegetation of Nicaragua," pp. 48-49.

spiny fish, sharks, cuttlefish, stingrays and very large mojarras and fresh sea bream and amberjacks and manatees."[183]

The interior highlands of Honduras rise to an average of 1,500m, above which isolated peaks reach 2,500m, with the highest land being located in western Honduras. Many of the mountains comprise short east-west parallel ranges often interrupted by cross ranges or by structural depressions or 'valles,' such as the 'valles' of Comayagua, Otoro, and Sensenti. These are generally located at between 500m and 1,200m. The valley of Comayagua in fact forms part of a major north-south structural depression that passes south from the Ulúa valley to the Bay of Fonseca. These rugged mountains are largely built of Palaeozoic metamorphic rocks, overlain in part by Cretaceous sedimentary rocks, particularly limestones. These rocks are exposed in the northern two-thirds of the serranías, but in the southern one-third they are covered by Tertiary volcanic rocks including andesitic plugs and dykes that form high peaks and have gold and silver deposits associated with them.

The rainfall in the mountain areas is generally lower than in the Caribbean lowlands, ranging between 1,000mm and 2,000mm a year, and there is a marked dry season from November to April when less than 60mm falls in each month. The interior valleys are located in the rain shadows of the surrounding mountains and as such they receive less rain (between 750mm and 1,250mm a year), although its seasonality is equally marked. The mountain soils are generally thin and poor, but the valley soils vary between fertile loams and sterile clay mixed with rock debris. The forest cover consists primarily of pines and oaks. The ocote (*Pinus oocarpa* Schiede) is the most common of the Honduran pines and it is found at lower mountain levels; on the higher mountain slopes *P. pseudostrobus* Lindl. is more abundant and it often forms pure stands. These pines are often found in association with oaks (*Quercus* sp.), which are abundant over 2,000m where they are covered with epiphytes. The oaks are found with laurels (*Lauracae*) and, in protected glens, with slender *Chamadorea* palms. The boundary of the pine forest is marked by the presence of liquidambar trees (*Liquidambar styraciflua* L.), which were exploited for resin throughout the colonial period. In 1580 the area around Tegucigalpa was described as "very mountainous with many very large pines and oaks and some cedars,"[184] whilst Antonelli and López de Quintanillas observed that the valley of Comayagua was "surrounded by forests not too high of many pines, oaks, cedars and trees which yield balsam and liquidambar and other woods." Although the pine trees show a preference for acidic soils, they are generally considered to be a disclimax associated with burning, the climax vegetation being a mixed hardwood forest.[185] The valleys themselves have a more arid climate, but the savannas that cover them have been maintained and extended by burning and, during the colonial period, by grazing. In many cases they have been degraded to the extent that they are now being invaded by thorny species such as carbón (*Mimosa tenuiflora* Willd.), espino blanco (*Acacia farnesiana* [L.] Willd.), and cacti (*Opuntia* sp. and *Cereus* sp). At the time of Spanish conquest woody species, such as the jícaro (*Crescentia alata* H.B.K.), would have been more common in the savannas. The fauna of the highlands is virtually unknown, but it appears to be poor in mammalian species. As early as 1544 Bishop Pedraza noted that tapir, ocelot, and

---

[183]CDIU 11:396 Pedraza 1544.

[184]AGI AG 39 Contreras 30.3.1580, PAT 183-1-16 Antonelli and López de Quintanillas 7.10.1590.

[185]Cook, *Vegetation Affected by Agriculture*, p. 22.; Johannessen, *Savannas*, pp. 44-48; Taylor, "Vegetation of Nicaragua," pp. 44-48.

puma were absent around Gracias a Dios and San Pedro, whereas they were found around Trujillo.[186] The fauna noted by early observers included deer, rabbits, squirrels, and game birds, such as turkeys, pheasants, guans, pigeons, and turtledoves,[187] which are animals that are generally associated with secondary rather than primary forest.

The Pacific lowlands comprise a narrow coastal plain that borders on the Bay of Fonseca. The bay itself is formed by a structural depression that breaks the volcanic axis, which runs northwest to southeast from Guatemala to Nicaragua. Honduras is thus free from the recent volcanic activity associated with neighboring countries, although volcanic islands are present in the Bay of Fonseca itself. Geologically the area is composed of Tertiary volcanic rocks, on which alluvium has been deposited by the Choluteca and the Nacaome rivers. The area receives about 1,500mm of rain, but there is a very marked dry season from November to May, when irrigation is required. The soils are generally thin and infertile and are covered with savanna and thorn scrub, similar to that already described for the interior basins. The coast itself is fringed with mangrove swamp, where oysters may be collected.

---

[186]CDIU 11:399, 401 Pedraza 1544.

[187]CDIU 11:389-90, 399, 401 Pedraza 1544; Vázquez de Espinosa, *Compendium and Description*, p. 246; Squier, *The States of Central America* (New York: Harper and Bros., 1858), pp. 212-15; Johannessen, *Savannas*, pp. 24-25.

# 3
# The Chiefdoms

At the time of Spanish conquest three chiefdom groups inhabited Honduras--the Lenca, Maya, and Chorotega. These groups were socially stratified. They were headed by hereditary chiefs, who ruled over a number of villages or communities whose total population sometimes reached tens of thousands. They were essentially agriculturalists, and their religious practices centered around priests, temples, and idols. In general terms they constituted larger, more complex, and more economically productive societies than their neighbors to the east. Although the Classic Maya reached the state level of organization, the culture of the Postclassic Maya in Honduras resembled that of chiefdoms.

Apart from a few documents contained in the Archivo General de Indias, Seville, the basic sources for reconstructing chiefdom culture at the time of Spanish conquest are the accounts of Herrera, Fr. Alonso Ponce, and early visitors to the north coast of Honduras, including Columbus and Cortés. With the exception of the accounts of the north coast that describe some of the characteristics of the Maya, and possibly the Pipil and Nahuatl, the majority of sources refer to the Lenca. Herrera's long description of the Indians of the "provincia de Higueras" near Cerquín clearly refers to the Lenca, and some observations made by Fr. Alonso Ponce of Lenca Indians in El Salvador could probably have been made about the Lenca in Honduras. There are few references to the culture of the Chorotega Indians in Choluteca, but there is abundant evidence of them in Nicaragua and Nicoya. Given the relatively small number of Chorotega Indians in Honduras, a long and detailed description of their culture cannot be justified here and the reader is referred to the recent analyses of Chapman and Newson.[1] Although the Chorotega differed from the Lenca and Maya in detail, typologically they were very similar. The following account is based largely on Herrera's description of the Lenca, which was the most extensive cultural-linguistic group in western and central Honduras.

The chiefdoms of western and central Honduras comprised between several thousands to tens of thousands of Indians. These populations were distributed in settlements ranging in size from several thousand in the case of the major administrative, market, and religious centers, down to a few hundred Indians in the case of small communities. Some of the largest settlements were the colonies of Mayan and Mexican traders. One of the first towns that the Spanish encountered in Honduras was the town of

---

[1]Chapman, *Los Nicarao*, pp. 76-96; Newson, *Indian Survival*.

Naco. Cortés considered it to be one of the four most important towns in the country, the other three being "Quimiotlán, Sula, Tholoma, and the smallest of these has over 2,000 houses, without other small villages which each one has subject to it."[2]  In 1539 Governor Montejo estimated that Naco had formerly possessed 10,000 men.[3]  Naco and Quimistán were clearly important towns in the urban hierarchy.  In 1535 Cerezeda estimated that Naco possessed 400 or 500 houses with about 1,500 Indians, and that it had as many or more subject to it, whilst Quimistán, which had 25 villages subject to it, had slightly less.[4]  These villages contained from 300 to 2,000 or more houses making the whole area from Naco to the sea a densely populated region.[5]  The existence of hierarchies of settlements has been testified by archaeological investigations in the Naco valley.[6]  There is little evidence, however, for the layout of settlements, with the exception of the town of Naco, where a cluster of large elite residences and public buildings, including a ball court, has been identified, all surrounded by smaller buildings.[7]

The Mexican colonies around Trujillo also attracted the attention of early visitors to Honduras, including Cortés and Díaz del Castillo, who observed that Papayeca and Chapagua served as regional centers for 18 and 10 villages respectively.[8]  In 1530 Cerezeda reported that around Trujillo villages of over 1,000 Indians had been reduced to a few hundred,[9] and the situation deteriorated even further such that in 1547 Bishop Pedraza observed that only 150 to 180 Indians were left in the villages around Trujillo, which had previously contained 2,000, 1,000, 800, 600, and 500 houses.[10]

Settlements in the rest of western and central Honduras were occupied by the Maya and Lenca.  In many respects the Postclassic Maya resembled the Lenca.  The major Maya center of Copán had been deserted, although it was probably visited occasionally for religious rites and ceremonies, including the burial of local chiefs.[11]  Archaeological evidence suggests that formerly the Maya occupied lowland sites,

[2]De Vedia, "Cartas de relación" 139 Cortés 3.9.1526.

[3]CDI 2:228 Montejo 1.6.1539.

[4]AGI AG 39 and RAHM CM A/107 4842 ff.160-191 Cerezeda 31.8.1535.  The original document says 25 but the transcript in the RAHM gives 45.

[5]AGI AG 39 and RAHM CM A/107 4842 ff.160-191 Cerezeda 31.8.1535.

[6]J.S. Henderson, "The Valley de Naco," p. 373.

[7]Ibid., p. 371.

[8]De Vedia, "Cartas de relación," 142-43 Cortés 3.9.1526; Díaz del Castillo, *Historia verdadera*, p. 228.

[9]ANCR CC 5309 Cerezeda 31.3.1530.

[10]AGI AG 164 Pedraza 1.5.1547.

[11]Longyear, *Copan Ceramics*, p. 71; G.R. Willey and R.M. Leventhal, "Prehistoric Settlement at Copán," in *Maya Archaeology and Ethnohistory*, eds. N. Hammond and G.R. Willey (Austin: University of Texas, 1979), p. 78.

whereas the Lenca were to be found in the uplands.[12] Whether they had been displaced there by the Maya is not clear. This pattern was reinforced in the colonial period when the Indians found security in the hills.[13] The Lenca still have a preference for upland sites today.[14]

The whole of western and central Honduras appears to have been highly populated, both at the time of conquest and throughout the colonial period. In 1535 Celis reported that in the jurisdiction of Gracias a Dios there were villages of "2,000 and 3,000 houses such as taloa, guarcha, cerquín and telulocelo," although he remarked that they were small compared to settlements in the Golfo Dulce.[15] What villages lacked in size, they made up for in numbers, for Gracias a Dios was founded in "a good area of many villages."[16] The Comayagua region also appears to have been highly populated. Stone remarks that "in pre-conquest times the Comayagua region must have been a mass of villages with the population running well into the thousands."[17] Further north the Ulúa valley was described in 1590 as having once been highly populated.[18] It was a stronghold of Indian resistance during the conquest period,[19] and when Alvarado established the town of San Pedro in 1536 he allocated nearly 150 villages in encomiendas, of which 18 were located in the Ulúa valley.[20]

There is little evidence for the form of settlements or houses. Family dwellings were probably similar to those in neighboring El Salvador, which were described by Fr. Alonso Ponce.[21] He observed that, "nearly all the houses of the Indians are made of adobe, covered with thatch, and even in the hot areas the walls are made of wood covered with plaster, although there are also some with flat roofs and terraces as in Mexico."

---

[12]Stone, *Central and Southern Honduras*, p. 120.

[13]Squier, *Notes on Central America*, p. 217.

[14]Johnson, "Central American Cultures," p. 62.

[15]AGI AG 49 Celis 10.5.1535.

[16]ANCR CC 5310 Cerezeda 14.8.1536.

[17]Stone, *Central and Southern Honduras*, p. 9.

[18]AGI PAT 183-1-16 Antonelli and López de Quintanillas 7.10.1590; Torquemada, *Monarquía Indiana*, p. 334.

[19]CDI 16:530-8 Testimonio de la fundación de la villa de San Pedro de Puerto Caballos 1536; R.S. Chamberlain, *The Conquest and Colonization of Honduras, 1502-1520*, Carnegie Institution Publication no. 598 (Washington, 1953), p. 57.

[20]AGI PAT 20-4-6 Repartimiento of San Pedro by Alvarado 15.7.1536.

[21]Ponce, *Relación breve*, p. 385.

Some houses in Mexican settlements, such as Papayeca and Chapagua,[22] also had houses built of "stone and mortar."[23]   Many villages possessed temples that contained idols. Herrera described those belonging to the Lenca as follows: "in the countryside they had some narrow houses, high above the ground, which contained their gods of stone, clay and wood, with faces of tigers and other animals."[24]

In addition to villages there were fortified hill sites, generally with access from one side only. The majority of these sites were not inhabited permanently, but the larger ones, notably Tenampua, did have accommodation and storage facilities, as well as ceremonial centers, for use in case of a prolonged attack.[25]   In 1539 Montejo described the hill site of Tenampua near Guaxerequi as "the strongest thing I have seen...and it was impossible to take it because inside it had water, firewood, cultivated fields and provisions; there were 220 large houses and some shrines and temples."[26]   Other famous hill sites included those of Cerquín, Calamuya, Quelepa, and Jamala.[27]

THE ECONOMY

In western and central Honduras agriculture was the most important subsistence activity, with hunting, fishing, and gathering playing secondary roles probably in that order of importance. Crafts were highly developed compared to the tribal groups to the east and trade was well established.   Agriculture and hunting were essentially male activities, whilst women were involved in river fishing and collecting.[28]   Nobles were probably exempt from routine subsistence activities, in which commoners and slaves were employed.[29]

---

[22]P.F. Healy, "Informe preliminar sobre la arqueología del periodo Cocal en el nordeste de Honduras," in *Fronteras de Mesoamérica*, XIV Mesa Redonda de la Sociedad Mexicana de Antropología, vol. 2 (Mexico, 1976), pp. 239-40, notes the presence of stonework at an archaeological site seven leagues from Trujillo and two leagues from the present-day village of Chapagua.

[23]CDI 14:236-64 Pareja 1525.

[24]Herrera, *Historia general* 9 dec.4 lib.8 cap.5:116.

[25]Longyear, *Southeastern Maya Frontier*, pp. 5-6; Stone *Central and Southern Honduras*, p. 106.

[26]AGI AG 39 and CDI 24:250-97 Montejo 1.6.1539.

[27]F. López de Gómara, *Hispania Victrix: historia general de las Indias* (Madrid: Imp. Sucesores de Hernando), p. 187; Stone, *Central and Southern Honduras*, pp. 47-56, 113.

[28]Torquemada, *Monarquía Indiana* 1:335; Herrera, *Historia general* 9 dec.4 lib.8 cap.3:107.

[29]Torquemada, *Monarquía Indiana* 1:346; Herrera, *Historia general* 9 dec.4 lib.8 cap.3:108.

There is little evidence of the nature of the land-holding system in pre-Columbian times, but lands were probably held under a system of communal ownership with lands being allocated to individual families for cultivation. It is doubtful if these lands were considered to be the private property of families; they are not regarded as such today.[30]

On these lands, crops would have been grown under a semipermanent system of cultivation. In western Honduras, where the soils were generally poor, lands would have been abandoned to fallow after only a few years of cultivation. Palerm has estimated that under a *barbecho* system of cultivation, which most closely approximates that practiced in this area, two to three times more land must lie fallow than is currently cultivated.[31] The land was cleared using stone axes and worked with digging sticks and a type of hoe that possessed hooks at the top and bottom to make the working of the soil easier.[32] On the cleared plots a variety of crops were intercropped, the most important of which were maize, beans, manioc, and sweet potatoes. Other crops such as cacao and cotton were cultivated in specially cleared and prepared plots. Techniques of irrigation do not appear to have been widely developed. Although a Maya dam has been found at Copán dating from between AD 650 and AD 800, irrigation was not extensive and canals appear to have been absent at the time of conquest.[33] Nevertheless, gardens and orchards were located along the banks of rivers, notably the Aguan, Ulúa, and Chamelecón, in order to take advantage of the fertilizing effect of floodwaters.[34] Root crops would have been harvested as need required, but maize and beans were probably harvested at less frequent intervals and stored. In addition to the cultivation of field plots, permanent gardens were maintained next to dwellings where a miscellany of fruit trees, gourds, and herb, spice, and dye plants were grown.

The most important food crops grown in western and central Honduras were maize, beans, manioc, and sweet potatoes. Maize (*Zea mays* L.) was by far the most important of these crops. It was probably introduced into southern Central America from

[30]D.Z. Stone, "The Northern Highland Tribes: The Lenca," in *Handbook of South American Indians*, vol. 4, Smithsonian Institution, Bureau of American Ethnology 143 (Washington, DC, 1948), pp. 212-13.

[31]A. Palerm, "Agricultural Systems and Food Patterns," in *Handbook of Middle American Indians*, vol. 6, ed. M. Nash (Austin: University of Texas Press, 1967), p. 38.

[32]RAHM CM 49 no.394 ff. 73-92 Fernández de Pulgar no date; Torquemada, *Monarquía Indiana*, p. 334.

[33]B.L. Turner and W.C. Johnson, "A Maya Dam in the Copán Valley," *American Antiquity* 44 (1979):299-305; G.R. Willey, R.M. Leventhal, and W.L. Fash, "Maya Settlement in the Copán Valley," *Archaeology* 31 (1978):36.

[34]A. de Alcedo, *Diccionario geográfico-histórico de las Indias occidentales o America*, vol. 2 (of 5) (Madrid: M. González, 1786-90) p. 368; Herrera, *Historia general* 9 dec.4 lib.8 cap.3:104.

Mexico in the Christian era, although a South American origin cannot be ruled out.[35] Many varieties of maize--dark purple, red, white, and yellow--were known,[36] and their productivity impressed early observers. In northern Honduras maize could be harvested every three months,[37] whereas further south near Gracias a Dios three sowings were possible.[38] It was claimed that in Honduras one *fanega* of seed could produce between 200 and 250 fanegas of maize.[39] This claim was probably exaggerated, however, since Oviedo's highest estimate of yields in Central America was only 150 fanegas for every one sown,[40] and Gibson has estimated that in the Valley of Mexico good yields were only 200 to one.[41] In Honduras maize bread was generally made by mixing ground maize with water, and salt if possible, to make a ball, which was then roasted;[42] the Mexican fashion of making tortillas does not appear to have been widespread in Honduras, although it may have existed amongst Mexican groups there. Drinks were also made from fermented maize.[43] Beans were widely grown in western and central Honduras. They probably included the common bean (*Phaseolus vulgaris* L.), the lima bean (*P. lunatus* L.), and the runner bean (*P. coccineus* L.). The jack bean (*Canavalia ensiformis* [L.] DC.), a native of Central America was probably grown also. Columbus

---

[35]For evidence of the early cultivation of maize in lower Central America see A.S. Bartlett, E.S. Barghoorn, and R. Berger, "Fossil Maize from Panama," *Science* 165 (1969):389-90; O. Linares, P.D. Sheets, and E.J. Rosenthal, "Prehistoric Agriculture in Tropical Highlands," *Science* 187 (1975):137-45. More recently Snarskis has reported the discovery of a carbonized maize cob belonging to the South American race Pollo on the Linea Vieja in Costa Rica, which was present in the first few centuries of the Christian era (M. Snarskis, "Stratigraphic Excavations in the Eastern Lowlands of Costa Rica," *American Antiquity* 41 (1976):348). It seems likely that the proximity of Honduras to Mexican sources would have facilitated the introduction of maize from that source, although a South American origin cannot be ruled out.

[36]Oviedo, *Historia general* 1 lib.7 cap.1:229.

[37]ANCR CC 5309 Cerezeda 31.3.1530; AGI PAT 183-1-16 Antonelli and López de Quintanillas 7.10.1590.

[38]Torquemada, *Monarquía Indiana* 1:334; Herrera, *Historia general* 9 dec.4 lib.8 cap.3:105-6.

[39]AGI PAT 183-1-16 Antonelli and López de Quintanillas 7.10.1590.

[40]Oviedo, *Historia general* 1 lib.7 cap.1:227.

[41]Gibson, *Aztecs*, p. 310.

[42]Torquemada, *Monarquía Indiana* 1:334; Herrera, *Historia general* 9 dec.4 lib.8 cap.3:106.

[43]Oviedo, *Historia General* 1 lib.7 cap.1:229.

noted that in Honduras red and white beans were cultivated in large quantities.[44] They appear to have been sown and harvested with maize three times a year.[45]

Compared to eastern Honduras, root crops played a less significant role in the economy. Root crops may be regarded as survivors of a former system of cultivation, which persisted in eastern Honduras at the time of conquest, but which in the west had been supplanted by seed-crop cultivation.[46] The most important root crops grown were manioc (*Manihot esculenta* Crantz) and sweet potatoes (*Ipomoea batatas* [L.] Lam.). Both sweet and bitter varieties of manioc were cultivated, and the root was boiled and roasted, as well as used in soups. It was also made into cassava bread and used in the preparation of drinks.[47] Sweet and starchy varieties of sweet potatoes, called *camotes* in Nahua and *ages* and *batatas* respectively in Taino, were both grown and could be harvested after three to six months. They were boiled, roasted, and used in stews.[48]

A variety of fruit trees were grown probably in household gardens.[49] The most important fruits cultivated were mammees (*Mammea americana* L.), nísperos or sapodillas (*Manilkara bidentata* [Mill.] Fosberg), pawpaws (*Carica papaya* L.), and jocotes (*Spondias purpurea* L. and *S. mombin* L.). The fruits that the Spanish called *hobos* or *ciruelas* were probably a species of *Spondias*. Other fruits grown in Honduras, which were recorded in sixteenth century accounts, were: guava (*Psidium guajava* L.), avocado (*Persea americana* Mill.), pineapple (*Ananas comosus* [L.] Merr.), pomegranate (*Punica granatum* L.), and sapote (*Calocarpum sapota* [Jacq.] Merr.).

Two other important plants grown in kitchen gardens were calabashes and peppers. Although it is possible that the bottle gourd (*Lagenaria siceraria* [Mol.] Standl) was cultivated in Honduras, probably most of the fruits used as vessels came from the calabash tree (*Crescentia cujete* L.). This tree was known as the *higuera* or *hibuera* by the Spanish and they were so abundant in western Honduras that the area was called

---

[44]Colón, *Vida del Almirante*, p. 278.

[45]Torquemada, *Monarquía Indiana* 1:334; Herrera, *Historia general* 9 dec.4 lib.8 cap.3:105-6.

[46]C.O. Sauer, "Cultivated Plants of South and Central America," in *Handbook of South American Indians*, vol. 5, Smithsonian Institution, Bureau of American Ethnology Bulletin 143 (Washington, DC, 1950), p. 509; A. Chapman, "An Historical Analysis of the Tropical Forest Tribes on the Southern Border of Mesoamerica," (Ph.D. diss., Department of Anthropology, Columbia University), p. 5.

[47]Oviedo, *Historia general* 3 lib.12 cap.11:393.

[48]RAHM CM 49 no.394 ff.73-92 Fernández del Pulgar no date; Torquemada, *Monarquía Indiana* 1:334; Herrera, *Historia general* 9 dec.4 lib.8 cap.3:105-6.

[49]For native fruit trees noted in the sixteenth century: CDIU 11:392-3 Pedraza 1544; Oviedo, *Historia general* 1 lib.8 cap.20:259-60, cap.22:261-2, cap.33:273-5, lib.12 cap.11:393; Díaz del Castillo, *Historia verdadera* 2:224; V.M. Patiño, *Plantas cultivadas y animales domésticos en América Equinoccial*, vol. 2 (of 4) (Calí: Imp. Departmental, 1963-69), p. 62.

Higueras.[50] The majority of gardens probably also possessed hot and sweet peppers (*Capsicum frutescens* L. and *C. annuum* L.). The former were used to flavor food and the leaves of the plant were added to soups and used to make sauces; the fruits of the latter were eaten whole.[51]

Two other crops that played important roles in the Indian economy were cacao and cotton. Cacao was introduced into Central America from Mexico and it was associated with central Mexican and Mayan traders. Its cultivation was concentrated in northwestern Honduras, particularly around the town of Naco. It was from this region and Soconusco that the Maya obtained cacao.[52] Thirty leagues of cacao groves existed on the coast to the west of the Ulúa valley,[53] and another center of cultivation existed in the Aguan valley.[54] Although much of the cacao was exported, some was consumed by local *caciques*; apparently it was not consumed by commoners in pre-Columbian times,[55] neither was it used as a medium of exchange. The localized production of cacao was reflected in the limited number of villages that paid tribute in cacao during the early colonial period. They included Naco, Coçumba, Tibonbo, Espoloncal, and Ticamay.[56] Cotton (probably *Gossypium hirsutum* L. and maybe also *G. barbadense* L.) was the most important fiber crop cultivated. An annual variety of cotton was probably grown and it was cultivated in large quantities in the sixteenth century.[57]

Wild animals were more abundant in the pre-Columbian period than at present and on the eve of conquest hunting appears to have been an important subsistence activity. The animals most commonly mentioned in early colonial sources included deer (the common deer [*Odocoileus virginiana*] and the small brocket deer [*Mazama*

---

[50]Alcedo, *Diccionario* 2:367; Herrera, *Historia general* 9 dec.4 lib.8 cap.3:104; Vázquez de Espinosa, *Compendium and Description*, p. 241; Sauer, "Cultivated Plants," p. 542; Chamberlain, *Conquest and Colonization of Honduras*, p. 29; Johannessen, *Savannas*, pp. 88-89.

[51]Herrera, *Historia general* 9 dec.4 lib.8 cap.3:105; Oviedo, *Historia general* 1 lib.7 cap.7:235-6; Díaz del Castillo, *Historia verdadera* 2:224.

[52]AGCA A3.16 511 5347 1588; Roys, *Indian Background*, p. 116; R.F. Millon, "Trade, Tree Cultivation and the Development of Private Property in Land," *American Anthropologist* 57 (1955):704; Chapman, "Tropical Forest Tribes," p. 145; J.F. Bergmann, "The Distribution of Cacao and Its Cultivation in Pre-Columbian America," *Annals of the Association of American Geographers* 59 (1969):86, 94-95.

[53]Ponce, *Relación breve*, p. 348; Vázquez de Espinosa, *Compendium and Description*, p. 246; Oviedo, *Historia general* 3 lib.13 cap.8:423.

[54]J. López de Velasco, *Geografía y descripción universal de las Indias* (Madrid: Tip. Fortanet for Real Academia de la Historia, 1894), p. 312.

[55]RAHM CM 49 no. 394 ff.73-92 Fernández del Pulgar no date; Herrera, *Historia general* 9 dec.4 lib.8 cap.3:106.

[56]AGCA A3.16 236 2421 Retasación 31.5.1583 (1548); AGI CO Treasury accounts 1555-6, 1562, AG 53 Petition on behalf of Pedro de Casa 1564, CO 989 Treasury accounts 1577; AGCA A3.16 511 5347 1588.

[57]Martyr, *Orbe Novo* 1:318.

*americana*]), tapirs (*Tapirus bairdii*), armadillos (*Dasypus novemcinctus*), anteaters (probably the lesser anteater [*Tamandua tetradactyla*] and the giant anteater [*Myrmecophaga tridactyla*]), opossums (*Didelphis marsupialis*), and monkeys.[58] Other species hunted probably included the agouti (*Dasyprocta aguti*), paca (*Aguti paca*), and peccaries (*Tayassu* spp.). 'Lions' and 'tigers'--probably pumas and jaguars respectively (*Felis concolor* and *F. onca*)--were commonly hunted for their skins, but they were only to be found in the higher mountain areas.[59] They were possibly traded with the Maya.[60] Herrera notes that the Lenca also ate a variety of smaller animals including iguanas, rats, frogs and toads, bats, scorpions, snakes, and a number of insects including locusts, ants, and spiders.[61]

The variety of animals hunted was paralleled by the diversity of techniques used to catch them. Fire, snares, and water-filled traps were used to capture animals, which were then killed with bows and arrows, lances, and spears.[62] Fr. Alonso Ponce recorded that animals were captured with an instrument consisting of a long stick with a loop at the end, which was placed at the entrance to a hole or nest, or used as a lasso.[63]

The only domesticated animals that appear to have been raised in Honduras were the mute dog and the turkey.[64] There is evidence that a trade in parrots existed with the Maya, the best parrots being raised in the Bay Islands, but it is not clear whether the birds were wild or semidomesticated.[65]

Fishing was a subsidiary economic activity in most chiefdoms, but along the north coast of Honduras and in the Bay of Fonseca it assumed greater importance. Indians there not only exploited the abundant sources of shellfish,[66] but they also ventured offshore exploiting a variety of marine environments. Amongst the species that have been found at the early Postclassic site of Selin Farm are sea catfishes (*Ariidae*), snooks

---

[58]CDIU 11:389, 401 Pedraza 1544; Torquemada, *Monarquía Indiana* 1:335; Herrera, *Historia general* 9 dec.4 lib.8 cap.3:106-7; Oviedo, *Historia general* 3 lib.12 cap.11:393.

[59]CDIU 11:389, 40l Pedraza 1544; Herrera, *Historia general* 9 dec.4 lib.8 cap.3:107, 109.

[60]Thompson, *Maya History and Religion*, p. 79.

[61]Herrera, *Historia general* 9 dec.4 lib.8 cap.3:106.

[62]Ibid., p. 107.

[63]Ponce, *Relación breve*, p. 380.

[64]CDIU 11:390 Pedraza 1544; Herrera, *Historia general* 9 dec.4 lib.8 cap.3:108.

[65]CDIU 11:390 Pedraza 1544; Herrera, *Historia general* 9 dec.4 lib.8 cap.3:106; Thompson, *Maya History and Religion*, p. 152.

[66]Baudez, *Central America*, p. 134; P.F. Healy, "Excavations at Selin Farm (H-CN-5), Colón, Northeast Honduras," *Vínculos* 4 (1978):63-64; J.W. Fox, "The Late Postclassic Eastern Frontier of Mesoamerica: Cultural Innovation along the Periphery," *Current Anthropology* 22 (1981):333.

(*Cetropomidae*), jacks (*Carangidae*), as well as ray fish (*Rajiformes*).[67] These are all littoral species that are found in estuaries and lagoons at least for part of the year. However, other species, notably snappers (*Lutjanus* sp.), tarpon (*Elopidae*), barracudas (*Sphyraena* sp.), and sharks (*Carcharinidae*) are all represented and these species are more commonly found in offshore waters. This suggests that the inhabitants of the site were skilled seamen and fishermen, and they were probably a Mexican or Maya group. There is archaeological evidence of a cluster of fishing groups, who were probably Maya, living on inland waterways and artificial canals near Trujillo.[68] Maya trading boats consisted of large canoes, about eight feet wide, hewn out from one tree trunk, and capable of conveying 25 men, plus women and children.[69] Fishing vessels probably also took a canoe-like form, as did those used on the Pacific coast. There, dugout canoes had curved sides for protection against the waves; they possessed rush mats to protect sailors against the sun and sea spray, and they were propelled by oars, although cotton sails were sometimes used.[70] River fishing, including the collection of river snails, also provided food.[71] River fishing was undertaken by damming rivers with earth and twigs, leaving a small exit where a net or cane trap was placed to capture the fish; trapped fish were also killed with arrows and lances.

The collection of wild fruits and vegetable products did not play a dominant role in the economy of Indian groups in western Honduras, where it was probably undertaken in times of shortage rather than as a regular activity.[72] Exceptions to this rule were the collection of honey, beeswax, gums, resins, and balsams. Honey and beeswax were collected from nests in trees and from under the ground,[73] and honey was mixed with water to make a beverage.[74] Balsams were used for medicinal purposes as were a whole variety of plants and trees, amongst which the most important were liquidambar (*Liquidambar styraciflua* L.) and *guayacán* or *lignum-vitae*, also called *palo sancto* or *brasil* (*Guaiacum officinale* L.).[75]

---

[67]Healy, "Selin Farm," p. 64; and idem, "The Paleoecology of the Selin Farm Site (H-CN-5): Department of Colón, Honduras," in *Civilization in the Ancient Americas: Essays in the Honor of G.R. Willey*, eds. R.M. Leventhal and A.L. Kolata (Albuquerque: University of New Mexico, 1983), pp. 41-44.

[68]Stone, *North Coast of Honduras*, p. 48.

[69]Colón, *Vida del Almirante*, p. 274.

[70]Ponce, *Relación breve*, pp. 375-76.

[71]Torquemada, *Monarquía Indiana* 1:335; Alcedo, *Diccionario* 2:368; Herrera, *Historia general* 9 dec.4 lib.8 cap.3:107; Stone, *Central and Southern Honduras*, p. 44.

[72]Herrera, *Historia general* 9 dec.4 lib.8 cap.3:106.

[73]Torquemada, *Monarquía Indiana* 1:334; Alcedo, *Diccionario* 2:368; Herrera *Historia general* 9 dec.4 lib.8 cap.3:105-7; Oviedo, *Historia general* 3 lib.31 cap.11:394.

[74]Herrera, *Historia general* 9 dec.4 lib.8 cap.3:107.

[75]AGI PAT 183-1-16 Antonelli and López de Quintanillas 7.10.1590; Ponce, *Relación breve* pp. 345, 348; Oviedo, *Historia general* 3 lib.31 cap.8:390, cap.11:393.

Compared to the tribes to the east, crafts in western and central Honduras were highly developed. Cotton was woven into blankets and clothes, and vegetable dyes, such as achiote, were used.[76] Women wore square cloths with one point covering the front and the other the back, whilst some had colored knee-length skirts and loose blouses, as in Mexico; men generally went naked, although chiefs and warriors wore loincloths and a shawl or poncho.[77] Elsewhere Herrera noted that warriors protected themselves with quilted cotton armor,[78] and wore feathers and skins of jaguars and pumas for decoration and in order to make themselves appear fierce.[79]

A variety of pottery bowls, jars, and cooking pots were manufactured, as were baskets and rush mats, which all became important items of tribute in the early colonial period.[80] Stone does not appear to have been used extensively for buildings, but it was worked to make idols. It was also used to make blades and points for arms and tools. There is archaeological evidence for obsidian working at Naco, with the obsidian probably being imported from highland Guatemala or central Mexico. Worked stone blades were traded with the Maya in Yucatán where flint was scarce.[81]

Honduras was known by the Maya as the land of "gold, feathers and cacao,"[82] but there is only scant evidence that its inhabitants smelted gold and silver. Ypsilantys de Moldavia makes the unsubstantiated suggestion that Lejamaní was a barrio of Comayagua where silversmiths and jewellers manufactured jewelry and ornaments for Aztec warriors and women.[83] The only possible evidence for the smelting of minerals in Honduras in pre-Columbian times is for copper smelting. A number of archaeological sites have yielded copper bells and Bartolomé Colón encountered Maya traders on the island of Guanaja who were carrying crucibles for smelting copper, as well as copper tools and bells. Since the traders were bound for Yucatán where copper is not found, it has been suggested that these items came from Honduras. It is more likely, however, that they were being imported from central Mexico.[84]

Trade in western and central Honduras appears to have been most active amongst the Maya; amongst the Lenca, trade was hampered by interchiefdom warfare, although it

---

[76]Herrera, *Historia general* 9 dec.4 lib.8 cap.3:108; Oviedo, *Historia General* 1 lib.8 caps.5 and 6:252-4.

[77]Herrera, *Historia general*, 9 dec.4 lib.8 cap.3:106 and cap.5:118.

[78]Ibid., 12 dec.6 lib.3 cap.19:279.

[79]Ibid., 9 dec.4 lib.8 cap.3:109.

[80]For example, AGCA A3.16 5346 Tasación for Caingala 27.2.1580.

[81]See p. 62; Lothrop, "The Word 'Maya'," p. 335; J.S. Henderson, "Pre-Columbian Trade Networks in Northwestern Honduras," *Journal of Field Archaeology* 3 (1976):342.

[82]Roys, *Indian Background*, p. 55.

[83]Ypsilantys de Moldavia, *Monografía de Comayagua*, p. 45.

[84]Colón, *Vida del Almirante*, pp. 374-75; Lothrop, "The Word 'Maya'," p. 355; Sauer, *Early Spanish Main*, p. 129; P.F. Healy, "The Archaeology of Honduras," in *The Archaeology of Lower Central America*, eds. F.W. Lange and D.Z. Stone (Albuquerque: University of New Mexico, 1984), pp. 149, 156, 159.

did occur at certain times of the year when peace was announced by the use of drums and rattles.[85] At those times they traded cotton cloth, birds, feathers, cacao, salt, and achiote.

Trade was an important activity amongst the Maya, particularly those living in northwestern Honduras centering on the Chamelecón and Ulúa valleys. Trade was probably conducted overland across the Omoa mountains to the Motagua valley, using trails that are still in use today, whilst the rivers themselves offered easy access to the coast.[86] Particularly important was the trade with Yucatán. The Maya of Chichén-Itzá maintained a trading post at Ascension Bay from where they embarked on trading expeditions to Honduras.[87] This trade was considered to be of such importance that Chetumal sent a fleet of fifty canoes to aid the Indians in northern Honduras against the Spanish.[88] The Maya were particularly interested in obtaining cacao, feathers, precious and nonprecious stones, and shells, which they exchanged for cotton cloth and feathers-- Thompson suggests those of Muscovy duck, which probably was not present in Honduras--as well as salt, honey, and slaves.[89]

Apart from occupying part of western Honduras, the Maya also possessed trading posts near Trujillo and on the Bay Islands. The traders who Bartolomé Colón met on the island of Guanaja possessed cacao, wooden swords with flint blades on both sides, as well as the copper items already mentioned.[90] In addition to Maya traders, it seems likely that Pipil traders were living in the valley of Naco and they probably had contacts with the Pipil on the Pacific coast.[91]

---

[85]Herrera, *Historia general* 9 dec.4 lib.8 cap.3:108, 12 dec.6 lib.3 cap.19:280.

[86]Díaz del Castillo, *Historia verdadera* 2:210; Henderson, "Valley de Naco," p. 363.

[87]Ponce, *Relación Breve*, pp. 407-408; A.M. Tozzer, *Landa's Relación de las cosas de Yucatán*, Papers of the Peabody Museum 18 (Cambridge, MA: Harvard University, 1941), p. 6.

[88]Tozzer, *Landa's Relación*, p. 8; Roys, *Indian Background*, p. 116; Chamberlain, *Conquest and Colonization of Honduras*, pp. 53-54.

[89]AGI AG 49 Celis 10.3.1535; Herrera, *Historia General* 9 dec.4 lib.8 cap.3:108; Tozzer, *Landa's Relacion*, pp. 94-96, 189; Stone, *North Coast of Honduras*, p. 15; Roys, *Indian Background*, p. 116; Scholes and Roys, *Maya Chontal*, pp. 3, 29, 34; Oviedo, *Historia General* 3 lib.31 cap.8:422; Chapman, "Port of Trade Enclaves," pp. 145-47; Thompson, *Maya History and Religion*, pp. 79, 128, 145, 151-53; Henderson, "Trade Networks," pp. 342-43; idem, "Valley de Naco," p. 366.

[90]Martyr, *Orbe Novo* 1:317; Colón, *Vida del Almirante*, pp. 274-75. These Indians were en route for Yucatán where neither copper nor flint is found (Lothrop, "The Word 'Maya'," p. 355), but Sauer (*Early Spanish Main*, p. 129) seems to think that they came from Yucatán, whence they brought cotton, together with flint or obsidian tools from central Mexico and copper bells and tools from Michoacán.

[91]Roys, *Indian Background*, p. 118; Henderson, "Valley de Naco," p. 190.

THE SOCIOPOLITICAL ORGANIZATION

The number of chiefdoms that existed in Honduras and the power they wielded is difficult to establish. In an attempt to oppose Spanish colonization in 1530 cacique Tapica tried unsuccessfully to unite 40,000 Indians in the province of Cerquín.[92] The task was later accomplished by Lempira, but only after he had conquered his enemies the Cares. Lempira was able to muster a fighting force of 30,000 warriors drawn from over 200 towns.[93] From these observations it would appear that the power wielded by Lempira was a recent phenomenon and that it arose largely out of the demand for cooperation created by the arrival of the Spanish. Prior to this time chiefdoms were probably smaller in size and independent to the extent that they were often at war with each other.

The reason given for warfare was that it was the custom, but it was also stimulated by the need to acquire slaves. Peace prevailed at certain times of the year when trading occurred, but those groups who spoke different languages were never at peace. They carried out attacks and ambushes, as well as open battles, and they possessed fortified hill sites to which they could retreat and withstand long sieges.[94] As a prelude to battle, ambassadors were sent under the pretext of making peace, but with the intention of ascertaining the size and nature of the enemy forces, after which war ensued. This practice resulted in many Spanish casualties, because soldiers were unprepared for war believing that the Indians had made peace.[95] The weapons they used were round cane shields, bows and arrows with needlelike flint points, and swords made of poisoned wood that inflicted wounds from which victims never recovered.[96]

The chiefdoms by definition were socially stratified and headed by chiefs. The position of chief was hereditary with the office passing from father to son.[97] Each village also had a minister of justice and four lieutenants, who presided over such things as war, government, lands, and marriages. They consulted with the priests over these matters and together advised the chief.[98] The priest was held in great veneration to the extent that only the most senior members of the society could communicate with him. Other officials included ambassadors who played an integral role in warfare.[99] Apart from the latter officials, military leaders do not appear to have been appointed; it seems

---

[92]Herrera, *Historia general* 9 dec.4 lib.8 cap.3:108-9.

[93]Herrera, *Historia general* 12 dec.6 lib.3 cap.19:278.

[94]Ibid., 9 dec.4 lib.8 cap.3:108.

[95]CDI 2:212-44 and CDI 24:250-97 Montejo 1.6.1539.

[96]Herrera, *Historia general* 9 dec.4 lib.8 cap.3:109.

[97]Ibid., cap.5:118.

[98]Ibid., pp. 116-17; Roys (*Indian Background*, p. 121) suggests that this organization suggests Mexican influence.

[99]Herrera, *Historia general* 9 dec.4 lib.8 cap.3:108.

that chiefs generally lead their people in battle.[100]  There are no references to craftsmen being exempt from routine subsistence activities, who might therefore have been classified as nobles.

The majority of people who comprised the chiefdoms were commoners. They carried out subsistence activities as well as participated in trade and war. It is uncertain whether they paid tribute in pre-Columbian times and if so what form it took; in the colonial period they paid tribute in cotton cloth and honey.[101]  Routine subsistence activities, such as cultivating and grinding maize, were also conducted by slaves. The slaves appear to have been captured in battle; indeed, one of the reasons given for war was the necessity to capture slaves. Slaves had their noses cut and if they resisted they were thrown over a precipice.[102]  There is no reference to enslavement occurring in recompense for crimes or in the case of poverty.

Crime was relatively uncommon in the chiefdoms. Theft was recompensed by the confiscation of the thief's possessions, except when the theft was great, in which case the thief had his ears and hands cut off.[103]  Since polygamy prevailed, adultery was not generally punished, although occasionally men had their earrings taken from them, were whipped, and had their possessions confiscated.[104]  Women were not punished because adultery was regarded as having taken place at the instigation of men.

Polygamy appears to have been general. In 1547 Bishop Pedraza observed that in the village of Coçumba near San Pedro each Indian had ten to twelve women.[105]  Marriages were arranged by the boy's father sending emissaries to the girl's father.[106]  In the case of a chief's son an old man was sent with gifts to give account of the qualities of the suitor and the deeds of his ancestors. A drunken fiesta was held and the next day the girl was wrapped in a blanket and conveyed on the shoulders of a man to the boy's home. They were accompanied by people dancing and singing. At each stream they stopped to get drunk and they were received with fiestas at each village. When they arrived at the future husband's home the women uncovered the girl and bathed her in flower water. She was then kept locked up for three days, after which she slept with her husband for three days during which there were fiestas; she then spent the following three nights in her parents-in-law's home before she returned to her husband and other fiestas were held. In the case of commoners, the boy's father sent an old woman with a dowry of four bags of cacao each containing 40 cacao beans. The girl's parents drank the cacao and on the following day they entrusted their daughter to the old woman together with the same amount of cacao. Fiestas were held at the home of the bride and bridegroom.

There is less evidence of birth and death ceremonies, and they appear to have been less elaborate. On the birth of a child, a woman retired to a secret place in the countryside,

[100]Ibid., p. 109, 12 dec.6 lib.3 cap.19:279.

[101]Ibid., 9 dec.4 lib.8 cap.3:105.

[102]Torquemada, *Monarquía Indiana* 1:346; Herrera, *Historia general* 9 dec.4 lib.8 cap.3:108.

[103]Herrera, *Historia general* 9 dec.4 lib.8 cap.5:118.

[104]Ibid.

[105]AGI AG 164 and RAHM CM A/111 4846 ff.222-46 Pedraza 1.5.1547.

[106]Herrera, *Historia general* 9 dec.4 lib.8 cap.5:116-7.

where she cut her own umbilical cord; it was believed that if anyone else cut it, the child would die. She then washed herself and the child in the stream.[107] When a man died his house was burnt,[108] and his widow moved to the home of her brother-in-law.[109]


## THE IDEOLOGY

Idolatry appears to have been well developed amongst the Lenca, although ritual and sacrifice do not appear to have been common. The Indians possessed temples in which idols, with the faces of jaguars or other animals made of stone, clay, and wood, were kept.[110] Amongst the gods who were revered were two known as the Great Mother and the Great Father, who ensured good health.[111] Others were petitioned for wealth, relief from poverty, food, success in rearing children, or a good harvest. A legendary figure, Coamiçagual, was highly revered and in her honor an annual ceremony was held. She was a white sorceress who had settled in Cesalcoquín, the most fertile part of the province of Cerquín, where there were many idols with the face of a lion (probably a puma) and a three-pointed stone with a deformed face at each point. This stone was believed to have been brought to the area by Coamiçagual and was considered to have been instrumental in assuring her victory in battles and in the extension of her empire. Although she was not married, she had three sons, who some thought were her brothers, and the province was divided between them when she returned to heaven in the form of a bird, amidst thunder and lightning.[112] Another god that was represented in the form of a round stone idol was to be found between Gracias a Dios and Chiquimula at Cerori. The idol was known as Izelaca and had two faces and many eyes. It was considered to know the present and the past and to be able to see everything. Blood from the penis of one Indian and from the circumcision of four twelve-year-old boys was offered to the idol. Sacrifices were also made of deer, 'chickens,' rabbits, peppers, and other items, with the blood from the foremost three being smeared over the idol.[113]

Guardian spirits were used extensively and without one it was considered impossible for a man to become wealthy. To obtain a guardian spirit, or *nagual*, a man would go to a remote area. Here he would speak with the spirits and sacrifice a dog or 'chicken.' Then he slept and whichever animal appeared to him in his dream or on awakening was regarded as his guardian spirit, to whom he subsequently prayed for

---

[107]Ibid., cap.6:122-3.

[108]Ibid., p. 123.

[109]Ibid., 9 dec.4 lib.8 cap.5:117-8.

[110]Ibid., p. 116.

[111]Torquemada, *Monarquía Indiana* 1:336; Herrera, *Historia general* 9 dec.4 lib.8 cap.4:112-3.

[112]Torquemada, *Monarquía Indiana* 1:336; Herrera, *Historia general* 9 dec.4 lib.8 cap.4:112-3.

[113]CDI 6:5-40 Palacios 8.3.1576.

wealth and success in life. This animal might be a puma, jaguar, coyote, lizard, snake, or bird. To seal the pact with the nagual the person conducted self-mutilation of either the tongue, ears, or other parts of the body.[114]

Fatalism seems to have pervaded beliefs to the extent that little help was given to the sick or dying.[115] Belief in dreams was strong and certain events were interpreted as omens: it was said that a woman who dreamt that she broke a calabash would be widowed, whilst one who broke a plate would lose her mother. Very often the life of a person was acted out to fulfill a dream.[116] Various other superstitions were held to. Eggshells were collected because it was thought that if they were discarded the young birds would die, whilst deer bones were kept for the purpose of encouraging good hunting. A child's clothes had to be washed by its mother and not in the river, because it was thought that the river would carry away the life of the child.[117]

There were two kinds of witches and sorcerers: those who were wise and could tell the future, who were respected by everyone; and those who cast evil spells. The latter were said to be able to transform themselves into pumas and jaguars, in which form they went around killing people.[118] This belief still exists amongst the Lenca today.[119]

Ceremonialism does not appear to have been highly developed amongst Indians in western and central Honduras. There were three major festivals a year and it is not clear whether they had any religious significance. Certainly they involved eating, drinking, and sexual indulgence. There were also celebrations at the beginning of each month. In common with Mexico, there were 18 months of 20 days each in a year.[120] Other religious ceremonies were those held in honor of the white sorceress, Coamiçagual, and the god Izelaca. There were animal and human sacrifices. Before going into battle the Lenca sacrificed birds and dogs, and even human beings. They extracted blood from the tongue and ears and looked to dreams to foretell what the outcome of the battle would be. Human sacrifice was not common, however, and they did not eat human flesh.[121]

---

[114]Herrera, *Historia general* 9 dec.4 lib.8 cap.4:112-3.

[115]Ibid., cap.5:118.

[116]Ibid., p. 119, cap.6:122-3.

[117]Ibid., cap.6:123.

[118]Ibid., cap.5:119.

[119]Stone, "Lenca," pp. 216-17; idem, *Central and Southern Honduras*, p. 110.

[120]Herrera, *Historia general* 9 dec.4 lib.8 cap.6:121; Roys, *Indian Background*, p. 121.

[121]AGI AG 164 and RAHM CM A/111 4846 ff.222-46 Pedraza 1.5.1547; Torquemada, *Monarquía Indiana* 1:335; Herrera, *Historia general* 9 dec.4 lib.8 cap.3:108.

# 4
# The Tribes

Apart from Columbus's description of the inhabitants of the north coast of Honduras in 1502, there are few accounts of the Indians of the northeast and east of the country during the sixteenth century since the greater part of the area remained unconquered and uncolonized. The earliest descriptions belong to missionaries who started work in the area in the early seventeenth century. Given the inadequacies of the early documentary record, the following reconstruction of tribal culture at the time of Spanish conquest makes critical use of information available from more recent ethnographic accounts.

Compared with their neighbors to the west, the Jicaque, Paya, and Sumu, who inhabited the east, formed smaller social units that were organized on an egalitarian basis. They subsisted on the products of agriculture, hunting, fishing, and gathering, but in general wild food resources played a more important role in the Indian diet than they did in the west. They did not possess temples or an instituted priesthood, rather their religion was based on animism and shamanism.

Tribal settlements were characterized by their smallness and uniformity of size, generally consisting of individual houses or small clusters of dwellings. Although the Indians possessed shrines, they were not easily distinguishable from ordinary dwellings. The lack of documentary references to them probably reflects this and the fact that Indians were reluctant to reveal them to outsiders. In fact, in 1600 Xicaque Indians in the Olancho valley (probably Payas) were said to possess "many shrines and houses of idols."[1] The Paya also possessed places of retreat in inaccessible parts of the mountains.[2] Nevertheless, the settlements lacked temple complexes and in general they were simple in form and undifferentiated in character.

Indians in eastern Honduras possessed permanent and temporary settlements. The permanence and location of settlements were influenced by the type of resources exploited by Indians. The subsistence of all groups inhabiting eastern Honduras consisted of a combination of agriculture, hunting, fishing, and collecting, with the emphasis on one or more of these activities varying throughout the area; the inland Paya and Sumu depended more on agriculture and collecting, whilst coastal groups exploited riverine and marine resources to some degree, and the Jicaque relied almost exclusively on wild food

---

[1]AGI AG 11 Dr. Criado de Castilla 15.5.1600.

[2]Goicoechea, "Relación sobre los indios gentiles," p. 307.

68

resources.[3] Whilst all groups appear to have possessed permanent settlements, temporary ones were more common amongst the inland groups, particularly those heavily dependent on hunting and gathering whose settlements were moved frequently in response to the availability of resources; other settlements may have been moved due to declining soil fertility, but settlements were moved less frequently than cultivated plots. The inland Sumu moved constantly in response to the availability of plantains, erecting temporary shelters that only lasted a few days,[4] whilst the Paya were said to move every five to eight days.[5] Nomadism was probably greatest amongst the Jicaque who depended to a greater degree on wild food resources. In 1584 they were described as "wandering rebellious about the hills with their wives and children without believing in the Catholic faith and without forming a settlement."[6] Although temporary settlements did exist in pre-Columbian times, nomadism, such as that just described amongst the Jicaque, undoubtedly increased during the colonial period as a result of the disruption caused by conquest and enslaving activities.

Although by the nineteenth century the Jicaque were living in the remote mountain areas,[7] in pre-Columbian times they probably lived in permanent settlements in the lowlands, preferring river valleys that gave them easy access to the sea. Vázquez recorded that the rancherías of the Paya were located in valleys,[8] and in 1674 Fr. Espino described their settlements in the Olancho valley as follows:

the houses in which they live consist of a few huts made from some broad leaves located on the banks of a river, they are very small; they are not all together, neither do they form a settlement, they have their huts on the banks of a river a league or two leagues apart.[9]

The dispersed nature of the settlement pattern is indicated in Sonnenstern's account of settlements along the Río Coco (Segovia) in 1869. He listed 13 settlements that together comprised 279 houses, and recorded that another 460 houses were dispersed in tributary valleys. He estimated that the average size of the household was five persons, but this may have been an underestimate.[10] Earlier in the century Fr. Goicoechea observed that in the Agalta mountains, where the Paya lived, houses were occupied by families of eight

[3]See pp. 69-78.

[4]AGI AG 223 Fr. Pedro de la Concepción 13.1.1699, AG 371 Fr. Ximénez 9.9.1748; Vázquez, *Crónica* 4:113-14.

[5]AGI AG 297 Fr. Betancurt 15.10.1698.

[6]AGI AG 39 Ponce de León 26.5.1584.

[7]AGI AG 963 Guardian of Recollects 10.1.1813, IG 1525 Recollect missionaries 7.1.1813.

[8]Vázquez, *Crónica* 4:158-59.

[9]BAGG 5:283-308 Fr. Espino 17.9.1674.

[10]*Límites entre Honduras y Nicaragua* (Madrid: Idamor Moreno, 1905), pp. 241-43 Sonnenstern 1869.

to 20 persons.[11]  In addition to individual family dwellings, there were multifamily lodges that contained a number of nuclear or extended families related by kinship or friendship. The documentary record suggests that such lodges were relatively few in number,[12] unless the term 'palenque,' which was generally used to refer to pallisaded settlements (such as those found amongst the Jicaque today),[13] was also applied to multifamily lodges. The lodges generally took a rectangular or oval form, and were open sided with wooden posts bearing heavily thatched roofs. Internally they were divided into individual family compartments. They also possessed attics that were used for storage and for sleeping, with beds rather than hammocks being used. Such houses are described fully in more recent ethnographic accounts of all three Indian groups.[14]


THE ECONOMY


In eastern Honduras Indians participated in agriculture, hunting, fishing, and gathering to various degrees. The inland Paya and Sumu relied to a greater degree on agriculture, although they also hunted, fished, and collected wild fruits and vegetables. Bancroft considered the Paya to be the best agriculturalists, whereas agriculture was poorly developed amongst the Jicaque, who depended almost exclusively on wild food

---

[11]Goicoechea, "Relación sobre los gentiles," pp. 303-15.

[12]For example, amongst the Sumu AGCA A1.12 78 646 no date.

[13]AGI AG 963 Guardian of Recollects 10.1.1813; Conzemius, *Ethnographical Survey*, p. 31; F. Termer, "La habitación rural en la América del Centro, a través de los tiempos," *ASGH* 11 (1935):398; V.W. Von Hagen, "The Jicaque (Torrupan) Indians of Honduras," *Indian Notes and Monographs* no. 53 (New York: Museum of the American Indian, Heye Foundation, 1943), pp. 39, 42.

[14]For the Jicaque: Von Hagen, "The Jicaque," pp. 42-43; A. Chapman, "Dual Organisation amongst the Jicaques of La Montaña de la Flor, Honduras," *34th International Congress of Americanists* (Vienna) (1962), p. 578; for the Paya: E.G. Squier, *Adventures on the Mosquito Shore* (New York: Worthington Co., 1891), pp. 293-94; and for the Sumu: H.A. Wickham, *A Journey amongst the Woolwa or Soumoo Indians of Central America* (London, 1872), p. 162; and idem, "Notes on the Soumoo or Woolwa Indians of Blewfields River, Mosquito Territory," *Journal of the Anthropological Institute* 24 (1895):199-200.

resources.[15]  In addition coastal groups probably exploited the lagoons and marine environment.

The only division of labor that existed was based on sex and age. Men generally hunted, fished, and cleared the land for cultivation. The latter activity was probably done on an exchange basis, with male relatives and friends helping each other to clear their individual family plots. Where agriculture played a more significant role in the economy men may also have been employed in cultivation, although it was primarily a female activity. Women planted, weeded, and harvested crops, as well as gathered wild fruits and vegetables and where possible shellfish and crabs. They also made pottery and wove cotton cloth.[16]

In pre-Columbian times crops were almost certainly grown under a system of shifting cultivation, as the majority of crops are today. Plots would have been cultivated for several years before being abandoned to fallow to enable the soil to recover some of its lost fertility.[17] As such agriculture required large expanses of land, and the continued forest clearance and burning associated with it resulted in the creation and extension of many grasslands in eastern Honduras.[18] Lands located near settlements were generally selected for cultivation, although sometimes plots were cultivated at longer distances for defensive reasons.[19] Plots were cleared using stone axes and fire, and digging sticks were used for planting. On the cleared plots a great variety of crops were generally grown. These plots were commonly referred to as *rozas*, *siembras*, or *milpas*. In addition there were other plots that were dominated by one crop such as manioc, plantains, maize, or cacao, in which case they were called *yucales*, *platanares*, *maizales*, and *cacaotales* respectively. Earlier this century Von Hagen noted that the Jicaque had larger plots for seed crops, and smaller ones for root crops, with their main crop manioc being grown in separate clearings.[20] Whilst plots were cleared and cultivated on a communal basis,

---

[15]For the Jicaque: AGI AG 164 Bishop of Honduras 27.2.1696; BAGG 7:80-115 Informes acerca de las misiones de Lean y Mulía 10.2.1761; for the Paya: BAGG 5:283-308 Fr. Espino 17.9.1674; Goicoechea, "Relación sobre los indios gentiles," pp. 303-15; and on the Bay Islands: RAHM CM A/66 24 no. 193 ff. 36-41 Descripción de las Islas Guanaxas 1.11.1639; for the Sumu: AGI AG 223 Fr. Pedro de la Concepción 13.1.1699, AG 371 Fr. Ximénez 9.9.1748; Vázquez, *Crónica* 4:114. For more recent accounts see: Squier, "Xicaque Indians," p. 760; H.H. Bancroft, *The Native Races of the Pacific States of North America*, vol. 1 (of 5) (San Francisco: A.L. Bancroft, 1883-86), p. 719; Squier, *Adventures*, p. 300; Conzemius, "Jicaques," pp. 164-65; and idem, "Los Indios Payas," pp. 289-91; Fr. M. Landero, "Los Taoajkas ó Sumos del Patuca y Wampú," *Anthropos* 30 (1935):38-41; Von Hagen, "The Jicaque," p. 47; Chapman, "Dual Organization," p. 578.

[16]Squier, *Adventures*, p. 298; Conzemius, "Los Indios Payas," pp. 289-90; and idem, *Ethnographical Survey*, pp. 39-40; Landero, "Los Taoajkas," pp. 38-40; Von Hagen, "The Jicaque," p. 49.

[17]For a description of the cycle of cultivation, see Palerm, "Agricultural Systems," pp. 29-34.

[18]Johannessen, *Savannas*, pp. 18-25, 104-106.

[19]For example, AGI AG Governor of Honduras 4.6.1616.

[20]Von Hagen, "The Jicaque," pp. 47-48.

individual families probably harvested crops from them as need required.[21] Root crops and plantains would have been harvested from nearby plots every few days, but more distant plots would have been visited less frequently. Seed crops, such as maize and beans, which were grown on a smaller scale, would have been harvested less frequently because they could be stored.

Early accounts indicate that a large variety of crops were cultivated in eastern Honduras. Columbus observed that on the north coast of Honduras "maize, yucca, ages and potatoes, all grow in this country as they do everywhere on the continent."[22] In 1579 a vecino of Trujillo reported that the Jicaque had "a lot of food, fish, maize, plantains, yuca and many other wild fruits,"[23] whilst in 1611 Fr. Verdelete reported that in the valleys of Olancho "were sown fields of sugar cane, many plots of plantains and cacao groves (which produce the cherished drink, which they call chocolate) there are many plots of camotes and yuca from which they make bread, pineapples, chile, cotton and many fruit trees."[24] These few descriptions suggest that root crops played a dominant role in the economy. Although seed crops, especially maize and beans, were grown in pre-Columbian times they were far less important in the economy in the east than they were in the west.

Although it is possible that root crops were domesticated in Central America, the consensus is that they were introduced from northern South America.[25] Chapman has suggested that the cultivation of sweet manioc was introduced into Central America by a lowland Chibchan group in the third millenium BC.[26] Root crops possess several disadvantages not shared by seed crops. First, root crops tend to be deficient in protein, fats, and oils so that supplements from hunting and fishing are needed to provide a balanced diet; seed crops can supply a greater variety of nutrients and can therefore release Indians from their dependence on wild food resources. Second, seed crops have greater storage capabilities, such that supplies acquired during periods of abundance can be used to overcome shortages. Since seed crops do possess certain advantages over root crops, why were they not adopted on a large scale on the Caribbean side of the isthmus? A number of authors have suggested that the Caribbean coast of Central America was isolated from contacts with Mesoamerica and the Central Andes, and that if any contacts

---

[21] Squier, *Adventures*, p. 298.

[22] Martyr, *Orbe Novo* 1:318.

[23] AGI AG Lopez 1579.

[24] AGI AG 175 Fr. Verdelete 29.4.1611. Although Verdelete is describing Taguzgalpa, he had just returned from an expedition to the Olancho valley and the description clearly refers to that area. The sugar cane, and possibly the cacao, were introduced during the colonial period.

[25] Sauer, "Cultivated Plants," pp. 40-48; D.R. Harris, "Agricultural Systems, Ecosystems and the Origins of Agriculture," in *The Domestication and Exploitation of Plants and Animals*, eds. P.J. Ucko and G.W. Dimbleby (London: Duckworth, 1969), pp. 3-15; D.W. Lathrap, *The Upper Amazon* (London: Thames & Hudson, 1970), pp. 47-60; Helms, *Asang*, pp. 24-27.

[26] Chapman, "Tropical Forest Tribes," p. 165.

did occur in Central America, they were effected via the Pacific coast.[27] However, such contacts were not altogether lacking, for maize was cultivated on the Caribbean coast and a Mexican colony probably existed in the area at the time of conquest. It seems more likely that maize was not adopted on a large scale at that time, because the cultivation of root crops and palms, supplemented by hunting, fishing, and gathering was not only better suited to the ecological conditions of the area, but provided the Indians there with a substantial and varied diet. As such there was no incentive for them to change their patterns of subsistence. It is possible that if Spanish conquest had not occurred when it did, the penetration of Mexican traders and colonists into the area might ultimately have resulted in the area being incorporated into the Aztec empire with demands for tribute and items of trade creating pressure for the adoption of new crops including maize.[28]

The most important crops grown in the colonial period were manioc and plantains, with manioc dominant in the coastal areas and plantains more important inland. Both varieties of manioc (*Manihot esculenta* Crantz) were cultivated. Oviedo recorded that in Honduras "the yuca is that which does not kill, and also of the other kind."[29] This suggests that sweet manioc was the dominant variety cultivated. Although cassava bread, which is normally made from bitter manioc, was produced, particularly in the Bay Islands, there is no archaeological evidence for the use of graters employed in the process of extracting the poisonous juices from the root. With the exception of the Paya, the sweet variety is more commonly cultivated by Indian groups today.[30] The secondary role of bitter manioc cannot be explained by climatic factors, although the two varieties do have slightly different requirements, and it is surprising given its higher starch content and the fact that in the form of bread it can be stored for long periods.[31] Chapman has proposed that the cultivation of sweet manioc represents an older agricultural tradition.[32] This is suggested by the wider distribution of sweet manioc cultivation and its simpler form of preparation; the more complex process of extracting the poisonous juices from bitter manioc developed later. She argues that after the introduction of sweet manioc to Central America in about the third millenium BC, the Caribbean coast of Central America remained a 'cultural backwater' that was bypassed by later developments. Sauer, however, maintains that there was ample time for the diffusion of techniques associated with the cultivation and preparation of bitter manioc. He suggests that a more likely

---

[27]Ibid., pp. 165-66; R.W. Magnus, "The Prehistory of the Miskito Coast of Nicaragua: A Study in Cultural Relationships," (Ph.D. Diss., Yale University, 1974), pp. 216-18; M.W. Helms, *Middle America: A Culture History of Heartlands and Frontiers* (Englewood-Cliffs, NJ: Prentice-Hall, 1975), pp. 117-18.

[28]Helms, *Middle America*, p. 119.

[29]Oviedo, *Historia general* 3 lib.31 cap.11:393.

[30]CDIU 11:394 Pedraza 1544; AGI AG 55 López 1579, PAT 183-1-16 Antonelli and López de Quintanillas 7.10.1590, AG 175 Fr. Verdelete 29.4.1611; RAHM CM A/66 ff.36-41 Descripción de las Islas Guanaxas 1.11.1639; Vázquez de Espinosa, *Compendium and Description*, p. 244. For recent accounts of its cultivation see: Conzemius, "Los Indios Payas," p. 292; and idem, *Ethnographical Survey*, p. 62; Von Hagen, "The Jicaque," p. 47.

[31]Sauer, "Cultivated Plants," p. 508.

[32]Chapman, "Tropical Forest Tribes," pp. 162-66.

explanation is that the Indians possessed adequate supplies of food from a variety of sources without having to adopt the crop, which in other areas satisfied the demand for a more substantial and reliable source of food.[33]

Although the plantain (*Musa paradisiaca* var. *normalis*) was an important source of food for Indians during the colonial period, it is a southeast Asian domesticate, and there is some dispute as to whether it reached Latin America prior to Spanish conquest. Nevertheless, the diversity of varieties present and its wide distribution in Latin America in the early sixteenth century suggest that it must have been introduced in pre-Columbian times.[34] Oviedo recorded the presence of a plant called 'plátano' in the West Indies and the fringing mainland of the Caribbean. He maintained that this fruit was different from the European variety, the banana (var. *sapientum*), which was introduced to Santo Domingo from the Canary Islands in 1516.[35] Bishop Pedraza also distinguished between two varieties of plantain cultivated in Honduras.[36] Although plantains are mentioned frequently in the documentary record, probably many were collected from wild sources rather than cultivated.[37] In 1798 the governor of Honduras claimed that the area inhabited by the Jicaque was so fertile that one *platanar* extended for 36 leagues along the banks of a river without cultivation.[38]

Other root crops grown probably included sweet potatoes, yautia, and possibly yams. The cultivation of sweet potatoes (*Ipomoea batatas* [L.] Lam.) was noted by the earliest observers,[39] but the cultivation of yautia (*Xanthosoma* sp.) went unnoticed although it was almost certainly cultivated in pre-Columbian times. It is generally found in association with sweet manioc and sweet potatoes, and it is cultivated by the Jicaque, Paya, Sumu, and Mosquito today.[40] There is some uncertainty as to whether yams were cultivated in the pre-Columbian period. It is possible that the New World yam (*Dioscorea trifida* L.) was cultivated in Central America prior to Spanish conquest,[41] but it is not mentioned in the early documentary record, and whereas the Sumu refer to yautia as

---

[33] Sauer, "Cultivated Plants," pp. 507-508.

[34] Ibid., p. 527.

[35] Oviedo, *Historia general* 1 lib.8 cap.1:247-48.

[36] CDIU 11:392 Pedraza 1544.

[37] For example, AGI AG 55 López 1579, AG 175 Fr. Verdelete 29.4.1611, AG 223 Fr. Pedro de la Concepción 13.1.1699, AG 343 1700; "Informe...acerca de la invasión que los indios Payas pretendían...17.2.1716," *RABN* 25 (1946):193-97.

[38] AGCA A1.12 118 2487 Anguiano 1.7.1798. Such large expanses of wild plantains were exploited by Indians in the Ríos Tinto and Plátano in the nineteenth century (*Límites*, 208 Echenique 1875).

[39] AGI AG Fr. Verdelete 29.4.1611; CDI 14:236-64 Pareja 1525; Martyr, *Orbe Novo* 1:318.

[40] Conzemius, "Jicaques," p. 165; idem, "Los Indios Payas," p. 291; idem, *Ethnographical Survey*, p. 62; Helms, *Asang*, p. 142.

[41] Sauer, "Cultivated Plants," p. 511.

wilis, they do not possess a native name for yams.[42] The yams that were cultivated on the Mosquito Shore during the seventeenth and eighteenth centuries were almost certainly Old World yams (*Dioscorea alata* L. and *Dioscorea bulbifera* L.) introduced from Africa.[43]

A distinctive feature of agriculture on the Caribbean coast of Honduras was the cultivation of the pejibaye palm (*Guilielma utilis* Oerst). It appears to have been domesticated in South America at an early date and although it was cultivated between the Aguan River and Panama, it was more commonly found in the southern part of this region.[44] Columbus noted the presence of seven kinds of palm on the north coast of Honduras,[45] and the pejibaye palm was probably cultivated there, at least on a small scale. The fruit would have been boiled or roasted, and made into an alcoholic drink.

Maize (*Zea mays* L.) was cultivated quite widely in eastern Honduras, but it appears to have been most commonly grown by the inland Paya and Sumu.[46] Maize does not appear to have been widely cultivated by the Jicaque, who in the nineteenth century did not possess a word for the crop and who appear to have adopted it only recently.[47] The maize was probably ground and boiled, sometimes mixed with ash, and used to make *tamales*; the Mexican technique of making tortillas has been adopted only recently. Archaeological investigations by Magnus on the Nicaraguan sector of the Mosquito Shore suggest that maize cultivation may have been more important in pre-Columbian times than at present.[48] This is also suggested by the presence of large stone *metates* associated with the grinding of maize in the valleys of the Aguan, Paulaya, Tinto,

---

[42]Conzemius, *Ethnographical Survey*, p. 62; Landero, "Los Taoajkas," p. 43.

[43]PRO CO 123/1 ff.55-79 Hodgson 1757; M.W., "Mosqueto Indian," p. 310; Dampier, *New Voyage*, p. 16.

[44]Sauer, "Cultivated Plants," p. 525; Stone, "Central American Ethnohistory," p. 218.

[45]Martyr, *Orbe Novo* 1:318; Colón, *Vida del Almirante*, p. 278.

[46]AGI AG 55 López 1579, AG 175 Verdelete 29.4.1611; BAGG 5:283-308 Fr. Espino 17.9.1674; AGI AG 164 Bishop of Honduras 27.2.1696, AG 223 Fr. Pedro de la Concepción 13.1.1699.

[47]Squier, "Xicaque Indians," p. 760; Conzemius, "Jicaques," p. 165; idem, *Ethnographical Survey*, p. 90; Von Hagen, "The Jicaque," pp. 14, 45-46; Roys, *Indian Background*, p. 119; D.Z. Stone, "Urgent Tasks of Research Concerning the Cultures and Languages of Central American Indian Tribes," *32nd International Congress of Americanists* (Copenhagen) (1958), p. 44; idem, "Eastern Frontier," p. 120.

[48]R.W. Magnus, "The Prehistoric and Modern Subsistence Patterns of the Atlantic Coast of Nicaragua: A Comparison," in *Prehistoric Coastal Adaptations: The Economy and Ecology of Maritime Middle America*, eds. B.L. Stark and B. Voorhies (New York: Academic Press, 1978), pp. 61-80.

and Plátano rivers in Honduras.[49] However, these areas have not been investigated scientifically and there are no dates for these artifacts. Beans are often associated with the cultivation of maize, and Columbus noted that beans were cultivated on the north coast of Honduras.[50] They probably included the common bean (*Phaseolus vulgaris* L.), the lima bean (*P. lunatus* L.), and the runner bean (*P. coccineus* L.). Nevertheless, there are relatively few references to them in the documentary record, and they were probably not widely cultivated.

A variety of edible fruits and a miscellaneous collection of plants providing herbs, spices, and dyes would have been grown in gardens attached to households rather than in more distant plots. Amongst the fruits grown were pineapples (*Ananas comosus* [L.] Merr.), pawpaws (*Carica papaya* L.), guavas (*Psidium guajava* L.), mammees (*Mammea americana* L.), and plumlike fruits called jocotes and hobos (*Spondias purpurea* L. and *S. mombin* L.).[51] It is worth noting that a number of fruits currently cultivated in eastern Honduras were not present in the pre-Columbian times; they included the coconut (*Cocos nucifera* L.), breadfruit (*Artocarpus communis* J.R. & G. Forst.), mango (*Mangifera indica* L.), and all of the citrus fruits (*Citrus* spp.).

Before discussing the contribution of hunting, fishing, and collecting to the economy a few comments should be made about three other crops that were probably cultivated in eastern Honduras in the pre-Columbian period: cotton, tobacco, and cacao. Both wild and cultivated forms of cotton were exploited by Indians in eastern Honduras. Probably the most important species cultivated was *Gossypium hirsutum* L., a Mexican domesticate, and possibly the Peruvian species, *Gossypium barbadense* L.[52] Columbus noted that some Indians on the north coast of Honduras wore red and white cotton cloths on their heads,[53] and in the early seventeenth century Paya Indians in the Olancho valley were said to make good cotton cloth.[54] Tobacco, probably *Nicotiana tabacum* L., a South American domesticate, was used both as a stimulant and for medicinal purposes. Amongst the Sumu tobacco leaves were mixed with masticated maize in water to make an alcoholic drink, whilst smoke was blown over a sick person to aid recovery.[55] The Jicaque made a paste from the green tobacco leaves and ground snail shells, which they

---

[49]H.J. Spinden, "The Chorotegan Culture Area," *21st International Congress of Americanists* (Göteborg) (1925), pp. 530, 533-39; Conzemius, "Los Indios Payas," pp. 301-302; idem, *Ethnographical Survey*, pp. 42-43; Strong, *Bay Islands*, pp. 168-79; idem, "Archaeology of Honduras," pp. 76, 83; Stone, *North Coast of Honduras*, pp. 19-52; Chapman, "Tropical Forest Tribes," pp. 67-71.

[50]CDI 14:236-64 Pareja 1525; Goicoechea, "Relación sobre los indios gentiles," pp. 303-15; Colón, *Vida del Almirante*, p. 278.

[51]CDIU 11:392-93 Pedraza 1544; AGI AG 175 Fr. Verdelete 29.4.1611; Colón, *Vida del Almirante*, p. 278.

[52]Sauer, "Cultivated Plants," pp. 533-35; P.C. Mangelsdorf, R.S. MacNeish, and G.R. Willey, "The Origins of Agriculture," in *Handbook of Middle American Indians*, ed. R.C. West, vol. 1 (Austin: University of Texas Press, 1964), p. 439-40.

[53]Colón, *Vida del Almirante*, p. 278.

[54]AGI AG 175 Fr. Verdelete 29.4.1611; BAGG 5:283-308 Fr. Ovalle 11.9.1675.

[55]AGI AG 371 Fr. Ximénez 9.9.1748; Vázquez, *Crónica* 4:114.

chewed to protect themselves from colds and fevers.[56]   Compared to the intensive cultivation of cacao (*Theobroma cacao* L.) in northwestern Honduras and in the Aguan valley, cacao was only grown on a small scale in eastern Honduras.   The majority of references to its cultivation are to the Olancho valley,[57] and it is possible that its cultivation was introduced there by Mexican traders, who it has been suggested founded a colony in the area.   The Indians there were certainly acquainted with the manufacture of chocolate in the seventeenth century.

Hunting played an important role in the economy of inland tribes.   The most important species hunted appear to have been deer (including the common or white-tailed deer [*Odocoileus virginiana*] and the small brocket deer [*Mazama americana*]), peccaries (mainly the white-lipped peccary [*Tayassu pecari*] but also the collared peccary [*Pecari tajacu*]), the tapir (*Tapirus bairdii*), rabbits (*Sylvilagus* sp.), and the hicatee turtle or land tortoise (*Chrysemys* sp.).[58]   More recent ethnographic accounts suggest that the agouti (*Dasyprocta punctata*), lape or paca (*Agouti paca*), monkeys (the capuchin monkey [*Cebus capuchinus*] and the spider monkey [*Ateles geoffroyi*]), and the armadillo (*Dasypus novemcinctus*) would have also been hunted.[59]   A large number of birds were hunted, but it is difficult to identify the actual species from the names recorded in the early colonial period.   Those most commonly mentioned were the pavo or curassow (*Crax rubra*), the perdiz or tinamou (*Tinamus major*), the paui or guan (*Penelope* sp.), and the chachalaca (*Ortalis* sp.), as well as ringdoves, turtledoves, wood pigeons, eagles, falcons, hawks, and parrots.[60]

All the groups were good hunters and hunted regularly.   The majority of animals were probably caught in the vicinity of plots where they came to forage, but hunting expeditions lasting several days would have exploited more distant hunting grounds.   A variety of hunting techniques were known in eastern Honduras, some of which were unfamiliar to Indians living in the west.   The main weapons used were bows and arrows, and lances and spears.[61]   In 1579 a citizen of Trujillo described the hunting equipment of

---

[56]AGI AG 457 Anguiano 1.7.1798.

[57]AGI AG 175 Fr. Verdelete 29.4.1611, AG 39 Reducción of Olomán 1616; BAGG 5:283-308 Fr. Espino 17.9.1674.

[58]CDIU 11:389-90 Pedraza 1544; BAGG 5:283-308 Fr. Espino 11.9.1674; AGI AG 223 Fr. Pedro de la Concepción 13.1.1699; Goicoechea, "Relación sobre los indios gentiles," pp. 303-15; Colón, *Vida del Almirante*, p. 278.

[59]Conzemius, "Los Indios Payas," pp. 289-90; idem, *Ethnographical Survey*, pp. 79-81; Landero, "Los Taoajkas," pp. 38, 40-41; Von Hagen, "The Jicaque," pp. 7, 45; Helms, *Asang*, pp. 115-17.

[60]CDIU 11:390 Pedraza 1544; AGI AG 223 Fr. Pedro de la Concepción 13.1.1699; Landero, "Los Taoajkas," p. 38; G. Benzoni, *La historia del nuevo mundo* (Caracas: Academia Nacional de la Historia, 1967), p. 58.

[61]For accounts of hunting equipment in colonial documents, see:  AGI AG 55 López 1579; BAGG 7:80-115 Informe...acerca de las misiones de Lean y Mulía 10.2.1761; Martyr, *Orbe Novo* 1:318.  For more recent accounts, see:  W.V. Wells, *Explorations and Adventures in Honduras* (New York:  Harper & Bros., 1857), p. 407; Conzemius, "Los Indios Payas," p. 290; idem, *Ethnographical Survey*, pp. 73-77; Von Hagen, "Jicaque," pp. 49-52.

the Jicaque as follows: "they have many arrows made with the teeth of sharks and other fish, and many staffs hardened by fire with sharp points, and different kinds of lances."[62] Other small arrows were tipped with blunt knobs of wood or wax and used to stun game, particularly birds. The blow gun, which was not known in the west, was used with arrows and clay pellets. There is also some evidence that poisoned arrows were used.[63] Fire was probably used as a hunting device in the dry season, although there is no mention of it in the documentary record.

There was an abundance of fish on the coast and in the lagoons and rivers of northern and eastern Honduras, and fishing clearly took place, but the activity is not described in detail in the documentary record and as such it is difficult to assess the contribution it made to the economy.[64] Whilst the rivers would have been exploited for fish, inland groups probably conducted expeditions to the lagoons and coast, particularly during the dry season when turtles would have been most abundant.[65] The main turtle species caught were the green turtle (*Chelonia mydas mydas*), the hawksbill turtle (*Eretomochelys* sp.), and the loggerhead turtle (*Caretta* sp.). The first was prized for its meat and the second for its shell; the last provided neither good meat or shell, but was probably exploited for its oil and eggs. On the coast and in the lagoons the Indians probably also exploited the manatee (*Trichechus manatus*). Magnus has suggested that fishing did not play such an important role in the economy of Indian groups living on the Mosquito Shore of Nicaragua in pre-Columbian times, when the settlement pattern consisted of permanent agricultural villages inland and temporary fishing stations on the coast.[66] This pattern of exploitation and settlement is likely to have been paralleled in eastern Honduras. A great variety of techniques were used to catch fish. Spears and harpoons were used for larger fish, whereas smaller fish were killed with hand spears and bows and arrows, with the points made of teeth or hardened wood. Apparently the Jicaque and Paya at least do not possess fishing lines and nets, but they do use stupefacients.[67] Marine fishing and most estuarine river fishing would have been undertaken from canoes, of which there were two kinds. One, called a dori or dory, was a keeled canoe that would have been used at sea and in the lagoons, whilst the other called a pitpan was a flat-bottomed canoe that would have been employed in the rivers.[68]

---

[62] AGI AG 55 López 1579.

[63] Wells, *Explorations*, p. 407.

[64] AGI AG 55 López 1579; CDIU 11:396 Pedraza 1544; BAGG 5:283-308 Fr. Espino 17.9.1674.

[65] AGI AG 449 Navarro 21.11.1758 (Report 1744). For recent accounts of turtling on the Mosquito Shore, see: J.J. Parsons, *The Green Turtle and Man* (Gainesville: University of Florida, 1962), pp. 30-34; B. Nietschmann, *Between Land and Water: The Subsistence Ecology of the Miskito Indians, Eastern Nicaragua* (London and New York: Seminar Press, 1973), pp. 152-80.

[66] Magnus, "Prehistoric and Modern Subsistence Patterns."

[67] Squier, *Adventures*, pp. 301-302; Conzemius, "Los Indios Payas," p. 290; Von Hagen, "Jicaque," pp. 52-55.

[68] Squier, *Adventures*, pp. 304-305; Conzemius, *Ethnographical Survey*, pp. 54-57.

The collection of wild fruits and vegetables played an integral role in the economy of Indian groups in eastern Honduras, as well as being a vital activity in times of shortage.[69] Truly wild plants, feral plants, and crops from abandoned plots would have all been exploited. Items collected included honey and wax from bees' nests in the forests. Honey was used to sweeten food prior to the introduction of sugar cane and beeswax was used as a glue in making arrows and spears.[70] Salt would have been obtained by evaporating sea water, but it was also manufactured by mixing the ashes of burnt pieces of a wild palm with water, and boiling it. By this method a very white but not very strong salt was produced.[71] A variety of resins, gums, and balsams were also extracted for medicinal purposes. Amongst the species exploited were sarsaparilla (*Smilax officinalis* H.B.K.), liquidambar (*Liquidambar styraciflua* L.), and lignum-vitae (*Guaiacum officinale* L.), but their frequent mention in the documentary record may reflect European interest rather than their importance to the Indians.[72]

Compared to western Honduras many crafts were poorly developed or unknown to Indians in the east. Whereas Indians in the west commonly wore cotton clothing, in the east cotton clothes were generally worn on festive occasions only. Both wild and cultivated cotton are likely to have been used in the manufacture of cotton cloth, which was probably woven using a simple horizontal loom.[73] In general the Indians went naked except for a small apron of bark cloth, which was also used for blankets and hammocks.[74] On the north coast of Honduras Columbus observed that the Indians were tattooed on the arms and body with patterns resembling animals and other figures, and on festive occasions they painted their faces black and other colors.[75]

Ropes, cords, hammocks, and bags were made from hennequen and a fiber extracted from the mahoe or majagua (*Hibiscus tiliaceus* L.).[76] Although some baskets

---

[69]For collecting amongst the Jicaque, see: BAGG 7:80-115 Informes acerca de las misiones de Lean y Mulía 12.2.1761; AGCA A1.12 118 2487 Anguiano 1.7.1798; for the Paya: AGI AG 164 Bishop of Honduras 27.2.1696; for the Sumu: AGI AG 223 Fr. Pedro de la Concepción 13.1.1699, AG 371 Fr. Ximénez 9.9.1748; Vázquez, *Crónica* 4:114.

[70]BAGG 5:283-308 Fr. Espino 17.9.1674; AGCA A1.12 118 2487 Anguiano 1.7.1798.

[71]BAGG 5:283-308 Fr. Espino 17.9.1674; AGI AG 371 Fr. Ximénez 9.9.1748.

[72]AGI AG 164 Bishop of Honduras 19.7.1620; BAGG 7:80-115 Informes acerca de las misiones de Lean y Mulía 24.11.1766; AGCA A1.12 118 2487 Anguiano 1.7.1798.

[73]BAGG 5:283-308 Fr. Ovalle 11.9.1675; Conzemius, "Los Indios Payas," p. 287; idem, *Ethnographical Survey*, pp. 54-57.

[74]BAGG 5:283-308 Fr. Espino 17.9.1674; AGI AG 164 Bishop of Honduras 27.2.1696, AG 223 Fr. Pedro de la Concepción 13.1.1699; Squier, "Xicaque Indians," p. 760; Conzemius, "Jicaques," p. 164; idem, "Los Indios Payas," p. 287; Von Hagen, "The Jicaque," p. 40.

[75]Conzemius, "Los Indios Payas," p. 284; Colón, *Vida del Almirante*, pp. 277-78.

[76]Conzemius, "Los Indios Payas," p. 287; Vázquez de Espinosa, *Compendium and Description*, p. 243.

were probably made for storage and transport, basketry was not highly developed;[77] calabashes were often used for such purposes. Kitchen utensils were made of wood, pottery, and stone. Bowls, spoons, pestles, and mortars would have been made of wood. Archaeological evidence indicates that pottery and stonework were quite highly developed in pre-Columbian times. Since then Indians have been losing the art of pottery making,[78] and they no longer work stone, although archaeological evidence in the form of stone bowls and elaborate three-legged metates up to six feet long, indicates that the art was once highly developed. More recently Indians have used simple, slightly hollowed out stones as metates.[79] It would appear that Indians in the east possessed no knowledge of metallurgy and thus did not exploit the rich and easily accessible alluvial gold deposits to be found in the region.

At the time of conquest trade appears to have been poorly developed. Regular trading on a large scale was discouraged by the bellicose relations that existed between the tribes. Any trade that did occur would have been conducted by barter and it is doubtful if any mediums of exchange were used. Von Hagen notes that amongst the Jicaque trade is usually conducted in a special house away from the settlement,[80] but this practice is likely to have emerged during the colonial period. Probably the most active trade occurred between coastal and inland groups that emphasized different economic activities. Coastal groups could have exchanged salt and sea shells for pottery, cotton goods, bark cloth, and hammocks. In addition Indians in eastern Honduras are likely to have traded with Mayan and Mexican traders who had established colonies in or on the fringes of the area. They probably exchanged dyes, feathers, and food, for cotton cloth.


## THE SOCIOPOLITICAL ORGANIZATION

The social organization of Indian groups in eastern Honduras was characterized by its simplicity. In general there was no form of permanent leadership, although deference to age was universal and councils of elders often acted as advisors to the community.[81] In the late seventeenth century or early eighteenth century the social organization of Indians living in eastern Honduras and Nicaragua was described by a missionary:

---

[77]Conzemius, "Jicaques," p. 165; idem, "Los Indios Payas," p. 288; Von Hagen, "The Jicaque," p. 46; Chapman, "Tropical Forest Tribes," p. 112.

[78]Conzemius, "Los Indios Payas," p. 288; idem, *Ethnographical Survey*, pp. 48-50; Von Hagen, "The Jicaque," p. 46.

[79]Conzemius, "Los Indios Payas," p. 286; idem, *Ethnographical Survey*, pp. 42-44; Von Hagen, "The Jicaque," p. 46; D.Z. Stone, "The Basic Cultures of Central America," *HSAI* 4:179-80.

[80]Von Hagen, "Jicaque," p. 49.

[81]AGI AGI 297 Fr. Betancurt 9.8.1698, AG 371 Fr. Ximénez 9.9.1748; Vázquez, *Crónica* 4:81; Squier, *Adventures*, pp. 297-98, 301; Landero, "Los Taoajkas," p. 43.

There is information that some nations in the extensive interior mountains are governed, some by leaders in the form of a republic and others by kinship and friendship, but it appears almost certain that they have not formed a republic, but that they have always lived without a head or leader, natural or elected, and that at best they have been subject, not recognizing any jurisdiction, to someone who emerges in ferocity or valor or industry or goodness, so that they should have captains in war and be governed in other things which are necessary, the necessity for which having ended they remain without law, king or court of justice.[82]

Nevertheless, it is possible that some form of emergent leadership existed. Juarros describes the activities of an old man in a community at Cabo de Gracias a Dios:

this old man, even in his idolatry, had employed himself in acts of kindness; he cultivated maize to distribute among those who were in distress; he composed strifes and settled disputes among his neighbours; besides performing many other kind offices where they wanted.[83]

On the other hand, the leadership observed amongst the Guaianes (probably Sumu) in 1699 was probably the result of contact. These Indians, who lived in the headwaters of the Ríos Guayape and Segovia, possessed four leaders--quin, quid, darim, and yambar-- who were respected because they had learned to read and write whilst they were employed by the English.[84]

Two other types of leadership existed in the form of shamans and military leaders. The shaman, who was also known as the sukya, wata, or punakpam, was highly esteemed and acted as a healer, diviner, sorcerer, and advisor, even to the elders.[85] Because Indian groups lived in a state of conflict or near conflict with each other, military leaders were often required.[86] They were generally chosen by the elders of the community on the basis of their military ability. They were held in great esteem but their leadership only lasted as long as conflict persisted, and if they did not provide good service they were replaced.[87]

---

[82]AGI AG 371 Fr. Ximénez 9.9.1748.

[83]Juarros, *Statistical and Commercial History*, p. 363.

[84]AGI AG 223 Fr. Pedro de la Concepción 13.1.1699.

[85]Henderson, *British Settlement of Honduras*, pp. 186-87; T. Strangeways, *Sketch of the Mosquito Shore, Including the Territory of the Poyais* (Edinburgh, 1822), p. 331; *Límites*, 179 Informe 1882 and 211-2 Echenique 1875; Conzemius, "Jicaque," p. 164; idem, "Los Indios Payas," pp. 296-97; idem, *Ethnographical Survey*, pp. 139-42; Landero, "Los Taoajkas," pp. 46-48; Chapman, "Tropical Forest Tribes," p. 123.

[86]AGI AG 12 Dr. Criado de Castilla 30.11.1608; BAGG 5:283-308 Fr. Espino 17.9.1674; AGI AG 963 Guardian of Recollects 10.1.1813; Juarros, *Statistical and Commercial History*, p. 365; Vázquez, *Crónica* 4:110.

[87]AGI AG 371 Fr. Ximénez 9.9.1748; Von Hagen, "The Jicaque," p. 56; Vázquez, *Crónica* 4:81.

The existence of continuous conflict within and between Indian groups can probably be explained by the lack of any true judicial authority to deal with crimes or to settle disagreements, so that offended parties often took justice into their own hands and disputes were settled by armed conflict; they were said to have little respect for human life, with murder being a common occurrence.[88] Chagnon has suggested that the state of chronic warfare in which Yanomamö villages on the borderland between Venezuela and Brazil exist may be attributable to the failure of Yanomamö institutions to govern effectively disputes arising within the villages resulting in village fission and the establishment of mutually hostile, independent villages.[89] Amongst the Guaianes there were apparently many occasions for conflict but, during the feasts that often preceded armed conflict, the women managed to hide their husbands' weapons.[90] Conflict between groups, which may have arisen in the way that Chagnon suggests for the Yanomamö, would have been sustained by crimes and their vengeance; groups often raided each other for wives and 'slaves,' and it is possible that conflicts arose over access to desirable areas for cultivation and hunting. Wars were conducted in the form of raids and amongst the Sumu festivals known as asan lauwana were held to provide men with some military training. Many of the ordeals at puberty and prior to marriage served to maintain men in good condition and able to withstand pain.[91] Weapons consisted of spears and bows and arrows.[92]

Evidence for birth, marriage, and death practices and ceremonies comes mainly from more recent ethnographic accounts, although some colonial documentation is available. During pregnancy women lived in a separate section of the house and at the time of birth retired to a hut not far from the hamlet. A lustration ceremony was then held to receive the mother and child back into the community. Infanticide was practiced on deformed children.[93]

Both monogamy and polygamy prevailed amongst Indians in eastern Honduras. Whilst the Sumu and Mosquito were polygamous, the Jicaque and Paya were monogamous, and amongst the Paya premarital intercourse was punished by death. Unfortunately there is little evidence for marriage rules; Fr. Espino noted that amongst the Paya marriage did not take place within the third degree of kinship. Neither did they allow marriages with members of other tribes and the offspring of such unions were killed.[94] Girls were generally betrothed at an early age and gifts were given to the girl's

---

[88]AGI AG 297 Fr. Betancurt 9.8.1698, 15.10.1698, AG 963 Guardian of Recollects 10.1.1813; *Límites* 213 Echenique 1875.

[89]N. Chagnon, "Yanomamö Social Organisation and Warfare," in *War*, eds. M. Fried, M. Harris, and R. Murphy (New York: Natural History Press, 1967), p. 112.

[90]AGI AG 223 Fr. Pedro de la Concepción 13.1.1699.

[91]Conzemius, "Los Indios Payas," p. 295; idem, *Ethnographical Survey*, pp. 81-82, 146.

[92]For example, BAGG 5:283-308 Fr. Espino 17.9.1674; AGI AG 223 Fr. Pedro de la Concepción 13.1.1699, AG 371 Fr. Ximénez 9.9.1748.

[93]*Límites*, 179 Informe 1882 and 213 Echenique 1875; Conzemius, "Los Indios Payas," p. 295; idem, *Ethnographical Survey*, pp. 150-52.

[94]BAGG 5:283-308 Fr. Espino 17.9.1674; AGI AG Bishop of Honduras 27.2.1696, AG 343 Fr. Herrera 8.2.1700, AG 371 Fr. Ximénez 9.9.1748; *Límites*, 212 Echenique 1875.

father by her father-in-law. Sometimes future husbands took up residence in their parents-in-law's house until they proved their suitability and the girls were old enough to leave their homes.[95] Pim and Seeman, however, recorded that amongst the Mosquito the husband generally remained in the bride's home, although some couples did establish separate residences.[96] Helms has suggested that matrilocal postnuptial residence is correlated with situations where men are absent from home for long periods and that it probably became more common on the Mosquito Shore after contact, when men became involved in raids, trade, and wage labor.[97]

On death, corpses were wrapped in bark cloth and buried in the floors of houses, sometimes together with their weapons, possessions, and food. They were then burnt or abandoned. In 1600 the president of the Audiencia reported that amongst the Jicaque the Spaniards had found "many houses with vaults where they bury the dead where there are the entire dried bodies with their food."[98] Sometimes a grave was dug away from the deceased's home but a hut was built over it, and in other cases Indians were buried in canoes that were cut in half to form a kind of coffin, or else canoes were placed over the grave.[99] The Jicaque apparently possessed walled cemeteries.[100]

*Mishla* feasts accompanied marriages and funerals and they were also held at harvest time, prior to expeditions or raids, or in order to settle disputes with neighbors. Mishla was often prepared in canoes. It was made from a variety of fruits and vegetables, including sweet manioc, sweet potatoes, maize, pineapples, and pejibaye fruits. During the colonial period introduced fruits such as bananas, coconuts, and sugar cane were also used. The fruits were crushed and left to ferment for several days to produce an intoxicating drink. Feasts were thus accompanied by drunken singing and dancing.[101]

[95]Conzemius, "Los Indios Payas," p. 295; Landero, "Los Taoajkas," p. 45.

[96]B. Pim and B. Seeman, *Dottings on the Roadside in Panama, Nicaragua and Mosquito* (London: Chapman & Hall, 1869), p. 307.

[97]M.W. Helms, "Matrilocality, Social Solidarity, and Culture Contact," *Southwestern Journal of Anthropology* 26 (1970):197-212; idem, *Asang*, pp. 24-27; and M.W. Helms and F.O. Loveland, eds., *Frontier Adaptations in Lower Central America* (Philadelphia: Institute for the Study of Human Issues, 1976), p. 14.

[98]AGI AG 11 Dr. Criado de Castilla 15.5.1600.

[99]BAGG 5:283-308 Fr. Espino 17.9.1674; *Límites*, 178 Informe 1882 and 212 Echenique 1875; Conzemius, "Los Indios Payas," p. 300.

[100]Von Hagen, "The Jicaque," p. 61.

[101]For example, *Límites*, 180 Informe 1882 and 218 Echenique 1875; Conzemius, "Los Indios Payas," pp. 300-301; idem, *Ethnographical Survey*, pp. 161-64; Goicoechea, "Relación sobre los indios gentiles," pp. 303-15; Chapman, "Tropical Forest Tribes," pp. 135-39.

## THE IDEOLOGY

In eastern Honduras observers noted the general absence of idols, priests, and forms of public worship.[102] The only references to the possession of idols concern the Paya. In 1600 the president of the Audiencia described Indians of the Olancho valley, who he called Xicoaques but who were probably Payas, as

> wild idolatrous people; there are many shrines and houses of idols and amongst them one more celebrated in which on a mound of stone and clay was a devil the size of a man stretched out and around about him more than two hundred others made of straw, with the inside and the face made of native paper all figures of the devil which surrounded the mound and were in contrast to the women who were of clay.[103]

The existence of large numbers of idols amongst the Paya was noted by missionaries in the seventeenth century; they claimed that the Indians kept the idols in secret places in the mountains and that each Indian had his own idol.[104] In 1526 the governor of Honduras reported that there were three main idols in the country, which were all made of green stone and took the form of a woman. One was to be found in a town four to five leagues from Trujillo, another on an island 12 leagues from the same town--probably on one of the Bay Islands--and the last in a village 30 leagues away.[105] On the basis of distance Stone argues that the last idol was located in the Olancho valley,[106] and their distribution suggests that they may have belonged to the Paya. The three idols were kept in temples, where sacrifices were made supervised by a priest called Papa, with whom the sons of leaders resided.

Some maintained that the Indians possessed no gods, whilst others recorded the belief in an ill-defined supernatural power. This being was said to have created the world and mankind and to be the origin of good as opposed to evil, but it was not honored by sacrifices, offerings, or public worship. According to recent ethnographic accounts it was known by different names by different Indian groups: Tomam by the Jicaque; Patatĭštahá by the Paya; and Ma-Papak or Ma-Papañki by the Sumu.[107] The Sumu appear to have associated the creator with the god of thunder. In the seventeenth century Indians living

---

[102]BAGG 5:283-308 Fr. Espino 17.9.1674; AGI AG 164 Bishop of Honduras 27.2.1696; BAGG 7:24-32 Fr. Joseph de Landa 31.7.1759; AGI AG 963 Guardian of Recollects 10.1.1813; Henderson, *British Settlement of Honduras*, p. 186; Strangeways, *Sketch of the Mosquito Shore*, p. 331.

[103]AGI AG 11 Dr. Criado de Castilla 15.5.1600.

[104]AGI AG 297 Fr. Betancurt 9.8.1698; ANH P5 L66 29.10.1698.

[105]AGI AG 39 and CS 1:169-191 Salcedo 31.12.1526; Herrera, *Historia general* 8 dec.4 lib.1 cap.6:40-41; Von Hagen, "The Jicaque," p. 18.

[106]Stone, *Central and Southern Honduras*, p. 18.

[107]*Límites*, 181 Informe 1882; Conzemius, "Los Indios Payas," p. 296; idem, *Ethnographical Survey*, p. 126; Landero, "Los Taoajkas," p. 49; Chapman, "Tropical Forest Tribes," p. 140.

between the Ríos Guayape and Segovia believed in a god or Gualahuana, which means mother of thunder, who had created the world and brought men into being from the hairs under her arms. She was said to have had two sons, who were the sun and moon. The sun had lived on the earth but retired to heaven angry when a crab ate his arm. The moon seeing his brother in heaven, made a fire and the sun seeing such a great light, went to see what it was and the moon laid hold of him and went with him to heaven.[108] They also believed in a number of supernatural beings, including the sun, moon, stars, and rainbow, which were thought to have had a former human existence on earth.[109] Greatest fear was reserved for evil spirits, which the Sumu called Woolsaw or Lasa and the Jicaque, Tsii.[110] There was also a large number of bush spirits associated with plants and animals of the forest. The presence and activities of animals in the forest were regarded as omens, and many stories were told surrounding them.[111]

The only religious figure amongst the tribes of eastern Honduras was the sukya, who acted as a healer and diviner, as well as advisor to individuals and the community. Conzemius recorded that amongst the Paya the office of sukya was hereditary passing to the most intelligent son or another close relative.[112] It is possible that the hereditary character of the office was a relatively recent phenomenon as it appears to be amongst the Sumu and Mosquito.

Religious ceremonies centered on the life cycle and they were generally accompanied by mishla feasts. The nature of burials indicates that they believed in an afterlife, for individuals were buried with their belongings and food. Amongst Indians living between the Ríos Guayape and Segovia in the seventeenth century a man was buried with his bow and lance and a woman with her grindstone. When a person died he or she went to hell and on the fourth day an old woman called Gualavana came with another person to clean the path from hell to enable the soul to pass to heaven.[113]

Some religious ceremonies were held at harvest and prior to battle or an expedition. They generally lasted several days and were accompanied by feasting, drinking, and music provided by bone flutes and pipes. Participants wore special clothes

[108]AGI AG 223 Fr. Pedro de la Concepción 13.1.1699. A version of this legend was recorded earlier in this century (Conzemius, *Ethnographical Survey*, p. 130).

[109]Conzemius, *Ethnographical Survey*, pp. 126, 136-37.

[110]AGI AG 963 Guardian of Recollects 10.1.1813; Henderson, *British Settlement of Honduras* p. 187; Strangeways, *Sketch of the Mosquito Shore*, p. 331; *Límites*, 177, 182 Informe 1882; Conzemius, "Los Indios Payas," pp. 296, 298; idem, *Ethnographical Survey*, pp. 127-28; Landero, "Los Taoajkas," p. 47; Von Hagen, "The Jicaque," p. 60.

[111]BAGG 5:283-308 Fr. Espino 17.9.1674; Conzemius, "Los Indios Payas," pp. 298-99; idem, *Ethnographical Survey*, pp. 132-34, 165-70.

[112]Conzemius, "Los Indios Payas," p. 297. It would appear that amongst the Sumu and Mosquito contenders for the office made prophecies and the individual whose prophecies came true was urged to became the sukya (Conzemius, *Ethnographical Survey*, pp. 140-42; Landero, "Los Taoajkas," pp. 46-47). It would appear therefore that the hereditary character of the position was rather vaguely established and depended to a degree on the ability of the office holder, thus suggesting that the hereditary aspect of the office was perhaps a recent development.

[113]AGI AG 223 Fr. Pedro de la Concepción 13.1.1699.

and painted their bodies, and sometimes wore masks and carried banners with the painted images of the sun, moon, and animals amongst other things. Self-mutilation of the ears, tongue, nose, and genitals was practiced and the blood was sipped to aid divination.[114] Although a number of religious ceremonies were held it appears that sacrifices were not common. Cannibalism was practiced but it is doubtful if it had any religious significance. War captives were often killed and eaten,[115] but their death probably signified no more than the annihilation of the enemy and the victory of the captors. Some were killed by having poles thrust up their torsos, but in this case the victims were not eaten. Reasons for these different practices are not known.

---

[114]Examples of such ceremonies include: BAGG 5:283-308 Fr. Espino 17.9.1674; AGI AG 297 Fr. Betancurt 9.8.1698; Goicoechea, "Relación sobre los indios gentiles," pp. 303-15; Conzemius, *Ethnographical Survey*, p. 89; Vázquez, *Crónica* 4:123-24.

[115]BAGG 5:283-308 Fr. Espino 17.9.1674; Lothrop, "The Word 'Maya'," p. 358 ref. to López de Gomara; Vázquez, *Crónica* 4:123-24, 167; Colón, *Vida del Almirante*, p. 277; Chapman, "Tropical Forest Tribes," pp. 144-46.

# 5
# The Aboriginal Population

## ABORIGINAL POPULATION ESTIMATES

The controversy that exists over estimates of the native population in the New World is more difficult to resolve in Central America because of the relative lack of documentary evidence and the speed with which the population declined.[1] Estimates of the size of the Indian population on the eve of discovery range from Kroeber's calculation of 100,000 for Honduras and Nicaragua together to Dobyns's estimate of between 10,800,000 and 13,500,000 for Central America.[2] Kroeber maintains that the estimates of early observers were exaggerated, a conclusion that he arrived at after examining the demographic history of Indian groups in the United States, particularly California. He assumed that the Indian population had grown at a regular rate since the time of conquest and derived his estimates by projecting the growth rate backwards from figures provided by Humboldt for the end of the eighteenth century. He thus disregarded the devastating impact of newly introduced diseases and the disruptive effect of conquest and colonization on the economic and social life of the Indians. Steward accepted Kroeber's conclusion that the estimates of contemporary observers were exaggerated and, on the basis of evidence provided by the contributors to the *Handbook of South American Indians*, he suggested that the population of Central America, excluding Guatemala, was 736,500 of which 392,500 were in Honduras, Nicaragua, and El Salvador together.[3] This estimate is somewhat lower than that of Rosenblat, who on the basis of readily available

---

[1]A modified version of this chapter appeared in L.A. Newson, "Demographic Catastrophe in Sixteenth-Century Honduras."

[2]A.L. Kroeber, *Cultural and Natural Areas of Native North America*, (Berkeley and Los Angeles: University of California, 1939), p. 166; Dobyns, "Estimating Aboriginal American Population," p. 415.

[3]Steward, *Comparative Ethnology*, p. 664.

documentary evidence has estimated that the native population of Central America was 800,000.[4] Alternative approaches have suggested that these estimates may be too low. Sapper, who had an intimate knowledge of Mexico and Central America, estimated that on the basis of climate, resources, and Indian technology the native population of Central America was between five and six million.[5] More recently Dobyns has reviewed the literature available for the demographic history of the hemisphere and concluded that insufficient account has been taken of the devastating impact of disease and suggests that the Indian population was between 20 to 25 times greater at the time of conquest than it was at its recorded nadir, which for many Indian groups in Latin America was in the middle of the seventeenth century. He estimates that the Indian population of Central America was 540,000 in 1650 thus giving between 10,800,000 and 13,500,000 Indians at the time of conquest.[6]

These estimates have been proposed on the basis of only a limited reading of the documentary sources, and only recently has archival research by Radell, MacLeod, and Sherman begun to yield more detailed evidence about the size of the Indian population at the time of conquest and during the early sixteenth century. These authors are not in complete agreement, however, over the interpretation of the documentary evidence, particularly that relating to the Indian slave trade. Radell has suggested that the population of Nicaragua was over one million at the time of discovery, given that up to 1548 between 450,000 and 500,000 were removed from the country as a result of the slave trade; 400,000 to 600,000 probably died of disease, in war, or fled the province; and 200,000 to 250,000 were probably residing in the central highlands to be decimated during the ensuing 20 to 30 years.[7] Denevan adopts this estimate in his calculation of the aboriginal population of Central America and suggests on the basis of incomplete comparative evidence that the population of Honduras and Belize was 750,000.[8] He proposes that the Indian population of Central America in 1492 was 5,650,000. Radell's estimate of the number of Indians exported as a result of the slave trade is comparable to the accounts of Las Casas and Oviedo, which indicate that 500,000 and 400,000 Indians respectively were enslaved.[9] Despite the convergence of estimates Sherman considers

---

[4]A. Rosenblat, *La población indígena y el mestizaje en América*, vol. 1 (of 2) (Buenos Aires: Editorial Nova, 1954), p. 102.

[5]K. Sapper, "Die Zahl und die Volksdichte der Indianischen Bevölkerung in Amerika vor der Conquista und in der Gegenwart," *21st International Congress of Americanists* (The Hague) (1924) 1:100.

[6]Dobyns, "Estimating Aboriginal American Population," p. 415.

[7]D.R. Radell, "The Indian Slave Trade and Population of Nicaragua during the Sixteenth Century," in *The Native Population of the Americas in 1492*, ed. W.M. Denevan (Madison: University of Wisconsin, 1976), pp. 67, 75.

[8]Denevan, *Native Population*, p. 291. His estimates for the Central American countries are: Guatemala 2,000,000; Honduras and Belize 750,000; El Salvador 500,000; Nicaragua 1,000,000; Costa Rica 400,000; and Panama 1,000,000.

[9]B. de Las Casas, *Breve relación de la destrucción de las Indias occidentales* (London: Schulze and Dean, 1812), pp. 43-45; Oviedo, *Historia general* 4 lib.42 cap.4:385.

these figures too high.[10] He maintains that the capacity of the ships was small and that in the early years of the trade only a small number of ships were involved, whilst in later years heavy cargo demands for space reduced that available for slaves. He suggests that a more realistic figure for the whole period from 1524 to 1549 would be 50,000 and this figure includes Indian slaves exported from the whole of Central America not just Nicaragua. He estimates that the aboriginal population of Central America was about two and one-quarter million. Although MacLeod does not provide an estimate of the Indian population of Central America, he does suggest that 10,000 slaves exported per year for the decade 1532 to 1542 would appear to be too low and 200,000 for the duration of the slave trade a conservative estimate.[11] It seems possible therefore that about one-half million Indian slaves were exported from Nicaragua, and a proportion of those would have come from Honduras. In addition, some Indian slaves were shipped from northern Honduras and the Bay Islands to the Caribbean islands, but the flow was undoubtedly much smaller than that which passed through Nicaragua. It will be suggested that between 100,000 and 150,000 Indians were exported from Honduras during the same period. Unfortunately none of the three authors mentioned proposes an estimate for the aboriginal population of Honduras and before doing so it is necessary to examine in detail the evidence available.

THE DOCUMENTARY AND CULTURAL-
ECOLOGICAL EVIDENCE

Although numerous archaeological sites have been uncovered in Honduras, the majority have not been investigated scientifically. It is impossible, therefore, to estimate the aboriginal population on the basis of archaeological evidence alone. The basic source of information is the documentary record, whilst cultural-ecological evidence may be used to indicate whether the numbers suggested by the documentary evidence could have been supported given the country's natural resources and the technology possessed by the Indians.

Contemporary observers were impressed by the size of the Indian population in Honduras, although few gave precise estimates. In 1539 the bishop of Honduras, Cristobal de Pedraza, wrote that when Gil González Dávila and Hernán Cortés had arrived in Honduras it had possessed almost as many people as Mexico, and in a later letter he described the country as having been as highly populated as Mexico and Peru.[12] In 1541 Benzoni recorded that the population of Honduras on the eve of conquest had

---

[10]W. L. Sherman, *Forced Native Labor in Sixteenth-Century Central America* (Lincoln: University of Nebraska, 1979), pp. 4-5. For a full discussion of the volume of the Indian slave trade, see pp. 74-82.

[11]MacLeod, *Spanish Central America*, p. 52.

[12]AGI AG 9 and RAHM CM A/108 4843 ff. 285-88 Pedraza to Crown 18.5.1539; AGI AG 164 Pedraza to Crown 1.5.1547.

been 400,000.[13] Unfortunately this is the only precise estimate made by a contemporary chronicler. It seems likely, however, that Benzoni's figure is an underestimate, for it was made after Pedro de Alvarado's brutal conquest of western Honduras and after the Indian slave trade had taken its heaviest toll. Prior to that time the country had been highly populated. In 1535 Andrés de Cerezeda reported that around the town of Naco alone there were 200,000 Indians, who could be of service,[14] whilst further south the legendary leader Lempira was able to muster a fighting force of 30,000 Indians to resist Spanish conquest.[15] There was clearly a large number of settlements in Honduras, although the majority did not exceed several thousand households. Cerezeda reported that all the way from Naco to the sea were villages with up to 2,000 houses,[16] whilst Stone believes that the abundance of archaeological remains in the Comayagua valley indicates that the population ran into the thousands.[17] Similarly, the hinterland of Gracias a Dios was densely populated,[18] with villages containing 2,000 and 3,000 houses.[19] It is also clear that eastern Honduras had a large population, but little was known about this unconquered and uncolonized area in the early sixteenth century, so that their numbers could not have been included in early population estimates. In 1548 there were said to be 27,000 pans working gold in the Río Guayape and by the end of the century 4,000 to 5,000 Indians had been found living between Trujillo and Cabo de Camarón.[20] There were thus dense populations in Honduras, for although the majority of settlements were small, what they lacked in size they made up for in numbers. As such Benzoni's estimate seems too low especially when the devastating impact of disease and the Indian slave trade are also taken into account. An aboriginal population of about 800,000, of which 200,000 were living in the uncolonized areas, seems not unreasonable and could easily have been supported given the province's natural resources and the nature of Indian economies.

Clark and Haswell have estimated that groups practicing shifting cultivation can achieve a population density of 20 persons per square kilometer, whilst simple agriculture can only support ten persons per square kilometer, and those dependent on wild food resources only 0.1 per square kilometer.[21] Indians in western and central Honduras practiced a form of shifting cultivation, though in the northern valleys and coastal plains where agriculture was more permanent in nature higher densities could have been

---

[13]Benzoni, *Historia del nuevo mundo*, p. 163. Johannessen believes that Benzoni was referring to tributary Indians and thus multiplies the figure of 400,000 by three to give a total population of 1,200,000 (Johannessen, *Savannas*, pp. 29-31).

[14]AGI AG 39 and RAHM CM A/107 4842 ff.160-91 Cerezeda to Crown 31.8.1535.

[15]Fuentes y Guzmán, *Recordación Florida* 2:145.

[16]AGI AG 39 and RAHM CM A/107 4842 ff. 160-191 Cerezeda to Crown 31.8.1535.

[17]Stone, *Central and Southern Honduras*, p. 9.

[18]AGI AG 39 Cerezeda to Crown 14.8.1536.

[19]AGI AG 49 Celis to Crown 10.3.1535.

[20]RAHM 9/4663 no. 15 Valverde to Crown, no date.

[21]G. Clark and M. Haswell, *The Economics of Subsistence Agriculture* (London: Macmillan, 1966), p. 37.

supported. In eastern Honduras the Indians practiced agriculture to some degree, but they were also dependent on hunting, fishing, and gathering; agriculture appears to have been most poorly developed amongst the Jicaque Indians. Nevertheless there were no Indian groups that were entirely dependent on wild food resources. It is suggested that the population density of the Jicaque was one per square kilometer, whilst other Indian groups in eastern Honduras, the Paya, and Sumu, could have achieved densities of ten per square kilometer. The total population supported by different Indian economies could thus have reached 1,396,858 or even higher, for, if anything, the population density estimates err on the low side, particularly for western and central Honduras. Hence, the proposed aboriginal population of 800,000 could have been supported easily given the province's natural resources and the subsistence patterns of the Indians.

Table 1

ESTIMATED ABORIGINAL POPULATION
BASED ON CULTURAL AND ECOLOGICAL EVIDENCE

|  | sq. kms. | Estimated density | Estimated population |
|---|---|---|---|
| Western and central Honduras[a] | 42,563 | 20 | 851,260 |
| Eastern Honduras[b] | 52,897 | 10 | 528,970 |
| Area occupied by the Jicaque[c] | 16,628 | 1 | 16,628 |
| TOTAL |  |  | 1,396,858 |

[a]Departments of Cortés, Santa Barbara, Copán, Ocotepeque, Lempira, Intibucá, Comayagua, La Paz, Francisco Morazán, Valle and Choluteca.

[b]Departments of El Paraíso, Olancho, Gracias a Dios, Islas de la Bahía, and half of Colón.

[c]Departments of Atlántida, Yoro, and half of Colón.

# Part III

## Spanish Conquest, 1522 to 1550

# 6
# Conquest, Slaves, and Gold

Although Honduras was discovered by Columbus on his fourth voyage in 1502, several decades passed before the country was brought under effective Spanish administration. Conquest and colonization were protracted because the province lacked the riches to attract high caliber conquistadors and the nature of the Indian societies themselves made conquest difficult. Conquest was therefore characterized by petty squabbles between rival conquistadors in which the Indians were often involved as innocent victims. The process of conquest and colonization involved the establishment of towns and the allocation of encomiendas and land grants. Since most conquistadors and colonists sought to return to Spain with enhanced financial and social positions within their short lifetimes, they looked for immediate sources of wealth. Encomiendas in Honduras were small and therefore generated only small incomes; they did, however, enhance the social standing of holders through the overlordship of Indians that they conferred. But the main sources of wealth during the first half of the sixteenth century were Indian slaves and minerals. Indian slaves were in great demand in the Caribbean islands and Panama where the Indian population had been decimated, whilst gold and silver commanded high prices in Europe. Both activities were dependent, however, on the availability of Indians whose rapid decline in the first half of the sixteenth century threatened the economic growth of the province in subsequent years. Although land grants were distributed to colonists, and they did enhance the social position of their owners, they could not provide the wealth that colonists sought, since the development of commercial agriculture required an investment of time and money, neither of which they could afford. It was not until the second half of the century, when profits from Indian slaves and minerals began to decline, that land was viewed as a source of income and as an outlet for profits that had been accumulated in slaving and mining.

DISCOVERY AND CONQUEST

In 1502 Columbus explored the Bay Islands and the coast from Cape Honduras, which he named Punta Caxinas, south to Panama.[1] Although it is clear that the Bay Islands and the north coast of Honduras were raided for slaves, two decades passed before further exploratory expeditions to the area were mounted. In 1522 a major expedition led by Gil González Dávila and Andrés Niño from Panama explored western Nicaragua as far north as the Bay of Fonseca.[2] Following the return of the expedition to Panama, the governor of Panama, Pedrarias Dávila (Pedro Arias de Avila), became anxious to possess the explored territory for himself. Whilst Gil González Dávila was in Santo Domingo organizing a new expedition to consolidate his claim to the territory, Pedrarias dispatched Francisco Hernández de Cordoba to establish his claim to the area.[3] Meanwhile several other claimants were arriving from the north. From Mexico Cortés sent one of his captains, Cristóbal de Olid, to take possession of Honduras and search for a sea link between the Atlantic and Pacific oceans. He arrived in 1524 but with the aim of claiming the territory for himself. Hearing of the intentions of Olid, Cortés sent another captain, Francisco de las Casas, to take possession of the area in his name. Finally in 1525 Cortés himself arrived in Honduras. Meanwhile in 1524 Gil González Dávila had arrived from Santo Domingo in an attempt to regain his rightful possession of the territory. It was thus in Honduras that rival conquistadors moving south from Mexico and Guatemala and north from Panama met and fought to gain control over the area. Efforts to pacify the Indians were thus accompanied by battles between the Spanish themselves and even between rival elements of the same faction, very often using Indians as fighting forces.[4]

The conquest of the area was made even more difficult by the presence of a large number of independent Indian groups, who at best formed weak confederacies. This meant that the Spanish could not achieve effective control through political alliances with a few native leaders, but had to conquer each group separately. No sooner had one group been pacified than it revolted.[5] It would appear that much of the resistance displayed by the Indians was a reaction to the ill treatment they received at the hands of the Spanish during and following conquest. In the 1530s Indian resistance was widespread in western Honduras, where it was coordinated by Coçumba whose fortress was located in the Ulúa

---

[1]S.E. Morison, *Admiral of the Ocean Sea: A Life of Christopher Columbus* (London: Oxford University Press, 1942), p. 596; Colón, *Vida del Almirante*, pp. 271-79; Sauer, *Early Spanish Main*, pp. 121-25.

[2]AGI PAT 20-1-3 and CS 1:84-89 Relación del viaje...no date (1522?), PAT 26-17 and CS 1:89-107 Gil González de Avila 6.3.1524.

[3]CS 1:128-33 Pedrarias Dávila no date (April 1525?).

[4]For a full account of the rivalries between conquistadors, see Bancroft, *Native Races*, 2:144-65; P. Alvarez Rubiano, *Pedrarias Dávila* (Madrid: Consejo Superior de Investigaciones Científicas, Instituto Gonzalo Fernández de Oviedo, 1954), pp. 319-77; C. Molina Argüello, *El gobernador de Nicaragua* (Sevilla: Escuela de Estudios Hispano-americanos, 1949), pp. 25-37; Chamberlain, *Conquest and Colonization of Honduras*, pp. 9-18.

[5]AGI AG 9 and CS 1:169-91 López de Salcedo 31.12.1526, AG 39 and CDI 2:212-44 Montejo 1.6.1539, AG 9 Audiencia 23.9.1547.

valley.[6] An appeal to Pedro de Alvarado in Guatemala to pacify the area resulted in the defeat of Coçumba and a momentary quietening of native resistance. But the pacification by Alvarado, with the help of Indian auxiliaries from Guatemala, was particularly brutal and it aroused hatred amongst the Indians of western Honduras. It was not long, therefore, before they began to muster for renewed resistance. This time it was estimated that 30,000 Indians were coordinated by the legendary Lempira, whose stronghold was the Peñol de Cerquín. The resistance displayed at Cerquín also encouraged revolts in the valley of Comayagua and the mountain districts of San Pedro. The wars against the Indians were hard and it was not until 1539 that Francisco de Montejo finally succeeded in conquering western and central Honduras before turning east to pacify the Olancho valley.[7] Although the resistance offered by the Indians in western and central Honduras was the most highly organized and difficult to suppress, the resistance of Indians in eastern Honduras was prolonged and in fact persisted throughout the colonial period. Revolts began in the late 1520s when Indians in the vicinity of Trujillo and the Olancho valley rebelled against ill treatment and enslavement, and in 1542, 1544, and 1546 there were further revolts in the mines of Olancho.[8] The uprising in 1544 appears to have been coordinated with revolts in Comayagua, San Pedro and Nueva Segovia and it may be that it was an attempt to revive the resistance that had been displayed between 1536 and 1539.


URBAN CENTERS


The difficult task of conquest was consolidated by the establishment of towns and cities, which acted as symbols of Spanish territorial possession and centers from which the surrounding countryside could be administered and colonized. The Spanish sought to locate towns where there were either minerals or dense Indian populations, or ideally both; the availability of land was not of paramount importance during the early colonial period since conquistadors and colonists sought wealth elsewhere and relied on Indians for their supplies of food. Many Spanish towns were founded next to well-established Indian towns; Trujillo was founded on the Indian site of Guaimura, and Comayagua on the Indian site of that name. During the first half of the sixteenth century towns were often abandoned or their sites changed for a wide variety of reasons, including Indian attack, mineral exhaustion, disease, or unfavorable physical conditions. In many cases, however, such reasons were given to justify site changes that were politically motivated; in 1544 the bishop of Honduras observed that the site of Gracias a Dios had been changed by Francisco de Montejo, not because of the poor physical conditions of the area

---

[6]AGI AG 49 Celis 20.6.1534, AG 39 Cerezeda 31.8.1535, AG 39 Cerezeda 14.8.1536, AG 402 cédula 30.7.1537; Chamberlain, *Conquest and Colonization of Honduras*, pp. 34-39, 53-57.

[7]AGI AG 39 and CDI 24:250-97 Montejo 1.6.1539; Fuentes y Guzmán, *Recordación Florida* 2:145; Herrera, *Historia general* 12 dec.6 lib.3 cap.19:279; F. Lunardi, *Lempira: El héroe de la epopeya de Honduras* (Tegucigalpa: Tipografía Nacional, 1941), p. 54; Chamberlain, *Conquest and Colonization of Honduras*, pp. 79-97, 224-25.

[8]CS 1:293-99 Castillo no date (1527?); AGI AG 49 and CS 2:404-40 Cerezeda 31.3.1530; RAHM CM A/111 4846 ff.145v.-146 García 8.2.1546; AGI AG 9 no author 21.2.1546; Chamberlain, *Conquest and Colonization of Honduras*, p 20.

Table 2

POPULATION OF SPANISH TOWNS IN HONDURAS TO 1550

| | Initial population | 1539[5] | 1542[6] | 1542[7] | 1544[8] | 1547[9] |
|---|---|---|---|---|---|---|
| Trujillo | 40 (1525)[1] Spaniards | 16 | | 25-30 | 50 | 50 |
| Puerto Caballos | ? | 6 | | 6-7 | 10 houses | |
| San Pedro | 30/39 (1536)[2] | 25 | 32 | 25-30 | 50 | 25-30 |
| Gracias a Dios | 95 (1536)[3] | 35 | 28 | 25-30 | 60 | 25-30 |
| Comayagua | 35 (1539)[4] | 35 | 39 | 25-30 | | 25-30 |
| San Jorge de Olancho | ? | | | 25-30 | 50 | 25-30 |

Numbers refer to vecinos unless otherwise indicated.

[1] RAHM CM A/105 4840 f.137v. 1529.

[2] CDI 16:530-38 and RAHM CM A/107 4842 f.271 26.6.1536 records 38 vecinos and Alvarado. Another document states that encomiendas were given to 30 vecinos (AGI AG 39 14.8.1536).

[3] CDI 1:20-29 20.7.1536 Repartimiento of Gracias a Dios, plus Alvarado and Spanish officials.

[4] CDI 24:250-97 1.6.1539.

[5] RAHM CM A/108 4843 f.202 3.11.1539 and AGI AG 9 4.11.1539.

[6] AGI AG 965 17.2.1542. A list of vecinos among whom an assignment of slaves were distributed.

[7] AHNM *Diversos - Documentos de Indias* 40 Nov. 1542 to 13.9.1543.

[8] CDIU 11:385-409 1544.

but because "it is in the style of governors to undo that which others have done and to re-found cities and towns."[9] The frequent abandonment and re-establishment of towns together with the reallocation of encomiendas and lands that often accompanied site changes created an atmosphere of instability, which did not encourage permanent settlement.

The fortunes of towns varied considerably and they were reflected in the size of their populations, shown in Table 2. In general those towns founded at an early date became the most important in the province primarily due to their administrative functions; few towns, apart from the ports, had a strong economic base. The governorship of Honduras was established under the jurisdiction of the Audiencia of Santo Domingo in 1526 and initially the governor resided in Trujillo. During the pacification of western Honduras in 1536 Pedro de Alvarado established Gracias a Dios as the capital of Honduras, seeing that it was located on a good route to Guatemala, where he lived. However, Montejo argued that Comayagua was a more suitable site for the capital city, because of its superior natural setting, its proximity to all mining areas and its central location on a major route between the Caribbean Sea and the Pacific Ocean. Pedro de Alvarado also recognized the need for a route linking the two seas, but emphasized the importance of establishing a town in the interior. The location of the capital was bound up with the dispute between Alvarado and Montejo over the governorship of Honduras, which was not settled until 1543 when the *Audiencia de los Confines* was established with initial jurisdiction over the provinces of Honduras, Nicaragua, Guatemala, Chiapas, Tabasco, Yucatán, Costa Rica, and Panama. The site chosen for the seat of the Audiencia was Comayagua, but when its officials arrived in Honduras they decided to reside in Gracias a Dios. The city was deemed to be more centrally located between Guatemala and Nicaragua and in an important mining area with dense Indian populations. Its life as the seat of the Audiencia was short-lived; within two years officials reported that people were abandoning the city and in 1548 the seat of the Audiencia was transferred to Santiago de Guatemala.[10] Meanwhile ecclesiastical affairs were centered on Trujillo. For over a decade the Crown had intended to erect a bishopric in Honduras, but this was not effected until 1545 when a see was established at Trujillo.[11] By 1550 there were also three Mercedarian convents in Honduras at Gracias a Dios, Tencoa, and Comayagua.[12]

---

[9]AGI AG 164 Bishop of Honduras 12.12.1544.

[10]AGI AG 9 Pedraza 18.5.1539, AG 39 and CDI 24:250-97 Montejo 1.6.1539. AG 43 Caceres 5.9.1539, AG 49 Lerma 31.10.1539, AG 402-2 cédula 13.9.1543, AG 9 and CS 11:22-24 Herrera 22.5.1544, AG 9 Oidores 30.12.1545, AG 9 no author 21.2.1546.

[11]AGI AG 9 and CDI 24:382-93 Audiencia 20.7.1545.

[12]J. Castro Seaone, "La expansión de la merced en América colonial," *Revista de Indias* 4 (1943):405-40.

## THE ENCOMIENDA

An encomienda was a grant of Indians to an individual, who in return for providing the Indians with protection and instruction in the Catholic faith could levy tribute and labor services from them.[13] Following the foundation of a town, Indians within its jurisdiction were assigned in encomiendas to its vecinos. Prior to the introduction of the New Laws conquistadors and later governors were given the right to grant encomiendas, although titles to them had to be approved by the Crown. After the issuing of the New Laws in 1542 the Audiencia de los Confines was given the responsibility for assigning encomiendas.[14] Initially encomiendas were granted to those who had assisted in conquest according to their merits and services. Government officials were initially allowed to hold encomiendas, such that many governors and their relatives and friends held many of the best encomiendas; colonists complained that many of those who had expended considerable effort and money in conquest had been overlooked when the encomiendas had been allocated. The first major change in the procedure for allocating encomiendas came with the New Laws, which forbade viceroys, governors and other government officials, monasteries, hospitals and *cofradías* from holding encomiendas. There appears to have been little opposition to this order, mainly because royal officials had anticipated the legislation and made over their encomiendas to their wives and children.[15]

Although encomiendas were granted following the foundation of a town in a newly pacified area, they often changed hands within the lifetime of encomenderos. In the early conquest period Indians in areas that had been pacified and who had been allocated in encomiendas often revolted, such that they were generally pacified by a different conquistador who reallocated them. A notable example of this was in 1536 when Alvarado pacified western Honduras and founded the towns of San Pedro and Gracias a Dios, nullifying the encomiendas that had been granted by Cerezeda when he founded Buena Esperanza in 1534.[16] The encomiendas allocated by Alvarado were then revoked by Montejo, who proceeded to distribute the Indians amongst the soldiers who had accompanied him on his campaigns. Even where no new campaigns were conducted, it was common for new governors to reallocate encomiendas to their relatives and friends,

---

[13]The encomienda had been used in Spain during the reconquest, but when it was introduced to America the institution was modified to overcome some of the shortcomings that had emerged in its operation in the peninsula. For example, the encomienda in the New World did not confer rights over land as it had done in Spain. For the Spanish background to the encomienda and its early history in the New World, see R.S. Chamberlain, *Castilian Backgrounds of the Repartimiento-Encomienda*, Carnegie Institution of Washington Publication no. 509 (Washington, DC, 1939), pp. 19-66; and L. Hanke, *The Spanish Struggle for Justice in the Conquest of America* (Philadelphia: University of Pennsylvania, 1949), pp. 19-20, 23-25, 86-87.

[14]AGCA A1.23 1511 f.56 and f.76 cédulas 30.6.1547, 18.8.1548; AGI AG 9 Audiencia 23.9.1547.

[15]AGCA A1.12.4 2195 15749 f.288 cédula 22.10.1541, A1.23 1511 f.17 cédula 7.9.1543; AGI AG 402-2 cédula 9.7.1546.

[16]Chamberlain, *Conquest and Colonization of Honduras*, pp. 146-56.

confiscating them from other encomenderos for alleged ill treatment or enslavement of Indians.

For these reasons the history of the encomienda during the first half of the sixteenth century was one of granting, confiscating or voiding, and regranting, and altogether it created an unstable basis for the development of the area. But the encomienda was an unstable institution not only because of the continual change of encomenderos, but also because of the nature of the institution itself. Encomiendas were initially granted to individuals for their lifetimes only, but from an early date encomenderos continually pressed the Crown to allow encomiendas to be held in perpetuity thus enabling them to pass them on to their descendants. It was argued that 'permanent' encomiendas would result in the better treatment of the Indians and encourage colonists to remain in the province. The Crown was reluctant to relinquish its control over the allocation of encomiendas, but in 1536 it did permit the inheritance of encomiendas for two generations.[17] This concession failed to satisfy encomenderos who continued to petition the Crown for encomiendas in perpetuity.[18] By that time, however, the Crown had decided to abolish the encomienda.

Under the New Laws issued in 1542 all encomiendas falling vacant were to pass to the Crown and no new grants were to be made. There was an immediate outcry: it was argued that colonists would leave the area because they could not survive without encomiendas; mining activities would cease since those who owned mines would have no sources of labor; and the Indians would be badly treated by corregidores appointed to administer Crown encomiendas since they were only interested in augmenting their small salaries at the expense of the Indians.[19] As a result of protests throughout the empire, in 1545 the part of the New Laws that effectively abolished the personal encomienda was revoked.[20] A few years later Audiencias were given the power to allocate vacant encomiendas, with the proviso that they were to reserve the best Indian towns and ports for the Crown.[21]

The number and size of encomiendas granted during the process of colonization depended on the number of soldiers and settlers who had been involved in conquest, most of whom aspired to become encomenderos, and the size of the Indian population; it is ironic that the areas that were the most difficult to conquer, and therefore involved larger fighting forces, were generally those that were sparsely inhabited by seminomadic tribes.[22]

It is not known how many encomiendas were granted when Trujillo was founded, but in 1540 the *cabildo* reported that there were only 14 or 15 vecinos who held

---

[17]AGCA A1.23 4575 f.29 cédula 23.2.1536; AGI AG 401-3 and CS 6:64-68 Carta acordada 18.10.1539. The succession was elaborated further in 1550 (AGI AG 393-3 cédula 7.7.1550).

[18]AGI AG 9, RAHM, CM A/111 ff.83-84 and CS 12:449-60 Audiencia 30.12.1545, AG 164 Pedraza 1.5.1547.

[19]AGCA A1.23 1511 f.35 cédula 20.10.1545.

[20]AGCA A1.23 1511 f.56 cédula 30.6.1547.

[21]AGCA A1.23 1551 f.65 cédula 23.4.1548; AGI AG 402-3 cédula 7.7.1550.

[22]AGI AG 9 Montejo 4.11.1539.

encomiendas with a total of only 150 Indians.[23] The two repartimientos made by Alvarado in western Honduras were more substantial in number and size. In San Pedro he assigned 38 encomiendas, excluding one that he took for himself, which included various villages in the Ulúa valley and the village of Naco containing 400 Indians.[24] In the vicinity of Gracias a Dios he created 99 encomiendas, but without an adequate knowledge of the area such that individuals were given encomiendas of places that did not exist or that had been deserted, or else the same village was given to a number of people under different names. In other cases the names of supposed villages turned out to be those of mountains and rivers.[25] In Comayagua the original allocation of Indians was altered in 1539 when the site of the town was changed. At that time 35 encomiendas were distributed.[26] It is not known how many encomiendas were made when the towns of San Jorge de Olancho and Nueva Salamanca were founded in 1540 and 1544 respectively but they were probably few in number and small in size; an encomienda in the jurisdiction of Nueva Salamanca that was given to Miguel de Casanos, who was described as one of the first conquistadors, comprised only 20 Indians.[27] In the early 1540s Lic. Bracamonte summarized the situation in Honduras as follows: there were six Spanish towns--Trujillo, Puerto Caballos, San Pedro, Gracias a Dios, Comayagua, and San Jorge de Olancho--which all possessed 25 to 30 vecinos, with the exception of Puerto Caballos, which only had six or seven. None of the vecinos were rich and the encomiendas they possessed were small, for the largest had less than 400 Indians and those encomiendas comprised of 150 and 200 Indians were regarded as good.[28] A list of encomiendas in the jurisdiction of Gracias a Dios, which was drawn up in 1544, includes 60 villages or *barrios* assigned to 32 encomenderos.[29] Unfortunately the number of tributary Indians in each village is not recorded, but the largest number of *tamemes*, or carriers, available to any one encomendero was 380, and only four encomenderos could use more than 200. Similarly tribute assessments for the jurisdiction of Comayagua drawn up in 1549 indicate that there were 24 encomenderos, but only three of them possessed more than 200 Indians and they came from several small villages. In both

---

[23] AGI AG 44 Cabildo of Trujillo 12.3.1540.

[24] CDI 16:530-38 and RAHM CM A/107 4842 f.271 Testimonio de la fundación...de San Pedro de Puerto Caballos 26.6.1536. A letter from Cerezeda to the Crown says that encomiendas were given to 30 vecinos (AGI AG 39 14.8.1536).

[25] CDI 1:20-29 Repartimiento de la ciudad de Gracias a Dios 20.7.1536; AGI AG 39, CDI 24:250-97 and RAHM CM A/108 4843 ff.239-57 Montejo 1.6.1539; R.S. Chamberlain, "The Founding of the City of Gracias a Dios, First Seat of the Audiencia de los Confines," *HAHR* 26 (1946):2-18.

[26] AGI AG 39, CDI 24:250-97 and RAHM CM A/108 4843 ff.239-57 Montejo 1.6.1539, AG 9 Montejo 4.11.1539.

[27] Chamberlain, *Conquest and Colonization of Honduras*, pp. 221-22.

[28] AHNM Diversos Documentos de Indias 40 Bracamonte 1542-43.

[29] AGI JU 299 Tasaciones 1544.

Table 3

NUMBER OF ENCOMIENDAS IN HONDURAS IN THE 1540s

| Villages or parcialidades | Gracias a Dios[1] 1544-45 | | Comayagua[2] 1549 | |
|---|---|---|---|---|
| | Number | Population | Number | Population |
| Under Crown | 2 | 200 | 6 | 350 |
| Granted in encomienda | 60 | 4,154 | 41 | 2,345 |
| Unknown | 2 | 0 | 3 | 50 |
| TOTAL | 64 | 4,454 | 50 | 2,745 |
| Encomiendas | | | | |
| Over 200 tributaries | 7 | 1,890 | 3 | 750 |
| 100 to 199 tributaries | 12 | 1,842 | 7 | 780 |
| 50 to 99 tributaries | 3 | 202 | 11 | 815 |
| Under 50 tributaries | 6 | 220 | 0 | 0 |
| Population not given | 4 | - | 3 | - |
| TOTAL | 32 | 4,154 | 24 | 2,345 |

[1]AGI JU 299 Population figures are tamemes or bearers and are not strictly comparable with the number of tributary Indians.

[2]AGI AG 128 The population was higher than indicated because only 40 of the 50 villages or parcialidades included figures for the number of tributary Indians.

areas the number of Indians paying tribute to the Crown was small.[30] Unfortunately similar comprehensive lists are not available for other parts of the province.

The possession of an encomienda entitled the encomendero to exact tribute and labor services from the Indians assigned to him. Until the middle of the 1530s the amount of tribute that could be exacted from the Indians was at the discretion of encomenderos. However, due to their excessive demands, in 1533 and 1534 the Crown ordered that official assessments be made in New Spain and Guatemala respectively, but due to continued warfare, political instability, and the reluctance of royal officials to implement the order, they were not made until the 1540s.[31]

When the Audiencia of Los Confines was established in 1543 new *tasaciones* were ordered for the area under its jurisdiction[32] and from that time onwards the responsibility for tribute assessments lay with the Audiencia. Under President Alonso Maldonado the amount of tribute payable by Indian villages in the jurisdiction of Gracias a Dios was assessed,[33] and it would appear that tasaciones were also made for villages in the jurisdiction of San Pedro and Comayagua.[34] Although no evidence of the amounts that were to be paid has been found, these assessments did include the number of tamemes that encomenderos could employ, despite the fact that the New Laws specifically forbade the employment of Indians as bearers. The Audiencia was reprimanded for having included tamemes in the tasaciones and as a result in 1547 the service of tamemes was commuted to tribute.[35] An examination of 12 villages in the jurisdiction of Gracias a Dios indicates that the service of tamemes was replaced at the rate of about one cotton blanket and sometimes, in addition, one chicken per Indian.[36] When Cerrato became president of the Audiencia in 1548 he reported that the Indians couldn't pay one-half of what was due even if they were doubled in number.[37] He therefore set about moderating the amount of tribute to be paid. It seems likely that Cerrato's assessments were based on earlier population counts, since they were made over a very short period during which time it would have been impossible to conduct a new survey. There are also doubts as to the completeness of the reassessment.[38] In 1549 it

---

[30] AGI AG 128 Libro de tasaciones 1549.

[31] AGCA A1.23 4575 f.28v. cédula 28.2.1536; Fuentes y Guzmán, *Recordación Florida* 2:256-58; Chamberlain, *Conquest and Colonization of Honduras*, p. 241; S. Rodríguez Becerra, *Encomienda y conquista: los inicios de la colonización en Guatemala* (Sevilla: Universidad de Sevilla, 1977), pp. 115-17; Newson, "Demographic Catastrophe," p. 237 n.23.

[32] AGCA A1.23 1511 f.25 cédula 23.10.1543; Remesal, *Historia general* 2:93.

[33] AGI JU 299 Tasaciones 1544.

[34] AGI AG 9 and CS 11:454-68 Herrera 10.7.1545.

[35] AGCA A1.23 1511 f.40 cédula 5.7.1546.

[36] AGI JU 299 Tasaciones 1544, 1547.

[37] AGI AG 9 and CS 14:344-50 Cerrato 28.9.1548.

[38] AGI AG 128 Libro de tasaciones 1549.

was noted that villages in the vicinity of San Pedro still needed to be reassessed,[39] and the only evidence that exists for Honduras is for the jurisdiction of Comayagua.

Until the 1540s there was no restriction on the amount of tribute and labor that could be exacted from the Indians, and demands made by encomenderos were often excessive. Although encomenderos did demand tribute, mainly in the form of foodstuffs such as maize and beans, they appear to have been more interested in using Indian labor. Perhaps the greatest burden that fell on the Indians was the provision of tamemes.[40] Because long-distance trade had been limited in pre-Columbian times and the wheel and draught animals had been absent, few roads existed that were suitable for use by the Spanish. As a result Indians were employed as carriers to the extent that in the first half of the sixteenth century they formed the basis of the transport system. An examination of tasaciones of villages in the jurisdiction of Gracias a Dios reveals that 19 of the 32 encomenderos were allowed to employ over 100 Indians as carriers and their only obligation was to provide them with food.[41] Sometimes these tamemes were hired out, particularly to miners and merchants. Montejo was said to have made 10,000 *pesos* through the hiring out of Indians as tamemes, whilst his son-in-law had made another 6,000 pesos.[42]

The employment of Indians as tamemes took a heavy toll on the Indian population. Although the loads that the Indians were required to carry were legally limited to one and one-half *arrobas*, they were often exceeded. In 1547 the bishop of Honduras complained that Indians had been forced to carry loads of three and four arrobas over distances of 50 to 60 leagues. Moreover, since the journey from Comayagua to San Pedro and Puerto Caballos involved travelling between different climatic zones, one-half of them did not return and at least one-third died or became ill on the journey.[43] Despite the ban on the employment of Indians as bearers in 1541, its implementation proved impossible given the lack of any alternative means of transport. Indian bearers were used primarily to transport goods between the ports, major cities, and mining areas, but in the early years of conquest they were also used on expeditions to carry supplies.[44] As well as being employed to move goods to and from the mines, Indians worked in the mines themselves. The death rate in the mines was high; in 1539 one-half of the Indians

---

[39]AGI AG 9 and CS 15:31-40 Cerrato 8.4.1549.

[40]The employment of tamemes is discussed at length by Sherman, *Forced Native Labor*, pp. 111-28.

[41]AGI JU 299 Tasaciones 1544.

[42]AGI AG 164 Pedraza 1.5.1547. Others who made substantial profits through the hiring out of Indians were Maldonado's cousin who made 2,000 pesos a year by hiring out Indians from his encomienda of the village of Macholoa, whilst his manservant made 800 to 1,000 pesos a year by similar means using Indians from the village of Coçumba (AGI AG 9 Cerrato 27.8.1554).

[43]AGI AG 164 Pedraza 1.5.1547; Rodríguez Becerra, *Encomienda y conquista*, p. 110. For detailed accounts of the employment of tamemes, see the residencia of the first Audiencia 1548 to 1550 (AGI JU 299).

[44]For example, J.A. Saco, *Historia de la esclavitud de los Indios en el nuevo mundo*, vol. 1 (of 2) Colección de Libros Cubanos vols. 18 & 19 (Havana: Cultural S.A., 1932), p. 173.

working in *cuadrillas* in the mines of Gracias a Dios died.[45]   Because of the high mortality rate in the mines, their employment in mining was forbidden in 1539, and encomenderos found guilty of employing them in mining were liable to have their encomiendas confiscated.[46]

In addition to performing particular tasks a number of Indians from each encomienda were assigned to work as household servants in the homes of encomenderos. Initially Indian slaves were employed as household servants or *naborías*, but increasingly encomenderos employed Indians from the villages they had been assigned. As household servants, these Indians were separated from their families and they were subject to considerable abuse by members of the household.[47]   In fact they were treated in much the same way as slaves to the extent that they were sometimes bought and sold, even though the practice was illegal.[48]   In 1548 it was reported that in many parts of the Audiencia there was not a vecino who did not possess five or six naborías and in 1550 the Crown ordered an investigation into the 'condition' of naborías.[49]

Although various types of service were banned during the 1540s, some were included in the tribute assessments drawn up in 1549.  In central Honduras 36 out of the 45 villages granted in encomiendas were obliged to provide Indians for personal service, the largest from any one village being seven and the average number about three.[50] Although the commutation of tribute to personal service was forbidden in 1549 and from that date was not included in tasaciones, there is no doubt that it was still demanded by encomenderos.[51]

The items that the Indians paid as tribute consisted of foodstuffs, vegetable products, chickens, honey, wax, liquidambar, and sarsaparilla, and a variety of craft manufactures.  The most important food crop paid as tribute was maize.  The tasaciones for 1544 indicated the number of fanegas of maize that should be sown by the community and the proportion of the harvest that had to be paid as tribute.  There appears to have been no constant relationship between the amounts of maize sown and harvested.  In most cases Indians were required to sow maize in their own villages, although a number of tasaciones stipulated that the plots were to be cultivated near the encomendero's place of residence or in the mining areas.[52]   The latter requirements obviously placed greater burdens on Indian communities.  The tribute assessments for 1549 only stipulated the amount of maize that should be sown and it is assumed that the total product of the harvest had to be rendered as tribute.  Naturally the amount of maize harvested from

---

[45]AGI AG 9 and CDI 24:298-310 Montejo 1.1.1539.

[46]AGI AG 44 Cabildo of Puerto Caballos 1.11.1539; AGCA A1.23 1511 f.40 cédula 5.7.1546, f. 93 22.2.1549.

[47]For example, AGI AG 164 Pedraza 1.5.1547, AGI AG 402-3 and CS 17:2-3 cédula 11.3.1550.

[48]AGCA A1.23 4575 f.49v. cédula 28.11.1540.

[49]AGCA A1.23 1511 f.91 cédula 15.12.1548, A1.23 4575 f.107 real cédula 7.6.1550.

[50]AGI AG 128 Libro de tasaciones 1549.

[51]AGCA A1.23 4575 f.94 cédula 22.2.1549.

[52]AGI JU 299 Tasaciones 1544.

equal amounts of seed sown varied from year to year, however, encomenderos were forbidden to claim recompense for years of bad harvest in years of abundance.[53] The same tasaciones regulated the amount of maize that was to be sown at about one fanega for every ten tributary Indians.[54] One-tenth of a fanega would have yielded between five and ten fanegas and this may be compared with about 20 fanegas required to support a family for one year.[55] Beans, which were generally intercropped with maize, and chili peppers were also paid as tribute. The Spanish also attempted to encourage the cultivation of wheat, but since Indians possessed neither draught animals or plows, where encomenderos demanded this crop as an item of tribute, they were required to provide them. Wheat became a significant item of tribute in Honduras where ecological conditions were suited to its cultivation; in 1544 18 of the 64 villages in the jurisdiction of Gracias a Dios paid tribute in wheat, as did nine villages in the jurisdiction of Comayagua in 1549.[56] One of the most successful sources of food that was introduced by the Spanish and that became an important item of tribute was the chicken, or *gallina de castilla*. Other items paid as tribute were cotton and cotton goods, and various kinds of pots and pans, jars for storage, rush mats, and wooden pans for panning gold.

## INDIAN SLAVERY

The Indian slave trade probably provided colonists with the largest and easiest profits.[57] The enslavement of Indians in Central America began before the area was colonized. The rapid decline of the Indian population in the Greater Antilles created an urgent demand for labor. The earliest recorded enslaving raid dates from 1515, when a ship from Cuba captured Indians on the island of Guanaja. On returning to Cuba the Indians escaped and sailed back to the Bay Islands. In the following year a second expedition comprising two vessels sailed to the Bay Islands to avenge the affront. They succeeded in capturing 500 Indians and, after some Indian resistance, the two ships

---

[53]AGCA 1.23 1511 f.121 cédula 7.8.1549.

[54]AGI AG 128 Libro de tasaciones 1549.

[55]Borah and Cook have estimated that 25 fanegas of maize were required per year to support a family in central Mexico at the time of Spanish conquest (W. Borah and S.F. Cook, *The Aboriginal Population of Central Mexico on the Eve of Spanish Conquest*, Ibero-Americana 45 (Berkeley and Los Angeles: University of California, 1963), pp. 90-91), whilst Gibson (*Aztecs*, p. 311) has suggested between 10 and 20 fanegas were needed in the colonial period.

[56]AGI AG 299 Tasaciones 1544, AG 128 Libro de tasaciones 1549.

[57]There are several excellent accounts of enslaving activities in Honduras: Saco, *Historia de la esclavitud*; W.L. Sherman, "Indian Slavery in Spanish Guatemala" (Ph.D. diss., University of New Mexico, 1967); and idem, *Forced Native Labor*.

finally arrived in Cuba with 400 slaves.[58] By 1525 when Cortés arrived in Honduras, the Bay Islands had been depopulated as a result of enslaving raids from Cuba, Española, and Jamaica.[59]

The attitude of the Spanish Crown towards Indian slavery fluctuated throughout the first half of the sixteenth century as it attempted to reconcile its humanitarian views towards the Indian with the practical needs of empire; it had been entrusted with the protection and conversion of the Indians by Pope Alexander VI in 1493, but it was being pressed by conquistadors and colonists for immediate rewards for their efforts in conquest and colonization, and at the same time had to deal with the practical problem of Indians who refused to submit to Spanish authority. In general the Crown upheld the freedom of Indians as subjects of the king of Spain and only permitted enslavement as a form of punishment for rebellion or for pagan practices, such as cannibalism, which were considered as crimes. It also allowed Spaniards to acquire Indian slaves from native owners, since under Christian owners their status did not deteriorate and they could be instructed in the Catholic faith. Indians enslaved for refusal to submit to Spanish authority were known as *esclavos de guerra* and those acquired from native owners were called *esclavos de rescate*. In the 1530s various attempts were made to control the enslavement of Indians, and although it was finally banned in 1542, it was not effectively prohibited in Central America until 1548 when Cerrato became president of the Audiencia.[60]

---

[58]Saco, *Historia de la esclavitud*, pp. 169-72; Herrera, *Historia general* 4 dec.2 lib.2 cap.7:111-14; A.A. Valladares, *Monografía del departamento de las islas de la Bahía* (Tegucigalpa: Talleres Tip. Nacional, 1939), p. 34; B. de Las Casas, *Obras escogidas*, 5 vols. (Madrid: Ediciones Atlas, 1957): lib.3 cap.92:392-93.

[59]De Vedia, "Cartas de relación," 147 Cortés 3.9.1526. Whilst condemning the depopulation of Honduras, Cortés actively gave his support to Indian slavery by giving his lieutenant Hernando de Saavedra license to barter with local caciques for slaves (CDI 26:185-94 Cortés 1525) and by branding Indians who rebelled with his own branding iron (AGI AG 39 and CS 1:169-91 López de Salcedo 31.12.1526).

[60]In 1530 the Crown, concerned about the ill treatment of Indians, ordered that no more slaves were to be taken in war or obtained from native owners by trade (AGCA A1.24 2197 15752 f.17v. cédula 2.8.1530; AGI AG 965 1531; V. de Puga, *Provisiones, cédulas, instrucciones para el gobierno de Nueva España* (Madrid: Ediciones Cultura Hispánica, 1945), pp. 65v., 66; S. Zavala, *Contribución a la historia de las instituciones coloniales en Guatemala* (Guatemala: Editorial Universitaria, 1967), pp. 13-14. Colonists complained bitterly and as a result esclavos de rescate and esclavos de guerra were permitted again in 1532 and 1533 respectively (AGCA A1.24 2197 15752 f.4 cédula 30.6.1532, f.5v. and AGI 393-1 cédula 19.3.1533; CDI 14:279-300 Testimonio del estado...Cabildo of Puerto Caballos 2.8.1536; Zavala, *Instituciones coloniales*, pp. 14-20; Sherman, *Forced Native Labor*, pp. 35-36). In order to try and restrict the number of Indians enslaved, in 1534 Indians were no longer allowed to possess Indian slaves (CDIU 10:192-203 cédula 20.2.1534). This effectively restricted the number of Indians that the Spanish could obtain from native owners. This was reinforced in 1536 by an order that forbade the acquisition of esclavos de rescate and ordered the drawing up of a list of slaves that had been obtained by trade (AGCA A1.23 4575 f.42 cédula 9.9.1536).

Apart from laws that stipulated the circumstances in which Indians could be enslaved, the Crown attempted to control the enslavement of Indians by specifying the procedures that were to be followed in making a slave. Before Indians could be sold as slaves, they had to be branded. In 1527 Indians who confessed to being slaves were branded on the face, whilst those who were sold as slaves were branded on the thigh and were supposed to be kept as naborías.[61] From 1526 the branding of slaves was to be supervised by royal officials, who also collected the royal *quinto*--one-fifth of the value of the slave. Those who branded slaves illegally were to suffer the death penalty and loss of property, but even these extreme punishments did not act as deterrents to illegal branding.[62] The Crown also attempted to control branding by limiting the number of branding irons. When royal branding irons were not in use, they were to be kept in a safe with three keys kept by three royal officials. Theoretically the only place in Honduras where branding could take place was Trujillo. However, it is clear that conquistadors made counterfeit irons and in some cases openly branded slaves with irons possessing their own marks.[63] In most cases the restrictions on the making of Indian slaves and the procedures to be followed were ignored, for although penalties existed, they were seldom imposed. For most Spaniards the risk involved in illegal enslaving activities was minimal and the profits to be made were high.

There were various circumstances in which Indians were enslaved. First, many expeditions aimed at subjugating the Indians or colonizing or exploring new areas resulted in the enslavement of large numbers of Indians. In 1527 the governor of Honduras, López de Salcedo, led a major expedition south to Nicaragua in order to establish his jurisdiction over that area. With him he took over 300 Indians slaves, including 22 caciques, who carried his personal effects and goods for sale in Nicaragua. On the way in the Olancho valley, he punished by death and mutilation 200 Indians who had taken part in a revolt. He continued south through the valley of Comayagua to León demanding supplies and Indian slaves from villages through which he passed. Altogether he enslaved 2,000 Indians, but most of them died on the journey; only 100 arrived in León.[64] Meanwhile Vasco de Herrera had usurped the authority of López de Salcedo's lieutenant in Trujillo and quelled an Indian rebellion caused by persistent Spanish

---

[61]RAHM CM A/105 4849 f.22 1527. Naborías were not true slaves since they could not be bought and sold publicly, but they were kept as household servants often for life (Sherman, *Forced Native Labor*, pp. 102-11).

[62]Sherman, *Forced Native Labor*, p. 384 n.1.

[63]AGI AG 49 and CS 2:404-40 Cerezeda 31.3.1530. Vasco de Herrera, the *regidor* of Trujillo, took with him the royal branding iron when he went on an expedition to Nicaragua and he also made two counterfeit irons with which he branded many slaves illegally. Similarly, Alonso de Cáceres appears to have used his own branding iron when he enslaved Indians in western Honduras (Sherman, *Forced Native Labor*, p. 65).

[64]CS 1:293-99 Castillo no date (1527?); AGI PAT 20-4 and CS 1:473-78 Testimonio...López de Salcedo 28.2.1529, AG 44 Cabildo of Trujillo 20.3.1530; RAHM CM A/106 4841 ff.50-1 Castillo 1531; Herrera, *Historia general* 8 dec.4 lib.1 cap.7:46-47; Sherman, *Forced Native Labor*, pp. 44-48. The details of the treatment meted out to the Indians by López de Salcedo make horrific reading: Indians were often killed by being roasted alive or being torn to pieces by dogs, whilst others were punished by having their limbs cut off. Those enslaved were put in neck chains and if they flagged on the journey, they were decapitated.

demands for Indian slaves. The suppression of the rebellion resulted in many villages being decimated such that around Trujillo "in the village which used to have 1,000 souls there are not 30."[65] Vasco de Herrera also conducted a slaving expedition to the valley of Naco where he enslaved 300 Indians. Pedro de Alvarado's conquest of western Honduras similarly resulted in the enslavement of many Indians. The expedition involved 3,000 Indian auxiliaries from Guatemala known as Achies or Aches, who were notorious for looting Indian villages and roasting people alive. The Bishop of Honduras, Cristóbal de Pedraza, reported that the expedition had resulted in 6,000 Indians being killed, enslaved, or sacrificed, of whom 3,000 had been enslaved and either taken to Guatemala or sold in the Caribbean islands.[66]

In addition to major expeditions during which thousands of Indians were enslaved, individuals or small groups of Spaniards continually harassed Indian villages to capture Indians or obtain Indian slaves by trade. The number of Indian slaves possessed by native owners was soon exhausted and caciques were forced to hand over free Indians.[67] Encomenderos also sold Indians from their encomiendas into slavery; profits from the sale of slaves were greater and more immediate than the income their tribute or labor yielded, and there was always the chance that they might receive another encomienda as colonization proceeded.[68]

The majority of Indians were enslaved for sale overseas; only a few were kept for personal use as household servants. They were not used to any large extent as agricultural laborers, but they were employed in mining. Initially the majority of slaves were exported to the islands of Española, Cuba, Jamaica, and Puerto Rico, but later as conquest and colonization proceeded they were exported further afield to Panama and Peru. In Panama the very rapid decline in the Indian population in the early colonial period created an acute shortage of labor. The first ship to sail from Nicaragua with Indian slaves for Panama left in 1526. At first slaves were exported via the island of Chira in the Gulf of Nicoya, but during the 1530s Realejo became the most important slave trading port.[69] It has been estimated that between 200,000 and 500,000 Indians were exported from Nicaragua up to 1542, and a proportion of those would have come from Honduras.

The New Laws of 1542 aimed at abolishing Indian slavery. The emancipation of slaves was the culmination of efforts by the Dominicans to ensure the good treatment of the Indians and it was encouraged by practical considerations. Slavery was a wasteful institution; many Indians were killed in enslaving raids and others died on their way to markets in the Caribbean, Central America, and Peru. Those that survived often had to

---

[65]AGI AG 49 and CS 2:404-40 Cerezeda 31.3.1530.

[66]AGI AG 9 and RAHM CM A/108 4843 ff.285-8 Pedraza 18.5.1539. For an account of losses sustained by individual villages, see: CDI 2:212-44 and CDI 24:250-97 Montejo 1.6.1539.

[67]AGI AG 49 and CS 2:404-40 Cerezeda 31.5.1530.

[68]For example, AGI AG 44 Cabildo of Trujillo 12.3.1540.

[69]CDIU 11:396-97 Pedraza 1544; AGI AG 164 Pedraza 1.5.1547. For an account of the Indian slave trade between Nicaragua, and Panama and Peru, see: MacLeod, *Spanish Central America*, pp. 51-55; Radell, "Indian Slave Trade," pp. 67-76; Sherman, *Forced Native Labor*, pp. 53-58, 74-82; Newson, "Demographic Catastrophe," pp. 228-29; and idem, "Depopulation of Nicaragua," pp. 270-75.

suffer further ill treatment and poor living conditions at their destinations. Not only was slavery very wasteful to human resources, but, since Indian slaves were exempt from tribute payment, it effectively reduced the income of encomenderos and the Crown.[70] However, when the New Laws were published the president of the Audiencia protested that it would lead to economic decline: the Crown would lose the quintos it received from the branding of slaves and from the gold that was mined by them, whilst the colonists had no other form of income or wealth.[71] In 1545 Las Casas observed that the New Laws were not being obeyed and it was not until 1548 when Cerrato arrived as president of the Audiencia that Indian slaves were effectively emancipated. Sherman attributes the successful enforcement of the New Laws to the courage and integrity of Cerrato himself, but it is doubtful if he would have succeeded had the circumstances not changed under which slavery had flourished.[72] The supply of slaves was drying up as the Indian population declined and at the same time the demand for slaves was falling; in Peru local sources of labor were beginning to be exploited and in Panama negro slaves, mules, and horses were being substituted for Indian labor. Meanwhile local demands for labor were increasing and colonists became concerned about the decline in the Indian population. Although the abolition of slavery also provided for the restitution of Indian slaves to their places of origin, very few were ever returned.[73]


MINING


The Spanish first discovered alluvial gold deposits in the vicinity of Trujillo not long after its foundation in 1525.[74] These deposits were worked only intermittently due to political upheavals and shortages of Indian labor, but prospecting continued and in 1534 a royal official in Trujillo reported that there wasn't a river or valley where gold had

---

[70]L.B. Simpson, *Studies in the Administration of New Spain IV: The Emancipation of the Indian Slaves and the Resettlement of the Freedmen, 1548-1553*, Ibero-Americana 16 (Berkeley and Los Angeles: University of California, 1940), pp. 3-4; MacLeod, *Spanish Central America*, pp. 52-56

[71]AGI AG 9 and CDI 24:421-22 Audiencia 30.12.1545.

[72]AGI AG 9 and CS 14:344-50, JU 301 and 302 1553. The enforcement of the New Laws in the Audiencia of Guatemala has been studied in detail by M. Bataillon, "Las Casas et le licencié Cerrato," *Bulletin Hispanique* 55 (1953):79-87; Sherman, "Indian Slavery"; idem, "Indian Slavery and the Cerrato Reforms," *HAHR* 51 (1971):25-50; and idem, *Forced Native Labor*, pp. 129-88; MacLeod, *Spanish Central America*, pp. 108-19.

[73]Despite numerous orders that the Indian slaves should be returned to their places of origin (for example, AGI IG 423-20 and CS 7:464-66 and 535 cédulas 24.7.1543, 28.9.1543) probably very few were. A list of 821 slaves freed in Panama in 1550, included 158 from Nicaragua, 18 from Guatemala, and 5 from Honduras. The largest number came from Cubagua (272) (Simpson, *Administration of New Spain*, p. 17).

[74]AGI AG 9 and CS 1:169-91 López de Salcedo 31.12.1526; Oviedo, *Historia general* 3 lib.12 cap.7:388.

not been found.[75] From 1531 gold deposits near Gracias a Dios were worked at intervals,[76] and in 1535 gold was also being mined in the Quimistán valley, near Buena Esperanza, Naco, and San Pedro.[77] In 1539 silver deposits were discovered near Comayagua[78] and in the following year miners with their cuadrillas, or gangs of laborers, left for the Olancho valley to search for gold, which they found in abundance.[79] The early years of mining were characterized by political instability and deposits were not worked on a regular basis. The peak years of production were between 1540 and 1565, after which output declined as the rich alluvial gold deposits were exhausted. In 1537 28,000 to 30,000 pesos of gold were produced[80] and between 1540 and 1542 109,000 pesos were smelted in Trujillo, San Pedro, and Gracias a Dios together.[81] During the latter period a further 100,000 pesos of Honduran gold were smelted in Guatemala. From that time onwards until the mid 1560s the gold deposits of the Guayape valley in Olancho dominated production. From that valley alone the treasurer of Guatemala, Francisco de Castellanos, claimed that up to 1560 two million pesos of gold had been extracted.[82]

Work in the mines was undertaken by gangs, or cuadrillas, which excavated stream bottoms and valley terraces moving on from one area to another as the deposits were exhausted. The cuadrillas varied in size between 20 to 100 workers, a number of whom were women who provided food for the male laborers. The average size of locally owned cuadrillas appears to have been about 20 workers, but those from Guatemala were larger, often comprising 60 to 100 people.[83] In 1537 30 cuadrillas belonging to citizens of Guatemala, many of them royal officials, were working in Honduran mines, and about the same time another 20 cuadrillas were owned by vecinos of San Pedro.[84] Initially the

---

[75]AGI AG 49 Barrientos 25.7.1534.

[76]AGI PAT 183-15 Sobre minas...en Gracias a Dios 8.5.1531.

[77]AGI AG 49 Celis to Crown 10.5.1535, AG 39 Cerezeda 31.8.1535; CDI 14:297-300 Cabildo of Puerto Caballos 12.8.1536.

[78]CDI 2:212-44 and 24:250-97 Montejo 1.6.1539.

[79]Chamberlain, *Conquest and Colonization of Honduras*, pp. 517-20.

[80]AGI AG 52 Lerma 1.6.1537.

[81]AGI AG 49 Royal officials 21.7.1542, AG 49 Celis 14.3.1542. The treasury accounts give a total of 179,103 pesos of gold for the period 1539 to July 1542, whilst the figures given by Celis are 24,000 pesos for 1540, 40,000 pesos for 1541 and 45,000 pesos for 1542. See also AGI PAT 180-1-74 Relación de las fundiciones...1539-1541.

[82]Chamberlain, *Conquest and Colonization of Honduras*, p. 234; AGI PAT 63-22 Probanza of Castellanos 1560, copy made 1623.

[83]AGI AG 39 Cerezeda 31.8.1535, AG 39 Cerezeda 14.8.1536; Sherman, *Forced Native Labor*, p. 72.

[84]AGI AG 52 Lerma 1.6.1537, AG 43 Cáceres 5.9.1539; CDI 24:352-81 García 1.2.1539, AG 9 Anon. 21.2.1546, AG 44 Cabildo of Gracias a Dios 6.9.1547; Chamberlain, *Conquest and Colonization of Honduras*, p. 122; Sherman, *Forced Native Labor*, p. 32.

gold mined in Honduras by Guatemalan miners was taken to Guatemala for smelting and taxing, with the result that the taxes entered the royal coffers in Guatemala. In order to control the exploitation of Honduran mines by Guatemalan miners, in 1537 the governor of Honduras, Francisco de Montejo, restricted the working of Guatemalan cuadrillas to specific areas and ordered that any gold they extracted should be smelted on Honduran soil.[85] Guatemalan miners complained and withdrew their cuadrillas with the result that production fell dramatically. It was estimated that prior to the introduction of the restrictions 60,000 pesos had been mined in one mining period, or *demora*, of nine months, whereas in the subsequent two years only 8,000 pesos of gold had been mined instead of a possible 150,000 pesos.[86] It was noted that there were only six or seven vecinos in Honduras with sufficient resources to undertake mining.[87] The dependence of Honduran mining on Guatemalan miners had been clearly demonstrated and as a result the restrictions on the areas that could be worked by Guatemalan miners were removed. However, the stipulation that the gold produced there should be smelted and taxed in Honduras remained.[88]

The cuadrillas were composed of Indians working in the personal service of encomenderos, together with Indian and negro slaves. Initially Indians formed the bulk of the workforce, but they were partially replaced by negro slaves as the Indian population declined and official restrictions on the employment of Indians in mining were introduced. From the earliest years of mining miners requested the Crown for shipments of negro slaves, but few appear to have arrived.[89] One consignment arrived in 1542, when 165 negro slaves were divided among the citizens of Gracias a Dios, San Pedro, and Comayagua, but there is no indication where they were employed.[90] Probably the majority of negro slaves that worked in the Honduran mines belonged to citizens of Guatemala and El Salvador. In 1543 there were said to be 1,500 negro slaves working in the Guayape valley and 2,000 in the country as a whole.[91] Since there were said to have been between 20,000 and 27,000 pans working gold in the Guayape valley at the peak of

[85] AGI AG 9 Montejo 27.7.1537.

[86] AGI AG 44 Cabildo of Gracias a Dios 10.8.1539.

[87] Oviedo, *Historia general* 3 lib.12 cap.7:389-90.

[88] AGI AG 9, CDI 2:212-44 and 24:250-97 Montejo 1.6.1539, AG 49 Royal officials 20.9.1547. For a full discussion of the dispute between the governor of Honduras and Guatemalan miners see Fuentes y Guzmán, *Recordación Florida* 2:165-67; Chamberlain, *Conquest and Colonization of Honduras*, pp. 111-15; Oviedo, *Historia general* 3 lib.12 cap.7:389-90.

[89] AGI AG 44 Cabildo of Trujillo 30.3.1530 request for 200 slaves, AG 49 Barrientos 25.7.1534 request for 100, AG 49 Celis 14.3.1542 request for 3,000 for Olancho, AG 49 Royal officials 4.5.1548 request for 200 for silver mines, AG 44 Pedraza, no date, request for 500 slaves for the mines.

[90] AGI AG 965 Royal officials 17.2.1542.

[91] AGI AG 9 and CDI 24:343-51 Maldonado 15.1.1543; RAHM CM A/110 Royal officials 20.2.1543.

production,[92] which was in the 1540s, it is clear that negro slaves only accounted for a small proportion of the workforce and that efforts to ban the employment of Indians in mining had so far been unsuccessful.


## AGRICULTURE

Although land grants did bestow some social status on recipients, the development of commercial agriculture required an investment of time and money before any profit could be realized. Capital was required for the importation of crops, animals, tools, and equipment for simple processing, as well as for the provision of adequate forms of transport, a particular problem in Honduras, and for the development of port facilities for the import and export of goods. The realization of profits was retarded in some cases by the long maturation of crops grown, whilst transportation difficulties made the production of bulky and highly perishable crops impossible. Commercial agriculture was not therefore regarded as a primary source of wealth, and its development appears to have been geared towards the domestic market for food. Initially colonists were supported by food imports from Spain and the Caribbean islands or by crops produced by the Indians and made available to them directly in the form of tribute or illegal exactions, or indirectly through local markets. As Indian supplies declined with the Indian population, colonists began to develop agriculture using the remaining sources of Indian labor; the importation of negro slaves for agricultural production was not a feasible proposition given its low profitability compared to other activities at that time.

Grants of land were initially distributed by the conquistador and later by the town council, or cabildo. Grants of land were theoretically limited to three *caballerías* or five *peonías*, but it is unlikely that these precise dimensions were adhered to in practice.[93] Furthermore, it is doubtful that the Spanish recognized Indian landholding rights, although there is a lack of evidence on the matter. In many cases the Spanish usurped

---

[92]AGI PAT 183-1-16 Antonelli and López de Quintanillas 7.10.1590, PAT 63-22 Probanza of Castellanos 1560, copy made 1623; RAHM 9/4663 no. 15 Relación geográfica of Valverde 24.8.1590; Ponce, *Relación breve*, p. 349. Authors of these accounts give different estimates of the numbers employed in mining ranging from 20,000 to 27,000.

[93]W.S. Stokes, "The Land Laws of Honduras," *Agricultural History* 21 (1947):149. The dimensions of caballerías and peonías appear to have varied throughout the colonial period. In the West Indies they were measured in terms of the number of *montones* that could be constructed, and a caballería was twice the size of a peonía. However, measurements specified in the Ordinances of 1573 indicated that caballerías were to be 5 times the size of peonías. A peonía consisted of a house plot of 50 by 100 feet; 100 fanegas of land for wheat or barley; 10 fanegas for maize; 2 *huebras* of land for a garden and 8 for trees; pasture land for 10 pigs, 20 cows, 5 horses, 100 sheep, and 20 goats. A caballería was to consist of a house plot of 100 by 200 feet and the rest was to be equivalent to 5 peonías (J.M. Ots Capdequí, *España en América: el régimen de las tierras en la época colonial* (Mexico: Fondo de Cultura Económica, 1959), pp. 20-28). In the middle of the eighteenth century a caballería was equivalent to 111 acres, whilst an *estancia* for *ganado mayor* was 6 3/4 caballerías and one for *ganado menor* was one-half of that (AGI AG 264 Ventas y composiciones de tierras 1749-51).

Indian lands, although they also made use of the extensive savanna areas that the Indians had not fully exploited. In pre-Columbian times the Indians had lacked suitable domesticated animals to raise and had not possessed effective tools to cultivate their lands.[94] The alienation of Indian lands became a more significant problem later in the colonial period when the value of land was realized.

Although colonists came to depend on native crops for their subsistence, they did introduce a number of crops from Europe, which they tried to encourage the Indians to cultivate. Two staple crops were introduced into Honduras with different degrees of success. Wheat (*Triticum aestivum* L.) was grown fairly successfully in the cooler highlands around Gracias a Dios and Comayagua. Two harvests a year were possible although the second was not as large as the first: the first harvest took place in August and then the land was burnt, plowed, and sown again.[95] Rice (*Oryza sativa* L.) was introduced by the Spanish at an early date, but it did not prosper.[96] Probably the most successful crops introduced from the Old World during this period were citrus fruits, many of which were introduced by Cortés from Santo Domingo.[97] Other fruits introduced during the first half of the sixteenth century were pomegranates, bananas, figs, and vines. Vegetables introduced by the Spanish, to Trujillo at least, included radishes, lettuces, aubergines, melons, cucumbers, chickpeas, onions, garlic, parsley, mint, coriander, spinach, rape, carrots, artichokes, and many others.[98] Although a great variety of crops were introduced, they would only have been grown on a small scale in the provision grounds and gardens of Spanish households.

Export crops remained insignificant in the economy during the first half of the sixteenth century. Although cacao continued to be produced in northwestern Honduras, its commercial production appears to have been overshadowed by that in other parts of Central America, notably Soconusco and Zapotitlán.[99] The only crop that the Spanish attempted to produce commercially in the early sixteenth century was sugar cane. In 1544 it was being cultivated around Trujillo, but solely for the domestic market.[100]

Horses, cattle, sheep, and pigs were all introduced into Central America by the earliest explorers and colonists; horses were essential for conquest and other animals were required to maintain the Spanish in the New World. Most of the livestock introduced

---

[94]Johannessen, *Savannas*, pp. 27, 109-11.

[95]CDI 2:212-14 and CDI 24:250-97 Montejo 1.6.1539; AGI AG 49 Lerma 31.10.1539, AG 9 Herrera 22.5.1544, AG 9 and CS 11:22-24 Herrera 22.5.1544, AG 164 Bishop of Honduras 12.12.1544; CDIU 11:397, 401 Pedraza 1544.

[96]AGI AG 39 Cerezeda 31.8.1535.

[97]AGI AG 49 Barrientos 25.7.1534; CDI 2:212-44 and CDI 24:250-97 Montejo 1.6.1539; AGI AG 49 Lerma 31.10.1539, AG 164 Bishop of Honduras 12.12.1544; CDIU 11:387-88, 391-92, 398, 401 Pedraza 1544.

[98]CDIU 11:393 Pedraza 1544.

[99]MacLeod, *Spanish Central America*, pp. 68-95.

[100]CDIU 11:393 Pedraza 1544.

were imported from the Caribbean islands.[101]   Cattle in particular thrived on the formerly underutilized savannas and on the lands left deserted by declining Indian populations.  The savannas were disease-free and, with the exception of the jaguar, predators were absent.  The grass was considered to be too high for sheep, which did not prosper,[102] but in the first half of the sixteenth century the raising of cattle, horses, and pigs was widespread in Honduras.[103]   The meat produced was of good quality and the relatively small demand for it meant that, despite shortages of fodder in the dry season, cattle in particular multiplied rapidly.[104]

## REGIONAL VARIATIONS IN SPANISH ACTIVITIES

The institutions and activities described above did not affect Honduras uniformly, but their introduction and importance were influenced by the distribution of the Indian population and natural resources, particularly minerals.  The presence of fairly dense Indian populations, particularly in western and central Honduras, which could be distributed in encomiendas or used to supply the Indian slave trade, encouraged the conquest of those areas at an early date.  But the conquest of western and central Honduras was difficult not only because was it the main area where rival conquistadors fought over territorial possession, but because no overriding political structure existed through which the Spanish could gain control.  As such each group had to be conquered separately and the maintenance of political control required high administrative inputs. Since these were seldom provided, there were constant Indian rebellions, which were further encouraged by demands for tribute and labor.  In eastern Honduras conquest and colonization were not undertaken with the same enthusiasm and in fact they were prolonged throughout the colonial period.  The introduction of the encomienda in these areas would have required considerable managerial inputs, which in most cases could not be justified given the small profits that could be made from the tribute and labor of the Indians; only in the mining areas was it considered desirable to control the local Indian population through the allocation of encomiendas.  However, the encomiendas that were granted were always few in number and small in size, and having exhausted local supplies of labor, the mines were worked by Indian slaves imported from other provinces and by negro slaves.

Although it is clear that Spanish activities were concentrated in western and central Honduras, it does not follow that the cultures that existed there were more profoundly affected by conquest and colonization.  The cultural changes that were experienced by different Indian groups were also influenced by the nature of the Indian groups themselves.  Because of the greater similarity of Spanish culture to those to western and central Honduras, the cultural changes demanded by them were less

---

[101]AGI AG 49 Cerezeda 31.3.1530, AG 44 Cabildo of Trujillo 20.3.1530; CDIU 11:389 Pedraza 1544; Johannessen, *Savannas*, pp. 36-37.

[102]CDIU 11:388 Pedraza 1544.

[103]AGI AG 49 Lerma 31.10.1539, AG 164 Bishop of Honduras 12.12.1544; CDIU 11:388, 399-402 Pedraza 1544; AGI AG 43 Cabildo of Comayagua 9.4.1551.

[104]CDI 24:463-73 Cerrato 28.9.1548.

fundamental and the larger size of the societies meant that demographic losses could be sustained more easily without cultural strains developing; the Indian cultures in eastern Honduras were more vulnerable to change and threatened to a greater degree by the types of changes that Spanish conquest and colonization demanded.

# 7
# The Cultural and Demographic Cost of Conquest, 1502 to 1550

During the first half of the sixteenth century changes in Indian culture were brought about directly as a result of Spanish conquest and colonization, and indirectly as a result of population decline. These changes were largely destructive, but there were regional variations in the degree of deculturation and depopulation that were related to the distribution of Spanish activities and to the nature of the Indian cultures themselves; whilst Spanish activities were concentrated in the western and central regions of the country, Indian groups in the east were more vulnerable to the changes that Spanish conquest and colonization precipitated.

## THE CHIEFDOMS

As will be demonstrated, the Indian population in western and central Honduras experienced a very rapid decline. This resulted in the disappearance of many villages and a reduction in size of many others. Montejo claimed that as a result of the conquest of the valley of Naco by Cerezeda not one of the 27 to 28 villages in the valley remained, whilst Alvarado's conquest of western Honduras resulted in the depopulation of many villages in the vicinity of Gracias a Dios: Talua was reduced from 400 houses to 40; Carcamo from 500 to 20; Araxagua from 250 to 40; Yopoa from 270 to 30; and Lepaera from 400 to 70 or 80.[1] Indian villages were depopulated not only as a result of conquest and enslaving raids, but because the Indians, particularly around Naco and Gracias a Dios, abandoned their homes and fled to the hills.[2] In some cases the Spanish tried to force the

---

[1] AGI AG 39, CDI 2:212-44 and CDI 24:250-97 Montejo 1.6.1539.

[2] AGI AG 39 and CS 1:169-91 Salcedo 31.12.1526, AG 49, RAHM CM A/105 4840 ff. Cerezeda 31.3.1530, AG 39 Cerezeda 31.8.1535, AG 39, CDI 2:212-44 and CDI 24:250-97 Montejo 1.6.1539, AG 44 Cabildo of Puerto Caballos 1.11.1539, AG 164 Pedraza 12.12.1544; Benzoni, *Historia del nuevo mundo*, p. 163; Sherman, *Forced Native Labor*, p. 45.

Indians to return to their villages,[3] but they generally relied on hunger driving them back to their homes in the lowlands.[4]

Apart from the disruption to the Indian economy brought about by the decline in the population and the redistribution of settlements, there was a number of other ways in which the arrival of the Spanish affected Indian subsistence patterns. First, the distribution of land grants to colonists reduced the area available for Indian subsistence activities, particularly agriculture and hunting. Second, the time available for the Indians to attend to their own subsistence needs was reduced as a result of Spanish demands for labor and tribute. Third, the Spanish introduced many new plants and animals from both the Old World and other parts of the New, as well as new techniques. Fourth, the pattern of trade that had been established in the colonial period was disrupted and reoriented.

The establishment of Spanish towns and the allocation of land grants within their jurisdictions meant that much of the land that the Indians had cultivated or exploited in pre-Columbian times was usurped; in Honduras the Spanish do not appear to have given legal recognition to pre-Columbian landholding rights, except in very general terms. Apart from directly usurping Indians' lands, the Spanish also pressured Indians to sell them their lands at very low prices.[5] Despite the fact that the Crown passed laws to protect Indians' rights to their lands, they were largely ineffective. Although it is sometimes suggested that the Spanish effectively occupied lands that were left vacant by declining Indian populations, there was no direct correlation between the alienation of Indians' lands and the decline in the population they supported.

The availability of labor for subsistence activities was drastically reduced by the decline in the Indian population and by the demands the Spanish made on Indian production. Labor inputs into subsistence activities were most dramatically reduced near the major towns where Spanish demands on Indian labor were the highest and where the Indian population experienced the greatest decline. Although the impact of declining Indian populations was mitigated to a certain extent by the existence of fewer consumers, population loss reduced the ability of Indian production to meet the demands made upon it by weakening the social organization of Indian communities. This made the cooperation required at critical stages in the cycle of cultivation difficult to organize. This was aggravated by the employment of large numbers of Indians in some form of personal service, which often involved them in prolonged absences from their villages. These absences had particularly serious consequences when they coincided with periods of land clearance, sowing, and harvest. During those periods Indians were often required to work the lands of their encomendero and parish priest, leaving them little time to attend to their own plots. Whilst labor inputs into production decreased, the demands made upon it increased. First, the Indians had to pay a proportion of their agricultural produce in tribute, which was often substantial. In the case of maize, Indians were often liable to pay the equivalent of about one-quarter to one-half of their annual family needs.[6] Since tithes were only payable on crops introduced from Europe, the Indians generally

---

[3] AGI AG 39, CDI 2:212-44 and CDI 24:250-97 Montejo 1.6.1539. Montejo claimed that he had secured the return of Indians to their villages after Alvarado's conquest of western Honduras.

[4] AGI AG 49, RAHM CM A/105 4840 ff.277-80 Cerezeda 31.3.1530; RAHM CM A/111 4846 ff.222-6 Pedraza 1.5.1547.

[5] AGCA A1.23 4575 f.103v. cédula 29.4.1549, f.110v. cédula 9.10.1549.

[6] See the discussion of the tasaciones for the proportion of production paid as tribute.

remained exempt from tithe payment, although a proportion of the tribute they paid was used to support the local church and clergy.[7] Nevertheless, they were required to pay for special masses and for ceremonies such as baptisms, confirmations, marriages, and burials. They were also obliged to provide hospitality in the form of food and shelter for official and nonofficial travellers, and this imposed a considerable burden on those villages located on major routeways.

Declining labor inputs and increased demands on Indian production had a number of effects on Indian subsistence. First, the decreased time available for subsistence activities and the reduced availability of land to exploit possibly resulted in the recultivation of lands rather than the clearance of new ones, with a resulting decline in soil fertility and hence crop yields. At a time when demands on production were increasing, the result would have been dietary deficiencies and food shortages. Second, the time-consuming nature of hunting, fishing, and gathering may have led to a decline in the importance of those activities, to the extent that they were undertaken only in times of severe food shortage. Third, the reduction in the diversity of economic activities would have been paralleled by a reduction in the diversity of crops grown, with low-yielding species such as starchy varieties of sweet potato, and those requiring high labor inputs being dropped from the assemblage of crops grown.[8] Conversely, there was an increase in the importance of the major subsistence crops, maize and beans, which were adopted by the Spanish as staples and as major items of tribute. The increased demand for maize could not always be met, however, even though maize and cassava were imported from the Bay Islands.[9] As such, there were often severe shortages of maize, which resulted in prices sometimes reaching 20 pesos a fanega.[10]

The probable loss in the variety of crops grown by the Indians was compensated for in part by the introduction of domesticated plants and animals, which either came from Europe or from other parts of the New World from which they had not diffused in pre-Columbian times. It is uncertain to what extent these newly introduced domesticates were adopted by the Indians. It seems likely that citrus fruits would have been added easily to the variety of fruit trees they already cultivated. Other crops such as wheat and sugar cane would not have been adopted so readily, because of the difficulty of fitting them into native systems of cultivation. Apart from the chicken, which became an important source of food as well as an item of tribute, other forms of livestock were not adopted to a large degree during the early colonial period, even though it was suggested that the Indians should be encouraged to acquire them, particularly pigs and sheep.[11] Even if ranching was not widely practiced by the Indians at this time, Indians were often forced to raise and tend livestock owned by encomenderos and priests.[12] The effects of the introduction of livestock were not wholly beneficial to Indian subsistence; very little

---

[7]C.H. Haring, *The Spanish Empire in America* (New York: Harbinger Books, 1963), p. 266.

[8]Sauer, *Early Spanish Main*, p. 54.

[9]AGI AG 39 Las cosas que se han remediado, no date.

[10]CS 1:293-99 Castillo, no date.

[11]AGI AG 402-3 and CS 15:106 cédula 9.10.1549.

[12]See personal service and CS 15:104 cédula 9.10.1549.

attention was paid to the management of livestock, which was allowed to range freely, often overrunning Indian plots.

The decline of Indian production undoubtedly led to a decline in trade within Honduras. The high levels of demand for agricultural produce and craft items would have left the Indians with little surplus to trade. In addition, long-distance trading links, particularly with Mexico, would have been broken with the destruction of the major trading colonies at Naco and on the north coast, whilst the demand for goods in Mexico probably declined with the changing power and needs of the elite groups there.[13]

The impact of conquest and colonization on the social organization of Indian groups was equally pervasive. Rivalries between Indian groups probably diminished in significance as the threat of Spanish domination increased, although there is no evidence for the emergence of a military or political organization that cut across traditional loyalties; Lempira was only able to muster a fighting force of 30,000 after he had defeated them in battle.[14] Although Indian solidarity was fostered to a certain degree by conquest, its ultimate effect was to weaken the social structure of chiefdoms through the imposition of Spanish institutions and through the decline in the Indian population it induced.

Throughout the New World the Spanish sought to gain control of Indian communities through their native leaders. They found that once the Indian leaders had accepted their authority and been converted to Christianity the rest of the population would follow.[15] They reinforced the authority of caciques by recognizing their noble rank and by allowing them and their eldest sons certain privileges. These included exemption from tribute payment and routine labor. Initially they were also allowed to possess slaves and they were permitted to wear Spanish dress, ride horses, and carry arms.[16] Spanish officials received constant orders from the Crown not to undermine the authority of natural leaders, by removing them from office and placing their own nominees in their place or by employing them in tasks inappropriate to their status.[17] Having achieved political control, the Spanish sought to maintain it by ordering that schools be provided in Spanish towns for the sons of Indian leaders.[18] Indian leaders thus became intermediaries between Spaniards and Indians. The native councils were eventually replaced by elected cabildos or town councils modelled on those established in Spanish towns. The councils consisted of elected officials, who received salaries that were paid out of the tribute paid by the community;[19] the former also had the authority to

---

[13]Chapman, "Port of Trade Enclaves," pp. 119-20.

[14]See Chapter 3.

[15]CDI 14:279-300 Testimonio del estado...1536; Fuentes y Guzmán, *Recordación Florida* 2:110.

[16]C. Gibson, "The Transformation of the Indian Community in New Spain," *Journal of World History* 2 (1955):587; and idem, *Aztecs*, p. 150. For the cédula allowing them to possess slaves, see AGCA A1.23 4575 f.22 20.2.1534.

[17]AGCA A1.23 1511 f.59 cédula 26.8.1547; AGI AG 402-3 and CS 15:106 cédula 9.10.1549.

[18]AGI AG 9 cédula 24.9.1545, AG 402-2 and CS 13:490-91 cédula 10.9.1546.

[19]AGI AG 402-3 and CS 15:106 cédula 9.10.1549.

make arrests and punish minor offenses. They were thus used to enforce Spanish rules and laws.

The majority of the Indians were regarded as commoners. They were distinguished by their lack of social privileges and by the fact that they were required to pay tribute and perform labor services. Specialist craftsmen were treated no differently from commoners and the official status of military and religious leaders disappeared as their roles were taken over by Spanish functionaries. Nevertheless, during the early conquest period they probably continued to command some respect within their communities. Since the Spanish only recognized the noble status of caciques and their eldest sons and did not differentiate between other Indians, a degree of social levelling occurred amongst those of non-noble birth.

Indian slaves formed the lowest class in Indian society until slavery was abolished in 1542. Slaves were owned by caciques, who often sold them to the Spanish, sometimes enslaving Indians in their own communities for that purpose, even though it was illegal.[20] As large numbers of Indian slaves were sold to the Spanish, the size of this class within Indian communities declined.

Other social changes occurred at the family level. In pre-Columbian times polygamy had been widely practiced, but the Spanish regarded it as a sin and sought to suppress it.[21] They also insisted that married couples did not live with their parents in order to prevent incest and adultery. It is difficult to assess the degree of success they achieved, but the Indians would not have been impressed by the example set by the Spaniards themselves. Many Spanish officials, encomenderos and priests entered into casual relationships with Indian women, taking advantage of them when they were working in their personal service.[22] Family cohesion was also weakened as individual members were killed during conquest, enslaved, and transported to other provinces, or were absent for prolonged periods whilst performing some form of labor service. These factors would have encouraged instability in marriage, and contributed to the existence of many one-parent families and large numbers of orphans. There is no evidence to suggest that marriage residence rules changed during the early colonial period, although it seems likely that the Spanish would have encouraged patrilocal residence as they did patrilineal descent.[23]

The Spanish were horrified by many of the religious practices of the Indians in western and central Honduras and as far as possible attempted to eradicate them and impose Christianity. Temples were destroyed or converted into churches, and idols were replaced by crosses and statues of the Virgin Mary. They were also appalled by many of the Indian ceremonies, which often involved sacrifices and drunken dancing, and they attempted to suppress them in favor of more sober Christian ones.[24] Mass baptisms were common in the early years of conquest and exploration, but it is doubtful if true conversion ever took place. The process of conversion was continued by priests provided either by the Crown or by encomenderos, but the task of conversion was not easy. Some

---

[20]AGCA A1.23 4575 f.22 cédula 20.2.1534, A1.24 2195 f.188 cédula 31.1.1538.

[21]CDI 24:513-57 López 9.5.1550.

[22]AGI AG 164 Pedraza 1.5.1547, AG 402-2 and CS 17:2-3 cédula 11.3.1550.

[23]Gibson, "Indian Community in New Spain," p. 587.

[24]AGI AG 164 and RAHM CM A/111 4846 ff.222-6 Pedraza 1.5.1547; Fuentes y Guzmán, *Recordación Florida* 2:110.

blamed the failure of Indians to adopt Christianity on the incapacity and obstinacy of the Indians,[25] but clearly the task was made more difficult by the resentment that their ill treatment by the Spanish aroused.[26]

## THE TRIBES

Unfortunately there is little evidence of the cultural changes amongst tribal groups in eastern Honduras, although undoubtedly some changes did occur as a result of enslaving raids and the establishment of mining enterprises in Olancho. Those areas most profoundly affected were the coast around Trujillo and the Olancho valley, with the interior regions affected to a much lesser degree.[27] Fear of enslaving raids often drove Indians to retreat inland. In 1544 Bishop Pedraza reported that Indians around Trujillo had retreated 14 and 15 leagues inland, so that villages that had formerly possessed 1,000 and 1,500 houses did not have one Indian left.[28]

In most cases the retreat inland would have resulted in at least a minor restructuring of the economy, generally forcing Indians to become more dependent on wild food resources. Since enslaving raids would have resulted in greater losses in the male population, and since hunting was essentially a male activity, there may well have been serious food shortages. Even where Indians remained in effective occupation of their lands, declining labor inputs may have seriously affected production, given that agriculture was organized on a communal basis requiring heavy labor inputs at critical times in the shifting cultivation cycle. Nevertheless, Indians in eastern Honduras did not suffer such widespread alienation of their lands, since the Spanish did not settle there permanently in large numbers. Similarly, although new crops and animals were introduced by the Spanish when Trujillo and San Jorge de Olancho were established,[29] their adoption was discouraged by their localized distribution and the lack of Spanish interest in developing agriculture.

The loss of individuals as a consequence of enslaving raids would have influenced the social organization of Indian villages, but there is a lack of evidence of social changes such as the re-evaluation of marriage rules. At the societal level intertribal warfare may have declined as hostilities were directed against the Spanish. However, the status of military leaders was probably enhanced by the increased role they were forced to play in opposing Spanish colonization. The status of shamans probably continued since the lack of effective Spanish colonization would have retarded the introduction of parish priests and, as a result, limited Indian conversion.

---

[25]Herrera, *Historia general* 9 dec.4 lib.8 cap.6:123.

[26]Benzoni, *Historia del nuevo mundo*, pp. 165-66.

[27]RAHM CM A/107 4842 ff.7-9 Barrientos 25.7.1534; AGI AG 49 Lerma 31.10.1539; Benzoni, *Historia del nuevo mundo*, pp. 163-64.

[28]CDIU 11:397 Pedraza 1544.

[29]Crops, cattle, and horses were sent to San Jorge de Olancho for the support of the population following its foundation (CDIU 11:402-3 Pedraza 1544).

DEMOGRAPHIC COLLAPSE

It has been estimated that the aboriginal population of Honduras was about 800,000. By 1539, according to Bishop Pedraza, the Indian population of Honduras had been reduced to 15,000, whilst in 1541 Benzoni maintained there were only 8,000.[30] Neither of these accounts probably took into consideration Indians living in the east of the country. Unfortunately there are no more detailed accounts of the Indian population until the 1540s when lists were drawn up for the purpose of tribute assessment. Although the Crown ordered that official assessments, or tasaciones, be drawn up in the 1530s, and it is possible that some were made, the earliest evidence of assessments for Honduras is for 1544.[31] These tasaciones were made by the *oidores* Rogel, Herrera, and Ramírez. Although it appears that these oidores covered a large part of the country, only the tasaciones for the jurisdiction of Gracias a Dios have been found. These assessments are contained in the *residencia* of the first Audiencia undertaken by its president, Alonso López de Cerrato, from 1548 to 1550.[32] Although the assessments do not indicate the number of Indians in each of the 64 villages listed, they do state the number of Indian carriers, or tamemes, each was to supply, as well as the number that was required to provide 'servicio ordinario'--to work as household servants--and render other services such as tending livestock, supplying fish on Fridays and holy days, and making pans for washing alluvial gold. Together the 64 villages supplied 4,354 tamemes and 373 Indians for other kinds of service. It is assumed that the tamemes were adult males, whether married or single, as were probably the majority of other Indians who provided services. This number thus represents only a proportion of the total Indian population to be found in the area. In addition not all villages were required to provide tamemes or services. As such, it is difficult to estimate accurately the total Indian population from these figures, but it seems likely that it would not have been below 15,000.[33] This suggests that the figures for the Indian population given by Bishop Pedraza and Benzoni in 1539 and 1541 respectively were underestimates. When Cerrato became president of the Audiencia in 1548 he reported that the Indians couldn't pay one-half of what was due even if they were doubled in number.[34] He thus set about moderating the amount of tribute and personal service the Indians paid. His reassessments constitute one of the best sources of

---

[30]AGI AG 9 and RAHM CM A/108 4843 ff.285-8 Pedraza to Crown 18.5.1539; Benzoni, *Historia del nuevo mundo*, p. 167.

[31]Newson, "Demographic Catastrophe," p. 237 nn. 23 and 24.

[32]AGI JU 299 Residencia of the first Audiencia 1548 to 1550. It appears that tasaciones were also made of villages in the jurisdictions of San Pedro and Comayagua (AGI AG 9 Herrera 10.7.1545), but there is no detailed evidence of them.

[33]The service of tamemes had been banned in 1541 (AGCA A1.23 4575 f.50 cédulas 28.1.1541, 31.5.1541). Following a reprimand from the Crown in 1546 (AGCA A1.23 1511 f.40 cédula 5.7.1546) in 1547 the service of tamemes was removed from the tribute assessments for villages in the jurisdiction of Gracias a Dios (AGI JU 299 Residencia of the first Audiencia 1548 to 1550).

[34]AGI AG 9 Cerrato 28.9.1548.

information about the Indian population in Central America in the sixteenth century.[35] Unfortunately, the *Libro de tasaciones* does not include assessments for all of Honduras. Tasaciones are only available for the jurisdiction of Comayagua and even then the population of only 38 of the 48 villages listed is included. These villages had a total of 2,745 tributary Indians. Given that the tasaciones regulated the amount of maize to be sown at about one fanega per ten tributary Indians, it is estimated that the tributary population for nine villages where the population is not stated but where the amount of tribute is indicated, was about 485. This gives a total tributary population for the jurisdiction of 3,230.[36]

The term *tributario* referred to married male Indians only, for it was not until 1578 that other able-bodied males such as widowers and single men were made liable for tribute payment.[37] Unfortunately there are no accounts of the structure of Indian populations in Honduras that could be used to obtain a figure for the total Indian population from the tributary population. In a discussion of the demographic changes experienced by Indians in Nicaragua during the sixteenth century, I have suggested that a multiplication factor of four might be applied to the tributary population of that country extracted from the same *Libro de tasaciones*.[38] In the absence of evidence to the contrary for Honduras, and given that similar factors operated in the conquest period in the two areas, the same multiplication factor may be used. This would give a total Indian population of about 12,920 for the jurisdiction of Comayagua in 1549. Comayagua and Gracias a Dios, whose population has already been estimated at not less than 15,000 in 1544, were the most densely settled areas in Honduras during the first half of the sixteenth century, whilst the northern part of the country suffered severely from enslaving raids. As such, an estimate of about 40,000 Indians in the Spanish-settled area at the end of the period seems reasonable. Population estimates for the second half of the sixteenth century suggest that about 20 percent of the population of the settled area would have been living in eastern Honduras (Tables 14 and 15). This would mean that the population of western and central Honduras declined from about 600,000 at the time of Spanish conquest to about 32,000 in the mid-sixteenth century, a depopulation ratio of about 18.8:1. It is virtually impossible to estimate losses in the eastern part of the country due to the lack of evidence, although it is clear that it lost population as a result of conquest, enslaving raids, and disease.

---

[35]AGI AG 128 Libro de tasaciones 1548 to 1551.

[36]This excludes the village of Ynquibiteca for which no tribute assessment is indicated.

[37]*Recopilación* 2 lib.6 tit.5 ley 7:226-27 5.7.1578.

[38]Newson, "Depopulation of Nicaragua," p. 265.

CAUSES OF THE DECLINE

The causes of the decline in the Indian population were manifold, complex, and interwoven. Contemporary observers identified three major factors--the Indian slave trade, conquest, and disease--but the overwork and ill treatment of the Indians and the severe disruption to Indian economies and societies brought about by conquest and colonization contributed significantly to the decline in the Indian population, and miscegenation also took its toll.

Comments have already been made concerning estimates of the numbers of Indians involved in the slave trade, particularly in Nicaragua, and here it is only necessary to emphasize its importance in contributing to the decline in the Indian population in Honduras and to note that it did not affect all areas equally. The worst affected areas were the hinterlands of the ports, notably Trujillo, whilst it was noted that those Indians living in inland areas were protected by their remoteness from the coast.[39] When Cortés arrived in Honduras in 1525 the Bay Islands had already been depopulated as a result of enslaving raids from Cuba, Española, and Jamaica[40] and in 1527 2,000 Indians from the neighboring coast of Trujillo were enslaved by the governor, López de Salcedo, and taken to Nicaragua.[41] In 1530 Andrés de Cerezeda complained that Vasco de Herrera had made war on Indians in the vicinity of Trujillo and had enslaved so many Indians that in villages that had possessed 1,000 souls only 30 were left.[42] Thus in 1547 Bishop Pedraza reported that around Trujillo villages with populations of several thousands had been reduced to 150 and 180 people, whilst one village located five leagues from the town that had possessed 900 houses had been completely depopulated such that the only survivor was the daughter of the cacique who had hidden under a boat.[43] The area around Naco was also badly affected. Bishop Pedraza maintained that when Andrés de Cerezeda entered the valley of Naco there had been between 8,000 and 10,000 men, but by 1539 there were only 250 left.[44] By 1586 the "great province of Naco" had been reduced to less than ten Indians.[45] Given this scale of depopulation it is reasonable to suggest that about 100,000 to 150,000 Indians were enslaved and exported from Honduras, both to the Caribbean islands and Guatemala, as well as south through Nicaragua to Panama and Peru.

Conquest and enslavement went hand in hand so it is difficult to estimate the numbers that were killed in battle as opposed to those who were enslaved; the impression given is that conquest was a more significant factor in the decline of the Indian population in Honduras than it was in neighboring Guatemala and Nicaragua, where the Spanish

---

[39]CDIU 11:400 Pedraza 1544.

[40]De Vedia, "Cartas de relación," 147 Cortés 3.9.1526.

[41]CS 1:293-97 Treasurer of Honduras, no date but probably 1527. Of the 2,000 enslaved only 100 arrived in Nicaragua alive.

[42]AGI AG 49 Cerezeda 31.3.1530.

[43]AGI AG 164 Pedraza 1.5.1547.

[44]Sherman, *Forced Native Labour*, p. 380 reference to AGI PAT 170-45.

[45]Ponce, *Relación breve*, p. 349.

achieved political control through the existing political structure.[46]  Particularly disruptive was the conquest of western Honduras by Pedro de Alvarado, which resulted in 6,000 Indians being killed, enslaved, or sacrificed.[47]  This was only one of the many campaigns that were conducted in Honduras and as such it seems reasonable to suggest that between 30,000 and 50,000 Indians were killed as a result of conquest.

Diseases were undoubtedly a major factor in the decline of the Indian population of Honduras. Epidemic diseases attracted most attention from contemporary observers, but there were other unrecorded diseases, particularly intestinal ones such as typhoid, paratyphoid, bacillary and amoebic dysentery, hookworm, and other helminthic diseases, which took their toll and increased the susceptibility of Indians to more deadly diseases. The first recorded epidemic in Middle America was in 1520 when smallpox was introduced into Mexico.[48]  In 1520 and 1521 Guatemala was ravaged by a disease but it is uncertain whether it was smallpox; it has been suggested that it was influenza.[49]  The only reference to disease spreading further south at this time comes from an account written in 1527, which stated that it was necessary to introduce slaves to "Panama City, Nata and the port of Honduras" because smallpox had killed off the Indians there.[50]  In 1531 Guatemala and Nicaragua appear to have been ravaged by a disease, probably some form of plague,[51] but the only reference to its presence in Honduras comes from Herrera, who said that two years before the major outbreak of measles, which was in 1533, "there was a general epidemic of pains in the side and stomach, which also carried away many Indians." The measles epidemic appears to have hit Honduras badly. Herrera describes the epidemic:

---

[46]For a comparison of the conquest of Honduras and Guatemala, see S. Rodríguez Becerra, "Variables de la conquista: los casos de Honduras y Guatemala," in *Primer reunión de antropólogos Españoles*, ed. A. Jiménez (Sevilla: Universidad de Sevilla, 1975), pp. 127-33.

[47]AGI AG 9 and RAHM CM A/108 4843 ff.285-8 Pedraza 18.5.1539.

[48]A.W. Crosby, *The Columbian Exchange: Biological and Cultural Consequences of 1492* (Westport, CT: Greenwood, 1972), p. 47.

[49]F.W. McBryde, "Influenza in America during the Sixteenth Century (Guatemala: 1523, 1559-62, 1576)," *Bulletin of the History of Medicine* 8 (1940):296-302; Thompson, "Maya Central Area," p. 24; Crosby, *Columbian Exchange*, p. 51; MacLeod, *Spanish Central America*, p. 98; Veblen, "Native Population Decline," p. 490.

[50]CDHCR 4:7-11 Instrucciones a los procuradores de la ciudad de Granada 10.7.1527; Crosby, *Columbian Exchange*, p. 51.

[51]MacLeod, *Spanish Central America*, p. 98, identifies the disease as pneumonic plague but the symptoms of the disease, especially as described for Nicaragua where the Indians developed swollen glands (AGI AG 9 and CS 3:68-78 Castañeda 30.5.1531), suggest that it was bubonic plague.

At this time there was such a great epidemic of measles in the province of Honduras spreading from house to house and village to village, that many people died; and although the disease also affected the Spaniards...none of them died...This same disease of measles and dysentery passed to Nicaragua where also many Indians died.[52]

In Honduras Oviedo maintained that the measles epidemic and other diseases had killed one-half of the population and the most susceptible were those who were servants in Spanish households or workers on Spanish estates.[53] Since diseases do not act uniformly but are affected by environmental factors such as population density, the degree of interpersonal contact, sanitation, dietary habits, and immunity, it seems likely that there would have been great spatial variations in the proportion of Indians killed by the disease, and the estimate of one-half of the population is likely to have been a local maximum. Over a decade later in 1545 an epidemic of either pneumonic plague or typhus struck Mexico and Guatemala, but it does not appear to have spread further south at that time.[54] In fact there is little evidence of either of these diseases in Honduras throughout the colonial period and it seems likely that, with the exception of the highlands in the west of the country, they were unable to survive in the warmer climatic conditions. Nevertheless, it is clear that a substantial proportion of the decline in the Indian population can be attributed to successive waves of disease.

There is some controversy over the origins of the tropical diseases yellow fever and malaria and whether either was present in Central America in the sixteenth century. Yellow fever is generally considered to be an introduction from the Old World. The first agreed epidemic of yellow fever occurred in Yucatán and Cuba in 1648; Ashburn effectively argues that the skin coloration recorded in the sixteenth century was the result of starvation rather than yellow fever.[55] Recent zoological and historical evidence, however, suggests that sylvan yellow fever may have been present in Latin America in pre-Columbian times.[56] If this was the case then outbreaks of the disease in the tropical coastal lowlands of Central America in the sixteenth century cannot be ruled out. Nevertheless it was only at a later date that these coasts, and particularly Panama, earned the reputation of being unhealthy.[57] Similar comments may be made with respect to malaria. It now seems certain that malaria was introduced from the Old World. This is based on the fact that Indian populations in Latin America do not produce polymorphisms resistant to malaria, whereas those in Africa do, and the fact that in Latin America the

---

[52]Herrera, *Historia general* 10 dec.5 lib.1 cap.10:72. Ashburn (*Ranks of Death*, p. 91) translates "*cámaras de sangre*" as dysentery.

[53]Oviedo, *Historia general* 3 lib.31 cap.6:388.

[54]AGI AG 9 and CDI 24:442-47 Maldonado 31.12.1545; H. Zinsser, *Rats, Lice and History* (New York: Bantam, 1960), pp. 194-95; Thompson, "Maya Central Area," p. 24; MacLeod, *Spanish Central America*, p. 98; McNeill, *Plagues and Peoples*, p. 209.

[55]Ashburn, *Ranks of Death*, pp. 130-34; Duffy, *Epidemics*, p. 140; McNeill, *Plagues and Peoples*, p. 213.

[56]Denevan, ed., *Native Population*, p. 5.

[57]Sauer, *Early Spanish Main*, p. 279.

malarial parasites are relatively unspecialized and have a restricted number of hosts thus suggesting their more recent appearance there.[58]

As long as the Indian population could be seen to provide an inexhaustible supply of labor, little attention was paid to its preservation, with the result that Indians were subject to ill treatment and forced to work long hours in poor conditions on inadequate diets and under threat of punishment for shortcomings. Many of the tasks in which Indians were employed were strenuous and contributed directly to illness and death; particularly important in sixteenth-century Honduras were the transportation of goods and mining. Indians were forced to travel with heavy loads over long distances, which often traversed climatic zones with the result that they fell ill and died.[59] In 1547 Bishop Pedraza reported that 500 tamemes who had been hired out by Governor Montejo had died and that in general one-half of the Indian porters that travelled from Comayagua to San Pedro and Puerto Caballos did not return, one-third dying or becoming ill on the journey.[60] Despite a ban on the employment of Indians as tamemes in 1541, the lack of paved roads and the difficult communications made the implementation of the order impossible.[61] Indian carriers were used primarily for moving goods between the ports, major cities, and mining areas, but in the early years of conquest they were also used on expeditions to carry supplies. In 1527 López de Salcedo on an expedition to Nicaragua took with him 4,000 Indian carriers of whom no more than six returned.[62] Conditions in the mines were also bad to the extent that they stimulated Indian revolts[63] and persuaded the Crown to ban the employment of Indians in mining in 1546.[64] Other tasks in which Indians were employed, whilst not contributing directly to the death rate, were exhausting, and with the poor diets that were provided, contributed to the susceptibility of the Indians to illness and disease. The burden of work which fell on the Indians was also increased directly and indirectly by the demands that were made for tribute, the repartimiento, and other goods and services. Whilst each demand or exaction may have been small, together they combined to keep the Indians in continual labor like "frightened deer" leaving them little time to attend to their own subsistence needs.[65]

Although very few contemporary observers attributed the decline in the Indian population to the economic, social, political, and ideological changes brought about by Spanish conquest and colonization, it is clear that their effects were considerable. Disruption to Indian economies led indirectly to food shortages and famines and hence to a decline in the Indian population. Many Indians fearing attack and enslavement, or later

---

[58]Dunn, "Antiquity of Malaria," pp. 385-93; Wood, "Late Introduction of Malaria," pp. 93-104.

[59]AGI AG 9 and CDI 24:343-51 Maldonado 15.1.1545; AGI AG 164 Pedraza 1.5.1547; AGI AG 968B Pedraza, no date; AGI AG 44 Cabildo of Gracias a Dios 16.2.1548.

[60]AGI AG 164 Pedraza 1.5.1547.

[61]See n. 33.

[62]Saco, *Historia de la Esclavitud* 1:173.

[63]For example, CDI 24:352-81 García 1.2.1539; AGI AG 9 Anon 21.2.1546.

[64]AGCA A1.23 1511 f.40 cédula 5.7.1546.

[65]AGI AG 164 Pedraza 1.5.1547.

excessive tribute and labor demands, abandoned their lands and fled to the hills, where they attempted to survive on wild fruits, vegetables, fish, and game. Unaccustomed to such a form of livelihood many of them suffered malnutrition and some died.[66] Others remained in their villages, but they could not maintain food production as their lands were alienated and labor inputs declined.[67]

There is some evidence to suggest that the breakdown in the social organization of Indian communities and the psychological impact of conquest also contributed to the decline in the Indian population. Whilst diseases and famines took their toll on the youngest and oldest sections of the community, enslavement, ill treatment, and overwork largely affected the adult male population probably resulting in an imbalance in the sex ratio. It is uncertain, however, whether this imbalance affected the birth rate, but it seems likely that the endless tiring work that the Indians were forced to carry out might have dampened their desires to procreate, particularly since additional children would have placed increased burdens on already inadequate food resources. Furthermore, Indians did not wish to bear children that would be born into slavery. These factors resulted in Indians practicing birth control by abstaining from sexual intercourse and inducing miscarriages, as well as practicing infanticide.[68] Apart from infanticide, the infant mortality rate would have risen as a result of malnutrition increasing their susceptibility to the newly introduced diseases.

Although miscegenation occurred during the sixteenth century it did not make as significant a contribution to the decline in the Indian population as it did in succeeding centuries. The degree of miscegenation was dependent on the intensity of contact between the races and it was stimulated by the predominance of men amongst the white and negro sections of the population. Miscegenation was most common in the towns, where many Indians were ordered to work and where many lived as servants in Spanish households. It was also common in mining areas of Olancho where in 1543 it was estimated that there were 1,500 negroes working gold in the Guayape valley.[69] Later, as agriculture developed, miscegenation became common on rural estates, where negroes and persons of mixed race were often employed as overseers.

---

[66]Ibid.; AGI AG 968B Pedraza, no date; AGI AG 44 Cabildo of Gracias a Dios 16.2.1548; AGI AG 56 Contreras 20.4.1582; AGI AG 39 Albardez to Crown 29.4.1598.

[67]AGI AG 39 and CDI 24 pp. 250-97 and RAHM CM A/108 4843 ff.239-57 Montejo 1.6.1539; AGI AG 164 Pedraza 1.5.1547.

[68]Although there is little documentary evidence for such practices in Honduras, they are well documented for neighboring Nicaragua and the experiences of the two countries, particularly when the Indian slave trade was at its height, are likely to have been similar (AGI JU 293 and CS 7:151-224 Petition against the conduct of Castañeda 16.11.1541; CDHCR 6:199-211 Rodríguez 9.7.1545; Saco, *Historia de la esclavitud* 2:168).

[69]AGI AG 9 and RAHM CM A/110 4845 f.108v. and CDI 24:343-51 Maldonado 15.1.1543; RAHM CM A/110 4845 oficiales reales 20.2.1543.

# Part IV

## Western and Central Honduras, 1550 to 1821

During the first half of the sixteenth century the Spanish found immediate sources of wealth in gold mining and the Indian slave trade, but by mid-century the gold deposits had been exhausted and the rapid decline of the Indian population had led to an effective cessation of the slave trade. Similarly, the value of encomiendas declined as tribute fell with the Indian population and as the right of encomenderos to exact labor services was withdrawn.

Due to the limited opportunities for wealth creation in Honduras, many colonists left the province, whilst those who remained turned their attention to the development of agriculture and to a lesser extent mining. Since agriculture could not be developed without sources of labor, the Indian population, although very much reduced in size, continued to be an important factor determining the character of agricultural production and favoring its concentration in the center and west of the country. Meanwhile, mining activities in Tegucigalpa and Choluteca, which employed labor imported from neighboring regions, extended Spanish colonization to the east and south. Although many urban dwellers moved to the countryside to reside on their estates and to supervise mining activities, the towns and cities, as centers of secular and ecclesiastical administration and as major concentrations of Spanish settlers, remained identifiable elements in the colonial settlement pattern and important centers of influence on Indians living in the surrounding rural areas.

Spanish activities affected Indian communities through the demands they made on Indian lands, labor, and production. Whilst the influence of silver mining and the towns was felt through the demands they made on Indian labor, agriculture also competed with Indian communities over the use of land. The major demands on Indian production emanated from the towns, where Spanish officials, the clergy and the majority of encomenderos resided. Although official levies, such as tribute and support for the local clergy, remained significant drains on Indian production, other unofficial demands in the form of forced sales and purchases, as well as direct exactions, added to these burdens. The increased level of demand on Indian production and labor, coupled with the alienation of Indian lands, reduced the viability of many communities, driving individuals to become wage laborers. In new economic and social environments they gradually lost their cultural and racial identity.

# 8
# Estate Agriculture

Of all Spanish activities agriculture probably had the most pervasive effects on Indian life. It developed to supply the needs of the domestic market and to support trade through the province, although it also provided some products, such as indigo, tobacco and hides, for export to Spain. The types of agriculture practiced varied spatially with local physical conditions and they made varying demands on Indian lands and labor. The impact of agricultural activities not only varied with the type of agriculture practiced, but also with the level of production; hence the promotion of agricultural development at the end of the eighteenth century resulted in an intensification and spatial expansion of production, which increased pressure on Indian communities.

The growth of Spanish interest in agriculture and the movement of landowners to the countryside have been viewed as responses to the high cost of living in the towns and the lack of opportunities for wealth creation there. MacLeod sees the Spanish as retreating into a semisubsistence form of existence in the rural areas, where they raised a few cattle and grew some maize, and sometimes cultivated a small amount of indigo that could be sold.[1] Chevalier and Wolf have made similar arguments for the emergence of the landed estate in Mexico.[2] They argue that in Mexico the retreat into self-sufficiency occurred as a result of an economic depression that was related to the decline in the mining industry and trade with Spain. Whilst Borah accepts that Mexico experienced an economic depression during the seventeenth century, he sees the hacienda emerging in response to increased demands for food at a time when its availability decreased as a result of the decline in the Indian population. Thus high prices for food acted as a stimulus to the development of haciendas.[3] Frank also sees haciendas growing in

[1] MacLeod, *Spanish Central America*, pp. 217-21.

[2] Wolf, *Shaking Earth*, pp. 202, 204; F. Chevalier, *Land and Society in Colonial Mexico* (Berkeley and Los Angeles: University of California, 1963), pp. 48, 66, 180.

[3] W. Borah, *New Spain's Century of Depression*, Ibero-Americana 35 (Berkeley and Los Angeles: University of California, 1951), pp. 32-33.

response to the profits to be made in agriculture.[4]  The evidence from Honduras is far from clear.  Whilst it seems likely that the movement to the countryside was a response to the lack of opportunities for wealth creation in the towns, not all of those who moved to the countryside retreated into a subsistence existence.  There were some wealthy ranchers and indigo producers, with the latter making sufficient profits to be able to incorporate fines as part of their costs of production.  In fact most haciendas had some market orientation.  Indigo, hides and later tobacco were produced for export to Spain, while livestock and subsistence crops, notably maize, were raised to supply the domestic market in the towns, ports, and mining areas, and were exported to neighboring provinces.  Nevertheless, there were some estate owners who only scraped a living in the way that MacLeod had suggested.

A prerequisite for agricultural development was the acquisition of lands.  Although land grants had been given to early settlers, the majority were concentrated around the towns of which they were vecinos, and it was not until the second half of the sixteenth century that the colonized area expanded with lands being granted in more remote parts of the country, particularly to the east and south.  In many cases the acquisition of lands by the Spanish conflicted with Indian claims to lands and it had other less direct disruptive effects on the Indian economy, all of which will be discussed in detail later.

Evidence for the size, location, and cost of lands granted in Honduras is extremely fragmentary, so that it is difficult to obtain a comprehensive view of their character and distribution over time.  The General Index of Land Titles for Honduras is undoubtedly incomplete, but on the other hand the accompanying table probably contains some duplication since it is difficult to ascertain from the index whether a particular land title represents a new grant or a new owner.[5]  Apart from the General Index of Land Titles, a small number of land titles for the period 1701 to 1726 are to be found in the AGCA *legajos* 1572-1585 and other evidence is available for 1713 and 1732 from the lists of *media anatas* paid on lands when the titles were granted.[6]

Throughout the second half of the sixteenth century and the seventeenth century most land grants were between 3 and 6 caballerías (333 to 666 acres).  Some smaller grants were also made in the already settled areas of Comayagua and Gracias a Dios.  In both these areas there appears to have been a mixture of small grants (18 of under 2 caballerías) and estancias (11 with the specified dimension of 6 3/4 caballerías), with the rest falling in between.  Grants made in Choluteca and Tegucigalpa were slightly larger in size and this may reflect the slightly later colonization of those areas or the poorer quality of the land there.  In the eighteenth century the general size of land grants appears to have increased with over one-half of the grants being over 6 caballerías and 30 percent over 10 caballerías.  At that time smaller land grants were made in the already settled areas, whilst larger grants were given in the relatively unoccupied regions of Olancho and San Pedro.  The small size of the land grants in Yoro may be related to the presence of a large number of persons of mixed race, who would have possessed smaller capital resources with which

---

[4]A.G. Frank, *Mexican Agriculture, 1521-1630:  Transformation of the Mode of Production* (Cambridge:  Cambridge University Press, 1979), p. 56.

[5]*Indice general de los títulos de tierras que se encuentran en el Archivo Nacional* (Tegucigalpa:  Instituto Nacional Agrario, 1969).

[6]AGCA A1.24 1572 to 1585 various folios of títulos de tierras 1701 to 1726; AGI AG 252 media anatas on lands 1713 to 1732.

to purchase lands. To what extent this pattern has been influenced by the availability of documentary evidence is not known.

Information relating to the price of land is very fragmentary, but it would appear that prices rose only slightly during the colonial period and that variations in prices were largely related to the quality of the land. Thus at the turn of the seventeenth century a caballería of good land in Gracias a Dios sold for 20 pesos, whereas one that was suitable

Table 4

SIZE AND DISTRIBUTION OF LAND GRANTS 1600 TO 1821

| Jurisdiction | 1600-1720 | 1721-1821 | 1600-1720 | 1721-1821 | 1600-1720 | 1721-1821 |
|---|---|---|---|---|---|---|
| | Number of grants | | Area in caballerías | | Average size | |
| Comayagua | 35 | 25 | 82.5 | 125.5 | 2.4 | 5.0 |
| Tegucigalpa | 87 | 120 | 524.0 | 1,470.5 | 6.0 | 12.3 |
| Choluteca | 59 | 76 | 372.0 | 1,029.0 | 6.3 | 13.5 |
| Gracias a Dios | 33 | 96 | 139.25 | 880.75 | 4.2 | 9.2 |
| San Pedro | 9 | 14 | 30.0 | 399.0 | 3.3 | 28.5 |
| Olancho | 12 | 83 | 30.5 | 1,205.75 | 2.5 | 14.5 |
| Yoro | 9 | 22 | 39.5 | 134.5 | 4.4 | 6.1 |
| TOTAL | 244 | 436 | 1,217.75 | 5,245.0 | 5.0 | 12.0 |

Source: *Indice General de los Títulos de Tierras*

The figures do not include titles to Indian *ejidos*, but do include titles to other lands owned by Indians, either individually or communally. Units of less than one-fourth caballería have not been included in the calculations. A caballería in Central America is equivalent to about 111 acres.

The jurisdictions cover the following present-day departments: Comayagua (Comayagua and La Paz); Tegucigalpa (Francisco Morazán and El Paraíso); Choluteca (Valle and Choluteca); Gracias a Dios (Intibucá, Lempira, Ocotepeque, and Copán); San Pedro (Santa Barbara); Olancho (Olancho and Colón); Yoro (Yoro and Atlántida).

for grazing was valued at 9 pesos, and poor land that could only be used for sowing some maize and raising a few cattle cost only 3 to 4 pesos.[7]

During the sixteenth century the main agricultural areas were located around the major towns of Comayagua, Gracias a Dios, San Pedro, and Trujillo;[8] in 1586 there were 37 estancias in the valley of Comayagua and 18 in the valley of Agalteca.[9] Livestock raising appears to have begun in Choluteca in the sixteenth century,[10] but the evidence provided by land grants indicates that many lands in this area were acquired in the first half of the seventeenth century,[11] such that Vázquez de Espinosa was able to describe the area as, "a country with large cattle and mule ranches, and a few indigo laboratories."[12] The colonization of the jurisdiction of Tegucigalpa really began in the second half of the sixteenth century with the development of silver mining, such that by the middle of the seventeenth century many estancias had been established in the surrounding valleys.[13] Towards the end of the seventeenth century there appears to have been an expansion south and east into the valleys of Yeguare, Jamastrán, and Cuscateca.[14] Further north in Olancho colonization did not occur until a later date. Following the collapse of mining in the Guayape valley only a few cattle ranches remained,[15] and the agricultural colonization of the area did not begin in earnest until the latter part of the seventeenth century; all the land titles listed for this area in the General Index of Land Titles are dated after 1682.[16] A description of Olancho at the end of the seventeenth century indicates that whilst a number of estancias clustered around San Jorge de Olancho and the village of Manto, the rest were scattered throughout the countryside separated from each other by

---

[7]AGCA A1.45 392 3768 1691, 3770 1693, 3771 1707, 3775 1704. Prices of land in different regions in 1743 were: Gracias a Dios 7 pesos; Tegucigalpa 5 pesos; Choluteca 5 to 8 pesos; San Pedro 5 pesos (AGI AG 264 Ventas y composiciones de tierra 1743) and for 1779 to 1784: Comayagua 6 to 15 pesos; Gracias a Dios 8 pesos; Olancho 6 to 9 pesos (AGCA A1.73 388 3623 to 3636).

[8]López de Velasco, *Geografía y descripción universal*, pp. 307-13; A.E. Gómez, *Esbozo de historia económica de Honduras* (Tegucigalpa: Universidad Autónoma de Honduras, 1967), p. 56.

[9]Ponce, *Relación breve*, pp. 345, 347.

[10]Ibid., p. 340; López de Velasco, *Geografía y descripción universal*, p. 300.

[11]*Indice general de los títulos de tierras*, list of land grants for Choluteca and Valle.

[12]Vázquez de Espinosa, *Compendium and Description*, p. 235.

[13]AGI IG 1530 Aguilar, no date; Serrano y Sanz, *Relaciones históricas*, p. xv; Vázquez de Espinosa, *Compendium and Description*, p. 244.

[14]*Indice general de los títulos de tierras*, list of land grants for Francisco Morazán.

[15]Serrano y Sanz, *Relaciones geográficas*, 468 Pineda 1594; Vázquez de Espinosa, *Compendium and Description*, p. 243.

[16]*Indice general de los títulos de tierras*, list of land grants for Olancho.

vast stretches of unoccupied land.[17] During the eighteenth century agricultural colonization extended mainly to the east, particularly in the jurisdictions of Olancho and Tegucigalpa, such that by the end of the century lands were owned as far as the headwaters of the Black River and the Guayape valley.[18] Further south new developments in the mining industry appear to have stimulated the development of livestock raising, particularly around Danlí, whilst miners themselves acquired small holdings within the mining area for growing provisions.[19] It is interesting to note that whilst the average size of land grants in Tegucigalpa was 12.3 caballerias, over 20 percent were of only 2 to 3 caballerías. These holdings are likely to have been owned by miners or by some of the many mulattoes who lived in the area.[20] In the west a substantial number of land grants were made during the eighteenth century, but given the relatively dense Indian settlement of this area, they resulted in the infilling of an already occupied area, rather than the colonization of a new region. Further north in San Pedro, however, it was noted that there were virgin lands and others suitable for irrigation, but it was impossible to produce commercial crops because of the shortage of labor; like others, such as Choluteca, which was suitable for the cultivation of indigo, it had to fall back on the less labor-demanding activity of livestock raising.[21]

Agricultural development suffered considerably from shortages of labor and capital. From 1549 Indians were no longer required to perform labor services for their encomenderos and the repartimiento was introduced with the aim of ensuring a supply of labor for all approved tasks.[22] These tasks included most agricultural activities, but work in sugar mills and indigo works was banned. Unfortunately, there were never enough Indians to supply all the demands made upon them, initially due to the decline in the Indian population, and later due to competing demands from mining and defense. For the majority of estate owners the introduction of negro slaves on a large scale was not an economic proposition. Although estate owners complained bitterly about the lack of negro slaves to perform agricultural tasks, there were few requests for imports, except in the sixteenth century when commercial enterprises were being established; their complaints were largely used to justify forms of Indian labor that were unacceptable to the Crown. Since the repartimiento failed to supply estate owners with the agricultural labor they required, employers soon resorted to encouraging Indians, aided by various forms of coercion, to work for them as free laborers. By the end of the seventeenth century free labor had emerged as the dominant labor system, with many Indians having taken up residence on estates and with the authorities in a powerless position to force them to return to their villages. Estate owners not only encouraged Indians to work for them as free employees, but where possible they employed free negroes and persons of mixed race. By the end of the seventeenth century most estates probably possessed a few negro slaves, who were employed mainly as household servants, a few free negroes and

---

[17]AGCA A1.12 46 416 Dean and Cabildo of the Cathedral of Comayagua 21.5.1698.

[18]AGI AG 578 Cadiñanos 20.10.1791.

[19]For example, AGCA A3.9 157 3040 Miners of San Joseph de los Cedros 2.9.1752.

[20]BAGG 7:210-20 Autos formados...23.8.1765.

[21]BAGG 7:228-48 Informes sobre las subdelegaciones ..24.12.1793, 20.7.1794.

[22]The characteristics of the repartimiento and free labor are discussed in more detail in Chapter 11.

other persons of mixed race, who undertook supervisory activities, and a larger number of Indian workers, mostly free laborers, who were either resident on the estate or worked as day laborers.[23] Altogether, however, the number of agricultural laborers available never satisfied the demand for them, partly because of competing demands for labor, but also because of the absolute shortage of workers.

Part of the reason why landowners failed to attract labor was that they were unable to pay high wages due to the limited profitability of their enterprises. Many documents describe *hacendados* in Honduras as poor and lacking capital.[24] By the beginning of the nineteenth century many landowners were burdened with *capellanías*, mortgages, and other debts. Landowners even had to secure loans to continue production from year to year. This was particularly common in indigo production, where producers were forced to rely on merchants for credit, which they repaid in the form of crops. To reduce the dependence of indigo producers on merchant credit, in 1782 a Monte Pío was established to provide loans at 4 percent interest to be repaid in cash.[25] In a similar way the governor of Honduras tried to persuade the Crown, without success, to establish a similar form of credit for tobacco producers.[26] Other producers turned to the funds of cofradías and Indian communities to obtain loans, but until the end of the eighteenth century, when attempts were made to provide loans for smaller producers, the majority of those who received them were large landowners who possessed the necessary collateral. Nevertheless many of the loans were never repaid and landowners often died in debt and estates went out of production.[27]

Towards the end of the eighteenth century the Crown took specific steps to promote agricultural development. In order to encourage the cultivation of crops for export to Spain, sales taxes (*alcabala*) and export-import taxes (*almojarifazgo*) were often removed.[28] In addition, in the early nineteenth century the commercial production of particular crops was promoted by the abolition of tithes and sales taxes on new plantings of indigo, cacao, sugar, cotton, and coffee for ten years to run from the day of the first harvest,[29] whilst in 1792 taxes on the importation of tools and machinery for the

---

[23]AGCA A1.1 2 42 13.4.1793. It was said that landowners were too poor to employ overseers.

[24]AGCA A1.1 2 42 13.4.1793; AGI AG 501 Anguiano 10.5.1804; ANH P14 L45 Mallol 28.6.1820; AGCA A1.1 2 60 9.6.1821.

[25]R.S. Smith, "Indigo Production and Trade in Colonial Guatemala," *HAHR* 39 (1959):194-95.

[26]AGI IG 1525 Lindo 10.5.1803.

[27]AGI AG 501 Anguiano 10.5.1804.

[28]For example, these taxes were removed on cotton in 1786 (AGI AG 472 real orden 14.3.1786).

[29]AGCA A1.23 1542 f.215v. cédula 15.11.1803, A1.38 1745 11, 716 f.685 cédula 15.11.1803.

processing of sugar and coffee had been removed.[30] Individual *cédulas* were also issued for the promotion of particular crops, such as cochineal.[31]

The types of agriculture that were practiced varied spatially with local physical conditions and the availability of Indian labor. Because ranching was less demanding in labor than many other agricultural activities and because it could be established easily on the preexisting grasslands, it became one of the most important economic activities in the province. The most important animals raised were cattle, followed by mules and horses; a few sheep were also raised. Cattle were raised for their hides and tallow, which were exported, and for meat, which was consumed locally and in the neighboring provinces of Guatemala and El Salvador.[32] Some dairy cattle were also kept for butter and cheese.[33] Livestock raising began in the Comayagua valley and Choluteca. The former area produced good quality animals due to the healthy climate, abundant water to sustain good pastures, and the presence of saline outcrops, which ensured that cattle wounds healed quickly and did not become infected.[34] In 1590 it was estimated that there were 30,000 head of cattle in the valley of Comayagua,[35] and it was said that six or seven of the richest cattle owners held such power over the city's affairs that it was impossible to pass ordinances prohibiting cattle from grazing in the valley in order to develop the production of maize and wheat.[36] Although the Comayagua valley and Choluteca continued to raise livestock throughout the colonial period, in the eighteenth century major livestock-producing areas emerged in Olancho and eastern Tegucigalpa; in 1743 the jurisdiction of Tegucigalpa was said to possess 40,000 cattle.[37] By 1804 the province as a whole possessed about one-half million cattle.[38]

The raising of mules and, to a lesser extent, horses also contributed to the development of a flourishing livestock industry. As well as being used in sugar milling

---

[30]AGCA A3.5 1105 20,007 f.188 cédula 4.3.1792.

[31]AGCA A1.77 91 1056 Alcalde Mayor of Tegucigalpa 17.1.1818, ANH UC real orden 22.7.1818, 31.8.1818.

[32]BAGG 1:29-39 Letona 20.7.1743, BAGG 2:462-73 Autos formados...13.10.1765. For a description of the operation of the cattle fair in Guatemala at the end of the eighteenth century, see Newson, *Indian Survival.*

[33]AGI AG 164 Cabildo eclesiástico of Comayagua 10.2.1680, AG 364 Cabildo eclesiástico 22.2.1681.

[34]AGI AG 43 Cabildo of Comayagua 9.4.1551, PAT 183-1-16 Antonelli and López de Quintanillas 7.10.1590; Ponce, *Relación breve*, p. 345; López de Velasco, *Geografía y descripción universal*, pp. 300, 306, 312; Vázquez de Espinosa, *Compendium and Description*, pp. 235, 241, 244; Herrera, *Historia general* 9 dec.4 lib.8 cap.3:105.

[35]AGI PAT 183-1-16 Antonelli and López de Quintanillas 7.10.1590.

[36]In 1590 there were 46 haciendas in the Comayagua valley, of which 38 raised cattle and which it was estimated could produce 12,430 head a year. Many also raised mules, horses, and sheep (RAHM 9/4663 no.15 Valverde 24.8.1590).

[37]BAGG 1:29-39 Letona 20.7.1743.

[38]AGI AG 501 Anguiano 10.5.1804.

and to harvest indigo, they were also employed in the mines, and perhaps most important of all, they were used for transport. The mule-raising industry developed from the end of the sixteenth century and was of vital importance to the economy of Gracias a Dios and Choluteca, which supplied mules for the mule trains that travelled the route from San Salvador, San Miguel, Choluteca, through Nicaragua south to Costa Rica and Panama. At the beginning of the nineteenth century there were said to be 50,000 mules and horses in Honduras.[39] Some sheep were also raised in the cooler parts of Honduras but they were absent from Choluteca, where the climate was too arid to sustain good pasture.[40]

Although agriculture in Honduras was dominated by livestock production, at times a number of commercial crops, such as indigo and tobacco, were produced for export, whilst wheat and maize were grown for the domestic market. These crops were produced in different regions of the country and they made different demands on Indian lands and labor.

Although cacao had been produced in northwest Honduras in pre-Columbian times, its cultivation was not extended and developed during the colonial period. There was a small market for cacao in Mexico and Europe, and its production appears to have been dominated by the extensive cacao-growing areas of Soconusco and Zapotitlán. A major problem with the production of cacao in Central America was that it was labor intensive. Although cacao production is not normally demanding in labor, the cacao trees cultivated in Central America were not very hardy and they required constant attention.[41] In addition the establishment of cacao groves required high investments of capital, which showed no profit for seven to eight years when the cacao could be harvested. As a result the Spanish did not become involved in cacao production in Honduras, but they allowed its cultivation to remain in the hands of Indians from whom they obtained it in the form of tribute or trade; cacao remained a significant item of tribute in northwest Honduras into the seventeenth century and it was even exported.[42] By the end of the colonial period the commercial production of cacao appears to have ceased, such that by 1818 there was said to be not one cacao hacienda in the province due to the shortage of capital.[43] Nevertheless, there appear to have been abundant sources of good quality wild cacao around San Pedro and Ulúa, such that the local residents used it everyday.[44] Two products associated with cacao production in pre-Columbian times were vanilla (*Vanilla planifolia* Andr.) and achiote (*Bixa orellana* L.), which were used for flavoring and coloring chocolate respectively. They were cultivated in the same areas as cacao and in

---

[39]Ibid. For earlier accounts of the raising of mules and horses see: RAHM 9/4663 no.15 Valverde 24.8.1590, PAT 183-1-16 Antonelli and López de Quintanillas 7.10.1590, López de Velasco, *Geografía y descripción universal*, pp. 235, 241, 242, 244; Herrera, *Historia general* 9 dec.4 lib.8 cap.3:105.

[40]RAHM 9/4663 no.15 Valverde 24.8.1590; AGI AG 472 Estado de las siembras ...15.9.1786, AG 501 Anguiano 10.5.1804; AGCA A1.12 82 970 24.5.1814; ANH UC Zelaya 27.6.1820; López de Velasco, *Geografía y descripción universal*, pp. 306, 310, 312; Vázquez de Espinosa, *Compendium and Description*, pp. 241, 244.

[41]MacLeod, *Spanish Central America*, pp. 68-79.

[42]See the discussion of Indian tribute in Chapter 11.

[43]BAGG 7: 175-9 Anguiano 15.12.1818.

[44]AGI AG 578 Cadiñanos 20.10.1791, AG 501 Anguiano 10.5.1804.

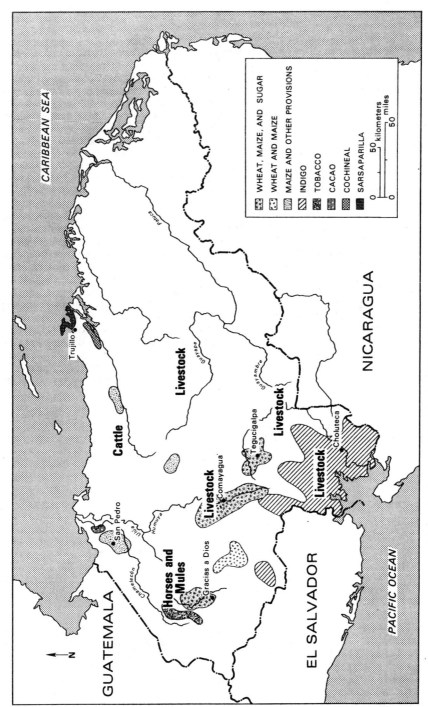

Figure 4. Commercial Agricultural Activities in the Colonial Period

the seventeenth century they were produced in sufficient quantities to allow their export.[45]

Although indigo dye was used by Indians in Honduras in pre-Columbian times,[46] it was not until the last quarter of the sixteenth century that its commercial production began. In 1558 samples of the plant, including details of its cultivation, were requested by the Crown in the hope that it could be developed as a source of blue dye for which there was a demand in Spain.[47] The most important indigo-producing areas in Central America were further north in San Salvador, and to a lesser extent in southeast Guatemala and Nicaragua, but indigo production also developed on a small scale in southern Honduras inland from the Bay of Fonseca in Gracias a Dios, Choluteca, and Tegucigalpa, with the parishes of Aguanqueterique and Guascorán being renowned for its cultivation. Some indigo was also produced in Comayagua and it was generally considered that its cultivation could be extended if labor were available.[48]

The species of indigo plant originally grown was probably *Indigofera suffruticosa* Mill., with the more common southeast Asian *Indigofera tinctoria* L. being introduced at a later date. The plant was known in Central America by its Nahuatl name *xiquilite*, whilst the dye it produced was known as 'añil' or 'tinta añil.' The cultivation of indigo plants and their processing to form blocks of dye are described in detail in contemporary accounts.[49] The cultivation of indigo began with the burning of the land over which the seeds were then broadcast and trampled into the soil by cattle or horses; it was not considered necessary to plow the land first. Sowing normally took place at the beginning of the rainy season, in April or May, in order to take advantage of the rains. An initial period of weeding was required when the plants reached about one foot in height, but subsequently the weeds were kept down by grazing livestock, which did not find the indigo plants a palatable source of food. The leaves of the plant were not picked in their first year of growth, but they were harvested in the July of the following year. In September the seeds were collected for future use. The plants could last for up to ten

---

[45]CDI 19: 239-304 Anon. 1677; AGI AG 164 Cabildo eclesiástico 10.2.1680, AG 26 Ramírez de Guzmán 4.4.1680; RPM 2537 I Descripción general, no date; AGI MP Guatemala 18 Onofre Nuñez 1723.

[46]MacLeod, *Spanish Central America*, pp. 176-77.

[47]AGCA A1.23 1511 f.237 cédula 14.6.1558.

[48]M. Rubio Sánchez ("El Añil o Xiquilite," *ASGH* 26 [1952]: 316-17) places the following areas in descending order of importance: El Salvador, Nicaragua, Guatemala, and Honduras. Vázquez de Espinosa (*Compendium and Description*, p. 236) suggested that Guatemala was the most important area followed by Nicaragua. For the cultivation of indigo in Honduras see also: AGCA A1.45 392 3757 título de tierra 20.5.1629; AGCA A1.53 375 3456 Visita de obrajes, Tegucigalpa 1721 to 1723; ANH P6 L90 Visita de obrajes 1725; BAGG 7: 45-67 1.6.1733, BAGG 1: 29-39 Letona 20.7.1743, BAGG 7: 462-73 Autos formados 3.2.1766; BM Add. 27,392K Map of the Musqueto Shore 30.12.1784; AGI AG 578 Cadiñanos 20.10.1791; BAGG 7: 228-48 Informe sobre las subdelegaciones ...20.7.1794; BAGG 7: 157-75 Anguiano 3.1.1800, BAGG 7: 175-9 Anguiano 15.12.1818, ANH P14 L45 Mallol 28.6.1820; AGCA A1.1 2 60 9.6.1821.

[49]AGI AG 13 Relación de la siembra y calidad de xiquilite...no date; AGCA A1.23 1514 f.194 cédula 1.11.1610; Vázquez de Espinosa, *Compendium and Description*, p. 236; Rubio Sánchez, "El Añil," pp. 317-18; Smith, "Indigo Production," pp. 181-84.

years, but the quality of dye they produced declined after three years. From this short description of its cultivation, it is clear that indigo possessed two advantages over other crops, particularly cacao. First, it could be easily combined with livestock raising, which had already proved its success in many areas into which indigo was introduced. Second, it required only a small investment of capital and a small seasonal supply of labor; this was a particular advantage in the sixteenth and seventeenth centuries when sources of labor were shrinking as the Indian population declined.

In order to make indigo dye, the leaves were cut in the early morning before they were dried out by the sun. Since it was desirable to start processing with freshly cut leaves it was necessary for the works to be located fairly close to the area of cultivation. Having been collected, the leaves were then placed in vats, known as *pilas* or *canoas*, and steeped in water for about 24 hours or until the water turned blue. Water from swamps or from warm springs was often used since it was considered to produce better dye. At this stage the water was drained into another vat, leaving behind the rotting leaves. The water was then beaten with wooden poles or sticks; initially the beating was done by Indians who stood in the water, but later beaters were driven by water- or horsepower. After several hours of beating, the dye was left to settle at the bottom of the vat or trough and then it was scooped out and placed in linen cloths to strain out the water. Finally, the dye was dried in the sun, before being divided into blocks for sale. Tasks of different degrees of skill were involved in the processing of indigo; relatively unskilled labor could be employed in bringing the leaves into the processing works in carts or on horseback, but the timing of the different processes involved in making the dye was a skilled job, particularly judging the point at which the beating of the liquid should stop and the dye be allowed to settle; over- or underbeating could adversely affect the quality of the dye.

Although indigo production possessed a number of advantages over many other forms of economic activity, it had one disadvantage that was noted from the beginning: the unhealthy character of the method of processing. The draining of the first vats, the removal of the rotting leaves, and the beating of the water in the second vats very often involved workers standing for several hours in warm water that gave off vapors and caused colds and other respiratory infections. In addition, the rotting leaves attracted insects that spread disease and helped to earn the *obrajes* the reputation of being unhealthy places of work.[50] Even though the construction of self-draining vats and the use of water- and horsepower helped to improve conditions in the processing plants, their reputation remained with them. The unhealthiness of indigo processing was recognized at an early date, and it resulted in the ban on the employment of repartimiento labor in obrajes in 1581.[51] Until 1601 Indians could volunteer to work in obrajes, but after that date the employment of Indians in indigo processing was banned completely;[52] even as late as 1791 the Crown was reiterating the ban on the employment of Indians in indigo manufacture.[53] Nevertheless, since negro slaves were expensive to purchase, the majority of indigo producers preferred to use Indian labor illegally and to employ other free persons of mixed race as they could. Following the total ban on the employment of Indians in obrajes in 1601, *alcaldes* were encharged with undertaking annual tours of inspection of indigo works and taking proceedings against those who were suspected of

---

[50]AGI AG 10 Audiencia 4.4.1580; Smith, "Indigo Production," pp. 185-86.

[51]AGCA A1.23 1513 f.594 cédula 15.5.1581.

[52]AGCA A1.23 4576 f.46 cédula 24.11.1601.

[53]AGCA A3.12 187 1901 Comments of Fiscal 30.3.1791.

having used Indian labor.  However, the threat of being fined or having a repartimiento suspended did not act as a deterrent to employers.  Many claimed that they had not used Indians inside the obrajes, but only to bring in the leaves from the fields, whilst others tried to shift the blame onto their overseers.  Generally, however, indigo producers accepted the fines that were imposed on them; they were not very high and they could often be reduced by bribing the inspector.  These fines were incorporated into the running costs of the enterprise and they represented a smaller outlay than the importation of negro slaves would have required.  With high profits to be made in indigo production, fines failed to check the illegal employment of Indians in obrajes, about which higher officials, ecclesiastics, and Indians themselves continued to complain.[54]  Indians were generally employed on a seasonal basis and they sometimes had to provide the animals on which they transported the bundles of indigo leaves to the obrajes; in 1689 most obrajes in the jurisdiction of Gracias a Dios employed five or six *sacateros*.[55]

Another dyestuff that became a minor export was cochineal.  Cochineal is produced from the dead bodies of insects that are raised on the tuna or nopal cactus, which itself might be wild or cultivated.  The techniques of cochineal production appear to have been developed by Indians in Mixteca and Oaxaca in pre-Columbian times, and those areas remained the most important centers of production during the colonial period.[56]  Spaniards showed a reluctance to become involved in the techniques of production, which consisted of raising and drying insects, and then converting them into blocks of dye at the rate of about 70,000 insects per pound; the Spanish preferred to allow the Indians to produce the cochineal and then obtain it from them by trade.[57]  It seems likely that the techniques of cochineal production were known to Indians in Honduras during pre-Columbian times, but if not, they were introduced soon after conquest.  In 1575, "tunas de grana" were said to be doing well in Honduras[58] and in 1595 the Crown ordered the authorities in Central America to encourage the planting of tuna cactuses for the production of cochineal.[59]  Small quantities were produced for export throughout the

---

[54]Fines appear to have been between 25 and 50 pesos (for example, visitas of obrajes P1 L90 (1657); P3 L40 (1676) L51 (1677), L69 (1677), L72 (1677), L78 (1678), L79 (1678), L85 (1678), L132 (1681); P4 L93 (1685), L140 (1689).  For the collusion between obrajeros and inspectors in other parts of the Audiencia, see MacLeod, *Spanish Central America*, pp. 186-90; and Smith, "Indigo Production," pp. 187-89.  Some repartimientos of Indians were suspended where obrajeros had employed Indians in the manufacture of indigo (See AGCA A3.12 186 1898 1791 and A3.12 187 1903 1791).

[55]AGCA A1.53 375 3454 Visita of obrajes 1689.

[56]R.L. Lee, "Cochineal Production and Trade in New Spain to 1600," *The Americas* 4 (1948):449-73; MacLeod, *Spanish Central America*, p. 174.

[57]MacLeod, *Spanish Central America*, p. 171.

[58]AGI AG 386-2 cédula 3.5.1595.

[59]AGCA A1.23 4588 ff.252-3 cédula 13.5.1595.

seventeenth century,[60] and by the end of the colonial period it was said to be found everywhere, although it was particularly abundant between Yoro and Trujillo.[61]

Although there were fertile lowlands with a suitable climate for sugar production and there were high hopes in the early sixteenth century that it could be produced commercially, it never provided for more than a small proportion of domestic needs.[62] There were two main reasons for this: first, as a bulky product the costs of transport rose rapidly with distance from markets, so that sugar produced in Central America could not compete in European markets with that produced in the nearer Caribbean islands; second, even if the profits from sugar production had been high, the establishment of a sugar mill required a high investment of capital and few residents in Honduras possessed the necessary financial resources. Many estates grew sugar on a small scale, but only a few, mainly in the jurisdiction of Comayagua and Tegucigalpa, appear to have concentrated on the production of sugar.[63] The sugar produced was mainly poor quality *rapadura* and it was consumed locally.[64] Another crop that achieved local importance, but not until the eighteenth century, was tobacco (*Nicotiana tabacum* L.). This was most suited for cultivation in humid areas and the main area of production was the Llanos de Santa Rosa de Copán, which produced excellent quality tobacco; some was also grown in Olancho.[65] The cultivation of tobacco appears to have been undertaken mainly by repartimiento labor. Its cultivation was said to be unhealthy, although it is not clear if this was because of the nature of the work or because it generally involved the Indians moving to humid areas to which they were not acclimatized.[66]

Before passing on to discuss the production of food crops it is worth noting one vegetable product that became an important item of export, but which was collected from wild plants: sarsaparilla. This was used for medicinal purposes, and particularly for the

---

[60]P. Chaunu, *Séville et l'Atlantique*, vol. 6 (of 8) (Paris: Colin, 1955-59), pp. 980-81; CDI 19:239-304 Proposiciones del Marques de Varinas 1677; AGI AG 40 Rodríguez Bravo 14.5.1688.

[61]AGI AG 501 Anguiano 10.5.1804.

[62]Gómez, *Esbozo de historia económica*, p. 50.

[63]BAGG 1:29-39 Letona 20.7.1743; BAGG 2:462-73 Autos formados...13.10.1765; BM Add. 27,392K Map of the Musqueto Shore 30.12.1784; AGI AG 578 Cadiñanos 20.10.1791; AGCA A3.12 187 1908 Milla 5.5.1795, A1.12 161 1695 Ribera and Perdomo 13.9.1802; ANH UC 8.6.1802.

[64]AGI AG 501 Informe de la provincia de Honduras 20.2.1816; BAGG 7:175-79 Anguiano 15.12.1818.

[65]AGI AG 778 6.11.1783, AG 777 Juan del Barrio 3.6.1784, Quintana 5.9.1786; AG 578 Cadiñanos 20.10.1791; BAGG 7:228-48 Informe sobre las subdelegaciones...20.7.1794, BAGG 7:157-75 3.1.1800; AGI AG 501 Anguiano 10.5.1804; Juarros, *Statistical and Commercial History*, p. 56.

[66]AGCA A3.16 517 5427 Village of Talgua 1787, A3.16 194 2010 10.5.1795, A3.16 194 2012 Matrículas of Yoro 1795.

treatment of syphilis. The plant grew in swampy areas, notably around Trujillo[67] which was said to produce "the best in the Indies."[68] The roots were collected from the plants by forced Indian labor.[69] The peak of production occurred in the 1580s when up to 4,429 *arrobas* were exported in one year.[70] Although production fell during the seventeenth century, probably due to the exhaustion of wild stocks of sarsaparilla and the uncertainty of European markets for the product, it still ranked as one of the most important exports of Honduras.[71]

When the Spanish turned their attention to agriculture their intention was to produce for external markets, mainly Spain, and to rely on the Indians to supply them with food. This clear-cut distinction in the orientation of Spanish and Indian production was never realized; commercial crops often found great difficulty in finding external markets, so that production tended to languish and shift to those for which there was an internal market. These included subsistence crops, particularly maize, beans, and wheat. Throughout the sixteenth and seventeenth centuries the Spanish relied on the Indians for their supplies of maize and beans, which they obtained through the sale of tribute or by trade.[72] Thus, the availability of maize depended not only on physical factors, such as climate, but also on the amount of Indian tribute paid and on the general level of Indian agricultural production, both of which suffered seriously as a result of the decline in the Indian population. There were other factors which also tended to make the level of production very variable and hence unreliable. They included whether or not *jueces de milpas*, who ensured that Indians planted food crops, were appointed and how much of the crop was bought up by merchants for export. Given the unreliability of supplies of maize, many estate owners began to plant a few subsistence crops themselves. Nevertheless the bulk of the maize and beans consumed by the Spanish was produced by the Indians. The same was not true of wheat.

The Spanish had a preference for wheat flour and as such tried to encourage its cultivation by Indians. However, the difficulties of introducing the techniques of cultivation to the Indians and the existence of good markets for the crop, encouraged the Spanish to establish their own wheat farms. The best areas for wheat cultivation were the

---

[67]AGI AG 44 Procurador of Trujillo, no date, AG 49 Romero 26.2.1595; CDI 19:239-304 Proposiciones del Marques de Varinas 1677, AG 164 Cabildo eclesiástico of Comayagua 10.2.1680, AG 29 Audiencia 21.2.1686, AG 40 Rodríguez Bravo 14.5.1688; RPM 2537 I Descripción general, no date; BNM 3047 ff.128-135v. no author, no date; López de Velasco, *Geografía y descripción universal*, p. 312; MacLeod, *Spanish Central America*, pp. 66-67.

[68]Vázquez de Espinosa, *Compendium and Description*, p. 244.

[69]For example, AGI AG 164 Bishop of Honduras 19.7.1620.

[70]Chaunu, *Séville and l'Atlantique*, vol. 6, p. 1024.

[71]CDI 19:239-304 Proposiciones del Marques de Varinas 1677; AGI AG 29 Audiencia 21.2.1686, AG 164 Cabildo eclesiástico of Comayagua 10.2.1680.

[72]See the discussions of tribute and changes in the Indian economy.

valleys surrounding the towns of Comayagua and Gracias a Dios.[73] Although the former area was more fertile, there wheat had to compete with cattle for the use of land. One or two harvests were possible a year and it was estimated that one fanega of sown wheat would produce a harvest of between 18 and 20 fanegas.[74] Despite this fairly low level of production compared to maize, wheat was produced in sufficient quantities to provide for the ports of Trujillo and Puerto Caballos, which were located in areas that were unsuitable for the cultivation of maize.[75] It was also exported to the neighboring provinces of San Salvador and San Miguel.[76] Sometimes merchants purchased the crop for export before it was harvested, thus resulting in shortages in Honduras itself and causing the price of wheat to rise from two pesos to seven and one-half pesos a fanega.[77] But even when there were no shortages of wheat, prices for the cereal were more than double that of maize, and to a large extent the Spanish became resigned to eating maize tortillas.

[73]AGI PAT 183-1-30 Herrera 5.4.1570, AG 44 Montoso Castillo 3.8.1590, PAT 183-1-16 Antonelli and López de Quintanillas 7.10.1590; RAHM 9/4663 no.15 Valverde 24.8.1590; RAHM CM 49 ff.73-92, no date; Torquemada, *Monarquía Indiana*, p. 334; Ponce, *Relación breve*, pp. 345, 348; López de Velasco, *Geografía y descripción universal*, pp. 307-10; Herrera, *Historia general* 9 dec.4 lib.8 cap.3:105.

[74]AGI AG 44 Montoso Castillo 3.8.1590, PAT 183-1-16 Antonelli and López de Quintanillas 7.10.1590.

[75]CDIU 17:182 1570.

[76]Torquemada, *Monarquía Indiana*, p. 334; López de Velasco, *Geografía y descripción universal*, pp. 307-309; Herrera, *Historia general* 9 dec.4 lib.8 cap.3:105.

[77]AGCA A3.12 509 5295 4.5.1710.

# 9
## Mining

Gold and silver production in Honduras never accounted for more than about 5 percent of that produced in Spanish America at any one time during the colonial period, but it was of considerable importance to the local economy and employed a significant proportion of the total workforce.[1]

In the early sixteenth century mining activities concentrated on the exploitation of alluvial gold deposits to be found in the Olancho valley and the valleys surrounding Trujillo and San Pedro, but mid-century production had declined. From the late 1550s to 1565 the gold smelted in Comayagua and San Pedro was worth about 3,000 pesos a year, but by the 1570s it had fallen to 1,000 pesos.[2] At that time there were only 50 negroes panning gold between Comayagua and Olancho.[3] A major shift in mineral production occurred when new deposits of silver were discovered at Guazucarán in the jurisdiction of Tegucigalpa in 1569 and at nearby Santa Lucía in 1578.[4] From that time onwards mineral production was dominated by silver mining. By 1581 other silver veins had been discovered at San Marcos, Agalteca, and Nuestra Señora de la O,[5] and during the seventeenth century ores were also being mined at San Juan, San Salvador, and San Antonio Yeguare, all in the jurisdiction of Tegucigalpa. The Tegucigalpa silver mines dominated mineral production throughout the colonial period, but from the end of the

---

[1]Parts of this chapter have appeared in L.A. Newson, "Labour in the Colonial Mining Industry of Honduras," *The Americas* 39 (1982):185-203; and idem, "Silver Mining in Colonial Honduras," *Revista de historia de América* 97 (1984):45-75.

[2]AGI CO 988 Cuentas 1557-1573.

[3]López de Velasco, *Geografía y descripción universal*, p. 313.

[4]AGI AG 8 Soto Pachón 10.4.1570, AG 10 Valverde 30.3.1580, AG 43 Cabildo of Valladolid (Comayagua) 17.4.1581, AG 39 Ponce de León 26.5.1584.

[5]AGI AG 55 Reynoso 12.4.1581.

seventeenth century important gold deposits were worked at El Corpus in Choluteca.[6] At the beginning of the eighteenth century new mines were opened up at Potrerillos and Cedros, but the two major discoveries of the century were at Opoteca near Comayagua in 1725 and at San Joseph de Yuscarán where mining began in 1744.[7] Alluvial gold deposits were also worked intermittently throughout the century at Olancho, Olanchito, Tencoa, and San Andrés de Zaragoza.[8]

The silver and gold was found in mineralized veins associated with volcanic intrusions mostly Tertiary in age. These veins were located in the metamorphic and sedimentary rocks that form the rugged interior highlands around Tegucigalpa and Comayagua.[9] Many of the silver ores, such as those at Santa Lucía, Agalteca, Cedros, and El Plomo, had associated lead deposits in the form of galena, which meant that they could be refined easily by smelting. Lead-free ores, however, were generally refined by the amalgamation process, which will be described in detail later.

Claims to deposits had to be registered with the authorities, who surveyed the area and established boundary markers, after which mining had to commence within a specified period. Although many claims were made to silver deposits, the majority were not worked. In 1581 a *visita* by the *Alcalde Mayor* of Tegucigalpa revealed that between 300 and 400 claims had been registered to mines in Guazucarán, but only three or four were being worked, whilst in Santa Lucía 500 to 1,500 mines had been registered and only 30 or 40 were working.[10]

The silver ores were worked only superficially. Ores found above the water table were weathered, which meant that they could be more easily extracted with simple tools

[6]Vázquez de Espinosa, *Compendium and Description*, p. 245, records that ores were discovered at San Juan in 1621. The San Salvador mines were discovered at the beginning of the seventeenth century; four mines were being worked there in 1648 (AGI AG 18 Testimonio del estado que tienen las minas de Tegucigalpa...Bernal del Cano 5.9.1648). The mines at San Antonio de Yeguare were not worked in earnest until the 1680s (G. Guardiola, "Apuntes acerca del mineral de San Antonio del Oriente," *RABNH* (1927):241-45; many mines were registered in that area during the decade (see ANH P4 and P6). The mines at El Corpus, which were renowned for gold rather than silver production, were discovered in 1682 (AGI AG 363 Bishop of Honduras 17.4.1696).

[7]ANH P7 L40, L46, and L47 1746-47; AGCA A3.9 506 5255 12.3.1766, A1.73 390 3662 Partial visita of Comayagua 1771, A3.9 176 1706 Morejon 10.2.1799; A.R. Vallejo, *Compendio de la historia social y política de Honduras* (Tegucigalpa: Tip. Nacional, 1926), p. 31; A. Batres Jáuregui, *La América Central ante la historia*, vol. 1 (of 2) (Madrid: Tip. Sánchez y de Guise, 1920), p. 412.

[8]AGI AG 231 Rivera 29.5.1737; BRP MA X ff.171-77v. Noticias de las minas 1749; AGCA A3.9 507 5264 Comandante de Omoa 19.2.1786, A3.9 176 1713 Fiscal 14.1.1805; AGI AG 501 Informe de la provincia de Honduras 20.2.1816.

[9]Roberts and Irving, *Mineral Deposits*, pp. 175-84.

[10]AGI AG 55 Reynoso 12.4.1581. The same pattern existed in other mining areas of the region: Agalteca: 100 to 200 claims to mines, only one being worked; San Marcos: 100 to 200 claims, four being worked; Nuestra Señora de la O: 20 claims, none being worked.

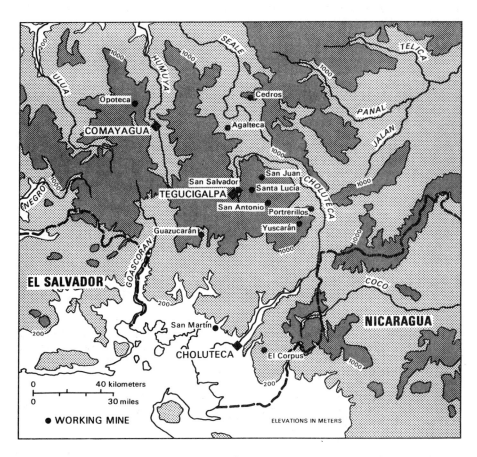

Figure 5. Colonial Silver Mines

than those below the water table.[11]   Also, the working of ores at greater depths involved the construction not only of deep galleries, but also drainage and ventilation shafts, all of which required high inputs of capital and labor.   As a result, few mines penetrated deeper than 50 *estados* (325 feet), even though rich deposits were often present at greater depths.[12]   Flooding was a serious problem that could only be overcome by the construction of sloping drainage adits, known as *taladros*, or by the use of vertical shafts and whims (*malacates*).   The construction of drainage shafts cost upwards of several thousand pesos,[13] so that whilst some were constructed in the more profitable mines, many more mines were abandoned as they became flooded.[14]

In general the rock in which the silver was found was hard and blasting powder was not generally available until the middle of the eighteenth century.[15]   Thus, in order to soften or crack the working surface of a lode, a technique known as fire-setting was used.[16]   Even in the eighteenth century, the high cost of gunpowder meant that blasting probably only supplanted fire-setting in areas of particularly hard rock, such as around Opoteca.[17]   The ore was extracted by *barreteros*, so named because they used a *barra*, or crowbar, and it was carried out of the mines by *tanateros* using large leather bags, or *tanates*.   Later whims were used for extracting the ore in some of the deeper mines.   The barreteros and tanateros formed two distinct classes within the mines: the extraction of the

---

[11]R.C. West, *The Mining Community in Northern New Spain:   The Parral Mining District*, Ibero-Americana 30 (Berkeley and Los Angeles:   University of California, 1949), p. 18.

[12]AGCA A3.17 1718 27685 Zelaya 27.7.1789; AGI AG 496 Miners of Yuscarán 30.7.1799; T.S. Floyd, "Bourbon Palliatives and the Central American Mining Industry, 1765-1800," *The Americas* 18 (1961):108.

[13]For example, AGI AG 770 Alcalde Mayor of Tegucigalpa 29.11.1785 gives the cost of constructing drainage shafts.   The cost of draining the El Corpus mines was estimated at between 20,000 and 30,000 pesos.   By 1816 the estimated cost had risen to 80,000 pesos (AGI AG 501 Informe de la provincia de Honduras...20.2.1816).

[14]See the visitas of the mines of San Antonio, Cedros, and Yuscarán ANH P6 L130 1730, P7 L3 1740, P8 L11 1763, P8 L27 1768, P9 L89 1774.   See also BPR MA X 286 ff.171-77v.  Noticias de las minas 1749; AGI AG 797 García 20.11.1790, AG 793 3.3.1816.

[15]R.C. West, "The Mining Economy of Honduras in the Colonial Period," *33rd International Congress of Americanists* (Costa Rica) 2:770-71; D. Brading, *Miners and Merchants in Bourbon Mexico, 1763-1810* (Cambridge:   Cambridge University Press, 1971), p. 133; D. Brading and H.E. Cross, "Colonial Silver Mining: Mexico and Peru," *HAHR* 52 (1972):550.

[16]This technique as practiced in the Guazucarán mines was described by Valverde (RAHM 9/4663 no. 15 Valverde 24.8.1590).

[17]There were numerous complaints from miners about the high price of blasting powder, particularly from miners in Opoteca (AGCA A1.30 222 2479 Visita by Orosco Manrique de Lara 1742, A3.9 214 5052 f.2 17.4.1742; BPR MA X ff.171-77v.  Noticias de las minas 1749; AGCA A3.9 506 5255 Teniente 12.3.1766; AGI AG 797 Caballos 20.11.1788, García 20.11.1790.

ores was a skilled job and as such barreteros earnt between two and three reals a day; tanateros on the other hand received only nine reals a week.[18]

Once the ore had been extracted, it was crushed and then refined by smelting or amalgamation. There were two kinds of refining works. First, there were small crude furnaces, where the ore was smelted after being crushed by hand. These works were generally owned by poor miners and they were often located near sources of wood. Second, there were the capital-intensive *haciendas de beneficio*, the most distinctive feature of which was the stamp mill that crushed the ores before they were smelted or amalgamated. The stamp mills comprised iron hammers that were operated by mules or water power. In the 1740s a new grinding machine called an *arrastre* was introduced. It consisted of a stone floor over which large stones were dragged by mules thereby reducing the ore to a fine power. Arrastres were generally used to crush ore prior to amalgamation;[19] at the peak of production in the Yuscarán area there were 60 arrastres and 17 mills in operation.[20]

There were two ways in which the silver ore could be refined. Ores with associated lead deposits could be refined by simply smelting them using charcoal, whereas lead-free ores had to be refined either by the amalgamation process using mercury, salt, and magistral (chalcopyrite), or by adding lead in the form of *greta* (lead monoxide) or *cendrada* (hearth lead). Greta was obtained from the lead-rich deposits at Agalteca and Cedros, or else it was imported from Guatemala.[21] Smelting took place in large furnaces that were fanned by bellows, which were operated by mules. The resulting compound was then burnt in smaller furnaces to separate the silver from the lead. Abundant supplies of wood were required for smelting; it was estimated that one arroba of wood was needed to smelt one *quintal* of ore.[22] There were several advantages to smelting rather than amalgamating ores: smelting was a simpler, more rapid process and it generally yielded larger quantities of metal from equivalent amounts of ore. Also, since the sale of mercury was one of the main ways by which the authorities could control the production and taxation of silver, smelting provided greater opportunities for tax evasion. Nevertheless, for a variety of reasons, which might include the poor quality of the ores or shortages of flux and wood, miners were often forced to amalgamate ores rather than smelt them. Nevertheless, even into the eighteenth century about one-half, or possibly

---

[18]AGCA A1.73 390 3662 Visita of the Opoteca mines 1771; ANH P20 L25 Arancel 1802.

[19]AGI AG 799 Talavera 4.6.1750; AGCA A3.12 186 1893 29.12.1758; AGI AG 464 Gálvez 1.6.1779.

[20]AGI AG 496 Miners of Yuscarán 30.7.1779, AG 793 Testimonio...1815.

[21]West, "Mining Economy of Honduras," p. 774; RAHM 9/4663 no. 15 Valverde 24.8.1590, AG 55 Reynoso 12.4.1581, AG 464 Gálvez 1.6.1779, AG 496 Gremio de Mineros de Tegucigalpa 18.10.1799.

[22]AGI AG 55 Reynoso 12.4.1581.

more, of the ores mined in Honduras were smelted, a much higher proportion than in Mexico and Peru, where the majority of ores were amalgamated.[23]

For the amalgamation process mercury, salt, and magistral were needed. The sale of mercury was a royal monopoly, but its price varied over time. During the sixteenth and seventeenth centuries the price of mercury was set at 60 pesos, excluding the costs of transport, but during the eighteenth century its price was often reduced by as much as one-half.[24] The mercury was issued on a credit basis with the recipients agreeing to return to the *Caja* a quantity of silver in proportion to their allocation of mercury; from each pound of silver the authorities expected to receive one mark of silver or one ounce of gold.[25] In this way officials attempted to keep an account of production and ensure that the Crown's fifth, or in the case of Honduras, its tenth (*diezmo*), was paid. The other important raw materials required for the amalgamation process were salt and magistral. Salt was obtained from the salt pans in Choluteca, where a small salt industry developed to supply the needs of the mining industry.[26] About one and one-half to two arrobas of salt were required to produce one mark of silver.[27] Magistral (chalcopyrite) was found with the deposits of silver.[28]

During the process of amalgamation the crushed ore was placed in piles together with the necessary mercury and salt and left to separate. It was periodically stirred by *repasadores*, who added extra mercury and salt as necessary. The whole process, which was supervised by an *azoguero*, took several weeks to several months, depending in part on the season, since cold weather retarded the chemical process, and in part on the quality

---

[23]Floyd, "Bourbon Palliatives," p. 110. Between 1771 and 1775, 50.1 percent of the quintos paid on silver were on amalgamated silver (see n. 119) and one remittance of 14,683 marks of silver from the Caja of Comayagua indicated that 8,194 marks had been produced by amalgamation (55.8 percent) and 6,489 marks by smelting (AGCA A3.17 1693 27269 Certificaciones que componen la cantidad de marcos...1769). However, a report from the previous year noted that whilst those who produced silver by amalgamation received two-thirds of the Indians who worked under the repartimiento, they only produced one-third of the silver (AGCA A3.9 174 1674 29.4.1768). For the proportion of silver produced by amalgamation in Mexico and Peru, see Brading and Cross, "Colonial Silver Mining," pp. 552-55.

[24]There are many cédulas setting the price of mercury in AGI AG 1 and 798. See also AGCA A3.7 1658 26944 f.1 cédula 10.8.1738, A3.17 1702 27425 f.88 cédula 6.2.1769, A3.9 506 5259 1772, A3.17 1723 27765 f.1 cédula 17.7.1773, A3.17 1718 27685 f.36 Zelaya 27.7.1789, A3.17 1735 27890 1794, A3.9 176 1707 2.5.1797; AGI AG 501 Anguiano 10.5.1804.

[25]AGCA A3.1 6 6 f.22 cédula 19.7.1735, A3.9 507 5260 Distribution of mercury 1758-1774.

[26]AGI AG 10 Lic. Caballos 12.3.1575, AG 64 Miners of Honduras 1617, AG 496 Miners of Yuscarán 30.9.1799.

[27]AGI AG 496 Gremio de Mineros de Yuscarán 18.10.1799; Vallejo, *Compendio de la historia*, p. 17.

[28]Roberts and Irving, *Mineral Deposits*, pp. 175-84.

of the ore and the skill of the azoguero. The resulting amalgam was then washed and finally burnt to separate the silver from the mercury.[29]

The techniques used in extracting and processing the ore remained very much the same throughout the colonial period. Although some technical innovations, such as the use of blasting powder and arrastres, were introduced in the eighteenth century, the technical knowledge available in the mines was minimal. There were a few requests for mining experts to come from Sweden or Mexico,[30] but miners generally considered themselves to be too poor to finance the establishment of a mining college for the instruction of mineralogy and metallurgy, as occurred in Mexico in 1792.[31] Even if the technical knowledge had been available, it is doubtful if miners would have possessed the necessary capital resources to finance the innovations required.

After the silver had been smelted or amalgamated it was supposed to be taken to the *casa de afinación*, where it was assayed and melted down to form silver bars or ingots of 130 and 135 marks.[32] It was then transferred to the Caja where it was taxed. When claims were made to mines, miners swore to bring all silver mined to the assay office on pain of death and loss of property.[33] Although the quinto was normally paid on silver produced in Spanish America, in order to encourage production, the silver produced in Honduras was only subject to the diezmo. On top of the diezmo miners also had to pay a seignorage tax of 1.5 percent when the silver was minted. This tax was later reduced to 1 percent during the period of the Bourbon reforms.[34]

One of the problems facing miners after they had produced the crude silver was exchanging it for money. From 1591 the Crown had authorized subtreasuries to exchange silver for coins,[35] but unfortunately the Caja at Comayagua never possessed sufficient coins to exchange. Throughout the sixteenth and seventeenth centuries coins were only minted in Mexico, Lima, and Potosí, and Central American trade with these areas was limited. In the seventeenth century most of the coins came from Peru and they were often debased and known as *moclones*. As a result miners resorted to the use of small slivers of silver cut from the silver bars they had produced or else they sold the silver to merchants. Although merchants generally offered lower prices than the treasury, they could provide

---

[29]West, *Mining Community*, pp. 31-33; P.J. Bakewell, *Silver Mining and Society in Colonial Mexico: Zacatecas, 1546-1700* (Cambridge: Cambridge University Press, 1971), pp. 140-44; and Brading, *Miners and Merchants*, p. 138, describe the amalgamation process in detail for Mexico. Brading estimates that about one-fourth of the mercury was lost in the process.

[30]AGI AG 464 Alcalde Mayor of Tegucigalpa 7.11.1778; AGCA A3.17 1718 27865 Zelaya 27.7.1789; AGI AG 797 García 20.11.1790, AG 501 Informe de la provincia de Honduras 20.2.1816.

[31]AGCA A3.17 1718 27685 Zelaya 27.7.1789.

[32]AGI AG 464 Gálvez 30.1.1780, AG 501 Informe de la provincia de Honduras 20.2.1816.

[33]*Recopilación* 2 lib.4 tít.23 ley 6 pp. 88-89 1535.

[34]Floyd, "Bourbon Palliatives," p. 117. In 1777 the quinto on gold was reduced to 3 percent (AGI AG 770 7.6.1778 [cédula 1.3.1777]).

[35]*Recopilación* 2 lib.4 tít.24 ley 2 pp. 93-94 1591.

miners with the immediate sources of cash they required to pay wages and discharge pressing debts.[36] The shortage of coinage in Honduras did not alter substantially after 1731 when a *Casa de Moneda* was established in Guatemala.[37] In 1750 the Crown attempted to break the control of the merchants over the mining industry by providing exchange facilities in the mining areas. However, there was never enough coinage available for exchange and alternative sources of credit were not provided.[38] As such merchants continued to provide a service for miners in arranging for the transport of silver to Guatemala and in supplying them with ready cash and goods in exchange; the alternative for miners was to organize the transport themselves. The latter was not a viable proposition for miners who possessed only a few bars of silver or who could not wait a year, the time taken to exchange silver for coins in Guatemala, before they received the cash they so desperately needed to continue production.[39] Miners generally sold their silver to merchants at the rate of six pesos three reals a mark for smelted silver and six pesos four reals a mark for amalgamated silver, and the silver could be exchanged in Guatemala at a profit of five to ten reals a mark depending on the quality of the silver.[40] Although miners resented the control of their operations by merchants, they realized that they could not continue production without the credit the merchants provided; the Crown was also unhappy with the arrangement, since much of the silver that passed into the hands of merchants was never exchanged at the Casa de Moneda, but was sold illegally to foreign traders.

In an attempt to encourage mining and ensure greater profits for the Crown, in 1780 a *Banco de Rescate*, which was independent of the Caja in Comayagua, was established in Tegucigalpa for the exchange of silver.[41] It was hoped that its proximity to the mining areas and the price of seven pesos a mark paid by the Banco would encourage a greater inflow of silver to the royal coffers. To encourage this process merchants were forbidden to trade in silver in the mining areas. Although a good idea in theory, the establishment of the Banco and the ban on the merchant trade in silver created new difficulties. The merchants had been the main sources of credit for the mining

[36]F. de P. García Peláez, *Memorias para la historia del Antiguo Reino de Guatemala*, vol. 2 (of 3) (Guatemala: Tip. Nacional, 1943-44), pp. 140-42; A.R. Vallejo, "Minas de Honduras," *Revista de la sociedad de geografía e historia de Honduras* 34, nos. 10-12 (1957):33; MacLeod, *Spanish Central America*, pp. 281-86.

[37]J.C. Díaz Durán, "Historia de la Casa de Moneda del Reino de Guatemala desde 1731 hasta 1773," *ASGH* 18 (1942):195-98; García Peláez, *Memorias* 2:144.

[38]For a discussion of Crown efforts to establish exchange facilities in the mining areas, see Newson, "Silver Mining," pp. 55-58.

[39]AGI AG 464 Alcalde Mayor 7.11.1778, AG 501 King to Audiencia 1817. The conflicts between Guatemalan merchants and agricultural producers, which were paralleled in the mining industry, are described in T.S. Floyd, "The Guatemalan Merchants, the Government and the Provincianos, 1750-1800," *HAHR* 41 (1961):90-110.

[40]ANH P7 L22 13.2.1744; BAGG 7: 210-20 and A1.17 1840 13999 Alcalde Mayor 23.8.1765, Valle 13.10.1765; AGCA A3.9 506 5255 12.3.1766; AGI AG 561 Garzón 14.10.1775.

[41]Floyd, "Bourbon Palliatives," pp. 117, 122; AGI AG 464 and 796 Instrucción que se ha de arreglar...30.1.1780.

industry, so that when they were banned from trading silver, the sources of credit for the industry dried up and silver production fell.[42] As a result of petitions from miners and following the suspension of the administrator of the Banco for corruption in 1791, the Banco was abolished, and in 1792 a subtreasury of the Caja of Comayagua was established where silver could be exchanged.[43] This subtreasury, known as the *Casa de Rescate*, persisted until the end of the colonial period, although its location was transferred with the Caja to Tegucigalpa in 1812.[44] The Casa was authorized to exchange silver with anyone who presented it, so that merchants once again became involved in the process of exchange.[45] Even though the removal of the ban on the merchant trade in silver probably resulted in more silver being lost through contraband trade, the proximity of the Casa to the mining areas should have encouraged a greater inflow of silver. Unfortunately the Casa never possessed enough coinage to exchange for silver. Coins came from the royal mint in Guatemala about three times in two years, and when they arrived they were exhausted within a very short period; in 1816 it was estimated that about 80,000 pesos had been exchanged in only eight days.[46] In 1813 it was suggested that the Casa de Moneda in Guatemala should be transferred to Comayagua, and the Casa in Tegucigalpa closed, after all the bulk of the silver produced in the *Reino de Guatemala* came from Honduras.[47] Nevertheless, the transfer did not take place, probably because of the domination of the silver trade by merchants from Guatemala.

It is clear that the whole process of obtaining coins from silver ores was a complex one in which many factors intervened to either stop production or, more commonly, to stifle the development of a flourishing mining industry. Most important in determining levels of production were labor and capital.

There was always a shortage of labor in the mining industry of Honduras. The small size of the Indian population and its dramatic decline during the first half of the colonial period limited the supply of labor, whilst Crown restrictions on the employment of Indian labor limited the types of mining activities in which Indians could be employed. Even when the Indian population began to increase in the eighteenth century, competing demands for labor meant that the supply of labor for the mining industry did not expand at a parallel rate. Changes in the types of labor employed in mining during the colonial

---

[42]Whilst quintos for the years 1777 and 1778 had averaged 33,453 pesos a year, from 1781 to 1785 they averaged only 13,540 pesos a year (AGI AG 744 Estado que manifiesta ...quintos de plata 1777 to 1785).

[43]AGI AG 797 García 20.11.1790; AGCA A3.17 1724 27781 13.5.1791, A3.9 158 3076 8.11.1792, A3.5 1105 20007 f.231v. cédula 1.6.1792, A3.17 1734 27880 20.12.1794.

[44]M. Wortman, "Government Revenue and Economic Trends in Central America, 1787-1819," *HAHR* 55 (1975):265.

[45]AGI AG 501 Anguiano 10.5.1804; Floyd, "Bourbon Palliatives," p. 123.

[46]AGI AG 501 Informe de la provincia de Honduras ...20.2.1816.

[47]BAGG 7: 74-80 and AGCA A1.17 2875 26357 Dictamen del Diputado 31.8.1813; AGI AG 501 King to Audiencia 1817.

period have been discussed in detail elsewhere,[48] so that only a brief summary will be made here.

From 1539 the employment of Indians in mining had been banned, and when Indian slavery and personal service were abolished, and the repartimiento introduced, this ban remained in force. Appeals by the Audiencia and miners to allow the employment of Indians in mining were unsuccessful until 1575 when the Crown finally agreed to allow Indians to work in the mines on a voluntary basis. However, they could not be employed in underground work, but only in providing the mines with food, charcoal, and pit-props.[49] The authorities tried to overcome labor shortages by importing negro slaves and encouraging the immigration of Spanish colonists, but the numbers that arrived were too few to solve the basic problem of the shortage of underground workers.[50]

The small number of negro slaves employed in mining during this period, compared to the mid-sixteenth century, was a reflection of the low profitability of mining, which meant that miners possessed neither the financial resources nor incentive to purchase expensive negro slaves, except on credit. The shortage of negro slave labor forced miners to press the Crown to allow the employment of Indians under the repartimiento. In 1590 the Alcalde Mayor was given the right to allocate Indians for work in the mines, although they could only be employed in work above ground.[51] Further representations by miners finally persuaded the Crown in 1601 to allow the repartimiento for mining for one year, during which time it was anticipated that negro slaves would be imported. If they could not obtain slaves, however, a secret meeting was to be held to determine whether the repartimiento should be prolonged for another year.[52] It was not until 1645, however, that the Crown finally agreed to the repartimiento of 100 Indians for the Tegucigalpa mines.[53] From that time onwards mining absorbed a large proportion of the Indians available for work under the repartimiento.

Although the repartimiento remained an important source of labor in the mines throughout the colonial period, at various times alternative suggestions were made for providing the mines with labor. These included the introduction of the *mita* as in Peru and the involvement of Indians in nearby villages in Nicaragua in the repartimiento.[54] Although by the 1760s the Indian population had begun to increase, so had the demands of other potential users. As the English threat to the Caribbean coast increased, defense made the greatest demands on repartimiento labor. Indians were required to build fortifications, particularly at Omoa, to provide the forts with supplies, to act as coast guards, as well as to form the ranks of the militia. In the late 1770s and 1780s during

---

[48]Newson, "Labour in the Colonial Mining Industry," pp. 185-203, and Chapter 11.

[49]AGI AG 386-2 Crown to Audiencia 27.4.1575. For an account of petitions made by local royal official and miners to allow the employment of Indians in mining, see Sherman, *Forced Native Labor*, pp. 232-33.

[50]Newson, "Labour in the Colonial Mining Industry," pp. 192-93.

[51]Zavala, *Instituciones coloniales*, p. 98.

[52]AGCA A1.23 1514 ff.33-4 Crown to Audiencia 24.11.1602; AGI AG 18 Bernal del Cano 5.9.1648.

[53]AGI AG 18 Bernal del Cano 5.9.1648.

[54]Newson, "Labour in the Colonial Mining Industry," pp. 196-97.

wars with the English, the demands of defense were so great that mining operations effectively ceased because of the shortage of labor.[55] Attempts to stimulate agricultural production, particularly tobacco cultivation, in the last quarter of the century, also created new demands for repartimiento labor.

With the decline in the availability of Indian labor under the repartimiento, miners were forced to turn to the employment of more expensive and less reliable free labor. Although a small number of skilled laborers, who were normally free laborers, were always required, particularly for the processing of the ores, miners generally preferred to employ Indian labor under the repartimiento since it was cheaper and more reliable. In order to attract free laborers, mine owners had to pay them higher wages than those they paid to repartimiento workers, and often offer them advances or a share of the profits.

Although free laborers were more costly in terms of wages and they were less reliable workers, they were essential in the absence of alternative sources of labor. In 1768 the ratio of free workers to Indians working under the repartimiento was about two or three to one. This is suggested by the fact that, remembering that free workers were paid higher wages, the wage bill for Indians working under the repartimiento in Yuscarán was about 1,000 pesos out of a total wage bill of 4,000 to 5,000 pesos.[56] In 1790 the total number employed in mining in Honduras was about 1,000 and since the number of Indians allocated under the repartimiento was generally 200 to 250, the ratio of free workers to Indians working under the repartimiento was an average of about four or five to one.[57] Thus by the end of the colonial period free workers constituted the dominant source of labor in the mines.

In Honduras there were a few wealthy miners with capital and access to sources of labor, whilst the majority of small producers eked out a living by depending on sources of credit; government investment in the industry was limited by the small income the Crown derived from the area, which was increasingly devoted to defense. Mining was a capital-intensive activity; money was needed to construct and maintain mining galleries, to build drainage and ventilation shafts, to purchase tools, animals, mercury, flux and charcoal, as well as to pay for the food and wages of mine workers. Hence there were only a small number of miners with sufficient resources to maintain their mines in working order and to establish a hacienda de beneficio. In 1590 there were four haciendas de beneficio in the Guazucarán mines and seven in the Tegucigalpa mines, and together they employed 182 negro slaves and 80 Indians working under the repartimiento.[58] By the middle of the seventeenth century the number of silver refineries does not appear to have changed substantially, although the numbers of workers they employed fell. In 1648 there were 12 *ingenios* working in the Guazucarán and Tegucigalpa mines and another two were under construction, but the seven ingenios working in the Santa Lucía and San Salvador mines employed only 24 negro slaves and 24 Indians working under the repartimiento.[59] With the discovery of new deposits in the eighteenth century, particularly at Yuscarán, the

---

[55]AGI AG 797 García 20.11.1790; AGCA A3.9 176 1707 2.5.1797.

[56]AGCA A3.9 174 1674 Alcalde Mayor of Tegucigalpa 29.4.1768.

[57]AGI AG 797 García 20.11.1790.

[58]RAHM 9/4663 no. 15 Valverde 24.8.1590.

[59]AGI AG 18 Bernal del Cano 5.9.1648.

number of refineries appears to have increased to about 40,[60] only to fall again to 25 towards the end of the century.[61]    Although the owners of haciendas de beneficio represented the elite of the mining industry, they were often described as poor and indebted.   As has been indicated, to a large extent miners depended on merchant credit.[62] Merchants not only provided capital for miners to continue production, but they also supplied the goods and materials required for the extraction and processing of ores, often issued on credit, all of which was repayable in silver.   The main creditors of the industry were foreign merchants, particularly from Guatemala.[63]   Although these merchants were keen to provide miners with short-term credit, they appear to have been less willing or unable to finance long-term developments in the industry.   In 1790 miners petitioned the Crown to establish a fund of 200,000 pesos to provide loans at a 4 percent rate of interest, but no silver bank was ever established in Honduras, as occurred in Mexico and Peru.[64] The continued dependence of miners on merchant credit, but only for day-to-day supplies, meant that technical developments were few and the industry remained undercapitalized up to the end of the colonial period.   In the absence of capital and with only limited sources of credit, miners tried to economize by working areas only superficially and by abandoning them as soon as they became flooded, and where possible by smelting ores rather than amalgamating them.

Due to shortages of labor and capital, mines were abandoned after only short periods of exploitation.   Many of the abandoned mines were later worked over by *gurruguces* who searched for rich ores they could refine without the use of mercury. Mine owners and the Crown alike objected to the activities of gurruguces.   Miners complained that they removed the rich ores left in the pillars supporting the mining galleries thereby causing them to collapse and making the mines unworkable; the Crown complained that the ore they extracted was often smelted without the knowledge of the authorities who were thus unable to tax the silver, which was often smuggled to Panama or to the Mosquito Shore for sale to the English.[65]   Although the activities of gurruguces were illegal, few were prosecuted.[66]   By the middle of the eighteenth century most of the

---

[60]AGCA A3.12 186 1893 29.12.1793.

[61]AGI AG 797 García 20.11.1790.

[62]Floyd, "Bourbon Palliatives," p. 107; M.L. Wortman, "The Bourbon Reforms in Central America, 1750-1786," *The Americas* 31 (1975):222.

[63]AGI AG 797 García 20.11.1790; AGCA A3.17 1734 27880 20.12.1794.

[64]AGI AG 797 García 20.11.1790; Floyd, "Bourbon Palliatives," p. 123; Brading and Cross, "Colonial Silver Mining," pp. 567-68.

[65]AGI AG 18 Bernal del Cano 5.9.1648, AG 19 Conde de Santiago 12.7.1656; ANH P3 L144 16.4.1681; AGCA A1.1 1 4 21.5.1708; AGI AG 449 Díaz Navarro 30.11.1758; AGCA A3.9 174 1682a Garzón 10.4.1775, A3.9 507 5263 8.6.1783; AGI AG 797 García 20.11.1790; West, "Mining Economy of Honduras," pp. 774-75.

[66]For an example of a prosecution see: ANH P8 L34 1769.

older mining areas were being worked over by gurruguces and by the end of the eighteenth century they were also operating in the abandoned mines of Yuscarán.[67]

Estimating silver production in Honduras is extremely difficult because of the numerous frauds and irregularities in which miners, merchants, and royal officials cooperated to their mutual advantages.[68] As a result official accounts of the amount of silver assayed and taxed can only suggest production trends. From official statistics it would appear that there was a peak of production in the late sixteenth century, whilst mining declined during the seventeenth century only to be revived again from the second quarter of the eighteenth century when new deposits of silver were discovered. During the remainder of the colonial period, silver production appears to have expanded very slowly, although there were a number of years when production fell as a result of labor shortages created by defensive demands.

In the early colonial period the peak of production occurred shortly after the discovery of silver deposits in the jurisdiction of Tegucigalpa, when in 1584 over 12,500 marks of silver were produced.[69] Treasury accounts of the taxes paid on silver and other documents suggest that production declined during the seventeenth century.[70] It is clear, however, that much of the silver refined in Honduras was exported from the province without being taxed.[71] Nevertheless, this fall in production is supported by the decline in the imports of mercury during the period,[72] although the ability of miners to smelt ores, rather than amalgamate them, makes mercury consumption an imperfect guide to levels of production.

With the discovery of new deposits of silver in the first half of the eighteenth century, silver production appears to have revived. Whereas in the late 1720s and early 1730s silver production in Honduras averaged about 8,000 marks a year,[73] the accounts of the Casa de Moneda between 1733 and 1748 indicate that about 24,000 marks were

---

[67]AGI AG 231 Rivera 29.5.1737; BAGG 1:29-39 Letona 20.7.1743; AGCA A3.9 186 1893 29.12.1758, A3.9 159 5592 27.2.1762, A3.9 174 1674 1772; ANH P12 L166 Visitas 1802.

[68]For irregular practices in the administration of the mines see Floyd, "Bourbon Palliatives," pp. 116-17, 122; Newson, "Silver Mining," pp. 68-69.

[69]AGI CO 988, 989, 991A, 992 Cuentas de la Real Hacienda 1560-1617.

[70]West, "Mining Economy of Honduras," p. 770.

[71]AGI AG 18 Bernal del Cano 5.9.1648, AG 19 Conde de Santiago 12.7.1656; AGCA A1.1 1 4 21.5.1708.

[72]Bakewell, *Silver Mining and Society*, p. 254.

[73]Between 1729 and 1736 royal officials at Comayagua taxed 54,463 marks of silver (AGI AG 236 Pedro de Rivera 29.5.1737). García Peláez, *Memorias* 2:144 notes that about 20,000 marks were produced in Honduras in January 1730 and another 8,000 marks were produced in the following March, but it is not clear over what time the silver had been collected.

being minted annually, with a peak of 38,000 marks being minted in 1739.[74] Clearly these figures include silver minted from other parts of the Audiencia as well as Honduras, although the bulk of the silver would have come from there. However, this increase in the amount of silver minted was more a function of improved facilities for exchanging crude silver in the mining areas, which effectively discouraged contraband trading and ensured a greater flow of silver into the royal treasuries, than it was to increased levels of production. With the withdrawal of exchange facilities from the mining areas, the amount of silver minted fell to about 15,000 marks. Production may have declined further in the following two decades. Between 1758 and 1774 70,921 marks of silver were produced by amalgamation in Honduras, thereby giving an annual production of 4,433 marks.[75] Although this figure may be doubled to take account of the silver smelted rather than amalgamated, it is still considerably less than that produced in the 1730s. Nevertheless, figures for the quintos (diezmos) paid on silver during the period 1771 to 1785 averaged 16,000 pesos a year, although there were considerable fluctuations in these taxes from year to year, which almost certainly reflected the state of war; they also include the quintos paid on gold, although these were minimal.[76] In 1785 it was estimated that the mines of Santa Lucía, Yuscarán, Cedros, and San Antonio produced about 9,300 marks a year.[77] Whilst this figure did not include the silver produced in a number of other smaller mining areas, it would appear to be an underestimate given that in the same year 104 bars of silver, equivalent to 13,250 marks, were assayed in the Casa de Rescate.[78] Figures for the number of silver bars either amalgamated or smelted that were assayed between 1785 and 1799 indicate a fairly steady level of production of about 14,000 marks a year, with if anything a slight decline towards the end of the period. At the official exchange rate of seven pesos a mark[79] production was therefore worth about 101,500 pesos a year, and 10,150 pesos in quintos to the Crown.

If official figures may be relied upon, silver production increased in the early nineteenth century. Squier recorded that the annual production of minerals in Central America was worth 146,255 pesos between 1795 and 1810, and it increased to 254,025 pesos in the years 1810 to 1825.[80] The former figure is fairly comparable with the figure

---

[74]AGI AG 236 Cuenta y razón de todo el oro y plata...desde 16.3.1733 a 1748, AG 231 Pedro de Rivera 5.2.1746. In the periods 1748-49 and 1752-55 the quintos paid on silver in Comayagua averaged nearly 10,000 pesos a year (AGI AG 725 Cuenta y tanteo de la Real Caja de Guatemala 1748 to 1755). At the exchange rate of six pesos six reals (AGI AG 236 Director of the Casa de Moneda 5.2.1746), this meant that about 1,480 marks were paid in quintos on 14,800 marks a year.

[75]AGCA A3.9 507 5260 Cuenta de satisfacciones...al real quinto 1758 to 1771.

[76]AGI AG 744 Estado que manifiesta...las Cajas Reales 1771-8, 1781-5.

[77]AGI AG 770 Alcalde Mayor 28.11.1785. Production figures for the individual areas were: Santa Lucía 3,500 marks, Yuscarán 4,000 marks, Cedros 600 marks, and San Antonio 1,200 marks.

[78]ANH UC Estado que manifiesta las barras de plata...1785 to 1799.

[79]AGI AG 464 and 796 Instrucción que se ha de arreglar la administración de la Casa y Fondo de Rescate 30.1.1780.

[80]Squier, States of Central America, p. 190.

of 532,158 pesos of silver minted and exported to Spain during the quinquennium 1798 to 1802, whilst the latter figure is similar to that of 250 bars of silver produced in 1816.[81] At that time the official rate of exchange was 7.5 pesos a mark, so that silver production was worth 253,125 pesos.

It is virtually impossible to calculate the amount of silver that was never taxed and hence total silver production. Nevertheless, it is clear that a considerable amount of the silver that was produced was never taxed and it either circulated within the mining areas or it was illegally exported from the province. Many factors contributed to the development of a contraband trade in silver. First, much of the silver produced in Honduras could be smelted in small crude furnaces without the use of mercury so that the authorities lacked an effective mechanism for keeping account of the amount of silver produced. Second, the absence of coinage in the area encouraged miners to use crude silver to pay their workers and to purchase the equipment and materials necessary to keep their mines in operation. Third, the small salaries paid to officials in the province encouraged them to seek alternative sources of income, one of which was participating in the illegal trade in silver. Fourth, the settlement of the English on the Mosquito Shore and in nearby Belize and Jamaica established suitable outlets for the silver as the Spanish fleet system broke down. Merchants and royal officials, rather than miners, appear to have been involved in this contraband trade. Most of the silver was smuggled to the north and east coasts of Honduras where it could be sold to the English for up to ten and eleven pesos.[82] It would appear that at times the Governor of the province, the Alcalde Mayor of Tegucigalpa, merchants, vecinos of Tegucigalpa and Comayagua, as well as parish priests living in villages on routes to the coast were all involved in the trade.[83] Intermittent efforts by the authorities in Guatemala to suppress contraband trading by fining and imprisoning those found guilty, proved ineffective. Even after the English evacuated the Mosquito Shore in 1787, contraband trading continued, such that in 1816 it was estimated that of every 250 bars of silver produced in Honduras only 210 arrived at the Casa de Moneda for minting, the rest finding its ways to Belize and Jamaica.[84]

[81]AGI 627 Larrazábal 20.10.1810.

[82]AGI AG 349 Testimonio...de trato ilícito con los ingleses 1745, AG 449 Díaz Navarro 30.11.1758, AG 450 Itinerario y navegación...23.12.1776, AG 796 Pilonass and Ortiz de Letona 28.1.1813; Floyd, *Anglo-Spanish Struggle*, pp. 60-61.

[83]AGI AG 349 Testimonio...de trato ilícito con los ingleses 1745, AG 236 Director of the Casa de Moneda 5.2.1746; MacLeod, *Spanish Central America*, pp. 254-57. See also A. Szaszdi de Nagy, "El comercio ilícito en la provincia de Honduras," *Revista de Indias* 17 (1967):271-83; M.L. Wortman, *Government and Society in Central America, 1680-1840* (New York: Columbia University Press, 1982), pp. 96-97.

[84]AGI AG 501 Informe de la provincia de Honduras 20.2.1816.

# 10
# Towns and Cities

With the development of agriculture, many colonists left the towns to reside on their estates. Nevertheless, Spanish settlers remained concentrated in the urban areas from whence they had powerful influences on Indian communities in the surrounding countryside through the demands they made on Indian labor and production. As such, the nearer an Indian village to a town, the greater the demands made upon it and the greater the changes that were brought about in its economic and social organization. This influence not only varied with the nearness of an Indian village to a town, but also with the size of the town; the larger the town the greater the demands that were made upon it. The size and importance of towns and cities varied during the colonial period. Many towns declined with the mining activities and Indian populations that had supported them; those that survived did so on the basis of their administrative functions. Only in the eighteenth century did other factors, notably economic and defensive ones, prove to be significant in determining the growth and size of towns and cities.

Towns and cities established in the early sixteenth century depended for their existence on the presence of minerals and large Indian populations. The Indians had provided not only the day-to-day necessities of domestic service and food, as well as a small income from the tribute they paid, but they had also been sold illegally as slaves. The exhaustion of mineral deposits and the decline in Indian populations thus threatened the existence of many towns. In 1586 Fr. Alonso Ponce recorded that the Indian population around San Pedro had declined such that "much gold was formerly mined in this city and there were in the city many rich and powerful men, but now there are few and they are poor."[1] A similar fate seems to have befallen the town of San Jorge de Olancho. In addition, the ports of Puerto Caballos and Trujillo declined relative to inland towns and the ports on the Pacific coast. During the early sixteenth century the former ports had flourished as ports of call for the Spanish fleets, but towards the end of the century they declined as the presence of foreign corsairs in Honduran waters increased and trade with Spain became irregular. Merchants who traded in Puerto Caballos or

---

[1] Ponce, *Relación breve*, p. 349.

Trujillo very often lived in San Pedro or Comayagua and travelled to the coast if and when the fleets arrived.[2]

The administrative functions of major cities helped to stem their decline, because there were always a number of posts to which vecinos could aspire, even if the most important officials were brought in from outside the province and generally from Spain. The existence of the posts also had a multiplier effect on employment opportunities within the city as a whole. Given the importance of the administrative functions of towns to their survival, and the fact that there appears to have been a relationship between the number and types of officials appointed and the decline in the Indian population, it is desirable to discuss their distribution in slightly more detail.

Comayagua remained the major administrative center of Honduras throughout the colonial period. The governor and treasury officials resided there, the latter travelling to the northern ports when the fleets arrived. The governor had deputies (*tenientes*) in the towns of Gracias a Dios, Trujillo, and Olancho, whilst Tegucigalpa and Choluteca at times formed separate *alcaldías mayores*.[3] In addition to these royal officials each of the towns possessed a cabildo consisting of two alcaldes (magistrates), an *alguacil* (constable), an *escribano* (notary), and a number of regidores (councillors), the number depending on the size of the town; in Honduras in the mid-seventeenth century the number varied between two and four. Often attached to the town councils were other officials such as an *alférez* (standard bearer), a *depositario general* (public trustee), and a *fiel ejecutor* (inspector of weights and measures).[4] Apart from *alcaldes ordinarios*, who had civil and criminal powers as courts of first instance within the towns' jurisdictions, and treasury officials, who collected tribute from *lavoríos*, contact between the majority of these royal and local officials and the Indians was probably small. The most important officials as far as the Indians were concerned were the tenientes and alcaldes mayores; corregidores do not appear to have been appointed widely in Honduras.[5] The tenientes and alcaldes mayores were originally charged with the collection of tribute from Crown villages, but later their powers were widened to include civil and criminal jurisdiction in

---

[2]López de Velasco, *Geografía y descripción universal*, p. 310; Serrano y Sanz, *Relaciones históricas*, pp. 466-67 Pineda 1594.

[3]López de Velasco, *Geografía y descripción universal*, pp. 306-13; BAGG 10: 5-19 Contreras de Guevara 20.4.1582; P. Gerhard, "Colonial New Spain, 1519-1786: Historical Notes on the Evolution of the Minor Political Jurisdictions," in *Handbook of Middle American Indians*, vol. 12, ed. H.F. Cline (Austin: University of Texas Press, 1972), pp. 134-35; C. Molina Argüello, "Gobernaciones, alcaldías mayores y corregimientos en el Reino de Guatemala," *Anuario de Estudios Americanos* 17 (1960):105-32. The Alcaldía Mayor of Tegucigalpa appears to have been established in 1579 and that of Choluteca in 1545, although the latter was under the gobernación of El Salvador until about the last quarter of the seventeenth century.

[4]J. Díaz de la Calle, *Memorial y noticias sacras y reales del imperio de las Indias Occidentales* (Madrid, 1646), pp. 125-30.

[5]Corregidores do not appear to have been appointed widely in Honduras. The corregimientos of Comayagua and Gracias a Dios were suppressed in 1573 because the Crown's income from tribute, from which they were paid, was insufficient to support them (AGCA A1.23 1512 f.433 cédula 26.5.1573). However, it would appear that a corregidor was appointed in Tencoa for a period during the seventeenth century (AGCA A1.23 f.233 cédula 4.6.1660).

cases between Indians and Spaniards and among Indians themselves, as well as the distribution of labor under the repartimiento.[6] They were generally appointed for five years and their salaries were small.[7] Nevertheless, the lack of remuneration that the posts provided and the short term for which they could be held, were compensated for by the profits they could generate. The almost exclusive control that tenientes and alcaldes mayores possessed over contacts between Spaniards and Indians placed them in a unique position to exploit both parties. They accepted bribes from vecinos for access to Indian labor under the repartimiento, as well as for support in court cases. From the Indians they exacted goods and services with little or no payment, and they forced them to buy items of little value at highly inflated prices. Thus in 1737 the Alcalde Mayor of Tegucigalpa was able to augment his small salary of 661 pesos to 8,000 pesos.[8] During their tours of inspection tenientes and alcaldes mayores also received bribes from miners and *obrajeros* to reduce or not impose fines.[9] Similar forms of bribes and exactions were made by jueces de milpas, who were appointed at times to ensure that Indians planted sufficient maize to prevent food shortages.

At the end of the eighteenth century administrative reforms were introduced that aimed at centralizing the administration and making it more efficient. In 1786 the governor and his deputies were replaced by an intendant and *subdelegados*. The intendant, whose seat was located in Comayagua, carried out combined political, judicial, and military functions, and was given jurisdiction over financial affairs.[10] Initially the Alcaldía Mayor of Tegucigalpa remained a separate administrative unit, but it was included as a subdelegación within the intendancy of Comayagua in 1788.[11] However, after complaints from the residents of Tegucigalpa and the surrounding mining areas, the Alcaldía Mayor was re-created in 1812. Nevertheless, the appointment was made from Comayagua and this provoked a revolt in Tegucigalpa fuelling the rivalry that already existed between the province's two most important cities.[12] The only area that formed a distinct administrative unit in the late eighteenth century was the north coast, which comprised a *comandancia* including Omoa, Trujillo, and the Bay Islands. Here disputes

---

[6]*Recopilación* 2 lib.5 tít. ley 3: 118 8.11.1550; C. Molina Argüello, "Comunidades y territorialidad en las jurisidicciones," in *Memoria del primer congreso venezolano de historia* (Caracas: Academia Nacional de la Historia, 1972), p. 451.

[7]*Recopilación* 2 lib.5 tít.2 ley 10: 118 15.7.1584.

[8]AGI AG 448 President of the Audiencia 23.11.1737. For the salaries attached to official posts in the seventeenth century, see Díaz de la Calle, *Memorial y noticias sacras*, pp. 125-30.

[9]See Chapter 8, pp. 145-46, and Chapter 11, p. 179.

[10]Wortman, "Bourbon Reforms," p. 236.

[11]AGI AG 575 12.8.1788.

[12]AGI AG 501 Informe de la provincia...20.2.1816; Vallejo, *Compendio de la historia*, pp. 15-18; Wortman, "Government Revenue," p. 236.

arose between the *comandante* and the intendant mainly over the supply of militia for the defense of the coast.[13]

Comayagua also attracted a large number of clergy, both secular and regular. It was not until the second half of the sixteenth century, however, that the site of the cathedral was transferred from Trujillo to Comayagua.[14] Most of the major towns in Honduras possessed Franciscan and Mercedarian convents, and Comayagua contained a hospital of San Juan de Dios.[15]

Whilst Comayagua remained the capital of Honduras throughout the colonial period, in the eighteenth century Tegucigalpa began to challenge its position as it developed with the mining industry. From a small population of 890 'personas de confesión' in 1743, the town increased to a total population of 5,739 in 1777 and 7,853 in 1821, and in recognition of its growing importance it was given the title of *villa* in 1768.[16] However, its rapid development was overlooked in 1786 and 1788, when the administrative reforms confirmed the priority of Comayagua and placed the Alcaldía Mayor under the jurisdiction of the intendant at Comayagua. This was resented by Tegucigalpa and several years later its citizens complained that it had resulted in the economic decline of the area. The new intendants, they said, were not interested in developing mining, and they imposed local taxes on agricultural produce such as indigo, sugar, and cattle, which only benefitted Comayagua. As such the area had gone into decline to such an extent that there were then only five or six shops in the town, whereas under the Alcaldes Mayores there had been 16 to 18.[17] Other observers confirmed this view, noting that the town was not as wealthy as it had been,[18] and that there were only a few miners, soldiers, and poor landowners living there.[19] To what extent the administrative reforms can be held responsible for the declining status of the town is not known; whilst local citizens resented being under the control of the intendant at Comayagua and blamed its decline on the administrative changes, it is also clear that silver production fell during this period due to labor being drawn off for employment in

---

[13]S. Salvatierra, *Contribución a la historia de Centroamérica*, vol. 2 (of 2) (Managua: Tip. Progreso-Managua, 1939), p. 14.

[14]The actual date of transferal is uncertain. Dates vary from 1558 (Vázquez de Espinosa, *Compendium and Description*, p. 240), to 1559 (CDI 8: 34 Décadas abreviadas...1559), 1561 (Díaz de la Calle, *Memorial y noticias sacras*, p. 127), and 1571 (CDI 8: 39 Décadas abreviadas...1571), but it seems that the Crown was not asked to agree to the transfer until 1570 and one document suggests that permission was given in 1573 (AGI PAT 183-1-30 Herrera 5.4.1570; CDIU 17:182 Indice de los papeles...16.11.1573).

[15]Díaz de la Calle, *Memorial y noticias sacras*, pp. 125-30; Vázquez de Espinosa, *Compendium and Description*, pp. 235-48.

[16]BAGG 1: 29-39 Ortiz de Letona 20.7.1743; AGCA A3.9 175 1689 Vecinos of Tegucigalpa 1762; AGI AG 595 Vecinos of Tegucigalpa 11.5.1768; AGCA A1.23 2590 21165 f.331 cédula 17.7.1768; "Padrón de la feligresía...1777," *RABNH* 29 (1949):194-95; AGCA A1.44 99 1160 Numero de almas...20.7.1821.

[17]AGI AG 973 Testimonio 1815.

[18]AGI AG 501 Anguiano 10.5.1804.

[19]AGCA A1.1 2 42 13.4.1793.

the militia. Despite these political and economic changes, the population of the parish of Tegucigalpa appears to have remained fairly stable and in 1821 it received the title of *ciudad*.[20]

Table 5

POPULATION OF URBAN CENTERS IN THE LATE COLONIAL PERIOD

|  | 1791 *almas* | 1804 Spanish and Ladino families |
|---|---|---|
| Comayagua | 10,530 | 574 |
| Tegucigalpa | 5,431 | 593 |
| Gracias a Dios | 4,262 | 413 |
| Choluteca | 3,856 | 331 |
| San Pedro | 357 | 56 |
| Olanchito | 1,354 | 250 |
| Trujillo | not included | 80 |
| Yoro* | 2,091 | 139 |
| Sonaguera* | 833 | 250 |
| Tencoa* | 3,582 | 144 |
|  | 32,296 | 2,830 |

* non-official urban status

Sources:
1791: AGI AG 578 Cadiñanos 20.10.1791. Figures refer to *almas* in urban parishes.
1804: AGI AG 501 Estado que manifiesta...1.5.1804. Figures do not include single persons in either category.

Not only did the establishment of the intendancy in Comayagua retard the growth of Tegucigalpa, but it failed to stem the continued decline of Comayagua. From being the capital city of the province it became a sleepy town that by the beginning of the nineteenth century contained only a few poor Spaniards who were reduced to living on charity. The Franciscan and Mercedarian convents were falling down, the cathedral and *caja real* were in a bad state of repair, and there was no doctor or chemist in the city. The

[20]R.E. Durón, *La provincia de Tegucigalpa bajo el gobierno de Mallol* (Tegucigalpa: Tip. Nacional, 1904), p. 171.

city had also gained the reputation of being unhealthy and poorly provisioned.[21] The reason given for the city's decay was the decline in agriculture and trade, which was often blamed on the laziness of the Indians. In 1802 the two parishes of the city together possessed a population of 5,369.[22] As Comayagua declined a number of suggestions were made about moving the site of the capital. Apart from the obvious alternative choice of Tegucigalpa, the site favored by the Intendant Anguiano was Santa Barbara. This settlement, although not large, was located in a healthy environment, surrounded by good agricultural lands, and had easy access to the coast for trade. Despite these discussions, Comayagua remained the capital city throughout the colonial period.[23]

The other major development at the end of the eighteenth century was the growth of Trujillo, which occurred after the Spanish had regained control of the north coast. Trujillo grew through the settlement of French negroes and Black Caribs there in 1796 and 1797 respectively.[24] The town appears to have been built from scratch; by 1804 a casa de comandante and a poor caja real had been constructed, but there was no church, hospital, warehouse, or customs house.[25] The newly arrived Spanish colonists, a few settlers from Comayagua, who were mainly artisans and traders, and public officials inhabited the center of the town, whilst the different groups of negroes formed separate barrios around it.[26] In 1821 it had a population of 898.[27]

The fortunes of other towns in Honduras during the eighteenth century varied with their economic bases. Choluteca and the newly developed settlements in the east flourished on livestock raising, although Olancho el Viejo was abandoned in favor of Olanchito as a result of earthquakes.[28] These settlements were predominantly mulatto and ladino in character. Gracias a Dios managed to survive on a variety of agricultural activities, the products of which were exported to neighboring Guatemala and El Salvador. However, it did lose population to Santa Rosa towards the end of the century. This was said to be due to the healthier climate in Santa Rosa, but it was more likely to have been due to the expansion of tobacco cultivation there.[29]

Although towns and cities remained important population centers and physically identifiable elements of the landscape, from the end of the sixteenth century many citizens took up residence in the rural areas. This movement appears to have begun earliest in the small peripheral towns where opportunities for wealth creation were

---

[21]AGCA A1.2 213 2417 Providencia dictadas...10.6.1809; AGI AG 501 Anguiano 10.5.1804; AGCA A1.17 2875 26357/8 Dictamen del Diputado 31.8.1813, A1.17 2875 26354 Informe...Anguiano 30.9.1811; AGI AG 973 Testimonio 1815.

[22]AGCA A1.11 48 471 10.11.1802.

[23]Vallejo, Compendio de la historia, pp. 61-71.

[24]See p. 257.

[25]AGI AG 501 Anguiano 10.5.1804.

[26]AGI 963 Ayzinenass 2.11.1813.

[27]AGCA A1.44 99 1159 Padrón que manifiesta los vecinos...31.1.1821.

[28]AGI AG 501 Anguiano 10.5.1804.

[29]Ibid.

restricted; Gracias a Dios and Choluteca lost some of their vecinos and encomenderos to the countryside in the sixteenth century.[30] By the end of the sixteenth century most of the vecinos of the northern ports of Puerto Caballos and Trujillo were also living on their estates inland. However, in the latter case, part of the stimulus to move was provided by attacks on the towns by corsairs.[31] The movement to the countryside continued throughout the seventeenth century and consisted primarily of landowners taking up residence on their estates; during the eighteenth century the migration continued but increasingly it was composed of landless persons, often of mixed race, who settled in Indian villages or on Indian lands they had rented or usurped. By the beginning of the nineteenth century only 32 percent of Spanish families in Honduras were living in the towns, of which one-third were living in Tegucigalpa and Comayagua together.[32]

Table 6

DISTRIBUTION OF SPANISH AND LADINO FAMILIES IN 1804

| Families | Towns | % | Rural areas | % | Valleys and haciendas | % | Mining areas | % |
|----------|-------|------|-------------|------|------------------------|------|--------------|------|
| Spanish  | 484   | 32.1 | 608         | 40.3 | 299                    | 19.8 | 117          | 7.8  |
| *Ladino  | 2,346 | 16.5 | 8,750       | 61.4 | 2,229                  | 15.6 | 931          | 6.5  |
| TOTAL    | 2,830 | 18.0 | 9,358       | 59.4 | 2,528                  | 16.0 | 1,048        | 6.6  |

Source: AGI AG 501 Estado que manifiesta...1.5.1804. Figures do not include single persons in either category.

[30]AGI AG 44 Cabildo of Gracias a Dios 18.11.1560; López de Velasco, *Geografía y descripción universal*, p. 300; MacLeod, *Spanish Central America*, p. 217.

[31]AGI AG 39 Alvarado 20.5.1601, AG 1 Council of the Indies 7.5.1602.

[32]AGI AG 501 Anguiano 10.5.1804.

# 11
# Demands on Indian Lands, Labor, and Production

The major influences that Spanish activities had on Indian communities emanated from the demands they made on Indian lands, labor, and production. The level of these demands varied both spatially and temporally, not only with economic, social, and demographic changes in the province, but also with modifications in Crown policy towards the Indians.

## DEMANDS ON INDIAN LANDS

Although the Crown recognized the rights of Indians to lands they possessed in pre-Columbian times, by the middle of the sixteenth century they were already being alienated. In 1549 and 1576 the Crown decreed that all lands taken from Indians should be returned,[1] and in 1550 ordered that Indians should be paid adequate sums for the land they rented out.[2] There were several ways in which Spaniards might acquire Indian lands: first, by illegally usurping it. This was probably the most common means by which they acquired land in the period immediately following the conquest, but later it was probably less contentious to obtain land through legal channels, for although the law was theoretically biased towards Indian possession, in practice it favored non-Indian petitioners.

The second means of acquiring land was through purchase followed by a request for a formal title to the land. Spaniards might purchase land from individual Indians or from caciques acting on behalf of the community. Often Indians were forced to sell their lands in order to meet tribute demands, and in such circumstances encomenderos were in an advantageous position to acquire it. In other cases Indians rented their lands, possibly for the same reason, and later a lessee might claim that the monetary transaction that had

---

[1] AGCA A1.23 4575 ff.103, 110v. cédula 29.4.1549, A1.23 1513 f.511 cédula 18.11.1576.

[2] AGCA A1.23 4575 f.122 cédula 4.8.1550.

taken place was a sale.[3] Most sales of Indian lands were in fact illegal, since although some Indians did own private holdings that they were free to sell, most lands were communally owned, with the Indians only possessing usufruct rights. Even though the sale of communal lands was illegal, there is no doubt that Indian leaders and members of the cabildo were bribed to sell lands either for private gain, or to meet tribute demands and other financial obligations of the community. This was particularly true in times of crisis such as during an epidemic or in the event of a poor harvest. The likelihood of land sales to non-Indians increased during the sixteenth century as the population declined and communal lands fell out of cultivation and reverted to the community for reallocation. Thus the availability of land increased at the same time as Indian communities were finding it increasingly difficult to meet their obligations with a decreased population. The sale of land provided an easy and immediate means of acquiring cash, which could be used to purchase food or to discharge obligations. In the 1530s the Crown sought to control the sale of Indian lands by ordering that all transactions should take place before a Spanish judge,[4] and later in 1571 it required that all Indian lands should be sold by auction over 30 days in order to allow higher bids to be made and prevent would-be purchasers from coercing Indians into selling their lands at low prices.[5] The deeds of sale of a piece of land formed the basis on which Spaniards then petitioned for a title to the land. Despite the previous decrees and the fact that it was specified that land titles would not be given where lands had been taken from Indians against their will,[6] there is no doubt that bribery and coercion were rife, and by this means many Spaniards did secure formal title to Indian lands.

The third means by which Spaniards might obtain lands was through declaring that an area was unoccupied and requesting a grant. The main stipulation was that the grant should not conflict with the claims or rights of other parties, and particularly those of Indians.[7] Before the grant was made the area had to be surveyed, the boundaries marked, and an inquiry held at which Indian communities and neighboring landlords could object. Although some communities did object, for example, in 1707 the village of Ojojona opposed the confirmation of a land title,[8] in many cases the silence of Indian communities at the inquiry could be bought.

A decisive piece of legislation was introduced in 1591, which consisted of two cédulas. The first ordered that all land that had been illegally occupied by Spaniards should be returned to the Crown. This by itself would have dealt a blow to the illegal occupation of Indian lands, but the second cédula declared that anyone who possessed land without a legal title could obtain one by payment of a fee, or *composición*.[9] At that time considerations of defense were uppermost in the Crown's mind and this was seen as

---

[3]Gibson, *Aztecs*, p. 274 notes this practice in the Valley of Mexico.

[4]Ibid., p. 281.

[5]*Recopilación* 2 lib.6 tít.1 ley 27: 195-6 24.5.1571, 23.7.1571, 6.5.1572, 18.5.1572.

[6]Ibid., lib.4 tít.12 ley 17: 43-4 30.6.1646.

[7]Ibid., ley 7: 41 6.4.1588 and ley 9: 41 11.9.1594.

[8]*Indice general de los títulos de tierras* (Francisco Morazán) Oposición de los naturales de este pueblo, 1707.

[9]AGCA A1.15 6943 f.37, A1.23 f.722, A1.23 4610 f.263 cédula 1.11.1591.

one way of raising revenue; the effect was to legitimize the illegal occupation of Indian lands.[16] The law not only applied to lands that had been illegally usurped, but also to those that were to be occupied in the future. A common means of obtaining land grants, therefore, particularly from the seventeenth century onwards, was to declare a tract of land unoccupied or uncultivated, that is to make a *denuncia*, and then pay the corresponding composición. The land was supposed to be held for ten years without detriment to a third party before a title could be obtained by the payment of a composición.[11] The major problem was that many of the lands regarded by the Spanish as unoccupied in fact played an important role in the Indian economy; the lands might be fallow as part of the shifting cultivation cycle, or constitute valuable hunting, fishing, and collecting grounds, or provide essential supplies of fuel, house-building materials and sometimes water. In fact all lands outside the legally protected minimum of 600 *varas* square and the one square league of ejidal land were regarded by the Spanish as fit for occupation, even though they might fall within the términos of a village; in the sixteenth century Indian communities generally regarded these lands as safe from alienation and did not, therefore, consider it necessary to obtain title to them. As suggested, one way around the problem was for the Indian community itself to make a denuncia and pay the corresponding composición. Legally Indian communities were to be favored over private individuals in this respect,[12] but the stronger financial position of most Spanish purchasers would have enabled them to pay higher composiciones and thus have their claims favored.

Pressure on Indian lands was probably greatest in the eighteenth century when the population began to increase and agricultural production expanded. In the early colonial period pressure on Indian lands was localized in the valleys around the major towns and two factors operated to reduce conflict between Spaniards and Indians over the use of land. First, the decline in the Indian population meant that Indian communities did not require such extensive lands for their subsistence, even though it is clear that their needs would not have declined in parallel with the population; second, one of the most important agricultural activities established by the Spanish was livestock raising and this generally exploited the pre-existing grasslands that had been unutilized or underutilized in pre-Columbian times. Nevertheless, as will be shown later, the alienation of lands severely affected Indian production and by undermining the subsistence base of Indian communities, it encouraged individuals to seek employment as wage laborers. This process accelerated from the end of the seventeenth century as the population began to increase and the economy expanded. At the same time the emerging mixed races entered into the conflict that already existed between Spaniards and Indians over the use and ownership of land. The majority of people of mixed race were originally landless, many of them being employed as overseers or workers either on haciendas or in the mines, or else as artisans in the towns. Over time, however, some appear to have accumulated small amounts of capital with which they were able to purchase or rent small holdings

---

[10]Ots Capdequí, *España en América*, p. 30; S. Martínez Peláez, *La Patria del criollo* (San José: Editorial Universitaria Centroamericana, 1975), pp. 149-53.

[11]*Recopilación* 2 lib.4 tít.12 ley 19: 44 30.6.1646. Previously petitions had been submitted after only five years (*Indice general de los títulos de tierras* Coray (Valle) Información hecha...a petición de Esteban de Amaya, 1585).

[12]*Recopilación* 2 lib. 4 tít.12 ley 19: 44 30.6.1646.

178

often from Indian communities;[13] those less fortunate probably became squatters on the margins of the already settled area. Finally, at the end of the eighteenth century, Crown efforts to promote agricultural production provided added stimulus for the acquisition of land.

## DEMANDS ON INDIAN LABOR

Throughout the colonial period Indians remained the most important source of labor in Central America, although the form of their employment changed. Until 1549 encomenderos could legally exact labor services from Indians charged to them, which meant that they had almost exclusive access to sources of labor. From that time onwards, however, the inclusion of personal service in tribute assessments and the commutation of tribute to personal service was strictly forbidden, except that up until 1812 government officials and the clergy were allowed to employ a small number of Indians to perform household duties.[14] The ban on personal service was repeated in the Ordinances of 1601 and 1609.[15]

The Crown intended that the abolition of personal service should open the way for the establishment of a free labor market to which both encomenderos and nonencomenderos would have access. Nevertheless, it was fearful that, if the Indians were given the freedom to work, they would refuse. As such a system of forced labor known as the repartimiento was introduced. Under this system Indians were to offer themselves for employment in approved tasks for stipulated periods for fixed wages. The repartimiento was to apply to all Indian communities, whether they paid tribute to an encomendero or to the Crown. Applications for the hire of Indian labor had to be made to the Audiencia, and the actual allocation of Indians was undertaken by a *juez repartidor*. The Indians then worked for the stipulated period at the end of which they received their pay and returned to their communities. Their places were immediately filled by a new group of Indians that had been collected and allocated in the same way. Since the hiring of Indian labor was open to any employer, the introduction of the repartimiento increased demands for labor and in part satisfied requests from nonencomenderos for access to it.

The early history of the repartimiento in Honduras is far from clear. In 1555 the repartimiento in the Audiencia of Guatemala required each Indian village to provide 2 percent of its tributary population to provide 'servicio ordinario,' that is, supplying households with food, water, and firewood and repairing the houses themselves. Indians were not supposed to be employed for more than a week at a time or more than half a day's journey from their homes. They were to be paid three reals a week plus food and extra for any time spent travelling to and from their places of employment.[16] During the

---

[13]For examples of conflicts over Indian lands, see: AGCA A1.45 368 3417 Común de labradores de Sabana Grande y Rincón 12.4.1780, A1.45 100 1166 Indians of Santa Ana Ula 13.10.1813; ANH P13 L13 7.5.1806.

[14]*Recopilación* 2 lib.6 tít.5 ley 24: 232 22.2.1549; AGCA A1.23 1538 10093 f.136 cédula 9.11.1812.

[15]AGCA A1.23 4576 39529 cédulas 24.11.1601, 26.5.1609.

[16]AGI AG 9 Ramírez and Quesada 25.5.1555.

late sixteenth century the repartimiento also provided Indians to work in 'public service,' which included the construction of public buildings, houses, and roads. On the other hand, repartimiento labor could not be used in the mines or to transport goods.[17] However, Indians could undertake these tasks voluntarily with the proviso that they could not work underground, but only in prospecting and supplying the mines with food, charcoal, and pit-props.[18]

Another activity that was banned because it was regarded as unhealthy was the manufacture of indigo dye, the process of which has already been described in detail.[19] Although from 1581 repartimiento labor could not be allocated for this task, until 1601 Indians could work in indigo obrajes on a voluntary basis.[20] From that time onwards, however, the employment of Indians in the manufacture of indigo was banned completely and alcaldes in indigo-growing districts were charged with making annual inspections of dye works and taking criminal proceedings against those who employed Indians illegally; in 1607 employers in Choluteca were being fined for using Indians to manufacture indigo, but the system of inspection does not appear to have been introduced into other parts of Honduras until later in the seventeenth century.[21] Numerous obrajeros were fined for having employed Indians in the manufacture of indigo, but most of the fines were between 25 and 50 pesos,[22] and they were an insufficient deterrent given the difficulty of securing alternative sources of labor and the very substantial profits to be made in indigo production. In the eighteenth century Indians also complained about the unhealthiness of tobacco cultivation, but their employment in this activity was never banned.[23]

Attempts to overcome some of the shortcomings of the repartimiento and place it on a more formal basis were made in the Ordinances promulgated in 1601 and 1609.[24]

---

[17] AGCA A1.23 1512 f.478 cédula 27.4.1575.

[18] AGI AG 39 Criado de Castilla 29.10.1598, AG 386-2 cédula 30.11.1599; J.J. Pardo, *Efemérides de la antigua Guatemala, 1541-1779* (Guatemala: Unión Tipográfica, 1944), p. 26.

[19] AGI AG 13 Relación de la siembra y calidad del xiquilite...1611; Rubio Sánchez, "El añil," pp. 318, 320; Smith, "Indigo Production," pp. 185-86; MacLeod, *Spanish Central America*, pp. 185-86. See Chapter 8, p. 145.

[20] AGCA A1.23 1513 f.594 cédula 15.5.1581, A1.23 4576 f.46 cédula 24.11.1601. The ban was reiterated in 1609 and 1627 (AGCA A1.23 4577 f.45 cédula 8.10.1631).

[21] AGI AG 14 Interrogatorio on the visita of Zúñiga 10.4.1620; MacLeod, *Spanish Central America*, p. 186. Although the governor fined individuals on a visita in 1615, inspections by alcaldes mayores do not appear to have been instituted in Tegucigalpa until 1676 (ANH P3 L40 Fines for using Indians in indigo manufacture 1676) and tours of inspection were being conducted in Gracias a Dios in 1689 (AGCA A1.53 375 3454 Visita of obrajes 1689).

[22] AGI AG 14 Interrogatorio on the visita of Zúñiga 10.4.1620; AGCA A1.53 375 3454 Visita of obrajes 1689; ANH P3 L40, 51, 69, 72, 77, 78, 79, 85, 132, P4 L93, 95, 109, 140 Proceedings against obrajeros 1676-1689.

[23] AGCA A3.9 194 2006 Juez comisario 10.5.1795.

[24] AGCA A1.23 4576 39529 cédulas 24.11.1601, 26.5.1609.

The former ordered that Indians should not be compelled to work, but because of the reluctance of Indians to offer themselves for employment, coercion was permitted once again in 1609. Indians still had to assemble at appointed places and the manner in which they were allocated did not alter; only the name of the officer in charge of the allocation was changed from juez repartidor to *juez comisario de alquileres*. The Crown also took the opportunity to reaffirm prohibitions on the employment of Indians in heavy tasks including mining, porterage, and working in textile workshops, sugar mills, and indigo manufacture. During the seventeenth century the collection of honey, wax, salt, and sarsaparilla were added to the list of prohibited tasks included in the 1601 and 1609 Ordinances.[25] Although the ban on the employment of Indians in mining had been reiterated in 1601, in the same year the Crown agreed to their employment for one year, during which time it was anticipated that negro slaves would be imported.[26] Since these slaves were not forthcoming and the labor shortages continued, in 1645 the Crown finally yielded to pressure from miners and agreed to the employment of Indians under the repartimiento.[27]

There is no clear indication of the proportion of the population that was required or actually worked under the repartimiento in the sixteenth and seventeenth centuries, but by the eighteenth century the repartimiento for agriculture, mining, and other approved tasks was regulated at one-quarter of the adult male population.[28] With the exception of Indian leaders and officials and those who were disabled, men were eligible for the repartimiento between the ages of 18 and 55 (later 50), although it was generally the younger sections of the community that were chosen for service. A few women were also allocated to provide food for workers, particularly for those employed in the construction of the fortifications at Omoa and in the mines. Theoretically the number of Indians exacted from a village at any one time depended on the size of the community as indicated in the tasación. The main problem with this method of assessment was that during the seventeenth century tasaciones often failed to keep pace with demographic changes and the number of Indians who became privately employed and resident on estates away from their homes increased. Although those listed were theoretically liable for the repartimiento, their employees were often able to bribe officials to release them from this duty, with the result that the burden of supplying a fixed number of workers fell on those that remained and with increasing frequency.[29] At the end of the eighteenth century Indians who were craftsmen or who possessed adequate lands to support a family and pay their tribute were exempt from the repartimiento.[30]

---

[25] AGCA A1.23 1560 10204 f.152 cédula 5.5.1649.

[26] AGCA A1.23 1514 ff.33-4 çédula 24.11.1602; AGI AG 18 Bernal del Cano 5.9.1648.

[27] AGI AG 18 Bernal del Cano 5.9.1648.

[28] AGCA A3.9 173 1656 Instancia de los mineros de Opoteca 1.1.1734, A3.9 156 3022 7.4.1736, A3.9 186 1886 17.5.1752, A3.9 173 1662 25.6.1752, A3.12 186 1893 Alcalde Mayor of Tegucigalpa 28.4.1760.

[29] ANH P5 L68 Alcalde Mayor of Tegucigalpa 3.5.1698.

[30] AGI AG 796 Intendant of Honduras 9.6.1809. In 1809 Indians in the city of Comayagua who were artisans or could sow half a fanega of maize and eight *medios* of beans were exempt.

The repartimiento functioned such that one-quarter of the adult male population would work on a specified task for about three weeks and would then be replaced by a similar number from the same village.[31] In effect this meant that an individual might be employed under the repartimiento for the equivalent of three to four months a year, not including the time that was spent in travelling to and from the place of work. The demands on Indian communities were particularly great when they coincided with sowing and harvesting, even though the repartimiento was supposed to be suspended for the months of April and May, and September and October, when Indians were to be free to attend to their own plots.[32]

Potential employers of Indians under the repartimiento were required to petition the Audiencia for the right to employ Indians from particular villages for a specified period, which in mining was normally three years.[33] Before the Audiencia agreed to assign Indians to particular employers certain conditions had to be satisfied. First, the tasks in which they were to be employed had to be approved; as already indicated Indians could not be employed in draining the mines or in other underground or dangerous work, whilst in agriculture they could not be employed in sugar mills or indigo workshops. Nevertheless there is abundant evidence that Indians were assigned to work in obrajes,[34] although on occasions when Indians objected, the repartimiento was withdrawn.[35]

Another stipulation was that Indians should not be employed at great distances from their homes. In 1563 the legal distance from which Indians could be drawn was set at ten leagues[36] and the 1609 Ordinances reiterated that Indians were to be chosen from villages near the place of their employment and they were not to cross climatic zones.[37] This limit was often exceeded illegally[38] and by 1648 the legal limit from which Indians could be drawn for work in the mines of Tegucigalpa had been extended to 20 leagues.[39] In the case of Indians employed in the defense of the north coast, the legal limit was later

---

[31]AGCA A3.9 155 2996 14.6.1661, 25.8.1662.

[32]AGCA A1.23 4576 39529 f.7 cédula 26.5.1609, A3.12 509 5290 Alcalde and regidor of the village of Teupacente 4.5.1639; ANH P2 L3 1669; AGCA A1.23 509 5293 Alcalde and regidor of Teupacente 2.1.1679.

[33]AGCA A3.12 509 5298 Vecinos of Tegucigalpa 20.6.1754, A3.12 186 1893 29.12.1758.

[34]See Chapter 8 n.54 for fines for employing Indians in these tasks; and AGCA A1.15 64 772 3.3.1762, A3.12 186 1898 13.9.1784, A3.12 186 1899 Romero 22.1.1784, A3.12 187 1911 Morejon and Lindo 8.1.1810.

[35]This was the case with several villages in the jurisdiction of Tencoa whose Indians had been employed in indigo production (AGCA A3.12 509 5301 26.4.1784 and 4.12.1784, A3.12 187 1901 30.3.1791.

[36]Recopilación 2 lib.6 tít.12 ley 3:286 2.12.1563.

[37]AGCA A1.23 4576 39529 cédula 26.5.1609.

[38]For example, AGI AG 167 Bishop of Honduras 6.7.1614.

[39]AGI AG 18 Bernal del Cano 5.9.1648.

extended to 45 leagues.[40] Petitioners often claimed, sometimes with the collusion of officials, that villages were nearer than they were.[41] When Indians objected to the distances they were forced to travel, their petition was sometimes upheld, but only where the distances far exceeded the legal limit. In 1774 the village of Langue was exempted from providing Indians for the mines located 60 leagues away,[42] whereas in 1785 the village of Lauterique located 50 leagues away was refused exemption.[43] In fact the 20-league limit was impracticable in the case of mining given the small size of nearby villages, so that it had to be extended. In 1777 the mines of Tegucigalpa employed 161 Indians from seven villages, none of which was located within 20 leagues of the mines and one was 50 leagues away.[44] Thus, the legal limit was often exceeded, but the law could be invoked at any time to suspend a repartimiento. This might arise where there was conflict between users, or where employers fell out of favor with officials administering the allocation of Indians.

Another condition for receiving Indians from particular villages for work under the repartimiento was that they should not have been allocated to another employer. In a situation of severe labor shortages this was clearly a problem. The most serious conflict that occurred was between miners and officials in charge of the defense of the north coast. Defensive demands also conflicted with those of estate owners in northern Honduras, and later with tobacco producers in western Honduras. Similarly there was competition between miners and farmers in the mining areas; a particular conflict arose between miners in the Mineral de Zaragoza and tobacco producers in western Honduras.[45] In general, however, mining and defense received preferential treatment in the allocation of Indians. Nevertheless, there were never enough Indians to supply the mining areas alone, so that there was even competition between mining districts, for example, between the miners of Yuscarán and Tegucigalpa in the middle of the eighteenth century, and even between miners within the same district.[46] The rule that was supposed to be followed was that miners who possessed the best mines and were in greatest need of labor were to be given priority.[47] Once allocated Indians could not be transferred to work on other tasks, and the employment of Indians in mines other than those to which they had been specifically allocated was also forbidden.[48]

---

[40] AGCA A1.23 4587 f.20v. cédula 6.6.1681.

[41] For example, in 1784 an owner of an indigo plantation in Tencoa and the governor conspired to obtain a repartimiento of Indian villages that they knew to be more than ten leagues away (AGCA A3.12 509 5301 4.12.1784).

[42] AGCA A3.9 174 1681 13.4.1774.

[43] AGCA A3.9 175 1690 7.7.1785.

[44] AGCA A3.9 174 1685 Alcalde Mayor of Tegucigalpa 1777.

[45] AGCA A3.9 174 1686 15.7.1776, A3.9 176 1713 Milla 14.1.1805.

[46] AGCA A3.9 174 1674 31.5.1766.

[47] AGCA A3.12 509 5298 Vecinos of Tegucigalpa 20.6.1754.

[48] AGCA A3.9 175 1698 Fiscal 10.9.1791; ANH P12 L66 Visita 1802, P13 L13 Village of Lepaterique 10.1.1807.

In employing Indians under the repartimiento employers agreed to pay them according to fixed rates of pay and to provide them with adequate food, as well as ensure that they are well treated and not overworked. In the sixteenth century Indians working under the repartimiento were paid about two or three reals a week,[49] but from the second half of the seventeenth century the average wage increased to between one and one and one-half reals a day.[50] In mining wages were generally one and one-half reals a day, but Indians employed in agriculture appear to have been paid only one real a day. Wages for travel time were regulated at one day's pay for each five leagues travelled, which was considered to be the distance that could be covered in a day.[51] Although work in the mines was generally paid at the rate of one and one-half reals a day, the rate of pay for travelling was normally only one real a day;[52] thus Indians from villages located 50 leagues from their place of employment were supposed to receive ten reals for the journey.[53] Despite official rates of pay, it is clear that they were not always adhered to; Indians from Chinacla sent to the Mineral of Opoteca were sometimes paid one and one-half reals a day, although more often they were paid only one real and young boys were normally paid only one-half real.[54] Often Indians were not paid or they received only half of what they were due, with the amount payable for travelling often ignored. Also, although Indians were supposed to receive their pay in money and individually, they were often paid in goods, crude silver or credit notes, and in some cases wages were paid to the officials of the village, such that the Indians themselves never received any pay.[55] Employers were also required to provide food for their employees, but this was often so inadequate that Indians had to take food with them. The main complaint was that employers did not provide them with meat, but only gave them beans and either tortillas or plantains.[56] Perhaps surprisingly the main complaints about overwork came from Indians who were employed in the towns and in agriculture. The general complaint was that they were forced to work from sunrise to sunset, with little time for rest, after which they were required to undertake additional tasks such as collecting firewood and hulling maize.[57] In other cases, such as where Indians were employed in cultivating tobacco, Indians were assigned tasks for each day, which if the weather was adverse they could not

---

[49] AGI AG 9 Ramírez and Quesada 25.5.1555.

[50] AGCA A3.9 155 2996 25.8.1662, A3.9 173 1656 Instancia de los mineros de Opoteca 1.1.1734, A1.30 222 2479 Visita of Comayagua 1742, A3.9 174 1671 Landa y Hualde 13.2.1766, A3.12 186 1887 Laurel 1772, A3.12 186 1898 Fiscal.

[51] AGCA A3.9 173 1656 Instancia de los mineros de Opoteca 1.1.1734.

[52] AGCA A1.30 222 2479 Visita of Comayagua 1742.

[53] AGCA A3.9 174 1685 Alcalde Mayor of Tegucigalpa 1777.

[54] AGCA A3.12 186 1895 Alcalde and village of Chinacla 28.6.1779.

[55] AGCA A3.12 509 5286 9.9.1639, A3.12 236 2425 1689, A1.23 1522 f.233 cédula 19.12.1687, A3.16 190 1940 Alcalde and village of Macholoa 8.8.1752, A1.15 64 772 3.3.1762, A3.12 186 1898 Fiscal 13.9.1784.

[56] AGCA A3.12 12 186 1887 Laurel 1772, A3.12 186 1895 28.6.1779.

[57] AGCA A3.12 187 1901 3.4.1789 and 14.8.1791, A3.12 187 1904 13.12.1793.

complete. As a result they were compelled to work longer hours on other days in order to fulfill the requirements.[58]

Once the Audiencia had agreed to the employment of Indians from specified villages by particular individuals, instructions were sent to alcaldes mayores, who were responsible for the allocation. On receiving Indians for employment, the employer was required to pay the alcalde mayor one-half real for each Indian he received, although in many cases the officials exacted more. Whilst employers could complain, and sometimes they did,[59] they were also aware that if they did not pay the extra demanded they would not obtain any workers.

Even after Indians had been allocated to an employer by the alcalde mayor there was no guarantee that they would arrive at their place of employment. Despite the threat of imprisonment Indians sometimes fled from their villages on the day they were assigned to work under the repartimiento.[60] Others escaped on the journey to work, so that overseers were employed to escort them at the rate of one-half real a day for each Indian.[61] Even when the Indians arrived at their place of employment there were still problems of discipline to be overcome. Mine owners complained that very often Indians fled stealing tools and goods.[62] The Indians were also described as insubordinate or lazy, and sometimes employers were forced to offer them advances in order to keep them content.[63] Despite the considerable problems involved in obtaining and keeping Indian employees under the repartimiento, most employers had no alternative source of labor. Before passing on to examine the alternatives that did exist for some, it is worth examining the employment of Indians in mining and other public services, which both received preferential treatment in the allocation of repartimiento labor.

From the mid-seventeenth century when the repartimiento of Indians for employment in the mines was permitted, mining probably absorbed a greater proportion of Indians available than other tasks. In 1662 120 Indians were drawn from 24 villages and allocated to 18 miners in Tegucigalpa.[64] In the 1730s the mines of Tegucigalpa employed 93 Indians under the repartimiento and those of El Corpus in Choluteca 50, whereas further north the Opoteca mines were worked by 170 Indians drawn from 13 villages within 25 to 30 leagues.[65] Although mining received preferential treatment in the allocation of repartimiento labor, the mines always suffered from shortages of labor. In 1752 the Alcalde Mayor of Tegucigalpa reported that one-quarter of the adult male population within the Alcaldía comprised only 225 Indians which was inadequate to meet

---

[58]AGCA A3.16 517 5427 Village of Talgua 27.11.1788.

[59]AGCA A1.23 1527 f.470 cédula 11.11.1750, A1.30 225 2508 Vecinos of Tegucigalpa 19.5.1748, A3.9 176 1701 Junta of miners of Opoteca 3.4.1793.

[60]ANH P9 L22 Romero 1774, P9 L53 Alcalde Mayor 24.9.1774.

[61]AGCA A3.12 186 1893 29.12.1758, A3.12 186 1887 10.3.1772.

[62]AGCA A3.16 174 1682 Alcalde Mayor of Tegucigalpa 1774.

[63]Ibid.; AGCA A3.16 187 1901 Vázquez 5.9.1789, A3.12 186 1898 Morejon 28.5.1784.

[64]AGCA A3.9 155 2996 14.6.1661, 25.8.1662.

[65]AGCA A3.9 156 3022 7.4.1736, A3.9 173 1656 Instancia de los mineros de Opoteca 1.1.1734.

Figure 6. Indian Villages and Mines Involved in the Repartimiento in the Mid-Seventeenth Century

miners' requirements. Since other villages in Honduras could not supply the Indians required because of their distant location, he pressed the Audiencia to provide Indians from the neighboring province of Nueva Segovia, where the villages of Somoto, Totogalpa, Telpaneca, Mozonte, and Yalaguina were located within 22 leagues of the nearest mines of Yuscarán and Potrerillos.[66] In June 1752 the Audiencia ordered that each of the first three villages should send 15 Indians to the mines of Honduras and a few months later it ordered that Mozonte and Yalaguina should send one-quarter of their tributary populations. The orders were not implemented, however, and although they were reiterated in 1762, four years later the Alcalde Mayor was still requesting Indians from the jurisdictions of Nueva Segovia and Comayagua, arguing that the 21 villages around Tegucigalpa could not meet the needs of three to four mines.[67] Another attempt to involve Indians in Nueva Segovia in 1777 was similarly unsuccessful.[68] In 1785 204 to 214 Indians were employed under the repartimiento in the nine mining areas, but over half of them were working in the Yuscarán mines (124-134), whilst other miners had to rely on scarce free labor.[69]

By the end of the century the problem of labor shortages had not been overcome, rather it had become more acute as a result of the new demands created by defense and the newly established tobacco industry. In the late 1780s officials in Tegucigalpa estimated that 3,000 more workers were required than were currently available, and they suggested that Indians should be relieved of contributing to the defense of the north coast and that Indians from the specified villages in Nueva Segovia should be sent to the mines of Yuscarán and Potrerillos.[70] There is no evidence that Indians from Nueva Segovia were ever sent to work in the mines of Honduras, although some did work there voluntarily.[71] Thus the repartimiento provided about 200 to 250 Indians for work in the mines, where they represented about one-quarter to one-fifth of the labor force;[72] the rest were persons of mixed race and Indians who worked as free laborers.

The other major employer of Indian labor under the repartimiento was defense. Indians were required to build fortifications, to perform guard duties, and to supply the forts with food. The main defensive operations were on the north coast, particularly at Omoa and Trujillo; in 1787 the defense of the north coast involved about 500 Indians, so that when their duties were completed and they were replaced by another group, about

---

[66]A3.9 173 1662 and A3.12 186 1886 Alcalde Mayor of Tegucigalpa 17.5.1752.

[67]AGCA A3.12 173 1662 Audiencia 25.6.1752, A3.12 186 1886 Fiscal of Audiencia 13.11.1752, A3.9 159 5592 27.2.1762, A1.17 1840 13999 3.1.1766.

[68]AGCA A3.9 174 1685 1777.

[69]AGI AG 770 29.11.1785.

[70]AGI AG 797 20.11.1788; AGCA A3.17 1718 27685 27.7.1789; AGI AG 797 García 20.11.1790.

[71]ANH P26 L29 Diligencias practicadas para reducir a poblado varias familias de indios en el partido de Choluteca 10.10.1774.

[72]See the discussion of free labor.

1,000 Indians were on the move.[73] Tours of duty lasted longer than in other activities; Indians involved in the construction of Fort Omoa worked for two months and those employed in defensive duties served for about four months.[74] In order to supply the number of Indians required, they had to be drawn from most parts of Honduras, even as far as the jurisdiction of Gracias a Dios. Villages in this area did manage to obtain relief from being sent to work on the building of Fort Omoa because of the long travelling distance involved, but they were still required to supply it with provisions.[75] The heavy demands that defense made on repartimiento labor brought severe complaints from other potential users, particularly miners, who advocated the establishment of fixed companies of coastguards comprised of free laborers.[76]

With the abolition of personal service, the Spanish turned their attention to the repartimiento for their supply of household servants. Unfortunately there are few references to the repartimiento being used as a source of labor in the towns. In the seventeenth century requests for Indian servants normally amounted to one female and one male Indian per household.[77] In the eighteenth century the village of Lejamaní did provide Indians for service in Comayagua. They were employed in building houses and working on small farms, haciendas, and slaughter houses, as well as acting as messengers and muleteers. However, it is clear that the service they provided should have been restricted to public works, such as constructing public buildings, hospitals and convents, since employment of Indians in the service of individuals was regarded as 'servicio personal' and was not approved for the purposes of the repartimiento.[78] Probably most of the labor requirements of the Spanish towns were met by voluntary labor or in the case of government officials and the clergy by personal service.

As early as the sixteenth century there is some evidence of employers turning away from the repartimiento as a source of Indian labor.[79] The repartimiento was unable to meet the demands made upon it and the rotational character of the system brought other disadvantages. The workers employed by any one individual changed constantly, so that an employer could not build up a skilled and permanent labor force. Also, he was obliged to pay his employees for the unproductive time they spent travelling to and from their place of work. Although it was more expensive to hire free workers these disadvantages of the repartimiento were overcome, as long as the workers remained in

---

[73]AGCA A3.17 1718 27678 14.10.1787. Another document mentions that 430 Indians were employed in the defense of Trujillo (AGCA A3.9 175 1693 21.8.1787).

[74]AGCA A3.12 186 1893 29.12.1758, A3.17 1718 27678 14.10.1787.

[75]AGCA A3.16 509 5300 24.11.1760, A3.12 186 1897 9.5.1780, A3.16 194 2010 10.5.1795, A3.16 194 2012 Dirección General de la Renta de Tabaco de Guatemala 18.7.1795.

[76]AGI AG 797 Cevallos 20.11.1788, García 20.11.1790; AGCA A3.17 1718 27678 14.10.1787, A3.17 27685 Zelaya 27.7.1789.

[77]AGCA A3.12 509 5282 Sevilla 2.5.1639, A3.12 509 5285 Escribano público 12.8.1639.

[78]AGCA A1.30 222 2479 Visita of Comayagua 1742, A3.12 187 1904 Governor of Honduras 12.5.1794.

[79]AGI PAT 183-1-16 Antonelli and López de Quintanillas 7.10.1590.

their employ. The wages paid to voluntary workers were often double those paid for similar work under the repartimiento. In addition, employers often agreed to discharge tribute debts or arrange for their exemption from the repartimiento; in the case of mining they also offered them a proportion of the profits or payment in crude silver.[80] Although employers offered higher wages to free laborers, which might be 50 to 100 percent higher than those paid to repartimiento workers, they were often insufficiently high to attract labor.[81] Once the Indians were in their employment, employers sometimes made them advances in order to bind them to their place of work through debts. This practice was illegal,[82] to the extent that hacendados could not advance workers more than three pesos otherwise they could not claim it back legally.[83] The whole process of attracting and retaining free labor was difficult for employers. One hacendado in the jurisdiction of Tegucigalpa claimed that it was impossible to get voluntary workers however much money was advanced, and even when it was possible the Indians worked reluctantly and refused to pay back their debts.[84] Employers generally complained that free workers came and went at will and were difficult to discipline.[85] In 1789 free workers in the mines of Tegucigalpa were described as "unreliable, truculent and insubordinate."[86] Free workers were therefore unreliable employees and in 1795 an official reported that vecinos were fed up of having to woo free workers and offer them higher salaries, when often they absconded leaving the work unfinished.[87] In fact they appear to have responded directly to incentives, moving freely from one place of employment to another according to which was able to offer the highest wages.[88] The essence of the problem from the employers' point of view was that there was a very real shortage of labor and free workers realized their bargaining power. Towards the end of the eighteenth century the problem was exacerbated by the absorption of a substantial number of potential free workers into the newly established militia and into occupations in the towns, whilst others

---

[80]AGCA A3.12 509 5284 Ortiz and Vázquez 14.1.1631; ANH P7 L23 1744, UC 23.1.1750; AGCA A3.9 174 1674 Alcalde Mayor of Tegucigalpa 25.5.1755; AGI AG 971 4.6.1814.

[81]AGCA A3.9 174 1678 Vega Lacayo to Alcalde Mayor of Tegucigalpa 1773, A3.12 186 1895 31.5.1777, A3.9 176 1706 Morejon 20.6.1799; AGI AG 501 Anguiano 10.5.1804. In 1777 miners in the Mineral of Opoteca paid barreteros working as free laborers four reals instead of two, and tanateros two reals instead of 1.5 reals.

[82]Pardo, *Efemérides*, p. 20, 2.6.1584; AGCA A1.23 1532 f.42 cédula 8.10.1631.

[83]AGI AG 796 Intendant of Honduras 9.6.1809.

[84]AGCA A3.12 186 1891 Rivera 2.11.1776. For other examples of salary advances see ANH P7 L23 Denuncias de minas 1744; AGCA A3.9 174 1674 Alcalde Mayor of Tegucigalpa 25.5.1755, A3.12 509 5299 10.9.1776; AGI AG 451 Instrucción de gobierno 23.9.1779.

[85]AGCA A3.9 506 5255 12.3.1766, A3.9 174 1681 13.4.1774.

[86]AGCA A3.17 1718 27685 Zelaya 27.7.1789.

[87]AGCA A3.12 187 1907 18.3.1795.

[88]AGI AG 231 Rivera 29.5.1737, A3.9 174 1674 29.4.1768, A3.9 174 1677 26.3.1772.

were content to survive on their small plots; the authorities blamed the lack of free labor on the laziness of the Indians.[89]

It is extremely difficult to estimate the numbers of Indians who were privately employed. Initially Indians who were servants and permanent residents in Spanish households were known as naborías. From the late sixteenth century onwards, however, the term naboría or lavorío was applied to those who were privately employed as well as household servants, and to all races. The enumeration of those who were privately employed was difficult, since they often moved freely between jobs in the towns, mines, and rural areas.[90] In 1801 and 1806 there were only 466 and 652 lavoríos respectively in the whole of Honduras, who accounted for 7.1 percent and 8.9 percent of the total adult Indian population.[91] These numbers undoubtedly underestimate the total number of Indian free laborers. In 1790 the total number of employees in mining in Honduras was estimated at 1,000, of which only 200 to 250 were employed under the repartimiento.[92] Free wage labor had thus become the dominant source of labor in the mines and, since the mines received preferential treatment in the allocation of Indians under the repartimiento, free wage labor must have been more significant in other economic activities.

Although personal service was abolished in 1549, during the late sixteenth and early seventeenth centuries at least encomenderos still possessed a privileged position in their use of Indian labor; there were numerous complaints from Indians and Spaniards, too numerous to mention, that encomenderos still employed Indians in their personal service often without payment and treating them like slaves. After 1549 only the most important government officials and members of the clergy were allowed to employ Indians in their personal service as servants, cooks, stablehands, and collectors of wood and fodder.[93] Personal service was abolished with the encomienda in 1812.[94]


DEMANDS ON INDIAN PRODUCTION


During the colonial period demands on Indian production remained, although it is difficult to judge whether they increased or decreased. What is clear is that the nature of demands changed. Whilst tribute probably constituted the major demand made upon Indian production in the early colonial period, other more subtle forms of exaction, some legal but others illegal, soon emerged to become considerable burdens on Indian communities. These exactions were undoubtedly a response to the decline in the value of

---

[89]AGCA A3.16 1700 Morejon 14.6.1793, A3.9 176 1706 Morejon 10.2.1799; AGI AG 501 Anguiano 10.5.1804; AGCA A3.12 187 1911 Morejon and Lindo 20.1.1810.

[90]AGCA A3.16 192 1966 2.7.1751.

[91]AGCA A3.16 255 5730 Estado de los curatos 8.7.1806 (23 villages in Honduras are not included).

[92]See discussion of the repartimiento and AGI AG 797 García 20.11.1790.

[93]For example, AGCA A1.30 232 2525 Indians of Tenambla 1758.

[94]AGCA A1.23 1538 10093 f.136 cédula 9.11.1812.

Indian tribute brought about by the decline in the Indian population itself, and by the increasing control over encomiendas exerted by the Crown.

Tribute was the most important legal exaction throughout the colonial period. The encomienda persisted longer in Central America than in many other parts of Spanish America, and when the administration of encomiendas was taken over by the Crown in the eighteenth century, Indian tribute constituted the most important source of Crown revenue from the area. During the colonial period the number of encomiendas assigned to private individuals declined. From a total of 79 private encomiendas in 1582, excluding Choluteca, the number fell to 26 in 1662. At the same time the proportion of villages and *parcialidades* being administered by the Crown increased from 13.5 percent to 65 percent.[95] In the early eighteenth century the Crown decided to take over the administration of the remaining encomiendas. In 1701 an order was issued that encomiendas of absent encomenderos were to revert to the Crown, and finally in 1718 the encomienda was abolished, although the latter order was not put into effect in the Audiencia of Guatemala until 1721.[96] Nevertheless, Indians continued to pay tribute to the Crown until the end of the colonial period, with the exception of a brief period between 1811 and 1816 when tribute payments were suspended.[97]

Until the 1530s encomenderos could levy as much tribute and labor services from Indians charged to them as they wished, but from that time onwards the Crown attempted to limit the amount of tribute payable and to regularize the manner in which it was assessed. Official assessments, or tasaciones, were made by oidores of the Audiencia, after they had visited the villages, counted the number of tributary Indians, and assessed the quality of the land and the type of crops produced by the communities.[98] Because of the expense involved in such official visits to distant parts of the Audiencia, such as Honduras, the responsibility for the count generally lay with governors and alcaldes mayores within their respective jurisdictions,[99] whilst the tribute assessments remained with the oidores. An enumeration was to be made every three years and whenever an encomienda was reassigned. After 1591 when the *servicio del tostón* was introduced, counts were supposed to be made annually.[100] The tasación was to be approved by the cacique and a copy of the tribute assessment was to remain in the Indian village, whilst

---

[95]BAGG 11: 5-19 Relación hecha...por el Gobernador de Honduras 1582; AGI AG CO 983A Escovar and Ferrera 29.12.1662. In 1582 of 215 villages and barrios only 29 were under the Crown, whereas in 1662 only 41 of 117 villages and barrios were allocated in private encomiendas (AGCA A3.16 511 5313 Oficiales de la Real Hacienda 23.1.1662).

[96]AGI AG 259 cédula 27.9.1721; Haring, *Spanish Empire*, p. 67.

[97]AGCA A1.23 2595 f.253v. cédula 13.3.1811, A1.23 1543 f.85 cédula 24.11.1815.

[98]*Recopilación* 2 lib.6 tít.5 ley 27: 233 11.7.1552.

[99]Ibid. leyes 55 and 56 23.12.1595, 13.6.1623, 9.10.1623, 2.10.1624; AGI AG 9 Audiencia of Guatemala 30.6.1560; AGCA A1.23 1517 f.203 cédula 30.9.1639.

[100]AGCA A1.23 1512 f.375 cédula 1.7.1567, A1.23 4581 f.28v. cédula 1.6.1571, A1.23 1515 f.52 cédula 12.12.1619. The servicio del tostón was a capitation tax of four reals payable by all tributary Indians.

other copies were to be lodged with the encomendero and the Audiencia.[101] A recount or reassessment could be requested at any time by any one of the three parties involved.[102] Since the process was long and the petitioner had to pay the costs, Indians soon became tired of wasting their time and money on entering into lawsuits that they never won.

During the sixteenth century visitas were conducted at extended intervals, but during the seventeenth century visits by oidores were rare and counts were generally undertaken by local officials and parish priests. The first official assessments were made in the 1530s, but the first attempt to draw up tasaciones for the whole of the Audiencia was made by Cerrato and the oidores Rogel and Ramírez in 1548 and 1549. Unfortunately the tasaciones are incomplete for Honduras; evidence only exists for the jurisdiction of Comayagua and it is uncertain whether other jurisdictions were assessed.[103] These tasaciones included personal service which was banned in 1549. As a result some reassessments were made in the early 1550s commuting the personal service to the payment of tribute in kind.[104] In 1554 villages in the jurisdiction of Gracias a Dios were assessed by the oidores Alonso Zorita and Tomás López. With the exception of villages located in the "mar del sur," they did not visit other parts of Honduras because they were too remote from Guatemala.[105] In 1559 Indian communities in Comayagua were still paying according to the 1549 tasaciones.[106] The tasaciones of Zorita and López were moderate compared to those made in about 1562 by the oidores Dr. Mexía and Jufre de Loaysa.[107] The latter assessments included a number of smaller items, such as chili, honey, wax, and rush mats, which had been omitted in the reassessments made after 1549. They also specified the amounts of maize and beans payable in terms of harvested crops rather than the amounts of seed sown, such that the Indians had to bear the risks of production. Furthermore, it would appear that the assessments were based on counts that included absentees.[108] As such it is not surprising that a visita of Honduras

---

[101]AGCA A1.23 1511 f.253 cédula 22.6.1559; Puga, *Provisiones* ff.127-28, ff. 152-53 8.6.1551.

[102]AGCA A1.23 4577 f.13v. cédula 12.12.1619.

[103]AGI AG 128 Libro de tasaciones 1549.

[104]For example, in 1551 the personal service of Indians in the village of Yoro was commuted to the product of two fanegas of maize (AGI CO 988 1.2.1551).

[105]AGI CO Tasaciones of Cerrato, Ramírez, Zorita, and López 1554, AG 9 Ramírez and Quesada 25.5.1555, AG 402-3 cédula 30.3.1557.

[106]AGI CO 988 Tasaciones of Cerrato and Ramírez 1549, 1559.

[107]Bancroft, *Native Races* 2:367; L.B. Simpson, *The Encomienda in New Spain: The Beginnings of Spanish Mexico* (Berkeley and Los Angeles: University of California, 1950), p. 152; A. de Zorita, *The Lords of New Spain* (London: Phoenix House, 1965), p. 36.

[108]AGI CO 988 Tasaciones 1562. For example, the village Rruruteca in the jurisdiction of Comayagua complained that the tribute assessment had been based on 34 tributary Indians, when in fact ten were absent (AGCA A3.16 511 5345 Autos de los indios del pueblo de Rruruteca 1581).

in the late 1570s found less than one-half of the Indians in the jurisdiction of Gracias a Dios than had been there when they were enumerated by Mexía and Loaysa, and less than one-third in San Pedro.[109] It is significant that the president of the Audiencia, Juan Núñez de Landecho, and the oidor Loaysa were both suspended from office in 1564.[110] There is no evidence for reassessments in the early 1570s, but when Lic. Valverde took office as president of the Audiencia in 1578, he immediately ordered a new count and an investigation into the treatment of Indians.[111] Possibly as a result of this order, the governor of Honduras, Alonso de Contreras visited the region in the late 1570s or early 1580s. His account lists the number of tributary Indians in the province, but it does not indicate the amount of tribute they paid.[112] The only other general assessment undertaken during the sixteenth century was made in 1587.[113] Evidence for this assessment is only available for Indian villages that were tributary to the Crown, but it seems likely that those paying tribute to encomenderos were also assessed. A feature of the 1587 assessment was the reduction in the number of tribute items to three--cotton cloth, maize, and chickens. This was in line with the order issued in 1552 that Indians should pay tribute in two or three items only.[114]

Evidence of tasaciones made in the seventeenth century is extremely fragmentary and it is mainly available from the accounts of tribute paid by individual villages. In 1609 the president of the Audiencia, Alonso Criado de Castilla, ordered a revision of tribute assessments following an investigation as to whether the amounts the Indians paid were excessive and whether they should pay tribute in cash.[115] It is uncertain, however, whether they were revised in Honduras before Gaspar de Zúñiga conducted a visita in 1615. This visita took two years and three months to complete, but unfortunately the only evidence available for the new tasaciones appears in the lists of encomiendas assigned after that date.[116] As in other parts of the Audiencia, it appears that by this time tribute assessments were being made on a per capita basis rather than being based on the overall size of the community. Piecemeal reassessments appear to have been made during the early seventeenth century; for example, villages in the jurisdiction of Gracias a Dios were enumerated in 1638,[117] but there is no evidence for a general reassessment for fifty years. Nevertheless, evidence for the assignment of encomiendas exists in two lists

---

[109] AGI AG 156 Cisneros 17.4.1583.

[110] Bancroft, *Native Races* 2:367-69.

[111] Simpson, *Encomienda in New Spain*, pp. 154-55; MacLeod, *Spanish Central America*, pp. 130-31.

[112] AGI AG 39 Contreras 20.2.1582; BAGG 11: 5-19 Relación hecha por el Gobernador de Honduras 20.4.1582; AGI AG 56 Contreras 20.4.1582.

[113] AGCA A3.16 236 2420 Tasaciones 1589.

[114] *Recopilación* 2 lib.6 tít.5 ley 22: 231-32 18.12.1552.

[115] AGCA A1.23 1514 f.131 cédula 26.5.1609.

[116] AGI AG Interogatorio on the visita of Zúñiga 10.4.1620. For details of tribute assessments in the seventeenth century see AG 98 to 106.

[117] AGCA A1.24 1558 10202 f.11 cédula 4.2.1638.

drawn up in 1662. One list includes encomiendas allocated within the Audiencia as a whole, whilst the other covers Honduras only.[118] For reasons of inaccuracy or differences in the actual dates of the tasaciones on which the lists were based, the two lists do not correspond exactly. The lack of visitas and reassessments during the seventeenth century was undoubtedly due to the high cost of conducting them, which could not be justified given the small tribute income the province yielded. This was made clear when following an order for a new enumeration in 1679, the Crown specified that the count was to be undertaken by ordinary vecinos rather than royal officials in order to reduce costs and eliminate fraud.[119] Nevertheless, the figures submitted to the Audiencia appear to have been drawn from *padrones* in the hands of exchequer officials rather than compiled from counts made by newly appointed enumerators. The account of the number of tributary Indians drawn up in 1683 lacks detail for Honduras, with the exception of the jurisdictions of Tegucigalpa and Choluteca where the number of tributary Indians is included for each village, but no account is given of the amount of tribute they paid.

From that time onwards until about the middle of the eighteenth century tribute assessments appear to have been made at irregular intervals and in most cases they were for limited areas within the province. The extended time intervals between assessments meant that Indians had to pay according to counts that were out of date, such that the burden of paying for those who were absent or dead fell on those that remained. The result was that although pressure was brought on Indian officials to pay the assessed tribute in full, most Indian villages fell into arrears. The book of tasaciones drawn up in 1753 indicates that assessments for the jurisdictions of Gracias a Dios, Tencoa, and San Pedro had been made within the previous few years, but some parts of Gracias a Dios and all of Olancho had not been counted for over ten years, whilst villages in Comayagua and Choluteca had various assessment dates between 1714 and 1745.[120]

Several changes were made in the form and methods of tribute assessment during the eighteenth century. From 1754 women were exempt from tribute payment. This necessitated the drawing up of new tribute assessments, which in Honduras were undertaken in 1759 and 1762.[121] Then in the following decade, a new system of enumerating Indians was introduced using specially appointed officials, *apoderados fiscales*, and parish priests.[122] The reason given for the change in the method of enumeration was to eliminate fraud, but another reason was the increasing difficulty of counting the number of Indians belonging to each village. Head counts undertaken in villages were clearly inadequate because many Indians did not reside there but lived on estates or in the towns and mining areas, as well as on isolated plots in the countryside. To obtain a complete list of the Indian population, therefore, it was necessary to refer to the registers of baptisms, marriages and deaths, kept in the parish churches. Although

---

[118]AGI CO 983A Escover and Ferrera 29.12.1662; AGCA A3.16 511 5313 Oficiales de la Real Hacienda 23.1.1662.

[119]AGI AG 29 Audiencia 14.5.1681 (cédula 21.6.1680), CO 815 1685. The latter document is badly burnt and extremely difficult to read.

[120]AGCA A3.16 192 1975 Tributarios de la provincia de Comayagua 1753.

[121]AGCA A3.16 2325 34320 Libro de tasaciones 1758 to 1763, A3.16 193 1985 to 1987 Tasaciones 1762.

[122]AGI AG 560 Instrucción 7.7.1767, 15.1.1771 (cédula 7.12.1776), Testimonio de la real cédula despachada...1778.

these records were inadequately kept and Indians could still escape the notice of the authorities, the new system did produce more accurate counts. A similar system had been introduced to Mexico in 1765 with some success, and it was modified for the Audiencia of Guatemala in 1767. One of the main problems of the new system was its time-consuming nature; the first enumeration using the new method took from January 1776 to February 1777. In order to mitigate the costs, subsequent counts were undertaken every five years rather than every three years, as had theoretically been the norm previously. By the end of the century the costs involved in making the counts were considerable; a count undertaken by six commissioners in Honduras between 1788 and 1796 cost 3,085 pesos. At the beginning of the nineteenth century it was estimated that it cost 30,000 pesos every five years to count Indians in the whole Audiencia and this may have represented as much as one-seventh of the Crown's annual income from tribute.[123] In order to dispense with the costs of drawing up tributary lists, the task was finally charged to parish priests and in 1805 instructions were drawn up for their guidance.[124]

Although new enumerations were to take place every five years, it is not clear that they were undertaken. Following the 1776 to 1777 enumeration, new tasaciones of villages in the jurisdiction of Comayagua appear to have been made in 1789 and 1796, but the coverage was incomplete.[125] In 1791 and 1797 new tasaciones were made for villages in the jurisdiction of Gracias a Dios,[126] but there is some doubt as to whether the Indians were actually recounted prior to being reassessed in 1791, since in 1792 the village of Ocotepeque complained that the Indians there had not been enumerated for 24 years.[127] Furthermore, it is uncertain whether any assessments were made in other parts of Honduras during this period, but a comprehensive count was undertaken in 1801.[128] Finally the counting of Indians by parish priests occurred systematically from 1806; complete lists of the number of tributary Indians in Honduras are available for 1806 and 1811.[129]

It would appear that in the early sixteenth century only male married Indians paid tribute. Early lists of tributary Indians refer to them as "indios tributarios" and it is assumed that they comprised married male Indians only.[130] This is suggested by the fact it was not until 1578 that the Crown ordered single persons to pay tribute because they

[123]AGCA A3.16 194 2023 20.11.1796, A3.16 255 5730 14.8.1811; Salvatierra, *Historia de Centroamérica* 2:157.

[124]AGCA A3.16 2327 34374 Instructions to parish priests 30.10.1805, AGCA A3.16 255 5730 14.8.1811.

[125]ANH Various expedientes in Paquetes 10, 11, 21, 22, 24 and Unclassified.

[126]AGCA A3.16 194 2005 20.7.1791, A3.16 194 2015 29.8.1796, A3.16 195 2038 Estado que manifiesta...el partido de Gracias a Dios 28.2.1798.

[127]AGCA A3.16 194 2006 15.3.1792.

[128]ANH P12 L20 18.1.1803; AGCA A3.16 255 5730 8.7.1806.

[129]BAGG 3: 221-5 Estado de los curatos 8.7.1806, A3.16 197 2096 20.11.1811.

[130]See Chapter 6.

were postponing marriage in order to avoid tribute payment.[131] By 1582 the order had not been put into effect in Honduras, for the list of tributary Indians drawn up by Governor Contreras at that time refers to them as "indios vecinos tributarios,"[132] but it was probably implemented soon after. Although single persons were liable to pay tribute, they paid only half the amount or less than that paid by full tributary Indians. Other groups of Indians who paid half tribute were those who were married to persons of a different race, or to Indians who were exempt from tribute payment by virtue of their age, status or disability, or to Indians who paid tribute in other villages or to those who were absent or classified as lavoríos. Those who were automatically exempt from tribute payment were caciques and their eldest sons, Indian officials, such as elected alcaldes and regidores, as well as those who assisted in the church, notably *fiscales, cantores, sacristanes*, and musicians.[133] Indians who had been recently converted were also exempt, except that they were required to pay the servicio del tostón, which was introduced in 1591. The period for which they were exempt was originally ten years, but by 1686 it had apparently been extended to 20 years.[134] Male Indians paid tribute between the ages of 18 and 55, and women paid up to the age of 50. It appears that in other parts of the empire women did not pay tribute, but it seems to have become 'the custom' for them to pay in the Audiencia of Guatemala,[135] at least until they were exempted in 1754. Women who were eligible to pay tribute, but who were married to men who were exempt from tribute payment, were exempt for the duration of their husbands' lives, but when they died they were liable to pay tribute as widows.[136]

Other forms of exemption from tribute payment had to be obtained from the Audiencia. Individuals could petition for exemption on the grounds of disablement or racial and social status. Due to increasing miscegenation, there were growing numbers of petitions for tribute exemption based on claims to non-Indian status. The rule that was followed was that a child was classified as having the same racial status as its mother, with the exception of a legitimate offspring of a Spanish father and Indian mother who was classified as a mestizo; the illegitimate children of such unions were classified as Indians and liable to pay tribute.[137] To obtain exemption from tribute as a non-Indian, the petitioner had to provide birth and marriage certificates. In many cases individuals were unable to do this, and it would appear that without the necessary documents their

---

[131]*Recopilación* 2 lib.6 tít. 5 ley 226-7 5.7.1578.

[132]BAGG 11: 5-19 Relación hecha por el Gobernador de Honduras 20.4.1582.

[133]AGCA A1.23 1512 f.407 cédula 18.5.1572; *Recopilación* 2 lib.6 tít. 5 ley 18: 230 17.7.1572.

[134]AGCA A1.23 4583 f.199 cédula 4.9.1551; AGI AG 39 Ortíz 16.12.1562; AGCA A1.23 4585 f.240 cédula 14.5.1686.

[135]AGCA A1.23 1524 10079 f.3 cédula 21.3.1702.

[136]*Recopilación* 2 lib.6 tít. 5 ley 18: 230 17.7.1572; AGCA A1.23 1512 f.407 cédula 18.5.1572.

[137]AGCA A3.16 193 2000 1789, A3.16 2327 34374 Instructions to parish priests 30.11.1805.

claims were unlikely to succeed.[138]   Other individuals who were craftsmen who were employed in the towns claimed exemption as lavoríos, whilst during the eighteenth century the establishment of the regular militia opened up opportunities for Indians to claim exemption under the *fuero militar*.[139]

There were other less formal ways in which Indians could avoid tribute payment. Indians were liable to pay tribute in the villages of their birth even though they might be resident elsewhere.  Indian officials charged with the collection of the tribute often found it difficult to locate absent Indians, particularly in the towns, such that over time they were probably dropped from tributary lists.  This led to conflicts between the absentees and their home villages, because the burdens of providing men to work on the repartimiento, and to carry out church and office-holding duties became heavier on those that remained.  Nevertheless, disputes between the two parties were generally concluded by the Crown reaffirming the right of an Indian to reside where he wished as long as he paid tribute in the village of his birth.[140]   Another way in which an Indian could gain tribute exemption was by avoiding being put on a tributary list.  Opportunities for this form of evasion increased as marriages between individuals from different villages became more common.  Generally the wife would take up residence in the home of the husband, and although their children were supposed to be included in the tributary list of the mother's village, it is clear many escaped the notice of enumerators.[141]   Similarly, individuals could claim that they paid tribute elsewhere when tributary lists for the villages in which they resided were drawn up.  That such evasion took place is clear from comparisons of the padrones, which indicate the place of birth of individuals, and the tributary lists for those villages, for often they do not correspond; that is, individuals listed as being born in a different village from that in which they resided are often absent from the tributary list of the village of their birth.

Whole villages could also claim exemption for periods of years in the case of disasters, such as epidemics, famines, earthquakes, and pirate attacks, and when the parish church required rebuilding.  All these claims had to be supported by a Spanish official and the local parish priest.  Some observers complained about the ease with which Indians obtained relief from tribute payment, but it is clear that in the case of famines at least, it was not always granted; very often communities were only allowed to defer payment for several years.[142]

---

[138]For example, AGCA A3.16 515 5415 1778, A3.16 515 5417 1778.  Many claims for exemption are to be found in the following legajos: AGCA A3.16 195-7 and 513-7.

[139]AGCA A3.16 Instructions to parish priests 30.10.1805, although such exemptions were not always granted--for example, AGCA A3.16 193 2003 Fiscal's comments on the case of Aguilar 1791.

[140]AGCA A1.23 1559 f.212 cédula 2.5.1642, A1.23 1567 f.167 cédula 3.3.1683, A1.23 1583 f.62 cédula 18.5.1719.

[141]Generally children of a married couple were to be included in the tributary list of the father's village, whilst children born to single women were to be registered in the mother's village (*Recopilación* 2 lib.6 tít.1 ley 10: 191-2 10.10.1618), but in Honduras children are not included in padrones where the mother is from another village, thus suggesting that the children became tributary in the mother's village regardless of whether the mother was married.

[142]AGCA A1.23 1524 f.189 cédula 2.8.1704.

Several changes in the nature of tribute payments were introduced during the late sixteenth century and seventeenth centuries. From 1549 tribute could no longer be commuted to personal service.[143] Although personal service did continue illegally, from that date it was not included in the schedule of items that each village had to provide. Most of the goods paid as tribute were either foodstuffs, notably maize, some beans, chickens, or craft manufactures. Some villages in the vicinity of San Pedro continued to pay tribute in cacao, and in the jurisdiction of Gracias a Dios a number of villages paid in wheat.[144] In general, however, a full tributary Indian paid four *piernas* of cotton cloth, one fanega of maize, and one or two chickens, whilst half tributaries paid half that amount. Whilst the simplification of tribute payments had the advantage of making their collection much easier, it had the disadvantage of taking no account of local conditions and therefore placed excessive burdens on Indians living in areas to which the crops were not ecologically suited. Probably for this reason, by the end of the seventeenth century the payment of tribute in cotton cloth in some Indians villages, notably in the jurisdictions of Comayagua and Gracias a Dios, had been commuted to a money payment.[145] In general, however, collectors put pressure on Indians to pay in kind since it afforded them opportunities to make illegal profits by regulating the value of tribute items well below market prices, at which they subsequently sold them, and by rendering to the royal coffers only the revenue yielded according to official prices. Also, when Indians possessed insufficient maize with which to meet their tribute demands, they were forced to buy it from officials at the highly inflated market prices, as were those Indians who did not practice agriculture, but who were employed as wage laborers.[146] Despite a number of royal orders to the effect that Indians should be free to pay their tribute in money or goods, officials continued to insist on payments in kind.

Although the amount of tribute payable was specified on a per capita basis and its value was regulated, there were variations in the amount paid by Indians in different regions of the country. In 1757 the amount payable by a full tributary Indian varied in value from 19 reals in Tencoa to between 11.5 and 13.5 reals in other parts of the province.[147] In 1787 the Audiencia considered the introduction of a uniform tax of three pesos a year,[148] but it finally decided to regulate it at 16 reals. Although the Audiencia attempted to introduce this uniform tax from the mid-1790s,[149] the list of tasaciones for Honduras for 1801 indicates that the majority of Indians were paying 17 reals (with the

---

[143]AGI AG 401-3 cédula 22.2.1549; AGCA A1.23 4575 f.94 cédula 22.2.1549; Zavala, *Instituciones coloniales*, p. 70.

[144]For example, AGCA A3.16 190 1928 Confirmation of encomiendas 10.5.1662, A3.16 511 5313 Oficiales reals 23.1.1662, A3.16 190 1930 Cargo...de tributos 1691-7.

[145]AGCA A3.16 511 5313 Oficiales reals 23.1.1662, A3.16 190 1930 Cargo...de tributos 1691-7.

[146]AGCA A3.16 513 5368 Pueblo of Cururu January 1734, A1.30 222 2479 Visita of Comayagua 1742.

[147]AGCA A3.16 2325 34320 Libro de tasaciones 1758 to 1762.

[148]AGCA A3.16 246 4912 20.7.1793 (cédula requesting information 27.7.1787).

[149]AGCA A3.16 194 2027 20.3.1797, Martínez Peláez, *Patria del criollo*, p. 232, 689 n.73.

exception of Tencoa, where individuals paid 21 reals), whilst in 1811 tribute payments ranged from 12.25 to 15 reals.[150] In addition to these payments in kind, all tributary Indians were required to pay a capitation tax of four reals, known as the servicio del tostón. This tax was introduced in 1591 to help fund the rising costs of defense.[151]

According to a royal cédula in 1551 Indians were not obliged to take their tribute to the residence of their encomendero or to the nearest town where a royal official resided.[152] Initially encomenderos or their representatives collected the tribute from Indian villages, whilst royal officials were responsible for its collection from those villages that paid tribute to the Crown. Because of the abuses perpetrated by the overseers and servants of encomenderos, they were banned from collecting tribute in 1553, and in 1605 the same order was applied to encomenderos as well. From that time on tribute from all Indian villages was collected by royal officials, and encomenderos were required to collect the amount they were due from the *Real Caja*.[153] However, royal officials were no less guilty of the charges made against the earlier collectors and the abuses continued. The actual responsibility for the collection of tribute from individuals lay with Indian leaders, who if they could not meet the necessary demands were liable to be fined or imprisoned. Once collected the items were sold in the marketplace and the revenue entered the royal coffers. It was a common practice for individuals, particularly royal officials with preferential access to tribute items, to monopolize them at low prices, and by creating shortages, cause prices to rise enabling them to make substantial profits.[154]

It is clear that there were considerable abuses of the tributary system. Collectors often took little notice of tasaciones, visiting Indian villages at harvest time and taking what they wanted.[155] They forced Indians to pay for those who were absent or dead, and when they failed to meet the demands, Indian leaders were either fined or imprisoned and the individual Indians who defaulted were required to compensate for their failure to pay tribute in other ways.[156] Sometimes an official would fix the price for the items that should have been paid, which was always above their true value, and require the Indians to pay in cash. To satisfy these demands Indians often had to seek wage labor or,

---

[150]AGCA A3.16 244 4871 Tasaciones 1.3.1804, A3.16 197 2096 Tasaciones 20.11.1811.

[151]*Recopilación* 2 lib. 6 tít. 5 ley 16: 228 1.11.1591; AGCA A1.23 1513 f.719 cédula 1.11.1591.

[152]Ibid., ley 44: 237 12.5.1551.

[153]AGCA A1.24 2195 f.99 cédula 17.4.1553, A1.24 2195 f.345 cédula 17.3.1553, A1.23 1514 f.777 cédula 22.12.1605, A1.23 1516 f.12v. cédula 12.12.1619.

[154]AGCA A1.23 1526 f.141 cédula 11.11.1719.

[155]AGCA A1.23 1516 ff.12-4 cédula 9.8.1631, A3.16 511 5318 27.11.1681.

[156]AGI AG 39 Contreras 20.2.1582, AG 56 Contreras 20.4.1582, AG 10 Valverde 25.3.1583, AG 164 Bishop of Honduras 20.4.1584; AGCA A3.16 192 1972 Testimonio de las diligencias practicadas en la cobranza de los tributos reals 19.6.1751. In an attempt to collect tribute arrears from about 30 villages in the jurisdiction of Gracias a Dios, nine Indian alcaldes were imprisoned and another forced to sell his goods to make good the deficit.

especially in the case of women, pay off their debts by working as servants.[157] These were only some of the exactions made by royal officials. Others were made in the form of labor and through trade. These demands are discussed elsewhere, but at this stage it is worth noting one group of Indians--lavoríos--who paid tribute of a different kind.

Prior to the introduction of the New Laws, many vecinos had Indians working as household servants and these were known as naborías. Since these Indians, later referred to as lavoríos, possessed no means of production, from 1575 they were liable to pay tribute in cash. In the early seventeenth century the amount payable was five tostones for a married couple and three tostones for a single person, but in the eighteenth century each tributary lavorío paid ten reals.[158] Lavoríos were free to reside where they wished, but they had to pay tribute in the towns in which they were registered, where it was collected by officials of the royal exchequer.

Alcaldes mayores and tenientes were probably the worst oppressors of the Indians. In their official capacities they came into the most sustained contact with Indians and as such they were in the best position to exploit them. Furthermore, they had the stimulus to do so given that the posts they held were only tenable for a few years and only commanded salaries of 150 to 200 pesos a year.[159] There were several ways in which alcaldes mayores and tenientes made profits at the expense of the Indians. One of the principal means was by trade, although it was illegal.[160] They forced Indians to sell them items, such as cotton, cacao, and other foodstuffs, at below market prices, which they then resold making substantial profits. They also forced Indians to buy items of low value, such as 'soap, candles and combs,' at high prices, sometimes offering Indians advances that were repayable at harvest time. This *repartimiento de generos* became a considerable burden on Indian communities and it continued throughout the colonial period despite orders prohibiting it. The result was that many Indians fell into the debt of alcaldes mayores and tenientes.[161] Officials also required Indians to sow milpas, to tend their horses and cattle, to weave cotton, and to carry out a multitude of services for which they were poorly paid, if at all. Not to belittle the hardships borne by Indians in Honduras, these exactions do not appear to have been as onerous as in neighboring Nicaragua. It was said that it was because the Indians in Honduras had little to trade, but probably more important, particularly in the mining areas, was that royal officials possessed alternative opportunities to make profits, notably in the illegal trade in silver.[162]

---

[157]AGCA A3.16 190 1940 Alcaldes of Tesigua 1714.

[158]*Recopilación* 2 lib.6 tít.5 leyes 8-10 15.2.1575 and 4.7.1594; AGI CO 992 Cargo de tributos 1615; AGCA A3.16 2325 34320 Libro de tasaciones 1762, A3.16 255 5730 8.7.1806.

[159]See Chapter 10.

[160]*Recopilación* 2 lib.5 tít. 2 ley 47: 125-6 10.7.1530 etc.; AGCA A1.24 4575 f.468v. cédula 21.4.1604.

[161]AGI AG 967 Regidores of Choluteca 12.11.1602, AG 14 Lic. Salmeron 20.5.1620; AGCA A1.23 1513 f.598 cédula 1582, A1.23 1520 f.242 cédula 11.8.1676, A1.23 4592 f.22 2.8.1679, A1.30 219 2466 Indians of Olancho El Viejo 4.12.1724, A1.15 64 770 Indians of Celilaca 2.6.1761; BAGG 2: 469-73 Rossa y Aguayo 3.2.1766.

[162]BAGG 2: 463-5 Cásseres 23.8.1765.

Jueces de milpas were appointed to ensure that Indians planted maize so that they would not suffer shortages of food. These officials were badly paid out of the *cajas de comunidad*, but their positions enabled them to supplement their incomes by levying goods and services from the Indians, as well as by forcing them to buy goods at high prices. The jueces de milpas were so notorious in their exploitation of the Indians that the Crown forbade their appointment in 1585.[163] Nevertheless, within the Audiencia of Guatemala jueces de milpas continued to be appointed, and it was not until 1619, when the order was repeated and an investigation of the conduct of all those who had been appointed since 1585 was ordered, that the Crown brought charges against two presidents of the Audiencia, Conde de la Gomera and Alonso Criado de Castilla, for having allowed the appointment of jueces de milpas.[164] During this period it would appear that over eighty jueces de milpas had been appointed in the Audiencia for periods ranging from one to five years. It is known that at least five were appointed in Honduras, but the figure may be higher because parts of the document in which the account appears are badly burnt. In Honduras they were paid 400 tostones. The charges against them were very similar: they traded with Indians charging them high prices for cheap goods; they forced them to sell goods cheaply or else exchange them for other, and often unwanted, goods at poor rates of exchange; they also obliged them to sow milpas of maize and cotton without payment, and to spin and weave cotton into cloth for which they provided them with insufficient cotton. The Indians were also required to provide food and lodging for the juez and his assistants on their tours of inspection. Apart from this the jueces do not appear to have conducted their duties conscientiously. Often they only surveyed the milpa de comunidad and a few other milpas nearby, and they meted out punishment at will. Despite the royal ban on the appointment of jueces, the Audiencia repeatedly petitioned the Crown to permit their appointment, particularly in times of food shortages. But the Crown did not relent and reaffirmed the order forbidding their appointment in 1630, 1640, 1632, 1640, 1644, and 1669.[165]

Parish priests were allowed to receive a certain amount of free goods and services. Although the Crown attempted to limit the amounts they could receive and require that Indians should be paid, priests often exacted more. Despite prohibitions against them, they also levied *derramas*, and like alcaldes mayores and other officials, they forced Indians to cultivate milpas, to tend their cattle, and to spin and weave cotton with little or no payment. At church festivals they demanded wine and food, particularly chickens, and

---

[163]AGCA A1.23 1515 f.231 cédula 8.6.1585; Pardo, *Efemérides*, p. 20 8.6.1585.

[164]The investigation of the conduct of jueces de milpas in the Audiencia of Guatemala makes interesting reading and it is contained in four legajos--CO 971A, 971B, 972A, and 972B, all of which are badly burnt and difficult to handle and read.

[165]AGCA A1.23 1515 f.231 and 4576 f.38v. cédula 28.5.1630, A1.24 2197 f.13 cédula 4.9.1640, A1.23 4582 f.113 cédula 14.11.1699; García Peláez, *Memorias* 1:235-37. Part of the reason why the Audiencia permitted their appointment was to appease would-be office holders; the Crown, however, tried to limit their appointment for financial reasons and to protect the Indians from exploitation (MacLeod, *Spanish Central America*, pp. 317-18). They were still being appointed in Honduras in the 1660s (ANH P2 L3 and L104 1662 and 1669).

for church services such as baptisms, marriages, and burials they demanded chickens and fruit, in addition to levying exorbitant fees illegally.[166]

Indians were also obliged to provide gifts for official visitors and food and lodging for travellers. Although the Crown tried to limit the number of visits undertaken by royal officials, the large number of officials who had different forms of jurisdiction within the same areas meant that visits by officials were frequent.[167] The problem was aggravated by the fact that many of the officials took large numbers of assistants and servants with them, although again the Crown attempted to limit their number.[168]

---

[166]For repeated orders against the levying of derramas and other exactions, see: AGCA A1.23 1513 f.619 cédula 3.11.1582, A1.23 1514 f.219 cédula 21.5.1611, A1.23 4577 39530 cédula 12.12.1619, A1.23 1521 f.235 cédula 19.6.1680 confirming cédula of 21.5.1678, A1.38 4778 41245 Ordenanzas 21.10.1683, A1.23 1526 f.98 cédula 7.2.1718.

[167]AGCA A1.23 4579 39532 f.86 cédula 17.8.1636; AGI AG 56 Merits of Cisneros 17.4.1583.

[168]AGCA A1.23 1513 f.580 cédula 17.6.1580.

# 12
# Cultural Changes in Western and Central Honduras

From 1550 the major cultural changes that occurred in western and central Honduras emanated from the expansion of agriculture and mining, and the gradual integration of the Indians into the economic and social life of the province. The latter could not occur, however, without the disintegration of Indian communities. The economic viability of Indian communities was undermined by the demands that were made on their lands, labor, and production, which weakened the subsistence base and encouraged individuals to desert their villages in search of wage labor. This process gathered momentum in the second half of the eighteenth century as the population increased and the commercial economy expanded. At the same time, the social organization of Indian communities was weakened by social levelling and emigration, which resulted in falling marriage and fertility rates. Meanwhile, the Spanish attempted to convert the Indians to Christianity, but the small number of clergy available and the dispersed character of the settlement pattern probably meant that the acceptance of Christian beliefs on anything more than a superficial level proceeded very slowly.

CHANGES IN THE SETTLEMENT PATTERN

During the colonial period the number of Indian villages in western and central Honduras (excluding Choluteca) fell from 145 in 1582 to 85 in 1811, with most of the losses occurring in the Ulúa valley and around San Pedro (Table 7). These losses were brought about by population decline, and to a lesser extent, by village amalgamations in the late eighteenth century. Whilst the number of villages fell throughout the colonial period, changes in the average size of Indian villages, expressed in terms of the number of tributary Indians, paralleled demographic trends, which showed a decline until the beginning of the eighteenth century, followed by an increase (Table 8). However, the increasing nucleation of the Indian settlement pattern towards the end of the eighteenth century, as suggested by the presence of fewer but larger villages, was more apparent than real, and it derives from the practice of assigning tributary Indians to particular villages for the purposes of tribute assessment and collection. In fact by that time a substantial

Table 7

NUMBER OF INDIAN VILLAGES IN HONDURAS
(excluding Choluteca) DURING THE
COLONIAL PERIOD

| Jurisdiction | 1582 | 1592 | 1602 | 1662 | 1684 | 1757 | 1770 | 1804 | 1811 |
|---|---|---|---|---|---|---|---|---|---|
| Comayagua | 57 | 58 | 55 | 45 | 43 | 40 | 32 | 35 | 34 |
| Gracias a Dios | 52 | 51 | 47 | 33 | 40 | 38 | 38 | 38 | 38 |
| Tencoa | 16 | 16 | 16 | 12 | 11 | 11 | 10 | 9 | 9 |
| San Pedro | 20 | 16 | 17 | 8 | 10 | 9 | 7 | 6 | 4 |
| Puerto Caballos | 4 | 4 | 4 | 0 | 2 | 1 | 0 | 0 | 0 |
| Trujillo | 18 | 13 | 13 | 4 | 1 | 3 | 2 | 2 | 2 |
| Olancho | 41 | 32 | 26 | 11 | 19 | 13 | 8 | 8 | 8 |

Jurisdictions have been transformed to coincide with those for 1592 for which the evidence is the most detailed and complete.

Sources:
BAGG 11: 5-19 Contreras Guevara 20.4.1582

AGI CO 989 Servicio del tostón 1592

AGI CO 991A Servicio del tostón 1602

AGCA A3.15.3 511 5313 List of encomiendas 1662

AGI AG 44 Condenaciones 1684

AGCA A3.16 2325 34320 Libro de tasaciones 1757

AGCA A1.73 390 3662 Extracto general de la visita 10.2.1771 and A3.16 174 1674 20.1.1771.

AGI AG 501 Estado que manifiesta las subdelegaciones 1.5.1804

AGCA A3.16 197 2096 Tasaciones 1811

Table 8

AVERAGE SIZE OF INDIAN VILLAGES IN HONDURAS
(excluding Choluteca) DURING THE COLONIAL PERIOD
IN TERMS OF THE NUMBER OF TRIBUTARY INDIANS

| Jurisdiction | 1582 | 1592 | 1602 | 1757 | 1770 | 1804 | 1811 |
|---|---|---|---|---|---|---|---|
| Comayagua | 30 | 34 | 24 | 43 | 62 | 60 | 71 |
| Gracias a Dios | 26 | 21 | 14 | 43 | 79 | 114 | 106 |
| Tencoa | 28 | 33 | 19 | 28 | 25 | 66 | 65 |
| San Pedro | 12 | 13 | 7 | 15 | 10 | 24 | 30 |
| Puerto Caballos | 20 | 22 | 17 | 6 | 0 | 0 | 0 |
| Trujillo | 19 | 23 | 16 | 13 | 60 | 44 | 42 |
| Olancho | 22 | 20 | 14 | 18 | 24 | 59 | 71 |

Jurisdictions have been transformed to coincide with those for 1592 for which the evidence is the most detailed and complete.

Sources:
BAGG 11:5-19 Contreras Guevara 20.4.1582

AGI CO 989 Servicio del tostón 1592

AGI CO 991A Servicio del tostón 1602

AGCA A3.16 2325 34320 Libro de tasaciones 1757

AGCA A1.73 390 3662 Extracto general de la visita 10.2.1771 and A3.16 174 1674 24.1.1771

AGI AG 501 Estado que manifiesta las subdelegaciones 1.5.1804

AGCA A3.16 197 2096 Tasaciones 1811

proportion of the Indian population no longer resided in nucleated settlements, but was to be found in the towns or else living on small plots or estates in the countryside.

At the time of Spanish conquest the Indian population of western and central Honduras was dispersed in small settlements throughout the countryside, and during the first half of the sixteenth century its dramatic decline reinforced this pattern as villages disappeared or were reduced in size. It was the Crown's intention that Indians should live in settlements of sufficient size to enable their administration and instruction in the Catholic faith,[1] hence in 1560 it was suggested that a process of *congregación* should begin in Honduras.[2] By 1584 the process had not been initiated, and as a result of further complaints about the difficulties of administering such a scattered population, the Crown ordered that Indian villages should be amalgamated.[3] It was envisaged that Indians from the smaller villages would move to the larger villages, which would form the nuclei of the new settlements. The task was considered to be difficult because of the reluctance of Indians to move and the likelihood of them fleeing into the interior if forced were applied. Maybe because of these difficulties, the order was never implemented; accounts of the number and size of villages at the end of the sixteenth century reveal no evidence of amalgamation.

The decline in the number and size of Indian villages during the late sixteenth and early seventeenth centuries can only partially be explained by the decline in the Indian population itself; another important factor was the dispersion of Indians to the surrounding countryside or towns, often to escape the burdens of tribute payment or the repartimiento, or to seek employment. As early as the beginning of the seventeenth century these movements had become so significant that during a visita in 1620, Zúñiga tried to force Indians to return to their villages, but to little effect.[4] The degree to which Indians began to desert their villages is difficult to estimate, since for tribute purposes Indians were enumerated in their places of birth rather than their current places of residence or employment. Although those Indians who were employed as wage laborers should have been reclassified as lavoríos and registered in their places of employment, their small number suggests that very few Indians in fact changed their tributary status. It seems likely therefore that the actual drift of the Indian population to Spanish centers of employment was greater than the available demographic accounts suggest. Indians migrated to the towns or sought permanent employment on local estates, whilst the mining areas also attracted settlement, with many Indians remaining there after working under the repartimiento.[5] In Choluteca, the El Corpus mining area contained many settlers from Nueva Segovia, but there were others from Comayagua, San Miguel, and San Salvador,[6] such that the surrounding valleys possessed "some tributary Indian

---

[1]AGCA A1.23 4575 f.16v. cédula 11.7.1572; *Recopilación* 2 lib.6 tít.3 ley 1:207; Remesal, *Historia general* 2:242-46.

[2]AGCA A1.23 1512 f.275 cédula 31.8.1560. MacLeod, *Spanish Central America*, p. 122, maintains that congregación had occurred in Chiapas, Verapaz, Guatemala, and Honduras before 1550, but I have been unable to find any evidence that it took place in Honduras.

[3]AGI AG 164 Bishop of Honduras 12.5.1582, AG 39 Ponce de León 26.5.1584, AG 164 Bishop of Honduras 20.4.1584; AGCA A1.23 1513 f.639 cédula 17.11.1584.

[4]AGI AG 14 Lic. Zúñiga 10.4.1620; AGCA A3.16.3 512 5358 Común of Nacaome 1631.

[5]ANH UC Vela 16.12.1812.

[6]ANH P26 L29 Diligencias practicadas para reducir a poblado...10.10.1774.

families in considerable number dispersed without any order, without allegiance to any village or regional centre."[7] Not only did Indians migrate in search of paid employment, but they also deserted their villages to eke out a living on small plots in the countryside. An account of the parish of Sulaco in 1689 reveals the nature of the settlement pattern, which was probably fairly typical in Honduras. At that time the parish contained 362 people, including men, women, and children, of whom 19 were Spanish, mestizo, or mulatto. The rest were Indians of whom 214 or 62.4 percent were to be found living in four Indian villages, 117 or 34.1 percent were scattered throughout the countryside, and 12 or 3.5 percent were living on estates.[8] Accounts of the jurisdiction of Tegucigalpa at the beginning of the eighteenth century also noted that many families did not possess houses in the villages, but they lived scattered throughout the countryside.[9] The effect of the progressive desertion of settlements was such that in the 1720s the Contador reported that in the jurisdiction of Comayagua there were 15 villages that, "today are extinct, some are inhabited by Indians from other villages and jurisdictions, in others only the name of the village remains with ladinos or two or three old and disabled Indians from whom it is not possible to collect tribute."[10] Although Ley 12 Tít.1 Lib.6 of the *Recopilación de las Leyes de las Indias* gave Indians the right to reside where they wished,[11] the law was often ignored. Nevertheless, efforts to force Indians to return to their villages, were generally unsuccessful. Searches of the countryside, particularly of estates by officials, with the support of Indian community leaders, often resulted in Indians fleeing further into the interior either temporarily or permanently, but where this was not possible temporary absence or occlusion within an estate often achieved the same effect.

The other source of change in the character of Indian villages was the expansion of the non-Indian population and its movement to the countryside. During the second half of the eighteenth century legislation was gradually introduced prohibiting the settlement of non-Indians in Indian villages, culminating with the ban on Spaniards residing in Indian villages in 1600.[12] Despite the introduction of legislation it would appear that non-Indians and particularly mulattoes and mestizos did take up residence in Indian villages to the extent that most Indian villages possessed at least one or two persons of either race. The main areas affected by influxes of non-Indians were those surrounding the major towns of Comayagua and Tegucigalpa. As early as 1723 villages in the jurisdiction of Comayagua were described as being full of ladinos,[13] such that by 1777 Indians formed only 38 percent of the total population of the area.[14] Similarly,

---

[7]ANH P26 L29 Diligencias practicadas para reducir a poblado...17.3.1774.

[8]AGCA A3.16 190 1923 Padrón de los pueblos...del curato de Sulaco 1689.

[9]ANH P18 L7 Visita de los pueblos...de Tegucigalpa 1703-4, P18 L5 Visita de los pueblos...de Tegucigalpa 1713.

[10]AGCA A3.16 191 1945 Contador of Comayagua 2.10.1723.

[11]AGCA A3.16 517 5425 Fiscal 21.5.1784.

[12]*Recopilación* 2 lib.6 tít.3 ley 21: 212 Various laws from 2.5.1563; AGI AG 39 Governor of Honduras, Carrança 1601.

[13]AGCA A3.16 191 1945 Contador of Comayagua 2.10.1783.

[14]AGI IG 1527 Estado y Padrón General...1777.

silver mining in Tegucigalpa attracted non-Indians so that a visita of the Alcaldía in 1743 revealed that the populations of Indian villages were very mixed,[15] and by 1777 only 22 percent of the jurisdiction's population was described as Indian.[16] In both areas the number of Indians relative to other racial groups appears to have declined even more in the last quarter of the eighteenth century.[17] By then the only areas in western and central Honduras that could be called Indian were Gracias a Dios and Tencoa. The intermixing of Indians and non-Indians in the rural areas persuaded the authorities to try and settle both groups in independent nucleated settlements. This involved moving Indians who were scattered throughout the countryside to already established Indian villages and amalgamating some of the smaller villages to form more viable settlements; it also involved establishing new settlements for non-Indians. Some of the new non-Indian settlements were completely independent of already existing settlements, but in many cases new barrios were added to already existing Indian villages. The process of establishing *reducciones* began in 1792 following a Crown order that Indians should not be allowed to live dispersed throughout the countryside but should form nucleated settlements. By 1793, 42 reducciones had been made and four were in the process of being formed,[18] and by the time the 1804 census was taken 134 reducciones were in existence, the majority in Comayagua, Tegucigalpa, and Gracias a Dios (106), of which 33 were located next to Indian villages.[19] The extent to which this program of establishing reducciones managed to segregate non-Indians from Indians is unknown, but it seems doubtful that within such a short time any real and permanent changes in residence patterns could have been achieved.

The dispersion of Indians from their villages and the expansion of the non-Indian population to the countryside meant that a very different settlement pattern existed at the end of the eighteenth century from that which had existed at the beginning of the colonial period, or indeed from that which had been envisaged by the Crown; it was no longer possible to distinguish by residence an urban Spanish republic from a rural Indian republic. At the beginning of the nineteenth century 16.1 percent of Spanish and ladino families in Honduras were living in Indian villages and a further 26.7 percent resided on haciendas or in other rural settlements.[20]

There is little evidence for changes in the size of households during the colonial period, since most censuses were made for the purpose of tribute assessment and thus they only include able-bodied adults; very few include the number of children. It was the Crown's intention that Indians should form nuclear family households in order to discourage immorality and this policy was reinforced by official inspections of dwellings. However, household sizes declined as much as a result of population decline as through the imposition of new patterns of residence. A visita of the village of Rruruteca in the jurisdiction of Comayagua in 1581 counted 18 households with a total population of 98,

---

[15]AGCA A1.17 210 5011 and BAGG 1:29-39 Alcalde Mayor of Tegucigalpa 20.7.1743.

[16]AGI IG 1527 Estado y Padrón General...1777.

[17]See the 1804 census, AGI AG 501 Estado que manifiesta las subdelegaciones...1.5.1804.

[18]AGCA A1.12 51 518 List of reducciones 12.8.1793.

[19]AGI AG 501 Estado que manifiesta las subdelegaciones... 1.5.1804.

[20]AGCA A1.1 2646 22150 Resumen General 7.5.1804.

of which 55 were adults and 43 were children. The average household size was therefore 5.4, generally consisting of two parents with two or three children, and in addition an elderly parent or the spouse of a married child.[21] Household sizes of some villages in the jurisdiction of Choluteca in 1683 were much lower ranging from 2.3 to 3.3 persons, with many families possessing no children or only one child.[22] By the eighteenth century, however, the population had begun to increase and visitas of Indian villages in the jurisdiction of Tegucigalpa revealed that there many families were living together.[23] It is clear that the ideal of nuclear family residence had not been achieved.


CHANGES IN THE ECONOMY


The major changes in the Indian economy during the colonial period emanated from the demands that were made on Indian lands, labor, and production, over which non-Indians gained increasing control. Although land grants had been allocated to vecinos when towns were founded, it was not until the second half of the sixteenth century that the alienation of Indian lands began in earnest. The Crown was anxious to protect Indian rights to their lands in order to preserve the Indian population and safeguard its tribute income. Indian leaders, in general, were also anxious to protect their villages' lands in order to discourage Indians from deserting their communities, a process that increased the burden of tribute payment and the provision of labor under the repartimiento on those that remained. The Crown and Indian leaders were thus united in the aim of preserving Indian communities and one way of achieving it was by providing them with adequate lands. Although the Crown passed protective legislation that specified the dimensions of village sites and communal land holdings, it was largely ineffective; the only way that Indian villages could safeguard their rights to their lands was through seeking a formal title in the same way as Spaniards. Although Indian communities were free to buy lands, most of them were too poor to do so. Most of lands purchased by Indians were in fact bought under the auspices of cofradías, rather than secular communities. Although it is clear that some Indian villages did increase the amount of land they held, more commonly they suffered alienation of part of their lands, such that Indian villages commonly found themselves with inadequate lands to support their populations; in 1821 the village of Aramecina in Choluteca complained that due to lack of lands in the vicinity of the pueblo its residents were forced to sow their milpas nine leagues away in the mountains.[24] Particularly vulnerable to encroachment were Indian lands in the vicinity of major towns. There were constant complaints that vecinos had either cultivated plots on their lands or more often had grazed their livestock there,

---

[21]AGCA A3.12 511 5345 Autos de los indios del pueblo de Rruruteca 1581.

[22]ANH, P4 L43, 44, 47, 48, 60 Visita of five villages in Choluteca 1683.

[23]ANH P18 L7 Visita de los pueblos...de Tegucigalpa 1703-4, P3 L7 Visitas of pueblos in Tegucigalpa 1744-5.

[24]AGCA A1.1 2 61 Pueblo of Aramecina 9.6.1821.

causing damage to crops and intermixing of herds.[25] Conflicts over the ownership and use of land increased during the eighteenth century as the population expanded and the landless mixed races emerged to increase the pressure on land. However, conflicts arose not only between Indians and non-Indians, but also between Indian villages. One dispute between the villages of Santa Ana and Ojojona appears to have continued throughout the eighteenth century.[26]

Although Indians were regarded as proprietors of the land they held at the time of Spanish conquest, with the rapid alienation of Indian lands, it became clear that some form of protective legislation was required that stipulated the minimum amount of land that an Indian community should hold. According to Gibson, in 1567 it was specified that each Indian village was to hold land within a 500 vara radius (c. 1/4 mile) and in 1687 this was increased to 600 varas.[27] At the same time the Crown tried to protect Indian holdings from being overrun by straying livestock. In 1550 a general order was issued stating that cattle ranches should not be established near Indian villages,[28] and in 1618 another decree specified that estancias de ganado mayor had to be located one and one-half leagues from already established Indian settlements.[29]

The majority of Indian lands were communally owned and they comprised ejidos and *pastos*, which were communal pastures, and *sementeras* or *labranzas*, which were cultivated lands. In addition most Indian communities originally possessed considerable stretches of *monte*, which was used for pasturing and exploited for building materials, wild vegetable products, and game. Ejidos could be assigned to Indian villages by the Audiencia for the raising of livestock,[30] and in 1573 it was stipulated that each Indian village should have one square league of 37 caballerías of land for its ejidos (approximately 4,110 acres).[31] In Honduras, however, it would appear that ejidos seldom reached these specified dimensions, although it is extremely difficult to draw any firm conclusions about the size of ejidos since they fluctuated in size with purchases, law suits, sales, etc. Furthermore, in some cases the term ejido referred to all communal lands, including cultivated lands, and in others only to pasture lands, and in general the documentary record does not specify the types of land included within the ejido. Nevertheless, the evidence for 66 ejidos in Honduras, which were either measured or for which titles were granted from the late seventeenth century onwards, indicates that only seven exceeded the minimum dimension of 37 caballerías, whilst 70 percent were under

---

[25]AGCA A1.30 222 2479 Partial visita of Comayagua 1742, A1.15 195 1949 Indians of Guascorán 1804, A3.9 176 1708 Alcaldes of Tiscagua 19.5.1801, A1.15 210 2371 Indians of Colosuca 1824.

[26]*Indice general de los títulos de tierras*, disputes between Santa Ana and Ojojona in the department of Francisco Morazán.

[27]Gibson, *Aztecs*, pp. 281, 285, 293.

[28]*Recopilación* 2 lib.4 tít.12 ley 12: 42 24.3.1550 and 2.5.1550.

[29]Ibid., 2 lib.6 tít.3 ley 20: 211-2 10.10.1618.

[30]AGCA A1.23 2347 17672 f.6v. cédula 26.4.1549.

[31]*Recopilación* 2 lib.6 tít.3 ley 8: 209 1.12.1573, 10.10.1618.

ten caballerías.[32] There appears to have been only a slight correlation between the size of ejidos and the size of the population. More important seems to have been the availability of land, for in Gracias a Dios few ejidos exceeded 10 caballerías, whereas in Olancho some were over 100 caballerías. The importance that the Crown attached to community lands is seen by the fact that as late as 1754 the Crown was insisting that *jueces subdelegados* should ensure that Indian villages had sufficient ejidos and pastos to support their communities.[33]

Although the aim of the Crown was to ensure that Indian villages had a minimum amount of pasture land, would-be purchasers interpreted it as a maximum. Thus, in 1679 in a dispute between the village of San Francisco de Catacamas and a neighboring landowner over the use of land for raising livestock, the latter was able to argue that Indian villages were only allowed to hold lands for one league around the village and that his cattle were to be found in a different area, which the Indians nevertheless claimed as part of their ejidos.[34] In most cases the limits of the ejido did not follow the geometric pattern that might be interpreted from the law, but naturally followed the configuration of the land, and in fact an ejido might be distributed in a number of parcels scattered over a wide area. Thus although the legal minimum was set in order to protect Indian lands from further encroachment, its effect was the opposite. Potential landowners viewed it as a maximum and any lands over and above the limit, even though they might be possessed legally by Indian communities, were regarded as fit for alienation.

Apart from communal pastures, Indian villages also held other lands within their jurisdictions, which were used for cultivation. Some of the land was worked communally, but it would appear that most was generally allocated to individuals for cultivation. During the sixteenth century crops raised for tribute payment were probably grown on communally worked plots, with the actual size of the plots being specified in the tasación and varying with the number of tributary Indians; it is not clear whether during the seventeenth century after the introduction of per capita tribute payments, items grown for tribute payment were grown on a communal basis or whether Indians grew them on the individual plots they had been allocated by the Indian cabildo. What is clear is that the Crown was anxious that Indian communities should have an income that could be used as security for overcoming disasters, such as an epidemic or harvest failure, and for meeting extraordinary demands, such as occurred when royal officials and priests visited the community. For these purposes in 1577 the Crown ordered that each village should establish a sementera or *milpa de comunidad*.[35] Each Indian was required to cultivate 10 *brazas* of land or each Indian community was required to sow one *fanega de sembradura* for every 100 Indians.[36] The relationship between the 10 brazas of land and

---

[32]*Indice general de los títulos de tierras*; AGI AG 252 Media anatas paid on lands 1712-32; AGCA A1.24 1576 10220 f.7 Título 15.1.1707, A1.24 1576 10220 f.322 Título 13.5.1707, A1.24 1579 10223 f.152 Título 1.6.1712, A1.24 1584 f.272 Título 12.6.1724.

[33]AGCA A1.23 1528 f.125 cédula 15.10.1754; Ots Capdequí, *España en América*, pp. 85-86.

[34]AGCA A1.45 368 3412 Escoto 22.3.1679.

[35]AGCA A1.23 1513 f.525 cédula 8.5.1577, A1.23 1524 f.164 cédula 2.8.1704.

[36]AGCA A1.23 1523 f.184-5 cédulas 26.3.1689, 27.11.1697, A1.38 4778 41248 Instrucción que ha de observar...20.2.1709; *Recopilación* 2 lib.6 tít.4 ley 31: 222 4.6.1582; García Peláez, *Memorias* 1:223.

the milpa de comunidad is far from clear. Whilst the product of these lands went into the caja de comunidad, it is not certain whether they were alternatives or whether the 10 brazas were worked individually and the milpa de comunidad communally. An account of the *bienes de comunidad* of villages in a number of provinces in Honduras in 1786 suggests that the situation varied from village to village; some communities had either a milpa de comunidad or sowed 10 brazas, whereas others had both and in some no distinction was made between the two.[37] Despite repeated orders that each Indian village should possess a caja de comunidad, it seems that villages that were small or too poor did not do so.[38] In other cases, especially where Indians were wage laborers or were absent working under the repartimiento, the contribution to the community fund was commuted to a per capita money payment, which in the eighteenth century was one and one-half reals.[39] Nevertheless, food shortages sometimes led the authorities to insist, though generally without effect, that the contribution should be made in agricultural produce.[40] By the beginning of the nineteenth century the community contribution had been raised differentially so that in the jurisdictions of Tegucigalpa, Olancho, and Gracias a Dios the Indians paid four reals, whilst elsewhere they paid three reals.[41] Its collection was suspended with the suspension of tribute payments between 1811 and 1815.[42] The contribution made by individuals and the income from the working of community lands formed only part of the total income of cajas de comunidad; other income was derived from the rent and sale of lands, and from the hire of draught animals.[43]

A caja de comunidad was administered by a cacique, a parish priest, and a Spanish official, who each possessed a key to the chest. Although the money was supposed to be used for community purposes, it is clear that these officials used its funds as their own private capital. The external control of community funds increased during the eighteenth century as a result of the establishment of central depositories or *arcas* for funds. Arcas were supposed to be established in each *cabecera* to house the community funds from all nearby villages.[44] The extent to which community funds were transferred to provincial centers is unknown; the only piece of evidence comes from villages in the jurisdiction of Gracias a Dios where in 1786 64 percent of their funds, which amounted to just over

---

[37] AGCA A1.30 237 2556 Bienes de comunidad 1786.

[38] AGCA A1.23 1523 f.184-5 cédulas 26.3.1689, 27.11.1679.

[39] AGCA A3.12 186 1898 19.4.1784, A1.30 239 2569 Commission to Barcena on the residencia of Vázquez y Aguilar 14.1.1789.

[40] ANH P22 L24 Alcalde Mayor of Tegucigalpa 3.11.1774; AGCA A3.12 186 1898 19.4.1784.

[41] ANH P13 L19 6.6.1807; AGCA A1.73 385 3513 Payments to the caja de comunidad 1817.

[42] AGCA A1.73 385 3514 Pueblo of Ojojona 7.10.1817, A1.73 385 3516 Pueblo of Santa Ana Ula 30.7.1817, A1.73 385 3518 Pueblo of Alubarén 2.10.1817.

[43] AGCA A1.30 237 2556 Bienes de comunidad 1786; Gibson *Aztecs*, p. 214.

[44] AGCA A1.30 239 2569 Commission to Barcena on the residencia of Vázquez y Aguila 14.1.1789.

3,586 pesos, were to be found in arcas in Gracias a Dios and Comayagua.[45] Even though community funds increased over time, the amount of money that remained under the control of Indian officials in their communities decreased as more and more was lent out to borrowers; in 1800 only 31.3 percent of the community funds in Honduras remained in the villages.[46]

Table 9

COMMUNITY FUNDS IN HONDURAS IN 1784

| Jurisdiction | Number of Cajas | Pesos | Reals | % of Total Funds |
|---|---|---|---|---|
| Comayagua | 19 | 2,798 | 7 | 21.9 |
| Gracias a Dios | 34 | 7,044 | 2.75 | 55.2 |
| Tencoa | 8 | 244 | 7.50 | 1.9 |
| San Pedro | 4 | 368 | 7 | 2.9 |
| Olancho | 4 | 1,981 | 5 | 15.5 |
| Yoro | 3 | 294 | 3 | 2.3 |
| Olanchito | 1 | 21 | 0 | 0.2 |
| TOTAL | 73 | 12,754 | .25 | |

Source: AGCA A1.73 390 3661 Estado que manifiesta los fondos 18.6.1784.

Community funds were supposed to be used to support the elderly, sick, widows and orphans, to maintain the church, and to establish schools. The funds also made good tribute arrears and contributed to the salary of the intendant, and generally acted as security in emergencies, such as epidemics, harvest failure, and enemy attack.[47] For other than very routine purposes Indian communities had to petition the Audiencia to use

[45]AGCA A1.30 237 2556 Bienes de comunidad 1786. The total community funds for other years were:

| 1771 | 7,872 pesos | AGCA A1.73 390 3662 Partial visita of Comayagua 10.2.1771 |
| 1784 | 12,754 pesos 1/4 real | AGCA 1.73 390 3661 Estado que manifiesta los fondos...18.6.1784 |
| 1800 | 17,613 pesos 3 reals | AGCA A1.73 390 3668 Estado de los bienes de comunidad 23.8.1800. |

[46]AGCA A1.73 390 3668 Estado de los bienes de comunidad 23.8.1800.

[47]AGCA A1.23 1531 f.336 cédula 5.11.1782; Gibson, *Aztecs*, p. 215.

their own funds.[48] In many cases permission was denied, either because the case for expenditure could not be justified or the existing funds were inadequate for the purpose. Whilst Indian communities found it increasingly difficult to use their funds, other groups, including officials and borrowers from different backgrounds, found it relatively easy to gain access to them. Indian officials, secular authorities, especially governors and their tenientes, and parish priests with privileged access to community funds often used them for their own private purposes, either by taking money direct from the cajas or by selling agricultural produce belonging to the community.[49] In some instances officials took money from the cajas in payment of goods distributed under the repartimiento de generos, even though the practice was illegal.[50] More commonly, however, community funds were used as loans to individuals. Request for loans had to be made to the Audiencia, and the granting of loans appears to have depended on the size of the funds; in 1784 a request by a vecino of Comayagua for a loan of 10,000 pesos to establish a mortgage company was refused because the funds from villages in the area were inadequate for the purpose (see Table 9).[51] Towards the end of the colonial period community funds were being widely used, to the extent that in 1815 the Audiencia authorized the use of community funds to provide loans to Indians and ladinos at 8 percent interest in order to encourage agricultural production.[52] Three years later it authorized the use of community funds for the development of cochineal.[53] Thus, the situation had been reached where community funds were no longer being used to support Indian communities, but for the general purpose of economic development. Indian communities were, therefore, subsidizing the essentially non-Indian sector, whilst individual Indians who required loans were having to pay interest on them, the capital for which they themselves had provided.

Cofradías, or religious brotherhoods, became important institutions in the economic, social, and religious life of Indian villages during the colonial period. Despite the financial burden that membership of cofradías imposed on Indians, they provided the Indians with a form of corporate identity at a time when outside influences were undermining their communities, and as their wealth increased, they provided them with a form of security and small degree of economic independence. It is not clear how the cofradías acquired their lands. Originally the lands may have formed part of a village's communal land, the product of which was designated for the celebration of particular

---

[48]For examples of petitions to use community funds see: AGCA A1.73 390 3509 Pueblo of Catacamas 26.6.1788, A3.16 517 5433 Pueblo of Opatoro, A1.73 390 3665 Común of Lejamaní 28.9.1802, A1.73 385 3511 Pueblo of Lepaera 1814, A1.73 385 3518 Pueblo of Alubarén 2.10.1817, A1.73 385 3520 Común of Macholoa 1818, A1.73 385 3526 Pueblo of La Iguala 25.2.1819, A1.73 385 3529 Ayuntamiento of Aguanqueterique 23.5.1821. Most of the petitions were for funds to build or rebuild churches and schools, as well as to overcome problems associated with harvest failure or epidemics.

[49]For example, AGCA A1.30 223 2483 Complaints against Governor Parga and his tenientes 1749.

[50]AGCA A1.30 239 2569 Commission to Barcena to take a residencia on Vázquez y Aguilar 14.1.1789.

[51]AGCA A1.73 390 3661 Estado que manifiesta los fondos 6.7.1784.

[52]AGCA A1.1 262 5763 f.1 cédula 23.6.1815.

[53]AGCA A1.77 91 1056 Alcalde Mayor of Tegucigalpa 17.1.1818.

saints. Likewise it is possible that individuals may have designated their own lands for the same purpose, receiving certain privileges in return. In addition cofradías purchased lands from funds accumulated from members' dues. Work on the land was undertaken by members of the brotherhood, and it would appear that such work exempted individuals from other community obligations, such as the repartimiento, leaving the burden of the latter to fall on non-members. This problem plus the fact that the income derived from the land was spent on drunken fiestas in celebration of various saints, at which officials observed they returned to their pagan state and committed "many offences against God," encouraged the Audiencia to try and limit the establishment of cofradías. From 1637 cofradías could not be established without permission. Nevertheless, they continued to be founded, and in 1663 the Audiencia reported that they had been established in such large numbers that in villages where there were no more than 100 Indians, there were 10 or 12 cofradías.[54]

Although separate cofradías were established for whites, ladinos, and Indians, most of the documents do not indicate the racial identity of their members. As such the following discussion draws on accounts of cofradías as a whole, which may not be wholly characteristic of Indian cofradías. It seems likely that cofradías, in terms of their assets, were most important amongst whites and ladinos, in the first case because of their greater financial resources, and in the second because ladino settlements did not have alternative sources of income that could be used to provide security in the event of disasters; in the case of Indian communities cajas de comunidad generally covered such emergencies. Although the origins of cajas de comunidad and cofradías were very different, in their economic organization they were very similar; so much so that there was often confusion as to which lands and animals were owned by the community and which by the cofradía. In 1804 the governor of Honduras was ordered to inform the Audiencia which haciendas belonged to each of the two groups.[55]

Originally founded to celebrate various saints and hold special services, the cofradías developed economic interests. The cofradías were administered by Indian *mayordomos*, who appear to have been unsalaried. They kept the accounts and supervised the sale and purchase of lands and agricultural produce. Keys to the chest in which the funds of the cofradía were kept were held by the alcaldes and the parish priests, again a parallel with the cajas de comunidad and indicating their close integration into the general community organization.[56] Although the administration of the cofradías was supposedly in the hands of Indian mayordomos, it is clear that in many cases the assets of the cofradías were disposed of by the parish priests; in 1803 Indians from the village of Tatumbla complained that the *cura* had sold all of the cofradía's cattle giving him an income of 500 pesos, which he then lent out at 150 percent interest.[57] One way in which parish priests controlled the sale of animals was by possessing the branding irons.[58]

Many cofradías owned land, but others possessed livestock, which they grazed on ejidos. During the eighteenth century, according to the General Index of Land Titles, seventeen land titles and surveys were made in favor of cofradías of all kinds. They were

[54]AGI AG 133 Frasso 20.4.1663.

[55]AGCA A1.24.41 4659 39893 cédula 1804.

[56]Anon., Curato de Tegucigalpa, *RABNH* 28 (1950), p. 389 (30.1.1783).

[57]AGI AG 917 Bishop of Honduras 18.9.1803.

[58]ANH UC Pueblo of Curarén 30.7.1818.

located in Comayagua, Choluteca, Tegucigalpa, and Olancho, and their average size was 11 caballerías, with little differences in size between the areas. Most of the land belonging to cofradías was given over to the raising of livestock, particularly cattle, horses, and mules, and Fr. Cadiñanos' accounts for 1791 indicate that cofradías generally possessed several hundred head of livestock. Probably the majority of cattle were consumed locally, although there is evidence that some were exported illegally from Gracias a Dios to Verapaz, whilst others found their way to the cattle fair at Jalpatagua.[59] Lands owned by cofradías were not always farmed by members of the cofradías themselves, but they were rented out to tenants. In addition the capital owned by cofradías was loaned at 5 percent rate of interest. From these sources, plus the dues paid by members, the cofradías received their income. The most wealthy cofradías were in Choluteca where they possessed enormous herds of cattle, and even in Gracias a Dios, which was not particularly renowned for cattle raising, it was said that there were haciendas with 2-4,000 head of cattle, "especially in haciendas belonging to cofradías."[60] There is no doubt that cofradías in Honduras were wealthier than those in the Valley of Mexico described by Gibson, who suggests that in a good year a cofradía would probably only make 10 to 20 pesos profit;[61] in Honduras many cofradías were sufficiently wealthy to make loans of several hundred pesos.[62] Furthermore, Fr. Cadiñanos noted that cofradías in Honduras had been much wealthier, but many of those who had received loans had died bankrupt, so that the loans were never repaid.[63]

The majority of cultivated lands owned by the community were worked individually as in pre-Columbian times. Land was allotted to the heads of families and could be inherited by male descendants. If there were no heirs or the holder moved to another village then the land reverted to the community for reallocation by the Indian cabildo. There were instances of favoritism and petty jealousies affecting the allocation and revocation of lands, so that in 1810 it was recommended that Indians should be given plots of land that were inalienable and could be inherited, since it was argued that this would provide them with an incentive to improve production.[64] This recommendation appears to have produced some effect a few years later. A decree issued in 1812 and repeated in 1820 ordered that all married Indians and those over 25 should be given lands as near as possible to Indian villages. The lands were not to be confiscated from individuals or Indian communities, except where the lands owned by the latter were extensive compared to the size of the population, when up to 50 percent could be used for the purpose.[65] The decree clearly reflects the dilemma that the authorities faced; whilst they clearly wished to develop agriculture, they also wanted to preserve the lands of

---

[59]AGCA A3.3 38 744 (Guatemala) 1791.

[60]Ibid.

[61]Gibson, *Aztecs*, p. 130.

[62]Archivo de Comayagua, Cofradías of Honduras. Unclassified material in the former cathedral of Comayagua gives examples of loans, e.g., 500 pesos from Ojojona and 1,200 pesos from Colama.

[63]AGI AG 578 Fr. Cadiñanos 20.10.1791.

[64]AGI AG 627 Larrazábal 20.10.1810; Martínez Peláez, *Patria del Criollo*, pp. 170-71.

[65]AGCA A1.23 1538 f.186 cédula 9.12.1812, A1.23 1543 f. 407 cédula 29.4.1820.

Indian communities in order to keep the Indians there. Unfortunately there is no evidence of the extent to which the decrees issued at the beginning of the nineteenth century resulted in the creation of private holdings from ejidal or other lands.

In addition to lands that were owned by the community by right, there were other lands, generally in the vicinity of the village, that had been purchased either by the community or by individual Indians. The opportunity for Indians to buy land during the colonial period was severely limited by their low income and consequent lack of savings. Although the evidence is scant, it is clear that most Indian purchasers of land were caciques and *principales*.[66]

Apart from the loss of land, perhaps the most important influence on Indian agriculture was the decline in labor inputs. During the last half of the sixteenth century and the first half of the seventeenth century the Indian population continued to decline and, although some legislation, such as the abolition of personal service, attempted to relieve the burden of work falling on those that remained, other forms of exploitation soon emerged to take their place. Although the payment of tribute remained a constant drain on Indian resources, the main complaints made by Indian communities were directed at the repartimiento and at the services and forced sales demanded by local priests, official visitors, and other Spanish officials, notably the tenientes and alcaldes mayores. The repartimiento in particular was incompatible with subsistence activities since it often necessitated the prolonged absence of Indians from their villages at critical times in the agricultural year. Although orders were issued that Indians were not to be employed at the times of land clearance, sowing, and harvest, they were largely ignored, such that, as one villager in the jurisdiction of Gracias a Dios described it in 1787, "if the land is cleared, it is not sown, and if it is sown, it is not weeded, and if it is weeded then the crop is not harvested, because this is the main time that we are burdened with the said repartimientos."[67] Although the impact of the repartimiento on sources of labor for subsistence activities was greatest at sowing and harvesting, it also affected production at other times of the year, when weeding, fencing, and the protection of crops from straying animals was necessary. There is no evidence to suggest that the repartimiento for different purposes affected Indian agricultural production in different ways, although it seems likely that the repartimiento for mining and defense might have had more adverse effects since they involved greater travelling distances and longer periods of absence. Nevertheless Indians working under the repartimiento in agriculture, mining, and defense complained equally that it affected their ability to provide for their own subsistence

---

[66]*Indice general de los títulos de tierras*; AGI AG 252 Media anatas paid on lands 1712-32; AGI AG 264 Ventas y composiciones de tierras 1748-51.

[67]AGCA A3.16 517 5427 Justicias y común...de Talgua 1787.

needs.[68] On top of this Indians were required to produce crops and items to meet tribute demands and to pay for the goods that were distributed under the repartimiento de generos, as well as to meet a whole variety of demands for personal service. As such the Indians complained that they suffered food shortages such that their wives and children starved, and they were forced to beg for food or sell their belongings to survive.[69]

Whilst the pressures on Indian lands and labor increased, there appear to have been few changes in the nature of production, including the types of crops and animals raised, and the techniques employed. Probably most Indian families cultivated a small milpa of maize and beans and many may have possessed a platanal, from which they obtained plantains. In addition they probably had a kitchen garden, where they raised spices, such as peppers and garlic, a few vegetables, and fruit trees. Small patches of sugar cane and cotton may also have been cultivated.

Due to tradition and the fact that it remained the major item paid as tribute by the Indians, maize continued to be the most important crop raised. Maize generally grew well throughout Honduras. Despite the decline in labor inputs, yields remained as high as 1:200 to 1:300.[70] Several authors indicated that in Honduras three or four sowings were possible,[71] but in most cases there were probably only two harvests a year. The first harvest in late August, September, or early October, was generally the largest, but the second harvest by virtue of its smaller size commanded higher prices. There were nevertheless many difficulties, excluding those of increasing shortages of land and labor already discussed, which intervened to cause shortages of the crop. Some of the difficulties were more widespread than others and some affected other crops as well as maize. The first problem, which affected maize in particular, was the shortage of rain during the growing season.[72] Although some maize was grown on irrigated lands in

---

[68]See cédulas AGCA A1.23 1517 f.3 25.5.1641 and A1.23 1563 f.209 7.3.1667. The complaints from the Indian villages include:
Teupacente AGCA A3.12 509 5293 4.5.1639; Villages of Tegucigalpa AGCA A3.12 509 5289 16.6.1649; Aguanqueterique ANH P2 L3 1669; Santa Ana Ula AGCA A3.16 511 5340 23.3.1721; Villages of Comayagua AGCA A1.30 222 2479 1742; Celilaca AGCA A1.15 64 770 2.6.1761; Chucuyuco AGCA A1.15 64 772 3.3.1762; Piraera, Erandique, Gualmoaca AGCA A3.12 86 1897 2.5.1780; Talgua AGCA A3.16 517 5427 1787; General AGCA A3.9 175 1693 21.8.1787; Macholoa AGCA A3.12 187 1901 1791; Texíguat AGCA A3.9 175 1697 17.6.1791; Lepaera AGCA A3.16 194 2012 1795; Puringla AGCA A3.12 187 1905 9.2.1795, 15.3.1797.

[69]AGCA A3.16 194 2012 Quejas de los indios de Lepaera 1795.

[70]AGI PAT 183-1-16 Antonelli and López de Quintanillas 7.10.1590, AG 44 Montoso Castillo 3.8.1590, AG 501 Anguiano 10.5.1804.

[71]Herrera, Historia general 9 dec.4 lib.8 cap.3: 105-6; Torquemada, Monarquía Indiana, p. 334; Alcedo, Diccionario 1: 367.

[72]AGI AG 501 Anguiano 10.5.1804; AGCA A3.16 197 2102 Villages in Choluteca 5.8.1816.

Comayagua and Tencoa,[73] irrigation was not widespread and the lack of rain generally resulted in a poor harvest and in maize having to be imported from Nicaragua.[74] Once the seed had been sown two other problems could beset the crop. First, the crop was sometimes devoured by plagues of locusts. This appears to have been a fairly common problem that affected other cereal crops and cotton.[75] Other threats to standing crops were straying livestock, particularly cattle, and birds.[76] Human factors also influenced the availability of maize. They included whether or not jueces de milpas had been appointed to ensure that the Indians planted sufficient maize, and the extent to which the crop was exported.[77] All of these factors resulted in considerable fluctuations in the price of maize, which in the eighteenth century varied between three and six pesos a fanega according to the season.[78] The unreliability of harvests and the fluctuating prices of maize encouraged the Indians to petition the Audiencia to pay tribute in cash rather than kind.

Other subsistence crops that had been commonly grown in the pre-Columbian period and which continued to be grown in the colonial period included beans, sweet and chili peppers, plantains, and sweet potatoes. Beans were an important item of tribute, though they were not levied so universally as maize, and occasionally chili peppers were also paid as tribute.[79] Although maize remained the Indian staple, it would appear that other crops, particularly root crops and fruit trees, which were less affected by problems of weather, locusts, and straying animals, assumed a more important role in the Indian diet during the colonial period. Plantains in particular are noted much more frequently in the documentary record of the eighteenth century. Many of the plantains were probably not cultivated in the true sense of the word, but grew wild and were harvested when needed, particularly in times of shortage.[80] Cultivated tree crops also constituted a

---

[73]AGCA A1.30 237 2556 Bienes de comunidad 1786; AGI AG 501 Anguiano 10.5.1804.

[74]BAGG 1:29-39 Alcalde Mayor of Tegucigalpa 20.7.1743; AGCA A3.16 197 2102 Villages in Choluteca 5.8.1816.

[75]ANH P22 L24 Alcalde Mayor of Tegucigalpa 3.11.1774; AGCA A3.16 515 5414 Alcaldes y común de Gualala 18.10.1777, A3.16 515 5416 Alcalde y común de Ylamatepeque 25.11.1777, A1.73 390 3665 Común de Lejamaní 27.9.1802.

[76]AGCA A1.45 368 3409 Pueblo of Aguanqueterique 1638, A3.12 187 1903 Pueblo of Chinacla 1791, A3.12 187 1905 Pueblo of Puringla 9.2.1795.

[77]See the discussion of jueces de milpas in Chapter 11 and ANH P2 L60 1672, P6 L40 17.7.1712.

[78]AGCA A3.3 136 1214 On provisions for Fort Omoa 1757, A3.16 194 2012 Quejas de los indios de Lepaera 25.2.1796; ANH P20 L25 Arancel 1802, P13 L12 Arancel 1810.

[79]AGI CO 988 Tasaciones 1562; AGCA A3.16 511 5345-6 Visitas of Rruruteca and Caingala 1581; RAHM CM 49 f.73-92 Fernández del Pulgar, no date (seventeenth century); Herrera, *Historia general* 9 dec.4 lib.8 cap.3: 105-6; Torquemada, *Monarquía Indiana*, p. 334.

[80]AGCA A3.12 509 5299 Governor of Comayagua 10.9.1776; AGI AG 501 Anguiano 10.5.1804.

source of food for the Indians, although most probably never possessed more than a few trees. Native fruit trees, such as papayas, annonas, jocotes, mammees, sapotes, nísperos, avocado pears, and pineapples, probably remained the most important trees cultivated, although a few introduced species such as the citrus fruits and banana, were probably adopted quite widely. Other introduced species such as apples, pears, peaches, and quinces were probably more common in European gardens. At the beginning of the nineteenth century, if not earlier, a number of trees of Asian origin were introduced into Central America through Trujillo. They included the now familiar mango (*Mangifera indica* L.), cinnamon (*Cinnamomum zeylanicum* Breyn.), and the breadfruit (*Artocarpus communis* J.R. and G. Forst).[81]

Cacao had played an important role in the economy in pre-Columbian times, when it had been a major item of trade between the Nahuatl traders of northern Honduras and the Maya, but its production declined markedly in importance during the colonial period. The main reason for the decline was the decrease in the Indian population, such that cacao groves could not be maintained. Nevertheless, Indians continued to cultivate small amounts for their own consumption, particularly in northern Honduras,[82] where they also paid tribute in cacao into the seventeenth century.[83] Thus many observers identified cacao as one of the most important crops grown in northern Honduras, particularly in the Ulúa and Aguan valleys.[84] There consumption became more widespread than it had been in pre-Columbian times when it had been restricted to the aristocracy;[85] in the eighteenth century one observer noted that the Indians drank chocolate twice a day, and sometimes three or four times a day, but by then most of the cacao was being collected from wild trees.[86]

Against the traditional staple maize, wheat made little headway. During the first half of the sixteenth century wheat cultivation was established in Honduras and the authorities tried to encourage the Indians to plant wheat by demanding that it should be paid as tribute. During the late sixteenth and seventeenth centuries, however, demands for tribute to be paid in wheat declined and by 1662 only one village in Honduras, La

---

[81]AGI AG 656 N273 f.197 Gaçeta de Guatemala 23.8.1802.

[82]AGCA A1.12 50 493 Autos...15.9.1710, A1.45 368 3414 Village of Nuestra Señora de la Candelaria nombrado Masca 6.3.1714.

[83]AGI CO 987 Tasaciones 1555-6, AG 53 Pedro de Casa 1564; AGCA A3.16 236 2421 Tasación of Espoloncal 31.5.1583, A3.16 311 5347 Indians of Naco 1588; AGI CO 990 Tasaciones 1598; AGCA A3.16 511 5313 List of encomiendas 1662, A3.16 190 1919 Tasación de Tatumbla 2.10.1662, A3.16 190 1928 Confirmation of the encomienda of Alonso de Oseguera 10.5.1662.

[84]AGI AG 44 Procurador of Trujillo no date (1577?); CDI 19:239-304 Proposiciones del Marqués de Varinas 1677; AGI AG 164 Cabildo eclesiástico of Comayagua 10.2.1680; López de Velasco, *Geografía y descripción universal*, pp. 310-12; Ponce, *Relación breve*, p. 348; Vázquez de Espinosa, *Compendium and Description*, p. 246.

[85]RAHM CM 49 f.73-92 Fernández del Pulgar, no date (seventeenth century); Herrera, *Historia general* 9 dec.4 cap.3:106-7; Torquemada, *Monarquía Indiana*, p. 335.

[86]AGI AG 578 Fr. Cadiñanos 20.10.1791, AG 501 Anguiano 10.5.1804, AG 656 N76 ff.225-7 Gaçeta de Guatemala 1798.

Guarcha, was paying in wheat.[87]  Two factors were probably responsible for the declining interest in developing Indian wheat production: first, the Spanish could obtain supplies of wheat from their own estates that were thriving in the area; second, wheat was produced by a completely different system of cultivation than maize.  The former required the clearance of special fields and the introduction of draught animals and plows. The availability of alternative supplies of wheat and the effort involved in teaching the Indians how to cultivate it discouraged Indian production.  From the Indians' point of view, there was no incentive to adopt wheat, whilst their own staple maize was easier to cultivate and produced much higher yields.  For the same reasons they did not adopt the cultivation of rice, although some was grown around Comayagua in the eighteenth century.[88]

It seems unlikely that techniques of cultivation changed very much during the colonial period.  Although metal tools, such as hoes, machetes, and knives, became more readily available, there is no evidence that the plow--the Mediterranean scratch plow--was adopted by the Indians for wheat cultivation.  Where the Indians were required to provide wheat as an item of tribute, encomenderos were obliged to provide the necessary tools and animals.[89]  On the negative side it is clear that techniques of irrigation fell out of use as the Indian population declined and could not maintain such intensive forms of production.

During the second half of the sixteenth century sources of animal protein increased as the Indians became familiar with European animals and started to raise them; by the eighteenth century livestock had achieved a prominent position in the Indian economy.  The chicken, which had been adopted most readily in the first half of the sixteenth century, continued to be an important source of food and item of tribute.  All Indian households were required to raise chickens and at the time of visitas those who did not possess them were fined.  Initially the Indians had been frightened of the larger domesticated animals, but in the process of tending the livestock of encomenderos and other Spaniards, they became more familiar with them and began to raise them themselves.  The raising of livestock by Indians was initially objected to by the Spanish who hoped to monopolize production, but in 1551 the Crown ordered that Indians were to be free to raise livestock as they wished;[90] by the eighteenth century probably most Indian villages possessed several hundred head of cattle, and some communities in Comayagua possessed sheep.[91]  Most of the livestock were communally owned and grazed on village ejidos, but small numbers may have been owned by private individuals. Accounts of animals belonging to Indian communities and to cofradías show clearly that more animals were owned by cofradías, although the evidence for cofradías includes non-Indian as well as Indian cofradías.  In the major livestock-raising areas herds of cattle

---

[87]AGCA A3.16 511 5313 List of encomiendas 1662.

[88]BAGG 1:29-39 Alcalde Mayor of Tegucigalpa 20.7.1743; AGI AG 472 Estado de las siembras 15.9.1786, AG 578 Fr. Cadiñanos 20.10.1791; AGCA A1.73 390 3665 Común de Lejamaní 27.9.1802, A1.17 2335 17517 Intendant Anguiano 15.12.1818.

[89]AGCA A3.12 511 5345-6 Visitas of Rruruteca and Caingala 1581.

[90]*Recopilación* 2 lib.6 tít.1 ley 22: 194 17.12.1551.

[91]AGCA A1.30 237 2556 Bienes de comunidad 1786.

belonging to cofradías sometimes exceeded 1,000.[92] The largest herds were to be found in Choluteca and eastern Honduras, although the largest number of cattle belong to cofradías was to be found in Tegucigalpa.

It would appear that the exploitation of wild plants and animals as sources of food declined considerably during the colonial period, although perhaps not as dramatically as the lack of documentary evidence might suggest. Undoubtedly the main reasons for this were the restriction of areas available for such activities, as a result of the establishment of haciendas, and the reduction in labor time available to carry them out. The need for the dietary supplements that these activities provided also declined as the availability of meat increased. Collecting, hunting, and fishing thus became activities that were undertaken either in times of shortage or where wild products had some commercial value. In the latter case, particularly important were sarsaparilla, honey, beeswax, and a variety of gums, resins, and balsams that were collected by the Indians particularly in northern Honduras.[93] Another commercial activity that exploited natural resources was salt making. This was concentrated in Choluteca and it supplied domestic needs, including those of the mining industry.[94]

A large number of activities were undertaken by the Indians not only to provide for their own needs, but also to meet tribute demands and the often illegal demands of Spanish officials and priests.[95] They included the manufacture of many household items such as rush and palm mats, wooden chairs, and a variety of cooking and storage vessels. They also produced cotton cloth, and shoes and sandals made from leather and rope. A craft that developed significantly during the colonial period was the working of leather. Although deer hides had been used for a variety of items in pre-Columbian times, during the colonial period leather became more generally available in the form of cattle hides, and the Indians learnt leather-working techniques from the Spanish. As well as being used for footwear, leather was important in the manufacture of riding equipment: bridles, saddles, reins, halters, leather seats, and saddle bags.[96]

As already noted some Indians preferred to subsist by earning wages as laborers either in the towns, on estates, or in the mines. Very few Indians would have been able to

---

[92]Compare AGCA A1.73 390 3662 Partial visita of Comayagua 10.2.1771, with AGI AG 578 Fr. Cadiñanos 20.10.1791.

[93]AGI AG 44 Procurador of Trujillo, no date, PAT 183-1-16 Antonelli and López de Quintanillas 7.10.1590, AG 49 Romero 26.2.1595, AG 164 Bishop of Honduras 19.7.1620; CDI 19:239-304 Proposiciones del Marqués de Varinas 1677; AGI AG 164 Cabildo eclesiástico of Comayagua 10.2.1680, AG 29 Audiencia 21.2.1686; BNM 3047 ff. 128-135v. no author, no date; BRP 2537 Descripción General I f.298, no author, no date; AGI AG 452 Relación de las providencias económicas 3.1.1804, AG 501 Anguiano 10.5.1804, AG 501 Informe de la provincia de Honduras 20.2.1816; Ponce, *Relación breve*, pp. 345, 348; Vázquez de Espinosa, *Compendium and Description*, pp. 308, 312; López de Velasco, *Geografía y descripción universal*, pp. 244, 246.

[94]AGI AG 257 Memorial de los pueblos...Valverde, no date; ANH P26 L44 3.6.1785, UC Vela 16.12.1812; AGCA A1.1 2 61 Pueblo de Aramecina 9.6.1821.

[95]AGCA A3.16 511 5345-6 Visitas of Rruruteca and Caingala 1581; AGCA A3.12 187 1901 Vázquez 5.11.1789; ANH UC Partido de Texíguat 29.5.1820, UC Zelaya 27.6.1820.

[96]AGCA A3.12 187 1901 Vázquez 5.11.1789; ANH UC Zelaya 27.6.1820.

live independent lives, for example as shopkeepers or artisans, but some may have managed to exist in the mining areas as gurruguces; the majority would have assumed routine occupations. On the whole most of those who were self-employed or possessed skilled jobs were ladinos. The types of occupations existing in the towns may be illustrated by a list of those found in Comayagua in 1809. There were carpenters, masons, lime-makers, grinders, silversmiths, weavers, tailors, shoemakers, tanners, muleteers, potters, and firework-makers.[97]

Whereas a proportion of extra-communal trade in pre-Columbian times was in luxury items and slaves, during the colonial period agricultural produce and craft products constituted the basis of trade. Indians were in theory free to market their produce where they wished and they were not required to pay the alcabala on goods they sold.[98] However, Indians were often coerced into selling their goods to Spanish officials, encomenderos, and priests at very low prices. The worst offenders were tenientes, alcaldes mayores, and jueces de milpas, who it was said were more like "traders and merchants" than royal officials.[99] Not only were Indians forced to sell their products at low prices, but in addition they were coerced into buying small manufactures, such as pieces of European cloth, tools, knives, combs, and candles, at high prices that had to be paid for in kind, sometimes with possessions such as cacao trees or horses. Although forced sales to Indians were forbidden by law, they continued throughout the colonial period and they were a bitter source of complaint by Indians.[100] In the middle of the eighteenth century each village in Tegucigalpa was forced to receive between 500 and 600 pesos of goods, mainly cloth, for distribution amongst its inhabitants. The Indians were given a year to pay, but it was said that they were so poor that all that they could offer in payment were "a few chickens, fish and fruit," such that they had to spend all the wages they had earned in the mines to pay for them.[101] Apart from Spanish officials and priests, there were other non-Indian traders who bought up Indian produce and in turn supplied the Indians with manufactures. Initially most of the traders were peripatetic, because they were only permitted to stay in each Indian village for three days,[102] but from 1632 at least non-Indians were permitted to establish shops and stalls in Indian villages as long as they paid an annual tax.[103] There were 30 to 35 commercial houses in Guatemala that received about 1,000 pesos worth of goods from Cadiz every year.[104] These goods were then distributed to merchants and traders for sale through shops in the

---

[97] AGI AG 796 Intendant of Comayagua 24.5.1809.

[98] *Recopilación* 2 lib.8 tít.13 ley 24: 503 31.8.1600.

[99] AGI AG 967 Regidores of Choluteca 12.11.1602.

[100] *Recopilación* 2 lib.8 tít.1 ley 25: 195 12.5.1551, 30.1.1567. For example, AGI AG 967 Regidores of Choluteca 12.11.1602; AGCA A1.23 1514 f.219 Guerra de Ayala 21.5.1611; AGI AG 164 Bishop of Honduras 20.10.1684; AGCA A1.30 223 2479 Visita of Comayagua 1742; AGI IG 1525 Anguiano 14.5.1797.

[101] BAGG 2: 462-73 Rossa y Aguayo 3.2.1766.

[102] *Recopilación* 2 lib.6 tít.3 ley 23: 212 21.11.1600.

[103] AGCA A1.23 1516 f.47 cédula 28.3.1632.

[104] AGI AG 627 Larrazábal 20.10.1800.

major towns and mining areas. Nevertheless, probably few of the items reached Indian hands unless under coercion from officials. Most European goods were extremely expensive; the wholesale price for European cloth was 60 percent higher than in Cadiz and the retail price 90 percent higher.[105] The most that Indians would have been able to afford was probably cloth woven in Guatemala or El Salvador that they could wear on festive occasions.[106] Indians not only complained about the prices that merchants and traders charged for their goods, but also the currency frauds that they committed. These included tampering with the item of exchange or setting artificially high exchange rates for cacao beans or silver coins.[107] Indians generally preferred to trade using cacao beans rather than metal coins, because there was greater possibility of fraud with the latter. Apart from trade with non-Indians, the Indians exchanged items between themselves by barter, rather than by sale or purchase. All that Indians had to sell were small quantities of food they had processed, such as cheese or sweets, and a few craft items, such as hats, baskets, pots, and leather articles.[108] Although Indians were free to hold their own markets, with the Indians possessing few items for sale and with trade being monopolized by officials, it is uncertain whether regular markets were held. If they were held, it is not known whether they were regulated according to pre-Columbian traditions or whether their periodicity changed to follow the Christian calendar.

## CHANGES IN THE SOCIOPOLITICAL ORGANIZATION

Changes in the social and political organization of Indian communities that had been initiated in the first half of the sixteenth century were consolidated subsequently. The legal status of caciques was more clearly specified and a large number of secular and ecclesiastical posts, to which Indians were either elected or appointed, were created in Indian villages. Whilst the existence of these posts maintained a hierarchical element in the social organization of Indian communities, the general effect of the changes was to bring about social levelling. At the family level of organization changes occurred in response to the decline in the Indian population and its increasing mobility, which brought about falling marriage rates and smaller families.

The reduction in the social status of Indian caciques vis-à-vis the rest of the Indian population and the general levelling of social classes continued. Although the social status of individuals was determined in part by the status their ancestors had held in pre-Columbian times, it was also affected by the political role they played. At the top of the social ladder were caciques, whose superior social position was reinforced by legal privileges. Nevertheless compared to the privileges they had possessed in pre-Columbian times these privileges were limited; they were no longer permitted to own Indian slaves or

---

[105]BAGG 7:157-75 20.1.1800.

[106]ANH UC Partido de Texíguat 29.5.1820.

[107]AGI AG 18 Bernal del Cano 5.9.1648, AG 19 Conde de Santiago 12.7.1656.

[108]ANH UC Zelaya 27.6.1820; AGCA A3.16 197 2117 Pueblos of Tencoa 1820, A1.1 2 61 Pueblo of Aramecina 9.6.1821.

to levy tribute and services from their communities.[109] Furthermore, even though caciques were given legal privileges, they were often ignored; caciques complained that their status was not recognized by Spanish officials who often forced them to perform tasks that were humiliating and caused them to lose respect in their communities.[110] Although the position of cacique was hereditary passing through the male line, the Spanish tried to gain control over the succession of office holders. First, the Crown ruled that caciques were to be of pure Indian descent and that any mestizos who held office, which was a reasonable possibility given the encouragement of marriages between Spaniards and Indian nobles in the early colonial period, were to be replaced.[111] Second, probably from the sixteenth century onwards governors began to appoint *indios gobernadores*, particularly when there was a problem of succession created by there being no male heir or the heir being too young to assume office.[112] Whilst the title of "indio gobernador" could be given to a cacique, it is clear that the faculty of Spanish officials to make such appointments opened the way for the imposition of Indian leaders or even non-Indians on Indian communities in denial of the hereditary claims of caciques.

Despite the gradual erosion of the powers and status of caciques they still held relatively privileged positions in Indian society, which were reinforced by their relative wealth. It is significant that the majority of Indians who purchased land in the colonial period were caciques and principales. Their wealth, although often reduced by the loss of land and tribute income, had its basis in the pre-Columbian period, and in the colonial period it was supplemented from community funds to which, in their official capacity, they had access and could use as their own private capital. They also received bribes from non-Indians for the rent or purchase of lands and for the use of Indian labor, and from Indians hoping for exemption from the repartimiento. Although the authorities tried to control the use of community funds and the sale of Indian lands by caciques by ordering that all transactions should be conducted in front of royal officials, they achieved little success and only occasionally were charges brought against caciques for malpractice.[113] Despite the reduction in the powers and status of caciques, their positions were still seen to be superior to that of the majority of Indians, to the extent that some commoners tried to establish themselves as caciques. The main advantages of the position were that it brought exemption from tribute payment and labor services.

Beneath the caciques and indios gobernadores in the social structure were the elected Indian officials, the alcaldes and regidores, who formed the cabildo modelled on those established in Spanish towns. Indian cabildos were probably introduced in the mid-sixteenth century and they were considered essential for the civilization of the Indians and to establish law and order.[114] The number of alcaldes and regidores elected in any one village was established by law; villages of under 80 houses were to have only one alcalde

---

[109]*Recopilación* 2 lib.6 tít.2 ley.3: 202 6.11.1538, 26.10.1541, 8.2.1588 and lib.6 tít.7 ley 10: 247 8.7.1577; AGI AG 128 Relación y forma que el Lic. Palacio...no date.

[110]AGI AG 520 Ordenanzas 28.6.1568.

[111]*Recopilación* 2 lib.6 tít.7 ley 6: 246 11.1.1576, 5.3.1576.

[112]Gibson, *Aztecs*, pp. 167-68, notes this practice in the Valley of Mexico.

[113]AGI AG 128 Relación y forma que el Lic. Palacio...no date.

[114]Ibid. Indian cabildos were introduced widely into neighboring Nicaragua in the 1550s (AGI AG 52 Lic. Cavallón 25.2.1555).

and one regidor, and those over 80 houses were to have two alcaldes and between two and four regidores depending on the size of the village.[115] When villages were too small to support a cabildo they were generally amalgamated.[116] Elections to the cabildo were to be made annually and Indians were not to serve for consecutive periods. Spanish officials were to ensure that people of bad character were not elected and they were to encourage the election of those who spoke Spanish. Although elections were theoretically free, they were open to manipulation by those with vested interests, such as local officials, encomenderos and priests, with the result that unpopular candidates might be appointed; in some cases no elections were held but candidates names were sent forward for approval. Despite the fact that all adult male Indians were eligible for election it seems likely that the posts circulated amongst a relatively small group of Indians and that they were often held for a number of consecutive years. Offices had to be confirmed by the Spanish authorities and for this purpose Indians often had to travel miles to Spanish towns to receive the vara--the insignia of office. The cabildo controlled all political affairs in the community in conjunction with the cacique. The tasks performed by the alcaldes and regidores were very similar, though the former acted as judges in local courts and were accorded greater respect; in the absence of a Spanish official they could even arrest non-Indians for committing offenses in Indian communities.[117] The most important duties undertaken by these Indian officials were the collection of tribute and the selection of Indians to serve under the repartimiento, but their other duties included the distribution of goods under the repartimiento de generos, the regulation of land sales and rents, the prevention and punishment of minor crimes, the maintenance of public buildings and roads, the supervision of markets, the provision of adequate water supplies, and the organization of public ceremonies. They also represented the community in its contacts with the Spanish administration over such matters as excessive tribute exactions or land encroachment.

The office of alcalde or regidor brought with it exemption from tribute payment and labor services. Through the access to community funds and Indian tribute that these offices provided, and through receiving bribes in the same way as caciques, these officials could also improve their financial status. Despite the advantages these positions bestowed on the holders, Indians were generally reluctant to stand for election. On the whole the social, political, and financial advantages that the offices offered were outweighed by the burden of work they imposed. The collection of tribute and the provision of labor under the repartimiento became more difficult as Indians began to desert their villages in search of employment elsewhere. Alcaldes were thus forced to travel around the countryside, sometimes with the help of *alguaciles de mandón*, searching for Indians who owed tribute and who were required for the repartimiento. The failure of alcaldes and regidores to submit the stipulated amount of tribute or quota of Indians to work under the repartimiento could result in them being fined, imprisoned or

---

[115]*Recopilación* 2 lib.6 tít.3 ley 15: 210 10.10.1618; AGCA A1.1 2 35 Testimony of elections in Tegucigalpa 1743.

[116]See the discussion of the amalgamation of Rocteca and Quelala in the jurisdiction of Comayagua (AGCA A3.16.3 513 5373 1739.

[117]*Recopilación* 2 lib.6 tít.3 ley 17: 211 11.8.1563.

having their goods confiscated.[118]  To most Indians office holding was yet another burden that had to be borne and the Indians often preferred to abandon their villages rather than assume office.  They were also discouraged by the fact that Indian cabildos, in enforcing Spanish laws and in organizing tribute collection and labor under the repartimiento, were regarded as institutions for their exploitation, rather than as platforms for the expression of their political views.

Other members of Indian cabildos were alguaciles, or local constables, escribanos, who looked after the community records, and standard bearers, or alféreces.  Some alguaciles had special responsibilities for the collection of tribute and for supervising the local hostelry and these were known as alguaciles de mandón and *alguaciles de mesón* respectively.  Officials of lesser importance who were not members of the cabildo were mayordomos, who were appointed to look after the community and cofradía lands, and cantores, sacristanes, and fiscales, who were attached to local churches and were appointed by the clergy.  Cantores and sacristanes assisted at services and looked after the ornaments and church buildings, whilst fiscales were appointed to summon people to mass.[119]  All of these officials were exempt from tribute payment and the repartimiento.

The Spanish only recognized the higher social status of caciques, their eldest sons and Indian officials, whilst social differences within the largest class, that of commoners, went unrecognized.  There were probably variations in the socioeconomic status of commoners, some of which may have had their origins in the pre-Columbian period, but these differences are not clearly revealed in the documentary record, and any that might have existed fade into insignificance when compared to differences between Indians and other races.

At the family level further changes in social organization occurred, although most of them were brought about not by the effective imposition of Spanish laws, but as a result of the broader demographic and economic changes that were occurring in Honduran society.  The Spanish tried to impose monogamy and Christian standards of morality in family life, by making bigamy illegal and punishing adultery.[120]  Legally Indians were free to choose their own marriage partners.[121]  Although this meant that they could choose non-Indian spouses, such unions were discouraged indirectly by other legislation that encouraged residential segregation.[122]  The number of Indians who did marry non-Indians was very small, at least in Indian communities; unfortunately there is no evidence for the character of Indian marriages in the towns, on estates, or in the mining areas, where one would expect such marriages to be more common.  The small percentage of Indians marrying non-Indian partners is evident from *padrones* of 11 villages in western Honduras for 1703 and 1722 which show that under 1 percent of

---

[118]AGCA A3.12 509 5289 Alcaldes and Indians of Pueblos in Tegucigalpa 18.6.1649, A3.16 192 1972 Testimonio de diligencias practicadas 19.6.1751, A3.16 527 5533 6.2.1767.

[119]*Recopilación* 2 lib.6 tít.3 leyes 6 and 7: 208-9 10.10.1618; AGCA A1.1 2 35 Testimony of elections in Tegucigalpa 1743.

[120]*Recopilación* 2 lib.6 tít.1 ley 4: 190 13.7.1530, lib.6 tít.1 ley 5: 190 17.12.1551. Sometimes Indians were imprisoned for bigamy. For example, AGCA A3.16 945 17642 Padron of Reitoca 5.9.1750.

[121]*Recopilación* 2 lib.6 tít.1 ley 2: 190 19.10.1514 etc.

[122]Ibid., 2 lib.6 tít.3 ley 21: 212 2.5.1563 to 12.7.1600.

couples comprised one partner of non-Indian race;[123] by the middle of the eighteenth century the percentage of mixed marriages in western and central Honduras had risen only slightly to just over 1 percent.[124] There was undoubtedly more contact between the races than these figures suggest, because many of the relationships between Indians and non-Indians were of a casual nature, but it is also clear that the number of mixed marriages was higher in some regions than others. For example, in the mid-eighteenth century over 5 percent of marriages in San Pedro were mixed marriages, and although figures are not available for the whole of the jurisdiction of Tegucigalpa, padrones for the three villages of Comayaguela, Tegucigalpa, and Tamara in 1751 suggest that about 6 percent of Indians were married to non-Indian spouses.[125]

The intermarriage rate amongst Indians was very high. Although Indians were free to choose their own marriage partners, it is clear that in the sixteenth century at least encomenderos put pressure on Indians to marry Indian spouses from their own villages in order to safeguard their tribute interests. On marriage a woman was legally bound to take up residence in her husband's village and their children were registered as potential tributaries in that village. Although this was not always the practice in Honduras, out-marriage by women often represented a loss of potential tribute.[126]

Marriage records for Honduras are not available from parish registers until the end of the eighteenth century, thus the following observations are based on padrones drawn up at single points in time generally for the purpose of tribute assessment. Unfortunately the information from the padrones declines after 1754 when women were exempted from tribute payment. Of particular interest are accounts of the number of Indians marrying out of their communities since this may give some indication of the stability or breakdown of communities. The best data available is for 11 villages in western

---

[123]AGCA A3.16 511 5327-5330, 5339, 5341-2, 5344, A3.16 512 5351, A3.16 514 5397-5399, 5402, 5405 1703 and 1722.

[124]AGCI A3.16 192 1975 Tasaciones 1741 and 1753, A3.16 2325 34320 Libro de tasaciones 1757 (both excluding Tegucigalpa). The latter figures only give marriage characteristics for men.

[125]AGCI A3.96 192 1966 Padrones of pueblos in the Real de Minas de Tegucigalpa 1751.

[126]Recopilación 2 lib.6 tít.1 ley 7: 191 10.10.1618; AGCA A3.16 194 2030 28.2.1797. See Chapter 11 n.141 for a discussion of this practice in Honduras.

Table 10

MARRIAGE PATTERNS IN 11 VILLAGES
IN WESTERN HONDURAS IN 1703 AND 1722

|  | 1703 | | 1722 | |
|  | Number | % | Number | % |
| --- | --- | --- | --- | --- |
| Men marrying women from the same village | 209 | 63.7 | 282 | .69.6 |
| Men marrying women from other villages and remaining in the village | 90 | 27.5 | 72 | 17.8 |
| Men marrying women from other villages and moving out of the village | 24 | 7.3 | 38 | 9.4 |
| Men marrying lavorías, other races, and tributary Indians | 5 | 1.5 | 13 | 3.2 |
| TOTAL | 328 | | 405 | |
| Women marrying men from the same village | 209 | 67.4 | 282 | 71.2 |
| Women marrying men from other villages and remaining in the village | 28 | 9.0 | 17 | 4.3 |
| Women marrying men from other other villages and moving out of the village | 62 | 20.0 | 70 | 17.7 |
| Women marrying lavoríos, other races, and nontributary Indians | 11 | 3.6 | 27 | 6.8 |
| TOTAL | 310 | | 396 | |

For sources see n. 123.

Honduras for 1703 and 1722.[127]  Although censuses were taken of 13 villages in 1703 and 1722, information for both dates is only available for 11 villages and the following comments will be based on these.  At both dates over 60 percent of the Indians chose partners from within their villages, though the percentage increased, perhaps surprisingly, in 1722.  Out-marriages accounted for nearly 35 percent of marriages in 1703 and fell slightly to about 27 percent in 1722 (Table 10).  An examination of the percentages in each category indicates that there was a high negative correlation between the size of the village and the number of out-marriages; the smaller the village, the larger the number of out-marriages.  Clearly this reflects the lack of potential marriage partners in small communities and the need for individuals to seek spouses elsewhere.  As such it is possible that the slight decrease in out-marriages may reflect the increased size of villages in 1722.  Differences between the total number of out-marriages by men and women do not appear to be very significant, but when changes of residence consequent upon marriage are considered then certain differences do emerge.  In 1703, of the 114 cases of men marrying women from other villages only 24 or 21 percent moved to their wives' villages, whereas of the 90 women marrying men from other villages 62 or 69 percent of them moved to their husbands' villages; the respective figures for 1722 are 35 percent and 80 percent.  This suggests that patrilocal residence was the rule, but it may reflect pre-Columbian traditions as much as the effective enforcement of Spanish laws.  Although the origins of marriage partners are indicated in the padrones, when they are crosstabulated they do not correspond.  This throws some doubt on the accuracy of the padrones as a whole, and suggests that the Indians may have been trying to avoid inclusion on tributary lists.  What is clear, however, is that the majority of out-marriages were taking place between members of neighboring villages within a region, rather than between people from different regions.  By the middle of the eighteenth century the degree of out-marriage does not appear to have changed significantly, but if anything it shows a slight decline.  In 1757 out-marriages accounted for only 10.8 percent in Comayagua,[128] and in 1751 the corresponding figure for a selected part of the jurisdiction of Tegucigalpa was 9 percent.[129]  Meanwhile, the 1757 figure for western and central Honduras as a whole (excluding Tegucigalpa) was 17 percent, which is a

---

[127]See n.123.  A similar correlation between the size of villages and the number of out-marriages is apparent in marriage patterns in six Indian villages in Choluteca in 1683:

| Village | Number of married couples | Number marrying out of village | % out-marriage |
|---------|---------------------------|--------------------------------|----------------|
| Nacaome | 7 | 5 | 71.4 |
| Texíguat | 221 | 22 | 10.0 |
| Yesguare | 14 | 2 | 85.7 |
| Colama | 5 | 5 | 100.0 |
| Linaca | 37 | 16 | 43.2 |
| Orocuina | 24 | 12 | 50.0 |

ANH P4 L43, L44, L45, L47, L48, L60 1683.

[128]AGCA A3.16 2325 34320 Libro de tasaciones 1757.

[129]AGCA A3.16 192 1966 Padrones of pueblos in the Real de Minas de Tegucigalpa 1751.

higher rate of out-marriage than that already noted for Comayagua and Tegucigalpa. The lower figures for the latter two regions may reflect the greater proximity of villages in those areas and the status of Tegucigalpa in particular as a region of immigration rather than emigration; the comparable figure for eastern Honduras was 40.3 percent.

The available evidence suggests that most people married, although the marriage rate appears to have fallen during the eighteenth century. In 1741-53 and 1757 the marriage rate was 89.3 percent and 90.3 percent respectively for the western and central areas,[130] though the latter figure refers to men only. By the 1770s the marriage rate had fallen to under 65.0 percent, with the lowest figure of 57.6 percent being recorded for Tegucigalpa,[131] where there were greater employment opportunities for single people. Most marriages, particularly for women, were contracted at an early date. In the sixteenth century Indians began to pay tribute when they married so that encomenderos put pressure on Indians to marry at an early age. Although this was forbidden in 1581,[132] it continued until the tributary status of individuals was made dependent on age rather than marital status.[133] It is worth noting that Indians also manipulated the former rule to their own advantage by postponing marriage and hence tribute payment.[134] Later most marriages were contracted at an early age; Indian girls often married in their early teens. The data for 11 Indian villages in western Honduras in 1703 reveals that of girls in the age group 10 to 14, 13.2 percent were married. The corresponding figure for boys was 1.6 percent. The earlier marriage of girls is also reflected in the age group 15 to 19 where 78 percent of the women were married and only 32 percent of the men; most men married in their early twenties.[135]

Most marriages were probably terminated by the death or prolonged absence of one partner; there is no evidence of Indians having gone through divorce proceedings. Many widowers and widows did remarry, but in most communities there were a large number of widows, often about three times as many widows as widowers, and this was no doubt a reflection of the longer life expectancy of women.[136] It seems likely that the prolonged and permanent absence of Indians performing a variety of tasks and services created instability in many marriages. Absentees very often had sexual relations with those they met in the course of their employment, many of whom were persons of mixed race, and as a result many never returned to their villages.[137] The impression given by

[130]See n.124.

[131]AGI IG 1527 Estado y Padrón General 1777.

[132]*Recopilación* 2 lib.6 tít.1 ley 3: 190 and AGCA A1.23 1513 f.391 cédula 17.4.1581.

[133]See the discussion of tribute assessments in Chapter 11.

[134]AGI AG 133 Frasso 6.5.1663.

[135]For sources, see n.123.

[136]For sources, see n.124. In the 1741 and 1753 tasaciones for western and central Honduras (excluding Choluteca), the number of widows totalled 386 and the number of widowers 124.

[137]For example, AGI AG 9 Diego de Robles 10.4.1556; AGCA A3.12 509 5288 29.1.1671.

the qualitative evidence is that relations between the sexes were a lot more flexible than the quantitative data suggest.

Unfortunately there is very little evidence for the size of families for the period under study. Most population counts were undertaken for the purpose of tribute assessment and do not include the number of children. Even where the numbers of children and tributary Indians are included, many of those who might have been defined as children on the basis of age would have been included in the latter category on the basis of their marital status. This is a greater problem with sixteenth century evidence; later tributary Indians were defined on the basis of age. Even where detailed censuses give the ages of individuals it is still not possible to estimate family size since the relationships between individuals are not specified. Once an individual married, he was generally listed as heading a separate household; thus a couple may have had a family of six children, but if say three of them were married they would have been registered as three separate family units and their parents listed as a family with three children. It is therefore impossible to calculate completed family size. Furthermore, the eighteenth century tributary lists generally do not include children born to women who came from other villages, so that many couples appear childless. The best that can be achieved is to calculate, where possible, the ratio of adults (generally over 18) to children, to get a general impression of family size and whether it was increasing or decreasing.

For western Honduras the earliest substantial evidence is for 11 villages for 1703 and 1722, for which it has been calculated that the average adult/child ratio was 1:0.76 and 1:0.77 respectively.[138] This ratio appears to have declined slightly towards the middle of the eighteenth century. The average ratio for nine villages in Comayagua in 1753 was 1:0.61, with individual villages ranging from 1:0.36 and 1:0.71.[139] The 1777 and 1778 censuses for Honduras differentiate between adults and children, although it is not certain at what age, or whether young married persons were included as adults rather than children. The average adult/child ratios for western and central Honduras as a whole

---

[138]See n.123.

[139]AGCA A3.16 514 5389, 5391-6, 5400-1 Padrones for nine villages in Comayagua 1753.

work out at 1:0.36 and 1:0.47 respectively.[140] Because of doubts as to the criteria used for classifying individuals in the censuses and the discrepancies between the two censuses taken only a year apart, these figures should be used with caution. Nevertheless, there is a suggestion that, along with the falling marriage rate, family size was declining. At the same time there may have been an increase in illegitimacy, with some children becoming orphans.[141]

Although the number of children who were described as orphans may be used as a guide to the high mortality rate and/or collapse of family structure, they are not consistently recorded in censuses. It is clear, however, that in the sixteenth century a large number of children were orphans and in the eighteenth century there appears to have been an increase in orphanage that may have been related to the decline in the marriage rate. The question of the upbringing of orphans was debated in the sixteenth century. A large number of orphans were adopted by Spaniards with the aim of raising them to be their household servants, such that it was said that each household possessed three or four orphans. This was considered to be undesirable by the authorities who argued that the Indians, after being raised in the towns, rarely returned to their villages but became vagrants or married mulattoes or negroes, and even if they did return, they had become so acculturated that they found it difficult to settle there.[142] The authorities were clearly concerned about the loss of the Indians' racial and cultural identity, because it represented a loss of tribute income. As a result the adoption of Indian orphans by Spaniards was forbidden in 1571 and the responsibility for raising them was placed on their nearest relatives.[143] It may be that the Christian practice of specifying godparents at the time of baptism eventually helped overcome the problem, though it is equally clear that Spaniards continued to adopt Indian orphans for use as servants and that priests were probably the worst offenders in this respect. Whereas in the early colonial period only 1 or 2 percent

---

[140]AGI AG 1527 Estado y Padrón General 1777 and Estado General que manifiesta...1778.

| Jurisdiction | Adult/Child Ratio | | % Single | |
|---|---|---|---|---|
| | 1777 | 1778 | 1777 | 1778 |
| Comayagua | 0.47 | 0.29 | 27.9 | 36.9 |
| Tegucigalpa | 0.35 | 0.40 | 42.4 | 45.6 |
| Gracias a Dios | 0.45 | 0.54 | 32.3 | 36.9 |
| Tencoa | 0.39 | 0.47 | 34.5 | 47.7 |
| San Pedro | 0.43 | 0.58 | 26.9 | 44.5 |
| Olancho | 0.42 | 0.76 | 36.3 | 34.7 |
| Yoro | 0.79 | 0.88 | 14.1 | 25.4 |
| Olanchito | 0.26 | 0.55 | 29.3 | 48.2 |
| Western & Central Honduras | 0.36 | 0.47 | 34.0 | 39.6 |
| Eastern Honduras | 0.39 | 0.70 | 30.3 | 38.5 |

[141]AGI AG 501 Anguiano 10.5.1804.

[142]AGCA A1.23 1512 f.378 cédula 24.5.1571.

[143]Ibid.; AGCA A1.38 4778 41245 Ordenanzas 21.10.1683.

of children were classified as orphans, this figure frequently passed 10 percent for individual villages in the eighteenth century. Unfortunately the evidence is not comprehensive enough to indicate any regional variations in the incidence of orphanage, but it does suggest that variations were related to village size, with the smallest villages possessing the largest number of orphans. The most comprehensive evidence available is for Comayagua and Tegucigalpa in the 1750s. In nine villages in Comayagua in 1753 orphans represented an average of 14.7 percent (range 0-50 percent) of children, and in Comayaguela, Tegucigalpa, and Tamara in 1751, 8.1 percent (range 7.5-13.5 percent).[144]

The social organization of Indians who were designated as lavoríos is difficult to determine because of the lack of documentary evidence. The majority lived in the urban areas or on Spanish estates. They may originally have been tributary Indians employed under the repartimiento, who were persuaded, or even forced, to stay there by employers, or they may have been raised as orphans. The origins of lavoríos are diverse and initially they consisted of a large number of single people--widows, unmarried men and women, and orphans.[145] Depending on the size of the community in which they found themselves they may have developed a distinct social identity; this would have occurred where the community was small. Within the urban areas Indian residences were probably concentrated in separate barrios, which over time formed separate parishes. Although the Indians may have lived in distinct residential areas, in the course of their employment they would have come into contact with people of non-Indian race and over time their marriage patterns would have changed. Lutz found that in Santiago de Guatemala, the distinctiveness of Indian barrios decreased over time as interracial marriages increased; in Oaxaca, on the other hand, where the demand for Indian labor was not as great, J.K. Chance found that the barrios remained distinct until the end of the colonial period.[146] In both these cases, however, the barrios were formed of existing Indian villages and they were not established specifically in response to Indians moving into the towns for employment. In general migrants to urban areas would have been isolated from their native communities and they would have become slowly integrated into the economy and social structure of the towns losing their racial and cultural identity. The same was probably true of the mining areas and rural estates. There is very little evidence for the social organization of lavoríos, because of the difficulties of enumerating such a dispersed population. Even where figures are available, they are for tributary lavoríos only, and they provide few guides to changes in marriage patterns and family size. It seems probable that the marriage rate amongst lavoríos would have been lower and family sizes smaller than amongst Indians residing in Indian villages. One piece of evidence for the parish of Tatumbla, near Tegucigalpa, for 1689 suggests that the average adult/child ratio was lower amongst lavoríos (1:0.81), than amongst tributary Indians (1:1.24) and even ladinos (1:0.91).[147]

---

[144]AGCA A3.16 192 1966 Padrones of pueblos in the Real de Minas de Tegucigalpa 1751; A3.16 514 5389, 5391-6, 5400-1 Padrones 1753.

[145]See for example the demographic composition of estates in the parish of Sulaco (AGCA A3.16 190 1923 Padrón...del curato de Sulaco 1689).

[146]C. Lutz, "Santiago de Guatemala, 1541-1773: The Socio-Demographic History of a Spanish American Colonial City," 2 vols. (Ph.D. diss., Department of History, University of Wisconsin, 1976); J.K. Chance, Race and Class in Colonial Oaxaca (Stanford: Stanford University Press, 1978).

[147]ANH P4 L136 Padrones of the curato of Tatumbla 1689.

CONVERSION TO CATHOLICISM

Although the task of converting the Indians to the Catholic faith had been charged to the Spanish Crown by Pope Alexander VI in 1493, it did not begin in earnest until political stability had been achieved, which in Honduras was not until the middle of the sixteenth century.

It was envisaged that members of the secular clergy should be responsible for the instruction of Indians in villages that had been granted as encomiendas, their salaries being paid for out of the tribute they paid to their encomenderos or the Crown. Due to the dispersed character of Indian settlements, a large number of parish priests were required to minister to the Indians and their daily task was difficult. Also, the small size and poverty of the Indian settlements meant that they could only offer low salaries to potential parish priests and consequently they failed to attract high-quality clerics, who in any case preferred a more comfortable existence ministering to the converted non-Indians in the urban centers. Because of the difficulty of attracting parish priests, therefore, regular clergy were permitted to minister to Indians who lived in tributary villages, even though it was the Crown's intention that missionaries should undertake the preliminary conversion of heathen Indians who remained outside Spanish control. However, the activities of the mendicant orders were supervised by the Bishop of Honduras whose permission was required to work in the region and with whom there were constant conflicts.[148] Despite the fact that tributary villages were often charged to the care of missionaries rather than parish priests, there was always a shortage of clergy in Honduras. The majority of priests were creoles, who had received little formal training because of the lack of seminaries and colleges in the area, and who it was said were more interested in supplementing their incomes by trading with the Indians than they were in converting them.[149]

For the purposes of religious administration Indian villages were grouped into partidos, each of which was assigned to a number of parish priests or missionaries. It was the Crown's intention that the Indians should be instructed in the faith independently of other races, but due to the lack of clergy, a parish priest might find himself responsible for the whole population, irrespective of race, distributed in towns, villages, and estates over a vast area. Although there was some reorganization of partidos to take account of demographic changes and the opening up of new areas of economic activity, especially the mines, the number of partidos remained fairly constant. Even a detailed investigation of the administration of parishes in Honduras in 1733 only resulted in the creation of one new parish, Camasca.[150] Similarly, there were few changes in the proportion of posts

---

[148]AGI AG 306-2 cédula 15.10.1581. See for example the conflict over the administration of the parishes of Cururu and Tatumbla between the Mercedarians and the Bishop (AGI AG 184 Testimonio...sobre el despojo de las doctrinas de Cururu and Tatumbla 1688).

[149]AGI AG 9 and CDI 24: 513-57 Lic. López 9.6.1550, AG 9 Oidores of the Audiencia 22.8.1559, AG 39 Relación de cartas 1575, AG 10 Audiencia 4.4.1580; AGCA A1.23 1513 f.534 Bishop of Honduras 15.12.1580; AGI AG 39 Alvara 1.4.1598; AGCA A1.23 1514 f.219 Guerra de Ayala 21.5.1611; AGI AG 501 Anguiano 10.5.1804.

[150]AGCA A1.12 50 497 Autos fechos para remediar la mala administración...1.6.1733, 22.10.1736. For other minor changes see: AGCA A1.11 48 471 Bishop of Honduras 10.11.1802, 5.2.1803, A1.12 49 489 Instancia of a vecino of Pespire 21.10.1019, agreed 13.11.1819.

held by the secular and regular clergy. In 1582 the Mercedarians were administering five partidos and the Franciscans one, which together contained about 50 villages with an estimated tributary population of about 1,800, which was about 35 percent of the total tributary population of Honduras at that time.[151] By 1591 there were 11 partidos of which seven were being administered by the missionary orders.[152] By 1661 the Franciscans were working in two partidos in Comayagua and Tegucigalpa consisting of eight villages containing about 300 Indians,[153] and in 1673 they were administering 10 villages in the partido of Choluteca from the convent of Nacaome.[154] Meanwhile the Mercedarians were administering 41 villages, mostly in western Honduras, with a total tributary population of 1,456,[155] and they continued to have charge of these villages into the eighteenth century.[156]

The task of converting the Indians was made difficult by several factors. First, the dispersed character of Indian settlements and the small number of clergy available meant that the Indians received only intermittent and hence superficial instruction in the Catholic faith. Although each partido may have had several priests working within its jurisdiction, each of them had to minister to several villages as well to individual families living on plots scattered throughout the countryside.[157] The problem was particularly acute in Honduras where villages were often widely separated and so small that they could not provide sufficient food and services to support visiting priests. In 1582 two Mercedarian friars were administering two partidos in the jurisdiction of Comayagua consisting of about 20 villages and 700 tributary Indians spread over a distance of 70 leagues.[158] Where Indian villages formed visitas, that is, where they were visited at intervals by clergy based in the main village of the partido, the regular instruction of the Indians was undertaken by cantores. Although these Indian officials existed in all Indian villages to provide music, to look after the ornaments, and to clean the church, in outlying areas they also helped to instruct the Indians in the Catholic faith.[159] Such methods of instruction were clearly unsatisfactory, however, and in Honduras the ecclesiastical authorities persuaded the Crown to order the amalgamation of Indian villages in 1584.

---

[151]AGI AG 164 Bishop of Honduras 12.5.1582.

[152]AGI AG 164 Bishop of Honduras 20.4.1591.

[153]AGI AG 181 Oficiales reales 24.9.1661.

[154]AGCA A3.2 825 15207 Doctrinas under the regular clergy 24.10.1673.

[155]Ibid.

[156]AGCA A1.18 211 5025 Relación histórica de la provincia de Nuestra Señora de la Merced 1740.

[157]Nolasco Pérez, *Mercedarias*, p. 101.

[158]AGI AG 164 Bishop of Honduras 12.5.1582.

[159]AGCA A1.23 1513 f.639 cédula 14.11.1584; *Recopilación* 2 lib.6 tít.3 ley 6: 209 10.10.1618.

Despite the order, there is no evidence that amalgamation took place and the difficulties of ministering to a dispersed population remained throughout the colonial period.[160]

The task of converting the Indians was also made difficult by the multiplicity of languages spoken by the Indians.[161] At best the secular clergy tried to instruct the Indians in "mexicana," which was used as a lingua franca throughout the area, but which it was claimed was only understood by a few men and virtually no women. The Mercedarians claimed that they taught the Indians in their native languages despite the variety of languages that were spoken in the area in which they worked.[162] The Mercedarians adopted the practice of removing a small number of children to convents where they were raised in the Catholic faith in order that they could return to their villages to help the priests preach to the Indians in their native languages.[163] The clergy also taught the Indians Spanish and in this task the mendicant orders were considered to be more successful.

The duties of priests were manifold. Apart from providing the Indians with regular instruction in the Catholic faith, they heard confessions, arranged for the celebration of special masses and festivals, and performed the ceremonies of baptism, marriage, and burial, keeping a record of them for census purposes. The regularity with which such activities were conducted varied with the size of the visita and the dispersion of the population within it. Apart from introducing the Indians to new religious beliefs and practices, the priests were also required to suppress idolatry, witchcraft, concubinage, drunkenness, and truancy, punishing offenders with flogging and imprisonment. In this task the clergy were aided by secular officials, in particular tenientes and alcaldes mayores.[164] However, as late as the early nineteenth century the authorities considered it necessary to issue a decree against "witchcraft and sorcery."[165]

Indians were not only required to accept the Catholic faith but they were also obliged to support the church financially. They were required to pay fees for the services performed, to contribute alms for charitable purposes, and to provide goods and services for the support of the local church and clergy. Although the clergy were not allowed to exact fees for baptisms and confessions, they could charge for marriages and burials.[166] From the seventeenth century at least there were fixed maximum rates for such services, which were laid down in *aranceles*. These rates varied from area to area and according to the type of service being performed. It is clear, however, that priests overcharged and did exact fees for baptisms and confessions. Also, from 1555 priests were not allowed to charge for performing the sacraments, so instead they requested Indians to contribute a

---

[160]See the discussion of changes in the settlement pattern.

[161]AGCA A1.23 1513 f.639 cédula 14.11.1584; AGI AG 39 Fr. Martínez 17.11.1621.

[162]AGI AG 184 Testimonio...que han seguido la religión de Nuestra Señora de la Merced 1688.

[163]Nolasco Pérez, *Mercedarias*, pp. 100, 119.

[164]AGI AG 9 Ramírez and Quesada 25.5.1555; AGCA A3.16 190 1920 Título de Alcalde Mayor 20.9.1666; ANH P2 L3 Visita de Aguanqueterique 1669.

[165]ANH UC cédula 28.5.1801.

[166]*Recopilación* 1 lib.1 tít.13 ley 7: 96 2.12.1578, tít.18 ley 10: 158 11.6.1578, tít. 7 ley 43: 67 16.8.1642.

*limosna*, or donation, to the church. Although such donations were meant to be voluntary, they soon became another compulsory levy on the Indians. Parish priests were also allowed to receive a specified amount of free goods and services, which was regulated according to the size of the parish, but often they exacted more.[167]

Another demand made upon the Indians came from the cofradías, or religious brotherhoods. Members of the cofradías paid dues, which were used for the holding of special masses and the celebration of saints' days, particularly the saint after whom the cofradía was named. The dues paid were often considerable and in some cases they exceeded the amount of tribute paid by the Indians. Since cofradías were normally distinct for different races, they emerged as institutions that supported the corporate identity of Indian communities.[168] Thus although the cofradías made demands upon the Indians, they were readily adopted by them. It is significant that cofradías did not emerge until the seventeenth century, and then very rapidly, probably in response to the breakup of native communities. Later cofradías became important landowners and the income they derived from their agricultural activities gave the Indians some measure of economic independence. Gibson has suggested that cofradías were also encouraged by parish priests as alternative sources of income for the church, at a time when the amount of tribute, and hence the money that entered the cajas de comunidad for the support of local churches, was falling.[169] Thus even though the membership of cofradías imposed certain financial burdens on its members, cofradías generally benefitted Indian communities and church alike, and as religious institutions they were acceptable to the Spanish authorities.

Although the imposition of Christianity affected the daily life of the Indians, it is difficult to assess the degree to which they accepted Christian beliefs. The outward symbols of religious adherence, such as temples and idols, were destroyed and replaced by churches and convents containing Christian images. However, Indian communities often managed to conceal their idols from the authorities and worship them in secret. Thus throughout the colonial period both secular and ecclesiastical officials continued to be instructed to suppress idolatry.[170] In the same way Christian services related to the life cycle and Christian calendar were introduced and pagan rites and ceremonies, including sacrifices, were banned. Parish priests became the dominant figures in the religious life of Indian communities, but they never wholly replaced the shamans who were still accorded respect and called upon to perform illicit ceremonies and heal the sick.[171] Thus although Christian symbols of religious adherence dominated aboriginal ones, Indian beliefs remained in essence aboriginal with aspects of Christianity grafted on to them. The Indians probably came to believe in the Virgin Mary and Jesus Christ, but as additions to the host of gods they already worshipped, such that the concept of monotheism, which Christianity demanded, went largely ignored.

---

[167]See Chapter 11, p.

[168]Gibson, *Aztecs*, p. 127.

[169]Ibid., p. 132.

[170]AGI AG 520 Ordenanzas 28.6.1568; AGCA A3.16 190 1920 Título de Alcalde Mayor 20.9.1666; ANH P2 L3 Visita of Aguanqueterique 1669.

[171]Herrera, *Historia general* 9 dec.4 lib.8 cap.6: 119.

# Part V

## Eastern Honduras, 1550 to 1821

Eastern Honduras, with the exception of the eastern fringes of the mining area of Tegucigalpa, held little attraction for the Spanish throughout the greater part of the colonial period. During the first half of the sixteenth century the rich alluvial gold deposits of Olancho had been exhausted and the Indian population, although never large, had been decimated. Although the open savannas offered excellent opportunities for livestock raising, it was not until the eighteenth century that they were colonized. The lack of incentives for the Spanish to effectively settle the area meant that only piecemeal efforts were made to bring the Indians there under Spanish control. In eastern Honduras the Indians were too small in number and too difficult to control to warrant the inputs of money and men necessary to civilize and convert them, but the English threat to the security of the Caribbean coast forced the Spanish to face up to this difficult task. They attempted to gain effective control over this area by military means and through the employment of missionaries; Crown support, both moral and financial, for missionary activities was greatest at times when imperial security was under threat. The history of Indians living in eastern Honduras was, therefore, essentially one of contact with either missionaries or with the English who settled on the Caribbean coast.

# 13
# The Missions

The main task of the missionary orders in Honduras was to convert the heathen Indians who remained outside Spanish control and administration in the eastern part of the country, often referred to as Taguzgalpa.  Initially the missionaries attempted to convert the Indians in their native areas, but the small number of missionaries available and the dispersed nature of Indian settlements made the task virtually impossible.  As such the missionaries attempted to congregate the Indians together in missions or reducciones.  In theory the missions were to be in the charge of missionaries for ten years, after which they were to pass to the administration of the secular authorities and the missionaries were to move on to convert heathen Indians in even more remote areas.

The two most important mendicant orders that worked in Honduras were the Mercedarians and the Franciscans.  The first missionaries to arrive in the area were Mercedarians, who established a convent in Comayagua in 1552 and by 1565 also possessed convents in Tencoa and Gracias a Dios.[1]  It was not until the 1570s, however, that the Franciscans arrived and established a convent at Trujillo; within the next thirty years others had been built in Comayagua, Agalteca, and Tegucigalpa.[2]  These convents were used as bases from which the missionaries embarked on converting Indians living in the east of the country.

There were some piecemeal efforts at converting Indians in eastern Honduras in the sixteenth century, but they appear to have been initiated and organized by the secular authorities with the help of missionaries, rather than by the missionaries themselves, and they were largely aimed at punishing and civilizing Indians who were harassing Spanish lands and settlements.  In 1584 Capt. Gregorio del Puerto led a punitive expedition against Indians near Trujillo,[3] and by the end of the century it was also reported that 500 "xicoaques" had been gathered together in the valley of Olancho by 12 soldiers and one missionary without the use of force.  The plan was to settle them in the Comayagua

---

[1] AGI AG 965 Fr. Ovalle 5.4.1565; Nolasco Pérez, *Mercedarias*, pp. 99-101.

[2] AGI AG 10 Audiencia 20.10.1577, Audiencia 4.4.1580, AG 167 Cabildo eclesíastico of Comayagua 20.4.1581, AG 39 Guerra y Ayala 21.5.1611.

[3] AGI AG 39 Ponce de León 26.5.1584, Governor of Honduras 22.4.1585.

valley.[4] Similarly, in 1616 a secular expedition against "indios infieles" resulted in 62 Indians being established in the newly founded village of El Dulcísimo Nombre de Jesús del Valle de Olomán.[5]

The first major attempt at converting Indians in eastern Honduras did not occur until the beginning of the seventeenth century, when it was initiated by Franciscans. After a preliminary reconnaissance of the area in 1604, Fr. Esteban Verdelete returned to Spain to obtain permission for eight missionaries to convert Indians in Taguzgalpa.[6] Arriving in 1608 the missionaries managed to persuade about 130 Indians to settle at Río de las Piedras in the Olancho valley, but because of dissensions among the Indians, the missionaries were forced to separate them into three groups--'taguacas,' 'lencas,' and 'mexicanos'--and administer them separately. In addition to conflicts among Indian groups within the mission, hostility also arose between the converted Indians in the missions and the unconverted Indians outside. The difficulties of maintaining control in the missions encouraged the missionaries to ask for military aid.[7] However, the 25 soldiers that arrived, through their use of force in bringing Indians into the missions, did little more than aggravate the conflicts that already existed. Finally in 1612 the Indians attacked the missions and killed two of the missionaries, including Fr. Verdelete.[8] Missionary efforts were suspended in this area until 1619 when a new attempt was made to reach the Indians of Taguzgalpa by approaching the area from the north coast. Two attempts at landing there were unsuccessful; in the first instance the boat was blown to Tabasco and in the second, difficult navigational conditions made landing impossible. Finally in 1622 Frs. Cristóbal Martínez de la Puerta and Juan de Vaena landed and in the following year they were joined by Fr. Benito López. Working amongst the Paya Indians, who were regarded as more docile than other Indian groups, they managed to establish seven villages: Asozegua, Yalamaha, Borbortabahca, Zuy, Barcaguez, Murahgui, and Xaragui. Nevertheless, they found great difficulty in keeping the Indians in the missions, and disillusioned with their work, they decided to move on to a place called Anavacas where the Guabas lived. A large number of the Guabas were reputedly mestizos, who were the offspring of Spaniards who had been shipwrecked on the coast, and who it was thought could perform an important role in converting the Indians. When they arrived they found only a few Guabas, and having converted them, they continued working amongst the "Xicaques" baptizing over 5,000 of them in the area between there and Trujillo. Their work was brought to an abrupt halt in 1623, however, when all three missionaries were killed by a neighboring Indian group of Albatuynas or Taguacas.[9]

---

[4] AGI AG 39 Alvarado 15.5.1600, AG 11 Criado de Castilla 15.5.1600, 30.4.1601.

[5] AGI AG 39 1616, 4.6.1616.

[6] AGCA A1.23 1514 ff.107-10 cédula 17.12.1607.

[7] AGI AG 175 Fr. Verdelete 29.4.1611, AG 183 Frs. Ovalle and Guevara 4.3.1681, AG 371 Fr. Ximénez 9.9.1748; CDHCN:92-122 Criado de Castilla 30.11.1608; Juarros, *Statistical & Commercial History*, pp. 347-54; Vázquez, *Crónica* 4:100-124.

[8] AGI AG 39 Alvarado 11.5.1610.

[9] AGI AG 183 Frs. Ovalle and Guevara 4.3.1681, AG 371 Fr. Ximénez 9.9.1748; Juarros, *Statistical & Commercial History*, pp. 354, 360-67; Vázquez, *Crónica* 4:86, 158-70; Vallejo, *Historia documentada*, pp. 29-30.

Conflict between the secular and regular clergy over the administration of the Indians appears to have retarded further missionary efforts until the 1660s. For example, in 1657 Fr. Baltazar de Torres, who had managed to convert 100 Indian families, was ordered to leave by the Bishop of Honduras.[10] However, the need to convert the Indians in eastern Honduras was brought to the fore again in the 1650s and 1660s when the Indians made repeated attacks on settlements in the valleys of Agalta, Jamastrán, and Olancho. In 1661 the Crown responded by charging the civilian Bartolomé de Escoto to conquer the Indians. Although he went with soldiers and arms, he managed to settle 300 Indians in four villages through offering them gifts.[11] Escoto then requested priests to administer these Indians, and since no secular clergy were available, the task was entrusted to the Franciscan friars Fernando Espino and Pedro Ovalle. By 1676 six villages had been established: Santa María, San Buenaventura, San Pedro, San Sebastián, San Felipe, and San Francisco, which together had 600 Indians.[12] San Pedro de Alcántara appears to have been established somewhat later, together with Santa Cruz near Nueva Segovia.[13] Several other villages were established about the same time in the valleys of Agalta and Olancho and were given the names San Miguel, San Bartolomé, San Pedro de Yara, and San Joseph.[14] Finally in 1699 the village of Purísima Concepción de San Diego was founded.[15] The history of these missions is virtually impossible to trace: some were abandoned as the Indians escaped to the hills or died as a result of epidemics, while others were amalgamated or their sites were moved (Figure 7).

At the same time Franciscans were working amongst Indians in the area between Trujillo and San Pedro south to the valley of Yoro, known as Lean, Mulía, and Locomapa (Figure 8). On the second of two *entradas*, which took place between 1689 and 1690, Don Rodrigo Navarro and Fr. Manuel Fernández managed to bring together 76 Indians settling them in the valley of Yoro. The number soon declined to 28 as Indians fled to the hills or died; it was said that they died of melancholy as a result of having been moved from their homes. As a consequence the settlement was moved to the Indians' home area and within a year 100 Indians had been gathered together.[16] It would appear that altogether six entradas were made and two villages were established called Nuestra Señora de la Candelaria and San Josef de Guaima which together had 300 Indians. The villages were administered by Fr. Fernández for 12 years until his death, after which he

---

[10]AGI AG 371 Fr. Ximénez 9.9.1748.

[11]AGI AG 39 Crown to Governor of Honduras 11.12.1674, Godoy y Ponce de León 15.3.1676; AGCA A1.23 1520 f.137 Merits of Escoto 11.12.1674; AGI AG 183 Frs. Ovalle and Guevara 4.3.1681.

[12]AGI AG 371 Fr. Ximénez 9.9.1748; Vázquez, *Crónica* 4:193.

[13]AGCA A3.1 800 14832 f.33 Frs. Santa Cruz and Mosquera 28.11.1690, A1.12 77 626 Fr. Magdalena 15.1.1693.

[14]AGI 183 Frs. Ovalle and Guevara 4.3.1681; AGCA A1.12 77 626 Fr. Magdalena 15.1.1693.

[15]AGCA A1.12 161 1688 1698; AGI AG 297 Fr. de la Concepción 13.1.1699, AG 343 Fr. Enríquez 20.1.1700.

[16]AGI AG 164 Bishop of Honduras 27.2.1696, AG 968A Crown 28.4.1697, AG 297 Testimonio sobre la reducción de los indios gentiles en la provincia de Comayagua 1698.

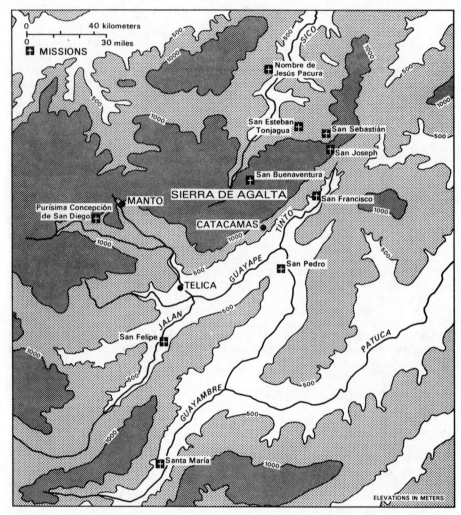

Figure 7. Approximate Location of Selected Missions in Olancho

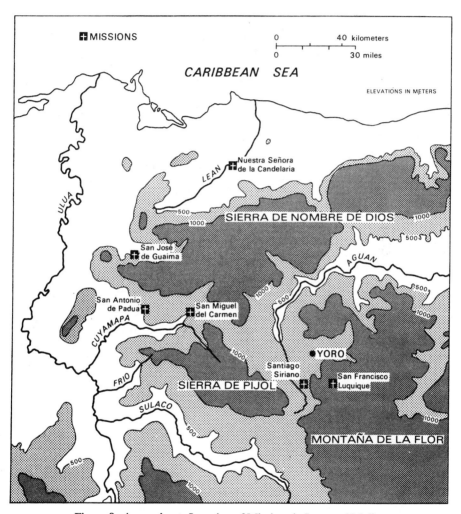

Figure 8.  Approximate Location of Missions in Lean and Mulia

was not replaced. As a result the Indians drifted away to the hills and others died, so that in 1737 there were only 30 left.[17]

The failure of missionary efforts up to the beginning of the eighteenth century to bring about the lasting conversion and civilization of Indians in eastern Honduras stemmed from the nature of the Indian groups themselves as well as from the strategies the missionaries employed to achieve their aims. The semi-nomadic existence of the Indians and the dispersed character of their settlements made the task of converting them extremely difficult, particularly given the small number of missionaries involved. Where possible the missionaries encouraged the Indians to settle in the missions by persuasion. Often they adopted the strategy of capturing and converting a small number of Indians who could then act as interpreters.[18] They also offered them trinkets, such as 'belts, beads and knives,' which in the early years of contact were highly appreciated; by the eighteenth century, however, the Indians were not so easily won over by such gifts, many of which they obtained from the Zambos-Mosquitos and English.[19] Indians became increasingly reluctant to move into the missions as Indians who had fled from the missions dissuaded others from joining and the missions were devastated by diseases.[20] As such the task of persuading the Indians to move into the missions became more and more difficult, and although some missionaries, such as Fr. Manuel Fernández, tried to convert the Indians by peaceful means, the numbers they converted were small, and in most cases the missionaries became resigned to the need for military support.[21] In some cases the expeditions, such as those carried out in the vicinity of Trujillo in the 1580s and in the valleys of Agalta and Olancho in the 1660s, were expressly punitive in their initial phases at least, but these were generally organized by the secular authorities rather than by the missionaries.

If the task of congregating the Indians together in mission villages was not easy, the task of maintaining them there was even more difficult. No sooner had the missions been founded than they started to lose population mainly through fugitivism. This was encouraged by the fact that the Indians were in general unfamiliar with a sedentary mode of existence and were said to yearn to return to the forests. Also, the Indians collected together in one mission village were often drawn from several communities, such that they often spoke different languages and in some cases were even hostile to each other. Hence, they often possessed few common interests that might have encouraged them to remain in the mission.[22] The missionaries responded to the problem of fugitivism in two ways: first, by using soldiers to prevent the Indians from fleeing; and second, by

---

[17]AGCA A1.11 50 492 Lázaro de Castro 1705, AG 230 Rivera 27.5.1737, AG 457 Anguiano 1.7.1798.

[18]For example, AGI AG 164 Bishop of Honduras 10.3.1680, Bishop of Honduras 27.2.1696.

[19]AGI AG 10 Lic. Palacios 20.11.1578, AG 12 Criado de Castilla 30.11.1608, AG 164 Bishop of Honduras 10.3.1680.

[20]AGI AG 297 Fr. de la Concepción 13.1.1699.

[21]AGI AG 39 Guerra de Ayala 11.5.1610, AG 223 Cabildo of Comayagua 21.1.1699.

[22]For example, AGI AG 164 Bishop of Honduras 27.2.1696, AG 343 1700; Juarros, *Statistical & Commercial History*, p. 366.

establishing the missions away from the Indians' home area.[23] The latter strategy was commonly used at the end of the seventeenth century, when Indians were forcibly settled in the Yoro valley[24] and when the mission of La Purísima Concepción de San Diego was established near Silca.[25] Unfortunately, these measures did not prevent the Indians from fleeing, and those that remained became depressed or ill due to the change of environment. An alternative strategy was to settle the neophytes amongst converted tributary Indians. This proved equally unsuccessful because the Indians fled.[26]

Following the death of Fr. Fernández, missionary activity lapsed until the middle of the eighteenth century when the English threat to the security of the Caribbean coast persuaded the Crown to give official support to missionary expeditions. In the eighteenth century missionary efforts were concentrated in two main regions: in the area known as Lean and Mulía, which was inhabited by Jicaque Indians; and in Olancho, including the areas around the Agalta and Tinto rivers, where the Paya were dominant.

The new missionary efforts were led by the Recollects, a Franciscan order recently established with the specific aim of converting heathen Indians. In 1747 Frs. Pedro de Alcántara and Joseph Ramiro began converting Jicaque Indians with the help of soldiers and mulattoes from the valley of Yoro. In 1748 they established the mission of San Miguel del Carmen in the Cerro de Pijol and in the following year Santiago Siriano was founded with local Indians and neophytes who had been moved from an earlier site at Santa Cruz because of the dangers of fugitivism. In 1751 the mission of San Francisco Luquique was founded. It was estimated that about 800 or 900 Indians were settled in these three missions. Their populations were dramatically reduced by a smallpox epidemic in 1751 when about 560 Indians died; Santiago Siriano lost no less than 290 of its population of 366.[27] The decline in the mission populations prompted the suggestion that the missions should be amalgamated. The site of San Miguel was proposed but it was considered unsuitable because of the hot, dry climate that not only created shortages of water, but was also distinct from the environment around Santiago Siriano and Luquique from which the Indians were being moved. Furthermore, given the proposed increase in the size of the mission, there were thought to be insufficient lands around the mission to dispense with the need for Indians to cultivate plots in the hills from which they were prone to flee.[28] By 1760 Santiago Siriano seems have disappeared, whilst the

---

[23]AGI AG 39 Alvarado 15.5.1600.

[24]AGI AG 223 Cabildo of Comayagua 21.1.1699, AG 164 Bishop of Honduras 27.2.1696.

[25]AGI AG 343 Fr. Enríquez 2.1.1700; AGCA A1.12 161 1688 1698.

[26]This strategy was tried by the Alcalde Mayor near the Condiaga valley (AGI AG 223 Cabildo of Comayagua 2.1.1700).

[27]AGI AG 371 Fr. Ximénez 9.9.1748; AGCA A1.12 334 7060 Testimonio...de los autos hechos en la misión y conquista de los indios Jicaques 1752; BAGG 6:159-171 and AGCA A1.12 117 2479 Teniente of Yoro 20.5.1750, Castillo, cura of Yoro 20.8.1751; BAGG 5:59-75 and AGCA A1.12 334 7061 Testimonio...de los gastos hechos en la misión y conquista de los indios Jicaques 1752; A1.12 6056 53627 Fr. Alcántara 4.2.1752, A1.11 118 2487 Visitas of missions of Lean and Mulía 1754; AGI AG 962 Informe on the Colegio de Propaganda Fide 23.12.1782.

[28]BAGG 7:3-45 Fr. Alcántara 1757.

missions of San Miguel and San Francisco Luquique possessed 127 and 104 Indians respectively, and registered 21 and 33 fugitives.[29] By the late 1760s discussions were still continuing about the amalgamation of the two missions, which in 1767 together contained 229 Indians. Finally in 1776 it was decided that they should be joined together at Luquique.[30] From that time onwards Luquique remained the only mission in the area until the end of the colonial period during which time it possessed about 300 Indians.[31]

Meanwhile in 1757, 25 leagues away the Recollects had begun collecting together Indians in the valley of Olomán, establishing a mission with the title of San Antonio de Padua. Starting with 60 Indians, their number had risen to 71 in 1760. At that time, however, desertions were beginning to be registered and by the end of that year the majority of the Indians had fled leaving only eight in the mission.[32]

The failure of the missions in Lean and Mulía, with the exception of Luquique, to become viable settlements was blamed on a number of factors. These included disease, the methods used to bring the Indians into the missions, and the contact the Indians had with other groups, particularly ladinos and the Zambos-Mosquitos.

There is no doubt that epidemics severely reduced the number of Indians in the missions and even contributed to the demise of several missions. In addition, the identification of the missionaries with disease discouraged the Indians from settling in the missions. Thus when the missionaries visited Indian villages they were often kept at a distance where they were required to leave any gifts. At the same time the Indians chewed a paste made of green tobacco leaves and lime in the belief that it protected them from infection.[33]

Whereas the missionaries could do little to prevent the occurrence of disease, they could be blamed for the harsh methods they used in collecting Indians into the missions. As in the seventeenth century, the missionaries employed soldiers, mulattoes and converted Indians from the surrounding areas to bring heathen Indians into the missions. These forces often used surprise tactics, capturing the Indians and transporting them as captives to the missions. Although the missionaries were not always happy with the methods employed by the soldiers and others, they regarded them as essential in the early stages of the missions' foundations both for establishing the missions and for their own

---

[29]AGCA A1.12 117 2479 Informes...acerca las misiones de Lean y Mulía 1760.

[30]AGCA A1.12 46 428 Fr. Chamorro 22.11.1767, A1.12 117 2472 and BAGG 1:213-56 Consulta de Fr. Ortiz 1768, A1.12 46 436 Fr. Iturvide 13.3.1776.

[31]For the number of Indians in the mission of Luquique see:

    --1777 321 IG 1527 Estado y Padrón general 1777
    --1779 290 IG 1527 Estado que manifiesta...1779
    --1797 265 CDHCR 10:258-65 Guardián of the Colegio de Propaganda Fide 3.11.1797
    --1804 290 AGI AG 501 Anguiano, Estado de la provincia de Honduras 1.5.1804
    --1810 279 AGI AG 963 Guardián of the Colegio de Propaganda Fide 10.1.1813.

[32]AGI AG 449 Bishop of Honduras 30.9.1758; AGCA A1.12 50 498 Autos...sobre haberse reducido a nuestra santa fé católica varias familias 1759, A1.12 117 2479 Informes...acerca las misiones de Lean y Mulía 1761-6, A1.12 118 2487 Cura de Cataguana 5.2.1761, Teniente de Dragones 30.6.1761.

[33]AGCA A1.12 118 2487 Cura of Cataguana 5.2.1761; BAGG 7:80-115 10.2.1761; AGI AG 457 Anguiano 1.7.1798.

protection. Some missionaries thought that once the missions had been established such forces would no longer be required, and that they could continue to attract Indians into the missions by persuasion; where Indians were particularly hostile, however, it was recognized that some form of guard would be required at all times. Soldiers were also needed to bring back Indians into the missions where the desertion rate was high.[34] The main critics of the use of force were the secular clergy and royal officials, and no doubt many of their criticisms grew out of their hostile attitude towards the regular clergy. In 1758 the Bishop of Honduras commented that he did not see how the missionaries justified their name since they did little more than carry out surprise attacks on Indians transporting them as prisoners to the missions. Such methods, it was said, were fruitless because they created resentment amongst the Indians thereby encouraging all those who were able to flee, to do so, leaving only the children and the old in the missions.[35] This sentiment was echoed by the governor, who added the practical note that even if a whole regiment was provided it would be insufficient to prevent the Indians from fleeing.[36] Because of the opposition of the secular authorities, it proved difficult for the missionaries to obtain military support. Although in 1758 the Recollects petitioned the Crown for an escort of 30 soldiers, they were refused and the missionaries were forced to pay for six from their own resources. A later petition for 20 soldiers, if the 30 could not be provided, was similarly refused.[37] The judgment at the end of the eighteenth century was that the use of force had been unsuccessful and that it had done nothing more than create resentment amongst the Indians and made further conversions more difficult; it was argued that the Indians could only be converted by peaceful means.[38] It is worthy of note that most of the criticisms of the missionaries were made by those who were not directly involved in the conversion process, and some had ulterior motives for not supporting their efforts.

No doubt part of the difficulty that the missionaries faced in attracting Indians to settle in the missions in the eighteenth century was the contact that they possessed with ladinos, mulattoes, negroes, and the Zambos-Mosquitos in the surrounding areas. These contacts were mainly trading contacts through which the Indians managed to secure most of the items that they had formerly obtained from the missionaries. The Indians thus had

---

[34]For a discussion of these arguments see: AGCA A1.12 334 7061 Testimonio de las diligencias...hechos en la conquista y misión de los indios Jicaques 1752; AGI AG 449 and BAGG 7:3-45 Bishop of Honduras 30.9.1758; AGCA A1.12 118 2487 Cura of Cataguana 5.2.1761, Teniente de Dragones 30.6.1761; BAGG 7:80-115 Informes sobre las misiones de Lean y Mulía 20.11.1761, 19.12.1761.

[35]AGI AG 449 and BAGG 7:3-45 Bishop of Honduras 30.9.1758.

[36]BAGG 7:80-115 Informes...sobre las misiones de Lean y Mulía 10.2.1761.

[37]AGI AG 919 and AGCA A1.23 1528 f.288 Guardián of the Colegio de Propaganda Fide 25.11.1758; AGCA A1.12 118 2487 Cura of Cataguana 5.2.1761.

[38]AGI AG 457 Anguiano 1.7.1798.

little incentive to settle in the missions and in addition those with whom they traded discouraged them from so doing.[39] Some of the lessons learnt from the failure of earlier attempts to convert the Jicaque Indians were incorporated in a plan drawn up in 1798.[40] At that time it was estimated that there were between 14,000 and 15,000 Indians in Lean and Mulía. It was accepted that the Indians could only be converted by peaceful means and that trade was very important to them. As such it was suggested that three missions should be established: two on the sites of the old missions of Guaima and Candelaria, where Fr. Fernández had achieved considerable success in converting the Indians by peaceful means, and the other at Cadena or Cangelica, which was the highest navigational point on the River Lean and which had been an important settlement where trade had been conducted with the English. In the establishment of each of these missions, a missionary was to be assisted by 15 ladino families provided with houses, lands, tools, and a small income for two years. These families were to set a good example to the Indians, as well as trade with them. It was hoped that the success of the missions would attract Indians from the mountains. There is no evidence that the plan was ever put into effect, probably because of its cost, which was estimated at 24,990 pesos. The plan is interesting, however, in that it shows the manner in which missionary activity adapted to changed circumstances.

Missionary efforts in Olancho occurred at intermittent intervals during the eighteenth century, but there is little precise evidence of the size and location of missions they founded. The work of the Franciscan Observants continued amongst Paya Indians in the first half of the eighteenth century, but by 1737 it appears that only two formal missions--San Buenaventura and San Sebastián--remained with a total population of 60.[41] Missionary activity continued in the valleys of Agalta and Río Tinto, where in 1750 there were two missions--San Buenaventura and San Francisco del Río Tinto--with populations of 97 and 100 Indians respectively.[42] However, it appears that there were other missionary settlements in various conditions of viability in the valley of Agalta at San Sebastián, San Joseph, San Bartolomé, and San Francisco.[43]

There appears to have been a lapse in missionary activity in Olancho shortly after this time, since documents indicate that it was resumed in 1767 under the Recollects. These missionaries appear to have re-established the mission of San Buenaventura and moved the Indians from the Río Tinto to a place known as Siguate where they were less exposed to attack by the Zambos-Mosquitos.[44] It would appear that a formal mission

---

[39]AGCA A1.12 118 2487 Teniente de Dragones 30.6.1761; BAGG 7:80-115 Informes...sobre las misiones de Lean y Mulía, no date; AGCA A1.12 6056 53630 Fr. Chamorro 30.8.1768; AGI AG 963 Guardián of the Colegio de Propaganda Fide 10.1.1813.

[40]AGI AG 457 Anguiano 1.7.1798.

[41]AGI AG 230 Rivera 27.5.1737, a reduction from 232 in 1711 (AGI AG 223 Testimonio sobre la nueva reducción de los indios de la nación Paia 1711).

[42]AGI AG 371 Fr. Segura de Iriaquez 20.5.1750.

[43]AGI AG 371 Fr. Ximénez 9.9.1748.

[44]AGI AG 456 Governor of Honduras 30.8.1767; AGCA A1.12 50 506 31.1.1768, A1.12 50 511 Governor of Honduras 1781; Lunardi, *Los Payas*, p. 9.

was not established at Río Tinto until 1776,[45] when it was suggested that those at San Buenaventura mission should move there; those at San Buenaventura were regarded as more nomadic and difficult to convert than those at Río Tinto. In 1777 there were 73 Indians at San Buenaventura and 81 at Río Tinto.[46] In the same year missionary activity in Olancho was resumed in the Olancho valley, when 225 Butucos Indians (probably Payas) voluntarily settled at Telica near Catacamas, seeking conversion and protection from the Zambos-Mosquitos. Some of them subsequently fled to the mountains, and to discourage further fugitivism the remaining Indians were transferred to the Marianí valley, five to six leagues from Comayagua.[47] Nevertheless the Indians still fled (twice) and it was resolved that they should be distributed amongst villages of converted Indians and vecinos of Comayagua. This plan was unsuccessful, however, since many of the Indians deserted back to Marianí.[48] Meanwhile, in 1780 an expedition to the Olancho valley by Capt. Arizabalaga resulted in the transference of a number of vagrant Paya Indians who were considered a security threat, to the barrio of Santa Lucía outside Comayagua. Although they were placed under official surveillance, in 1783 the majority (43) fled from Santa Lucía leaving only eight in the settlement. They were subsequently recaptured and transferred to the more distant village of Sensenti in the jurisdiction of Gracias a Dios from where it was more difficult for them to flee, and where it was hoped that they stem the demographic and economic decline of the region. In 1790 the Indians asked to be returned to Santa Lucía.[49]

Meanwhile there is a shortage of information on the state of the missions in Olancho; there is an account of Paya settlements in the Agalta valley, and at Petaste (near Río Tinto) and Aguaquire in 1790,[50] but only in 1794 is there mention of two new reducciones at the Río Tinto and Aguaquire.[51] The only other concerted missionary effort during the colonial period occurred in early nineteenth century when Fr. Antonio Martínez and Fr. Antonio Goicoechea managed to settle about 300 Indians in San Esteban Tonjagua and Nombre de Jesús Pacura; it was suggested that San Buenaventura, which presumably had survived from a previous period of missionary activity and only

---

[45]AGI IG 1527 Estado y Padrón general 1777, AG 450 Testimonio...sobre que se entregue el pueblo de San Buenaventura 6.3.1777.

[46]AGI IG 1527 Estado y Padrón general 1777. In 1778 San Buenaventura had 85 Indians (AGI IG 1527 Estado que manifiesta...1779).

[47]AGI AG 456 Governor of Honduras 31.7.1768.

[48]AGCA A1.12 50 511 Governor of Honduras 12.3.1781, A1.23 1531 10086 f.311 cédula 19.4.1782.

[49]AGCA A1.12 50 511 Governor of Honduras 12.3.1781, A1.12 50 514 and BAGG 6:115-34 Expediente sobre la traslación de los indios payas 18.9.1783, 20.9.1783; BAGG 6:127-33 17.12.1790; AGCA A1.12 51 517 4.4.1791.

[50]AGCA A1.12 51 517 30.4.1790.

[51]AGCA A1.11 48 464 Yrias 18.11.1794.

252

possessed 34 Indians, should be amalgamated with one of these.[52] This merger does not appear to have taken place before the missionaries left in 1807. In 1810 the care of the Indians in this area was charged to parish priests, although they did not arrive until 1817.[53]

---

[52]Goicoechea, "Relación sobre los indios gentiles," pp. 303-15, no date; Juarros, *Statistical & Commercial History*, p. 372; Conzemius, "Los Indios Payas," p. 279.

[53]Lunardi, *Los Payas*, pp. 12-13.

# 14
# The English

For both ideological and practical reasons Spain sought to prohibit the settlement of non-Castilians in the New World. This policy was consistent with the prevailing concept of absolute monarchy and was justified by the Papal Bulls of 1493, which gave Spain the exclusive right to christianize the native population west of an imaginary line later established by the Treaty of Tordesillas in 1494. The Spanish Crown also wanted to reserve its right to the resources of the New World in the belief that, if given access to them, foreign nations would be strengthened both economically and politically. Thus throughout the colonial period decrees were issued prohibiting foreigners from settling and trading in the New World.[1]

Foreigners first appeared in Honduras as aggressors and then as illegal traders and settlers. From the middle of the sixteenth century foreign corsairs led by the French and followed by the English attacked Spanish vessels and ports, notably Trujillo and Puerto Caballos. It was at these ports that the fleets took on board goods produced in Central America and supplied it with manufactures produced in Europe. Goods destined for Guatemala were transferred in Puerto Caballos for shipment to Bodegas. Because of the shallower water in the Golfo Dulce goods had to be conveyed on smaller craft and these were particularly vulnerable to attack by corsairs. Despite efforts to safeguard vessels and ports from attack by changing the routes of the ships, providing coastguards, and fortifying established ports, during the late sixteenth century raids became a fact of life.[2]

Several factors contributed to a lull in the activities of corsairs at the beginning of the seventeenth century; the Spanish concentrated their trading activities on the newly constructed and more easily defended port of Santo Tomás de Castilla in the bay of Amatique, whilst the attention of Europeans focused on the colonization of North

---

[1]L. Moreno, "Los extranjeros y el ejercicio del comercio en Indias," *ASGH* 14 (1938):441-54; R. Konetske, "Legislación sobre inmigración de extranjeros en América durante la epoca colonial," *Revista de sociología*, nos. 11-12 (1945), pp. 269-99.

[2]Floyd, *Anglo-Spanish Struggle*, pp. 12-16; MacLeod, *Spanish Central America*, pp. 156-57. There are numerous references to foreign attacks in the sixteenth century: AGI AG 52 1558, AG 9 Audiencia 22.8.1559, AG 394-4 cédula 5.5.1561, AG 386-2 cédula 26.5.1573, AG 39 López 20.5.1575, AG 39 Relación de cartas 1575, AG 55 López 1577, AG 43 Cabildo of Comayagua 7.4.1578, AG 10 Audiencia 17.3.1578; AGCA A1.23 1513 f.561 cédula 22.5.1579, AG 10 16.5.1583, AG 49 Romero 26.2.1595, AG 39 Carrança 27.8.1595, AG 10 no author 21.9.1595, AG 1 Council of the Indies 7.3.1596, AG 10 Audiencia 4.4.1596, AG 386-2 cédula 28.11.1596, AG 164 Bishop of Honduras 12.10.1598, AG 39 Alvarado 20.5.1603.

America, the Guianas, and the unoccupied islands in the Caribbean. The general stimulus for attacking Spanish settlements and trade routes was also reduced by European peace treaties with Spain.[3] Conversely the outbreak of war between England and Spain in 1625 encouraged the revival of piratical activities and renewed efforts at establishing settlements within Spanish territory as a means of weakening its power. Whilst attacks by corsairs continued on the northern coast of Honduras,[4] several English settlements were established by the Providence Company.[5] The English first settled in Providencia in 1629 and within five years they had occupied the islands of Tortuga and Roatán; they had also established settlements on the neighboring mainland at Cabo de Gracias a Dios, Bluefields, and Belize. Within a short time the Spanish managed to drive the English from the islands--from Tortuga in 1635, Providencia in 1641, and Roatán in 1642--but those on the Mosquito coast and in Belize remained. These setbacks for the English were in part compensated for in 1655 by the seizure of Jamaica, which became a vital base from which attacks and colonizing expeditions could be mounted. The most outrageous attacks were perpetrated on the major cities of Nicaragua, which the construction of Fort Inmaculada Concepión on the San Juan River failed to prevent.[6]

During the first half of the eighteenth century the English consolidated their position on the Mosquito Shore by making it a protectorate. In return for English protection, in 1739 the inhabitants of the Shore surrendered their territorial rights.[7] Despite the consolidation of the English position on the Shore, the number of non-Indian inhabitants does not appear to have increased substantially. The earliest settlements of non-Indians were at the Río Tinto or Black River, Cabo de Gracias a Dios, Bluefields, and Punta Gorda, although small numbers of Europeans were scattered all along the Shore.[8] When the Protectorate was established, the headquarters of the Superintendent were located at the mouth of the Black River and it was the northern part of the Mosquito coast that attracted most non-Indian settlers. In 1757 over three-quarters of the 1,124 inhabitants of the Shore lived in the Honduran sector.[9] During the next thirty years about

---

[3]Floyd, *Anglo-Spanish Struggle*, pp. 15-17.

[4]AGI AG 44 Cabildo of Trujillo 6.2.1643, AG 16 Dávila y Lugo 4.10.1643; BNM 3047 ff.128-135 no author, no date; AGCA A1.23 1520 10075 f.137 Merits of Escoto 11.12.1674.

[5]The activities of the Providence Company are described fully in A.P. Newton, *The Pioneering Activities of the English Puritans* (New Haven: Yale University Press, 1914), and summarized in Parsons, *Green Turtle*, pp. 5-13.

[6]Newson, *Indian Survival*.

[7]PRO CO 123/3 ff.185-8 no author, no date; Floyd, *Anglo-Spanish Struggle*, pp. 68-69.

[8]For the location of English settlements see AGCA A1.12 117 2473 18.9.1759; SHM Plano 5185 Sig. D-13-37 Clapp 2.9.1771; AGI AG 665 and CDHCN: 198-205 Gastelu 11.7.1776; MNM Bª-XI Cª-B n° 1 Hodgson and Hodgson 1782.

[9]PRO CO 123/1 ff.55-79 Hodgson 1757.

Table 11

INHABITANTS OF THE MOSQUITO SHORE IN 1757

| | Whites | Mulattoes & Mestizos | Negro Slaves | Indian Slaves | TOTAL |
|---|---|---|---|---|---|
| Brewer's Lagoon* | 3 | 16 | 19 | | 38 |
| Plantain River* | 2 | 14 | 10 | | 26 |
| Black River (eastern lagoon)* | 1 | 5 | 1 | 6 | 13 |
| Black River* | 31 | 17 | 254 | | 302 |
| Mistire Creek* | 9 | 51 | 127 | | 187 |
| Cape River* | 25 | 17 | 201 | | 243 |
| Cabo de Gracias a Dios | 6 | - | 28 | - | 34 |
| Sandy Bay | 5 | 7 | 3 | 8 | 23 |
| Bragman's Bluff | 11 | 6 | 8 | 20 | 45 |
| Pearl Key Lagoon | 2 | 2 | 3 | 11 | 18 |
| Corn Islands | 3 | 23 | 10 | 30 | 66 |
| Bluefields | 2 | 2 | 10 | 3 | 17 |
| Punta Gorda | 4 | 10 | 12 | 16 | 42 |
| Not Fixed | 50 | - | 20 | | 70 |
| TOTAL | 154 | 170 | 800 | | 1,124 |

Source: PRO CO 123/1 ff.55-79 Hodgson 1757.

*in Honduras

200 to 300 whites were living on the Mosquito Shore with 900 to 1,000 slaves.[10] The main interests of the English were trading in dyewood, mahogany, sarsaparilla, and turtleshell. In 1769, 800,000 feet of mahogany, 200,000 pounds of sarsaparilla, and 10,000 pounds of turtleshell were exported to England,[11] and in 1783 the export of these items was said to be worth £30,000.[12] Dyewood was exported to England, Holland, and North America, where it was used as a dye in the textile industries.[13] In addition to trading with the inhabitants for wood, the English also established wood-cutting enterprises in which they employed both negro slaves and the Zambos-Mosquitos. A few families established sugar plantations at Cabo de Gracias a Dios and further north in Honduras, whilst some possessed cacao plantations along the upper reaches of the Río Segovia and others raised livestock.[14]

By the second quarter of the eighteenth century it was recognized that an offensive was needed to root the English out of the Mosquito Shore. This was to be undertaken by two means: first, by strengthening coastal fortifications; second, by increasing missionary activity on the frontier with the aim of extending the area of Spanish control and creating a buffer zone between the rival nations. The failure of the latter strategy has already been described. The choice of a well-defended site from which an offensive could be mounted was a difficult one. Although the Spanish had control of Fort Inmaculada on the San Juan River, it was difficult to defend and it was an unsuitable site from which to launch an offensive. Trujillo was also considered to be unsuitable because it was difficult to fortify and because it was located too close to the English settlements at the Black River and on the Bay Islands, which the English seized in 1742. It was recommended, therefore, that the basis of the military offensive should be a new fort that would be established at Omoa. Although the establishment of Fort Omoa was recommended in 1744, work did not commence until 1752 and the fort was not completed until 1775. During the offensive between 1779 and 1783 the Spanish established themselves at Trujillo from whence they managed to retake Roatán and move to the Black River, which they held for a short time. Further south they managed to hold onto Fort Inmaculada. Further hostilities between the Spanish and the English were forestalled by the Treaty of Versailles in 1783 and the associated Mosquito Convention of 1786, in which the English undertook to evacuate the Mosquito Shore. In 1787, 517 freemen and 903 slaves were evacuated from the Shore mainly to Jamaica and Belize,[15] although it appears that 202 remained, of whom 46 were slaves who deserted during the

---

[10]MNM Bª-XI Cª-B n° 1 Hodgson and Hodgson 1782; PRO CO 123/3 ff.185-8 no author, no date; R. White, *The Case of the Agent to the Settlers on the Coast of Yucatan and the Late Settlers on the Mosquito Shore* (London: T. Cadell, 1793), p. 47.

[11]Edwards, "British Settlements," p. 211.

[12]ANHM Estado 4227 Fuertes 24.6.1784.

[13]MNM Bª-XI Cª-B n° 1 Hodgson and Hodgson 1782; Floyd, *Anglo-Spanish Struggle*, p. 58.

[14]AGI AG 665 and CDHCN:198-205 Gastelu 11.7.1776; BM Add. 12,431 f.202 Request for information from Col. Kimberley, no date; MNM Bª-XI Cª-B n° 1 Hodgson and Hodgson 1782; Long, *History of Jamaica* 1:318.

[15]PRO CO 123/5 ff.194-7 Return of the inhabitants of the Mosquito Shore 20.10.1787.

evacuation.[16] Although the English evacuated the Shore, they maintained contraband trading contacts with the Zambos-Mosquitos from Jamaica and Belize.[17]

From 1787 until 1800 the Spanish tried unsuccessfully to gain control of the Mosquito Shore by establishing colonies of Spanish immigrants at the Black River, Cabo de Gracias a Dios, and Bluefields.[18] Although 1,298 colonists were recruited in Spain and the Canaries (992 and 306 respectively) not all arrived: 22 died, 54 deserted before leaving Spain, and 290 died en route. Those who survived went mainly to Trujillo; a few went to the Black River and Cabo de Gracias a Dios, but none went to Bluefields. Unaccustomed to agricultural labor in the tropics, these settlements had a very precarious existence and consisted largely of soldiers supported by government rations; in 1791 there were 135 soldiers and only 3 colonists at Cabo de Gracias a Dios.[19] The threat of English attack finally resulted in the abandonment of Roatán and the colony at Cabo de Gracias a Dios in 1795, whilst an attack from the Zambos-Mosquitos in 1800 drove the Spanish from the Black River, so that Trujillo once again became the frontier town.[20]

Meanwhile other negro immigrants had arrived in the area. In 1796 French negroes, mainly artisans, who were fleeing from the political upheavals in Sainte Domingue, were given asylum in Honduras and settled in the vicinity of Trujillo.[21] In 1797 these negroes were joined by 1,490 Black Caribs from St. Vincent. The Black Caribs had posed a security threat in the Caribbean and as such they were transferred to Roatán from St. Vincent by the English. The Spanish promptly responded by moving them to Trujillo.[22] To these two groups were added the negro slaves who remained in the area once the English had evacuated the Shore.[23] The area around Trujillo thus took on a distinct racial charter.

---

[16]PRO CO 123/6 ff.82-5 Embarkations from the Mosquito Shore 1787.

[17]Floyd, *Anglo-Spanish Struggle*, pp. 162-82.

[18]ANH UC 19.5.1787.

[19]W.S. Sorsby, "Spanish Colonization of the Mosquito Coast, 1787-1800," *Revista de historia de América*, nos. 73-74 (1972), p. 149 n. 14.

[20]AHNM 4227 Families from Galicia and Asturias 31.10.1787; AGI AG 828 and 829 Families from Galicia and Asturias 1787, Families from Asturias 15.2.1788; Floyd, *Anglo-Spanish Struggle*, pp. 168-71; Sorsby, "Spanish Colonization of the Mosquito Coast," pp. 145-52.

[21]AGCA A1.12 51 519 22.12.1802; AGI AG 452 Relación de las providencias...3.1.1804; AGCA A1.17 2875 26354 Informe...de Anguiano ca. 1814.

[22]AGCA A3.16 194 2025 16.10.1797 and 23.9.1797; Floyd, *Anglo Spanish Struggle*, p. 184; W.V. Davidson, "Dispersal of the Garífuna in the Western Caribbean," *42nd International Congress of Americanists* (Paris) (1979) 6:467-74 ref. to p. 468.

[23]AGI AG 963 Ayzinenass 2.11.1813.

# 15
# Cultural Changes in Eastern Honduras

In eastern Honduras the cultural changes experienced by the Indians were extremely varied due to differences in the nature and intensity of contact with different outside groups. During the colonial period the area was colonized both from the already settled west and from the Caribbean coast. Colonization from the west took two forms. The eastern frontier of settlement was gradually pushed further east until it came to a halt in about the third-quarter of the sixteenth century largely because the mining industry, which had originally encouraged the settlement of the area, had declined and no other economic incentive existed there to stimulate the pushing back of the frontier. From the end of the sixteenth century, therefore, it was the missionary orders that carried the limits of colonization further east. Although some of the more successful missions were later taken over by the secular authorities, many settlements that were established by the missionaries were only short-lived. On the Caribbean coast contact with non-Indians did not occur until the middle of the seventeenth century and it was of a different kind. Contact was essentially with northern Europeans, negroes, and later people of mixed race. Meanwhile some Indians did not come into sustained contact with other races throughout the colonial period, although as the two waves of colonization converged from the west and the east, they formed a smaller and smaller group.

Although contact between Indians and other races was sustained in the case of Indians living in tributary villages and on the Caribbean coast, Indians who were brought under the control of the missionary orders experienced the most profound changes because the missionaries attempted to restructure their culture completely. Indians who remained outside the control or influence of Spaniards, missionaries, and other Europeans experienced only minor cultural changes brought about by intermittent contact with them and with other Indians who were under their control. Thus, despite the fact that there was increasing contact between the different groups, notably through trade and raids, particularly in the eighteenth century, it is useful to consider the cultural changes experienced by Indians in eastern Honduras under four headings: Tributary Indian villages; Missions; Indians outside Spanish control; the Mosquito Shore.

Because of the remoteness of eastern Honduras and the difficulties of accessibility within the region, the documentary evidence for this area is very fragmentary. Accounts by missionaries, which might be expected to provide more detailed information, are equally incomplete because the missions were short-lived. Evidence for the Indian population living outside Spanish control is, for obvious reasons, even more inadequate. Nevertheless, an attempt will be made to describe the cultural changes experienced by Indian groups living in eastern Honduras, although the inadequacy of the evidence should always be borne in mind.

## TRIBUTARY INDIAN VILLAGES

During the middle of the sixteenth century Spanish colonization was consolidated on the western fringes of eastern Honduras. A fairly large number of small villages were made tributary to individuals or the Crown, and Spanish forms of secular and ecclesiastical administration were introduced as in western and central Honduras. The process of cultural change experienced by these communities was thus broadly similar to that described for the latter areas, although there were a number of differences that stemmed from differences in the character of the Indian groups they affected, the local environments in which they lived, and the intensity of contact.

During the colonial period changes in the number and size of villages in eastern Honduras followed the pattern already described for the western and central parts of the country. In both areas the number of villages declined throughout the period, although the decline in the east was 84.1 percent, over double that to be found in the west and center of the province.[1] In common with the latter areas, the average size of villages, as measured by the number of tributary Indians, declined until the middle of the eighteenth century, after which it increased substantially.

The decline in the number of villages was brought about mainly by the decline in the Indian population, in part caused by enemy attacks and the migration of Indians to towns and estates. Enemy attacks took their heaviest toll on Indian villages located on or near the north coast of Honduras. From the sixteenth century onwards settlements there were attacked by Jicaque Indians; in the 1570s it was reported that the villages of Montexucar, Guacura, and Moaca in the jurisdiction of Trujillo had been depopulated by Jicaque Indians.[2] There were also periodic attacks by hostile Indians in the valleys of Olancho and Jamastrán and these prompted missionary activity in the area in the 1660s.[3] From the end of the sixteenth century raids by English and Dutch pirates added to these attacks by hostile Indians, although their efforts focused on Spanish rather than Indian settlements.[4] During the seventeenth century these Europeans often employed the Zambos-Mosquitos as fighting forces. By the beginning of the eighteenth century the Europeans had turned to trade rather than buccaneering, but the Zambos-Mosquitos continued to carry out raids, which resulted in a number of settlements being destroyed or abandoned as their sites were moved inland.[5] During the early eighteenth century the Zambos-Mosquitos attacked villages in northern Honduras as far as San Pedro,

---

[1]Table 7.

[2]AGI AG 55 López 1579.

[3]AGI AG 39 King to Governor of Honduras 11.12.1674, AG 39 Godoy y Ponce de León 15.3.1676.

[4]Floyd, *Anglo-Spanish Struggle*, pp. 14-15.

[5]The survivors of attacks on Utila, Tomala, and Chalachala were gathered together and settled at Agalteca, whose site had been moved inland at an earlier date (AGCA A1.12 50 497 Autos hechos para remediar la administración...1.16.1733, A3.16 193 1998 Indios de la Concepción de Agalteca 1778).

destroying the villages of Utila, Agalteca, and Lemoa,[6] whilst Catacamas in the Olancho valley was attacked three times.[7]

Indian villages also lost population due to migration. Indians sometimes deserted to the countryside, often to avoid tribute payment or the repartimiento, establishing individual dwellings in the hills.[8] This type of movement appears to have been more common in eastern Honduras than in the west, for here the Indians were more familiar with a semi-nomadic form of existence. Other Indians deserted to the towns and mining areas.

The major changes that occurred in the Indian economy were associated with the increasing importance of agriculture. Whereas in pre-Columbian times the Indians had practiced shifting cultivation based on an assemblage of crops in which root crops figured significantly, in the colonial period permanent cultivation became more common as did seed crops. Livestock also made their appearance, largely supplanting hunting and fishing as sources of protein; and for the first time Indian communities were required to produce surpluses to meet extracommunal demands.

In pre-Columbian times Indians in eastern Honduras had no concept of private property, but during the colonial period the Spanish introduced a land-holding system that brought concepts of private and communal ownership. Familiarity with the legal aspects of land holding during the colonial period may have enabled the Indians in the east to defend their lands more effectively when pressure on land increased in the eighteenth century; in western and central Honduras many Indian lands were alienated in the sixteenth century before the Indians became aware of the nature and operation of Spanish land laws. As the location of settlements and land holdings took on a more permanent character, so also did the system of cultivation, and this process was further stimulated by changes in the assemblage of crops grown and the introduction of livestock, which provided more reliable sources of food. Although cajas de comunidad and cofradías were both established in eastern Honduras, they were fewer in number and their capital assets were smaller than in the west.[9] In 1784 villages in eastern Honduras possessed only 18 percent of the total funds existing in cajas de comunidad in Honduras, and in 1791 the cofradías there possessed only 26 percent of the cattle owned by cofradías.

Changes in the nature of land holding were paralleled by changes in the allocation of labor to various economic activities. The major difference was that time had to be set aside to meet Spanish demands for tribute and labor. Although the amount of tribute paid by Indians in the east was no higher than in the west, it may have constituted a greater burden on Indian communities there, since the items demanded could not be produced easily given the local physical conditions. As in western and central Honduras, the repartimiento and other demands for labor services by Spanish officials and priests constituted unfamiliar burdens on sources of labor, reducing those available for subsistence activities. Many of the tasks in which Indians were employed were similar to

---

[6]Ibid.; AGCA A3.16 146 988 Justicias del pueblo de Agalteca 1702, A3.16 190 1932 Información sobre la entrada de los zambos...1702; CDHCN: 1-12 Audiencia 26.7.1704; CDHCN: 12-63 Bishop of Nicaragua 30.11.1711.

[7]AGCA A1.30 219 2466 Indians of Olancho El Viejo 4.12.1724, A1.73 390 3662 Partial visita of Comayagua 1771.

[8]AGCA A1.45 369 3429 11.1.1802.

[9]Table 9.

those in the west and they included household duties, building, repairing houses and roads, and preparing milpas, as well as working on cattle ranches and in mining.[10] Although the Indians complained about the burdens that all of these activities imposed, they do not appear to have been as great as those experienced in the west. This was almost certainly due to the remoteness and lower economic importance of the area resulting in the presence of fewer Spanish officials, priests, colonists, and travellers to make demands. It is possible, however, that the remoteness of the eastern region from official surveillance would have encouraged the greater exploitation of Indians, albeit by a smaller number of people, imposing burdens on communities that were excessive given their small size and their lack of familiarity with providing goods and services to meet extracommunal demands.

Although the assemblage of crops cultivated by the Indians in eastern Honduras did not alter significantly, the emphasis of production did. The items of tribute generally demanded by the Spanish were maize, beans, and cotton for spinning and weaving cloth.[11] Although these items were produced in small quantities in pre-Columbian times, the Indians had depended to a greater degree on the cultivation of root crops for their subsistence. Indeed in the sixteenth century, the Bay Islands produced large supplies of manioc for the city of Trujillo.[12] The need to pay tribute in the crops specified led to an increase in their cultivation. It is assumed that the Indians continued to cultivate indigenous fruit trees; there is no evidence that they adopted European fruits, such as the citrus fruits. A notable arrival in the area in the early colonial period was the coconut (*Cocos nucifera* L.), which became established in the Bay Islands and on the northern coast of Honduras.[13]

Domesticated animals, particularly cattle, spread rapidly on the extensive pastures found in eastern Honduras. Cattle were introduced at an early date and it was probably not long before the Indians began to raise them, sometimes in very large numbers;[14] in 1679 the cofradía of San Francisco Catacamas in the Olancho valley possessed 16,000 head of cattle.[15] Indian villages in this area may have developed a contraband trade in cattle with inland Indian groups who sold them to the Zambos-Mosquitos, or even with the Zambos-Mosquitos themselves.[16] More often, however, their herds were raided by these groups.[17] The Indians also raised horses and mules in small numbers and pigs

[10]Chapter 11, pp. 178-80, 184-87.

[11]Chapter 11, p. 197.

[12]AGI AG 44 Paez, vecino of Trujillo, no date; RAHM 9/4663 no.15 Valverde 24.8.1590; AGI PAT 183-1-16 Antonelli and López de Quintanillas 7.10.1590; RAHM CM A/66 Descripción de las Islas Guanajas 1.11.1639.

[13]RAHM CM A/66 Descripción de las Islas Guanajas 1.11.1639.

[14]Serrano y Sanz, *Relaciones históricas*, p. 468 (Pineda 1594).

[15]AGCA A1.45 368 3412 Pueblo of Catacamas 22.3.1679.

[16]Floyd, *Anglo-Spanish Struggle*, p. 61.

[17]AGI AG 302 Rivera 10.5.1737.

were found in the Bay Islands.[18] Meanwhile chickens became one of the most important sources of food and item of tribute.

The exploitation of wild food resources probably continued though at a reduced level of intensity as the areas that could be exploited were reduced in extent, labor inputs declined, and alternative sources of protein in the form of domesticated animals, particularly cattle and chickens, were adopted. Fishing remained an important activity in the Bay Islands and on the north coast of Honduras. After the abolition of fish tribute, six to eight Indians were employed to provide the city of Trujillo with fish and these Indians were exempt from all other forms of service.[19] In 1639 the Bay Island Indians were described as "great fishermen and sailors."[20]

Craft activities would not have varied significantly from the pre-Columbian period. As in western and central Honduras, certain pieces of household furniture, utensils, and cotton cloth were demanded as tribute. The spinning and weaving of cloth demanded as tribute may have led to its greater use by the Indians, particularly as the Spanish required more 'decent' forms of clothing than the bark cloth they normally wore.

In pre-Columbian times the Indians had produced little in the way of food surpluses or craft items for exchange, and any trade that occurred was by barter. During the colonial period trade probably expanded and it is possible that formal markets and mediums of exchange were introduced. However, goods were probably not exchanged freely in an open market, but trade was forced on the Indians by Spanish officials, who either coerced them into selling them agricultural produce and other goods at low prices, often paid for in kind, or into purchasing manufactures at high prices, often through the repartimiento de generos.[21]

Although the social and political institutions that the Spanish imposed on Indians in eastern Honduras were the same as those introduced in western and central Honduras, their effects were dissimilar because the groups they affected were different. Whereas in western and central Honduras the impact of Spanish rule was to bring about a degree of social levelling and changes in the political organization of communities, in the east Indian groups that had formerly been egalitarian underwent social differentiation and witnessed the introduction of a form of political organization, albeit weak, for the first time. Social differentiation occurred in two ways. First, whereas Indian leaders had only been elected on a temporary basis in pre-Columbian times, the position of the cacique was made permanent and hereditary, and caciques were differentiated from the mass of the common people by being granted certain privileges. Second, the introduction of Indian cabildos also resulted in the singling out of a small group of elected Indian officials who were accorded a higher social status. Thus, the colonial period witnessed a convergence in the social structure of Indian communities to be found in the east and west.

At the family level of organization the Spanish sought to impose monogamy and Christian standards of morality in marriage. They attempted to suppress polygamy and discourage the cohabitation of families in multifamily households. Polygamy was not widespread and it could be controlled relatively easily by parish priests. Most people

---

[18] AGI AG 10 Audiencia 17.3.1578; RAHM 9/4663 no.15 Valverde 24.8.1590; AGI PAT 183-1-16 Antonelli and López de Quintanillas 7.10.1590.

[19] AGI AG 53 Casa, vecino of Trujillo 1564; AGCA A3.13 527 5524 Romano 1586.

[20] RAHM CM A/66 Descripción de las Islas Guanajas 1.11.1639.

[21] Chapter 11, p. 199.

married, although the marriage rate fell during the eighteenth century. Tasaciones for Honduras for 1741 indicate that the percentage of adults who were married or who had been married was 87.7 percent, but by 1796 it had fallen to 76.5 percent.[22] These figures are not dissimilar to those noted for western and central Honduras. On the other hand the percentage of out-marriages appears to have been higher in the east. In 1702, 71.4 percent of marriages in the village of El Real were out-marriages, compared to 32 percent for 11 villages in western Honduras in 1703.[23] This is likely to have been higher than the norm, for in 1757 the average percentage of out-marriages in the east, although it is for men only, was 40.3 percent, which was over double the percentage noted for western and central Honduras at the same time.[24] Part of the reason for the higher percentage of out-marriages in the east was undoubtedly the small size of the villages, which restricted the choice of marriage partners. Similarly, the smaller villages possessed larger numbers of absentees (Table 12). This not only reflected the lack of marriage partners and employment opportunities there, but the attraction of other areas for settlement. Although the padrones for 1796 do not record the location of absentees consistently, some are noted as residing in Comayagua, Tegucigalpa, and the mining areas.[25] Just as the numbers of out-marriages and absentees were increasing, so also were the number of Indians marrying other races, although they were always few. In 1741 and 1757 such marriages accounted for under 2 percent of all marriages,[26] and by 1796 the proportion had only increased to 4.9 percent, and all except one had a mulatto spouse.[27] This increase is likely to have been due to the increased number of *libres* in the area, many of whom arrived from the middle of the century to form the militia for defense against the Zambos-Mosquitos.

There is only fragmentary evidence for family sizes in eastern Honduras and then only for the eighteenth century. The 1777 and 1778 censuses of Honduras indicate that the adult/child ratio was 1:0.39 and 1:0.70, which are both slightly higher than in the west.[28] In common with the west, however, there was a slight increase in the ratio towards the end of the century to 1:0.96.[29] A fairly high proportion of the children were orphans, although not as high as in the west; in 1796, 7.2 percent of the children in eastern Honduras were orphans, although the figure is distorted by the high figure of 29.2 percent for Agalteca.[30]

The religious affairs of Indians residing in tributary Indian villages in the east fell under the jurisdiction of the secular clergy and as such the comments made about the

---

[22]AGCA A3.16 192 1975 tasaciones 1741 and Chapter 12, n. 140 and Table 12.

[23]Compare Table 10 with El Real AGCA A3.16 511 5326 17.10.1702.

[24]AGCA A3.16 2325 34320 Libro de tasaciones 1757.

[25]Table 12.

[26]For sources see n. 22 and 24.

[27]Table 12.

[28]Chapter 12, n. 140.

[29]Table 12.

[30]Ibid.

Table 12

DEMOGRAPHIC CHARACTERISTICS OF TRIBUTARY
INDIAN VILLAGES IN EASTERN HONDURAS IN 1796-97

| | Total | Adults | Chil-dren | % Mar-ried | % Mar-ried to Other Races | % Adults Absent | % Adult/ Child | % Orphans |
|---|---|---|---|---|---|---|---|---|
| Parish of Manto | | | | | | | | |
| Manto | 112 | 69 | 43 | 56.5 | 16.7 | 23.2 | 0.62 | 11.6 |
| Jano | 264 | 151 | 113 | 70.9 | 2.2 | 3.8 | 0.75 | 11.5 |
| La Guata | 220 | 115 | 105 | 74.8 | 0.0 | 4.3 | 0.91 | 4.8 |
| Yocon | 36 | 25 | 11 | 60.0 | 33.3 | 8.0 | 0.44 | 0.0 |
| Sapota | 107 | 47 | 60 | 55.3 | 30.0 | 0.0 | 1.27 | 0.0 |
| Catacamas | 1091 | 534 | 557 | 76.4 | 4.5 | 3.2 | 1.04 | 3.8 |
| El Real | 105 | 51 | 54 | 56.9 | 0.0 | 2.0 | 1.05 | 11.1 |
| Parish of Yorito | | | | | | | | |
| Yorito | 286 | 121 | 165 | 87.6 | 0.0 | 0.0 | 1.36 | 0.6 |
| Sulaco | 44 | 28 | 16 | 78.6 | 22.2 | 7.1 | 0.57 | 0.0 |
| Parish of Yoro | | | | | | | | |
| Jocon | 316 | 161 | 155 | 82.6 | 9.6 | 0.6 | 0.96 | 0.0 |
| Parish of Sonaguera | | | | | | | | |
| Agalteca | 401 | 216 | 185 | 81.5 | 0.0 | 0.5 | 0.86 | 29.2 |
| TOTAL | 2982 | 1518 | 1464 | 76.5 | 4.9 | 3.6 | 0.96 | 7.2 |

Source: AGCA A1.94 2011, 2016-22 Padrones 1796-7.

organization of the Church and its impact on the economic, social, and political life of the Indians apply equally to eastern Honduras, but a few additional observations are worth making. In the east the task of converting the Indians to Christianity was made even more difficult by the dispersed nature of the settlement pattern, by the greater diversity of languages that were spoken by the Indians, and by the greater difficulty of attracting clergy to work in these remote and unattractive areas; in Olancho one parish priest was responsible for ministering to 36 villages dispersed over an area of 130 leagues with difficult relief, heavy rains, and dangerous rivers such that it was only possible to visit them in summer.[31] In many cases, therefore, many Indian villages were visited irregularly by poor quality priests, with little training and knowledge of Indian languages, who were more interested in trading with the Indians than they were in converting them. As such the adoption of Christianity by Indians living in eastern Honduras was even more superficial than it was in the west.

## THE MISSIONS

The level of missionary activity in eastern Honduras varied considerably during the colonial period and it was largely related to the threat of attack or invasion by foreigners and the Zambos-Mosquitos; at times when these threats were greatest, the Crown gave greater support to missionary activity. The work of the missionaries was severely hampered by the attacks of the Zambos-Mosquitos, by trading contacts the Indians possessed with outside groups and by the increased reluctance of Indians to move into and remain in the missions. As a result the missions were highly unstable; few survived more than a few years and even those that did often changed sites. Nevertheless, during the short life of the missions the missionaries attempted to reorganize the life of the Indians.

It was the Crown's intention that Indians should live in sedentary villages and not "scattered through the countryside like savages and brutes."[32] Mission villages were established as miniature versions of Spanish towns with the houses erected around a central plaza, on which were located the church and administrative buildings. The specific sites of missions sometimes changed as a result of attacks, whilst their general location varied over time according to which sites were considered more appropriate for effecting conversions.[33]

Although the location of the missions varied throughout the colonial period, they differed little in their economic and social organization. Prior to missionization, Indians in this area subsisted on manioc and plantains, though some groups relied more on maize and sweet potatoes. In addition they cultivated or exploited wild cacao to make chocolate. Agriculture was not practiced throughout the year; the rest of the time they

---

[31] AGI AG 164 Bishop of Honduras 12.5.1582. See also AGCA A1.12 46 416 Dean of the Cathedral of Comayagua 21.5.1698.

[32] AGCA A1.23 1513 f.639 cédula 17.11.1584.

[33] Chapter 13, passim.

subsisted on hunting, fishing, and gathering.[34] One of the main aims of the missionary orders was to 'civilize' the Indians and this meant congregating them into permanent nucleated settlements, where they could be taught the techniques of cultivation, livestock raising, and craft skills. Initially the Indians were fed on provisions, mainly maize and meat, which were imported by the missionaries, but at the same time they were given plots of land, tools, and animals, notably chickens, cattle, and some horses, with which to establish a permanent form of agriculture. It seems likely that a land-holding system similar to that found in tributary Indian villages was introduced in the missions; whilst the community owned the land, plots would have been allocated to individuals for cultivation, although pastures are likely to have been held in common even though many of the animals grazed on them were privately owned.[35] In 1713 an order specified that all reducciones were to have adequate "water, lands, and montes" as well as an ejido consisting of one league of land, for the grazing of livestock."[36] The similarity of the land-holding system in the missions to that in the tributary Indian villages is to be expected given that it was the intention that the missions would one day be secularized. The missionaries appear to have preferred open sites where the Indians could cultivate their plots and raise livestock. In areas where land was restricted, the Indians had to locate their plots in the hills, and this was considered undesirable since it afforded them opportunities to flee.[37]

Unfortunately there is no evidence for the organization of labor in the missions, although it seems likely that it would have been regulated by missionaries. The burden of work imposed on the Indians was probably not very great for the missions only aimed at self-sufficiency and the Indians were not required to meet the external demands of tribute payment and the repartimiento. Nevertheless, it is clear that the Indians resented work in the missions and preferred their semi-nomadic existence in the forests; most of the work in the missions was agricultural, whereas previously they had been involved in a greater variety of economic activities.[38]

There is little evidence for the character of agriculture in the missions, but that which exists suggests that maize was the dominant crop raised regardless of the area in which the mission was located.[39] For Indian groups living in areas that were not naturally suited for the cultivation the crop this would have been an innovation. In many

---

[34]Chapter 4, pp. 69-79; AGI AG 55 López 1579, AG 12 Criado de Castilla 30.11.1608, AG 175 Fr. Verdelete 29.4.1611, AG 39 On a reducción in the valley of Olomán 1616, Testimonio de una entrada 4.6.1616; BAGG 5: 283-308 Fr. Espino 17.9.1674; AGI AG 164 Bishop of Honduras 27.2.1696, AG 43 Fr. Henríquez 1700.

[35]AGI AG 223 Visita of the pueblo of Candelaria 20.8.1698; AGCA A3.1 800 14832 f.33 Frs. Santa Cruz and Mosquera 28.11.1690; AGI AG 297 Testimonio...sobre la reducción 1698; CDHCR 10: 258-65 Guardián del colegio de misioneros franciscanos 3.11.1797.

[36]AGCA A1.23 1525 10080 f. 254 cédula 15.9.1713, A1.12 50 499 12.3.1740.

[37]BAGG 7: 3-45 Informes acerca las misiones de Lean y Mulía 1757; BAGG 7: 80-115 Franco 10.2.1761.

[38]Chapter 4, pp. 69-70.

[39]AGI AG 223 Visita of the pueblo of Candelaria 20.8.1698; BAGG 5:283-308 Fr. Espino 17.9.1674.

cases the missionaries had to teach the Indians how to cultivate new crops and even the basic techniques of cultivation; in 1716 missionaries in the Catacamas valley were reported as showing the Indians how to establish milpas and plots for the cultivation of plantains, manioc, sweet potatoes, and sugar.[40] Also new to the Indians were domesticated animals, which proved vital sources of food for the missions, particularly in the initial stages of their foundation. They were also distributed to the Indians in order to encourage them to remain in the missions.[41] The raising of livestock supplanted hunting and fishing as sources of protein. Although the latter activities may have continued on a small scale, they were not encouraged or even permitted by the missionaries because of the opportunities they afforded for fugitivism. There is little evidence of food shortages in the missions and in most cases their failure to survive was attributable to other factors, such as attack by the Zambos-Mosquitos or desertion, rather than to inadequacies in the subsistence base.

In addition to instructing the Indians in agricultural techniques, the missionaries also taught the men to read, and the women "to sew, wash, cook and carry out other household duties."[42] They also taught them various crafts, notably the spinning and weaving of cotton. Although the Indians did manufacture small amounts of cotton in pre-Columbian times, most of their clothes were made of bark cloth and the missionaries considered them to be indecent.[43] The missionaries also trained the Indians to be carpenters and blacksmiths, and in 1797 Indians in the mission at Luquique manufactured riding equipment, such as saddle bags, reins, lassoes, and halters, which they sold in the surrounding area.[44] However, any trade with persons outside the missions was regulated by the missionaries, although Indians within the missions would have been able to exchange small items amongst themselves.

The impact of missionization on the social organization of Indian communities was profound and largely destructive. During the process of congregating the Indians into the missions many Indian communities were destroyed, and during the short life of the missions no form of community organization, independent of that imposed by the missionaries, emerged to encourage them to stay. As a result many Indians fled, leaving a socially fragmented population, which was unbalanced in terms of its age and sex structure, and which finally dispersed when the missionaries left.

During the process of missionization many Indian communities were broken up to the extent that the Indians collected together in one mission were often drawn from several communities. In some cases the Indians were so hostile to each other that they

---

[40]Anon., "Informe...acerca de la invasión que indios Payas pretendían hacer al pueblo de Catacamas...17.2.1716," *RABNH* 25 (1946): 193-97.

[41]AGCA A1.12 50 499 12.3.1740, A1.12 334 7060 Fr. Alcántara 25.5.1749, A1.12 334 7061 Testimonio...de los gastos hechos en la conquista de Lean y Yoro 1752; CDHCR 10: 258-65 Guardián del colegio apostólico de misioneros franciscanos 3.11.1797; Fr. Saldaña, "Del cuaderno y diligencias...de varios indios Xicaques en el valle de San Juan," *RABNH* 28 (1949): 97-101 8.6.1749.

[42]CDHCR 10: 258-63 Guardián del colegio apostólico de misioneros franciscanos 3.11.1797.

[43]BAGG 5: 283-308 Fr. Espino 17.9.1674; AGI AG 164 Bishop of Honduras 27.2.1696.

[44]CDHCR 10: 258-65 Guardián de colegio apostólico de misioneros franciscanos 3.11.1797.

had to be segregated out and settled in distinct missions. This occurred when missions were established in the Olancho valley by Fr. Verdelete at the beginning of the seventeenth century, and when Frs. Espino and Ovalle founded missions in the same valley and that of Agalta in the 1660s.[45] With missions containing fragments of former communities with few common interests and with dissension amongst them sometimes aggravated by contact with outside groups, such as the Zambos-Mosquitos and English, who encouraged them to escape, the task of integrating the Indians into a community was a formidable one. The process was not helped by the fact that the missionaries chose to supervise closely all aspects of Indian life, thus divesting the Indians of the faculty to regulate their own lives and establish some form of community organization. In most cases, therefore, when the missionaries died or left, the Indians dispersed, generally to resume their former way of life in the forests, and the mission settlements disintegrated. As such, few missions ever became secular settlements.

Within the missions a form of social structure was introduced. The absence of native leaders made it difficult for the missionaries to impose discipline in the missions.[46] This was overcome to some extent by the establishment of Indian cabildos, which aimed at instructing Indians in political affairs and prepare them for the role they were to play when the missions became secularized. In the eighteenth century Indians in the Franciscan missions elected alcaldes, regidores, and a fiscal on January 1 of each year.[47] Although Indian officials were supposed to be elected, in many cases they were probably chosen by the missionaries as being the most politically reliable.

Indian family life was profoundly affected by missionization. First, some family units were destroyed during the process of missionization, particularly where force was employed. Those brought into the missions generally came from a variety of communities and amongst them the old, women, and children, who were less able to escape, predominated. In 1699 over 50 percent of the Indians settled in the missions of Purísima Concepción de San Diego and Santa María de los Dolores were under 18 or over 50.[48] Similarly, in the case of the mission of San Miguel, established in Lean and Mulía about 1740, the initial population comprised 29 women and 54 children, but only 19 men.[49] Such imbalances in the age and sex composition of the missions did not alter much over time, because of the greater ability of able-bodied adults to flee. In 1711, 20 percent of the population of the four missions in the valleys of Olancho and Agalta, which had been established for 30 to 40 years, was under 18 and 40 percent over 50.[50] Fugitivism began as soon as the missions were founded. Following the establishment of a mission, the missionaries would often leave in search of new converts returning to find

[45]CDHCN: 92-122 Criado de Castilla 30.11.1608; BAGG 5: 283-308 Fr. Espino 17.9.1674; AGI AG 371 Fr. Ximénez 9.9.1748; Vázquez, *Crónica* 4: 113-23; Juarros, *Statistical and Commercial History*, pp. 350-52.

[46]For example, AGI AG 297 Fr. Betancurt 9.8.1698.

[47]CDHCR 10: 258-63 Guardián del colegio apostólico de misioneros franciscanos 3.11.1797.

[48]AGI AG 223 Testimonio...de la conversión de los indios Payas 1699.

[49]AGCA A1.12 50 499 26.2.1740.

[50]AGI AG 223 Testimonio...sobre la nueva reducción de los indios de la nación Paya 1711.

that the greater proportion of those settled in the mission had fled. This occurred shortly after the mission of Santa María de los Dolores was established in 1698, when 22 out of the 40 Indians settled there fled whilst the missionaries were absent converting other Indians.[51] Similarly, the population of another mission established in the valley of Yoro in the 1620s fell rapidly from 76 to 28 as a result of deaths and desertions.[52]

Many of the Indians who were collected into the missions were familiar with polygamy, which the missionaries regarded as a sin and sought to suppress. In 1773 it was suggested that missionary expeditions should be accompanied by women in order to demonstrate to the Indians that a man could be satisfied with one wife.[53] Although the missionaries probably achieved some temporary success in imposing monogamy, it appears that as soon as they left, the Indians returned to their own marriage customs and rites.[54] Even when they were in the missions, the missionaries found it difficult to control marriages between relatives that were permitted by Indian customs; a missionary in the mission of Santa María de los Dolores reported that the Indians were marrying "their cousins, nephews and nieces and their wives' daughters" (presumably by an earlier marriage).[55] The missions formed relatively closed communities so that the choice of marriage partners was fairly restricted, though small numbers appear to have married tributary Indians and even people of other races.[56]

The sizes of families within the missions seems to have been comparable to those in tributary villages in eastern Honduras. In the missions of San Miguel and Santa Cruz in 1749 the ratio of adults to children was 1:0.80 and 1:0.81 respectively.[57] Nevertheless, evidence for the mission of San Francisco Luquique suggests that such ratios were highly variable over time. For the dates of 1777, 1778, and 1797 the ratios were 1:0.87, 1:1.54, and 1:0.41.[58] Although there were probably differences in the method of recording at different dates, these variations probably also reflect the very unstable demographic and social composition of the missions. The ratio of children to adults may appear high given the disruption of family life caused by missionization and the depression that appears to have afflicted many Indians who were settled in

---

[51] AGI AG 223 Testimonio...sobre la conversión de los indios Payas 1699.

[52] AGI AG 968A Bishop of Honduras 27.2.1696.

[53] AGCA A1.23 1529 f.532-44 Diaz Navarro 18.5.1773.

[54] AGI AG 164 Bishop of Honduras 27.2.1696.

[55] AGI AG 223 Testimonio...de la conversión de los indios Payas 1699.

[56] AGI AG 183 Frs. Ovalle and Guevara 4.3.1681. For example, AGI AG 223 Testimonio...sobre la nueva reducción de los indios de la nación Paya 1711.

[57] AGCA A1.12 334 7060 Testimonio de...hechos en la misión y conquista de los indios Jicaques 1752.

[58] AGI IG 1527 Estado y Padrón General...1777 and Estado General que manifiesta...1778; CDHCR 10: 258-65 Guardián del colegio apostólico de misioneros franciscanos 3.11.1797.

missions,[59] but the ratio is inflated by adults deserting the missions, leaving orphans and children to be raised by relatives.[60] The declining size of households does suggest that fewer children were being raised than was the case prior to missionization. The missions established from the late 1660s in the valleys of Olancho and Agalta had initial household sizes of between 2.0 and 5.5 souls.[61] By 1711, however, household sizes in the same missions had generally fallen to between 2.8 and 3.6 persons.[62]

Table 13

DEMOGRAPHIC CHARACTERISTICS OF FRANCISCAN MISSIONS
IN THE VALLEYS OF OLANCHO AND AGALTA IN 1711

| Mission | 50 & over No. | % | 18-49 No. | % | Under 18 No. | % | Households No. | Ave. Size | Adult/ Child |
|---|---|---|---|---|---|---|---|---|---|
| Santa María de Paya | 6 | 13.0 | 19 | 42.2 | 20 | 44.4 | 13 | 3.46 | 0.80 |
| San Sebastián de Aguaquire | 17 | 19.8 | 34 | 39.5 | 35 | 40.6 | 31 | 2.77 | 0.69 |
| San Joseph de Aguaquire | 10 | 18.5 | 21 | 38.9 | 23 | 42.6 | 15 | 3.60 | 0.74 |
| San Buen-b aventura | 7 | 14.9 | 20 | 42.6 | 20 | 42.6 | 15 | 3.13 | 0.74 |
| TOTAL | 40 | 17.2 | 94 | 40.5 | 98 | 42.2 | 74 | 3.14 | 0.73 |

Source: AGI AG 223 Testimonio...sobre la nueva reducción...1711.

[59] AGI AG 223 Testimonio...de la conversión de los indios Payas 1699, AG 968A Bishop of Honduras 27.2.1696.

[60] AGI AG 223 Testimonio...sobre la nueva reducción de los indios de la nación Paya 1711.

[61] AGI AG 39 Godoy y Ponce de León 15.3.1676. The figures are: Santa María 2.0, San Francisco 5.5, San Pedro 4.4, San Sebastián 4.4. The number of houses is not given for San Buenaventura and San Felipe and even the other figures are rounded to the nearest 10, suggesting that they were very general estimates.

[62] AGI AG 223 Testimonio sobre la nueva reducción de los indios de la nación Paya 1711. The figures are: Santa María 3.5, San Sebastián 2.8, San Joseph 3.6, San Buenaventura 3.1.

The organizational structure of the Franciscan and Mercedarian orders and their aims, activities, and means of converting the Indians have already been described, so that comments here will be confined to discussing their impact on the religious beliefs and practices of the Indians. The absence of idols, temples, priests, and sacrificial ceremonies gladdened the hearts of the missionaries and suggested to them that the task of conversion would be relatively easy.[63] The absence of idols was, however, more apparent than real, particularly amongst the Paya, who were said to possess idols in secret places in the forest[64] and in such large numbers that each person possessed his own idol.[65] The initial optimism of the missionaries was soon dispelled, however, when the missionaries began to collect the Indians into the missions. The absence of community leaders made Indian conversions more difficult and protracted. The Indians were generally reluctant to move into the missions, although some were easier to convert than others; amongst the Jicaque they distinguished those of "genio alegre y despejado," who were easy to instruct, from those who were "crudos, agrestes y melancólicos," who were more difficult to convert.[66] As a result the missionaries often resorted to the use of force to bring the Indians into the missions. This aroused resentment and discouraged the Indians from adopting Christian beliefs, whilst their instruction was made even more difficult by the diversity of languages they spoke. As such the Indians only practiced Christianity under duress and the lack of true conversion is demonstrated by their constant desire to return to their homes in the hills, lured by the "voices of witches."[67] Even in the missions the Indians continued to adhere to their own customs; in 1698 Fr. Betancurt reported that although missions amongst the Paya had been in existence for 20 years the Indians didn't know about God or how to make the sign of the cross and they were "idolators, sorcerers and polygamists."[68] Finally, when the missionaries left, the Indians reverted to their former beliefs and ceremonies.[69] Thus, despite the apparent lack of religious beliefs in the east, the missionaries found the task of converting the Indians there a formidable one.


INDIANS OUTSIDE SPANISH CONTROL


During the seventeenth century Indian groups that lived outside Spanish control were affected by the activities of missionaries and the settlement of the English on the Mosquito Shore, and as time progressed contacts with the English, Zambos-Mosquitos,

---

[63]BAGG 5: 283-308 Fr. Espino 17.9.1674; AGI AG 164 Bishop of Honduras 27.2.1696.

[64]ANH P5 L66 29.10.1698.

[65]AGI AG 297 Fr. Betancurt 9.8.1698.

[66]AGI IG 1525 Misioneros apostólicos de Propaganda Fide 7.1.1813, AG 963 Guardián of the Colegio de Propaganda Fide 10.1.1813.

[67]BAGG 7: 3-45 Bishop of Honduras 31.7.1759.

[68]AGI AG 297 Fr. Betancurt 9.8.1698.

[69]AGI AG 164 Bishop of Honduras 27.2.1696.

and ladinos, who settled on the fringes of the colonized area, intensified. These contacts appear to have had significant, though varied, effects on the distribution of Indian settlements and economic activities; they appear to have had less significant effects on the social organization and ideology of these groups. Although this may reflect the inadequacy of the documentary record, more likely it stems from the economic nature of contacts; no direct attempts were made to alter the social organization or ideology of the Indians.

Despite the lack of precise information relating to the number and size of settlements in the area in the seventeenth century, it is clear that the area remained highly populated, even though some Indians were collected into the missions or were enslaved by the Zambos-Mosquitos. An entrada into the area between the Rivers Lean and Mulía in 1689 revealed 40 Indian villages,[70] and in 1699, 18 settlements of Guaianes were enumerated in the headwaters of the Río Segovia.[71] Nevertheless, the sites of settlements changed as the Indians retreated into the remote mountain areas to avoid contact with missionaries and the Zambos-Mosquitos, and in the case of the Jicaque they only returned to the coast during the turtle-fishing season.[72] In 1813 the settlements of the Jicaque were described as follows: "their villages are very many but small and dispersed in the highest parts of the mountains or in deep valleys in order to escape not only from Spanish domination but also from being surprised by thefts of women and children."[73] These settlements, of which there were 50 to 60, consisted of "groups of houses, which they call villages,"[74] and their sites were often moved as a result of bad omens, sickness, or death.[75] The Paya also appear to have retreated inland from the coast between Río Tinto and Cabo de Gracias a Dios, as the coast was occupied by the English and Zambos-Mosquitos.[76] At the beginning of the nineteenth century Fr. Goicoechea noted that Payas were living in the mountains of Agalta dispersed in families comprised of 8 to 20, and even more, persons.[77] Many of these movements inland would also have involved the abandonment of riverine sites that were most prone to attack; new settlements would have been located on the interfluves, where the soils would not have been so fertile and hence agriculture not so productive.

As contacts with outside groups increased and as the Indians moved inland, their economy changed. Whilst cultivation and hunting were still practiced, fishing probably declined in importance; indeed the Paya obtained fish by trade with the English on the

---

[70]Ibid.

[71]AGI AG 223 Fr. Pedro de la Concepción 13.1.1699.

[72]AGI AG 449 and CDHCN: 96-136 Diaz Navarro 30.11.1758; AGCA A1.12 118 2487 Anguiano 1.7.1798; Floyd, *Anglo-Spanish Struggle*, pp. 88-89.

[73]AGI IG 1525 Misioneros apostólicos de Propaganda Fide 1.7.1813, AG 963 Guardián of the Colegio de Propaganda Fide 10.1.1813.

[74]AGCA A1.37 2335 17514 Anguiano 1.7.1798.

[75]Squier, "The Xicaque," p. 760.

[76]Conzemius, "Los Indios Payas," p. 245.

[77]Goicoechea, "Relación sobre los indios gentiles," pp. 303-15.

coast.[78] Root crops, notably plantains, manioc, sweet potatoes, and the fruit of the pejibaye palm, remained the most important crops cultivated and collected. Plantains were particularly abundant such that platanares extended for leagues along river banks.[79] In some cases cultivation only supplied food for part of the year, the rest was provided by the collection of wild fruits and vegetables, and the hunting of peccaries, coati-mundis, armadillos, rabbits, and deer.[80] In order to supply goods demanded by traders, collecting and to a lesser extent hunting may have increased.

Trade had an important influence on economic activities. The Jicaque and Paya traded with the English and ladinos, and in addition the Paya traded with the Zambos-Mosquitos. Formerly the Zambos-Mosquitos had conducted enslaving raids amongst these Indians, but encouraged by the English, who preferred more peaceful contraband trading, they turned the relationship from one of enslaving and exacting 'protection money,' to one of trading and more formal forms of tribute exaction. In the 1720s the Zambos-Mosquitos defeated the Paya in battle and from that time on exacted tribute from them in the form of cattle.[81] The main items sought after by the English, Zambos-Mosquitos, and ladinos were sarsaparilla and other balsams, gums, and resins for medicinal purposes, and dyewoods.[82] In addition the Indians provided some agricultural products such as cacao, vanilla, and tobacco. Other items in high demand were gold and silver, which were smuggled over from Tegucigalpa, and cattle. The Indians did not raise the cattle themselves, but they generally obtained them by trading with ladinos, by raiding frontier estates, or by capturing feral cattle. In 1759 Paya Indians between Catacamas and Petaste were said to possess 1,000 head of cattle.[83] In return for these goods the Indians received European manufactures and firearms. As early as 1722 it was observed that the Paya possessed "300 guns, gunpowder and shot."[84] Most of the items they received, however, consisted of tools and trinkets. For example, the Jicaque Indians received from ladinos, "machetes, knives, razors, scissors, nets, fishing hooks, looking glasses, rings, glass beads, ribbons, rosaries and earrings."[85]

---

[78]AGCA A1.12 117 2473 Yarrince 18.9.1759.

[79]AGCA A1.12 118 2487 Anguiano 1.7.1798; Goicoechea, "Relación sobre los indios gentiles," pp. 303-15.

[80]Chapter 4, p. 76; and Goicoechea, "Relación sobre los indios gentiles," pp. 303-15.

[81]AGCA A1.12 134 1504 13.12.1722; AGI AG 501 Anguiano 10.5.1804; Long, *History of Jamaica* 1: 326-27; Henderson, *British Settlement of Honduras*, p. 190.

[82]For trade see: AGCA A1.12 134 1504 13.12.1722, A1.12 117 2473 Yarrince 18.9.1759; AGI AG 449 Lara y Ortega 18.9.1759; BAGG 7: 80-115 Informes acerca de las misiones de Lean y Mulía 24.11.1766; AGCA A1.12 118 2487 and AGI AG 457 Anguiano 1.7.1798; AGI AG 501 Anguiano 10.5.1804, Informe de la provincia de Honduras 20.2.1816, IG 1525 Misioneros apostólicos de Propaganda Fide 7.1.1813; Roberts, *Narrative of Voyages*, pp. 161, 166; Squier, *Notes on Central America*, pp. 147-48; Floyd, *Anglo-Spanish Struggle*, p. 61.

[83]AGCA A1.12 117 2473 Yarrince 18.9.1759.

[84]AGCA A1.12 134 1504 13.12.1722.

[85]AGCA A1.12 118 2487 Anguiano 1.7.1798.

Despite these increased contacts with outside groups, the social and political organization of Indians in this area does not appear to have changed significantly. They remained essentially egalitarian, "without god, nor law, nor king,"[86] and continued to appoint temporary leaders only as community requirements necessitated.[87] Although increased contacts with outside groups, either through raids or later through trade, would have increased the demand for leaders who could lead groups in defense or attack and could act as community spokesmen, there is no evidence that their positions became permanent. The only possible evidence of the existence of permanent leaders is a description of a Paya community living near the Río Tinto, which was said to be governed by an Indian called Phelipe.[88] The Spanish name indicates that the group had had contacts with Europeans, and he was probably no more than a temporary leader who acted as village spokesman when the need arose. In the absence of any permanent form of political organization, groups united in *palenques* according to kinship and friendship. These palenques often helped each other in defense or revenge, and sometimes they banded together against other groups of palenques belonging to the same stock.[89] There is no evidence for the existence of a lower class of slaves. Slaves were either sacrificed or sold to the Zambos-Mosquitos.[90]

Although the missionaries were outspoken in their criticisms of polygamous practices amongst inland Indian groups,[91] probably only a few individuals possessed more than one wife. The Indians were generally considered to be monogamous, although sometimes the elders had several wives.[92] Documentary evidence of marriage residence rules amongst these groups is lacking, but Helms has suggested that the neighboring Sumu may have been patrilocal. She contrasts them with the Zambos-Mosquitos, amongst whom matrilocality was the rule, which she argues was better adapted to the prolonged absence of men from their villages, which contact with the English fostered.[93] Despite contacts with outside groups and the loss of individuals, particularly women and children, to the missions or enslaving raids, the social organization of inland groups appears to have changed very little.

While the missionaries had little success in converting the Indians, some provided vivid descriptions of their religious practices. The missionaries were pleasantly surprised

---

[86]AGCA A1.23 1529 f.532-44 Díaz Navarro 18.5.1773.

[87]AGI AG 343 Fr. Herrera 8.2.1700, AG 371 Fr. Ximénez 9.9.1748.

[88]AGCA A1.12 117 2473 Yarrince 18.7.1759.

[89]AGI IG 1525 Misioneros apostólicos de Propaganda Fide 7.1.1813.

[90]Chapter 4, pp. 81, 85, and Chapter 15, p. 282.

[91]BAGG 5: 283-308 Fr. Espino 17.9.1674; AGI AG 164 Bishop of Honduras 27.2.1676, AG 343 Fr. Herrera 8.2.1700, AG 371 Fr. Ximénez 9.9.1748.

[92]Chapter 4, p. 81; Goicoechea, "Relación sobre los indios gentiles," pp. 303-15; AGI AG 963 Guardián del Colegio de Propaganda Fide 10.1.1813.

[93]Helms, "Matrilocality"; and idem, *Asang*, pp. 24-27.

to find that the Indians did not worship idols, even though they possessed gods.[94] An early nineteenth century account indicated that amongst the Jicaque, "there is no religion, nor god, nor idol, they know that there is a devil who they call malotaes, of whom they are afraid."[95] Another account of the same group noted that, "they are not so idolatrous as other Indians, they have sorcerers, they speak with the moon, and through them have other abuses such as a belief that they can foretell those who come and go, and without worship or knowledge of the true God."[96] Further details of beliefs in gods and spirits, as well as religious ceremonies have already been described,[97] and they probably changed little during the colonial period. This conclusion is backed by more recent ethnographic accounts that suggest that their religious practices have not been profoundly modified by Christianity.[98]

THE MOSQUITO SHORE

The cultural changes experienced by Indians living on the Mosquito Shore emanated from the settlement of Europeans and negroes on the Caribbean coast, which later became known as the Mosquito Shore. The permanent settlement of Europeans on the Shore did not occur until the 1630s, but prior to that time buccaneers of various nationalities temporarily camped on the coast, often provisioning themselves there before making attacks on the northern coast. The first negroes to arrive probably landed in 1641 as the result of a shipwreck;[99] there is some doubt as to the origin of the vessel but Holm has recently suggested that the slaves may have been fleeing from Providencia, which was recaptured by the Spanish in that year.[100] Subsequently, conflict arose between the newly arrived male negro slaves and the native Indians in which the negroes defeated them and took their women for wives, from which the so-called Zambos-Mosquitos emerged.[101] The negro contribution to this mixed racial group was maintained by the English, who introduced negro slaves from the Caribbean islands, especially Jamaica, to work on their plantations, and by runaway slaves both from the interior areas of

---

[94]BAGG 5: 283-308 Fr. Espino 17.9.1674, BAGG 7: 24-32 Fr. Joseph de Landa 31.7.1759; AGI AG 449 Bishop of Honduras 30.9.1758, AG 963 Guardián del Colegio de Propaganda Fide 10.1.1813.

[95]AGI IG Misioneros apostólicos de Propaganda Fide 7.1.1813, AG 963 Guardián del Colegio de Propaganda Fide 10.1.1813.

[96]BAGG 7: 24-32 Fr. Joseph de Landa 31.7.1759.

[97]Chapter 4, pp. 83-85.

[98]Conzemius, "Los Indios Payas," pp. 296-304; Von Hagen, "The Jicaque," pp. 59-60; Landero, "Los Taoajkas," pp. 46-47, 49-50.

[99]Chapter 2, p. 43; and AGI AG 299 Bishop of Nicaragua 30.11.1711.

[100]Holm, "Creole English," pp. 178-81.

[101]AGI AG 299 Bishop of Nicaragua 30.11.1711.

Honduras and Nicaragua, notably from the mining areas of Tegucigalpa and Comayagua, and also from plantations on the Caribbean coast and islands.

The arrival of Europeans and the emergence of the Zambos-Mosquitos resulted in changes in the settlement pattern on the Mosquito Shore. The area inhabited by the Zambos-Mosquitos expanded with the population, so that by the beginning of the nineteenth century they were dispersed in over 20 settlements, or rancherías, from the Río Tinto in Honduras south to Punta Gorda.[102] Whereas in pre-Columbian times the Indians had possessed temporary fishing settlements on the coast, due to the poor quality of the soils there, their permanent agricultural villages were located some distance inland; in some areas the soil was too sandy and in others it was covered with mangrove swamp. From the second half of the seventeenth century, however, it is clear that the Zambos-Mosquitos possessed some permanent settlements on the coast.[103] These settlements were more appropriately located to take advantage of the employment and trading opportunities offered by the English. The settlements were generally small, averaging between 50 and 150 persons, but there were larger settlements at Río Tinto, Cabo de Gracias a Dios, Sandy Bay, Pearl Lagoon, and Bluefields.[104] The only fortified settlement was that of the Mosquito king at Cabo de Gracias a Dios, which was surrounded by a wall and a deep ditch.[105] The settlements appear to have been racially mixed, with a few whites plus their slaves living in the same settlements as Indians. There is no evidence for the size of households, although it is clear that they lived in multifamily dwellings.[106]

The main aim of Europeans who settled on the Mosquito Shore was trade; they had no intention of directly altering the Indian economy. Nevertheless the demands they made on Indian labor and production did stimulate economic changes. The fact that Europeans came as traders rather than colonists, at least in the early years of the settlement of the coast, meant that only small stretches of Indian land were alienated. Even where they did establish sugar and cacao plantations, they often used areas that had not been cultivated by the Indians.[107] The English employed a small number of Indians as sailors and cabin boys on boats that traded between the coast and the Caribbean

---

[102]CDHCN: 63-77 Consulta de Consejo de Indias 8.7.1739; AGCA A1.17 335 7088 and CDHCN: 78-96 Rivera 23.11.1742.

[103]AGI AG 228 Lic. de Errera 29.4.1725; AGCA A1.17 335 7088 and CDHCN: 78-96 Rivera 23.11.1742; AGCA A1.17 4501 38303 Porta Costas 1.8.1790; BAGG 5: 157-75 5.3.1800; Roberts, *Narrative of Voyages*, pp. 115, 150; Dampier, *New Voyage*, p. 15; M.W., "Mosqueto Indian," pp. 300-301; Raveneau de Lussan, *Voyage into the South Seas*, pp. 285-87.

[104]MNM Bᵃ-XI Cᵃ-B n° 1 Hodgson and Hodgson 1782. Two other maps show the dispersion of the Zambos-Mosquitos along the coast: Mapa Ideal Particular de la Provincia de Nicaragua..., no date (MNM) and SHM 5185 Sig.D-13-37 Razón de los establecimientos que hay...John Clapp 2.9.1771.

[105]CDHCN: 63-77 Consulta de Consejo de Indias 8.7.1739.

[106]Chapter 4, pp. 68-69.

[107]They did, however, purchase some lands from the Indians (White, *Case of the Agent*, p. 51).

islands, particularly Jamaica,[108] but labor on plantations was undertaken by imported negro slaves. Nevertheless, trade did divert Indian labor into the acquisition of items, such as turtle shell, Indian slaves, cacao, sarsaparilla, and hard woods, which foreigners demanded.[109] The time expended in these activities reduced that available for subsistence and agriculture became a predominantly female activity.[110]

The economy of Indians living on the Shore was based on the cultivation of crops, heavily supplemented by fishing, and further inland by hunting. Cultivation generally took place several miles inland, because the lands on the coast were sandy and infertile. As settlements were increasingly located near the coast, although not actually on it, to take advantage of employment and trading opportunities Indians often had to travel inland to tend their plots. Even there crops took about a year to mature and the roots they produced were small. Those most commonly grown were plantains, manioc, sweet potatoes, and yams; maize was grown in small quantities and for the purpose of making beverages rather than bread.[111] In 1714 it was reported that the Mosquito lived on "fish, wild game, plantains and plants, roots and different vegetables, and from maize they make their drinks."[112] Plants were intercropped. Dampier described the cultivation plots of the Mosquitos as follows: "In the largest plantations they do not have above 20 to 30 plantain trees, a bed of yams, and potatoes, a bush of Indian pepper, and a small spot of pineapples."[113] During the seventeenth and early eighteenth centuries a few new crops were introduced into this area. In 1699 M.W. noted that bitter manioc was being grown from which the Indians made cassava,[114] and it seems likely that it was introduced to the Indians by foreign traders. By this time the coconut palm was well

---

[108]AGI AG 223 Fr. de la Concepción 13.1.1699.

[109]Ibid.; AGI AG 299 Bishop of Nicaragua 30.11.1711, AG 299 Testimony of five Indians...18.10.1707 (In Testimony for 1710); CDHCN: 12-63 Fiscal 5.6.1713; AGI AG 302 Vecino of Olancho 21.6.1718 (In Testimony for 1725); AGCA A3.16 1010 18564 f.103-4 Quijano 22.7.1776, A1.17 4501 38303 Porta Costas 1.8.1790; Roberts, *Narrative of Voyages*, p. 111.

[110]Conzemius, *Ethnographical Survey*, pp. 39-40; Helms, *Asang*, p. 23.

[111]For descriptions of the crops cultivated see: AGI AG 223 Fr. Pedro de la Concepción 13.1.1699; CDHCN: 12-63 Fiscal 5.6.1713, Aranzibia 14.1.1715; AGI AG 300 Informe de Consejo de Indias 25.2.1714, AG 299 Testimony of five Indians 18.10.1707 (In Testimony 1710); PRO CO 123/1 ff.55-79 Hodgson 1757; AGCA A1.1 118 2484 27.6.1790, A1.17 117 4501 38303 Porta Costas 1.8.1790; M.W., "Mosqueto Indian," pp. 308, 310; Esquemeling, *Buccaneers of America*, pp. 114, 235; Raveneau de Lussan, *Voyage into the South Seas*, p. 285; Henderson, *British Settlement of Honduras*, pp. 142, 179; Roberts, *Narrative of Voyages*, pp. 115, 128-30, 142; Young, *Narrative of a Residence on the Mosquito Shore During the Years 1839, 1840, 1841* (London: Smith, Elder & Co., 1842), pp. 107-08.

[112]AGI AG 300 Informe de Consejo de Indias 25.2.1714.

[113]Dampier, *New Voyage*, p. 16.

[114]M.W., "Mosqueto Indian," p. 301.

established on the Caribbean coast.[115] There is no evidence that the negroes who settled on the coast introduced any African domesticates, unless the yams recorded by Dampier were of an African variety. Indeed Raveneau de Lussan noted that around Cabo de Gracias a Dios the Indians taught the shipwrecked negroes to plant maize, bananas, and manioc and also to make a drink called *hoon* from an indigenous palm tree (probably the pejibaye palm).[116]

Due to the poor soils, there were considerable problems with food shortages. These were overcome in part by fishing and by Indians venturing into the mountains to hunt and collect wild fruits. Although the Europeans introduced domesticated animals, particularly cattle and horses, to the Mosquito Shore, they were not widely adopted by the Indians. Thus, in 1707 the economy of the Mosquito was described as follows: "they subsist on plantains and other edible roots and there is no domesticated meat only wild meat, that they usually eat, fish, some chickens and beans."[117] Although the Indians possessed many ingenious methods for capturing animals and fish, undoubtedly the guns and fishing equipment they obtained from the English made such activities more efficient. Firearms were greatly sought after by the Indians, to the extent that men were said to offer their wives to sleep with the English in order to acquire muskets.[118] However, in general they were acquired in exchange for turtle shell and Indian slaves.[119] It is worth noting here that firearms were not only used in hunting, but also in warfare and for the capture of Indian slaves. In 1721 the governor of Costa Rica reported that the Mosquito used firearms "like fish in the sea and birds in the air" such that they could compete with Spaniards in war.[120] At sea the Mosquito used canoes that were generally made by inland groups who traded them in a half-finished state with those who lived on the coast.[121] Archaeological evidence indicates that these developments in fishing equipment and marine transport enabled the Indians to expand their fishing activities to offshore waters.[122]

Many of the characteristics of trade between the English and the Zambos-Mosquitos have already been described and it is clear that this trade dominated over that between the Indians themselves. Generally speaking European manufactures, notably guns, gunpowder, a variety of tools including fishing equipment, and European cloth were exchanged for turtle shell, cacao, and Indian slaves, although other wild products

---

[115]Ibid.

[116]Raveneau de Lussan, *Voyage into the South Seas*, p. 285.

[117]AGI AG 299 Testimony of five Indians...18.10.1707 (In Testimony 1710), AG 300 Informe de Consejo de Indias 25.2.1714; CDHCN: 12-63 Aranzibia 14.1.1715.

[118]AGI AG 223 Fr. Pedro de la Concepción 13.1.1699.

[119]Ibid.; CDHCN: 12-63 Fiscal 5.6.1713, Aranzibia 14.1.1715; Vázquez, *Crónica* 4:81.

[120]AGI AG 301 Governor of Costa Rica 15.12.1721.

[121]PRO CO 123/1 ff.55-79 Hodgson 1757; BAGG 7: 157-75 5.3.1800; Henderson, *British Settlement of Honduras*, p. 180; Roberts, *Narrative of Voyages*, pp. 119-21, 156.

[122]Magnus, "Prehistoric and Modern Subsistence Patterns."

such as honey, wax, and sarsaparilla were also traded.[123] The acquisition of items for trade with the English, sometimes obtained through trade with inland groups, appears to have consumed a large proportion of the Zambos-Mosquitos' time. No mediums of exchange appear to have been used, neither were formal markets established.

From the mid-seventeenth century the sociopolitical organization of Indians living on the Mosquito Shore changed so much that in 1809 Henderson was able to remark that, "Neither the Poyers or the Towkcas possess anything like the civilization of the Mosquito people."[124] Throughout the period the main influence on life of the Indians was the English, even though they evacuated the Shore in 1787. Relationships between the races appear to have been very good to the extent that one observer noted that the English "let them eat at their table."[125] The alliance between the English and the Zambos-Mosquitos resulted in the imposition of leaders on what had formerly been an egalitarian society. In pre-Columbian times Indians living on the Mosquito coast had been essentially egalitarian with temporary leaders chosen to lead expeditions against hostile neighbors; at other times they had no form of government.[126] After contact, according to Conzemius (quoting Exquemelin), the Mosquito selected leaders in times of war, but those who were preferred were those who had sailed with the buccaneers.[127] This reflects the friendship that had developed between the Mosquito and the English, and the prestige they accorded the latter, on whom they were dependent for the firearms that were essential for their domination of the coast.

In addition to the temporary war leaders, the English established a number of official positions in order to substantiate their claims to the Shore. They attempted to create the Kingdom of Mosquitia, with a king at its head. The date of the origin of the kingship is uncertain; it had certainly been established by 1687 when the chief at Cabo de Gracias a Dios was crowned King Jeremy I.[128] From that time onwards the king was chosen by the governor of Jamaica, theoretically from a list of candidates. The governor of Jamaica later found it desirable to extend the support of the Zambos-Mosquitos and established a number of other offices along the coast: a general was established at Black River, a governor at Tuapí Lagoon, and an admiral at Pearl Lagoon. Nevertheless it was

---

[123]AGI AG 223 Fr. Pedro de la Concepción 13.1.1699; CDHCN: 12-63 Fiscal 5.6.1713; AGI AG 300 Informe de Consejo de Indias 25.2.1714, AG 302 Rivera 10.5.1737; AGCA A1.12 117 2473 Yarrince 18.9.1759; AGI AG 665 and CDHCN: 198-205 Diario de Antonio de Gastelu 11.7.1776; AGCA A1.17 4501 38303 Porta Costas 1.8.1790; BAGG 7: 157-75 5.3.1800; AGCA A1.17 2875 26357 Dictamen del Diputado 31.8.1813, A1.17 2875 26354 Informe rendido...Anguiano ca.1814; Strangeways, *Sketch of the Mosquito Shore*, p. 337; Roberts, *Narrative of Voyages*, pp. 108, 116-18; Young, *Residence on the Mosquito Shore*, p. 82; Squier, *Notes on Central America*, pp. 147-48; Vázquez, *Crónica* 4: 81; Floyd, *Anglo-Spanish Struggle*, pp. 58, 60-61.

[124]Henderson, *British Settlement of Honduras*, p. 190.

[125]AGCA A1.12 117 2473 Yarrince 18.9.1759.

[126]M.W., "Mosqueto Indian," pp. 301, 307; Dampier, *New Voyage*, p. 17; Esquemeling, *Buccaneers of America*, p. 234.

[127]Conzemius, *Ethnographical Survey*, p. 101.

[128]M.W., "Mosqueto Indian," p. 302; M.W. Helms, "The Cultural Ecology of a Colonial Tribe," *Ethnology* 8 (1969): 78.

the king who commanded the greatest respect. He resided in a thatched palace at Sandy Bay during the turtle season and in another palace on the Río Segovia for the rest of the year. From the early eighteenth century at least, the king was generally a zambo or mulatto, whereas further south the governor at Tuapí Lagoon was generally a Mosquito Indian.[129] Originally the position of king was not hereditary, but when the English evacuated the coast the most important positions appear to have become hereditary. In 1809 Henderson observed that, "The government of the Mosquito Indians is hereditary; and a very exact and perfect idea of British law of succession is entertained by them."[130] There was some rivalry between the king and the governor, and also between less important leaders amongst the Mosquito branch of the Zambos-Mosquitos.[131] Many of those who held office were in fact related. Even though all the Zambos-Mosquitos were under the authority of the king, they were divided up into parcialidades and battalions of about 100 to 150 Indians, which were under the command of captains.[132] It is uncertain how they were selected, but they were probably those who had demonstrated the greatest dexterity in raiding and warfare. The most important officials received British army uniforms and other insignia, which they continued to wear long after the English had evacuated the coast.[133]

The king, governor, and many lesser captains were clearly able to muster large fighting forces and the former were undoubtedly respected as key men in relations with the English. At first their power does not appear to have been very extensive such that Hodgson observed that they undertook no action without consulting the elders and that their directions were followed rather than their orders obeyed.[134] By the end of the century, however, it was considerable. In 1793 it was said that the king was respected and feared, and at the beginning of the nineteenth century Henderson described the power of leaders as follows:

> Legislative and judicial power resides exclusively in the will of him who governs. The king, or chief is completely despotic. Whenever he dispatches a messenger, his commands are always accompanied by his cane; this establishes credibility of the bearer and a sudden compliance with the purport of his errand. In this way decrees are enforced, the punishment due to offence remitted or the severest sentence annexed to it carried into instant execution.[135]

---

[129]CDHCN: 63-77 Consulta de Consejo de Indias 8.7.1739; Floyd, *Anglo-Spanish Struggle*, pp. 62-64.

[130]Henderson, *British Settlement of Honduras*, p. 183.

[131]Floyd, *Anglo-Spanish Struggle*, pp. 123-25, 172-82; Newson, *Indian Survival*.

[132]BM Add. 17,566 f.169 Relación de las poblaciones...19.1.1746; AGCA A1.12 117 2473 Yarrince 18.9.1759; MNM Bª-XI Cª-B n° 1 Hodgson and Hodgson 1782; Edwards, "British Settlements," p. 210.

[133]Henderson, *British Settlement of Honduras*, pp. 146, 182.

[134]PRO CO 123/1 ff.55-79 Hodgson 1757.

[135]CDHCN: 44-66 25.8.1793; Henderson, *British Settlement of Honduras*, pp. 185-86.

Although these high officials had extensive powers, it is doubtful that they exercised them in domestic disputes, which were more commonly resolved by village elders or sukyas.

During the eighteenth century the high officials may have been supported by the tribute that was levied from defeated tribes. It is not clear when such exactions began; they may have begun as compensations for goods that might have been acquired during raids, which the English were anxious to discourage for political reasons.[136] Items paid as 'tribute' included cattle, turtle shell, canoes, hammocks, and cotton lines.[137]

Whilst political leaders were imposed on an essentially egalitarian society, there were other ways in which the society may have become differentiated. Through the acquisition of firearms the Zambos-Mosquitos were able to dominate their Indian neighbors, carrying out raids, and seizing Indian slaves. These raids were an extension of the intertribal conflicts that had occurred in pre-Columbian times, but they were intensified by the Zambos-Mosquitos who, having acquired firearms, were able to carry out raids with impunity. Roberts noted that "These Indians used to make frequent incursions on the neighbouring Cookras, Woolwas and Toacas bordering on the Spanish territory for the purpose of seizing and selling them for slaves to the settlers and chief men of different parts of the Mosquito Shore."[138] The Zambos-Mosquitos regarded all inland Indian groups as fit for enslavement and they generally referred to them as *Alboawinneys*, meaning slavemeat in Miskito (*alba* = slave and *wina* = meat).[139] The majority of men enslaved would have been sold to Europeans, whilst the women would have been kept as wives, and the children brought up as their own.[140] As such Indian slaves probably did not form a distinct social class, but they were either exported or rapidly absorbed into Mosquito society.

From the observations of early visitors to the Mosquito coast it would appear that the newcomers adopted the customs of the indigenous inhabitants, such that any changes in family structure emerged indirectly as a result of contact. The Mosquito were polygamous marrying as many wives as they could support; on the Isla de Mosquitos each man was said to have 6 or 7 wives,[141] whilst one king had 22.[142] Initially the

---

[136]AGCA A1.12 134 1504 13.12.1722; AGI AG 501 Anguiano 10.5.1804; Long, *History of Jamaica* 1: 326-27; Henderson, *British Settlement of Honduras*, p. 190; Floyd, *Anglo-Spanish Struggle*, pp. 66-67.

[137]Roberts, *Narrative of Voyages*, pp. 100, 116; see also n. 82.

[138]Ibid.

[139]M.W., "Mosqueto Indian," pp. 305, 307; Dampier, *New Voyage*, p. 16; Holm, "Creole English," p. 176.

[140]CDHCN: 1-12 Audiencia 26.7.1704; AGI AG 299 Bishop of Nicaragua 30.11.1711, AG 301 Governor of Costa Rica 15.12.1721.

[141]AGI AG 299 Bishop of Nicaragua 30.11.1711; CDHCN: 12-63 Aranzibia 14.1.1715; M.W., "Mosqueto Indian," p. 309; H. Sloane, *A Voyage to the Islands of Madera, Barbados, Nieves, S. Christophers and Jamaica* (1707), p. lxxvii.

[142]Henderson, *British Settlement of Honduras*, p. 187; Strangeways, *Sketch of the Mosquito Shore*, p. 331.

Mosquito had no concept of adultery,[143] but by the nineteenth century it was considered a crime such that the offending man had to pay the husband an ox or if he could not pay, the fine was paid by his village's headman and the offender had to pay it off by serving a period of servitude.[144] The Mosquito lived in extended family or multifamily units, although there is little evidence for precise family sizes. One account written in the seventeenth century noted that each family was composed of 10 or 12 people, but it is not clear whether they were large nuclear families or extended families.[145] The rapid expansion of the Zambos-Mosquitos in the second half of the seventeenth century from their origin in the 1640s to 5-6,000 in 1711 suggests a high fertility rate.[146] This would have been encouraged by the practice of polygamy aided by the capture of wives and children from other Indian groups.[147]

The documentary evidence is unclear about the marriage residence rules that operated on the Shore. The only comment on the matter was made by Dampier in the seventeenth century, who recorded that on marriage a couple built a separate house, but this clearly did not occur in all instances as the existence of multifamily houses indicates.[148] Helms has suggested that there was a tendency to matrilocality stimulated by changes in the Indian economy from the seventeenth century.[149] Although in pre-Columbian times men would have been absent from their homes whilst on hunting and fishing expeditions and in times of war, their absences increased with the arrival of Europeans in the area. Not only were the Mosquito drawn to working for Europeans particularly as sailors and to obtaining goods for trade with them, but the acquisition of firearms enabled them to carry out more effective raids and as such they increased in frequency. In situations where the absence of men from their communities is prolonged, it is advantageous in terms of cultural continuity for the men to move to their wives' villages or homes on marriage, so that a stable consanguineal core of women may remain to stabilize the community. Should patrilocality prevail in communities where men are absent from their homes for long periods, the deserted wives tend to drift back to their parents' home so that the composition of the community tends to be unstable. Matrilocality is also an advantage where the husbands are chosen from outside the community, as was the case on the Mosquito coast. Helms suggests fairly convincingly that formerly individual families foraged together for part of the year but with more distant expeditions being mounted the men probably left their families at home thereby initiating matrilocality, which later became institutionalized.

---

[143]M.W., "Mosqueto Indian," p. 309.

[144]Henderson, *British Settlement of Honduras*, p. 186; Strangeways, *Sketch of the Mosquito Shore*, pp. 331-33.

[145]CDHCN: 12-63 Aranzibia 14.1.1715.

[146]AGI AG 299 Bishop of Nicaragua 30.11.1711.

[147]AGI AG 301 Governor of Costa Rica 15.12.1721.

[148]Compare Dampier, *New Voyage*, p. 16, with evidence for multifamily houses in Chapter 4.

[149]Helms, *Asang*, pp. 23-26.

There is no evidence that Europeans living on the Mosquito Shore attempted to convert the Indians to Christianity; certainly the recent descriptions of their religion indicate only superficial influences of Christianity.[150]

---

[150]Chapter 4, pp. 83-84; Henderson, *British Settlement of Honduras*, p. 187; Strangeways, *Sketch of the Mosquito Shore*, p. 331.

# Part VI

## Demographic Change, 1550 to 1821

# 16
# The Indian Population, 1550 to 1821

## INDIAN POPULATION ESTIMATES

A number of parish registers listing baptisms, marriages, and burials do exist for some parishes in Honduras towards the end of the eighteenth century, but the coverage is patchy.[1] As such, estimates of the Indian population during the colonial period have to rely on lists of Indians drawn up for the purposes of tribute assessment. A major disadvantage of using such lists, excluding the problem of accuracy and possibilities of exaggeration or depression of numbers, is that they only give the numbers of tributary Indians, thereby excluding those exempt by virtue of their age, status, or physical disability. Therefore, any accounts of the total population derived from these counts, including those made by Spanish officials, involve problems of estimation.

The tribute paid by Indians in Honduras was reassessed by the oidores Alonso Zorita and Tomás López in 1554 and by the oidores Dr. Mexía and Jufre de Loaysa in 1562, but there is no evidence of the number of tributary Indians they counted, only the amount of tribute they paid. Since the amount of tribute assessed by Mexía and Loaysa was considered to be much heavier than that of their predecessors it is impossible to use the tasaciones as indicators of demographic change.[2] However, Batres Jáuregui suggests that in 1561 the bishopric of Comayagua contained 145 villages with a population of 10,000 Indians,[3] and although he does not cite the source of his information, it may have been one of these reassessments.

López de Velasco's *Geografía y descripción universal de las Indias* is often used by historians to obtain an overview of social and economic conditions in Latin America in the early 1570s, but the population figures he gives for Central America should be used with caution. It is almost certain that the figures he gives for individual villages in the jurisdiction of Comayagua were taken from the tributary lists drawn up in 1549. Only summary figures are given for other jurisdictions and their origin is unknown. It is possible that they were based on other tributary lists that were drawn up at the same time but that have since been lost, but more likely they were based on later tasaciones or general estimates. The figure of 10,000 tributary Indians for Olancho is the same as that

---

[1] For example, there are a number of parish registers dating from the mid-eighteenth century in the Archivo de la Curia Eclesiástica de Comayagua and in the Cathedral archive in Tegucigalpa. Many of the parish registers have been microfilmed by the Church of Jesus Christ of the Latter Day Saints and are to be found in the manuscript collection of the Genealogical Society of Utah, Salt Lake City.

[2] Chapter 11, pp. 191-92.

[3] Batres Jáuregui, *América Central* 2: 367.

recorded in an unsigned and undated document in the Biblioteca Nacional in Madrid and it is clearly an error or wild guess.[4]

The next general assessment occurred at the end of the 1570s, when Lic. García de Valverde took office as president of the Audiencia and in 1578 ordered a general survey into the treatment of the Indians.[5] Unfortunately there are no detailed accounts of the numbers of Indians counted during this reassessment, although one report from Francisco Cisneros charged with part of the visita of Honduras said that in the jurisdiction of Gracias a Dios there were only 2,400 Indians, whereas at the time they had been counted by Loaysa there had been 5,000. He also noted that the Indian population in the jurisdiction of San Pedro had been reduced by two-thirds.[6] Probably in connection with the visita ordered by Valverde, the governor of Honduras, Alonso de Contreras visited the country in the late 1570s and early 1580s. His account written in 1582 lists the number of tributary Indians in each village and they sum to 5,106.[7] Another letter from the Bishop of Honduras written in the same year lists 5,400 *vecinos naturales*, but it only gives the total figures by jurisdiction.[8] In both accounts many of the figures are multiples of five or ten suggesting rounding or estimation rather than accurate counting.[9]

---

[4]López de Velasco, *Geografía y descripción universal*, pp. 307-13. The source of his information for jurisdictions other than Comayagua is likely to have been different from the tasaciones made in 1548 to 1551, since all of those recorded in the libro de tasaciones are included in detail by López de Velasco; he only gives summary figures for other jurisdictions. His summary figure of 2,600 for the jurisdiction of Comayagua does not correspond to the total for the individual villages, which is 1,955. The latter figure is somewhat smaller than the total of 2,745 found in the tasaciones for 1549, but this is because the population of about one-fifth of the villages is not included by López de Velasco. Where the population of the villages is recorded in both accounts, it is the same. The document in the Biblioteca Nacional, Madrid is reproduced in CDI 15: 409-572 no author, no date.

[5]Chapter 11, p. 192.

[6]AGI AG 56 Cisneros 20.4.1582.

[7]BAGG 11: 5-19 Contreras 20.4.1582.

[8]AGI AG 164 Bishop of Honduras. There are two copies of the same letter with different dates: 10.5.1582 and 12.5.1582.

[9]Using the Bishop's account, MacLeod, *Spanish Central America*, p. 59, calculates the total number of vecinos naturales at 4,840. This is clearly a miscalculation, although it is not possible to identify the source of the error. Sherman, *Forced Native Labor*, p. 351, gives the total as 5,840. He appears to have erred in transcribing the figure for Olancho, which he gives as 400 and which is clearly 460 in the document, and to have counted Agalteca and Tegucigalpa as separate jurisdictions instead of as parts of the jurisdiction of Comayagua, so that those areas have been double counted.

Table 14

INDIAN POPULATION ESTIMATES FOR HONDURAS,
1571 TO 1582

| Jurisdictions | 1571-74[a] Velasco's account tributarios | 1582[b] Governor's account tributarios | 1582[c] Bishop's account vecinos naturales | |
|---|---|---|---|---|
| | | | Indiv. | Summary |
| Comayagua | 2,600 | 1,723 | 1,640 | 1,800 |
| Gracias a Dios | 3,000 | 1,769 | 2,160 | 2,100 |
| San Pedro | 700 | 415 | 330 | 330 |
| Puerto Caballos | | 60 | 120 | 120 |
| Trujillo | 600 | 413 | 90 | 590 |
| Olancho | 10,000 | 726 | 460 | 460 |
| TOTAL | | 5,106 | 5,300 | 5,400 |

[a] López de Velasco, *Geografía y descripción universal*, pp. 307-13.
[b] BAGG 11: 5-19 Contreras 20.4.1582.
[c] AGI AG 164 Bishop 10.5.1582 and 12.5.1582.

In 1590 the surveyor Francisco de Valverde drew up an account of the tributary population of Honduras as part of a proposal for the construction of a road from Trujillo to the Bay of Fonseca. Two accounts of the Indian population exist, one of which includes the number of tributary Indians for each village, and with the exception of the jurisdiction of Olancho, the coverage is complete and includes Choluteca.[10] The detailed account contains a number of summation errors and the more general account, which was probably based on the former, possesses several errors of transcription. The summary figures give a total population of 5,695 with a further 663 in Choluteca.

[10]RAHM 9/4663 no.15 Relación geográfica of Valverde 24.8.1590 and AGI MEX 257 Memorial de todos los pueblos...Valverde, no date.

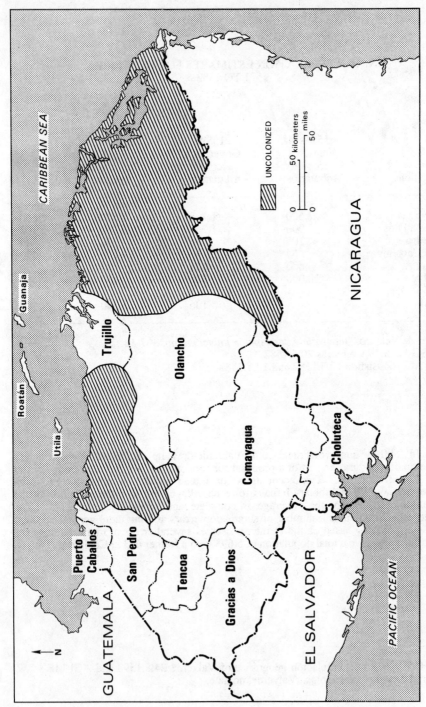

Figure 9. Approximate Boundaries of Jurisdictions at the End of the Sixteenth Century

Table 15

INDIAN POPULATION ESTIMATES FOR HONDURAS CIRCA 1590

| Jurisdictions | Relación[a] 24.8.1590 indios | Memorial[b] no date indios casados tributarios | |
|---|---|---|---|
| | | Indiv. figs. | Summary figs. |
| Comayagua | 1,061 | 1,666 | 2,061 |
| Gracias a Dios | 2,188 | 1,888 | 2,188 |
| San Pedro | 376 | 376 | 363 |
| Puerto Caballos | 104 | 104 | 104 |
| Trujillo | not given | 510 | 510 |
| Olancho | 470 | 464 | 469 |
| TOTAL | 4,199 | 5,008 | 5,695 |
| Choluteca | 663 | 663 | 663 |

[a] RAHM 9/4663 no. 15 Relación geográfica, Francisco de Valverde, 24.8.1590.
[b] AGI MEX 257 Memorial de todos los pueblos...Francisco de Valverde, no date.

The most detailed and comprehensive accounts of the Indian population for the end of the sixteenth century are contained in the treasury accounts for that period. In 1591 the Crown introduced a capitation tax known as the servicio del tostón to help pay the costs of defense.[11] Each tributary Indian was required to pay one tostón a year in two installments of two reals. The treasury accounts list the number of tostones paid by each Indian village and thus they may be used as a rough guide to the size of the tributary population. Accounts of the income from the servicio del tostón for Honduras are more or less complete for 1592 to 1602, and they are available for the jurisdiction of

[11] AGCA A1.23 1513 f.719 cédula 1.1.1591.

Comayagua until 1614.[12] The figures are an imperfect guide because some Indians only paid for one-half of the year, because they either ceased to pay tribute or became tributary during the year, whilst others avoided payment completely. As such, the figures if anything slightly underestimate the size of the tributary population and it is possible that part of the decline in income from 4,734.5 to 3,035.5 tostones between 1592 and 1602 could be attributed to tax evasion. Although the income from the servicio del tostón is an imperfect guide to the size of the tributary population, the figures are fairly consistent with other reports of the size of the Indian population already discussed.

References to the Indian population in the seventeenth century only refer to the numbers of tributary Indians for the whole province; in no case is there a detailed breakdown of jurisdictions within the province. In 1626 royal officials complained that there was insufficient labor to work the mines, maintaining that there were only 3,000 Indians in the province.[13] Although the figure could refer to the total Indian population, it probably referred to tributary Indians since the miners were interested in able-bodied Indians to work in the mines. This is given further weight by the fact that in 1647 it was estimated that the jurisdiction of Tegucigalpa alone possessed 1,500 "indios de tributo," whilst in 1657 the bishopric of Honduras was said to comprise 145 villages with 8,000 Indians.[14] These documentary references to different categories of Indians makes comparisons of the figures extremely difficult, although it would appear that the rapid decline experienced in the sixteenth century had been halted and that during the mid-seventeenth century at least, the population was entering a period of stability.

Between 1683 and 1684 the Audiencia drew up a detailed account of the population within its jurisdiction, with the numbers of Indians taken from the most recent tasaciones.[15] With the exception of the jurisdictions of Tegucigalpa and Choluteca, there is no detailed breakdown of the Indian population on a village basis. Instead, the province of Comayagua was said to contain 3,676 "indios casados que hacen otros tantos tributarios enteros," which were distributed in 126 villages. This figure clearly did not include widowers, widows, single persons, and those exempt on the basis of their disablement, race, or social status. Evidence from the padrones for 11 villages in western Honduras in 1703 and 1722 gives the average ratio of *casados* to the total population as

---

[12]AGI CO 989, 990, 991A, and 992 Treasury accounts 1592 to 1614. The accounts for the whole country from 1592 to 1602 show a steady decline in income as follows:

| 1592 | 4,734.5 tostones | 1596 | 3,619 | 1600 | 3,094.5 |
|------|------------------|------|-------|------|---------|
| 1593 | incomplete       | 1597 | -     | 1601 | 2,924.5 |
| 1594 | 4,055.5          | 1598 | 3,302 | 1602 | 3,035.5 |
| 1595 | -                | 1599 | -     |      |         |

[13]AGI AG 49 Oficiales reales 23.7.1626.

[14]BNM 3025 ff.46-47v. 4.5.1647 and BNM 2023 f.313v. Noticias Sacras de Indias 1657, probably written by Díaz de la Calle.

[15]AGI CO 815 Razón de las ciudades...1683. The document also includes an estimate for the partido of Olancho, suggesting that it contained 3,180 tributarios distributed in 137 villages. This figure is clearly an error of transcription. The number of villages in that region was small and they were almost certainly included in the figure for the province of Comayagua, which comprised 126 villages. Another list of 126 villages in Honduras in 1684 includes the villages in eastern Honduras (AGI AG 44 Condenaciones...1684).

about 1:3.3.[16] Using this ratio the Indian population in 1683 may be estimated at about 12,131. To this figure should be added those for Tegucigalpa and Choluteca, for which the numbers of casados, *viudos*, and *viudas* are included. The document is badly burnt at the edges and as such the account for Tegucigalpa only includes readable figures for 14 of the 16 villages in the jurisdiction.[17] The number of casados recorded for the 14 villages sum to 407 and, if a further 12.5 percent is added to take account of the 2 villages for which data is not available, the total number of casados may be estimated at 458. Unfortunately little evidence is available for the ratio of casados to the total population for this area. Only 2 padrones exist for Tegucigalpa and Comayaguela in 1687 and in these the ratio of casados to the total population is 1:4.0 and 1:3.6.[18] In the absence of more comprehensive evidence, the number of estimated casados may be multiplied by 3.8 to give an estimated total Indian population of 1,740. The slightly higher multiplication factor for this region is justified, since it seems likely that with the greater employment opportunities in Tegucigalpa, the proportion of single persons in the population would have been higher. The number of casados recorded for Choluteca was 350, but this number excludes those in 5 small villages for which population is not recorded, and for which a further 20 casados may be added.[19] Fortunately, 6 padrones exist for villages in Choluteca in 1683 and they indicate that the ratio of casados to the total Indian population was 1:3.1. Using this multiplier, the total Indian population may be estimated at 1,147. This gives an estimated total Indian population in tributary Indian villages of 15,018.

To complete the estimate for the total Indian population of the colonized areas in Honduras, it is necessary to add an estimate for the numbers of lavoríos. Although a separate barrio for lavoríos existed in Comayagua at the beginning of the seventeenth century, there are no accounts of the population living there.[20] In addition there were small numbers of lavoríos scattered throughout the countryside working on estates or living in the mining areas. In 1689 the village of Tatumbla, located in the vicinity of the Tegucigalpa mines, contained a total population of 142, of which 87 were lavoríos. However, the latter accounted for only 3.3 percent of the total population of the parish,

---

[16]AGCA A3.16 511 5327-30, 5339, 5341-2, 5344, A3.16 512 5351, A3.16 514 5397-9, 5402, 5404 Padrones of 11 villages in western Honduras in 1703 and 1722. In 1703 the number of casados was 429 and the total population 1,429, and in 1722 the corresponding figures were 519 and 1,709.

[17]According to AGI AG 44 Condenaciones...1684 there were 16 villages in the jurisdiction of Tegucigalpa.

[18]ANH P4 L107 Padrón of Tegucigalpa 1687 and P4 L104 Padrón of Comayaguela 1687.

[19]The 6 padrones for villages in Choluteca in 1683 (ANH P4 L43, 44, 45, 47, 48, 60 1683), on which the account was clearly based, suggest that there were some errors in transcription. Thus the padrón for Linaca indicates that there were 23 rather than 33 casados, so a correction has been made for the number of casados in the calculation. Also, a figure of 213 casados has been included for Tesigua (Texíguat), the figure being unreadable in AGI CO 815.

[20]AGI CO 992 Treasury accounts for lavoríos 1615.

which comprised many ladinos.[21] It is likely that many of those who were resident in the parish's valleys were in fact employed as wage laborers and as such should have been designated as lavoríos; their status is unclear. A similar account of the more northerly parish of Sulaco in 1689 indicates that 3.5 percent of the Indian population resided on estates, although again their status is not defined.[22] In the absence of further evidence, it may be suggested that lavoríos accounted for about 3.5 percent of the total Indian population in tributary villages, such that a further 526 should be added to the estimate for tributary Indian villages to give a grand total of 15,544.

Although the missionary orders were active in Honduras in the seventeenth century, the missions they founded were generally short-lived. As such it is difficult to ascertain any long-term demographic trends amongst the Indians subject to their control. The earliest two attempts at converting Indians in the Olancho valley at the beginning of the seventeenth century only succeeded in settling small numbers of Indians in missions; Alonso de Oseguera's expedition resulted in the conversion of 500 "xicoaques," whilst Fr. Verdelete only managed to settle 130 Indians (excluding children) at Río de las Piedras.[23] A third expedition at the beginning of the seventeenth century revealed that the number of Indians who were still outside Spanish control were considerable. As already indicated, between 1622 and 1623 missionaries working amongst the Paya Indians managed to settle 700 Indians in seven villages and to baptize another 5,000.[24] These Indians remained outside Spanish control from 1623, when the missionaries were killed, until missionary activity was resumed in the last quarter of the century by the Franciscans. The latter succeeded in converting a large number of Indians, although the precise number is difficult to estimate given that the missions they founded suffered from fugitivism and were often abandoned or amalgamated. One account suggests that they made three entradas: in the first they gathered together 1,500 Indians; and in the second, 1,600, but about one-half of the Indians were the same as those encountered in the first entrada; and in the third, 200.[25] Whatever their initial populations, it is clear that the missions lost population as soon as they had been established, to the extent that they were maintained through the addition of new converts. Whilst the missionaries probably came into contact with several thousand Indians during the first 40 years they were active in northeast Honduras, by 1711 four of the remaining missions contained only 232 Indians.[26] To this figure should be added the populations of Santa María de los Dolores and Purísima Concepción de San Diego, which were still in existence but for which information is not available for the same date. In addition to the missionary efforts already described, from 1689 other missionaries were working inland between Trujillo and San Pedro. After several efforts at establishing missions, largely frustrated by Indian desertions, 300 were finally settled in their home area at Nuestra Señora de la Candelaria

---

[21]ANH P4 L136 Padrón of the parish of Tatumbla 1689.

[22]AGCA A3.16 190 1923 Padrón of the parish of Sulaco 1689.

[23]AGI AG 11 and 39 Criado de Castilla 15.5.1600, AG 371 Fr. Ximénez 9.9.1748; Juarros, *Statistical and Commercial History*, pp. 347-54.

[24]AGI AG 371 Fr. Ximénez 9.9.1748; Juarros, *Statistical and Commercial History*, pp. 347-54.

[25]AGI AG 230 Rivera 27.5.1737.

[26]AGI 223 Testimonio...sobre la nueva reducción 1711.

and San Josef de Guaima.[27] Altogether the maximum number of Indians in the missions at any one time probably did not exceed 2,000 (Table 16).[28]

It is clear from missionary accounts that substantial numbers of Indians, who were to attract more attention in the eighteenth century, existed outside Spanish control. Contemporary observers stressed the highly populated character of eastern Honduras; it is not without significance that López de Velasco guessed that there were 10,000 tributary Indians in the jurisdiction of Olancho,[29] and that at the end of the sixteenth century it was estimated that south of the Cabo de Camarón and east from Olancho and Segovia there were between 4,000 and 5,000 Indians.[30] Even into the seventeenth century, the highly populated character of Honduras was worthy of note; in 1611 Fr. Verdelete described the Olancho valley as "muy poblados de gente,"[31] and there is evidence of substantial Indian populations in Lean and Mulía, where in 1689 an entrada revealed 40 Indian villages.[32] These accounts are based on only limited contacts with Indians in these areas, and late eighteenth century estimates suggest that the population must have been considerably higher given that it continued decline throughout the colonial period as the intensity of contacts with Europeans and other groups increased.

It is worth noting at this stage that from the middle of the seventeenth century the Zambos-Mosquitos began to emerge on the Caribbean coast.[33] In 1672 the buccaneer Exquemelin described the Mosquito Indians as a nation of 1,600 to 1,700,[34] and from this small beginning they grew rapidly in number. In 1707 it was suggested that there were some 1,000 men under the protection of the English, and about 2,000 to 3,000 women and children,[35] and in 1711 the Bishop of Nicaragua reported that the Zambos-Mosquitos comprised between 5,000 and 6,000 almas.[36] Although the Zambos-Mosquitos are often referred to as Indians, they constitute a mixed racial group and as such their numbers are not included in estimates for the Indian population.

Thus, by the end of the seventeenth century it would appear that there were about 47,544 Indians in Honduras (Table 21). This figure must be regarded as a very rough estimate, since the evidence on which it is based is very slender. Furthermore, the inadequacies in the documentary record do no permit any regional breakdown of the

---

[27]AGI 230 Rivera 27.5.1737.

[28]A number of the accounts written at later dates, often with the purpose of relating the history of a missionary order, tend to suggest rather higher mission populations.

[29]López de Velasco, *Geografía y descripción universal*, p. 313.

[30]RAHM 9/4663 no. 40 Valverde, no date.

[31]AGI AG 175 Fr. Verdelete 29.4.1611.

[32]AGI AG 164 and 968A Bishop of Honduras 27.2.1696.

[33]Chapter 2, pp. 42-43.

[34]Esquemeling, *Buccaneers of America*, p. 234.

[35]AGI AG 300 Informe de Consejo de Indias 25.2.1714, but the document includes a testimony made in 1707.

[36]AGI AG 299 Bishop of Nicaragua 30.11.1711, AG 302 Santaella Malgarejo 3.4.1715.

figures. Nevertheless, it is clear that the Indian population had declined dramatically, probably by about 94.1 percent from an estimated aboriginal population of 800,000.

Compared to the seventeenth century, there is an abundance of demographic data for the eighteenth and early nineteenth centuries. Tasaciones were made at irregular intervals during the second quarter of the eighteenth century, but the first list that covers the whole country, excluding Choluteca was drawn up in 1757 following the exemption of women from tribute payment in 1754 (Table 17). Many of the tasaciones included in the 1757 list were in fact based on earlier assessments with the number of women tributaries excluded. A new set of tasaciones were drawn up in 1760 and the figures they provide are probably more reliable guides to the number of tributaries at that time. Unfortunately, these tasaciones do not include villages in Tegucigalpa. The figures included in these eighteenth century tribute assessments indicate that the tributary population fell slightly at the beginning of the century, after which it increased rapidly. In 1683 the number of casados in tributary villages (excluding Tegucigalpa and Choluteca) was 3,676, and according to tasaciones dated between 1741 and 1753 the number of casados (here taken to be the number of married couples, as was the case with the 1683 account) had decreased slightly to 3,192, probably due to the falling marriage rate.[37] When the total number of male tributaries for 1741/1753 is compared to that of 1760, there is a marked increase of 21.7 percent from 3,659 to 4,452. An important feature of demographic change during this period is that all regions were registering increases in their Indian population, though according to the tasaciones for 1757, 94.9 percent of the total tributary population was to be found in western and central Honduras, with Gracias a Dios alone possessing 47.6 percent.

Up to 1760 there are few accounts of the total Indian population. In 1743 a visita of the alcaldía mayor of Tegucigalpa, including Choluteca, recorded that there were 2,337 "almas de confesión y comunión" in Indian villages,[38] but it is not clear how they were defined.[39] Perhaps more interesting is the comparison it contains between the

---

[37]Although the 1683 account lists 3,676 "indios casados que hacen otros tantos tributarios enteros," it is clear from a comparison of padrones for Choluteca, on which the 1683 figures for Choluteca were based, that the number of couples were counted, rather than only the number of Indians married to spouses from the same village. Thus it would seem wrong to compare the figure of 3,676 with the figure of 2,458 casados enteros obtained from the tasaciones drawn up between 1741 and 1753.

[38]BAGG 1: 29-39 Ortiz de Letona 20.7.1743. The summary figure for the number of Indians is given as 1,337, but it has clearly been wrongly transcribed, since the figures for the individual parishes sum to 2,337. Similarly the summary figures for other races differ from the individual figures. The summary figures are: Spaniards 406, mulattoes 742, and negroes . . .177.

[39]Cook and Borah, *Essays* 2: 53-55, suggest that almas de confesión y comunión were generally those over about the age of 12, who comprised about 60 percent of the total population. They therefore use a multiplication factor of 1.67. This would give a total Indian population in the alcaldía of 3,903. Later accounts of the area suggest that this figure may be too low. In 1743 the parish of Tegucigalpa contained only 258 almas, yet padrones for 1751 (AGCA A3.16 192 1966 1751) indicate that there was a total population of 981, of which 307 were tributary Indians. Although the Indian population was increasing during the 1740s, it was not as great as these figures suggest, so that it seems likely that the number of almas noted in the 1743 visita were equivalent to the number of tributary Indians.

Table 16

MISSION POPULATIONS FROM THE MID-SEVENTEENTH CENTURY

Olancho missions

| 1674 | 300+ persons | Baptized and settled in 4 villages AGI AG 39 11.12.1674 |
|---|---|---|
| 1675 | 428 persons de todas edades | In San Sebastián, San Pedro Apostol, San Felipe, Santa María, San Francisco BAGG 5: 283-308 17.9.1675 |
| 1675 | c. 600 almas | In the above 5 missions plus San Buenaventura and San Pedro de Alcántara. Does not include 100 adults who had died since missions founded. AGI AG 371 9.9.1748 |
| 1676 | 460 almas | In the same missions, excluding San Pedro de Alcántara AGI AG 39 15.3.1676 |
| 1676 | 1,073 almas | In the 7 missions AGI AG 371 9.9.1748 |
| 1683 | 800 almas | In the 7 missions AGI AG 371 9.9.1748 |
| 1690 | 6,000 almas | Up to then 6,000 had been baptized and settled in 9 missions AGI AG 371 9.9.1748 |
| 1696 | 7-800 persons | In San Sebastián, San Francisco, San Buenaventura, San Joseph, and San Pedro de Yara AGI AG 164 27.2.1696 |
| 1698 | 209 | Only 3 missions left: San Buenaventura, San Francisco, and San Sebastián AGI AG 297 9.8.1698 |
| 1698 | 700 Indians excluding children | Settled in Santa María de los Dolores ANH P5 L66 29.10.1698; AGCA A1.12 161 1688 1698 |
| 1699 | 40 Indians | In Santa María de los Dolores AGI AG 223 1699 |
| 1699 | 281 Indians | In Purísima Concepción de San Diego AGI AG 223 1699 |
| 1700 | 431 Indians | In Purísima Concepción de San Diego. 241 settled plus 190 new converts AGI AG 343 2.1.1700 |
| 1710 | c.1,500 Indians | In San Sebastián, Santa María, San Joseph, and San Buenaventura AGI AG 371 20.5.1750 |
| 1711 | 232 Indians | Individual counts for the above 4 missions AGI AG 223 1711 |
| 1722 | 301 almas | In the above 4 missions, plus 24 Piriries not living in a formal settlement AGCA A1.12 134 1504 13.12.1722 |
| 1737 | 60 persons | In San Buenaventura and San Sebastián. Estimate 3,000 Indians in the area AGI AG 230 and 343 27.7.1737 |
| 1750 | 197 Indians | In San Buenaventura and San Francisco del Río Tinto AGI AG 371 20.5.1750 |
| 1767 | 225 Indians | Butucos Indians came down from the mountains seeking conversion AGI AG 456 30.8.1767 |
| 1777 | 154 Indians | In San Buenaventura and San Francisco del Río Tinto AGI IG 1527 1777 |
| 1778 | 85 Indians | In San Buenaventura AGI IG 1527 1778 |
| 1805? | 300 Indians | In San Esteban de Tonjagua and Nombre de Jesús Pacura Fr. Goicoechea, "Relación sobre los indios gentiles," pp. 303-15 |

## Lean and Mulía Missions

| | | |
|---|---|---|
| 1699 | 300 Indians | In Nuestra Señora de la Candelaria and San Josef de Guiama after 6 entradas AGI AG 230 27.5.1737, AG 457 1.7.1798 |
| 1737 | c.30 Indians | Left from entradas in the seventeenth century AGI AG 230 27.3.1737 |
| 1748 | 184 Indians +607 | San Miguel del Carmen and Santiago Siriano, to which 607 were collected AGCA A1.12 118 2487 1754 |
| 1751 | 54 persons | In San Francisco Luquique AGCA A1.12 118 2487 1754 |
| 1748-51 | 8-900 Indians | Many documents refer to the establishment of the above 3 missions. In 1751 500-560 of them were killed in an epidemic BAGG 6: 159-71 20.8.1751; AGCA A1.12 6056 53627 4.2.1752, A1.12 117 2472 1768; AGI AG 962 1782; AGCA A1.12 51 526 20.11.1819 |
| 1754 | 172 Indians | In San Miguel and Santiago Siriano AGCA A1.12 118 2487 1754 |
| 1760 | 331 adults | In San Miguel, San Francisco Luquique, and San Antonio Olomán AGCA A1.12 117 2479 1760 |
| 1761 | 300 inhabitants | In San Miguel, San Francisco Luquique, and San Antonio Olomán AGI AG 962 1782 |
| 1767 | 229 Indians | In San Miguel and San Francisco Luquique (123 and 106) AGCA A1.12 46 428 22.11.1767 |
| 1768 | 210 Indians | Left of the original 900 converted AGCA A1.12 117 2472 1768, AG 962 1782 |
| 1777 | 321 Indians | In San Francisco Luquique AGI IG 1527 |
| 1778 | 290 Indians | In San Francisco Luquique AGI IG 1527 |
| 1797 | 265 Indians | In San Francisco Luquique CDHCR 10: 258-65 3.11.1797 |
| 1804 | 290 Indians | In San Francisco Luquique AGI AG 501 1.5.1804 |
| 1810 | 279 Indians | In San Francisco Luquique AGI AG 963 10.1.1813 |

Table 17

TRIBUTARY POPULATION OF HONDURAS IN THE MID-EIGHTEENTH
CENTURY

| | 1741-53 | | | 1757 | | 1760 | |
|---|---|---|---|---|---|---|---|
| | Casados enteros | Male casados | Trib. males | Casados enteros | Trib. males | Casados enteros | Trib. males |
| Comayagua | 650 | 730 | 839 | 596 | 804 | 775 | 898 |
| Tegucigalpa | | | | 776 | 1,046 | | |
| Gracias a Dios | 1,475 | 1,913 | 2,114 | 1,629 | 2,308 | 2,322 | 2,676 |
| Tencoa | 144 | 263 | 300 | 144 | 306 | 239 | 305 |
| San Pedro | 37 | 61 | 120 | 41 | 132 | 139 | 213 |
| Olancho | 78 | 138 | 166 | 85 | 180 | 150 | 183 |
| Yoro | 14 | 23 | 32 | 14 | 37 | 19 | 50 |
| Olanchito | 60 | 64 | 88 | 11 | 31 | 81 | 127 |
| TOTAL | 2,458 | 3,192 | 3,659 | 3,296 | 4,844 | 3,725 | 4,452 |

Sources:
1741-53    AGCA A3.16 195 1975
1757       AGCA A3.16 2325 34250        1759
1760       AGCA A3.16 2325 34250 1762 and A3.16 193 1985-7 (Two villages
           missing in Gracias a Dios)

Table 18

TRIBUTARY POPULATION OF HONDURAS IN THE LATE COLONIAL
PERIOD

|  | 1770 | 1801 | 1804 | 1806 | 1811 |
|---|---|---|---|---|---|
| Comayagua | 881 | 831 | 995 | 807 | 1,085 |
| Tegucigalpa | 1,286 | 1,427 | 1,430 | 1,369 | 1,536 |
| Gracias a Dios | 2,958 | 4,012 | 4,343 | 3,734 | 4,023 |
| Tencoa | 250 | 529 | 590 | 493 | 586 |
| San Pedro | 71 | 103 | 146 | 109 | 120 |
| | | | | | |
| Olancho | 169 | 375 | 381 | 357 | 442 |
| Yoro | 56 | 128 | 148 | 119 | 135 |
| Olanchito | 100 | 74 | 75 | 70 | 71 |
| | | | | | |
| Western and Central Honduras | 5,376 | 6,902 | 7,504 | 6,512 | 7,350 |
| Eastern Honduras | 325 | 577 | 604 | 546 | 648 |
| | | | | | |
| TOTAL | 5,701 | 7,479 | 8,108 | 7,058 | 7,998 |

Sources:
1770    AGCA A1.73 390 3662 and A3.16 174 1674
1801    AGCA A3.16 244 4871
1804    AGI AG 501 1.5.1804
1806    BAGG 3: 221-25 8.7.1806
1811    AGCA A3.16 197 2096.

There were no Indians in the subdelegación of Trujillo.

Table 19

TOTAL INDIAN POPULATION OF HONDURAS IN THE LATE COLONIAL
PERIOD

| | Total Indian Population | | | % Indian | | |
|---|---|---|---|---|---|---|
| | 1777 | 1778 | 1804 | 1777 | 1778 | 1804 |
| Comayagua | 4,387 | 4,308 | 3,875 | 38.4 | 39.9 | 28.0 |
| Tegucigalpa | 6,779 | 8,015 | 4,842 | 20.7 | 22.0 | 12.7 |
| Gracias a Dios | 19,490 | 23,633 | 19,845 | 71.0 | 71.9 | 49.5 |
| Tencoa | 2,708 | 2,736 | 2,714 | 67.2 | 68.8 | 48.3 |
| San Pedro | 410 | 581 | 640 | 19.6 | 23.7 | 18.6 |
| Olancho | 1,005 | 1,305 | 1,523 | 19.7 | 22.6 | 19.8 |
| Yoro | 368 | 448 | 661 | 13.4 | 12.5 | 13.3 |
| Olanchito | 1,025 | 929 | 283 | 40.0 | 42.9 | 14.3 |
| Western & Central Honduras | 33,774 | 39,273 | 31,916 | 43.4 | 45.4 | 30.0 |
| Eastern Honduras | 2,398 | 2,682 | 2,467 | 23.0 | 23.3 | 15.8 |
| TOTAL | 36,172 | 41,955 | 34,383 | 41.0 | 42.8 | 28.2 |

Sources:
1777 & 1778    AGI IG 1527 Figures for Indians exclude those in the missions, and the
percentages exclude the clergy and army
1804    AGI AG 501 1.5.1804 Figures for Indians exclude lavoríos and Indians
in the missions.

There were no Indians in the subdelegación of Trujillo.

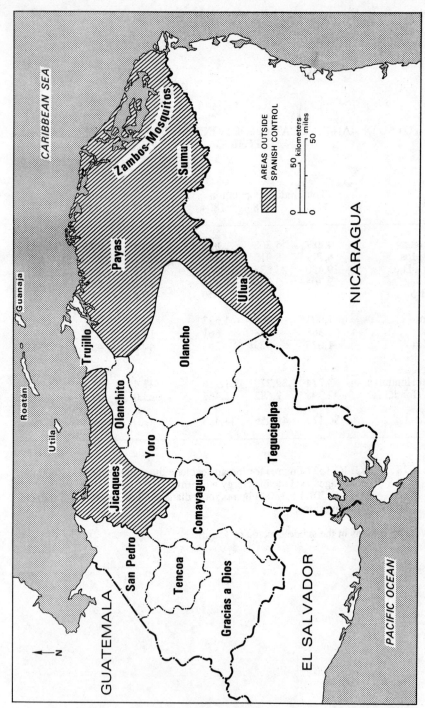

Figure 10. Approximate Boundaries of Jurisdictions at the Beginning of the Nineteenth Century

number of Indians and other racial groups. At that time there were 408 Spaniards, 662 mestizos, and 5,107 mulattoes and negroes in the alcaldía, such that Indians comprised only 27.5 percent of the total population. An indication of the total Indian population in 1757 may be gained by applying the ratio of tributary Indians to the total Indian population obtained from padrones of nine Indian villages in Comayagua in 1753.[40] The ratio of tributary Indians to the total Indian population averaged 1:4.7, although it ranged between 1:2.8 to 1:5.1. The tasaciones based on these counts appear to have been included in the list of tributary Indians drawn up in 1757, so that in the absence of other evidence, it seems reasonable to multiply the tributary population of 4,844 for that date by 1:4.7 to give an estimated total Indian population of 22,767. This is probably an underestimate, however, since as previously indicated many of the 1757 tasaciones had been drawn up at earlier dates, some fifteen to twenty years before, during which time the Indian population had increased.

Several comprehensive lists of tributary Indians by village exist for the latter part of the eighteenth and the beginning of the nineteenth centuries (Table 18), but only one account, that for 1804, also includes the total number of Indians in each village. In addition there are several censuses that give the size of the total Indian population, although not always on a village basis.

A visita by the Governor Don Antonio Ferrandis between July 1770 and February 1771 recorded that there were 5,701 tributary Indians in Honduras (excluding Choluteca), an increase of 17.7 percent on the figure for 1757, with the increase being most marked in Tegucigalpa, Gracias a Dios and Olanchito.[41] In the mid-1770s the new method of enumerating tributary Indians using special commissioners was introduced. Counts undertaken between 1775 and 1776 revealed that there were 5,121 tributary Indians in the province of Comayagua, and 795 in the alcaldía mayor of Tegucigalpa.[42] This suggests an increase of 4.2 percent on the 1771 figures. Unfortunately there is no further breakdown of the figures by jurisdiction or village. It is likely that the returns for 1775-76 were used in compiling the censuses ordered by the Crown in the latter year.

On 10 November 1776 the Crown ordered the compilation of censuses for all Spanish overseas territories. Orders were sent to both the secular and religious authorities instructing them to draw up separate censuses. Unfortunately, the detailed returns for Honduras have not survived, but two summary tables compiled by the Bishop for 1777 and 1778 have survived (Table 19),[43] whilst the total number of inhabitants was recorded in the *Gaçeta de Guatemala* in 1802, and listed by Juarros in his *Statistical and*

---

[40]AGCA A3.16 514 5389-5401 Padrones for Guajiquiro, Cacauterique, Cururu, Opatoro, Tambla, Similatón, Jaitique, Miambar, Chapoluca 1753.

[41]AGCA A1.73 390 3662 Estado general de la visita 10.2.1771. The figures for the tributary population of Tegucigalpa are taken from AGCA A3.9 174 1674 24.6.1771 and are based on tasaciones drawn up in 1768-69.

[42]AGI AG 560 Testimonio de la real cédula despachada...1778.

[43]AGI IG 1527 Estado y padrón general...1777 and Estado general que manifiesta...1778. For the background to the 1776 census see D. Browning, "Preliminary Comments on the 1776 Census of the Spanish Empire," *Bulletin of the Society of Latin American Studies* 25 (1974): 5-13.

*Commercial History of the Kingdom of Guatemala.*[44] The Bishop's summary tables indicate that in 1777 there were 36,172 Indians and in 1778, 41,955 (both excluding those in the missions).[45] Such an increase in the Indian population within one year is unlikely, so the difference probably reflects a more significant difference in the dates of the two counts, although when they might have been taken remains unknown; one census was probably based on the 1775-76 enumeration, but it is uncertain which one. The censuses reveal the concentration of the Indian population in the jurisdiction of Gracias a Dios, which in 1777 contained 53.8 percent of the total Indian population of the province, whilst western and central Honduras as a whole still contained over 90 percent of the total Indian population. Not only did Gracias a Dios contain the largest number of Indians, but its population was the most 'Indian' in Honduras. Whereas in 1777, 70 percent of the population of Gracias a Dios was Indian, in all other jurisdictions, with the exception of Tencoa, Indians accounted for under 40 percent of the population, with the figure falling to about 20 percent in Tegucigalpa. Before passing on to examine later censuses, it should be noted that the figures for the total population recorded in the *Gaçeta* and in Juarros do not correspond with those on the Bishop's summary tables. The former published accounts give populations of 56,275 for Comayagua and 31,455 for Tegucigalpa and a further 413 for Omoa, giving a grand total of 88,143, whereas the Bishop's tables give populations of 90,138 and 100,294 for 1777 and 1778 respectively. The reason for the discrepancy is that the former accounts were probably based on the returns of the secular, rather than the religious, authorities.[46]

Another royal decree issued on 18 October 1776, instructed the religious authorities to collect the ecclesiastical tax of the *Bula de Santa Cruzada*, which had originally been levied for financing the Crusades. The cost of *bulas*, or indulgences, varied according to the race and social class of the individual. The return for the province of Honduras in 1778 recorded that only 27,856 people were capable of purchasing bulas, and the governor noted that the parish priests had included in their returns many people who were either too young or had insufficient means to purchase them, so that the total should be reduced.[47] The account is not particularly useful since not all parish priests distinguished between the races and others failed to make any return. Nevertheless, a summary table drawn up in the following year estimated that 40,790 persons should have been able to purchase bulas, of which 1,790 were Spaniards, 23,000 mulattoes and mestizos and 16,000 Indians (39.2 percent).[48]

---

[44]AGI AG 656 Gaçeta de Guatemala vol.6 no. 256: 100 26.4.1802 and Juarros, *Statistical and Commercial History*, p. 497. Another account in BM Add. 17,577, no date, gives the population of Honduras in 1778 as 87,730.

[45]The total population included in the document does not correspond to the sums achieved by adding the figures for the individual jurisdictions. The figures included in Table 19 correspond to the latter figures, excluding those Indians in the missions.

[46]R. Barón Castro, *La Población de El Salvador* (Madrid: Consejo Superior de Investigaciones Científicas, Instituto Gonzalo Fernández de Oviedo, 1942), p. 229, comes to the same conclusion.

[47]AGCA A3.29 1749 28130 Estado y plano que demuestra las personas...1778.

[48]AGI AG 562 Estado de las Bulas de Santa Cruzada 23.7.1779.

In 1786 an account of the adult population was drawn up in connection with a proposal to expand tobacco cultivation.[49] The adult population was used as an indicator of the size of the market for tobacco. The figures included in the account were based on documents found in the *Secretaría*, but it is not clear to which date they refer, although they are clearly different from those included in the 1777 and 1778 censuses (Table 20). In 1786 the adult Indian population was 22,873 and this may be compared with the figure of 25,416 adults recorded in the 1777 census, thereby indicating a decline of 10 percent. This is likely to have been due to the major smallpox epidemic at the beginning of the 1780s, although the increase of 9.6 percent in the ladino population between the two dates suggests that some losses in the Indian population may have been due to miscegenation.

Another major census of Honduras was compiled in 1791 by Bishop Cadiñanos whose visita took one and one-half years to complete. His long account gives details of the geography of each parish, but unfortunately it only records the number of almas and does not give any breakdown of the population according to race, sex, or age.[50] His figures for the individual parishes sum to 96,421, but the total number of almas noted in the summary table is given as 93,501. The latter figure has been reproduced by many contemporary, and even more recent, authors.[51] Of the latter figure 86.2 percent of the total number of almas were living in western and central Honduras.

Returning to the discussion of the number of tributary Indians, the next complete list of tributary Indians available is for 1801.[52] At that time the total number of tributary Indians was 7,479, an increase of 31.2 percent on the figure for 1770 (Table 18). This general trend is backed up by evidence of changes in particular regions. An account of the partido of Gracias a Dios by the *contador* compared the number of tributary Indians in 1791 and 1797, indicating an increase from 3,454 to 3,867 respectively.[53] The latter figure is likely to have been fairly accurate since the enumeration of Indians in Gracias a Dios took a year to complete and used evidence from the parish registers. This suggests that the Indian population was recovering from the impact of epidemics and it confirms the trend noted for the country as a whole. Similarly, the padrones for eastern Honduras for 1796 and 1797 give a tributary population of 604 Indians, which represents an

---

[49]AGI AG 777 Quintana 5.9.1786.

| Adults | 1777 | 1786 | % change |
|--------|------|------|----------|
| Spanish | 4,044 | 3,704 | -8.4 |
| Ladino | 35,054 | 36,702 | +9.6 |
| Indian | 25,416 | 22,873 | -10.0 |

[50]AGI AG 578 Cadiñanos 20.10.1791.

[51]For example, AGI AG 627 Larrazábal 20.10.1810, AG 656 Gaçeta de Guatemala vol. 6 no.286: 301 22.11.1802; Juarros, *Statistical and Commercial History*, p. 12; Salvatierra, *Historia de Centroamérica* 2: 121; Rosenblat, *Población indígena*, p. 142.

[52]AGCA A3.16 244 4871 Tasaciones 1801.

[53]AGCA A3.16 195 2038 Estado que manifiesta el numero de indios tributarios...28.2.1798.

Table 20

ADULT POPULATION IN HONDURAS IN 1786

| | Spanish | Ladinos | Indians | TOTAL | % Indians |
|---|---|---|---|---|---|
| Comayagua | 198 | 4,641 | 3,116 | 7,995 | 39.2 |
| Tegucigalpa | 1,433 | 20,114 | 5,677 | 27,224 | 20.9 |
| Gracias a Dios | 1,223 | 5,496 | 10,918 | 17,637 | 61.9 |
| Tencoa | 515 | 1,074 | 1,341 | 2,930 | 45.8 |
| San Pedro | 113 | 518 | 246 | 877 | 28.1 |
| | | | | | |
| Olancho | 69 | 3,156 | 921 | 4,146 | 22.2 |
| Yoro | 48 | 2,446 | 267 | 2,761 | 9.7 |
| Olanchito | 105 | 986 | 387 | 1,478 | 26.2 |
| | | | | | |
| Western & Central Honduras | 3,482 | 31,843 | 21,298 | 56,623 | 37.6 |
| Eastern Honduras | 222 | 6,588 | 1,575 | 8,385 | 18.8 |
| | | | | | |
| TOTAL | 3,704 | 38,431 | 22,873 | 65,008 | 35.2 |

Source: AGI AG 777 5.9.1786.

The subdelegación of Trujillo was not included.

increase of 85.8 percent over the figure of 325 recorded for 1770.[54] Although the Indian population of Tegucigalpa also increased between the same dates, the increase was marginal being only 0.9 percent.[55] With the large population of Spaniards and ladinos in this area, it seems likely that miscegenation was cutting into the Indian population and retarding the increase that it was experiencing elsewhere.

Perhaps the most useful census of Honduras drawn up in the colonial period was compiled by Intendant Anguiano in 1804.[56] It is particularly interesting because it gives the total populations and number of families by race, and for the Indian population it gives both the total population and the number of tributary Indians for each village (Tables 18 and 19). There is a slight discrepancy in the total number of persons as indicated in the summary figures (127,620) and that obtained by summing the individual figures (126,363), but with respect to the Indian population the figures are consistent (34,383). It is worth commenting that, whilst the Indian population comprised 28.0 percent (35,392, including 719 lavoríos and 290 mission Indians) of the total population, another document written in the same year indicating the residence of families in the *gobierno* of Comayagua records that only 16.1 percent of the population lived in Indian villages.[57] This suggests that about 12 percent of the Indian population must have been living in the towns or other rural settlements, and the figure of 12 percent should be increased to compensate for the number of non-Indians who were living in Indian villages and contributed to the 16.1 percent. According to the 1804 census Indians accounted for nearly 50 percent of the population in Gracias a Dios and Tencoa, but in the east and in the jurisdiction of Tegucigalpa they averaged under 20 percent. The population of 34,383 in tributary villages represents a slight loss of 4.9 percent since 1777, although this figure masks the slight increase of 2.8 percent in the east. If the number of tributary Indians in 1804 are compared to those for 1770, then both areas show increases.[58] Although these increases are likely to be slightly exaggerated due to the earlier date of the figures with which those for 1804 are being compared, the percentage

---

[54]AGCA A3.16 194 2016-22 Padrones for the parishes of Manto, Yoro, Yorito, and Sonaguera 1796-97.

[55]ANH P11 L44, 49, 55, 56, and P24 L25 Various padrones of villages in the jurisdiction of Tegucigalpa 1796. Excluding the villages in Cedros, Nacaome, and Choluteca, the tributary population only increased from 869 in 1770 to 877 in 1796.

[56]AGI AG 501 Estado que manifiesta las subdelegaciones...1.5.1804.

[57]AGCA A1.1 4646 22130 Resumen general de las familias 7.5.1804. Of a total of 13,028 families in the gobierno of Comayagua 2,095 were living in Indian villages, 7,449 in towns or reducciones, and 3,484 in valleys and haciendas. The account, which covers the whole of the Reino de Guatemala, is incomplete for Honduras, since it excludes the subdelegación of Trujillo.

[58]

| | Total Indian Population | | % | Tributary Population | | % |
|---|---|---|---|---|---|---|
| | 1777 | 1804 | change | 1777 | 1804 | change |
| Western & Central | | | | | | |
| Honduras | 33,774 | 31,916 | -5.5 | 5,376 | 7,504 | +39.6 |
| Eastern | | | | | | |
| Honduras | 2,398 | 2,682 | +2.8 | 325 | 604 | +85.8 |
| TOTAL | 36,172 | 34,383 | -4.9 | 5,701 | 8,101 | +40.4 |

figures do suggest that the tributary population was increasing faster than the total Indian population. This suggests that the population as a whole was entering a period of stabilization. This trend is confirmed by two lists of tributary Indians drawn up in 1806 and 1811 (Table 18).

The list of tributary Indians drawn up in 1806 and based on counts made by parish priests, shows that within two years the number of tributary Indians had declined dramatically by an average of 13.0 percent, with the decline being most marked in the western and central regions.[59] All of the figures entered on the list for 1806 are lower than those recorded for 1804 and 1811 and it may be that this sharp decrease represents a difference in the method of enumerating or recording the number of tributary Indians. Nevertheless, the general downward trend in the tributary population from 1804 is confirmed by the 1811 figures.[60] At that date there were 7,998 tributary Indians, which was a slight decrease of 110, or 1.4 percent, since 1804, although again if this figure is broken down, the western and central regions were still losing population (-2.1 percent), whilst the east was still increasing (+7.3 percent).

Unfortunately later censuses do not distinguish between the races, so that the only account of the Indian population after 1811 is for Olancho in 1821. At that date 2,892 Indians were living in Olancho villages, indicating a 90 percent increase over the population recorded in 1804.[61] The proportion of the total population (12,194) that it represented had fallen only slightly to 23.7 percent, so that the population as a whole was clearly increasing.

The numbers of Indians who had left their villages and resided at or near their places of employment increased during the eighteenth century. As already indicated, in 1804 the Indian population accounted for 28.0 percent of the total, but only 16.1 percent of families lived in Indian villages. Even discounting the fact that the figure may be distorted by differences in the size of families between racial groups or conversely that a proportion of those who lived in Indian villages may not have been Indian, it is clear that a substantial proportion of the Indian population lived in towns, on estates, or in the mining areas. Nevertheless the majority of these Indians do not appear to have changed their status from being tributary Indians to being lavoríos, since the number of lavoríos

---

[59]BAGG 3: 221-5 Estado de los curatos...8.7.1806.

[60]AGCA A3.16 197 2096 Tasaciones 1811.

[61]AGCA A1.44 99 1155 Estado general de la población del partido de Olancho El Viejo 28.2.1821.

recorded is very small.[62] It should also be remembered that by this time some lavoríos were non-Indians. For example, in 1792 mulattoes living in the Suyapa valley who had been employed in the army were designated as lavoríos.[63] There were four main settlements of lavoríos at Barrio de la Caridad and Barrio del Calvario, adjacent to Comayagua and Gracias a Dios respectively, in the valley of Suyapa and at Masaguara. In addition a large number were scattered throughout the jurisdiction of Tegucigalpa, where employment opportunities existed in the mines and supporting agricultural activities. In the 1804 census there were 187 tributary lavoríos in the four major settlements, with a total population of 719.[64]

During the eighteenth century the Indian population gradually increased, with the exception of a period in the 1780s when the country was ravaged by disease. Into the nineteenth century the Indian population began to stabilize, with the western and central areas showing a slight decline, but the east continuing to increase, although the absolute increase was small and the pattern of change varied within the region. During the eighteenth century there was little change in the size of the Indian population in the jurisdictions of Gracias a Dios and Tencoa, but the number of Indians declined markedly in the jurisdiction of Tegucigalpa, although the population as a whole increased. This was almost certainly due to the fertility rate failing to keep pace with miscegenation.

Despite bursts of missionary activity by the Franciscan Recollects in Lean and Mulía and by the Franciscan Observants in Olancho during the eighteenth century, the numbers of Indians resident in the missions in both areas together probably never exceeded 1,000 (Table 16). At the beginning of the nineteenth century 300 Indians were settled in the Olancho missions.

For the second half of the eighteenth century there are a number of estimates of Indians living outside Spanish control in the interior mountain areas. In 1752 Fr. Alcántara, who was in charge of the conversion of Indians in Lean and Mulía, reported

---

[62]Some of the figures available for the number of lavoríos are:

|                 | 1791 | 1797 | 1801 | 1806 | 1811 |
|-----------------|------|------|------|------|------|
| Comayagua       |      |      | 69   | 81   | 83   |
| Tegucigalpa     |      |      | 303  | 423  | 454  |
| Gracias a Dios  | 138  | 172  |      | 142ᵃ | 288  |
| San Pedro       |      |      | 2    | 0ᵃ   |      |
| Olancho         |      |      | 4    | 6    | 4    |

ᵃIncomplete

Sources:
1791, 1797    AGCA A3.16 195 2038 Estado que manifiesta el numero de indios tributarios...28.2.1798.
1801          AGCA A3.16 244 4871 tasaciones and A3.16 255 5730 tasaciones
1806          AGCA A3.16 255 5730 tasaciones
1811          AGCA A3.16 2096 tasaciones.

[63]AGCA A3.16 195 2036 Alcaldes y común de indios lavoríos del valle de Suyapa 8.3.1799.

[64]AGI AG 501 Estado que manifiesta las subdelegaciones...1.5.1804.

that there were about 3,000 Indians living in the mountains.[65] A later survey of the area by the subdelegado Don Antonio Manzanares in 1798 revealed that there were 1,535 "hombres de armas," but suggested that to obtain the total population this figure should be multiplied by eight, since each man had two or three wives.[66] Thus, the total population was estimated at 12,280 "chicos y grandes." On the basis of this information Intendant Anguiano reported that there were 14,000 to 15,000 almas living in the region, excluding those in the very remote mountain areas.[67] By 1804 he estimated that their number had increased to 16,000.[68] Von Hagen has suggested that this figure was exaggerated,[69] but it seems reasonable, if the continued decline of the Jicaque into the nineteenth century is taken into account. In the mid-nineteenth century Squier reported that there were about 7,000 Jicaques living in Honduras, and in the 1920s Conzemius estimated that there were between 1,200 and 1,500.[70] There is less evidence for the number of Indians living in and to the north of Olancho, but in general it suggests that there were fewer than in Lean and Mulía. In 1737 there were said to be 3,000 unconverted Indians in the partido of Olancho, despite the fact that they had been reduced in number as a result of wars with the Zambos-Mosquitos.[71] In 1804 Intendant Anguiano estimated that there were between 10,000 and 12,000 Paya Indians.[72] Conzemius has considered this figure to be an overestimate,[73] although the fact that at the beginning of the nineteenth century Fr. Goicoechea observed that amongst the Paya, the women were very fertile, such that they often bore four children within the first four years of marriage,[74] suggests that the population was increasing rapidly. If Intendant Anguiano's accounts of the Jicaque and Paya are accepted, then the total number of Indians outside Spanish control in eastern Honduras may be estimated at between 24,000 to 28,000, to which should be added a further 590 who were in the missions.

Although there were spatial variations in the racial character of the Zambos-Mosquitos, the coast they inhabited from Trujillo in northern Honduras to Punta Gorda in southern Nicaragua was regarded as a common cultural area. As such most population estimates of the Zambos-Mosquitos cover the whole area and it is difficult to calculate the numbers that were to be found in Honduras. The figures as a whole illustrate the rapid expansion of the Zambos-Mosquitos from a localized origin near Cabo de Gracias a

---

[65]AGCA A1.12 6956 53267 Fr. Alcántara 4.2.1752.

[66]AGCA A1.12 118 2487 Manzanares 13.4.1798. There is some doubt as to the validity of his observation, since the Jicaque are generally considered to be monogamous.

[67]AGI AG 457 and IG 1525 Anguiano 1.7.1798.

[68]AGI AG 501 Anguiano 1.5.1804.

[69]Von Hagen, "The Jicaque," pp. 26-28.

[70]Squier, "Xicaque Indians," p. 760; Conzemius, "Jicaques," p. 163.

[71]AGI AG 230 and 343 Rivera 27.5.1737; Long, History of Jamaica 1:326-27.

[72]AGI AG 501 Anguiano 1.5.1804.

[73]Conzemius, "Los Indios Payas," p. 254.

[74]Fr. Goicoechea, "Relación sobre los indios gentiles," pp. 303-15.

Dios in the mid-seventeenth century, which was achieved through the domination of neighboring Indian groups made possible by the acquisition of firearms.

In 1731 an account by Don Carlos Marenco recorded that there were about 7,000 Zambos-Mosquitos "bien armados" at Cabo de Gracias a Dios, whilst there were six other settlements, four at Punta Gorda and two on the Río San Juan;[75] a later account by the corregidor of Sebaco and Chontales suggested that in 1730 there had been 12,000 to 14,000 Zambos-Mosquitos.[76] In response to an order in 1734 to draw up plans for a coastal offensive, Pedro de Rivera reconnoitered the coast recording that there were 27 settlements of Zambos-Mosquitos with some English, with a total population of only 2,000 "armados de todas armas," though in 1743 it was reported that there were 10,000 "hombres de armas" on the coast.[77] Perhaps the most reliable account was written by Hodgson in 1757.[78] He had resided on the coast for 17 years and he estimated that there were not above 8,000 souls, of whom 1,500 were able to bear arms. Two years later a Spanish spy reported that there were 3,000 Zambos-Mosquitos in the vicinity of the Río Tinto "bien armados y diestros en el fusil."[79] A detailed account of the population of the Mosquito Shore is included in a map drawn by Robert Hodgson the Younger and his son William Pitt Hodgson in 1782. The map gives the location of settlements and their populations by race for 1761, indicating that there were 3,521 "indios,"[80] of whom about 30 percent were to be found on the Honduran sector of the coast. Three accounts in the 1770s give much larger estimates.[81] Edwards includes an account that estimated that in 1773 there were 7,000-10,000 "fighting men" and similarly White recorded that there were 10,000 "Mosquito warriors." Long, however, maintained that on the coast there were "six to seven thousand men, so that the whole number possibly amounts to between twenty and thirty thousand." The numbers of fighting men are given some credibility by the fact that the king of the Zambos-Mosquitos offered the English 5,000 "indios" to help in the war against the rebels in North America, whilst another account in 1778 also suggested the total number of Zambos-Mosquitos was not above 30,000.[82] However, another British account indicated a smaller population of between 1,500-2,000 capable of bearing arms and about four to five times that number of women and children.[83]

---

[75]CDHCR 9: 187-205 Informe on the Zambos-Mosquitos 16.2.1731.

[76]AGCA A1.17 210 5018 Corregidor of Sebaco and Chontales 8.7.1743.

[77]AGI AG 302 Rivera 10.5.1737; AGCA A1.17 335 7088 Rivera 23.11.1742; AGI AG 303 Averiguación en razón de la fortificación...en la Isla de Roatán 26.2.1743.

[78]PRO CO 123/1 ff.55-79 Hodgson 1757.

[79]AGI AG 449 and AGCA A1.12 117 2473 Yarrince 18.9.1759.

[80]MNM Bª-XI-Cª-B n°-1 Hodgson and Hodgson 1782.

[81]Long, *History of Jamaica* 1: 316; PRO CO 123/3 ff.1-6 White 16.1.1784; Edwards, "British Settlements," p. 210.

[82]AGI AG 665 and CDHCN: 198-205 Diario de Antonio de Gastelu 11.7.1776; Anon, *The Present State of the West Indies* (London: R. Baldwin, 1778), p. 48.

[83]BM Add. 12,431 f.202 Request for information from Capt. Kimberley, no date; Henderson, *British Settlement of Honduras*, p. 190.

Altogether it seems likely that at the beginning of the nineteenth century the Zambos-Mosquitos numbered between 15,000 and 30,000.

Using figures from the 1804 census and other estimates made here, the total Indian population of Honduras at the beginning of the nineteenth century was about 62,692, which represents an increase of about 31.9 percent over that calculated for the end of the seventeenth century (Table 21). The increase was mainly registered in tributary Indian villages, where it appears that the population more than doubled during the century. However, amongst the tributary villages increases were uneven. They were most marked in Gracias a Dios and Tencoa, whereas in Tegucigalpa the increase was marginal. In the east the increase was also marked, but in relative rather than absolute terms. Meanwhile, Indian groups outside Spanish control continued to lose population as many came into sustained contact with outside groups for the first time. At the beginning of the nineteenth century the Indian population was only 7.8 percent of the size it had been at the time of Spanish conquest and represented less than 30 percent of the total population of the country.

Table 21

INDIAN POPULATION ESTIMATES FOR COLONIAL HONDURAS

|  | End of the seventeenth century | Beginning of the nineteenth century |
| --- | --- | --- |
| Tributary Indians | 15,018 | 34,383 |
| Lavoríos | 526 | 719 |
| Missions | 2,000 | 590 |
| Outside Spanish control | 30,000 | 27,000 |
| TOTAL | 47,544 | 62,692 |

FACTORS UNDERLYING DEMOGRAPHIC CHANGE

The major factors responsible for the decline in the Indian population changed after the mid-sixteenth century. Whereas conquest and the Indian slave trade had taken a heavy toll on the Indian population in the first half of the sixteenth century, by 1550 political stability had been achieved and the slave trade had effectively ceased. Also, although there were many instances of overwork and excessive demands for goods and services, the New Laws introduced in 1542 went some way towards improving the treatment of the Indians to the extent that the proportion of the decline that can be attributed to these causes decreased. The most significant factors that contributed to the continued decline of the Indian population through the seventeenth century were disease, the disruption of Indian economies and societies, and miscegenation. The latter assumed greater importance in the eighteenth century, undermining increases in the Indian population that were fostered by greater economic and social stability, and by increased immunity to disease, although it still took its toll.

Once political stability had been achieved casualties resulting from wars between Indians and non-Indians accounted for an insignificant proportion of the decline, although two areas of conflict still existed. First, Indians were sometimes killed during missionary expeditions and, second, from the last quarter of the seventeenth century the Zambos-Mosquitos conducted enslaving raids inland from the Mosquito coast particularly amongst the Paya and Sumu.[84]

Throughout the colonial period disease continued to take its toll on the Indian population, although its demographic effects were not as devastating because many Indians, especially in western and central Honduras, had built up a degree of immunity to disease, particularly to smallpox and measles. However, in the remoter eastern parts of the province, where the Indians were gradually brought under Spanish control by missionaries, the initial impact of disease was devastating. Unfortunately there are few references to the actual numbers contracting or dying of different diseases so it is difficult to be precise about their impact. The epidemiography of Honduras is difficult to trace, but the evidence that exists suggests that the country did not suffer as badly as Guatemala from the impact of disease (Table 22). Pneumonic plague and typhus, which both prefer cooler climatic conditions,[85] were amongst the most important diseases that ravaged highland Guatemala at regular intervals during the colonial period.[86] Although these diseases may have ventured into western Honduras, they were generally unsuited to the warmer conditions to be found in the province.

In the early seventeenth century Guatemala was badly ravaged by smallpox, followed by typhus and pneumonic plague. The pneumonic plague epidemic was vividly described by the president of the Audiencia Alonso Criado de Castilla, who observed that it did not affect Spaniards, but was worst amongst hispanicized Indians and those who

---

[84]For example, AGCA A3.16 146 988 Justicias y Pueblo de Agalteca 6.8.1702, A3.16 190 1932 Información sobre la entrada de los zambos...1702; AGI AG 217 Audiencia 31.8.1704; AGCA A1.12 50 7493 Autos...hiciese mudar el pueblo de Jetegua 7.7.1709, 15.9.1710, A1.30 219 2466 Indians of Olancho El Viejo 4.12.1724; AGI AG 231 Rivera 10.9.1738; AGCA A3.16 193 1998 Real contaduría 6.5.1789.

[85]The origin of pneumonic plague is uncertain but it has been suggested that it develops when a person suffering from a respiratory infection contracts bubonic plague. Plague flourishes between 10°C and 30°C, with pneumonic plague found at the lower end of the temperature range and bubonic plague at the higher end of the range, though not over 30°C or in dry conditions. Pneumonic plague tends to be a winter disease and when the climate becomes warmer and drier it changes to bubonic plague (Pollitzer, *Plague*, pp. 418, 483, 510-13, 535-38; Shrewsbury, *Bubonic Plague*, pp. 1-6; MacLeod, *Spanish Central America*, pp. 8-9; McNeill, *Plagues and Peoples*, p. 124. Similarly, Ashburn notes that typhus is generally associated with poverty where inadequate housing, clothing, and sanitation encourage the spread of disease by lice and rats. In hot, moist coastal regions where little clothing is worn and washing can occur frequently, the disease is unlikely to spread. By contrast in cold, dry uplands, where water is scarce so that bathing and the washing of clothes occurs less frequently, unhygienic conditions are fostered that encourage the spread of disease (Ashburn, *Ranks of Death*, pp. 81, 95-96.

[86]F. Solano Pérez-Lila, "La Población indígena de Guatemala (1498-1800)," *AEA* 26 (1969): 315; MacLeod, *Spanish Central America*, pp. 98-100; Veblen, "Native Population Decline," pp. 497-98; W.G. Lovell, "Historia demográfica de la Sierra de los Cuchumatanes: 1520-1821," *Mesoamérica* 4 (1982): 296-97.

Table 22

EPIDEMIC DISEASES 1600 TO 1821

| | | |
|---|---|---|
| 1617 | smallpox, measles, & typhus | AGI AG 64 1617 |
| 1670s | "pestes y enfermedades" | (Gracias a Dios) AGI AG 164 28.7.1675 |
| 1690s | smallpox and measles | (Olancho missions) AGI AG 164 27.2.1696, AG 223 and 297 13.1.1699 |
| 1714 | "epidemia" | (Comayagua) AGCA A3.16 191 1945 15.7.1724 |
| 1720s | smallpox | (Comayagua) AGCA A3.16 513 5373 22.6.1739 |
| 1727-28 | measles | (Comayagua) AGCA A3.16 513 5373 22.6.1739, A3.16 513 5376 2.3.1743 |
| 1730s | "continuadas pestes y enfermedades" | (Comayagua & Olancho)AGCA A3.16 192 1955 14.8.1739, 29.12.1739 |
| 1733 onwards | "continuadas epidemias de pestes" | (Comayagua) AGCA A3.16 514 5385 1745 |
| 1746-53 | "gran peste" | (Gracias a Dios & Tencoa) AGCA A3.16 192 1972 22.7.1750, 4.6.1751, A3.16 192 1974 1.7.1752, A3.16 192 1981 26.10.1753. |
| 1750-51 118 | smallpox | (Missions of Lean y Mulía) AGCA A1.12 |
| | | 2487 10.3.1754, 12.3.1754, A1.12 117 2479 20.8.1751, A1.12 6056 53627 4.2.1752 |
| 1774 | measles | (Tegucigalpa) AGCA A3.9 174 1680 28.5.1774 |
| 1777 | smallpox | (Comayagua) AGCA A1.1 10 9.2.1781 |
| 1780-82 | smallpox | Major epidemic. AGI AG 568 6.6.1783; AGCA A3.16 516 5422 1785 |
| 1788 | measles | (Olancho) AGCA A1.45 385 3509 8.2.1788 |
| 1788 | "pestes y enfermedades" | (Gracias a Dios) AGCA A3.16 193 2001 12.8.1794 |
| 1789 | "epidemia pestilenciosa" | (Tencoa) AGCA A3.16 193 2002 18.11.1791 |
| 1801-08 | "pestilencia" | (Gracias a Dios) AGCA A3.16 196 2091 22.11.1808 |
| 1804 | "enfermedades y peste" | (Comayagua) AGCA A3.16 517 5435 1805 |
| 1809 | yellow fever | (Trujillo) AGCA A1.46 107 1315 20.9.1809 |
| 1816 | smallpox | Major epidemic. AGCA A3.16 197 2100, 2102, 2103, 2108 1816; ANH P15 L47 2.10.1816 and UC 1816. |

lived in the coldest areas.[87] This disease does not appear to have spread further south, but in 1617 smallpox, measles, and typhus were reported as having killed many Indians in Honduras.[88] During the seventeenth century the impact of disease was most devastating amongst the Indians who were collected into the missions. In the 1690s smallpox and measles were introduced into Honduras by missionaries. The disease probably came from Guatemala, which suffered epidemics between 1693 and 1694, and it was so devastating that it discouraged other Indians from settling in the missions and encouraged those who remained to flee.[89] Other reports of diseases are so vague that it is impossible to identify them, let alone assess their impact. It would appear that during the 1670s western Honduras was afflicted by "enfermedades y pestes."[90]

During the eighteenth and early nineteenth centuries, there seem to have been relatively few epidemics, although this may reflect the inadequacy of the documentary record. The most notable epidemics were in 1727-28, 1746-53, 1780-82, and 1816, and they were all either smallpox or measles. In addition there were a number of diseases generally referred to as 'epidemias' and 'enfermedades.' Most of the diseases appear to have spread southwards from Guatemala, but the evidence is too fragmentary to obtain a clear picture of the areas that were affected, and whether there was any regional or urban/rural variations in mortality rates.

During the 1720s there was an outbreak of smallpox and in 1727-28 an epidemic of measles.[91] The latter was probably the same disease that was afflicting Guatemala at the same time.[92] There are a number of documents written in the 1730s that refer to the inability of Indians to pay tribute due to the decline in the population as a result of "continuadas pestes y enfermedades."[93] There is no mention of a specific disease and it is possible that the complaints were a retarded response to the measles epidemic just noted. Alternatively, it is possible that the smallpox epidemic in Guatemala in 1733 did spread further south.[94] There are further references to a "gran peste" in western Honduras between 1746 and 1753. This disease was not recorded elsewhere in the province, and given the cooler climatic conditions in western Honduras, it may well have been typhus,[95] which ravaged Guatemala in the early 1740s.

---

[87]CDHCN: 92-112 Dr. Criado de Castilla 30.11.1608.

[88]AGI AG 64 Miners of Honduras 1617.

[89]AGI AG 164 Bishop of Honduras 27.2.1696, AG 223 Fr. Pedro de la Concepción 13.1.1699.

[90]AGI AG 164 Bishop of Honduras 28.7.1675.

[91]AGCA A3.16.3 513 5373 22.6.1739, A3.16.3 513 5376 2.3.1743.

[92]Veblen, "Native Population Decline," p. 498.

[93]AGCA A3.16 192 1955 Alcalde of Caingala 14.8.1739, Teniente of Olancho 29.12.1739, A3.16 514 5385 Alcalde of Quelala 1745.

[94]Veblen, "Native Population Decline," p. 498.

[95]AGCA A3.16 192 1972 22.5.1750, 4.6.1751, A3.16 1974 1.7.1752, A3.6 192 1981 Cuenta de cobranzas de tributos 26.10.1753.

Between 1750 and 1751 smallpox appears to have struck the missions again; there is no evidence of it reaching epidemic proportions in other parts of the province. In Lean and Mulía, the mission of San Miguel lost 106 of its 241 Indians and Santiago Siriano lost 290 of its 366 inhabitants,[96] whilst one account noted that altogether the disease had claimed 560 of the 860 mission Indians in the area.[97]

During the 1770s there are two references to outbreaks of disease in Honduras: one of measles in villages in the jurisdiction of Tegucigalpa and the other of smallpox in Comayagua.[98] Probably the major epidemic of the century occurred between 1780 and 1782. This was a smallpox epidemic that affected all parts of Honduras. The epidemic was so devastating that accounts were drawn up of the numbers that had died in the outbreak. In eighteen parishes in Honduras a total of 521 tributary Indians died out of a total tributary population of 5,121.[99] The figures for the individual villages listed in the different accounts of the epidemic vary slightly, but the differences do not alter the overall pattern.[100] If the numbers of tributary Indians dying in the epidemic figures are compared with the number of tributary Indians included in the nearest comparable tasaciones (those for 1770), it would appear that the mortality rate varied little between the regions, with the exception of the high mortality rate in Tencoa, but there were considerable variations within the regions (Table 23). There are only partial accounts of the mortality rate amongst non-tributary Indians, but it is clear that the death rate was greater amongst those under the age of eighteen.[101] Where the number of males under

---

[96]AGCA A1.12 118 2487 Visita of San Miguel del Carmen 10.3.1754, Visita of Santiago Siriano 12.3.1754.

[97]AGCA A1.12 117 2479 Cura of Yoro 20.8.1751, A.1.12 6056 53627 4.2.1752.

[98]AGCA A3.9 174 1680 Alcalde Mayor of Tegucigalpa 28.5.1774, A1.1 1 10 9.2.1781.

[99]AGI AG 568 Testimony on relief of tribute due to the smallpox epidemic 6.6.1783, AG 743 12.5.1784.

[100]AGI AG 568 Testimony on relief of tribute due to the smallpox epidemic 6.6.1783; AGCA A3.16 5422 Account of those dying of smallpox 1785. See also AGCA A3.16 191 1993 19.1.1784.

[101]AGCA A3.16 516 5422 1785. Where the numbers of women and children dying are included the figures are:

|  | Tributary males | Males under 18 | Women |
|---|---|---|---|
| Comayagua (2 parishes) | 35 | 168 | 225 |
| San Pedro | 5 | 13 | 31 |
| Gracias a Dios | 305 | 1,018 | - |

The figure for Gracias a Dios is probably slightly too low since some villages only included males between the ages of 10 and 18, so that tributary Indians probably accounted for a slightly lower percentage of total number of deaths than the figures suggest.

Table 23

## THE IMPACT OF THE 1781-82 SMALLPOX EPIDEMIC

| | Tributary Indians | | | |
| | no. dying | no. in 1770 | % loss | range of % loss |
|---|---|---|---|---|
| Comayagua | 55 | 629 | 8.7 | 0.0-48.0 |
| Gracias a Dios | 347 | 2,531 | 13.7 | 0.0-53.1 |
| Tencoa | 72 | 199 | 36.2 | 11.9-100.0 |
| San Pedro | 5 | 53 | 9.4 | 13.0-24.0 |
| Olancho | 12 | 169 | 7.1 | 0.0-25.0 |
| Yoro | 2 | 56 | 3.6 | 0.0-5.0 |
| Olanchito | 25 | 100 | 25.0 | |
| Western & Central Honduras | 479 | 3,412 | 14.0 | |
| Eastern Honduras | 39 | 325 | 12.0 | |
| TOTAL | 518 | 3,737 | 13.9 | |

Sources:
1770     AGCA A1.73 390 3662 (Villages have been excluded for which information on the numbers dying of smallpox are not available).
1781-82  AGCA A3.16 516 5422 1785

18 and women are included, only 8.5 percent of the total number of deaths were of tributary Indians. Thus it may be estimated that the total number of Indians who died in the epidemic was somewhere around 6,100. The impact of this epidemic was so devastating that it remained clear in the minds of Indians well into the nineteenth century.[102]

This epidemic was shortly followed by a measles epidemic. It originated in Guatemala probably about 1786, but it did not appear in Honduras until 1788.[103] Unspecified epidemics occurred in Opoa in 1788 and in Yamala in 1789 and it seems likely that they were also measles.[104] There are a number of accounts of unspecified diseases occurring at intervals at the beginning of the nineteenth century, but they do not appear to have reached epidemic proportions.[105] Finally, there was another outbreak of smallpox in Honduras in 1816.[106] Despite the fact that vaccination had begun in Honduras in 1815,[107] the death toll in some areas was very high; in the parish of Cerquin in the jurisdiction of Gracias a Dios it was estimated that 900 people died.[108] In Choluteca, comparing the tributary list with the number of deaths from smallpox in 1816, the mortality rate was about 18.0 percent.[109]

It is assumed that the tropical diseases--yellow fever and malaria--were introduced sometime during the seventeenth century, but because of the lack of documentary evidence for the Caribbean coast, no precise dates can be given for their introductions or any assessment made of their impact on the Indian population there, although it must have been considerable. The first definitely identifiable outbreak of yellow fever occurred in Trujillo in 1809 and it was described as follows: "This colony [Trujillo] is infested with the disease they call vomito prieto [black vomit], it is so malignant that it scarcely gives those who are suffering it time to receive the sacraments, because then they lose their minds and begin to emit blood through the mouth, and from these symptoms death follows."[110] Although yellow fever is unlikely to have spread

---

[102]AGCA A3.16 197 2098 Pueblo de Ocotepeque 5.6.1810.

[103]AGI AG 472 President of the Audiencia 15.9.1786; AGCA A1.45 385 3509 Pueblo of Catacamas 8.2.1788.

[104]AGCA A3.16 193 2001 Pueblo of Opoa 12.9.1794, A3.16 193 2002 Pueblo of Yamala 18.11.1791.

[105]AGCA A3.16 517 5435 Pueblo of Comayaguela 1805, A3.16 196 2092 Pueblo of Chucuyuco 22.11.1808.

[106]AGCA A3.16 197 2100 Pueblos of Petoa, 2102 Partido of Nacaome, 2103 Yambalanguira, 2108 Lauterique all 1816; ANH P15 L47 Sobre verificar el padrón de Tegucigalpa 2.10.1816, ANH UC Indians of the parish of Choluteca 1816.

[107]ANH P15 L57 1815.

[108]ANH UC Pueblo of Quesailica 1816.

[109]The number of deaths in Aguanqueterique, Curarén, Alubarén, Reitoca and Tambla was 59, which was 18.2 percent of the tributary population of 324 in those villages in 1811 (AGCA A3.16 197 2096 Tasaciones 1811; ANH UC Indians of the parish of Choluteca 1816.

[110]AGCA A1.46 107 1315 20.9.1809.

inland due to the cooler climate there, it is uncertain whether it spread east and south along the Mosquito coast.

The evidence for the impact of disease is very fragmentary so that it is difficult to ascertain any regional variations in their impact. What seems to have been the case is that diseases preferring cooler climates, such as typhus, probably did not spread very extensively in Honduras. Comparing the evidence for Honduras with Veblen's chart of diseases in Totonicapán in Guatemala,[111] it would appear that the former was largely spared from *tabardillo* (typhus) epidemics. Whilst the documentary record might be incomplete for Honduras, it is doubtful that it would not have recorded one of the five epidemics that occurred in Guatemala if they had spread further south. In contrast it is likely that yellow fever epidemics were restricted to the north coast of Honduras, possibly spreading to the Mosquito Shore, being dependent on high temperatures. The only other regional variation in the impact of disease in the late colonial period is the considerably higher mortality rate from smallpox in the missions, where the Indians had little, if any, immunity to disease. There appears to have been little correlation between the size of the settlement and the percentage of the tributary population dying in particular epidemics; it seems more likely that other environmental factors, such as the climate, availability of food, character of the water supply, housing conditions, the presence of vectors for transmitting the disease and the immunity of the population, would have had more important influences on the spread of disease and its impact on particular populations.

Although Indian communities gradually adjusted to the realities of Spanish conquest and colonization, the demands that were made on them continued to undermine their viability, contributing to their continued decline and retarding their recovery. The burden of work that fell on the Indians in providing tribute and in meeting the repartimiento quota and other demands for goods and services was considerable. Although each exaction may have been small, together they combined to keep the Indians in continual labor leaving them little time to attend to their own subsistence needs. The employment of labor under the repartimiento was particularly damaging when the tours of duty coincided with sowing and harvest, but even in the intervening periods, it resulted in crops being left untended and exposed to straying cattle. Complaints about the disastrous impact of the repartimiento on Indian agriculture are numerous in the documentary record. The repartimiento was not, however, the only institution that made demands on Indian labor; labor was needed to produce items for tribute payment, and to provide the numerous services and goods required by secular and ecclesiastical officials. These demands on Indian labor and coupled with the alienation of their lands contributed to food shortages, such that in the seventeenth century, the Lencas in western and central Honduras were said to be constantly fighting hunger.[112] Food shortages and famines not only contributed directly to an increase in the mortality rate, but they increased the susceptibility of Indians to diseases that often followed in their wake. Although drought, plagues of locusts, and the excessive export of maize contributed to food shortages, it is clear that many resulted from the inability of Indians to either sow or harvest their crops. Although it is clear that crop shortages occurred, they were mitigated to a certain extent by the raising of domesticated animals, particularly chickens and cattle, the latter often raised communally or by cofradías.

In addition to undermining the subsistence base, some tasks in which Indians were employed were injurious to health and directly contributed to the death rate.

---

[111]Veblen, "Native Population Decline," p. 498.

[112]RAHM CM 49 394 ff.73-92 Fernández del Pulgar, no date.

Although the Ordinances promulgated in 1601 and 1609 reaffirmed prohibitions on the employment of Indians under the repartimiento as porters, and in mining, indigo manufacture, and sugar milling amongst other things, they were often infringed, and in the case of mining the repartimiento was reintroduced in Honduras in 1645.[113] One heavy task in which repartimiento labor was employed throughout the colonial period was in the construction of coastal fortifications, notably Fort Omoa. It was claimed that the employment of Indians in its construction had resulted in the depopulation of the surrounding area, and reduced the population of the province as a whole by half.[114] In many cases it was not the task itself that directly contributed to the mortality rate, but the fact that Indians were often required to work in areas to which they were not acclimatized, with the result that many fell ill. The most common complaints came from Indians living in the highland areas, particularly around Gracias a Dios, who were often forced to work in the construction of forts on the hot and humid north coast[115] or else in tobacco cultivation in the cool and humid *llanos* of western Honduras.[116] When a padrón of the village of Opoa was drawn up in 1795, it was observed that the Indians had once been healthy, but because of their employment in the llanos they were falling ill, "with sores, leprosy, fever, stomach infections and many other illnesses."[117]

In general the repartimiento was resented as a form of labor, for apart from being employed in arduous tasks in areas to which they were not acclimatized, Indians were often ill treated, overworked, and poorly fed to the extent that some died. Nevertheless, cruelty appears to have become more localized than it was in the early colonial period. The endless tiring work the Indians were required to undertake also contributed to the falling fertility rate. In 1584 the Bishop of Honduras reported that as a result of overwork "mothers kill their children at birth because they say they wish to free them from the misery they suffer."[118] It might be supposed that Indians were treated as free laborers, since employers would have found it necessary to provide them with better wages and working conditions in order to attract them and maintain them in their employment. Nevertheless, the fact that many employers failed to attract free laborers suggests that their working conditions were not significantly better than those of other Indians.

Although changes also occurred in the social organization of Indian communities, it is difficult to assess their precise demographic impact. The rapid decline of the Indian population in the sixteenth century resulted in the breakdown of many communities and

---

[113]See Newson, "Demographic Catastrophe," pp. 232-35; and idem, "Labour in the Colonial Mining Industry," pp. 185-203. For the 1601 and 1609 Ordinances see AGCA A1.23 4576 39529 24.11.1601, 26.5.1609, and for later prohibitions see A1.23 1516 f.179 cédula 15.4.1640.

[114]AGCA A3.12 509 5300 14.11.1760; AGI AG 546 Notes on a journey of the President of Guatemala 1.11.1768; AGI AG 797 García 20.11.1790.

[115]AGCA A3.16 390 5300 14.11.1760; AGI IG 1525 Testimonio 10.10.1803.

[116]AGCA A3.16 194 2010 Padrón del Pueblo de Opoa 29.5.1795, A1.12 51 521 Vecinos mas distinguidos...de los Llanos 12.3.1804, A3.16 197 2099 Pueblos of Tencoa 12.10.1812.

[117]AGCA A3.16 194 2010 Padrón del pueblo de Opoa 29.5.1795.

[118]AGI AG 164 Bishop of Honduras 20.4.1582.

the prolonged absence of individuals working under the repartimiento or as free laborers increased the breakdown of marriages and the propensity of Indians to marry spouses from outside their communities. Thus following conquest the fertility rate declined markedly, only to begin to increase again in the eighteenth century, by which time miscegenation was gathering momentum and reducing its impact.

Meanwhile Indians outside Spanish control experienced different degrees of economic and social change. Those collected into the missions were the most profoundly affected. The aim of the missionaries in eastern Honduras was to create self-sufficient communities based on agriculture, but the short life of most missions meant that this goal was seldom achieved. In the initial stages of their foundation, the Indians were maintained by imported provisions and as such they led a precarious existence, often thrown back on wild food resources for survival. Later, as agriculture became established, the missions became more economically stable, largely as a result of the development of livestock raising. Even so, the mission populations declined, not only because of fugitivism, but also because of the low fertility rate, probably psychologically induced. In 1819 a report by a missionary working amongst the Jicaque noted that, "each year more die than are born, because of the sterility of women, who in their palenques on the contrary experience great fecundity."[119]

Outside the missions contacts with ladinos and with the Zambos-Mosquitos created demands for a variety of wild products, diverting Indian labor into the acquisition of these items and away from subsistence. This loss in food production was not compensated for by trade, which returned only cheap manufactures, tools, and trinkets to the Indians. Nevertheless, there is no evidence of food shortages in these areas. This contrasts with the Mosquito Shore, where agriculture had always been difficult, and much of the food consumed by Indians was obtained from wild food resources. With the expansion of the population and its increased contacts with Europeans several changes occurred: agriculture became more inadequate to meet the demands made upon it; labor was withdrawn from fishing into the collection of wild animal and vegetable products in demand by Europeans; but this fall in food production was probably compensated for in part by the introduction of livestock, and by the acquisition of firearms, which made hunting more efficient. That the balance was on the negative side, however, can be seen by references to food shortages on the coast.[120] Nevertheless, the decline in the Indian population on the Mosquito Shore may be attributed more to the rapid expansion of the Zambos-Mosquitos, than to inadequacies in the subsistence base.

During the colonial period miscegenation accounted for an increasing proportion of the decline in the Indian population as the intensity of contact between the races increased and the population of mixed races rose. During the seventeenth century, accounts generally distinguished between Spaniards, mestizos, mulattoes, and negroes, but in the eighteenth century less distinction was made between the latter three groups, which were often referred to collectively as ladinos. The majority of ladinos were mestizos and mulattoes, in a ratio of about one to three, but small numbers of negroes and zambos were also included in this category. Due to the predominance of mulattoes amongst the non-Indian population, the mixed races including negroes, were often referred to as *pardos*.

During the colonial period the non-Indian population increased substantially. The greatest increase was in the eighteenth century, although part of the increase was

---

[119]AGCA A1.12 51 526 20.11.1819.

[120]AGCA A1.17 4501 38303 Porta Costas 1.8.1790; Roberts, *Narrative of Voyages*, pp. 115, 150.

probably due to Indians being reclassified as ladinos. In the 1620s according to Vázquez de Espinosa, there were 560 vecinos in Honduras, including Choluteca, distributed in six cities.[121] On the other hand, in 1646 Díaz de la Calle recorded that there were only 230 Spaniards, excluding Tegucigalpa and Choluteca (which Vázquez de Espinosa noted together contained 160 vecinos), but including San Pedro with 30 Spaniards, which Vázquez de Espinosa excluded.[122] By 1683 the number of Spaniards had not changed significantly. At that time there were 531 in the whole province, representing nearly 35 percent of the total non-Indian population of 1,555 (Table 24).[123] These latter figures almost certainly referred to adults, if not only male adults, and they may be compared with an adult population of Spaniards and ladinos of 38,498 in 1777. At that time the total non-Indian population was 52,793 (including Omoa) and by 1804 it has risen to 85,550.[124]

This increase in the non-Indian population was the result of natural increase and miscegenation, for the province attracted few immigrants, although some did arrive from the mid-eighteenth century onwards. The first to arrive were about 300 negro slaves imported to work on the construction of Fort Omoa.[125] Then in 1787, following the evacuation of the Mosquito Shore by the English, over 1,000 colonists from Spain and the Canary Islands were settled on the Shore.[126] Meanwhile, 1,500 Black Caribs from St. Vincent were transferred to Trujillo from Roatán, where they had been deposited by the English,[127] and these were joined by several hundred negro slaves fleeing from the revolution in Sainte Domingue.[128] In 1804 Intendant Anguiano estimated that there were 200 French negroes, 300 English negroes, and 4,000 Black Caribs around Trujillo.[129]

Clearly the degree of the miscegenation depended on the intensity of contact between the races. The Crown tried to minimize interracial contact by passing laws that prohibited non-Indians, with the exception of a small number of authorized secular and ecclesiastical officials, from residing in Indian villages and barrios. Although these laws were partially successful, opportunities for interracial contact existed in the towns, estates, and in the mining areas, where Indians were employed either under the

---

[121]Vázquez de Espinosa, *Compendium and Description*, pp. 235-47.

[122]Díaz de la Calle, *Memorial y noticias sacras*, pp. 125-29.

[123]AGI CO 815 Razón de las ciudades...1683.

[124]AGI IG 1527 Estado y Padrón General...1777, AG 501 Estado que manifiesta las subdelegaciones...1.5.1804.

[125]AGI AG 970 Diligencias practicadas...compra de 100 negros 1757; AGCA A1.23 1540 f.54 14.6.1765; Floyd, *Anglo-Spanish Struggle*, p. 110.

[126]Chapter 14, p. 257.

[127]AGCA A3.16 194 2025 List of Caribs...23.9.1797, 16.10.1797; Floyd, *Anglo-Spanish Struggle*, p. 184; Davidson, "Dispersal of the Garífuna," p. 468.

[128]AGI AG 452 Relación de las providencias económicas...3.1.1804.

[129]AGI AG 501 Estado que manifiesta las subdelegaciones...1.5.1804, AG 963 Ayzinenass 2.11.1813.

Table 24

## NON-INDIAN ADULT MALE POPULATION OF HONDURAS IN THE SEVENTEENTH CENTURY

| | Spanish officials | Spaniards | Other[a] officials | | Other races |
|---|---|---|---|---|---|
| Comayagua | 13 | 144 | 3 | 177 | pardos & morenos |
| Tegucigalpa | 5 | 130 | | 300 | mestizos, mulattoes & negros |
| Gracias a Dios | 9 | 72 | | 40 | mestizos & mulattoes |
| Tencoa | 1 | 26 | | | |
| San Pedro | 2 | 24 | 3 | 76 | pardos & morenos |
| Choluteca | 2 | 50 | | 130 | mestizos, mulattoes & negroes |
| Yoro | 3 | | 3 | 167 | pardos & morenos |
| Olancho el Viejo | 4 | 30 | | 30 | mestizos, 64 mulattoes & negroes |
| Olanchito | 1 | 9 | | 2 | mestizos, 24 mulattoes |
| Trujillo | | 6 | | 5 | mulattoes |
| TOTAL | 40 | 491 | 9 | 1,015 | |

[a]The racial status of these officials is uncertain.

Source: AGI CO 815 Razón de las ciudades...1683.

repartimiento or as private employees. Since employment under the repartimiento was normally temporary, the intensity of contact with other groups was probably less than where Indians were permanently employed as free laborers and often resided in their places of employment. It is clear therefore that as more and more Indians turned to private employment, the likelihood of the loss of Indian population through miscegenation increased.

Just as Indians were being attracted to centers of employment, so non-Indians were dispersing to the countryside. This dispersion involved landowners taking up residence on their estates and, from during the eighteenth century, the settlement of the expanding population of mixed races in the rural areas, including Indian villages. In Olancho in 1802 it was estimated that there were only 1,500 Indians, whilst the number of Spaniards and ladinos who had settled there had risen to 10,000.[130] The dispersion of non-Indians from the urban centers included the militia, composed primarily of mulattoes, who were stationed on the north coast and in the east. Thus, by the end of the eighteenth century, the races were no longer racially segregated, and although following an order in 1792, the authorities initiated a program of establishing distinct settlements for the mixed races, it is doubtful if they achieved much success.[131]

Despite the movement of non-Indians to the countryside, the majority of non-Indians were concentrated in and around the major cities, notably Comayagua and Tegucigalpa. Most Spaniards and mestizos resided in the towns where they held official positions, or were merchants or landowners. The majority of artisans were probably mulattoes, whilst a small number of negro slaves may have been kept as domestic servants. The relatively large negro slave population that had existed in the sixteenth century declined markedly with the exhaustion of the gold placer deposits in Olancho, the majority being transferred to more profitable enterprises in neighboring Central American provinces and even to Colombia.[132] During the remainder of the colonial period, mining was insufficiently profitable to justify the importation of negro slaves on a large scale.[133] Although the negro slave population in the mining areas declined, runaway slaves and descendants of those who had been employed in gold mining remained in small numbers to give the region a distinct racial character. Some became independent miners or gurruguces,[134] whilst others survived by hunting feral cattle and later they developed a contraband trade with those living on the Mosquito Shore.[135] In addition to negro slaves, small numbers of free negroes were employed as overseers of estates, although the majority were mulattoes.[136]

Due to miscegenation the proportion of ladinos was highest in the jurisdictions of Tegucigalpa and Comayagua, and in the east and north where the mulatto militia were

---

[130]AGCA A1.45 369 3429 Pueblo of Sapota 11.1.1802.

[131]Chapter 12, p. 208.

[132]AGI AG 43 Cabildo of Comayagua 9.4.1551, AG 64 Miners of Honduras 1617.

[133]Newson, "Labour in the Colonial Mining Industry," pp. 185-203.

[134]ANH P3 L144 Miners of Tegucigalpa 16.4.1681; AGCA A1.1 1 4 21.5.1708.

[135]AGI AG 63 Villavicencio, vecino of Choluteca 1615, CDHCN: 96-136 Díaz Navarro 30.11.1758; AGI AG 457 Anguiano 1.7.1798; Floyd, *Anglo-Spanish Struggle*, p. 60.

[136]AGCA A3.12 509 5300 Pueblo of La Iguala 29.1.1770.

stationed (Table 25). Consequently, in 1804 the proportion of Indians in all these areas remained under 30 percent (Table 19). In contrast, in those areas where there were few profitable economic enterprises and consequently few non-Indians, the Indians comprised nearly 50 percent of the population. Throughout the nineteenth century the jurisdictions of Gracias a Dios and Tencoa remained the most 'Indian' in Honduras.[137]

Table 25

TOTAL POPULATION BY RACE IN 1777

|  | Indians | Ladinos | Spaniards | TOTAL |
|---|---|---|---|---|
| Comayagua | 4,387 | 6,621 | 428 | 11,436 |
| Tegucigalpa | 6,779 | 23,529 | 2,497 | 32,805 |
| Gracias a Dios | 19,490 | 6,923 | 1,052 | 27,465 |
| Tencoa | 2,708 | 678 | 643 | 4,029 |
| San Pedro | 410 | 1,578 | 109 | 2,097 |
| Olancho | 1,005 | 3,968 | 130 | 5,103 |
| Yoro | 368 | 1,441 | 99 | 2,753 |
| Olanchito | 1,025 | 2,232 | 153 | 2,565 |
| Omoa | - | 485 | 227 | 712 |
| Western & Central Honduras | 33,774 | 39,329 | 4,729 | 77,832 |
| Eastern Honduras | 2,398 | 8,126 | 609 | 11,133 |
| TOTAL | 36,172 | 47,455 | 5,338 | 88,965 |

Source: 1777 AGI IG 1527 Figures exclude Indians in the missions, the clergy and 604 negroes at Omoa.

[137]Squier, *Notes on Central America*, pp. 123, 144, 217.

# Part VII

---

# Conclusion

# 17
# Counting the Cost of
# Conquest and Colonization

On the eve of Spanish conquest Honduras was inhabited by Indian groups representative of two cultural types: chiefdoms and tribes. The chiefdoms inhabited western and central Honduras, although they had a few outliers further east. These Indian groups were socially stratified and they formed dense populations that were supported by intensive forms of agricultural production. Eastern Honduras was inhabited by essentially egalitarian tribes who subsisted on a combination of shifting cultivation, hunting, fishing, and gathering. Historical, cultural, and ecological evidence suggests that at the time of Spanish conquest the Indian population of the province was about 800,000, of which 200,000 were living in the east of the country.

During the first half of the sixteenth century the distribution of Spanish activities was influenced by the distribution of the Indian population and minerals. Initially Spaniards were attracted to western and central Honduras by the existence of large Indian populations that could be distributed in encomiendas or used to supply the Indian slave trade. However, the conquest of these areas was difficult and prolonged due to conflicts between rival conquistadors and the absence of any unifying political structure through which the Spanish could gain control. As such conquest brought heavy Indian casualties and it was several decades before political stability was achieved. During conquest the Spanish founded towns and proceeded to distribute encomiendas within their jurisdictions. Contact between Spaniards and Indians was greatest in the vicinity of the towns where the Indians suffered most from ill treatment and overwork, and their communities experienced the most profound economic and social changes. Spanish demands for tribute and labor put strains on Indian subsistence resulting in food shortages and famines, which in turn increased the susceptibility of Indians to deadly Old World diseases. Meanwhile, the dramatic decline in the Indian population undermined the social structure of communities and the psychological impact of conquest contributed to a lowering of the fertility rate. The larger concentrations of Indians in western and central Honduras also made it an attractive area for enslaving activities. The Indian slave trade in Honduras was never as important in Honduras as it was in neighboring Nicaragua, but it contributed significantly to the decline in the Indian population.

As a result of conquest and colonization the Indian population of western and central Honduras was reduced to about 32,000 in 1550. This amounts to a reduction of nearly 95.0 percent and a depopulation ratio of 17.8:1. As would be expected this ratio is higher than that recorded in the highland states of Central Mexico and the Central Andes,

Table 26

ESTIMATED INDIAN POPULATION CHANGE IN HONDURAS DURING THE
COLONIAL PERIOD

Population Estimates

| | Aboriginal population | Circa 1550 | End 17th century | Beginning 19th century |
|---|---|---|---|---|
| Western & central Honduras | 600,000 | 32,000 | 15,544* | 32,635 |
| Eastern Honduras | 200,000 | 100,000 | 32,000 | 30,057 |
| Area under Spanish control | | 8,000 | 2,000 | 3,057 |
| Area outside Spanish control | | 92,000 | 30,000 | 27,000 |
| TOTAL | 800,000 | 132,000 | 47,544 | 62,692 |

Percentage Change

| | Aboriginal to 1550 | 1550 to end 17th century | End 17th to beginning of 19th century | Aboriginal to beginning of 19th century |
|---|---|---|---|---|
| Western and central Honduras | -94.7 | -51.4 | +110.0 | -94.6 |
| Eastern Honduras | -50.0 | -68.0 | -6.1 | -85.0 |
| Area under Spanish control | | -75.0 | +52.9 | |
| Area outside Spanish control | | -64.4 | -10.0 | |
| TOTAL | -83.5 | -64.0 | +31.9 | -92.2 |

* This figure includes villages in eastern Honduras that were under Spanish administration, but they were small in size and number.

but it is also higher than the depopulation ratios for chiefdoms such as the Chibcha.[1] In all these cases the ratio of decline within the first 30 to 40 years of conquest was less than 5:1. The depopulation ratio for Honduras is also slightly higher than the ratio of 13.3:1 calculated for chiefdoms in neighboring Nicaragua during the same period,[2] but the difference in the depopulation ratios for the two areas is small and could be accounted for by errors of estimation. One of the main reasons why there were higher levels of decline amongst chiefdom groups in Honduras and Nicaragua was the Indian slave trade. Although the impact of the Indian slave trade was not as great in Honduras, the Indians suffered a more difficult conquest, which resulted in greater population losses and caused greater disruption to Indian communities (Table 26).

Although the smaller concentrations of Indians in eastern Honduras were less attractive as sources of tribute, labor, and slaves, the existence of easily workable alluvial gold deposits in Olancho encouraged the early settlement of that part of the region. There the Spanish attempted to control the Indians and exploit them as sources of labor through the introduction of the encomienda. However, the encomiendas granted were few in number and small in size, and the labor they provided, which proved difficult to control, was inadequate to meet the demands of miners. As such miners resorted to the employment of Indian slaves from other parts of Honduras or other provinces, and where possible to the importation of negro slaves. Indians in eastern Honduras were also less desirable as sources of slaves, since although slavery could be justified easily by their resistance to Spanish rule, their smaller numbers and their more nomadic mode of existence meant that enslaving expeditions produced fewer rewards and involved greater efforts than in other parts of the province. Although the level of Spanish activity in eastern Honduras was lower than in the west, enslaving raids and colonization in the vicinity of Olancho took their toll on the Indian population, as did newly introduced diseases. It is virtually impossible to estimate the decline in the Indian population in the east during the first half of the sixteenth century, but it may have been reduced by about one-third or one-half.

During the second half of the sixteenth and the seventeenth centuries the Indian population continued to decline, reaching its nadir at the end of the period when there were only about 47,500 Indians left in the province. In western and central Honduras the Indian population was halved, but the relative importance of different factors responsible for the decline changed. The Indian slave trade had been abolished and the treatment of the Indians gradually improved with legislation. Apart from epidemic diseases, which continued to take their toll, the main sources of cultural and demographic change during

---

[1]Cook and Borah's figures for the decline of the Indian population in Central Mexico until 1548 give a depopulation ratio of 4.4:1 (the actual figures are 27,650,000 on the eve of Spanish conquest to 6,300,000 in 1548) (Cook and Borah, *Essays* 1: 82, 115). Depopulation ratios for the Chibcha are: for Tunja (1537 to 1564) 1.4:1 (232,407 at the time of Spanish conquest to 168,440 in 1564) (J. Friede, "Algunas consideraciones sobre la evolución demográfica en la provincia de Tunja," *Anuario Colombiano de historia social y de la cultura* 2 (1965): 13) and for the Sabana of Bogotá (1537 to 1592-95) 2.2:1 (120,000 to 160,000 at conquest and 62,791 (excluding the city of Bogotá) in 1592-95) (Villamarin and Villamarin, *Indian Labor*, pp. 83-84). The degree of decline was slightly less in the Central Andean highlands where between 1525 and 1571 the Indian population declined from 4,641,200 to 1,349,190, a depopulation ratio of 3.4:1 (C.T. Smith, "Depopulation of the Central Andes in the Sixteenth Century," *Current Anthropology* 11 (1970): 459). See also N.D. Cook, *Demographic Collapse: Indian Peru, 1520-1620* (Cambridge: Cambridge University Press, 1981).

[2]Newson, *Indian Survival*.

this period were Spanish demands on Indian communities and their response to them. Demands for tribute and for labor under the repartimiento were a constant drain on Indian production and labor, but probably more oppressive were the unofficial exactions made by Spanish officials, encomenderos, and priests. These forms of direct exploitation were coupled with demands for lands and labor that arose with the establishment of estates and the development of commercial agriculture. Indian labor was also required in the towns and by the silver mining industry. Reductions in Indian lands and in labor time to work them resulted in decreased production at a time when external demands upon it were increasing. The result was that Indians abandoned their villages and sought employment as wage laborers in order to subsist and escape tribute demands and other exactions. In the towns, on estates, and in the mining areas they came into sustained contact with the non-Indians and began to lose their racial and cultural identity.

Whilst western and central Honduras continued to be the focus of Spanish activities, colonization was extended in eastern Honduras by the establishment of missions. Although the missions were generally short-lived, they radically altered the economic, social, and political life of Indians living in them and indirectly they affected the communities from which the Indians were drawn. Meanwhile, on the Mosquito Shore cultural changes were brought about indirectly by the presence of the English and from the mid-seventeenth century by the emergence of the Zambos-Mosquitos whose expansion cut into the Indian population. During the seventeenth century these more extensive contacts with different non-Indian groups and the widespread introduction of Old World diseases that accompanied them probably resulted in the Indian population being reduced by two-thirds between 1550 and 1700.

During the eighteenth century the Indian population in both regions increased, reaching a peak in the first decade of the nineteenth century after which it began to decline again. The increase was most marked in western and central Honduras, where the population more than doubled (+110.0 percent). This increase may be related to the absence of the most destructive forces that had been present in the early colonial period, the improvement in sources of food, and the effective establishment of a new social and political order. However, the expansion of the non-Indian population into the countryside put additional pressure on Indian lands, labor, and production, so that conditions were still bad enough to encourage Indians to abandon their communities in search of wage labor. This process resulted in more frequent contacts between the races, with Indians being gradually absorbed into the growing population of mixed races. Thus, although the Indian population increased during the eighteenth century, the rate of increase was slow, and finally at the beginning of the nineteenth century miscegenation outstripped the rate of natural increase converting the increase into a decline.

During the eighteenth century the Indian population in eastern Honduras continued to decline. Areas that had been outside Spanish control during the previous century declined by about 10 percent as they were encroached upon by Spanish colonists and missionaries on the one hand, and the Zambos-Mosquitos on the other. Some of the losses contributed to the 52.9 percent increase in the Indian population in the Spanish-settled area and to the growth of the Zambo-Mosquito population on the Mosquito Shore. The increase in the Spanish-settled area was not as marked as in western and central Honduras, probably because there were greater opportunities for racial mixing. Although in 1804 the numbers of Spaniards and ladinos were smaller in eastern Honduras, they accounted for 84.2 percent of the total population of the area; in western and central Honduras they accounted for a smaller proportion of the population and in some areas nearly 50 percent of the population remained Indian.[3]

---

[3] AGI AG 501 Estado que manifiesta las subdelegaciones...1.5.1804.

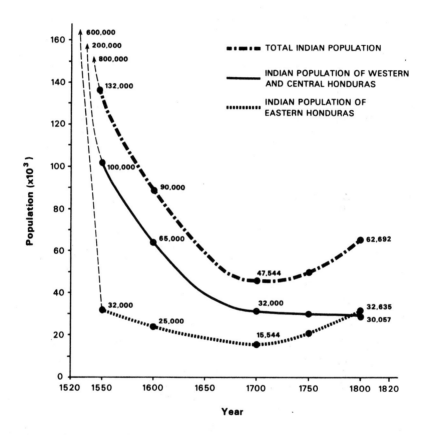

Figure 11. Estimated Indian Population Change During the Colonial Period

During the colonial period the Indian population of Honduras was reduced by over 90 percent, although a more marked decrease in the sixteenth century and early seventeenth centuries was mitigated by an increase in the eighteenth century. Overall the decline during the colonial period was most marked in western and central Honduras. This may appear to be contrary to what was predicted at the beginning of the study: it was suggested that the chiefdom groups would have a greater chance of surviving contact than the tribal groups in the east. The major reason for this unpredicted outcome is that at the end of the colonial period nearly 90 percent of the Indian population in eastern Honduras had not been brought under Spanish control and therefore experienced the profound cultural and demographic changes that followed contact in other parts of the province. It is significant that although the Indian population of eastern Honduras declined less during the colonial period, at the end of the colonial period it was still declining.

Although the nature of Indian cultures at the time of Spanish conquest did influence their level of survival in a positive way--for example, the intensive nature of agricultural production and the hierarchical social structure of the chiefdoms enabled the Spanish to control and exploit the Indians without having to modify their basic economic and social structures--it had one major negative effect. The dense Indian populations associated with the more highly developed chiefdoms provided the only source of profit in the province in the early colonial period. The Indians were used to supplying the Indian slave trade and those that were left in the second half of the sixteenth century formed the basic source of labor for the development of commercial agriculture and mining. The existence of sources of Indian labor and the more fertile soils and mineral deposits in central Honduras combined to make this area the continued focus of Spanish activities with the capital city and major towns being located there. In 1777 88.6 percent of the Spanish population lived in western and central Honduras together with 82.9 percent of the ladino population (Table 25), and it was here that contacts between Indians and non-Indians were most intense and demands on Indian communities therefore greater.

Within western and central Honduras, however, there were important regional variations in demographic change. The highlands of Gracias a Dios and Tencoa, which were highly populated at the time of Spanish conquest, suffered heavy casualties during the conquest of the province, but these areas possessed few resources to attract colonists, such that during the colonial period fewer demands were made on Indian communities and there were fewer contacts between the races. As such, these areas remained the most 'Indian' in Honduras at the end of the colonial period, with Indians accounting for nearly 50 percent of the population (Figure 12). The central regions of Comayagua and Tegucigalpa were also highly populated at the time of Spanish conquest, but here the administrative and economic centers of the province were located. As a result the Indian population was overworked and ill treated, and Indian communities were undermined through demands on their lands, labor, and production. These factors contributed to the decline in the Indian population and encouraged Indians to become wage laborers, in which capacity they came into contact with other races losing their racial and cultural identity. In these areas Indians comprised under 30 percent of the population at the beginning of the nineteenth century. Indian survival was even lower in Choluteca and the coastal lowlands of northern Honduras where the Indian population was decimated during the first half of the sixteenth century, largely as a result of the Indian slave trade. In Choluteca it was replaced by a growing population of mixed races which was attracted into indigo and livestock-raising enterprises.

Similarly, in eastern Honduras there were variations in demographic change. As has been demonstrated a large proportion of the Indian population still remained outside Spanish control at the end of the colonial period and, although it had declined as a result

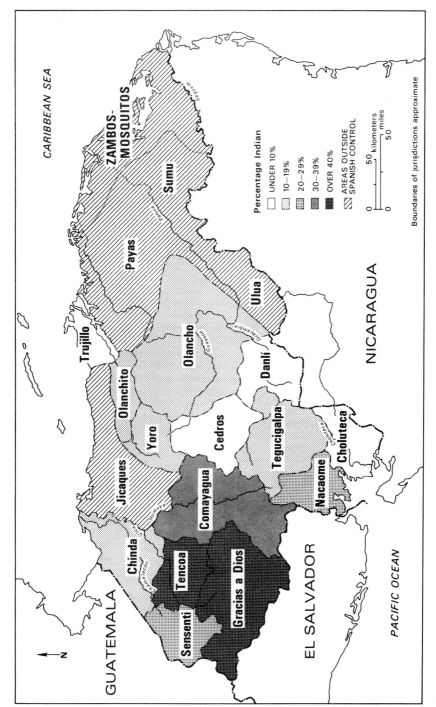

Figure 12. Distribution of the Indian Population in 1804

of the introduction of Old World diseases and contacts with outside groups, it had survived to a fairly high degree. In contrast, the Indian population of the Olancho and Aguan valleys was decimated during the early sixteenth century when Indians were employed either as slaves or forced labor in panning alluvial gold. These depopulated valleys later became the focus of ladino settlement in the eighteenth century, such that at the end of the colonial period the number of Indians there was small and they accounted for less than 20 percent of the total population.

In Honduras Spanish conquest and colonization resulted in clear regional variations in Indian survival, which were influenced by two major factors: the nature and distribution of the Indian population at the time of Spanish conquest and the attractiveness of human and natural resources in different parts of the province. Indian survival was favored in more complex and productive societies and where few resources existed to attract conquistadors and colonists; in less well-developed societies and where there were abundant natural resources, Indian survival was more problematic. These factors combined to produce not only regional variations in Indian survival at the end of the colonial period, but also distinct colonial experiences.

# Glossary

| | |
|---|---|
| Alcabala | A sales tax |
| Alcalde | A magistrate |
| Alcalde Mayor | A Spanish official with political and judicial authority over a district |
| Alcalde Ordinario | A magistrate who was a member of a cabildo |
| Alférez | A standard bearer |
| Alguacil | A constable, police officer |
| Alguacil Mayor | Chief constable, usually attached to a cabildo |
| Alguacil de Mandón | Constable charged with locating Indians with the purpose of collecting tribute from them |
| Alguacil de Mesón | Constable charged with supervising inns |
| Alma | Soul |
| Almojarifazgo | Import and export duty |
| Añil | Indigo |
| Apoderado fiscal | Spanish official appointed for a specific purpose; special commissioner |
| Arancel | List of fixed prices or fees |
| Arca | A treasury chest |
| Arrastre | Mill for grinding silver ore to a fine powder prior to amalgamation |
| Arroba | Weight equivalent to about 25 pounds |

| | |
|---|---|
| Audiencia | High judicial court and governing body of a region, and by extension the area under its jurisdiction |
| Azoguero | Supervisor of the amalgamation process |
| Banco de Rescate | Exchange bank |
| Barra | Crowbar |
| Barretero | Miner employed in extracting ore from a face |
| Barrio | District or suburb of a town |
| Batea | Wooden pan for washing alluvial gold |
| Bienes de comunidad | Community assets |
| Braza | A linear measure equivalent to 2 varas (ca. 1 yd. 30 ins.) |
| Bula | A papal bull |
| Caballería | An area measurement, in this region about 111 acres |
| Cabecera | The main village of a district generally with several other villages under its jurisdiction |
| Cabildo | Municipal council |
| Cacique | Indian leader or chief |
| Caja | Strongbox or chest |
| Caja de comunidad | Community chest |
| Canoa | Vat for making indigo dye |
| Cantor | Singer. In Indian villages they also provided Christian instruction |
| Capellanía | Endowed fund, sometimes of land or property, used to generate income for the church |
| Casa de afinación | Refining and assay house |
| Casa de Moneda | Mint |
| Casa de Rescate | Exchange House |
| Casado/a | A married person |

| | |
|---|---|
| Casado entero | A male Indian married to a female Indian from the same village or barrio |
| Cédula | Decree |
| Cendrada | Hearth lead |
| Ciudad | City |
| Cofradía | Religious brotherhood |
| Comandante General de Armas | Spanish official in charge of military affairs |
| Composición | Payment of a fee to regularize illegal or irregular occupation of land |
| Congregación | Forced resettlement of secular communities |
| Contador | Treasurer |
| Corregidor | Royal official with administrative and judicial authority |
| Corte | A type of indigo, of poorer quality |
| Cuadrilla | Gang of workers |
| Demora | Period during which mines were worked |
| Denuncia | An accusation or a claim to unoccupied land |
| Depositario General | Public trustee |
| Derrama | Collection made for the support of a bishop whilst conducting a visita |
| Diezmo | A tenth or tithe |
| Ejido | Communal lands |
| Encomendero/a | Holder of an encomienda |
| Encomienda | Grant of Indians given to an eminent colonist as a personal reward for merits or services. In return for the protection and instruction provided by the encomendero, the Indians were required to pay tribute in the form of goods, money, and until 1549, labor services |
| Enfermedades | Illnesses, disease |
| Entrada | Expedition, military or religious, into unexplored or unconquered territory |

| | |
|---|---|
| Epidemia | Epidemic, disease |
| Esclavo de guerra | Indian slave taken in war or rebellion |
| Esclavo de rescate | Indian slave obtained by trade |
| Escribano | Notary |
| Españoles | Spaniards |
| Estado | A linear measurement of 2.17 yards |
| Estancia | Ranch for livestock. Generally 6 3/4 caballerías for ganado mayor and half of that for ganado menor |
| Fanega | Measure of capacity, about 1 1/2 bushels |
| Fiel ejecutor | Inspector of weights and measures |
| Fiscal | Attorney general |
| Flor | A type of indigo, of good quality |
| Fuero | The fuero eclesiástico and the fuero militar bestowed certain privileges on clerics and soldiers respectively, including exemption from tithe payment and trial in civil courts |
| Gallina de castilla | A chicken |
| Ganado mayor | Cattle, horses, and mules |
| Ganado menor | Pigs, sheep, and goats |
| Gobernación | Area under the jurisdiction of a gobernador |
| Gobernador | Governor |
| Greta | Lead monoxide |
| Gurruguces | Poor independent miners |
| Hacendado/a | Owner of a hacienda |
| Hacienda | Landed estate or wealth in general |
| Hacienda de beneficio | Refinery |
| Indio gobernador | Indian leader appointed during the colonial period |

| | |
|---|---|
| Intendente | Royal official with extensive powers. Appointed in the last quarter of the eighteenth century |
| Juez | Judge or inspector |
| Juez de comisión | Judge or inspector appointed for a specific purpose |
| Juez de milpas | Inspector charged with ensuring that Indians grew maize |
| Juez repartidor | Spanish official in charge of the allocation of Indians under the repartimiento |
| Labranza | Cultivated plot |
| Ladino | A non-Indian. Generally persons of mixed race, including Indians who had experienced a degree of cultural and racial change |
| Lavorío | Originally an Indian who worked as a household servant. Later an Indian living in a non-Indian settlement, who was not included in an encomienda and who paid a distinct form of tribute |
| Legajo | A bundle, in this case, of documents |
| Libre | Free man or woman |
| Limosna | Alms, charity |
| Llanos | Grasslands or savannas |
| Mayordomo | Overseer or manager |
| Media anata | Payment equivalent to half a year's income. Often paid on the acquisition of encomiendas or land grants, and on receipt of public office |
| Mestizo | Offspring of an Indian and a European |
| Metate | Mortar for grinding maize |
| Milpa | Plot cultivated in maize, often with beans |
| Moclón | Debased silver coin from Peru |
| Monte | Uncultivated land or scrub, often used for sources of fuel and timber |
| Moreno | Brown-skinned person, lighter than a pardo |
| Mulatto | Offspring of a negro and a European |

| | |
|---|---|
| Naboría | See Lavorío. Naboría was the more commonly used term in the first half of the sixteenth century |
| Obraje | Workshop, in this case for making indigo dye or textiles |
| Oidor | Spanish official. Judge and member of the Audiencia |
| Padrón | Detailed list of inhabitants of a settlement, Indian or Spanish |
| Palenque | Multifamily house, possibly a fortified settlement |
| Parcialidad | Suburb of a town or village or kinship group within an Indian community |
| Pardo | Dark-skinned person, generally used to refer to a mulatto in the eighteenth century |
| Partido | Subordinate administrative unit |
| Pastos | Pastures |
| Peonía | An area measure. 5 peonías were originally equivalent to 1 caballería |
| Peso | Monetary unit comprised of 8 reales |
| Peste | Disease, generally referred to smallpox |
| Pestilencia | Pestilence, disease |
| Pierna | Linear measurement equivalent to about a yard (33 ins.) |
| Pila | Vat for making indigo dye |
| Platanar | Plot of wild or cultivated plantains |
| Principal | Indian leader, generally with less authority than a cacique |
| Quinto | A tax of one-fifth of the value of an item. Paid on Indian slaves and silver amongst other things |
| Ranchería | A small rural settlement |
| Rapadura | Poor-quality sugar |
| Real | Monetary unit comprised of 34 maravedís. 8 reals constituted 1 peso |
| Reducción | Settlement formed of nonconverted Indians or by amalgamation of several Indian settlements |

| | |
|---|---|
| Regidor | Councillor attached to a cabildo |
| Repartimiento | Draft labor system whereby each Indian village was to make available a quota of its tributary Indians to work in approved tasks for specified periods |
| Repartimiento de generos | Forced distribution and sale of goods amongst Indians generally by royal officials and the clergy |
| Repasador | Person employed in mixing mercury with silver ore |
| Reservado/a | Indian exempt from tribute payment by virtue of his/her age, status, or physical incapacity |
| Residencia | A judicial review of a Spanish official's conduct at the end of his term of office |
| Roza | Cultivation plot |
| Sacatero | Collector of indigo leaves |
| Sacristán | Sacristan |
| Sarampión | Measles |
| Secretaría | Secretary's office |
| Sementera | A sowing. There were two sowings(and hence harvests) a year. The first was known as the primera sementera and the second the segunda sementera |
| Servicio del tostón | A capitation tax of 4 reals on each tributary Indian introduced in 1591 to help pay for the costs of defense |
| Sobresaliente | A type of indigo, of good quality |
| Subdelegado | Royal official in charge of a partido and under the authority of an intendente |
| Tabacal | Plot cultivated in tobacco |
| Tabardillo | Typhus |
| Taladro | Sloping drainage adit |
| Tamal | Maize dough steamed or baked in a leaf |
| Tameme | An Indian carrier or porter |
| Tanate | Leather bag |
| Tanatero | Miner employed in carrying ore from the mine |

| | |
|---|---|
| Tasación | An official assessment of the amount of tribute to be paid by an Indian village |
| Teniente | Governor's lieutenant |
| Términos | The limits of a jurisdiction |
| Tierra caliente | Area with a hot climate |
| Tierra fría | Area with a cold climate |
| Tierra templada | Area with a temperate climate |
| Tortilla | Maize bread made in the form of thin, round flat cakes |
| Tostón | 4 reals or half a peso |
| Vara | A linear measure of about a yard (33 ins) or a staff of office |
| Vecino | Householder in a Spanish town |
| Vecino natural | Indian householder in Indian village |
| Villa | Town |
| Viruelas | Smallpox |
| Visita | Tour of inspection of an area |
| Viudo/a | Widower/widow |
| Zambo | Offspring of an Indian and a negro |

# Bibliography

The most important archives for this study were the Archivo General de Indias in Seville and the Archivo General de Centro América in Guatemala City. The Archivo General de Indias (AGI) is particularly important for the sixteenth century, for which few documents have survived in Central America. The most important sections for this study proved to be the Audiencia de Guatemala, Patronato, Justicia, and Contaduría. A large number of documents from the AGI for the period 1522 to 1550 have been published in a seventeen-volume collection, the *Colección Somoza* (CS). Although this collection focuses on the history of Nicaragua, it includes many transcripts useful for the study of other regions in Central America. The Archivo General de Centro América (AGCA) contains important documents of a more local character dating from the mid-sixteenth century onwards. When this study was conducted the archive was well catalogued, but more recent scholars have experienced some difficulty in locating relevant materials. The most important section researched for this study was that dealing with Honduras, although some documents in the Guatemala and Nicaragua sections yielded additional information. Further research was conducted in the Archivo Nacional de Historia (ANH) in Tegucigalpa. This archive contains many unclassified documents and research there tends to be time-consuming, though not unrewarding.

A number of other archives in Spain yielded valuable information. The most important was the Real Academia de la Historia (RAHM) in Madrid and in particular its Colección Muñoz. All of the other archives, including the Biblioteca Nacional, the Biblioteca del Palacio Real, the Archivo Histórico Nacional, the Museo Naval, and the Servicio Histórico Militar, contained a small number of important documents, most of which were geographical descriptions of the area. Essential for the history of the Mosquito Shore were documents contained in the British Museum (BM) and the Public Record Office (Colonial Office) (PRO) in London.

Apart from the *Colección Somoza* already mentioned, there are a number of collections of published documents of varying degrees of usefulness. The most valuable is the 11-volume *Boletín del Archivo del Gobierno*, published by what is now the Archivo General de Centro América. A small number of documents in the *Colección de documentos para la historia de Costa Rica* was useful, as were others in the *Colección de documentos referentes a la historia colonial de Nicaragua*, although in the latter case the documents are poorly transcribed and should be used with caution. The *Relaciones históricas y geográficas* published by Serrano y Sanz also contains useful material on eastern Honduras. As for most studies of early colonial history, the two Spanish collections of unedited documents (CDI and CDIU) contained a few essential documents for the early sixteenth century.

346

To establish the nature and distribution of Indian cultures at the time of Spanish conquest the following accounts were invaluable: Herrera, Martyr, Oviedo, Ponce, and Torquemada. None of these accounts covers the eastern part of the country and the earliest descriptions of the area are to be found in the seventeenth-century travel accounts of Dampier, de Lussan, Exquemelin, and M.W. The early Central American histories by Fuentes y Guzmán, Remesal, and Vázquez also constitute important sources of information for the early history of the area.

Alcedo, A. de. *Diccionario geográfico-histórico de las Indias occidentales ó América.* 5 vols. Madrid: Manuel González, 1786-89.

Alvarez Rubiano, P. *Pedrarias Dávila.* Madrid: Consejo Superior de Investigaciones Científicas, Instituto Gonzalo Fernández de Oviedo, 1954.

Ashburn, P.M. *The Ranks of Death: A Medical History of the Conquest of America.* New York: Coward-McCann Inc., 1947.

Bakewell, P.J. *Silver Mining and Society in Colonial Mexico: Zacatecas, 1546-1700.* Cambridge: Cambridge University Press, 1971.

Ball, A.P. "Measles." In *A World Geography of Human Diseases,* edited by G.M. Howe, pp. 237-54. London and New York: Academic Press, 1977.

Bancroft, H.H. *The Native Races of the Pacific States of North America.* 5 vols. San Francisco: A.L. Bancroft, 1883-86.

Barón Castro, R. *La población de El Salvador.* Madrid: Consejo Superior de Investigaciones Científicas, Instituto Gonzalo Fernández de Oviedo, 1942.

Bartlett, A.S.; Barghoorn, E.S.; and Berger R. "Fossil Maize from Panama." *Science* 165 (1969):389-90.

Bataillon, M. "Las Casas et le licencié Cerrato." *Bulletin Hispanique* 55 (1953):79-87.

Batres Jáuregui, A. *La América Central ante la historia.* 2 vols. Madrid: Tip. Sánchez y de Guise, 1920.

Baudez, C.F. *Central America.* London: Barrie and Jenkins, 1970.

Benedict, R. "Two Patterns of Indian Acculturation." *American Anthropologist* 45 (1943):207-12.

Bennet, C.F. "A Review of Ecological Research in Middle America." *Latin American Research Review* 2 (1967):3-27.

Benzoni, G. *La historia del nuevo mundo.* Biblioteca de la Academia Nacional de la Historia 86. Caracas: Academia Nacional de la Historia, 1967.

Bergmann, J.F. "The Distribution of Cacao and Its Cultivation in Pre-Columbian America." *Annals of the Association of American Geographers* 59 (1969):85-96.

Black, F.L. "Infectious Diseases in Primitive Societies." *Science* 187 (1975):515-18.

Bolton, H.E. "The Mission as a Frontier Institution." *American Historical Review* 23 (1917):42-61.

Borah, W. *New Spain's Century of Depression.* Ibero-Americana 35. Berkeley and Los Angeles: University of California Press, 1951.

_____. "America as Model: The Demographic Impact of European Expansion upon the Non-European World." *35th International Congress of Americanists* (Mexico) (1964) 3:379-87.

Borah, W., and Cook, S.F. *The Aboriginal Population of Central Mexico on the Eve of Spanish Conquest.* Ibero-Americana 45. Berkeley and Los Angeles: University of California Press, 1963.

Brading, D.A. *Miners and Merchants in Bourbon Mexico, 1763-1810.* Cambridge: Cambridge University Press, 1971.

Brading, D.A., and Cross, H.E. "Colonial Silver Mining: Mexico and Peru." *Hispanic American Historical Review* 52 (1972):545-79.

Brasseur de Bourbourg, C.E. *Histoire de nations civilisées du Méxique et de l'Amérique-Centrale.* 4 vols. Paris: A. Bertrand, 1857-59.

Brinton, D.G. *The American Race.* New York: N.D.C. Hodges, 1891.

Brown, A.W.A. "Yellow Fever, Dengue and Dengue Haemorrhagic Fever." In *A World Geography of Human Diseases*, edited by G.M. Howe, pp. 271-317. London and New York: Academic Press, 1977.

Browning, D. "Preliminary Comments on the 1776 Census of the Spanish Empire." *Bulletin of the Society for Latin American Studies* 25 (1974):5-13.

Cámara Barbachano, F. "El mestizaje en México." *Revista de Indias* 24 (1964):27-85.

Campbell, L.R. "The Linguistic Prehistory of the Southern Mesoamerican Periphery." In *Las fronteras de Mesoamérica.* XIV Mesa Redonda de la Sociedad Mexicana de Antropología, vol. 2, pp. 157-83. Mexico, 1976.

_____. "Distant Genetic Relationship and Diffusion: A Mesoamerican Perspective." *42nd International Congress of Americanists* (Paris) (1978) 4:595-605.

Carr, A.F. "Outline for a Classification of Animal Habitats in Honduras." *Bulletin of the American Museum of Natural History* 94 (1950):563-94.

Castro Seaone, J. "La expansión de la merced en América colonial." *Revista de Indias* 4 (1943):405-40.

Chagnon, N. "Yanomamö Social Organisation and Warfare." In *War*, edited by M. Fried, M. Harris, and R. Murphy, pp. 109-59. New York: Natural History Press, 1967.

Chamberlain, R.S. *Castilian Backgrounds of the Repartimiento-Encomienda.* Carnegie Institution of Washington Publication no. 509. Washington, DC, 1939.

_____. "The Founding of the City of Gracias a Dios, First Seat of the Audiencia de los Confines." *Hispanic American Historical Review* 26 (1946):2-18.

_____. *The Conquest and Colonization of Honduras, 1502-1550.* Carnegie Institution of Washington Publication no. 598. Washington, DC, 1953.

Chance, J.K. *Race and Class in Colonial Oaxaca.* Stanford: Stanford University Press, 1978.

Chapman, A. "Port of Trade Enclaves in Aztec and Maya Civilizations." In *Trade and Market in Early Empires*, edited by K. Polanyi, C.M. Arensberg, and H.W. Pearson, pp. 114-53. New York: The Free Press, 1957.

_____. "An Historical Analysis of the Tropical Forest Tribes on the Southern Border of Mesoamerica." Ph.D. dissertation, Department of Anthropology, Columbia University, 1958.

_____. *Los Nicarao y los Chorotega según las fuentes históricas.* Serie Historia y Geografía 4. San José: Universidad de Costa Rica, 1960.

_____. "Dual Organisation Amongst the Jicaques of La Montaña de la Flor, Honduras. *34th International Congress of Americanists* (Vienna) (1962):578-84.

Chaunu, P. *Séville et l'Atlantique.* 8 vols. Paris: Colin, 1955-59.

Chevalier, F. *Land and Society in Colonial Mexico.* Berkeley and Los Angeles: University of California Press, 1963.

Clark, G.M., and Haswell, M. *The Economics of Subsistence Agriculture.* London: Macmillan, 1966.

348

Cockburn, J. *A Journey Overland, from the Gulf of Honduras to the Great South Sea.* London: C. Rivington, 1735.

Coe, M.D. "Costa Rican Archaeology and Mesoamerica." *Southwestern Journal of Anthropology* 18 (1962):170-83.

*Colección de documentos inéditos relativos al descubrimiento, conquista y organización de las antiguas posesiones españolas de América y Oceanía.* 42 vols. Madrid, 1864-84.

*Colección de documentos inéditos relativos al descubrimiento, conquista y organización de las antiguas posesions españolas de Ultramar.* 25 vols. Madrid, 1885-1932.

*Colección de documentos para la historia de Costa Rica.* Comp. by L. Fernández. 10 vols. Paris: Imp. Dupont, 1881-1907.

*Colección de documentos referentes a la historia colonial de Nicaragua.* Recuerdo del Centenario de Independencia Nacional, 1821-1921. Managua: Tip. y Enc. Nacionales, 1921.

*Colección Somoza: documentos para la historia de Nicaragua.* Edited by A. Vega Bolaños. 17 vols. Madrid, 1954-57.

Colón, H. *Vida del Almirante Don Cristóbal Colón.* Biblioteca Americana, Cronistas de Indias. Mexico: Fondo de Cultura Económica, 1947.

Conzemius, E. "The Jicaques of Honduras." *International Journal of American Linguistics* 2, nos. 3-4 (1921-23):163-70.

_____. "Los Indios Payas de Honduras: estudio geográfico, etnográfico y lingüístico." *Journal de la société des américanistes* 19 (1927):245-302.

_____. "On the Aborigines of the Bay Islands." *22nd International Congress of Americanists* (Rome) (1928):57-68.

_____. "Notes on the Miskito and Sumu Languages of Eastern Nicaragua and Honduras." *International Journal of American Linguistics* 5 (1929):57-115.

_____. *Ethnographical Survey of the Miskito and Sumu Indians of Honduras and Nicaragua.* Smithsonian Institution, Bureau of American Ethnology, Bulletin 106. Washington, DC, 1932.

Cook, N.D. *Demographic Collapse: Indian Peru, 1520-1620.* Cambridge: Cambridge University Press, 1981.

Cook, O.F. *Vegetation Affected by Agriculture in Central America.* US Department of Agriculture Bureau of Plant Industry Bulletin, 145. Washington, DC, 1909.

Cook, S.F. "The Demographic Consequences of European Contact with Primitive Peoples." *Annals of the American Academy of Political and Social Sciences* 237 (1945):107-11.

Cook, S.F., and Borah, W. *The Indian Population of Central Mexico, 1531-1610.* Ibero-Americana 44. Berkeley and Los Angeles: University of California Press, 1960.

_____. *Essays in Population History: Mexico and the Caribbean.* 3 vols. Berkeley and Los Angeles: University of California Press, 1971-79.

Crosby, A.W. "Conquistador y Pestilencia: The First New World Pandemic and the Fall of the Great Indian Empires." *Hispanic American Historical Review* 47 (1967):321-37.

_____. *The Columbian Exchange: Biological and Cultural Consequences of 1492.* Westport, CT: Greenwood, 1972.

_____. "Virgin Soil Epidemics as a Factor in the Aboriginal Depopulation of America." *William and Mary Quarterly* 33 (1976):289-99.

Curato de Tegucigalpa. "Estado que demuestra los individuos de esta feligresía." *Revista del archivo y biblioteca nacionales* (Honduras) 28 (1950):389.

Dampier, W. *A New Voyage Round the World.* London: A & C Black, 1937.
Davidson, W.V. "Dispersal of the Garífuna in the Western Caribbean." *42nd International Congress of Americanists* (Paris) (1979) 6:467-74.
Denevan, W.M., ed. *The Native Population of the Americas in 1492.* Madison: University of Wisconsin Press, 1976.
Deutschmann, Z. "The Ecology of Smallpox." In *Studies in Disease Ecology*, edited by J. May, pp. 1-13. New York: Hafner Publishing Co., 1961.
Díaz de la Calle, J. *Memorial y noticias sacras y reales del imperio de las Indias occidentales.* Madrid, 1646.
Díaz del Castillo, B. *Historia verdadera de la conquista de la Nueva España.* 2 vols. Mexico D.F.: Editorial Porrua, 1960.
Díaz Durán, J.C. "Historia de la casa de moneda del reino de Guatemala desde 1731 hasta 1773." *Anales de la sociedad de geografía e historia* (Guatemala) 18 (1942):191-224.
Dixon, C.W. *Smallpox.* London; Churchill, 1962.
Dobyns, H.F. "An Outline of Andean Epidemic History to 1720." *Bulletin of the History of Medicine* 37 (1963):493-515.
_____. "Estimating Aboriginal American Population." *Current Anthropology* 7 (1966):395-449.
____. *Native American Historical Demography: A Critical Bibliography.* Bloomington and London: Indiana University Press, 1976.
Duffy, J. *Epidemics in Colonial America.* Port Washington and London: Kennikat, 1972.
Dunn, F.L. "On the Antiquity of Malaria in the New World." *Human Biology* 37 (1965):385-93.
Durón, R.E. *La provincia de Tegucigalpa bajo el gobierno de Mallol.* Tegucigalpa: Tip. Nacional, 1904.

Edwards, B. "Some Account of the British Settlements on the Mosquito Shore." In *The History, Civil and Commercial of the British West Indies.* 5th ed. 5 vols. 5:202-14. London, 1819.
Epstein, J.F. "Late Ceramic Horizons in Northeastern Honduras." Ph.D. dissertation, Department of Anthropology, University of Pennsylvania, 1957.
____. "Dating the Ulua Polychrome Complex." *American Antiquity* 25 (1959):125-29.
Esquemeling, J. *The Buccaneers of America.* Translated by W.S. Stallybrass. London: Routledge and Sons, 1924.

Floyd, T.S. "The Guatemalan Merchants, the Government and the Provincianos, 1750-1800." *Hispanic American Historical Review* 41 (1961):90-110.
____. "Bourbon Palliatives and the Central American Mining Industry, 1765-1800." *The Americas* 18 (1961):103-25.
_____. *The Anglo-Spanish Struggle for Mosquitia.* Albuquerque: University of New Mexico, 1967.
Fox, J.W. "The Late Postclassic Eastern Frontier of Mesoamerica: Cultural Innovation along the Periphery." *Current Anthropology* 22 (1981):321-46.
Frank, A.G. *Mexican Agriculture, 1521-1630: Transformation of the Mode of Production.* Cambridge: Cambridge University Press, 1979.
Friede, J. "Algunas consideraciones sobre la evolución demográfica en la provincia de Tunja." *Anuario colombiano de historia social y de la cultura* 2 (1965):5-19.
Fuentes y Guzmán, F.A. *Historia de Guatemala: Recordación Florida.* Biblioteca 'Goathemala,' vols. 6-8. Guatemala: Sociedad de Geografía e Historia, 1932-33.

Furtado, C. *Economic Development of Latin America: A Survey from Colonial Times to the Cuban Revolution*. Cambridge: Cambridge University Press, 1970.

García Peláez, F. de P. *Memorias para la historia del antiguo reino de Guatemala*. 3 vols. Guatemala: Tip. Nacional, 1943-44.

Gasco, J. "Demographic Trends in the Soconusco, 1520-1970." Paper presented at the 44th International Congress of Americanists, Manchester, 1982.

Gates, W.E. "The Distribution of the Several Branches of the Mayance Stock." *Carnegie Institution of Washington Yearbook* (1920) Appendix 12:605-15.

Gerhard, P. "Colonial New Spain, 1519-1786: Historical Notes on the Evolution of the Minor Political Jurisdictions." In *Handbook of Middle American Indians*. vol. 12. Edited by H.F. Cline, pp. 63-137. Austin: University of Texas Press, 1972.

____. *The Southeast Frontier*. Princeton: Princeton University Press, 1979.

Gibson, C. "The Transformation of the Indian Community in New Spain." *Journal of World History* 2 (1955):581-607.

____. *The Aztecs under Spanish Rule*. Stanford: Stanford University Press, 1964.

Girard, R. *Los Chortís ante el problema Maya*. 5 vols. Mexico D.F.: Instituto Indigenista Interamericano, 1949.

Godelier, M. "The Concept of 'Social and Economic Formation': The Inca Example." In *Perspectives on Marxist Anthropology*, edited by M. Godelier, pp. 63-69. Cambridge: Cambridge University Press, 1977.

Goicoechea, Fr. J.A. de. "Relación sobre los Indios gentiles de Pacura." *Anales de la sociedad de geografía e historia* (Guatemala) 13 (1937):303-15.

Gómez, A.E. *Esbozo de historia económica de Honduras*. Tegucigalpa: Universidad Nacional Autónoma de Honduras, 1967.

Goodwin, G.G. "Mammals of Honduras." *Bulletin of the American Museum of Natural History* 79 (1942):107-95.

Greenberg, J.H., and Swadesh, M. "Jicaque as a Hokan Language." *International Journal of American Lingustics* 19 (1953):216-22.

Guardiola, G. "Apuntes acerca del mineral de San Antonio de Oriente." *Revista del archivo y biblioteca nationales* (Honduras) 6 (1927):241-45.

Hanke, L. *The Spanish Struggle for Justice in the Conquest of America*. Philadelphia: University of Pennsylvania Press, 1949.

Haring, C.H. *The Spanish Empire in America*. New York: Harbinger Books, 1963.

Harris, D.R. "Agricultural Systems, Ecosystems and the Origins of Agriculture." In *The Domestication and Exploitation of Plants and Animals*, edited by P.J. Ucko and G.W. Dimbleby, pp. 3-15. London: Duckworth, 1969.

Harris, M. *Patterns of Race in the Americas*. New York: Walker and Co., 1964.

Healy, P.F. "The Archaeology of Southwest Nicaragua." Ph.D. dissertation, Department of Anthropology, Harvard University, 1974.

____. "Informe preliminar sobre la arqueología del periodo Cocal en el nordeste de Honduras." In *Las fronteras de Mesoamérica*. XIV Mesa Redonda de la Sociedad Mexicana de Antropología. vol. 2, pp. 237-44. Mexico, 1976.

____. "Los Chorotega y Nicarao: evidencia arqueológica de Rivas, Nicaragua." In *Las fronteras de Mesoamérica*. XIV Mesa Redonda de la Sociedad Mexicana de Antropología, vol. 2, pp. 257-66. Mexico, 1976.

____. "Excavations at Selin Farm (H-CN-5), Colón, Northeast Honduras." *Vínculos* 4 (1978):57-79.

____. *Archaeology of the Rivas Region, Nicaragua*. Waterloo, Ont.: Wilfrid Laurier U.P., 1980.

_____. "The Paleoecology of the Selin Farm Site (H-CN-5): Department of Colón, Honduras." In *Civilization in the Ancient Americas: Essays in the Honor of G.R. Willey*, edited by R.M. Leventhal and A.L. Kolata, pp. 35-54. Albuquerque: University of New Mexico Press, 1983.

_____. "The Archaeology of Honduras." In *The Archaeology of Lower Central America*, edited by F.W. Lange and D.Z. Stone, pp. 113-61. Albuquerque: University of New Mexico Press, 1984.

Heath, G.R. "Notes on Miskuto Grammar and on Other Indian Languages of Eastern Nicaragua." *American Anthropologist* 15 (1913):48-62.

Helbig, K.M. *Antiguales (Altertümer) der Paya-Region und die Paya-Indianer von Nordost-Honduras.* Hamburg: Hamburgische Museums für Volkerkunde und Vorgeschichte, 1956.

_____. "Die Landschaft von Nordost-Honduras." *Petermanns Mitteilungen Ergänzungschaft* 286. Gotha, 1959.

Helms, M.W. "The Cultural Ecology of a Colonial Tribe." *Ethnology* 8 (1969):76-84.

_____. "Matrilocality, Social Solidarity, and Culture Contact." *Southwestern Journal of Anthropology* 26 (1970):197-212.

_____. *Asang: Adaptations to Culture Contact in a Miskito Community.* Gainesville: University of Florida Press, 1971.

_____. *Middle America: A Culture History of Heartlands and Frontiers.* Englewood-Cliffs, NJ: Prentice-Hall, 1975.

Helms, M.W., and Loveland, F.O., eds. *Frontier Adaptations in Lower Central America.* Philadelphia: Institute for the Study of Human Issues, 1976.

Henderson, Capt. G. *An Account of the British Settlement of Honduras...to Which Are Added Sketches of the Manners and Customs of the Mosquito Indians.* London: C.R. Baldwin, 1809.

Henderson, J.S. "Pre-Columbian Trade Networks in Northeastern Honduras." *Journal of Field Archaeology* 3 (1976):342-46.

_____. "The Valley de Naco: Ethnohistory and Archaeology in Northwestern Honduras." *Ethnohistory* 24 (1977):363-77.

Henderson, J.S., et al. "Archaeological Investigations in the Valle de Naco Northwestern Honduras." *Journal of Field Archaeology* 6 (1979):169-92.

Herrera y Tordesillas, A. de. *Historia general de los hechos de los castellanos en las islas i tierra firme del Mar Océano.* 17 vols. Madrid: Real Academia de la Historia, 1934-57.

Holm, J. "The Creole English of Nicaragua's Miskito Coast: Its Sociolinguistic History and a Comparative Study of its Lexicon and Syntax." Ph.D. dissertation, Department of Linguistics, University College London, 1978.

Holt, D., and Bright, W. "La lengua paya y las fronteras lingüísticas de Mesoamérica." In *Las fronteras de Mesoamérica.* XIV Mesa Redonda de la Sociedad Mexicana de Antropología. vol. 2, pp. 149-56. Mexico, 1976.

Howe, G.M., ed. *A World Geography of Human Diseases.* New York and London: Academic Press, 1977.

*Indice general de los títulos de tierras que se encuentran en el Archivo Nacional.* Tegucigalpa: Instituto Nacional Agrario, 1969.

"Informe....acerca de la invasión que Indios Payas pretendían hacer al pueblo de Catacamas." *Revista del archivo y biblioteca nacionales* (Honduras) 25 (1946):193-97.

Jacobs, W.R.  "The Tip of the Iceberg:  Pre-Columbian Indian Demography and Some Implications for Revisionism."  *William and Mary Quarterly* 3rd Ser. 31 (1975):123-32.

Jiménez Moreno, W.  *Síntesis de la historia pre-Tolteca de Mesoamérica esplendor del Mexico antiguo.*  2 vols.  Mexico: Centro de Investigaciones Antropológicas, 1959.

_____.  "El mestizaje y la transculturación en Mexiamérica."  In *El mestizaje en la historia de Ibero-América.*  Mexico D.F.: Instituto Panamericano de Geografía e Historia, Comisión de Historia, 1961.

Johannessen, C.L.  *Savannas of Interior Honduras.*  Ibero-Americana 46.  Berkeley and Los Angeles: University of California Press, 1963.

Johnson, F.  "The Linguistic Map of Mexico and Central America."  In *The Maya and Their Neighbors,* edited by C.L. Hay et al., pp. 88-114.  New York: D. Appleton Century Co. Inc., 1940.

_____.  "Central American Cultures."  In *Handbook of South American Indians.* vol. 4, pp. 43-68.  Smithsonian Institution, Bureau of American Ethnology Bulletin 143.  Washington, DC, 1948.

Juarros, D.  *A Statistical and Commercial History of the Kingdom of Guatemala.*  Translated by J. Baily.  London, 1823.

Kaufman, T.  "Mesoamerican Indian Languages."  *Encyclopedia Britannica.*  15th ed. vol. 11, pp. 954-63.  Chicago: Benton, 1974.

Kirchhoff, P.  "Mesoamérica."  *Acta americana* 1 (1943):92-107.

Konetske, R.  "Legislación sobre inmigración de extranjeros en América durante la época colonial."  *Revista de sociología,* nos. 11-12 (1945), pp. 269-99.

Kroeber, A.L.  *Cultural and Natural Areas of Native North America.*  University of California Publications in Archaeology and Ethnology 38.  Berkeley and Los Angeles:  University of California Press, 1939.

Landero, Fr. M.  "Los Taoajkas ó Sumos del Patuca y Wampú."  *Anthropos* 30 (1935):33-50.

Las Casas, B. de.  *Breve relación de la destrucción de las Indias occidentales.*  London: Schulze and Dean, 1812.

_____.  *Obras escogidas.*  5 vols.  Biblioteca de Autores Españoles nos. 95-96, 105-06, 110.  Madrid: Ediciones Atlas, 1957-58.

Lathrap, D.W.  *The Upper Amazon.*  London: Thames and Hudson, 1970.

Lauer, W.  "Klimatische und Planzengeographie Grundzüge Zentralamerikas."  *Erdkunde* 12 (1959):344-54.

Lee, R.L.  "Cochineal Production and Trade in New Spain to 1600."  *The Americas* 4 (1948):449-73.

Lehmann, W.  *Zentral-Amerika.*  2 vols.  Berlin: Dietrich Reimer, 1920.

León-Portilla, M.  *Religión de los Nicarao.*  Instituto de Investigaciones Históricas. Serie Cultura Náhautl, Monografías 12.  Mexico: Universidad Nacional Autónoma de Mexico, 1972.

*Límites entre Honduras y Nicaragua.*  Madrid: Idamor Moreno, 1905.

Linares, O.; Sheets, P.D.; and Rosenthal, E.J.  "Prehistoric Agriculture in Tropical Highlands."  *Science* 187 (1975):137-45.

Long, E.  *A History of Jamaica...An Account of the Mosquito Shore.*  3 vols. London: T. Lowndes, 1774.

Longyear, J.M.  *Cultures and Peoples of the Southeastern Maya Frontier.*  Carnegie Institution of Washington, Division of Historical Research, Theoretical Approaches to Problems, no. 3.  Washington, DC, 1947.

\_\_\_\_. *Copan Ceramics: A Study of Southeastern Maya Pottery.* Carnegie Institution of Washington Publication no. 597. Washington, DC, 1952.

López de Gómara, F. *Hispania Victrix: historia general de las Indias.* Historiadores Primitivos de Indias vol. 1, Biblioteca de Autores Españoles no. 22. Madrid: Imp. los Sucesores de Hernando, 1918.

López de Velasco, J. *Geografía y descripción universal de las Indias.* Madrid: Tip. Fortanet for Real Academia de la Historia, 1894.

Lothrop, S.K. *Pottery of Costa Rica and Nicaragua.* Contributions from the Museum of the American Indian, Heye Foundation. vol. 8, 2 parts. New York, 1926.

\_\_\_\_. "The World 'Maya' and the Fourth Voyage of Columbus." *Indian Notes.* vol. 4, no. 4, pp. 350-63. New York: Museum of the American Indian, Heye Foundation, 1927.

\_\_\_\_. "The Southeastern Frontier of the Maya." *American Anthropologist* 41 (1939):42-54.

\_\_\_\_. "South America as Seen from Middle America." In *The Maya and Their Neighbors,* edited by C.L. Hay et al., pp. 417-29. New York: D. Appleton Century Co. Inc., 1940.

Lovell, W.G. "The Historical Demography of the Cuchumatán Highlands, Guatemala, 1500-1821." In *Studies in Spanish American Population History,* edited by D.J. Robinson, pp. 195-216. Boulder, CO: Westview Press, 1981.

\_\_\_\_. "Historia demográfica de la sierra de los Cuchumatanes, 1520-1821." *Mesoamérica* 4 (1982):279-301.

Lucena Salmoral, M. "El indofeudalismo Chibcha como explicación de la fácil conquista Quesadista." In *Estudios sobre política indigenista española en América.* vol. 1, pp. 111-60. Valladolid: Universidad de Valldolid, 1975.

Lunardi, F. *Lempira: el héroe de la epopeya de Honduras.* Tegucigalpa: Tip. Nacional, 1941.

\_\_\_\_. *Los Payas, documentos curiosos y viajes: esbozo de un capítulo de la historia de Honduras.* Tegucigalpa: Tip. Nacional, 1943.

Lutz, C. "Santiago de Guatemala, 1541-1773: The Socio-Demographic History of a Spanish American Colonial City." 2 vols. Ph.D. dissertation, Department of History, University of Wisconsin, Madison, 1976.

McBryde, F.W. "Influenza in America During the Sixteenth Century (Guatemala: 1523, 1559-62, 1576)." *Bulletin of the History of Medicine* 8 (1940):296-302.

MacLeod, M.J. *Spanish Central America: A Socioeconomic History, 1520-1720.* Berkeley and Los Angeles: University of California Press, 1973.

\_\_\_\_. "An Outline of Central American Demographics: Sources, Yields and Possibilities." In *The Historical Geography of Highland Guatemala,* edited by R. M. Carmack, J. Early, and C. Lutz, pp. 3-18. Institute of Mesoamerican Studies, Publication no. 6. Albany: SUNY Press, 1982.

\_\_\_\_. "Ethnic Relations and Indian Society in the Province of Guatemala, ca. 1620-ca. 1800." In *Spaniards and Indians in Southeastern Mesoamerica: Essays on the History of Ethnic Relations,* edited by M.J. MacLeod and R. Wassertrom, pp. 189-214. Lincoln and London: University of Nebraska, 1983.

McNeill, W.H. *Plagues and Peoples.* Oxford: Basil Blackwell, 1976.

MacNeish, R.S. "Preliminary Archaeological Investigations in the Sierra de Tamaulipas, Mexico." *Transactions of the American Philosophical Society* 48 (part 6) (1958).

\_\_\_\_. "Ancient Mesoamerican Civilization." *Science* 143 (1964):531-37.

\_\_\_\_. "The Origins of New World Civilization." *Scientific American* 211, no. 5 (1964):29-37.

Magnus, R.W. "The Prehistory of the Miskito Coast of Nicaragua: A Study in Cultural Relationships." Ph.D. dissertation, Department of Anthropology, Yale University, 1974.

_____. "The Prehistoric and Modern Subsistence Patterns of the Atlantic Coast of Nicaragua: A Comparison." In *Prehistoric Coastal Adaptations: The Economy and Ecology of Maritime Middle America*, edited by B.L. Stark and B. Voorhies, pp. 61-80. New York: Academic Press, 1978.

Mangelsdorf, P.C.; MacNeish, R.S.; and Willey, G.R. "The Origins of Agriculture." In *Handbook of Middle American Indians*. vol. 1. Edited by R.C. West, pp. 427-45. Austin: University of Texas Press, 1964.

Manson-Bahr, P.H. *Manson's Tropical Diseases*. London: Cassell & Co., 1948.

Martínez Peláez, S. *La patria del criollo*. San José: Editorial Universitaria Centroamericana, 1975.

Martyr D'Anghera, P.H. *De Orbe Novo*. Edited by F. MacNutt. 2 vols. London and New York: Knickerbocker Press, 1912.

Mason, J.A. "The Native Languages of Middle America." In *The Maya and Their Neighbors*, edited by C.L. Hay et al., pp. 52-87. New York: D. Appleton Century Co. Inc., 1940.

Matson, G.A., and Swanson, J. "Distribution of Hereditary Blood Antigens among Indians in Middle America: Part V in Nicaragua." *American Journal of Physical Anthropology* 21 (1963):545-49.

May, J., ed. *Studies in Disease Ecology*. New York: Hafner Publishing Co., 1961.

Membreño, A. *Hondureñismos: vocabulario de los provincialismos de Honduras*. Tegucigalpa: Tip. Nacional, 1897.

Millon, R.F. "Trade, Tree Cultivation and the Development of Private Property in Land." *American Anthropologist* 57 (1955):698-712.

Molina Argüello, C. *El gobernador de Nicaragua*. Sevilla: Escuela de Estudios Hispanoamericanos, 1949.

_____. "Gobernaciones, alcaldías mayores y corregimientos en el reino de Guatemala." *Anuario de estudios americanos* 17 (1960):105-32.

_____. "Comunidades y territorialidad en las jurisdicciones." In *Memoria del primer congreso Venezolano de historia*, pp. 445-56. Caracas: Academia Nacional de Historia, 1972.

Moreno, L. "Los extranjeros y el ejercicio del comercio en Indias." *Anales de la sociedad de geografía e historia* (Guatemala) 14 (1938):441-54.

Morison, S.E. *Admiral of the Ocean Sea: A Life of Christopher Columbus*. London: Oxford University Press, 1942.

Newson, L.A. *Aboriginal and Spanish Colonial Trinidad: A Study in Culture Contact*. London and New York: Academic Press, 1976.

_____. "Demographic Catastrophe in Sixteenth-Century Honduras." In *Studies in Spanish American Population History*, edited by D.J. Robinson, pp. 217-41. Boulder, CO: Westview Press, 1981.

_____. "The Depopulation of Nicaragua in the Sixteenth Century." *Journal of Latin American Studies* 14 (1982):253-86.

_____. "Labour in the Colonial Mining Industry of Honduras." *The Americas* 39 (1982):185-203.

_____. "Silver Mining in Colonial Honduras." *Revista de historia de America* 97 (1984):45-76.

_____. "Indian Population Patterns in Colonial Spanish America." *Latin American Research Review* 20 (1985):41-74.

_____. *Indian Survival in Colonial Nicaragua.* University of Oklahoma Press, forthcoming.

Newton, A.P. *The Colonizing Activities of the English Puritans.* New Haven: Yale University Press, 1914.

Nietschmann, B. *Between Land and Water: The Subsistence Ecology of the Miskito Indians, Eastern Nicaragua.* London and New York: Seminar Press, 1973.

Nolasco Pérez, P. *Historia de las mercedarias en América.* Madrid: Revista 'Estudios,' 1966.

Ots Capdequí, J.M. *España en América: el régimen de las tierras en la época colonial.* Mexico: Fondo de Cultura Económica, 1959.

Oviedo y Valdés, G. Fernández de. *Historia general y natural de las Indias, islas y tierra firme del Mar Océano.* 5 vols. Biblioteca de Autores Españoles, nos. 117-21. Madrid: Ediciones Atlas, 1959.

"Padrón de la feligresía de la parroquia de San Miguel de Tegucigalpa...1777." *Revista del archivo y biblioteca nacionales* 29 (1949): 194-95.

Palerm, A. "Agricultural Systems and Food Patterns." In *Handbook of Middle American Indians.* vol. 6. Edited by M. Nash, pp. 26-52. Austin: University of Texas Press, 1967.

Pardo, J.J. *Efemérides de la antigua Guatemala, 1541-1779.* Guatemala: Union Tiográfica, 1944.

Parsons, J.J. "The Miskito Pine Savannas of Nicaragua and Honduras." *Annals of the Association of American Geographers* 45 (1955):36-63.

____. *The Green Turtle and Man.* Gainesville: University of Florida Press, 1962.

Patiño, V.M. *Plantas cultivadas y animales domésticos en América equinoccial.* 4 vols. (I Frutales, II Plantas Alimenticias, III Plantas Medicinales, IV Plantas Introducidos). Cali: Imprenta Departmental, 1963-69.

Pendeleton, R.L. "General Soil Conditions in Central America." *Proceedings of the Soil Science Society of America* 8 (1943):403-07.

Pim, B., and Seeman, B. *Dottings on the Roadside in Panama, Nicaragua and Mosquito.* London: Chapman and Hall, 1869.

Pinkerton, J. *A Modern Atlas.* Philadelphia: T. Dobson, 1812.

Pollitzer, R. *Plague.* World Health Organisation Monograph Series no. 22. Geneva: WHO, 1954.

Ponce, Fr. A. *Relación breve y verdadera de algunas cosas que sucedieron al padre fray Alonso Ponce en las provincias de Nueva España.* 2 vols. Madrid: Imp. Viuda de Calero, 1873.

Popenoe, W. "Plant Resources of Honduras." In *Plants and Plant Science in Latin America,* edited by F. Verdoorn, pp. 273-75. Waltham, MA: Chronica Botanica, 1945.

Portig, W.H. "Central American Rainfall." *Geographical Review* 55 (1965):68-90.

*The Present State of the West Indies.* London: R. Baldwin, 1778.

Puga, V. de. *Provisiones, cédulas, instrucciones para el gobierno de la Nueva España.* Madrid: Ediciones Cultura Hispánica, 1945.

Radell, D.R. "The Indian Slave Trade and Population of Nicaragua during the Sixteenth Century." In *The Native Population of the Americas in 1492,* edited by W.M. Denevan, pp. 67-76. Madison: University of Wisconsin Press, 1976.

Raveneau de Lussan, S. de. *Journal of a Voyage into the South Seas in 1684 and the Following Years with the Filibusters.* Translated by M.E. Wilbur. Cleveland: A.H. Clark, 1930.

*Recopilación de las leyes de los reynos de las Indias.* 3 vols. Madrid: Gráficas Ultra, 1943.

Remesal, Fr. A. de. *Historia general de las Indias occidentales, y particular de la gobernación de Chiapa y Guatemala.* 2 vols. Guatemala: Sociedad de Geografía e Historia, 1932-33.

Rivet, P.; Stresser-Péan, P.; and Loukotka, C. "Langues du Méxique et de l'Amérique." In *Les Langues du Monde,* edited by A. Meillet and M. Cohen, pp. 1069-97. Paris: Centre National de la Recherche Scientifique, 1952.

Roberts, O.W. *Narrative of Voyages and Excursions on the East Coast and in the Interior of Central America.* Edinburgh: Constable and Co., 1827.

Roberts, R.J., and Irving, E.M. *Mineral Deposits of Central America.* US Geological Survey, Bulletin 1034. Washington, DC, 1957.

Robinson, D.J., ed. *Studies in Spanish American Population History.* Boulder, CO: Westview Press, 1981.

Rodríguez Becerra, S. "Variables de la conquista: los casos de Honduras y Guatemala." In *Primer reunión de antropologos españoles,* edited by A. Jiménez, pp. 127-33. Sevilla: Universidad de Sevilla, 1975.

_____. *Encomienda y conquista: los inicios de la colonización en Guatemala.* Sevilla: Universidad de Sevilla, 1977.

Rosenblat, A. *La población indígena y el mestizaje en América.* Buenos Aires: Editorial Nova, 1954.

Roys, R.L. *The Indian Background of Colonial Yucatán.* Carnegie Institution of Washington Publication no. 548. Washington, DC, 1943.

Rubio Sánchez, M. "El Añil o Xiquilite." *Anales de la sociedad de geografía e historia* (Guatemala) 26 (1952):313-49.

Saco, J.A. *Historia de la esclavitud de los Indios en el nuevo mundo.* 2 vols. Colección de Libros Cubanos, vols. 18 and 19. Havana: Cultural S.A., 1932.

Saldana, Fr. "Del cuaderno y diligencias practicadas a la casa y población de varios Indios Xicaques en el valle de San Juan, jurisdicción de la misión de Cataguana...8.6.1749." *Revista del archivo y biblioteca nacionales* (Honduras) 28 (1949):97-101.

Salvatierra, S. *Contribución a la historia de Centroamérica.* 2 vols. Managua: Tip. Progreso-Managua, 1939.

Sangster, G. "Diarrhoeal Diseases." In *A World Geography of Human Diseases,* edited by G.M. Howe, pp. 145-74. London and New York: Academic Press, 1977.

Sapper, K. "Beitrage zur Physichen Geographie von Honduras." *Zeitschrift der Gesellschaft für Erdkunde zu Berlin* (1902):33-56, 143-64, 231-41.

_____. "Die Zahl und die Volksdichte der Indianischen Bevölkerung in Amerika vor der Conquista und in der Gegenwart." *21st International Congress of Americanists* (The Hague) (1924) 1:95-104.

Sauer, C.O. "Cultivated Plants of South and Central America." In *Handbook of South American Indians.* vol. 5, pp. 487-543. Smithsonian Institution, Bureau of American Ethnology Bulletin 143. Washington, DC, 1950.

_____. *The Early Spanish Main.* Berkeley and Los Angeles: University of California Press, 1966.

Schmidt, K.P. "Honduras." In *Naturalist's Guide to the Americas,* edited by V. Shelford, pp. 601-602. Baltimore: Ecological Society of America, 1926.

Scholes, F.V., and Roys, R.L. *The Maya Chontal Indians of Acalan-Tixchel: A Contribution to the History and Ethnography of the Yucatan Peninsula.* Carnegie Institution of Washington Publication no. 560. Washington, DC, 1948.

Schuchert, C. *Historical Geology of the Antillean-Caribbean Region.* London: Wiley, 1935.

Serrano y Sanz, M. *Relaciones históricas y geográficas de América Central.* Colección de Libros y Documentos Referentes a la Historia de América, vol. 8. Madrid: Librería General de V. Suarez, 1908.

Service, E.R. "Indian-European Relations in Colonial Latin America." *American Anthropologist* 57 (1955):411-25.

Sharer, R.J. "The Prehistory of the Southeastern Maya Periphery." *Current Anthropology* 15 (1974):165-87.

Shea, D.E. "A Defense of Small Population Estimates for the Central Andes." In *The Native Population of the Americas in 1492*, edited by W.M. Denevan, pp. 157-80. Madison: University of Wisconsin Press, 1976.

Sherman, W.L. "Indian Slavery in Spanish Guatemala." Ph.D. dissertation, Department of History, University of New Mexico, 1967.

_____. "Indian Slavery and the Cerrato Reforms." *Hispanic American Historical Review* 51 (1971):25-50.

_____. *Forced Native Labor in Sixteenth-Century Central America.* Lincoln and London: University of Nebraska Press, 1979.

Shrewsbury, J.F. *A History of Bubonic Plague in the British Isles.* Cambridge: Cambridge University Press, 1970.

Simpson, L.B. *Studies in the Administration of New Spain IV: The Emancipation of the Indian Slaves and the Resettlement of the Freedmen, 1548-53.* Ibero-Americana 16. Berkeley and Los Angeles: University of California Press, 1940.

_____. *The Encomienda in New Spain: The Beginnings of Spanish Mexico.* Berkeley and Los Angeles: University of California Press, 1950.

Sloane, H. *A Voyage to the Islands of Madera, Barbados, Nieves, S. Christophers and Jamaica.* 2 vols. London, 1707.

Smith, C.T. "Depopulation of the Central Andes in the Sixteenth Century." *Current Anthropology* 11 (1970):453-64.

Smith, R.S. "Indigo Production and Trade in Colonial Guatemala." *Hispanic American Historical Review* 39 (1959):181-211.

Snarskis, M.J. "Stratigraphic Excavations in the Eastern Lowlands of Costa Rica." *American Antiquity* 41 (1976):342-53.

Solano Pérez-Lila, F. de. "La población indígena de Guatemala (1492-1800)." *Anuario de estudios americanos* 26 (1969): 279-355.

_____. "Castellanización del Indio y areas del castellano en Guatemala." *Revista de la universidad de Madrid* 19, no. 73 tomo III (1971):289-340.

Sorsby, W.S. "Spanish Colonization of the Mosquito Coast, 1787-1800." *Revista de historia de América*, nos. 73-74 (1972), pp. 145-53.

Spinden, H.J. "The Chorotegan Culture Area." *21st International Congress of Americanists* (Göteborg) (1925):529-45.

Squier, E.G. *Notes on Central America.* New York: Harper and Bros., 1855.

_____. *The States of Central America.* New York: Harper and Bros., 1858.

_____. "The Xicaque Indians of Honduras." *The Athenaeum* 1624 (1858):760-61.

_____. *Honduras; Descriptive, Historical and Statistical.* London: Trübner and Co., 1870.

_____. *Adventures on the Mosquito Shore.* New York: Worthington Co., 1891.

Stern. S.J. *Peru's Indian Peoples and the Challenge of Spanish Conquest: Huamanga to 1640.* Madison: University of Wisconsin Press, 1982.

Steward, J.H., ed. *Handbook of South American Indians: The Marginal Tribes.* vol. 1. Smithsonian Institution, Bureau of American Ethnology Bulletin 143. Washington, DC, 1946.

358

_____. *Handbook of South American Indians: The Circum-Caribbean Tribes.* vol. 4. Smithsonian Institution, Bureau of American Ethnology Bulletin 143. Washington, DC, 1948.

_____. *Handbook of South American Indians: The Comparative Ethnology of South American Indians.* vol. 5. Smithsonian Institution, Bureau of American Ethnology Bulletin 143. Washington, DC, 1949.

Steward, J.H., and Faron, L.C. *Native Peoples of South America.* New York: McGraw-Hill, 1959.

Stokes, W.S. "The Land Laws of Honduras." *Agricultural History* 21 (1947):148-54.

Stone, D.Z. "The Ulua Valley and Lake Yojoa." In *The Maya and Their Neighbors,* edited by C.L.Hay et al., pp. 386-94. New York: D. Appleton Century Co. Inc., 1940.

_____. *Archaeology of the North Coast of Honduras.* Memoirs of the Peabody Museum. vol. 9, no. 1. Cambridge, MA: Harvard University Press, 1941.

_____. "A Delimitation of the Area and Some of the Archaeology of the Sula-Jicaque Indians of Honduras." *American Antiquity* 7 (1942):376-88.

_____. "The Basic Cultures of Central America." *Handbook of South American Indians.* vol. 4, pp. 169-93. Smithsonian Institution, Bureau of American Ethnology Bulletin 143. Washington, DC, 1948.

_____. "The Northern Highland Tribes: The Lenca." *Handbook of South American Indians.* vol. 4, pp. 205-17. Smithsonian Institution, Bureau of American Ethnology 143. Washington, DC, 1948.

_____. "Los grupos mexicanos en la América Central y su importancia." *Antropología e historia de Guatemala* 1 (1949):43-47.

_____. *Estampas de Honduras.* Mexico City: Impresora Galve S.A., 1954.

_____. "Urgent Tasks of Research Concerning the Cultures and Languages of Central American Indian Tribes." *32nd International Congress of Americanists* (Copenhagen) (1956):43-47.

_____. *The Archaeology of Central and Southern Honduras.* Papers of the Peabody Museum 49, no. 3. Cambridge, MA: Harvard University Press, 1957.

_____. "The Eastern Frontier of Mesoamerica." *Mitteilungen aus dem Museum für Volkerkunde im Hamburg* 25 (1959):118-21.

_____. "Synthesis of Lower Central American Ethnohistory." In *Handbook of Middle American Indians.* vol. 4, ed. R. Wauchope, pp. 209-33. Austin: University of Texas Press, 1966.

_____. "Nahuat Traits on the Sula Plain, Northwestern Honduras." *38th International Congress of Americanists* (Stuttgart-München) (1968) 1:531-36.

_____. *Pre-Columbian Man Finds Central America.* Cambridge, MA: Peabody Museum Press, 1972.

Strangeways, T. *Sketch of the Mosquito Shore, Including the Territory of the Poyais.* Edinburgh, 1822.

Strong, W.D. *Archaeological Investigations in the Bay Islands, Spanish Honduras.* Smithsonian Institution, Miscellaneous Collections, vol. 92, no. 14. Washington, DC, 1935.

_____. "Anthropological Problems in Central America." In *The Maya and Their Neighbors,* edited by C.L. Hay et al., pp. 377-94. New York: D. Appleton Century Co. Inc., 1940.

_____. "The Archaeology of Honduras." *Handbook of South American Indians.* vol. 4, pp. 71-120. Smithsonian Institution, Bureau of American Ethnology 143. Washington, DC, 1948.

_____. "The Archaeology of Costa Rica and Nicaragua." In *Handbook of South American Indians*. vol. 4, pp. 121-42. Smithsonian Institution, Bureau of American Ethnology Bulletin 143. Washington, DC, 1948.

Strong, W.D.; Kidder, A.J.; and Paul, J.D. *Preliminary Report on the Smithsonian Institution-Harvard University Archaeology Expedition to North-Western Honduras 1936*. Smithsonian Institution Washington, Miscellaneous Collections, vol. 97, no. 1. Washington, DC, 1938.

Swadesh, M. "Lexicostatistic Classification." *Handbook of Middle American Indians*. vol. 5, edited by N.A. McQuown, pp. 79-116. Austin: Texas University Press, 1967.

Szaszdi de Nagy, A. "El Comercio ilícito en la provincia de Honduras." *Revista de Indias* 17 (1967):271-83.

Taylor, B.W. "An Outline of the Vegetation of Nicaragua." *Journal of Ecology* 51 (1963):27-54.

Termer, F. "La habitación rural en la América del centro, a través de los tiempos." *Anales de la sociedad de geografía e historia* (Guatemala) 11 (1935):391-409.

Thomas, C., and Swanton, J.R. *Indian Languages of Mexico and Central America and Their Geographical Distribution*. Smithsonian Institution, Bureau of American Ethnology Bulletin 44. Washington, DC, 1911.

Thompson, J.E.S. "Sixteenth and Seventeenth Century Reports of the Chol Mayas." *American Anthropologist* 40 (1938):584-604.

_____. *An Archaeological Reconnaissance in the Cotzumalhua Region, Escuintla, Guatemala*. Carnegie Institution of Washington Publication no. 574. Washington, DC, 1948.

_____. "The Maya Central Area at the Time of Spanish Conquest and Later: A Problem in Demography." *Proceedings of the Royal Anthropological Institute of Great Britain and Northern Ireland for 1966*. (1967), pp. 23-37.

_____. *Maya History and Religion*. Norman: University of Oklahoma Press, 1970.

Torquemada, Fr. J. de. *Monarquía Indiana*. 3 vols. Madrid: Nicolas Rodríguez, 1723.

Tozzer, A.M., ed. *Landa's Relación de las cosas de Yucatán*. Papers of the Peabody Museum no. 18. Cambridge, MA: Harvard University, 1941.

Turner, B.L., and Johnson, W.C. "A Maya Dam in the Copán Valley, Honduras." *American Antiquity* 44 (1979):299-305.

Valladares, A.A. *Monografía del departamento de las islas de la Bahía*. Tegucigalpa: Tip. Nacional, 1939.

Vallejo, A.R. *Compendio de la historia social y política de Honduras*. 2nd ed. Tegucigalpa: Tip. Nacional, 1926.

_____. *Historia documentada de los límites entre la república de Honduras y las de Nicaragua, El Salvador y Guatemala*. New York, 1938.

_____. "Minas de Honduras." *Revista de la sociedad de geografía e historia de Honduras* 34 (1957):32-40; 35 (1957):35-44, 99-104; 35 (1958):158-63.

Vázquez, F. *Crónica de la provincia del Santísimo Nombre de Jesús de Guatemala*. 4 vols. Biblioteca 'Goathemala,' vols. 14-17. Guatemala: Sociedad de Geografía e Historia, 1937-44.

Vázquez de Espinosa, A. *Compendium and Description of the West Indies*. Smithsonian Institution of Washington, Miscellaneous Collections vol. 102. Washington, DC, 1942.

Veblen, T.T. "Native Population Decline in Totonicapán, Guatemala." *Annals of the Association of American Geographers* 67 (1977):484-99.

de Vedia, D.E. "Cartas de relación de Fernando Cortés." In *Historiadores primitivos de Indias*. vol. 1, pp. 118-53. Biblioteca de Autores Españoles 22. Madrid: de los Sucesores de Hernando, 1918.

Vellard, J. "Causas biológicas de la disaparición de los Indios americanos." *Boletín del Instituto Riva-Agüero* 2 (1956):77-93.

Villamarin, J.A., and Villamarin, J.E. *Indian Labor in Mainland Colonial Spanish America*. Newark: University of Delaware Press, 1975.

Vivó Escoto, J.A. "Weather and Climate of Mexico and Central America." In *Handbook of Middle American Indians*. vol. 1. Edited by R.C. West, pp. 187-215. Austin: University of Texas Press, 1964.

Von Hagen, V.W. "The Mosquito Coast of Honduras and Its Inhabitants." *Geographical Review* 30 (1940):238-59.

———. "The Jicaque (Torrupan) Indians of Honduras." *Indian Notes and Monographs*, no. 53. New York: Museum of the American Indian, Heye Foundation, 1943.

W., M. "The Mosqueto Indian and His Golden River." In *A Collection of Voyages and Travels*, edited by A. Churchill. vol. 6, pp. 297-312. London: T. Osborne, 1752.

Wallerstein, I. *Mercantilism and the Consolidation of the European World-Economy, 1600-1750*. New York and London: Academic Press, 1980.

Wells, W.V. *Explorations and Adventures in Honduras*. New York: Harper and Bros., 1857.

West, R.C. *The Mining Community in Northern New Spain: The Parral Mining District*. Ibero-Americana 30. Berkeley and Los Angeles: University of California Press, 1949.

———. "The Mining Economy of Honduras in the Colonial Period." *33rd International Congress of Americanists* (Costa Rica) (1959) 2:767-77.

White, R. *The Case of the Agent to the Settlers on the Coast of Yucatan and the Late Settlers on the Mosquito Shore*. London: T. Cadell, 1793.

Wickham, H.A. *A Journey among the Woolwa or Soumoo Indians of Central America*. London, 1872.

———. "Notes on the Soumoo or Woolwa Indians of Blewfields River, Mosquito Territory." *Journal of the Anthropological Institute* 24 (1895):198-208.

Willey, G.R., and Leventhal, R.M. "Prehistoric Settlement at Copán." In *Maya Archaeology and Ethnohistory*, edited by N. Hammond and G.R. Willey, pp. 75-102. Austin: University of Texas Press, 1979.

Willey, G.R.; Leventhal, R.M.; and Fash, W.L. "Maya Settlement in the Copán Valley." *Archaeology* 31, no. 4 (1978):32-43.

Wolf, E. *Sons of the Shaking Earth*. Chicago and London: University of Chicago Press, 1959.

Wood, C.S. "New Evidence for a Late Introduction of Malaria into the New World." *Current Anthropology* 16 (1975):93-104.

Wortman, M.L. "Government Revenue and Economic Trends in Central America, 1787-1819." *Hispanic American Historical Review* 55 (1975):251-86.

———. "Bourbon Reforms in Central America, 1750-1786." *The Americas* 31 (1975):222-38.

———. *Government and Society in Central America, 1680-1840*. New York: Columbia University Press, 1982.

Ximénez, Fr. F. *Historia de la provincia de San Vicente de Chiapa y Guatemala*. 6 vols. Guatemala: Sociedad de Geografía e Historia, 1929-1971.

Young, T. *Narrative of a Residence on the Mosquito Shore During the Years 1839, 1840, 1841*. London: Smith, Elder & Co., 1842.

Ypsilantys de Moldavia, J. *Monografía de Comayagua, 1537-1937*. Tegucigalpa: Tip. Nacional, 1937.

———. *Monografía de la parroquia del Señor San Miguel de Heredia de Tegucigalpa*. Tegucigalpa: Tip. Nacional, 1944.

Zavala, S. *New Viewpoints on the Spanish Colonization of America*. Philadelphia: University of Pennsylvania Press, 1943.

———. *Contribución a la historia de las instituciones coloniales en Guatemala*. Guatemala: Editorial Universitaria, 1967.

Zinsser, H. *Rats, Lice and History*. New York: Bantam, 1960.

Zorita, A. de. *The Lords of New Spain*. London: Phoenix House, 1965.

# Index

Merchants, 167-68, 223-24; as sources
of credit, 140, 157-59, 162
Mercury, 155-57, 163
Mesoamerica, 18-20, 71
Mestizos: migration to countryside of,
207; populations of, 255, 296, 303-4,
321, 323; occupations of, 324
Metallurgy: pre-Columbian, 61, 79. *See
also* Gold; Copper
Metates (grindstones), 74-75, 79
Mexía, Dr. Antonio, oidor, 191-92, 287
Mexican culture, 31, 56, 66
Mexican languages, 31
Mexican place-names, 31
Mexican traders. *See* Pipil; Nahuatl
Mexico, 9, 56, 96, 122, 135, 146, 156-
57, 162, 216; population of, 4, 88,
329; epidemics in, 128-29
Migration: of non-Indians to rural areas,
133, 135-36, 167, 172-73, 207-8, 324;
from Indian villages, 203, 206-7, 332;
of Indians to mines, 206-7, 261, 264;
of Indians to rural areas, 206-8, 261;
of Indians to towns, 206, 261, 264
Military leaders. *See* War leaders
Militia, 188, 264, 324-25
Mines and mining, 111-14, 151-65, 239,
329; and the development of towns,
97, 167, 170; Indian labor in, 105-7,
111-14, 159-61, 179-86, 189, 319-20,
336; and depopulation, 105-6, 130,
336; labor in, 106-7, 111-14, 116,
151, 154-55, 159-63, 331;
distribution of, 111-12, 151-53, 185;
techniques in, 112, 152, 154, 157,
162; negro labor in, 113-14, 131, 151,
160-61, 180, 324, 331; and
agricultural development, 138-39;
administration of, 152, 163; claims to,
152, 152n.6, 152n.10; capital
investment in, 154, 154n.13, 155,
157, 159, 161-62; and merchant
credit, 157-59, 162; and merchant
trade in silver, 157-59. *See also*
Gold; Silver
Mint, 159, 164-65
Mishla, 82
Missions and missionaries, 9-11, 13,
239, 241-52, 273; as parish priests,
235-36; and the use of military force,
239, 241-42, 246-47, 248-49;
populations of, 241-52 passim, 271,

294-95, 297-98, 309, 312; difficulties
in establishing, 241-42, 243-51
passim; in the Agalta valley, 241-44,
247, 250-52, 269-71; in the Olancho
valley, 241, 243-44, 250-52, 269-71,
294, 297; and conflicts with the
secular clergy, 242-43; attacks by
Indians on, 242-43; in Lean and
Mulía, 243, 245, 247-48, 250, 298,
314; in the valley of Yoro, 243, 245-
48, 250, 270; sites of, 243-52, 266-
67; methods of conversion used by,
246-50; and disease, 246-48, 314-17,
319; impact on Indians of, 259, 266-
72, 331; agriculture in, 267-68, 321;
social organization of, 268-71, 321;
and contacts with English, 269; and
contacts with Zambos-Mosquitos,
269; marriage patterns in, 270; family
size in, 270-71, 321
Mixed races: occupations of, 131, 139-
40, 145, 186; and demand for land,
136, 177-78, 210; move to
countryside, 173, 207-8; on the
Mosquito Shore, 259. *See also*
Ladinos, Mestizos; Morenos;
Mulattoes; Pardos; and Zambos
Montejo, Francisco de, governor, 52, 54,
97-100, 104, 113, 119, 130
Morenos, 323
Mosquitia: kingdom of, 280-81
Mosquito Convention, 256
Mosquito king, 280-81
Mosquito Shore: Europeans on the, 254-
56, 276-77; population of the, 255.
*See also* Zambos-Mosquitos,
population of
Mulattoes, 207, 264, 321, 324;
population of, 255, 303-4, 321, 323.
*See also* Ladinos
Mules, 141-43, 155, 262
Multifamily houses, 68-69, 277, 283

Naborías, 106, 109, 189. *See also*
Lavoríos
Nacaome, 25, 230n.127, 236
Naco, 19, 32-33, 52, 58, 61, 102, 110,
112; as a trading center, 33, 62, 122;
population of, 52, 90, 119, 127
Nahuat-speakers: migration of, 30-31

## Dellplain Latin American Studies
## Published by Westview Press